PRAISE FOR
*PREPARE THE WAY OF THE LORD*

*Prepare the Way of the Lord* is a remarkable achievement in the genre of "Introduction to the Old Testament." Reed Lessing and Andrew Steinmann have managed to balance overviews of classic Christian and Jewish positions on such matters as date and authorship with a fair and concise review of historical-critical scholarship and its current perspectives.

Charts, bibliographical data, literary analysis, and concise commentary combine to enrich the reader's entrance into the Old Testament world. The description of issues surrounding the Pentateuch is exemplary and sets a high standard that is maintained throughout the volume. The student of the Old Testament—whether clergy, seminarian, or laity—will benefit greatly from the thorough, yet manageable, overviews. Particularly refreshing is the consistent fidelity to the Old Testament texts themselves. This fidelity leads the authors to a clear defense of historic positions, but with an informed and articulate discussion of the prevailing alternatives. *Prepare the Way of the Lord* will surely become the standard introduction to the Old Testament in confessional Lutheranism and other Christian communities with a high regard for the authority of Sacred Scripture.

—Dean O. Wenthe, PhD
Professor of Exegetical Theology
President Emeritus
Concordia Theological Seminary, Fort Wayne, IN

To read the Bible is to risk a thrilling adventure through wild jungles with thunderous cataracts and soaring timbers teeming with life. Some turn its pages like those who would make rain forests into concrete wastelands for billboards and bobos. Others, and we thank God for the likes of Drs. Steinmann and Lessing, come to the forest with a gleaming eye and forward lean, eager to plunge in, to explore the glories and relish the sights and smells and sounds, for there is always more to see. This book will take you on a life-changing expedition through the Book of books. Your guides are as faithful as they are courageous, and you will not regret your time on this excursion with these authors. Enjoy!

—James M. Hamilton, PhD
Associate Professor of Biblical Theology
The Southern Baptist Theological Seminary

Lessing and Steinmann offer us a readable, but scholarly, up-to-date introductory textbook for Old Testament study, connecting the plan of salvation in Jesus Christ with Old Testament history from Genesis to Malachi. With numerous maps, tables, and helpful exegetical insights, this book will serve seminary students well for years to come, and, because of the book's frequent insights from the New Testament, pastors will benefit from reading the appropriate chapter before preaching on an Old Testament text.

—Joel D. Heck, ThD
Professor of Theology
Concordia University Texas

This book is a rich seminary-level introduction to the Old Testament rooted in the Reformation exegetical principles of humanistic arts, *sola Scriptura*, *solus Christus*, and *sola gratia*. It judiciously engages scholarship to inform a deeper understanding of God's Word. Its focus, though, is the canonical text and its theological messages. Each chapter highlights theological themes that percolate within a biblical book and spins two golden threads that run throughout this testament: Christ and sin and grace. Drs. Lessing and Steinmann have written an Old Testament introduction that seminarians can fruitfully use to prepare them to proclaim God's Law and Gospel.

—Scott A. Ashmon, PhD
Associate Professor of Old Testament and Hebrew
Director of Core Curriculum
Concordia University, Irvine, CA

It is a privilege to recommend *Prepare the Way of the Lord* by Lessing and Steinmann. The authors have written an excellent introduction to the Old Testament for seminary students. They lead the readers into every book of the Old Testament by providing historical and archaeological background, by discussing its literary features, and by highlighting its theological accents. They also interact with the most influential hypotheses and secondary literature in a fair, evenhanded, and insightful way. Throughout their introductory remarks they show how the entire Old Testament leads to Jesus Christ and his work in the past during his earthly ministry, in the present through the church, and in the future at his Second Advent.

—Paul R. Raabe, PhD
Professor of Old Testament
Concordia Seminary, St. Louis, MO

Unswervingly loyal to the witness of the Old Testament in its self-affirmation as the Word of God, the authors demonstrate at the same time a thorough understanding of contemporary critical scholarship and the fallacies on which much of it rests. Their objective, however, is not primarily polemical but pedagogical, addressing the complex issues attendant to understanding the Hebrew Scriptures while showing how they testify to Christ and the Gospel. In both they are eminently successful.

—Eugene H. Merrill, PhD
Distinguished Professor of Old Testament Studies Emeritus
Dallas Theological Seminary, Dallas, TX

Lessing and Steinmann, two prolific Old Testament scholars, have produced an excellent introduction to the Old Testament which will be much used, especially in the seminary classroom, in the years ahead. Drawing on their own previous scholarship, as well as on that of their peers in the field, and on their years of teaching, they cover all the important topics, including those which are controversial. While they are fair in their representation of the various sides, they also clearly come through with conservative, Lutheran conclusions. Especially admirable is their emphasis on the Messianic theme throughout the Old Testament.

—Walter A. Maier III, PhD
Associate Professor, Exegetical Department
Concordia Theological Seminary, Fort Wayne, IN

# PREPARE THE WAY OF THE LORD

# PREPARE THE WAY OF THE LORD

## AN INTRODUCTION TO THE OLD TESTAMENT

### R. REED LESSING
### AND
### ANDREW E. STEINMANN

**Peer Reviewed**

CONCORDIA PUBLISHING HOUSE · SAINT LOUIS

Peer Reviewed

Published by Concordia Publishing House
3558 S. Jefferson Ave., St. Louis, MO 63118–3968
1-800-325-3040 • www.cph.org

Text copyright © 2014 R. Reed Lessing and Andrew E. Steinmann

Scripture quotations are the authors' translation.

The maps and captions in this publication are adapted from *The Lutheran Study Bible*, copyright © 2009 by Concordia Publishing House. All rights reserved.

This work uses the SBL Hebrew Unicode font developed by the Font Foundation, under the leadership of the Society of Biblical Literature. For further information on this font or on becoming a Font Foundation member, see http://www.sbl-site.org/educational/biblicalfonts.aspx

Cover art © Shutterstock, Inc.

Manufactured in the United States of America

Library of Congress Cataloging-in-Publication Data

Lessing, R. Reed (Robert Reed), 1959-
  Prepare the way of the Lord : an introduction to the Old Testament / R. Reed Lessing and Andrew E. Steinmann.

    pages cm
  ISBN 978-0-7586-2832-9
  1. Bible. Old Testament--Criticism, interpretation, etc. I. Title.

BS1171.3.L465 2014
221.6'1--dc23                              2013018216

2 3 4 5 6 7 8 9 10          23 22 21 20 19 18 17 16 15 14

# CONTENTS

CONTENTS

# MAPS AND TABLES

# ABBREVIATIONS

| | |
|---|---|
| *Ag. Ap.* | Josephus, *Against Apion* |
| *Ant.* | Josephus, *Antiquities of the Jews* |
| *B. Bat.* | Talmud, Tractate *Baba Bathra* |
| LXX | Septuagint and allied Greek Old Testament versions |
| *Mak.* | Talmud, Tractate *Makkot* |
| MT | Masoretic Text of the Old Testament |
| *m. Yad* | Talmud, *mishnah Yadayim* |
| NT | New Testament |
| OT | Old Testament |

## Old Testament Books

| | | | |
|---|---|---|---|
| Gen | Genesis | 2 Chr | 2 Chronicles |
| Exod | Exodus | Ezra | Ezra |
| Lev | Leviticus | Neh | Nehemiah |
| Num | Numbers | Esth | Esther |
| Deut | Deuteronomy | Job | Job |
| Josh | Joshua | Ps | Psalms |
| Judg | Judges | Prov | Proverbs |
| Ruth | Ruth | Eccl | Ecclesiastes |
| 1 Sam | 1 Samuel | Song | Song of Songs |
| 2 Sam | 2 Samuel | Isa | Isaiah |
| 1 Kgs | 1 Kings | Jer | Jeremiah |
| 2 Kgs | 2 Kings | Ezek | Ezekiel |
| 1 Chr | 1 Chronicles | Dan | Daniel |

| Hos | Hosea | Nah | Nahum |
|-----|-------|-----|-------|
| Joel | Joel | Hab | Habakkuk |
| Amos | Amos | Zeph | Zephaniah |
| Obad | Obadiah | Hag | Haggai |
| Jonah | Jonah | Zech | Zechariah |
| Mic | Micah | Mal | Malachi |

## New Testament Books

| Matt | Matthew | 1 Tim | 1 Timothy |
|------|---------|-------|-----------|
| Mark | Mark | 2 Tim | 2 Timothy |
| Luke | Luke | Titus | Titus |
| John | John | Phlm | Philemon |
| Acts | Acts | Heb | Hebrews |
| Rom | Romans | Jas | James |
| 1 Cor | 1 Corinthians | 1 Pet | 1 Peter |
| 2 Cor | 2 Corinthians | 2 Pet | 2 Peter |
| Gal | Galatians | 1 John | 1 John |
| Eph | Ephesians | 2 John | 2 John |
| Phil | Philippians | 3 John | 3 John |
| Col | Colossians | Jude | Jude |
| 1 Thess | 1 Thessalonians | Rev | Revelation |
| 2 Thess | 2 Thessalonians | | |

## Apocrypha

| 1 Macc | 1 Maccabees | 1 Esd | 1 Esdras |
|--------|-------------|-------|----------|
| 2 Macc | 2 Maccabees | 2 Esd | 2 Esdras |

# PREFACE

In June of 2010 when Edward Engelbrecht of Concordia Publishing House asked to meet with us over lunch during an LCMS professors meeting at Concordia Theological Seminary in Fort Wayne, Indiana, neither one of us suspected that he would propose we collaborate on the production of a new OT isagogics book for seminary students. While we knew each other for many years by that point, and counted each other as friends, we had never had a chance to work together. Collaborating on this volume has been a rewarding and enriching experience, one that we are grateful to Ed and CPH for proposing and supporting.

The writing of a work covering the entire OT is not an easy task for any biblical scholar. It is difficult, if not impossible, for any one person to be an expert on all the issues in every book of the Hebrew canon, and even two cannot possibly claim to have intimate knowledge of each book from Moses to Malachi. Nevertheless, we are thankful that the Lord has provided us with knowledge and talents that we came to perceive as complementary, making for a fruitful partnership on this volume.

The goal of any introduction of the OT is to prepare students to read Israel's texts with understanding and insight. Twenty-first century scholarship offers a myriad of ways to read them. How does the beginning student make sense of it all? What is helpful and what is detrimental to evangelical faith? And how do conservative scholars respond to critical views of the OT? To be sure, this information may be found elsewhere, yet there is value in having one volume that discusses the most important issues. This book interacts with these scholars in a respectful way while providing evangelical assessments that foster historical and theological confidence in the OT.

At the outset a number of decisions were made that led to the product you have before you. It was decided that each chapter that treats an OT book should have sections on authorship and literary features as well as historical, archaeological, and textual issues (where appropriate). Of course, these chapters discuss theological emphases. In addition, a section that treats the key biblical themes of sin and grace is always included. Some comments are brief; others go into some detail, such as discussions of genre under literary features and the importance of a book's theological themes as they develop in the Bible. Chapters may end with a comment or two on how literary forms, historical backdrop, and theology, though separated in this book, are finally three parts of a unified whole. Our goal is to provide a bridge between the ancient text and its meaning and application today.

Since this is intended to be an OT introduction for seminary students seeking to enter the Christian ministry, this book was designed from the beginning to be Christocentric in keeping with the ancient Christian conviction that everything written about the Messiah in the Law, Prophets, and Psalms finds its fulfillment in Jesus (Luke 24:44). Thus, in every chapter that treats a specific OT book there will be a section about Christ in that book.

Early on it was decided that an introductory chapter on the canon and its formation was essential. In addition, we recognized that the Pentateuch needed not only chapters on each individual book but also a chapter introducing and evaluating Pentateuchal criticism since the Enlightenment. As we progressed, we also saw the need for chapters introducing the prophetic books as a whole and one summarizing more recent scholarship on the Book of the Twelve Prophets.

Another early decision was to have only a limited bibliography for each chapter. Given the widespread availability of search engines, dedicated databases, and online library catalogs, anyone who wishes to compile a list of studies on any book of the OT can do so quickly and with relatively little effort, eliminating the need for large bibliographies in an OT introduction. Instead, we have included in the bibliographies only those works that are prominently mentioned in each chapter or which we consulted with some frequency in our research. In our book when a scholar's work is referenced in the first instance in a chapter by complete name (not simply by surname), then there will be no bibliographic entry for that work at the end of that chapter. If a scholar is referenced only by surname in the first instance, that scholar's work will be listed in the bibliography.

We also decided to eschew the use of footnotes. Reading experts have demonstrated that most readers do not consult footnotes regularly. Moreover, we wanted to resist the temptation to place extended discussions in footnotes. Anything we deemed worthy of discussion for students beginning their seminary studies in the OT ought to be in the text itself. Only quotations are footnoted. In the same vein, we cite only chapter and verse numbers as they appear in English versions, and not the variant numbers used in some parts of the Masoretic text.

At times it is necessary to refer to the years of the reigns of the Egyptian pharaohs. Especially in the earlier period there are continuing discussions among Egyptologists as to the exact dates of these reigns. While we do not endorse any particular view, to simplify matters we have followed the dates given in one recent work, that of Hornung, Krauss, and Warburton (*Ancient Egyptian Chronology*. Leiden: Brill, 2006). For justification for the dates in biblical history given in this book, please see Steinmann's explanations in *From Abraham to Paul: A Biblical Chronology* (St. Louis: Concordia, 2011). In those chapters that rely heavily on this resource, it is also included in that chapter's bibliography.

Finally, we would like to thank those who helped us along the way during the time we spent working on this book. They include Edward Engelbrecht, Paul McCain, Laura Lane, and Sarah Steiner at Concordia Publishing House. It is our privilege to have been asked to write this work and our joy to have worked together on it. We chose the title *Prepare the Way of the Lord* based on Isa 40:3 and echoed in all four Gospels (Matt 3:3; Mark 1:3; Luke 3:4; John 1:23). It is our prayer that it will serve the Christian church in preparation of pastors and others in her service as they, like John, point others to Christ through the proclamation of God's Word as revealed to Moses and the prophets.

*Soli Deo Gloria*

R. Reed Lessing, Concordia Seminary, St. Louis
Andrew E. Steinmann, Concordia University Chicago

1

# THE OLD TESTAMENT CANON

The OT is a collection of books. The word used to describe the set of books that comprise this collection is *canon*. Derived from the Greek word κανών, *measuring rod*, a canon is a corpus of authoritative and divinely inspired books accepted as such by an overwhelming majority in a religious community. Several religious traditions recognize the OT canon, though they may differ on the order in which the books are to be listed or whether some additional books are to be placed alongside those that others accept.

## THE HISTORY OF THE CANON AS A COLLECTION

While the way in which the books of the OT came to be collected is shrouded in the history of ancient Israel, it is clear that at least two centuries before Christ (and perhaps earlier) the collection we now know as the OT had formed. The Wisdom of Jesus Ben Sira, written around 180 BC, made use of nearly every book of the OT, even mentioning the twelve minor prophets (Hosea–Malachi) as a unit. The NT recognizes an OT canon (although it does not use that term to describe it). It often mentions "the Scriptures" (e.g., Matt 21:42; Acts 17:2; Rom 15:4) and quotes from them with the formula "it is written" (e.g., Matt 2:5; John 6:31; Gal 4:27). The NT divides the OT into small units, most commonly the Torah (the five books of Moses) and the Prophets (the rest of the OT). The NT, like Ben Sira, mentions the collection of the twelve minor prophets (Acts 7:42). It treats every book of the Hebrew OT as Scripture except Esther, and no book outside this collection is ever treated as Scripture by the NT writers. For instance, Song of Songs is most likely quoted as Scripture at John 7:38 (though the quotation is also similar to Isa 58:1), and the Twelve Minor prophets as a group are referenced as Scripture at Acts 7:42 ("in the book of the Prophets"). It appears that Luke 10:26–27 in quoting "the Law" combined elements of Deut 6:5, Lev 18:5, and Josh 22:5, treating all three equally as part of God's inspired Word. Nehemiah, which is treated as Scripture at least as early as Ben Sira, was also known to the NT writers (Matt 1:5, 12; Luke 1:5). By the late first century Josephus (AD 37—c. 100), a Jewish historian and younger contemporary of Jesus, wrote about the OT canon and outlined its contents, giving a description that corresponds to the Hebrew OT we know today.

Many higher critical scholars dispute that the OT canon was a recognized collection in Jesus' day. For instance, McDonald argues that it was not recognized in its present form until sometime in the fourth century. He claims that NT quotations of certain Jewish books such as Ben Sira (Mark 10:19; 2 Tim 2:19), 1 Enoch (Jude 14), and the Assumption of Moses (Jude 9) demonstrate that the OT canon was still a fluid concept in the first century. However, Steinmann has examined these and demonstrated that the supposed quotations of Ben Sira may well be periphrastic quotations of OT books instead. The citations in Jude appear to be actual quotations from 1 Enoch and the Assumption of Moses. However, in neither case are these books quoted *as Scripture.* Note that the NT at times quotes works that clearly are not Scripture. For example, Paul quotes Aratus (Acts 17:28), Menander (1 Cor 15:33), and Epimenides (Tit 1:12). It is an unsound procedure to hold that whenever a NT writer adopts phraseology or concepts from a source, he considered that source to be authoritative revelation—although this appears to be exactly what McDonald assumes.

However, if we look at the places where NT authors quote "Scripture" (ἡ γράφη/τὰ γράμματα), "the Torah" (ὁ νομός), or "the Prophets" (οἱ προφῆται) or use the formula "it is written" (γέγραπται), we find that they only quote books found in the OT canon, and that the majority of the OT books are quoted at least once. Every book of the Hebrew OT is quoted by these formulas except Judges, Ruth, Chronicles, Ezra, Nehemiah, Esther, Obadiah, and Zephaniah. When we combine these citations with texts which refer to passages from the OT, without directly quoting them (such as the reference to the

Minor Prophets as a collection at Acts 7:42), every book except Esther is referenced.

Moreover, several passages in the NT *assume* that a definitive collection known as *Scripture* or *the Torah and the Prophets* was accepted by most Jews and early Christians. For instance, Jesus told some Jews:

> You study the Scriptures because you think in them you have eternal life. They testify about me. (John 5:39)

Jesus could hardly claim that the Scriptures testified about him if there was not a general and widespread agreement about the content of the scriptural canon in his day. The same assumption can be found in other NT passages (cf. Matt 5:17; Luke 24:44; John 1:45; Acts 18:28; 28:23; Rom 3:21; 1 Cor 15:3–5; 2 Tim 3:15–17). Thus, there is good evidence to hold that the OT canon had been accepted some time before the first century AD and that its contents were most likely identical to the Jewish canon (and, therefore the Protestant OT).

During the time of Jesus and Josephus, the OT did not exist as a book, but as a collection of scrolls. In the early centuries of the church's history, bound books became popular, and people began to put the books of Scripture together within the covers of a single volume. At this time Christians, who seldom knew or read Hebrew, relied on Greek translations of the OT books. Along with these translations of various books of the OT, they also read other Jewish books in Greek. By the third century many Christians, especially in the West, began to accept these additional books as part of the OT canon. However, Jews and other Christians continued to treat only the books of the Hebrew OT as Scripture.

During the Middle Ages, most Christians in Western Europe accepted the wider canon that included the additional books, while Christians in the East were divided over their status. At the time of the Reformation, Martin Luther and other reformers began to question the canonical standing of the additional books. When Luther translated the Bible into German, he removed them from their accepted place in the OT and placed the books between the OT and NT as worthy reading, but not Scripture. The same procedure was followed in English Bibles, such as the King James Version when it was first published in 1611.

Luther and the Reformers argued that no Jew in Jesus' day recognized the additional books as Scripture, and the NT evidence demonstrates that Jesus and his apostles accepted only the books of the Hebrew OT. The additional books were labeled Apocrypha (from a Greek word that means *hidden*). In reaction to the Protestant view, the Roman Catholic Church reaffirmed their canonical status, labeling them *deuterocanonical*, "second canon." Eventually, most Protestant Bibles omitted the Apocrypha altogether (since this made Bibles cheaper and less bulky) while Roman Catholic Bibles continue to include the deuterocanonical books within the OT.

## THE CANON IN VARIOUS RELIGIOUS TRADITIONS

| Jewish (24 books) | Protestant (39 books) | Roman Catholic (46 books) |
|---|---|---|
| *Torah* | *Pentateuch* | *Pentateuch* |
| Genesis | Genesis | Genesis |
| Exodus | Exodus | Exodus |
| Leviticus | Leviticus | Leviticus |
| Numbers | Numbers | Numbers |
| Deuteronomy | Deuteronomy | Deuteronomy |
| *Prophets* (Former Prophets) | *History* | *History* |
| Joshua | Joshua | Joshua |
| Judges | Judges | Judges |
|  | Ruth | Ruth |
| Samuel | 1 Samuel | 1 Samuel |
|  | 2 Samuel | 2 Samuel |
| Kings | 1 Kings | 1 Kings |
|  | 2 Kings | 2 Kings |
| (Latter Prophets) | 1 Chronicles | 1 Chronicles |
| Isaiah | 2 Chronicles | 2 Chronicles |
| Jeremiah | Ezra | Ezra |
| Ezekiel | Nehemiah | Nehemiah |
| *The Book of the Twelve* |  | Tobit |
| Hosea |  | Judith |
| Joel | Esther | Esther (with additions) |

4

| | | |
|---|---|---|
| Amos | | 1 Maccabees |
| Obadiah | | 2 Maccabees |
| Jonah | *Poetry & Wisdom* | *Poetry & Wisdom* |
| Micah | Job | Job |
| Nahum | Psalms | Psalms |
| Habakkuk | Proverbs | Proverbs |
| Zephaniah | Ecclesiastes | Ecclesiastes |
| Haggai | Song of Songs | Song of Songs |
| Zechariah | | Wisdom of Solomon |
| Malachi | | Ecclesiasticus (Ben Sira, Sirach) |
| *Writings* | *Prophets* | *Prophets* |
| Psalms | (Major Prophets) | (Major Prophets) |
| Job | Isaiah | Isaiah |
| Proverbs | Jeremiah | Jeremiah |
| Ruth | Lamentations | Lamentations |
| Song of Songs | | Baruch (including the Letter of Jeremiah) |
| Ecclesiastes | Ezekiel | Ezekiel |
| Lamentations | Daniel | Daniel (with additions) |
| Esther | (Minor Prophets) | (Minor Prophets) |
| Daniel | Hosea | Hosea |
| Ezra-Nehemiah | Joel | Joel |
| Chronicles | Amos | Amos |
| | Obadiah | Obadiah |
| | Jonah | Jonah |
| | Micah | Micah |
| | Nahum | Nahum |
| | Habakkuk | Habakkuk |
| | Zephaniah | Zephaniah |
| | Haggai | Haggai |
| | Zechariah | Zechariah |
| | Malachi | Malachi |

## THE JEWISH CANON

The Jewish canon, often called the Tanak, an acronym for the three major divisions of its books (Torah, Nevi'im [Prophets], Kethuvim

[Writings]), consists of twenty-four books. The first major division, the Torah, encompasses the five books attributed to Moses. The second division, the Prophets, is divided into two sections. The former prophets are made up of books primarily concerned with the history of Israel. The latter prophets contain the messages of individual prophets. The twelve prophets are counted as one book—hence the title "The Book of the Twelve"—since in ancient times this entire collection could be written on one scroll. The Writings contain other books, including poetry, wisdom, and historical narratives.

Steinmann has argued that this arrangement of the canon probably arose after the first century in response to Jewish liturgical practices. Before this time all of the books outside the Torah were generally grouped together as "the Prophets," as evidenced by the NT and other first century BC and first century AD documents (e.g., Matt 5:17; 7:12; Luke 16:16, 29; John 1:45; Acts 13:15; 26:22; Rom 3:21). Later Jewish liturgical practice used a cycle of readings for each Sabbath from the Torah and the Prophets. Books that were not part of this cycle—those that were never read in worship or read only on certain festival days—became part of the Writings.

## THE PROTESTANT OT

The Protestant OT of thirty-nine books is identical in content to the Jewish canon, although the books are arranged and counted differently. Samuel, Kings, and Chronicles are divided into two books each. The twelve are reckoned as twelve books instead of one while Ezra and Nehemiah are counted as two books instead of one.

The Pentateuch (from Greek for *five volumes*) is identical to the Jewish Torah. The books that in the first century were called "the Prophets" are divided into three sections. The first presents the history of Israel in roughly chronological order from Joshua, Moses' successor, to Esther. The second division is comprised of the major poetic books of the OT (including the wisdom books). The third section contains the messages of the prophets. The larger prophetic books plus Lamentations are called the Major Prophets, while the small books are called the Minor Prophets. (The distinction between major and minor is based on size, not on the importance of the prophet's message.)

## THE ROMAN CATHOLIC OT

The arrangement of the Roman Catholic OT is similar to that of the Protestant OT. The Pentateuch begins the collection, making the books of Moses foundational in the Jewish canon and in all Christian canons. The remaining books are once again divided into three sections of history, poetry, and prophets, with the deuterocanonical books placed in the sections where they most logically fit. The forty-six books of the Roman Catholic canon include not only seven additions, but also expansions to Daniel and Esther that are found in the Greek versions of those books.

## ABOUT THE APOCRYPHA/DEUTEROCANONICAL BOOKS

While Roman Catholics are often familiar with the books they call *deuterocanonical*, many other Christians are not acquainted with them. Among Christians from the Western traditions, Episcopalians are most likely to have heard these books read in worship, although many traditional Lutheran lectionaries once included readings from Sirach and the Wisdom of Solomon.

All of these books date from the period between the end of the OT in Ezra's day and the birth of Christ. Although some originally were written in Hebrew or Aramaic, the oldest surviving complete versions are in Greek.

### *Additions to the Historical Books*

**Tobit** relates the title character's devotion to the Torah and Israelite customs in Nineveh during Israel's captivity there. His family suffers a number of misfortunes, but God's angel guides his life and blesses his family. Written about 200 BC in Hebrew, the only surviving complete versions are in Greek and Syriac (a dialect of Aramaic).

**Judith** relates the wiles of a daughter of Israel as she single-handedly rallies her people to victory over the Assyrians after slaying the Assyrian general Holofernes. Judith was probably written around 150 BC.

**Additions to Esther** are from the Greek version of this book. These embellishments make Esther a more pointedly religious book and temper its apparent lack of theology by mentioning God, who is never mentioned in the Hebrew version. The Greek additions may date from about 160 BC.

**1 Maccabees** tells the history of the Jewish revolt against the Seleucid kings of Syria and the struggle against Jewish absorption into the Hellenistic world from 167 to about 127 BC. The rebellion was brought on by Syrian kings and their attempt to stamp out any distinctly Jewish way of life. The book relates the forty-year struggle led by the priestly Hasmonean family of Matthias and his sons, especially Judas and Simon, who were known as the *Maccabees,* "hammers." The author admires these Jewish heroes and their commitment to Jewish customs and beliefs. Written in Hebrew about 100 BC, the book was preserved only in Greek.

**2 Maccabees** covers the period from 167 to 151 BC, overlapping the history related in 1 Macc 1–7. Instead of writing a strict history, the author relates selected incidents from this period to illustrate the heroism of the Jews and the protection they receive from God. Much more overtly theological than 1 Maccabees, 2 Maccabees was originally written about 124 BC in Greek. Much of it is based on an earlier work by Jason of Cyrene.

## *Additions to the Wisdom Books*

**Wisdom of Solomon** was written by a Hellenized Jew who was familiar with Greek culture. He probably lived in Alexandria, Egypt, and wrote about 50 BC. The first part of the book is devoted to encouraging Jews in Egypt to remain faithful in a culture that encouraged pagan worship and mocked the Jews and their trust in the God of Israel. The second part of the book purports to be Solomon speaking in praise of Wisdom. Since Wisdom is personified as God's agent in the world and as sharing his nature, the Wisdom of Solomon is an important link in Jewish thought between Proverbs' portrayal of Wisdom (Prov 8) and Jesus as the incarnate Wisdom of God (1 Cor 1:24, 30).

**Ben Sira** is known as Sirach in Greek or Ecclesiasticus in Latin. This book contains the wisdom of Jesus Ben Sira, a scribe who trained others in wisdom in Jerusalem. It comprises mostly pithy sayings about worldly wisdom, common sense, and good behavior. Ben Sira was originally written in Hebrew between 190 and 180 BC. In 132 BC it was translated into Greek by Ben Sira's grandson. The Greek version includes the translator's prologue.

## Additions to the Prophets

**Baruch and the Letter of Jeremiah** contain four documents, two prose and two poetry. These works tell us about Jewish devotion to God's law and their messianic hopes in the Babylonian exile. Although attributed to Baruch, a scribe to the prophet Jeremiah, the book of Baruch was probably written in the first century BC. However, the sixth chapter, the Letter of Jeremiah, was written up to one century earlier.

**Additions to Daniel,** which are extant only in the Greek translation of Daniel and probably date from the second century BC include:

*The Prayer of Azariah*: An addition to Dan 3, the prayer is purported to be by one of the three young Judeans condemned to be cast into a furnace by Nebuchadnezzar.

*The Song of the Three Young Men*: Also an addition to Dan 3, this song was supposedly sung in praise to God by the three men in the furnace. The Song of the Three Young Men has had a special place in Christian liturgical use, often used as a psalm or song in worship in Roman Catholic, Episcopalian, and Lutheran churches.

*Susanna*: Often included as chapter 13 in Greek Daniel, this short story tells how Daniel, as a boy in the Babylonian captivity, rescued Susanna, who was condemned to death by a plot of certain Judean elders because she had refused to commit adultery with them.

*Bel and the Dragon*: The first part of chapter 14 in Greek Daniel is a brief account of Daniel's wisdom in action as he proves that the priests of the Babylonian god Bel (Marduk) are frauds and that Bel is a false god. The second part of chapter 14 in Greek Daniel is a brief story in which Daniel destroys a dragon (a large snake) worshipped by the Babylonians, thereby proving that it is a false god. Because he demolishes their god, some Babylonians force their king to throw Daniel in a lion's pit. However, Daniel is rescued from the pit where he was protected by an angel who brought him the prophet Habakkuk.

### EASTERN ORTHODOX OT CANONS

In Eastern Christianity, especially in the churches of the Orthodox tradition, there is a mixed view concerning the Apocrypha. While all of these churches accept the books in the smaller canon recognized by Jews and Protestants, many members of Eastern Orthodox churches also affirm some or all of the books of the Apocrypha. A few churches among the Eastern traditions accept additional books. For instance, Ethiopic Christians have traditionally included a second century Jewish book known as Jubilees as part of their OT canon.

## CONCLUSION

The OT canon has been recognized as such since before the time of Jesus, and Jesus and the apostles, as well as extra-biblical sources, testify to this. However, these facts do not mean that there were no changes in the OT canon after that time. Clearly, there are developments in the way that the canon was arranged, as evidenced by the differing orders of the biblical books in Christian and Jewish Bibles. Moreover, within Christianity there were later historical currents that led some Christians to view additional books as canonical, although none of these were universally accepted in the church, and none of them were ever accepted by Jewish communities. From antiquity the canon consisted of "the Torah and the Prophets," books which pointed to the promised Savior (John 1:45; 5:23; Acts 28:23; Rom 3:21), and it is these canonical books that are universally accepted by the church as Scripture, even among Christians who would acknowledge additional books in the OT canon.

## SELECT BIBLIOGRAPHY

Aune, David E. "On the Origins of the 'Council of Javneh' Myth," *Journal of Biblical Literature* 110 (1991): 491–93.

Barr, James. *Holy Scripture: Canon, Authority, Criticism.* Philadelphia: Westminster, 1983.

Ellis, E. Earle, *The Old Testament in Early Christianity: Canon and Interpretation in the Light of Modern Research.* Grand Rapids: Baker, 1991.

Leiman, Sid A. *The Canonization of Hebrew Scripture: The Talmudic and Midrashic Evidence.* Transactions of the Connecticut Academy of Arts and Sciences 47. 2nd ed. New Haven: Connecticut Academy of Arts and Sciences, 1991.

Lewis, Jack P. "What Do We Mean by Jabneh?" *Journal of Bible and Religion* 32 (1964): 125–32.

McDonald, Lee Martin. *The Biblical Canon: Its Origin, Transmission, and Authority.* Peabody: Henderson, 2007.

Steinmann, Andrew E. *The Oracles of God: The Old Testament Canon.* St. Louis: Concordia, 1999.

Sundburg, Albert C. Jr. *The Old Testament Canon of the Early Church.* Harvard Theological Studies 20. Cambridge: Harvard, 1964.

Vasholz, Robert I. *The Old Testament Canon in the Old Testament Church.* Ancient Near Eastern Texts and Studies 7. Lewiston: Edwin Mellen, 1990.

2

# THE ORIGIN OF THE PENTATEUCH

In both Jewish and Christian arrangements of the canon, the first five books form the foundation upon which the OT Scriptures are built. They relate the early history of God's people from creation to the death of Moses, maintaining a plotline that flows from one book into the next. Yahweh's promises to Israel's patriarchs lead to the formation of God's special people (e.g., Exod 19:5–6). The land that is pledged to Abraham, Isaac, and Jacob (cf. Gen 12:7; 15:7, 18; 24:7; 26:3; 48:4) drives the narrative from Genesis to Deuteronomy as Israel moves from Canaan to Egypt and then back toward Canaan. In various ways from Exodus to Deuteronomy, the people that are descended from Jacob's sons in Genesis are set apart from the rest of the nations as a "kingdom of priests and a holy nation" (Exod 19:6).

Yet, despite this continuity of plot and theme, no other books of the OT have been more discussed in relation to various theories of their authorship and growth as a collection. While more conservative Christians have maintained that these books are essentially the work of Moses, for the past 250 years critical scholars have searched for other ways to explain the origin of the Pentateuch. In this chapter we will explore the various ways in which the Pentateuch's composition has been explained before moving on to subsequent chapters that examine its individual books.

These five books collectively are called Torah (תורה) in Hebrew. This word, often translated "law," derives from the verbal root ירה, meaning teach or instruct. Thus, torah signifies teaching. Christians have called these books the Pentateuch from the Greek words for "five volumes."

# MOSES AND THE PENTATEUCH

## MOSES' QUALIFICATIONS AS AN AUTHOR

From antiquity the Pentateuch has been ascribed to Moses. Certainly Moses, as he is presented to readers of Exodus, is qualified to write such a work. The exodus from Egypt took place in 1446 BC when Moses was about 80 years old. This places his early life in Egypt during the eighteenth dynasty, and he was probably in the pharaonic court during the reigns of Ahmose (c. 1539–1515), Amenhotep I (c. 1514–1494 BC), and Tutmose I (c. 1494–1483). During this era Egypt enjoyed great power and international prestige. Contacts with other peoples and cultures were commonplace and would have served to broaden the education of Moses and other princes in the Egyptian court. During this period even uneducated Semitic slaves were writing on the walls of Egypt's turquoise mines at Serabit el-Khadim in the southwest Sinai Peninsula. It would have been even more likely that Moses learned to read and write, and he would have been familiar with the various genres that appear in the Pentateuch: historical narrative, genealogies, law codes, and speeches.

Moreover, Moses would have had time to write the Pentateuch during the long forty-year wandering of the Israelites in the Sinai wilderness. The book of Numbers concentrates on the first and last years of this period, relating few incidents from the other thirty-eight years. During this time Moses could have written the bulk of Genesis, Exodus, Leviticus, and Numbers. Most of Deuteronomy was written by Moses, including portions called "this teaching" (Deut 31:9) and "this song" (Deut 31:22). Deut 1–33 could have been put in final written form by someone who listened to these sermons, perhaps Joshua, Moses' assistant, who is portrayed as literate in the book that bears his name (Josh 24:26).

## TRADITIONAL VIEW OF THE PENTATEUCH AS THE WORK OF MOSES

### *The Witness of the Pentateuch Itself*

Several passages in the Pentateuch itself indicate that Moses wrote at least a few passages. Yahweh instructed Moses to write an account of Israel's victory over Amalek (Exod 17:14). Moses also recorded God's words to Israel at Mount Sinai (Exod 24:4). After he smashed the first tablets of the covenant that had been inscribed by the finger of God (Exod 31:8), Moses wrote a duplicate set (Exod 34:27). At Yahweh's behest, Moses maintained the list of campsites that Israel used during its forty years in the wilderness (Num 33; esp. v. 2). Moses wrote the song he composed about God's work for Israel (Deut 31:22; cf. Deut 32–33). Perhaps the most comprehensive statements about the authorship of the Pentateuch are found in Deut 31, where twice we are told that Moses wrote "this Torah" (Deut 31:9, 24).

## The Witness of the Rest of the OT

The OT regularly refers to the Pentateuch, and Moses is usually associated with it as its author. Yahweh instructed Joshua to do everything according to the Torah that Moses had commanded (Josh 1:7). Moreover, this "scroll of the Torah" was to be Joshua's meditation "day and night" (Josh 1:8). Later Joshua built an altar following the instructions in "the scroll of the Torah of Moses" (Josh 8:31; cf. Exod 20:25). Joshua also read every word from this Torah of Moses to Israel, especially the blessings and curses (Josh 8:34–35; cf. Deut 11:26, 29; 30:1, 19).

The book of Kings also affirms Moses' authorship of the Pentateuch. When David was near death, he instructed Solomon to keep God's commandments that were written in Moses' Torah (1 Kgs 2:3). Upon his accession to Judah's throne, Amaziah obeyed the command written in the "Book of the Torah of Moses" by not executing children of murderers for their fathers' sin (2 Kgs 14:6; cf. Deut 24:16; 2 Chr 25:4). Josiah turned to Yahweh "with all his heart and with all his soul and with all his might" according to "the Torah of Moses" (2 Kgs 23:25; cf. Deut 6:5).

The post-exilic books of the OT also testify to Moses' authorship of the Torah (2 Chr 23:18; 30:16; 35:12; Ezra 3:2; 6:18; 7:6; Neh 8:1; 13:1). It is noteworthy that Malachi, the last of the OT prophets, quotes God exhorting Israel to remember "the Torah of my servant Moses" which included the statues and regulations commanded at Horeb (Mal 4:4; cf. Exod 20:3–17; Deut 4:9–10).

## The Witness of the NT

The NT recognizes Moses as the author of the Pentateuch. It refers to the "the law of Moses" nine times (law = νομός = תורה;

Mark 12:26; Luke 2:22; 24:44; John 7:23; Acts 13:39; 15:5; 28:23; 1 Cor 9:9; Heb 10:28; cf. John 1:45) and the "book of Moses" once (Mark 12:26). At times the Pentateuch is simply called "Moses" (Luke 16:29, 31; 24:27; Acts 21:21). The Torah is frequently quoted as "Moses wrote" (Mark 12:19; Luke 20:28; John 1:45; 5:46), "Moses said" (Matt 22:24; Mark 7:10; Acts 3:22; 7:37; 26:22; Heb 7:14; 12:21), "Moses allowed" (Matt 19:8; Mark 10:4), or "Moses commanded" (Matt 8:4; 19:7; Mark 1:44; 10:3; Luke 5:14; John 8:5).

In this regard the Gospel of John is most pointed in assigning the Pentateuch's composition to Moses. John 1:17 says "the Law was given through Moses." Jesus is quoted as ascribing the Torah to Moses, a point his Jewish opponents did not dispute (John 7:19–23). This Johannine passage is most significant, since it may assign the covenant of circumcision to Moses and may be referring to Gen 17 (although it could be argued that Jesus is referring to Lev 12:3). Since Genesis is entirely about events before Moses was born, the case for Mosaic authorship of this book is more vulnerable to challenge than the other books of the Pentateuch. Yet Jesus confidently asserted Moses' writing of the first book of the Torah.

## Post-Mosaic Additions and Glosses in the Pentateuch

Given the witness of the OT and NT to Moses' authorship of the Pentateuch, it is not surprising that the traditional position of both Christians and Jews for most of the last two thousand years has been to affirm the Mosaic origin of these books. Nevertheless, it has long been recognized that the text of the Pentateuch transmitted to us contains a limited number of statements reflecting later editorial additions and changes.

The most evident of these is the account of Moses' death at Deut 34:1–12. Since this passage ends with a notice that no prophet like Moses had arisen again in Israel (Deut 34:10–12), it appears as if it was added a number of years after Moses had died. Already in antiquity the rabbis taught that this addition was appended to Deuteronomy by Joshua (B. Bat. 14b).

Perhaps Joshua or some other contemporary of Moses added the observation that Moses was the most humble man on earth (Num 12:3). In this context humility appears to refer to Moses' lack of assertiveness, especially in the face of criticism by his siblings (Num 12:1–2). If this is the case, it would be unlikely that Moses would assert his timidity by placing this parenthetical comment into the narrative. However, this addition need not be post-Mosaic if added by Joshua, since Joshua was Moses' assistant (Exod 24:13; 33:11; Num 11:28). He could have been entrusted with recording Moses' words as dictated to him. (Thus, Joshua may also be the author of the note at Num 13:16 where we are told that Moses renamed Hoshea son of Nun as "Joshua," a variant of Hoshea.)

A number of short notices in the Pentateuch appear to be later glosses that were added to explain historical circumstances. Gen 36:31 seems to have been appended sometime after the monarchy was established in Israel:

> These are the kings who ruled in the land of Edom before any king reigned over the Israelites.

A series of comments about the Rephaim and Anakim in Deut 2–3 appear to have been inserted after the period of the Judges, since they mention Israel's conquest of Canaan, the Philistines' invasion of southwest Canaan, Og's bed being in Rabbah "to this day," and the judge Jair.

> Formerly the Emim lived there, a very numerous people and tall as the Anakim. Like the Anakim they are also counted as Rephaim, but the Moabites call them Emim. Previously the Horites also lived in Seir, but the people of Esau dispossessed them and destroyed them from before them and settled in their place, as Israel did to the land of their possession, which Yahweh gave to them. (Deut 2:10–12)

> It is also counted as a land of Rephaim. Rephaim formerly lived there, but the Ammonites call them Zamzummim. They are a very numerous people and tall as the Anakim. However, Yahweh destroyed them before the Ammonites, and they dispossessed them and settled in their place, as he did for the people of Esau, who live in Seir, when he destroyed the Horites before them and they dispossessed them and settled in their place even to this day. As for the Avvim, who lived in villages as far as Gaza—the Caphtorim [i.e., Philistines], who came from Caphtor, destroyed them and settled in their place. (Deut 2:20–23; cf. Jer 47:4; Amos 9:7)

Only King Og of Bashan was left from the Rephaim. His bed was made of iron and was more than thirteen feet long and six feet wide. It is still in the Ammonite city of Rabbah. (Deut 3:11)

All that portion of Bashan is called the land of Rephaim. Jair the Manassite took the entire region of Argob, that is, Bashan, as far as the border of the Geshurites and the Maacathites. He called the villages after himself, Havvoth-jair, as it is to this day. (Deut 3:13; cf. Judg 10:4)

In addition to these notices, it appears as if a later scribe updated place names throughout the Pentateuch. This includes:

Dan (Gen 14:14; Deut 34:1)—This city was called Laish until the tribe of Dan conquered and renamed it (Judg 18:29).

Hebron (Gen 13:18; 23:19; 37:14; Num 13:22)—It is not known when this city, originally called Kiriath Arba (Gen 23:2; 37:27, cf. Josh 14:15; Judg 1:10), was renamed. It was rebuilt in the nineteenth year of Rameses XI (c. 1087; i.e., during the latter part of the period of Israel's judges). So, perhaps, this was the date when it was given a new name. This would also mean that the last words in Num 13:22 are also a post-Mosaic scribal updating ("Now Hebron was rebuilt seven years before Zoan in Egypt").

Hormah (Num 14:45; 21:3; Deut 1:44)—This city was called Zephah until the tribes of Judah and Simeon conquered it (Judg 1:17).

Ramesses (Gen 47:11; Exod 1:11; 12:37; Num 33:3, 5)—This city and the surrounding region were not known by this name before the reign of Rameses II (1279–1213 BC). Rameses rebuilt the city of Avaris and renamed it Pi-Ramesses, making it his capital. The region is normally called *Goshen* in the Pentateuch (e.g., Gen 45:10; 48:28; 47:1; Exod 8:22; 9:26).

One other possible place name that could be included is Bethel, which was called Luz before Jacob renamed it (Gen 28:19). However, it is called Bethel twice before Jacob's day (Gen 12:8; 13:3). It is possible that Moses called it Bethel proleptically in these earlier passages,

assigning an earlier date

since by his day Israel had applied this name to this locale for over 400 years. On the other hand, it appears that the Canaanites continued to call the city Luz until the Joseph tribes (Ephraim and Manasseh) conquered it (Judg 1:23–26). Thus, it is possible that *Bethel* in Genesis is also a later scribal updating (cf. esp. Gen 35:6).

It is often suggested that the references to Philistines and the region of Philistia (Gen 10:14; 21:32, 34; 26:1, 8, 14–15, 18; Exod 13:17; 15:14; 23:31) are other examples of scribal updating in the Pentateuch, since many scholars identify this people with the Sea Peoples who were expelled from Egypt and settled on the coast in southwest Canaan in the twelfth century, over 300 years after Moses. However, the name *Philistine* probably means *migrant* or *foreigner* (as it is often translated in the LXX; ἀλλόφυλος). Thus, the reference to Philistines and a region called Philistia in the Pentateuch may be speaking of non-Canaanites who came from the Mediterranean to live on Canaan's coast. They may or may not have been ethnically related to the later Sea Peoples who invaded this area.

With the exception of Deut 24 and Num 12:3, which give no reliable clue as to the date when they could have been added to the Pentateuch, all of the other scribal changes appear to be no earlier than the period of the Judges. In addition, Gen 36:31 was probably written no earlier than the establishment of the Israelite monarchy under Saul (c. 1049). However, nothing requires them to be later than the reign of David or Solomon, especially since Gen 36:31, when mentioning kings ruling over "the Israelites" (בני ישראל), appears to have been written before the division of the kingdom after Solomon's death.

Scholars who accept the Bible's attribution of the Pentateuch to Moses commonly agree that these small changes in the text were made after his day. Nevertheless, they affirm that the Torah, as it has come down to us, is essentially the work of Moses.

## THE DOCUMENTARY HYPOTHESIS

### FROM EARLY DOUBTS TO THE OLDER DOCUMENTARY HYPOTHESIS

Although from antiquity the great majority of Christians and Jews accepted Moses as the author of the Pentateuch, doubts were sporadically raised. The Nazarenes, a Jewish-Christian sect concentrated in the Transjordan and mentioned by some church fathers in the fourth century, rejected Mosaic authorship. The Andalusian Islamic philosopher Ibn Hazm of Cordova, Spain (AD 994–1064) believed that Ezra was the primary author of the Pentateuch. In Reformation era Germany, Andreas Karlstadt (1480–1541) argued that if Moses did not write about his death, then he did not write any of the Pentateuch.

## First Serious Challenges to Mosaic Authorship

During the Enlightenment a number of doubts about authorship arose. In his work *Leviathan* (1651) the English deistic philosopher Thomas Hobbes held that Moses wrote only those portions of the Pentateuch that were directly attributed to him, and the rest of the Torah was written much later. Benedict Spinoza, a Jewish philosopher, published a more influential challenge to Mosaic authorship in 1670. Spinoza noted that throughout much of the Pentateuch Moses is referred to in the third person. He concluded that a few portions of the Torah came from Moses' pen, but most of it was written by Ezra. The Roman Catholic priest and philosopher Richard Simon (1638–1712) argued that the Pentateuch's several styles combined with chronological difficulties in the text (see discussion above) prove that Moses could not have written it. Instead, it was composed by a later author who relied on earlier sources.

## The Rise of Source Criticism

Influenced by the work of Spinoza and Simon, the French physician Jean Astruc published a book in 1753 that set the stage for the higher critical source criticism of the Pentateuch. Astruc examined Genesis and concluded that Moses had compiled it from earlier sources. Three observations made by Astruc would prove pivotal in later discussions of the Pentateuch's origin. First, he noted that certain events are recorded more than once (e.g., the creation in Gen 1:1–2:3 and then again in Gen 2:4–25, and the two supposedly interwoven flood accounts in Gen 6:9–9:17). Second, he saw that God was most often referred to either as *Elohim* (God in English translations) or *Yahweh* (LORD in English translations). Finally, he noted that some events are reported in the Pentateuch out of chronological order, placed earlier in the text than one would expect.

Astruc divided Genesis into four columns, labeled A through D. In column A he listed passages where *Elohim* was used. Column B contained passages that mentioned *Yahweh*. Column C had passages that repeated events from either column A or B but did not use a divine designation. The final column contained texts that related history foreign to that of the Israelites. Astruc theorized that Moses had originally placed these four columns side-by-side, but a later copyist mistakenly combined them into a continuous narrative, creating the current text of Genesis.

In 1780–83, in a three-volume work on the OT, Johann Gottfried Eichhorn apportioned Genesis and the beginning of Exodus into two sources: the J source or Yahwist (*Jahwist* in German) and the E source or Elohist. He suggested Leviticus could also be divided between these two. Eichhorn further separated the flood account into two sources and held that, in addition to their differing on the use of divine epithets, they also could be distinguished by characteristic words and phrases. This introduced the strategy of using literary style to locate sources behind the text of Genesis. Initially Eichhorn held that Moses edited these sources, but in later editions he ruled out Mosaic authorship altogether.

In 1798 Karl David Ilgen published a work suggesting that Genesis was composed from seventeen different source documents. These seventeen, however, derived from only three authors: a first Elohist, a second Elohist, and the Yahwist. Ilgen was the first scholar to propose that there was more than one source underlying the Pentateuch that used Elohim to refer to God. However, this concept would lie dormant for another five decades until it was advocated again by Heinrich Ewald and Hermann Hupfeld (see below).

The position advocated with variations by Astruc, Eichhorn, and Ilgen came to be known as the *Older Documentary Hypothesis.* It was a theory confined to examining Genesis and the initial chapters of Exodus and said little about the origin of the rest of the Pentateuch. However, it laid the foundation for later source criticism and introduced heavy reliance on two criteria for determining sources that lay behind the text of the Torah: the presence of different divine names in Genesis, and the recognition of supposedly duplicate accounts of the same events.

## THE FRAGMENTARY HYPOTHESIS

While the Older Documentary Hypothesis was reaching its zenith, another school of thought was taking root and led to what became known as the Fragmentary Hypothesis. No longer content to look for sources behind Genesis alone, scholars expanded their search to include the entire Pentateuch. The Torah's sources were thought to be preserved in incomplete and disconnected form—mere fragments strung together like beads on a string.

An early proponent of this approach was the Scottish Roman Catholic theologian Alexander Geddes. During the last decade of the eighteenth century he argued that the Pentateuch was compiled during Solomon's reign by a redactor (editor) from various fragments of texts. The sources came from two Israelite traditions, one that used *Elohim* to refer to God and the other that used *Yahweh*. Some of the pieces were as old as or older than Moses. In his analysis Geddes included the book of Joshua and argued that with the five books of the Pentateuch it formed a "Hexateuch."

In 1802 Johann Severin Vater further developed the Fragmentary Hypothesis. According to Vater, the book of Deuteronomy formed the nucleus around which the Pentateuch coalesced. He introduced the concept that part of Deuteronomy was the "Book of the Torah" discovered in the temple in Josiah's day (2 Kgs 22). This conjecture would become a pivotal part of the later Documentary Hypothesis.

The Fragmentary Hypothesis was at least partially supported by Wilhelm Marin Lebrecht DeWette in his 1805 doctoral thesis. DeWette argued that the entire book of Deuteronomy was the scroll discovered in the temple by the high priest Hilkiah. It had been written by the command of King Josiah to support his program of centralizing worship in Jerusalem. With DeWette's work, a third major source was now part of the discussion of the origin of the Pentateuch: D or the Deuteronomist.

In 1807 DeWette rejected the fragmentary approach to Genesis and the early chapters of Exodus. Instead, he argued that this portion of the Pentateuch came mainly from the Elohist with supplemental material from a Yahwist. The rest of the Pentateuch (except Deuteronomy), however, was compiled from fragmentary texts. Eventually DeWette would reject the Fragmentary Hypothesis altogether.

## THE SUPPLEMENTARY HYPOTHESIS

After a couple of decades, scholars became dissatisfied with the Fragmentary Hypothesis and turned their speculations in another direction, asserting that the Pentateuch, or the Hexateuch, was formed from a main document augmented by additions from other sources. This became known as the Supplementary Hypothesis.

The first major work to propose this supplementary theory was published in 1823 by Heinrich Ewald. Arguing against DeWette's fragmentary approach, Ewald asserted that the significant literary unity evident in Genesis suggested that the Hexateuch had derived from a basic Elohist document. This E source was supplemented by a J source. In 1840 DeWette endorsed the concept of a supplemented E source.

In 1840 Ewald, in his *Geshichte des Volkes Israel bis Christ* (*History of the People of Israel until Christ*), modified his views. He declared that E, J, and D did not account for the entire Pentateuch. Ewald now believed that there were two E documents. One of these he called the Book of Origins, because it explained the origins of Israel's basic practices such as the Sabbath and circumcision. This source supposedly was written by a Levite during Solomon's reign. Ewald called the other E document the Book of Covenants. It was composed in Judah in the era of the judges. These two continuous E sources were combined by a redactor. Later this work was supplemented with J material by a Yahwistic redactor. Ewald had now combined the Supplementary Hypothesis with the Older Documentary Hypothesis.

Although the Supplementary Hypothesis did not gain many supporters, it was important for two reasons. First, it abandoned the fragmentary approach which had multiplied sources to an extreme that was unsustainable by almost any construal of the evidence. Second, it came to recognize two E sources, one of which had a Levitical origin and would eventually become the P source of the New Documentary Hypothesis.

## THE NEW DOCUMENTARY HYPOTHESIS

### First Efforts to Form a New Hypothesis

In 1853 Hermann Hupfeld returned scholarship to a purely documentary approach to the composition of Genesis. Although he

23

revived the basic outlines of the Older Documentary Hypothesis, he also incorporated the results of subsequent studies. Hupfeld theorized that there were three sources behind Genesis: E1, an older "foundation document," E2, a document that resembled J, and, of course, J. E1 lay behind many of the earlier chapters of Genesis and was priestly in origin. Later critical scholars would call it P.

The next year Eduard Riehm revived DeWette's view that Deuteronomy was composed independently from the rest of the Pentateuch. His suggestion quickly gained widespread approval. When combined with Hupfeld's theory and extended to the entire Torah, the result was the New Documentary Hypothesis. It held that the Pentateuch came from four sources combined by a redactor. The order of the sources was: First Elohist (P); Second Elohist (E); Yahwist (J); Deuteronomist (D). Although the basic outlines of the Documentary Hypothesis were now in place, scholars continued to debate the order of the four basic sources.

## The Graf-Wellhausen Hypothesis

While DeWette and Ewald had been refining the Supplementary Hypothesis, an important study on biblical theology was published in Berlin by Wilhelm Vatke. Though this work would not play an important role in the debate over the origin of the Pentateuch for some decades, it would eventually prove critical in the coalescence of the theory in the work of Graf and Wellhausen.

Vatke adopted the philosophical system of Georg Wilhelm Friedrich Hegel. Hegel posited that history developed in stages which he called thesis, antithesis, and synthesis. An original prevailing worldview is called the thesis. Eventually that worldview is challenged by an alternate view, the antithesis. These two competing views are eventually eclipsed by a new worldview that incorporates insights from both the thesis and the antithesis. This synthesis becomes the new thesis, and the process continually repeats itself.

According to Hegel, religion developed in line with this three-stage process. During the first period religion is in a natural phase in which God and nature are equated (thesis). A second phase follows during which God is regarded as a personal spirit (antithesis). In the third phase God is perceived to be an infinite spirit (synthesis). Vatke arranged texts from the OT into this scheme. Judges and the early monarchy were the first phase, the thesis. This was followed by the prophets and the later monarchy (antithesis). Finally came the post-exilic period (synthesis). According to Vatke, the Pentateuch fit into the third stage, since in it Israel's legislation was institutionalized. *It was the product of the Israelite state, not the basis for it.* Although considered radical in the early nineteenth century when they were first proposed, Vatke's ideas would have a profound impact later on Wellhausen.

In 1866 Heinrich Graf endorsed DeWette's view that Deuteronomy was composed in Josiah's time. In addition, following the lead of his teacher, Eduard Reuss, Graf argued that E was the latest rather than the earliest of the four documents that lay behind the Pentateuch. Moreover, the P material was later than D, and the references to the tabernacle in P were fictional. The tabernacle had never existed, but its description in the Pentateuch was based upon the post-exilic temple in Jerusalem.

Graf's contemporary, the Dutch scholar Abraham Kuenen, provided the most convincing argument for the unity and lateness of P. In addition, Kuenen asserted that J was older than E. His defense of the order J then E has prevailed to this day among critical scholars.

With the work of Hupfeld, Graf, and Kuenen the stage was set for Wellhausen, who began publishing his theory in a series of articles in 1876 and 1877. Eventually these resulted in his book *Prolegomena to the History of Israel,* which went through six editions. Wellhausen's studies crystallized the Documentary Hypothesis into its classic form with the order of the documents being J, E, D, and P. His work was heavily influenced by Vatke's Hegelian approach which appeared to go hand-in-hand with the evolutionary model of Charles Darwin as propounded in his *Origin of the Species* (1859). Wellhausen's theory that Israelite religion evolved from naturalistic animism to advanced monotheism met with almost immediate adoption by all critical scholars, and by 1900 had become the standard model for explaining the origins of the Pentateuch.

## The Classic Form of the Documentary Hypothesis

Wellhausen proposed that Moses had created Israel from loosely related tribes by forming them into a community with common interests. Moses also gave them a common religion centered on a national deity. Wellhausen further postulated that Israelite religion developed into a more complex form as the Israelites adopted religious practices from the Canaanites. Finally, the Israelites transformed their simple religion into strict monotheism. This, Wellhausen said, was the work of the prophets, especially Amos. The prophetic conception of monotheism led to the centralization of religion and worship in Jerusalem and, ultimately, to the construction of the temple.

The Pentateuch developed along parallel lines according to Wellhausen. Initially, various groups that came to be part of Israel had their own stories about the Patriarchs and Moses. These early oral and written sources were used first by the Yahwist. The Yahwist produced much of the material in Gen 2 to Num 24. He compiled the traditions of the southern tribe of Judah sometime between 950 and 850 BC. The Yahwist emphasized God's nearness to mankind, using anthropomorphic language (i.e., God is described in human terms; he has eyes, ears, can see, etc.). Being from Judah, the Yahwist recorded his version of Israel's ancient history to support David's dynasty. In addition, the Yahwist calls the mountain of God "Sinai."

A century or two after the Yahwist, a second writer recorded Israel's ancient history by placing in writing another version of Israelite oral tradition from the perspective of the northern tribes of Israel. Between 750 and 700 BC the Elohist produced his own compilation of the stories in Gen 2 to Num 24. Because he was from the northern tribes, he stressed stories that took place at the northern shrines in Bethel and Shechem as well as stories that highlighted the tribes that came from Joseph—Ephraim and Manasseh. The Elohist supposedly emphasized prophetic revelation, used refined speech about God, and portrayed him as speaking to people in dreams. The Elohist called the mountain of God "Horeb."

About a century after the E document was written, a redactor wove these two sources together to form JE. Many critical scholars admit that this person was so successful that in some passages in the Pentateuch it is impossible to determine whether a passage originally came from J or E.

In the early seventh century, shortly before the time of Josiah (641–609 BC), the Deuteronomist began to write his view of Israelite traditions and law into a document that became the bulk of Deuteronomy. This author stressed worship at a central shrine (i.e., the temple in Jerusalem). He also had a prosaic, preachy style due to his heavy moralism communicated through long sermons. He emphasized that one should serve God from a heart filled with love. The Deuteronomist also asserted that God would deal with Israel through blessings for those who believe and curses for those who fail to believe. (Later scholars would call this style "Deuteronomistic" and use it to describe the style of other portions of the OT, such as Judges–Kings and particularly Jeremiah.) Wellhausen argued the now well-established conjecture of DeWette that when the Torah was discovered in the temple in the days of King Josiah (2 Kgs 22), it was not the entire Pentateuch but only D that was found, since it had been recently written and hidden in the temple archives.

During the Babylonian exile, about 550 BC, Israel's priests began to write down their view of the origin of Israel's religion, especially as it pertained to priestly duties. Since the people in the captivity were from Judah, these priests stressed worship life from Judah's viewpoint. They emphasized approaching God only through proper worship, used majestic language, and were especially concerned about the details of genealogies, covenants, holy days, sacrifices, and ceremonies. This resulted in the Priestly document P. Ezra was the main compiler and editor of the legal and ceremonial material in P, but Ezekiel was the author of the "Holiness Code" (Lev 17–26). According to Wellhausen, P is primarily to be found in Leviticus. However, Gen 1 is also said to be the work of the priestly writers.

Eventually someone combined P with JE to form the continuous narrative we know today as Genesis, Exodus, Leviticus, and Numbers. In the fifth century BC, when P was combined with JE, Deuteronomy was added to this collection to complete the Pentateuch. Wellhausen believed that between 400 and 200 BC additional minor changes were made, and by the beginning of the second century BC the Pentateuch was complete.

## EXPLORING THE ORIGIN OF THE DOCUMENTS THAT COMPRISE THE PENTATEUCH

### Form Criticism

Once the Documentary Hypothesis became the standard explanation of the Pentateuch's origin, critical scholars turned their attention to the pre-literary stages of its development. They sought to get behind the supposed written source documents to the oral traditions they assumed preceded literary production.

The pioneering work in this investigation was done by Gunkel in the early years of the twentieth century. He called this *Gattung-forschung* (research concerning literary types) or *Literaturgeschichte* (history of literature), but it has become known as form criticism (*Formgeschichte*). Gunkel believed that in the text of Genesis it is possible to observe different types or forms that represent basic oral accounts that were incorporated into the documents that formed the Pentateuch. Among these are:

Etiological stories—how a custom or institution became established

Etymological stories—how a person or place received its name

Cultic legends—explanation of the origin of a sanctuary

Ethnological legends—explanation of the relationships between ethnic groups

Gunkel noted the episodic nature of many of the stories in Genesis and argued that these accounts, which he called *Sagen* (legends or fables), were collected to form the documents that in turn were woven together to make the Pentateuch. *Sagen* must have been transmitted orally according to Gunkel. He also distinguished between *Sagen* and history. *Sagen* were poetic, recounted supernatural events, and focused on the individual, rather than on national history.

Gunkel also attempted to date individual *Sagen*. He assumed that the more primitive a society was, the less developed was its sense of morals, ethics, and spirituality. Thus, a *Sage* that mixed religious and profane elements was thought to be older than one that contained only religious elements.

Gunkel's method was developed by other German scholars, most notably Alt. In his study he attempted to explain the evolution of Israelite religion up to the time of the monarchy. In addition, Alt distinguished between two types of laws: casuistic (i.e., beginning, "if a person . . . ") and apodictic (i.e., beginning, "you shall [not] . . . ").

## Tradition Criticism

Closely related to form criticism is a method that has been called *tradition criticism* or *tradition history* (*Überlieferungsgeschichte* or *Traditionsgeschichte*). This approach also traces its beginning to the work of Gunkel. In his study of Genesis, he proposed that individual *Sagen* were collected to form cycles of legends (*Sagenkränze*). According to Gunkel, it was possible to discern such cycles in Genesis, such as an Abraham-Lot cycle (Gen 12–19), a Jacob-Esau cycle (Gen 25:19–28:22; 32:1–33:20), a Jacob-Laban cycle (Gen 29–31), and a Joseph cycle (Gen 37–50). Since he believed the Joseph cycle in Gen 37–50 was less episodic, he labeled it a *novella.*

Gunkel's student, von Rad, established tradition criticism as an important interpretive method. Von Rad theorized that J was composed via an outline of Israel's history contained in early creeds that were used in cultic celebrations (e.g., Deut 6:20–24; 26:5–9; Josh 24:2–13). These creeds were supposedly first employed when celebrating the Festival of Weeks at Gilgal during Israel's early years in Canaan. They contained three main topics: the Aramean origin of the patriarchs, the exodus from Egypt, and the possession of the land. Von Rad also proposed that the tradition producing both the theophany and covenant at Mount Sinai (Exod 19–24) and the book of Deuteronomy were derived from an autumn festival held at Shechem. These two traditions were combined to form J. In addition, von Rad dated J earlier than Wellhausen had. It came from David's time in the later part of the tenth century and was intended to unify the nation under Davidic rule.

Von Rad's method was further developed by Noth. Since J and E were supposed to be parallel traditions from Judah and Israel, Noth thought that they must have derived from a common tradition or *Grundlage* (G; "foundation"). Whenever J and E appear to be similar, it should be possible to trace their origins to G. According to Noth there were five major themes in J (in contrast to von Rad's three): the exodus from Egypt, guidance to the land, the promise to the patriarchs, provision in the wilderness, and revelation at Mount Sinai. These five traditions were combined in an early stage of Israel's history to form J when the twelve tribes became federated in an *amphictyony*, a term used to describe a cultic association of twelve tribes in ancient Greece or Italy that worshiped at a central shrine. Each tribe was supposed to maintain the shrine for one month every year.

Noth's method assumes that most of the Pentateuch originally circulated orally. It also presupposes that the Documentary Hypothesis was a correct reconstruction of the literary history of the

Pentateuch. In addition, Noth assumed that shorter units of tradition were older, and longer ones were younger. Thus, Gen 24, a rather long unit, must be late. Finally, Noth assumed that during the transmission of tradition the main characters were changed, with lesser-known figures being replaced by better-known ones. Thus, Moses, who appears to be the main character in Exodus to Deuteronomy, has actually replaced other original characters. He did not actually lead Israel out of Egypt. The elders of Israel—not Moses—originally confronted Pharaoh in Egypt. Likewise, according to the original tradition behind the text, at Mount Sinai God spoke only to the elders.

## Problems with Form and Tradition Criticism

This brief discussion of these two methods should serve to point out their major drawback: both are highly speculative. Scholars propose a theoretical origin for the supposed documents that make up the Pentateuch, but like the product of a spider spinning a web, the result is mostly air between the very thin cords that hold the theory together.

There are other problems, however. Critics employing these methods are often quick to offer rationalizations for features of texts that they cannot explain by other means. This raises the question about whether another explanation, which they refuse to consider, might better account for these features without atomizing the text or resorting to highly speculative historical conjectures about its development. Moreover, the assumptions supporting the principles used to date the traditions are suspect. For instance, many scholars have pointed out that length is not a reliable indicator of a text's age.

### CRITICISM OF THE DOCUMENTARY HYPOTHESIS

Despite its popularity and influence, source criticism of the Pentateuch has consistently been opposed by conservative scholars. During the second half of the nineteenth century in Germany, E. W. Hengstenberg and his student C. F. Keil defended the Mosaic authorship of the Pentateuch. In England the prominent archaeologist A. H. Sayce, who had rejected his earlier endorsement of source criticism, pointed out several fallacies in the Documentary Hypothesis. In the United States, William Henry Green of Princeton Theological Seminary noted that Wellhausen's methodology was inconsistent and at times contradictory. In addition, he also demonstrated that the Documentary Hypothesis did not fully explain the biblical data.

## Flaws of the Documentary Hypothesis

One of the major concerns about the Documentary Hypothesis is its subjective nature of identifying the four source documents. Despite the declaration of possessing the "assured results of higher criticism," none of the alleged documents that make up the Pentateuch have ever been found. Moreover, critical scholars have not been able to agree among themselves as to the content of each document. One scholar may assign a particular verse to E while another scholar assigns it to P. Even more telling is the continued division of the four "basic" documents into other sources. As we have seen, Noth proposed a G document that lay behind both J and E. Von Rad divided P into P(a) and P(b). In the early 1920s, the German scholar Otto Eissfeldt claimed to have isolated an L (Lay Source) document within J that preserved the nomadic ideals of the Rechabites (cf. Jer 35). In 1927 the American Jewish scholar Julius Morgenstern claimed to have identified a K (Kenite) document that influenced the reforms of Judah's king Asa at the beginning of the ninth century BC. In 1941 Harvard Professor Robert Pfeiffer proposed the recognition of an S (Mount Seir) document drawn from texts that were earlier assigned to J and E in Gen 1–38.

Conservative scholars have argued that the Documentary Hypothesis's view of the growth of the Pentateuch has no parallel in ancient Near Eastern literature. To counter this, Tigay demonstrated that the Gilgamesh Epic, a poem from ancient Mesopotamia, was compiled from earlier independently-circulated Sumerian stories until it reached its final form in the neo-Assyrian period (1300–1000 BC). However, Tigay's analysis does not reveal a process similar to the weaving together of various strands (J, E, D, and P) as in the Documentary Hypothesis. It simply shows how independent stories were linked together in a serial fashion. At best, Tigay has provided support for form-critical analyses that posit a linking together of stories to produce the theoretical J or E documents.

Another weakness of the Documentary Hypothesis is its reliance upon the use of vocabulary to distinguish various documents. The most obvious use of this criterion is the division of sources based on the divine epithets *Yahweh* and *Elohim*. However, source critics also developed extensive lists of words and phrases for each of the four primary source documents. Driver supplies an extensive and often-used catalogue in his OT introduction.

There are numerous problems with using vocabulary in this manner. For instance, two passages from different source documents that are addressing the same subject may use similar vocabulary because of their content. Source critics may view two words as synonyms and assign them to different traditions. Yet, two words are seldom exactly synonymous, and their use may be determined by the different nuances in their denotations or connotations rather than by different authorship. Finally, even words or phrases that are assigned to one document may appear frequently in another. The phrase "land of Canaan" is usually said to be characteristic of P (e.g., Gen 12:5; 17:8). Even so, it appears frequently in passages said to derive from both J and E (e.g., Gen 42: 5, 7, 13, 29, 32 [all J]; 44:8 [E]).

In the end, differentiation of the source documents by vocabulary results in a circular argument. A word may be assigned to a particular source. If that word occurs in a text assigned to a different source for other reasons, source critics will often claim that it is an intrusion into the text rather than questioning their assignment of the vocabulary item in question. Instead, one probably ought to conclude that the term in question should not be used for source analysis.

Many scholars have noted that the use of divine names has an additional weakness—in ancient Near Eastern literature it is common for a deity to be referenced by more than one name. This phenomenon occurs in both Egyptian and Mesopotamian texts. However, no one suggests that these texts are compiled from interwoven source documents.

It appears more likely that the use of divine epithets in the OT is at least partially due to theme and context. It is conventional for critics to view Gen 1–2 as two creation accounts with the first assigned to P (Gen 1:1–2:3) and the second being a conflation of J and E (Gen 2:4–25). The more generic name *Elohim* is often used to emphasize God's general relationship to his creatures, which explains its use in Gen 1. God's proper name *Yahweh* highlights his covenant relationship with individuals and groups. Since Gen 2 focuses on both God's creative activity and his relationship with Adam and Eve, it is not surprising that the compound *Yahweh Elohim* is used in this chapter. Therefore, no source explanation is necessary to account for the use of divine names in these chapters.

Moreover, even critical scholars admit that later redactors may have changed the particular divine name in some cases. Gen 22:11, 14; 28:21; and 31:49 are usually assigned to E, yet all use *Yahweh*. This has been explained as an example of redactional activity. If this is the case, how can we be at all certain that the divine names are any indication of source documents behind the current text of the Pentateuch?

The identification of duplicate events, often called *doublets,* is another basic method to differentiate sources in the Documentary Hypothesis. These doublets are said to fit into two main categories: The same event may be described in two separate episodes (e.g., Abraham pretending Sarah is only his sister, Gen 12:10–20 [assigned to J]; Gen 20:1–18 [assigned to E]). On the other hand, one account may be said to have resulted from the intertwining of two distinct sources (e.g., the flood narrative, Gen 6–9).

Both of these assumptions present difficulties. For instance, the account in Gen 20:1–18 presupposes that the reader is already familiar with Gen 12:10–12. This is evident from Gen 20:2 which makes no sense unless one has already read Gen 12:11–13. A better explanation, therefore, is that the author of Genesis is relating two different but related incidents, and he wants to highlight Abraham's continued insecurity concerning Sarah and the birth of an heir (cf. Gen 15:1–3; 17:15–19, esp. 17:18).

In the case of intertwined accounts, it is often held that the story of the sale of Joseph in Gen 37 is such an example. Gen 37:28 refers to the buyers as both Ishmaelites and Midianites, indicating to source critics that two sources have been conflated. However, Kitchen has shown that *Ishmaelite* and *Midianite* are overlapping terms and refer to what is essentially the same group (cf. Judg 8:22–26). The two terms may have been used by the author for variation. Often it is textual details like this that the source critics use to divide single accounts into doublets when no such procedure is necessary. It often results in ripping apart a text into two accounts so that neither presents a coherent narrative or so that the result is two narratives without literary texture or depth.

Finally, as noted above, the Documentary Hypothesis is heavily dependent upon the Hegelian philosophy of history and Darwinian notions of evolution. Contemporary historians no longer employ Hegelian historical analysis, since they acknowledge that events and the development of movements and ideas do not follow any such rigid, prescriptive pattern. Moreover, it is impossible to demonstrate that religion evolves in a Darwinian fashion from more primitive forms to more advanced forms. Theological developments are also difficult to predict. Religious groups often revive older movements in new guises or acquire new theological outlooks akin to those discarded long ago. These observations undercut the conceptual and theoretical foundation upon which the Documentary Hypothesis was constructed.

## MORE RECENT HIGHER CRITICAL CHALLENGES TO THE DOCUMENTARY HYPOTHESIS

From the end of the nineteenth century through the first three quarters of the twentieth century there was little challenge to the Documentary Hypothesis from critical scholars, although conservative scholars continued to object to its assumptions, methods, and conclusions. Higher Critical studies during this era discussed the extent and content of the four source documents. Some scholars challenged whether E ever existed as an independent document. Cross argued that P was not a document but the work of a redactor who expanded JE. Nevertheless, the basic conclusions of the Documentary Hypothesis about the sources and growth of the Pentateuch were assumed. This began to change at the end of the twentieth century with some critical scholars themselves objecting to the theory.

### F. V. WINNETT AND HIS STUDENTS

An early attempt at a different source analysis was offered by Winnett in 1949. He saw only three sources in the Pentateuch: J (a Mosaic tradition from the Northern Kingdom contained in Exodus and Numbers), P, and D. He divided Genesis into three sections: the primeval history (Gen 1–11), the patriarchal narratives (Gen 12–36), and the Joseph cycle (Gen 37–50). Winnett dated J to the early post-exilic period. It was supplemented by an Elohistic writer to create a more favorable impression of Abraham. He also proposed a rather complicated history of Genesis with additional E and J supplements.

The most significant new source analysis came from Van Seters, a student of Winnett. In his study of the wife/sister incidents in Gen 12, 20, and 26, he concluded that there were three stages in the development of the Abraham cycle, with the last and most significant being the Yahwist (J), whose work dated to the exilic period. The work of this Yahwist, however, is not the same as the J source of the Documentary Hypothesis. Instead, it is roughly equivalent to E and to the texts traditionally assigned to the redactor who combined J and E. Van Seters rejects the existence of pre-exilic sources for the Tetrateuch (Genesis–Numbers), and he holds that the Yahwist created it mostly from his imagination. Two main arguments are advanced by Van Seters in defense of his position: non-priestly texts show signs of dependence on Deuteronomistic and priestly traditions; the historiographical form of the non-priestly portions of the Pentateuch exhibit characteristics of sixth and fifth century BC historiographical writings around the Mediterranean, especially the works of the early Greek historians. In later studies Van Seters argues that the non-priestly Pentateuch is essentially a unified work and that the Pentateuch as a whole postdates all the Deuteronomistic (i.e., Joshua—Kings) and prophetic books of the OT.

## RHETORICAL CRITICISM OR LITERARY CRITICISM

In 1969 James Muilenburg published an article entitled "Form Criticism and Beyond." In it he proposed a new approach that he called *rhetorical criticism.* Form criticism, in Muilenburg's view, does not pay enough attention to the final form of the text, but looks for building blocks that make up the text. Thus, form criticism overlooks or ignores the structural patterns in a pericope. On the other hand, rhetorical criticism attempts to appreciate interrelationships of various units and an author's use of repetition and other artistic devices. Because scholars who engage in rhetorical criticism are searching for how a text holds together rather than for ways in which a text can be broken apart into supposed sources, they tend to see evidence that argues against the results of source criticism.

In 1975 Fokkelman published a literary analysis of a number of passages in Genesis. He pointed out the artistry evident in these passages when one examined them holistically. For instance, Fokkelman studied the Tower of Babel account (Gen 11:1–9) and demonstrated that it was skillfully constructed in an hourglass pattern.

In 1981 Alter pointed out the exquisite artistry found in the Joseph accounts in Gen 37–50. For instance, the repetition of the imperative verb *recognize* at Gen 37:32 and Gen 38:25 (הכר־נא) ties these two chapters together although they appear at first glance to be two unrelated narratives (in Gen 37 Joseph is sold into slavery, while in Gen 38 Judah sires Perez and Zerah by his daughter-in-law Tamar). In fact, the verbal root *recognize* plays an important role again in Gen 42 when Joseph encounters his brothers for the first time in Egypt (Gen 42:7, 8). In another case the verbal root *guarantee* or *pledge* (ערב) plays a pivotal role in Judah's character development from being selfish to selfless (Gen 38:18; 43:9).

Other texts throughout the Pentateuch offer similar glimpses of authorial deftness. The plagues in Egypt are skillfully narrated and arranged in three groups of three plagues before the final climactic one, the death of the firstborn sons (Exod 7:9–12:30).

The practitioners of rhetorical criticism (sometimes called *literary criticism* since it is similar to the critical reading of any kind of literature) have differing views of their work in relationship to the Documentary Hypothesis. Fokkelman believes that his analysis undermines the Graf-Wellhausen theory. In contrast, Alter is indifferent or ambivalent about source criticism and its findings; he is content simply to point out the literary artistry of the final form of the text no matter how it came into being.

Rhetorical criticism calls into question the source analysis of the Documentary Hypothesis. How did a later redactor or series of redactors pull together disparate sources into such skillfully written narratives? Even if later editors worked with earlier sources, after they applied their art of recounting the stories, how can anyone be certain that the editors have not thereby obscured sources so much that any recovery of them is doubtful? Is positing, instead, that these texts are the product of a single author a more likely explanation for their origin? Is this not more probable than proposing a complicated growth of the text through work of multiple redactors working with contrasting source materials?

Barton has called this "the trick of the disappearing redactor."

The trick is simply this. The more impressive the critic makes the redactor's work appear, the more he succeeds in showing that the redactor has, by subtle and delicate artistry, produced a simple and coherent text out of the diverse materials before him; the more also he reduces the evidence on which the existence of those sources was established in the first place. No conjuror is required for this trick: the redaction critic himself causes his protégé to disappear. . . . Thus, if redaction criticism plays its hand too confidently, we end up with a piece of writing so coherent that no division into sources is warranted any longer.[1]

## R. RENDTORFF AND E. BLUM

Beginning in 1969 in Germany, where much of the work on the Documentary Hypothesis was accomplished, Rendtorff began to challenge it. He perceived an inherent conflict between the Graf-Wellhausen theory and later developments in form and tradition criticism. Rendtorff argued that there were no continuous J or E documents within Genesis. Instead, since the book was made up of larger independent units, such as the Jacob-Esau cycle (Gen 25:19–28:22; 32:1–33:20) or the Joseph account (Gen 37–50), each had its own author.

In further writings, Rendtorff proposed abandoning the Graf-Wellhausen theory altogether, since he believed it was not the best way of explaining the composition of the Pentateuch. His attack had five major components: First, he noted considerable disagreement among scholars as to the exact formulation of the Documentary Hypothesis. These, he believed, called into question the entire approach. Second, he observed that tradition-critical studies suggested that the Pentateuch was made up of larger units, which he believed were independently authored and not woven together from sources such as J, E, or P (e.g., patriarchal narratives in Genesis; the Sinai account in Exodus, Israel's wanderings in the wilderness in Numbers). Third, Rendtorff noticed that it is impossible to reconstruct continuous, coherent narratives from material assigned to J or P. Fourth, he exposed the vocabulary fallacy of the Documentary Hypothesis's literary criteria, remarking that words and expressions normally understood to be characteristic of one source are often found in passages that are assigned to other sources. Finally, he noted that disparate types of material were often allocated to one source (e.g., P

---

[1] John Barton, *Reading the Old Testament: Method in Biblical Study* (2nd ed.; London: Darton, Longman & Todd, 1996), 57.

is said to have contained narratives, genealogies, and laws). Rendtorff doubted whether a single coherent source document could contain such an assortment of genres.

Rentdorff's student, Blum, further developed his teacher's rejection of J and E. He discarded the concept of parallel source documents in favor of a supplementary theory that traces the growth of the Pentateuch from the early days of Israel under Jeroboam I (931–910 BC) to the post-exilic period.

### R. N. WHYBRAY

Perhaps one of the most trenchant evaluations of the Documentary Hypothesis came from Whybray. He examined the underlying assumptions and methods of the Graf-Wellhausen theory and offered a number of pointed criticisms of it. Whybray noted that the Documentary Hypothesis assumes a consistency of repetitions that is unparalleled in ancient literature. That is J, E, and P can supposedly be distinguished because they avoid contradictions—they always appear to the critic to be internally consistent. Perceived inconsistencies indicate different sources. The Graf-Wellhausen theory ignores or discounts the possibility that these duplicates may occur in one document as part of the literary scheme of the author. For instance, Abraham's deception about Sarah must come from two different sources according to the critics.

Using an argument long employed by more conservative scholars, Whybray complained that the fracturing of the Pentateuch into sources often destroys its literary artistry and produces texts that are hopelessly pedestrian. He noted that vocabulary differences may not be due to source differences but to variations due to subject matter, desire to avoid repetition, or even unconscious deviation common to human communication. Finally, he criticized the supposed four source texts of the Documentary Hypothesis as having no single style or consistent theology despite the claims of such by its supporters.

## RECENT DEFENDERS
## OF THE DOCUMENTARY HYPOTHESIS

Although there have been attacks on the Documentary Hypothesis from critical scholars for over a quarter century, the theory is not without its many defenders. In Germany some scholars have bolstered it by advocating some form of the classic Wellhausen presentation with minor adjustments. Others have worked with the model but have narrowed the scope of the J source and relegated E to a redactional layer rather than a distinct source. In Australia, Anthony Campbell has risen to the defense by maintaining Noth's view of the Documentary Hypothesis. In the United States, Friedman offered a justification of the theory that proposed P was earlier than D, transforming the order of the four basic sources to JEPD. He also listed every passage in the Pentateuch according to its presumed source. For Genesis through Numbers he classified them as J, E, P, and R (redactor). For Deuteronomy he classified the sources as First Deuteronomist, Second Deuteronomist, E (a few verses in Deut 31, 33, and 34), P (only Deut 34:7–9), and "other," most notably the "Law Code" in Deut 12:1–26:15.

Most recently, Baden has taken up the defense of the Documentary Hypothesis as the most likely explanation for the origin of the Pentateuch. He argues that J and E were separate sources, since Deuteronomy quotes each separately. They were not redacted into one work until the final editing of the Pentateuch. Moreover, he has challenged the insights of literary criticism by claiming that it is not enough to demonstrate that the final text displayed literary artistry in order to disprove the Documentary Hypothesis. One must also show that the proposed underlying sources could not have displayed the same type artistry. Instead, Baden believes that literary criticism and classic source criticism can be viewed as parallel disciplines.

## CONCLUSION

To this day there remains a divide between conservative Christian and Jewish scholars and their higher critical counterparts as to the origins of the Pentateuch. The traditional view that Moses was the author of Genesis–Deuteronomy is still maintained and defended. Those who hold this position believe that the witness of the Pentateuch, the rest of the OT, the NT, and Jesus himself is determinative.

The higher critical search for the origin of the Pentateuch that occupied scholars in Europe for two centuries and resulted in the Documentary Hypothesis has a checkered history. Even so, it has become the dominant theory in critical scholarship. This happened because of the convergence of a number of factors: the popularity of Hegelian philosophy during the latter part of the nineteenth century, the cultural acceptance of Darwinian-like evolutionary approaches to areas beyond biology, and the opinion of many scholars that there are contradictions and inconsistencies in the Pentateuch that cannot be explained if it originated from one author. Each of these assumptions is problematic. Hegel's philosophy has been proven false. Darwinian theories often cannot account for human historical interactions that do not lead inexorably to new and better developments. What critical scholars see as contradictions and inconsistencies, conservative scholars claim are misreadings of the text or mishandlings of its literary features. Where conservatives believe the text can be harmonized, critics assert that the text is being unnecessarily and inappropriately aligned in order to obscure its difficulties.

The majority of critical scholars continue to accept some form of the Documentary Hypothesis despite a vocal minority within their ranks that has argued against it. However, these detractors among the critics are not advocating a return to a Mosaic Torah. Instead, they propose new theories to account for the Pentateuch's completion in the post-exilic era.

The main problems with the Documentary Hypothesis pointed out for over a century by conservative scholars have not been overcome. There is no firm consensus on the exact identification of the sources or on their content or nature. The methods used to isolate sources— vocabulary, content, duplicates, and the like—are problematic, and even some higher critical scholars have voiced these objections. The supposed source documents—J, E, D, and P—remain theoretical with no historical evidence to confirm that they actually existed. Most important, the Documentary Hypothesis calls into doubt the veracity of the scriptural witness and the words of Christ himself: "If you believed Moses, you would believe me, for he wrote about me" (John 5:46).

## SELECT BIBLIOGRAPHY

Alt, Albrecht. "The God of the Fathers." In *Essays on Old Testament History and Religion.* Oxford: Blackwell, 1966. Translation of *Der Gott der Väter.* Stuttgart: W. Kohlhammer, 1929.

————. "The Origin of Israelite Law." In *Essays on Old Testament History and Religion.* Oxford: Blackwell, 1966. Translation of *Die Ursprünge des israelitischen Recht.* Leipzig: S. Hirzel, 1934.

Alter, Robert. *The Art of Biblical Narrative.* New York: Basic Books, 1981.

Baden, Joel. *J, E, and the Redaction of the Pentateuch.* Forschungen zum Alten Testament 78. Tübingen: Mohr Siebeck, 2009.

———. "The Tower of Babel: A Case Study in the Competing Methods of Historical and Modern Literary Criticism." *Journal of Biblical Literature* 128 (2009): 209–24.

———. *The Composition of the Pentateuch: Renewing the Documentary Hypothesis.* The Anchor Yale Bible Reference Library. New Haven: Yale, 2012.

Barton, John. *Reading the Old Testament: Method in Biblical Study.* Revised and enlarged ed. Louisville: Westminster, 1996.

Blum, Erhard. *Die Komposition der Vätergeschichte.* Wissenschaftliche Monographien zum Alten und Neuen Testament 57. Neukirchen-Vluyn: Neukirchener, 1984.

———. *Studien zur Komposition des Pentateuch.* Beihefte zur Zeitschrift für die Alttestamentliche Wissenschaft 189. Berlin: Walter de Gruyter, 1990.

———. "Pentateuch—Hexateuch—Enneateuch? Or: How Can One Recognize a Literary Work in the Hebrew Bible?" In *Pentateuch, Hexateuch, or Enneateuch? Identifying Literary Works in Genesis through Kings.* Edited by Thomas B. Dozeman, Thomas Römer, and Konrad Schimd. Ancient Israel and Its Literature. Atlanta: Society of Biblical Literature, 2011.

Carr, David M. "Controversy and Convergence in Recent Studies of the Formation of the Pentateuch." *Religious Studies Review* 23 (1997): 22–31.

Cross, Frank Moore. "The Priestly Work." In *Canaanite Myth and Hebrew Epic.* Cambridge: Harvard University, 1973.

Driver, S. R. *An Introduction to the Literature of the Old Testament.* 9th ed. Edinburgh: T&T Clark, 1913.

Fokkelman, J. P. *Narrative Art in Genesis: Specimens of Stylistic and Structural Analysis.* Studia Semitica Neerlandica 17. Assen: Van Gorcum, 1975.

Friedman, Richard Elliott. *Who Wrote the Bible?* New York: Harper and Row, 1987.

Gunkel, Hermann. *The Legends of Genesis, the Biblical Saga and History.* New York: Schocken, 1964. Translation of *Die Urgeschichte und die Patriarchen: das erste Buch Mosis.* Göttingen: Vandenhoeck & Ruprecht, 1911 [1st ed., 1901].

———. *Genesis.* Macon: Mercer University, 1997. Translation of *Genesis: übersetz und erklärt.* 3d ed. Göttingen: Vandenhoeck & Ruprecht, 1910.

Kitchen, Kenneth. *Ancient Orient and Old Testament.* Chicago: InterVarsity, 1966.

Noth, Martin. *A History of Pentateuchal Traditions.* Englewood Cliffs, NJ: Prentice-Hall, 1972. Translation of *Überlieferungsgeschichte des Pentateuch.* Stuttgart: W. Kohlhammer, 1948.

Rendtorff, Rolf. "Traditio-Historical Method and the Documentary Hypothesis." *Proceedings of the World Congress of Jewish Studies* 5 (1969): 5–11.

———. *The Problem of the Process of Transmission in the Pentateuch.* Journal for the Study of the Old Testament Supplements 89. Sheffield: JSOT, 1990. Translation of *Das überlieferungsgeschichtliche Problem des Pentateuch.* Beihefte zur Zeitschrift für die Alttestamentliche Wissenschaft 17. Berlin: Walter de Gruyter, 1977.

———. "The 'Yahwist' as Theologian? The Dilemma of Pentateuchal Criticism." *Journal for the Study of the Old Testament* 3 (1997): 2–10.

Tigay, Jeffrey H. *Empirical Models for Biblical Criticism.* Philadelphia: University of Pennsylvania, 1985.

Van Seters, John. *Abraham in History and Tradition.* New Haven: Yale, 1975.

———. *Prologue to History: The Yahwist as Historian in Genesis.* Louisville: Westminster, 1992.

———. *The Life of Moses: The Yahwist as Historian in Exodus–Numbers.* Louisville: Westminster, 1994.

von Rad, Gerhard. "The Problem of the Hexateuch." In *The Problem of the Hexateuch and other Essays.* Edinburgh: Oliver and Boyd, 1966. Translation of *Das formgeschichte Problem des Hexateuch.*

Beiträge zur Wissenschaft vom Alten und Neuen Testament 24. Stuttgart: W. Kohlhammer, 1938.

Wellhausen, Julius. *Prolegomena to the History of Ancient Israel.* Edinburgh: Meridian, 1957. Translation of *Prolegomena zur Geschichte Israels.* 6th ed. Berlin: de Gruyter, 1927. [1st ed. 1879 under the title *Geschichte Israels I.*]

Whybray, R. N. *The Making of the Pentateuch: A Methodological Study.* Journal for the Study of the Old Testament Supplement Series 53. Sheffield: JSOT, 1987.

Winnett, Frederick V. *The Mosaic Tradition.* Toronto: Toronto University, 1949.

3

# GENESIS

Sooner or later all people become curious about their origins and the origin of the world in which they live. The book of Genesis answered those questions for Israel. The Hebrew title of this book is derived from its first word, בראשית, "in the beginning." The English title comes from the Greek designation of the book as Γενέσεως, which means *origin* or *source.* Both of these titles are apt descriptions of the book, since it tells of the beginning of the created world and the origin of the people of Israel. Most important, Genesis relates the source of God's promise of the Savior and traces this pledge from Eve through the line of Abraham down to his great-grandson Judah.

## AUTHORSHIP, COMPOSITION, AND DATE

Proponents of the Documentary Hypothesis maintain that Genesis is a product of a process that wove together three sources: J, E, and P. Most notable among the supposed P material in Genesis is Gen 1:1–2:3. This so-called "First Creation Account" is placed in opposition to Gen 2:4–25, which is said to give the J source version of creation combined with some material from E. Much of the rest of Genesis is divided between the J and E sources according to most critics. This theory holds that Genesis, as it has come down to us, is a product of a final priestly redactor during the post-exilic period. The methods used to isolate these sources and chart the growth of the book of Genesis have always been opposed by conservative scholars and, in more recent decades, have been questioned by some critical scholars. For further details see chapter 2 on the origins of the Pentateuch.

While conservative scholars continue to attribute the composition of the Pentateuch to Moses, Genesis presents the greatest challenge for connecting it with Israel's great prophet. All of the accounts in Genesis take place long before Moses, with the latest event in the book—the death of Joseph—taking place more than three centuries before Moses' birth. Moreover, no statement in the rest of the OT or in the NT explicitly connects any passage in Genesis with Moses as its author. Nevertheless, the rest of the Pentateuch presumes knowledge of the narratives in Genesis. For instance, it quotes or alludes to Genesis, assuming that the reader will understand these references as deriving from the OT's first book. Without knowledge of the specific phrasing of these references to Genesis, these allusions often would be meaningless to readers of Exodus, Leviticus, Numbers, and Deuteronomy. This is especially true of the accounts of Israel's patriarchs and God's promises to them concerning the land of Canaan and the great nation that would come from them (e.g., Exod 2:24; 6:8; 32:13; 33:1; Lev 26:42; Num 32:11; Deut 1:8; 6:10; 9:5, 27; 29:13; 30:20; 34:4). Another example is the prophecies of Balaam in Num 23–24, which reference the patriarchal promises and cannot be fully understood without knowledge of the wording used in Genesis:

### Balaam's References to the Patriarchal Promises

"Who is able to count Jacob's dust?" (Num 23:10; cf. Gen 13:16; 15:5)

"Yahweh their God is with them." (Num 23:21; cf. Gen 17:8)

"A people rise like a lioness; they rouse themselves like a lion." (Num 23:24; cf. Gen 49:9)

"He crouched; he lay down like a lion and like a lioness. Who will arouse him?" (Num 24:9; cf. Gen 49:9)

"May those blessing you be blessed and those cursing you be cursed." (Num 24:9; cf. Gen 12:3)

"A star will come from Jacob, a scepter will arise from Israel." (Num 24:17; cf. Gen 49:10)

Such references to Genesis strongly imply that it was available to those who would read the rest of the Pentateuch. Moses must have written Genesis, since he was responsible for the rest of the Torah (cf.

2 Chr 23:18; 30:16; 35:12; Ezra 3:2; 6:18; 7:6; Neh 8:1; 13:1; Mal 4:4).

The sources for Moses' knowledge of events before his time are never directly mentioned in Genesis. They may have included oral traditions, written records, or even direct revelation from God (for he also revealed the plan of the tabernacle to Moses; cf. Exod 25:9).

In 1936 Wiseman suggested that the key to uncovering the sources for Genesis lay in the Hebrew word *tôledôth* (תולדות) meaning *generations, family records,* or *descendants.* According to Wiseman, ten sections of Genesis are marked with the formula, "[and] these are the descendants of" (אלה תולדות [ו]; Gen 2:4; 6:9; 10:1; 11:10, 27; 25:12, 19; 36:1, 9; 37:2). Another begins, "this is the book of the descendants of" (זה ספר תולדת; Gen 5:1). Wiseman posited that the *tôledôth* formula represented the end of a tablet commissioned by the man whose name it contained. This corresponded to the common practice in the ancient Near East of ending a text with a note that recorded the name of the scribe who had written it and the time when the tablet was composed. Thus, according to Wiseman, the first source tablet ended at Gen 5:1 with "these are the generations (or 'family records') of Adam."

The major drawback of Wiseman's proposal is that the text that follows each of these *tôledôth* formulas more naturally belongs with the notice than the material that precedes it. Thus, at Gen 25:19, "these are the descendants of Isaac" is followed by accounts about his sons Esau and Jacob (Gen 25:20–35:29). At Gen 36:1, "these are the descendants of Esau" is followed by an account concerning Esau's descendants (Gen 36:2–8). Then at Gen 36:9, "these are the descendants of Esau, father of the Edomites in the mountains of Seir" is followed by a genealogy of Esau's descendants and a record of Edomite kings (Gen 36:10–43). For this reason and others, most scholars have rejected Wiseman's conjecture. Nevertheless, Wiseman correctly drew attention to what appears to be an organizing principle of Genesis—the *tôledôth* formula. It is a valuable literary device. Genesis has twelve sections, separated by the eleven instances of that formula, that extend from the creation account into the clearly historical patriarchal age, tying all the chapters together in one unified historical account.

## LITERARY FEATURES OF GENESIS

### NARROWING THE FOCUS

Genesis begins with all of creation and ends with the sons of Jacob in Egypt. This broad sweep of Israel's pre-history narrows its focus from the universe to the twelve patriarchs. It begins with creation, focusing on the earth (Gen 1:1–2:3). Having given this bigger picture, it constricts the reader's view to the creation of humans and their fall into sin (Gen 2:4–3:24). Next it traces one line of Adam's descendants—the sinful line of Cain (Gen 4:1–26). Once it has told the reader about this part of Adam's family, Genesis moves its attention to another son of Adam that Moses wants to spotlight: Seth and his righteous descendant Noah (Gen 5:1–6:8). This establishes a general pattern for the rest of the book—a wider view, then a subsidiary line or lines of descendants is briefly traced, and finally the emphasis is narrowed by placing the focus on the progeny to whom God will extend his favor.

### *Narrowing the Focus in Genesis*

| *Main Line* | *Subsidiary Line* |
|---|---|
| Earth (1:1–2:3) | |
| Adam (2:4–3:24) | Cain's descendants (4:1–24) |
| Adam to Noah (4:25–5:32) | Sinful humans (6:1–8) |
| Noah (6:9–9:29) | Noah's descendants (10:1–11:9) |
| Shem to Abraham (11:10–25:11) | Ishmael's descendants (25:12–18) |
| Isaac (25:19–35:29) | Esau's descendants (36:1–43) |
| Jacob and his sons (37:1–50:26) | |

### GOD'S ELECTION BY GRACE

The literary structure of Genesis also highlights the work of God as the reader follows the increasing attention given to the line from Adam to Israel. The Almighty created the world and all that is in it by his all-powerful word (Gen 1). He alone chose to create humans and endowed them with mastery of the world (Gen 2). When they sinned, he not only pronounced judgment and banned them from Eden, but he also gave them hope of victory over the tempter through the

Descendant of Eve (Gen 3; esp. Gen 3:14–19). God's favor for Noah (Gen 6:8), who is characterized as righteous (Gen 6:9) and faithful (Heb 11:7), caused God to protect Noah and his family from the deluge (2 Pet 2:5). God chose Abram and called him to be the father of a great nation (Gen 12:1–3). Yahweh did not deviate from his choice, although Abram's faith was less than ideal in trusting that Yahweh would bring forth his promise (Gen 12:11–20; 15:3; 20:1–13). God did not take his promise from Isaac, even when he repeated the deceptive practices of his father (Gen 26:7). Yahweh chose the younger Jacob over his brother Esau (Gen 25:33). God's choice of Judah as the bearer of the messianic promise (Gen 49:8–12) was not made because he had always behaved admirably (cf. Gen 38). Moreover, as Genesis draws to a close, Joseph reminds his brothers (and also the readers of the book) of Yahweh's plan to preserve the chosen people of God (Gen 50:20).

In most cases, God did not choose as humans would have chosen. Instead, he often chose younger sons over older ones—Isaac over Ishmael, Jacob over Esau, Judah over Reuben.

Yahweh's choice of Jacob's twelve sons and their descendants as his special people is also underscored by the eleven *tôledôth* formulas, which serve to divide the book into twelve sections but also link those sections into one unified history leading to the survival of the twelve clans of Israel in Egypt.

## Outline of Genesis

I.  Creation (1:1–2:3)
II.  The origin and spread of sin (2:4–4:26)
    A.  The creation of humans (2:4–25)
    B.  The fall into sin (3:1–24)
    C.  The consequences of sin (4:1–26)
III.  The family of Adam (5:1–6:8)
    A.  Genealogy from Adam to Noah (5:1–32)
    B.  Noah's righteousness among sinful humanity (6:1–8)
IV.  Noah and his family (6:9–9:29)
    A.  The flood leads to God's covenant with Noah (6:9–9:17)
    B.  Noah's prophecy concerning his sons (9:18–29)

V. The family of Noah (10:1–11:9)

    A. Genealogies: Noah's descendants through his three sons (10:1–32)

    B. Sin at the tower of Babel (11:1–9)

VI. The family of Shem: Genealogy from Shem to Terah (11:10–26)

VII. The family of Terah (11:27–25:11)

    A. Terah and his sons (11:27–32)

    B. The call of Abram (12:1–9)

    C. Abram in Egypt—he deceives Pharaoh (12:10–20)

    D. Abram and Lot separate (13:1–18)

    E. Abram rescues Lot (14:1–16)

    F. Melchizedek blesses Abram (14:17–24)

    G. Yahweh's covenant with Abram (15:1–20)

    H. Abram fathers Ishmael by Hagar (16:1–16)

    I. Yahweh's covenant and its sign: circumcision (17:1–27)

    J. Abraham's three visitors (18:1–33)

        1. Yahweh promises Abraham a son (18:1–15)

        2. Abraham pleads for Sodom (18:16–33)

    K. Lot rescued from Sodom (19:1–29)

    L. Lot's sons by his daughters (19:30–38)

    M. Abraham in Gerar—he deceives Abimelech (20:1–18)

    N. The birth of Isaac (21:1–7)

    O. Hagar and Ishmael sent away (21:8–21)

    P. Abraham's covenant with Abimelech (21:22–34)

    Q. The near sacrifice of Isaac (22:1–19)

    R. News of Nahor's family (22:20–24)

    S. Sarah's death and burial (23:1–20)

    T. Isaac marries Rebekah (24:1–67)

    U. Abraham's other sons (25:1–6)

    V. Abraham's death (25:7–11)

VIII. The family of Ishmael (25:12–18)

IX. The family of Isaac (25:19–35:29)

A. The birth of Esau and Jacob (25:19–26)

B. Esau sells his birthright (25:27–34)

C. Yahweh's promise to Isaac (26:1–5)

D. Isaac among the Philistines (26:6–33)

    1. Isaac deceives Abimelech (26:6–11)

    2. Conflict over wells (26:12–22)

    3. Yahweh blesses Isaac at Beersheba (26:23–25)

    4. Isaac's covenant with Abimelech (26:26–33)

E. Esau's Hittite wives (26:34–35)

F. Jacob deceives Isaac in order to receive the blessing (27:1–46)

G. Jacob leaves for Paddan-aram (28:1–9)

H. Yahweh's promise to Jacob at Bethel (28:10–22)

I. Jacob meets Rachel (29:1–12)

J. Jacob deceived by Laban (29:13–30)

K. The birth of Jacob's sons (29:31–30:24)

L. Yahweh blesses Jacob: his flocks increase (30:25–43)

M. Jacob leaves Paddan-aram (31:1–21)

N. Jacob and Laban (31:22–55)

    1. Laban pursues Jacob (31:22–35)

    2. Jacob's covenant with Laban (31:36–55)

O. Jacob returns to Canaan (32:1–33:20)

    1. Jacob sends word to Esau of his return (32:1–23)

    2. Jacob wrestles with God (32:24–32)

    3. Jacob meets Esau (33:1–20)

P. The rape of Dinah (34:1–31)

Q. Yahweh again blesses Jacob at Bethel (35:1–15)

R. Rachel's death (35:16–20)

S. Reuben's sin (35:21–22a)

T. Israel's sons (35:22b–26)

U. Isaac's death (35:27–29)

X. Esau's family in the hill country of Seir (36:1–8)

XI. Esau's family: Genealogy from Esau and a list of Edomite kings (36:9–43)

XII. The family of Jacob (37:1–50:26)

  A.  Joseph's dreams (37:1–11)

  B.  Joseph sold into slavery (37:12–36)

  C.  Judah's sons by Tamar (38:1–30)

  D.  Joseph in Potiphar's house (39:1–20)

  E.  Joseph in prison (39:21–40:23)

    1.  God blesses Joseph (39:21–23)

    2.  Joseph interprets dreams in prison (40:1–23)

  F.  Joseph becomes Pharaoh's administrator (41:1–57)

    1.  Joseph interprets Pharaoh's dreams (41:1–36)

    2.  Joseph given high rank by Pharaoh (41:37–45)

    3.  Joseph as administrator (41:46–55)

  G.  The famine brings Joseph's brothers to Egypt (42:1–45:28)

    1.  Jacob's sons' first trip to Egypt (42:1–26)

    2.  Jacob's sons return to him (42:27–38)

    3.  Jacob's sons return to Egypt with Benjamin (43:1–34)

    4.  Joseph is reunited with his brothers (44:1–45:28)

      a.  Joseph accuses his brothers of theft (44:1–17)

      b.  Judah's plea for Benjamin (44:18–34)

      c.  Joseph reveals himself to his brothers (45:1–15)

      d.  Pharaoh invites Jacob and his sons to live in Egypt (45:16–28)

  H.  Jacob goes to Egypt (46:1–47:12)

    1.  God sends Jacob to Egypt (46:1–7)

    2.  Jacob's family as they enter Egypt (46:8–27)

    3.  Pharaoh welcomes Jacob (46:28–47:12)

  I.  Pharaoh acquires all of the land in Egypt (47:13–26)

  J.  Jacob settles in Goshen (47:27–31)

  K.  Jacob blesses Joseph's sons (48:1–22)

  L.  Jacob's final blessings for his sons (49:1–28)

M.  Jacob's final words and death (49:29–33)

N.  Jacob's burial in Canaan (50:1–14)

O.  Joseph forgives his brothers (50:15–21)

P.  Joseph's death (50:22–26)

## HISTORICAL AND ARCHAEOLOGICAL ISSUES

### NEAR EASTERN CREATION ACCOUNTS

In 1849 among the ruins of the library of Ashurbanipal (685–c. 627), the last great king of the Assyrian empire, Austen Henry Layard, discovered an ancient Mesopotamian creation myth in Nineveh (modern Mosul, Iraq). Named *Enuma Eliš* (English translation: "when on high") after its first words, the seven tablets containing the text of this myth were first published in 1876. Almost immediately scholars proposed that this creation myth provided the conceptual background for the creation account in Gen 1. This connection is still advocated by many, including some evangelicals (e.g., Walton).

The *Enuma Eliš* begins with the divinized primordial waters: Apsû, representing fresh waters, and Tiamat, representing the oceans. There is a conflict between Tiamat and the other gods, who reside in her body. Eventually Marduk engages Tiamat in battle, killing her and ripping her body into halves, which he uses to form the earth and the sky. Marduk then creates the yearly calendar, the sun, moon, stars, and weather. He also slays Tiamat's son Kingu, and from his blood he creates humans to serve the gods.

Some of the alleged parallels to Gen 1 are obvious. The primordial waters and their division between earth and sky are prominent at the beginning of both accounts (cf. Gen 1:2–8). The creation of the sun, moon, and stars and their connection to the reckoning of time is found in both (cf. Gen 1:14–18). Humans are formed from a dead god's blood in *Enuma Eliš*. However, the supposed parallel is not part of the creation account in Gen 1; it is not mentioned until Gen 2:7.

There are several problems, however, with holding that *Enuma Eliš* provides the Near Eastern background for Gen 1. For instance, it is often claimed that Tiamat and the Hebrew word for the primordial waters, *tᵉhom* (תהום; Gen 1:2), are cognates. Yet this etymological connection remains controversial. If Tiamat is derived from *tᵉhom,* then the latter should have a middle consonant 'aleph and not a hē, as well as a feminine ending. Most now accept that the Hebrew does not come directly from the Akkadian, but that both words derive independently from a common proto-Semitic root, *tiham*. Moreover, there is no divine conflict in the Genesis account as in *Enuma Eliš* (see below). Most important, there is no consensus on the date of the composition of the Babylonian myth. Some date it to the time of the Babylonian king Hammurabi in the eighteenth century. Others date it more broadly to sometime in the Kassite Era (eighteenth to sixteenth centuries). Still other Assyriologists place it as late as 1100. If the later date is accepted, it would post-date the work of Moses by some three centuries, reversing the direction of dependence from Genesis to *Enuma Eliš*.

Recently, Johnston has argued that Genesis is less related to the Assyrian creation myth and is, instead, purposely written to refute Egyptian creation myths. Building on work by A. H. Sayce and, more recently, Hoffmeier, he notes that the general sequence of events from the Old Kingdom (twenty-seventh through twenty-second centuries) *Pyramid Texts* and *Coffin Texts* is very similar to Genesis and that these myths were still current in the Middle and New Kingdom periods (twenty-first through seventeenth centuries and sixteenth through eleventh centuries respectively). The sequence is:

### *Parallels between Egyptian Creation Myths and Genesis 1:1–2:23*

| *Pyramid and Coffin Texts* | *Genesis 1:1–2:23* |
|---|---|
| 1. Lifeless watery deep | 1. Lifeless watery deep |
| 2. Breath/wind (Atum) moves on the waters | 2. Breath/wind of God moves on the waters |
| 3. Creation of light (Atum) | 3. Creation of light |
| 4. Emergence of primordial hill | 4. Creation of firmament in the midst of the waters |
| 5. Procreation of the sky (Shu) | 5. Creation of the sky when waters were raised above the firmament |

| | |
|---|---|
| 6. Formation of heavenly waters (Nut) by separation | 6. Formation of heavenly waters by separation |
| 7. Formation of dry ground (Geb) by separation | 7. Formation of dry ground when waters were gathered |
| 8. Humans accidentally created by tears of Atum | 8. Sun and moon created to rule day and night |
| 9. Sun created to rule the world as the image of Re | 9. Creation of humans to rule the world as the image of God |

A similar sequence is found on the Egyptian *Shabaka Stone* (inscribed in the eighth or seventh centuries) which preserves the Memphite Theology of the New Kingdom period. One additional parallel from this text with Gen 1 is that at the end of creation the Egyptian god Ptah rests at the end of his work, just as God rests at the end of his work at Gen 2:2–3. Intriguingly, Moses (1526–1406) lived during the early New Kingdom period.

Johnston suggests that Gen 1 is a polemic against Near Eastern creation mythology in general and Egyptian mythology in particular. According to this theory, Moses would have not only been relating the correct account of the origin of the world, but he was also refuting ancient Egyptian polytheism and creation models which competed against monotheistic faith in Yahweh for the loyalty of Israel after exposure to Egyptian religion during their long sojourn in the land of the Nile.

## PRE- AND POST-DILUVIAN GENEALOGIES

There are two major genealogies that link Adam to Abraham. The pre-diluvian genealogy from Adam to Noah (Gen 5:1–32) and the post-diluvian genealogy from Shem to Abram and his brothers (Gen 11:10–26). These genealogies display two unique features: (1) The age of the ancestor at the birth of his progeny is listed. For example, "Nahor lived twenty-nine years and fathered Terah" (Gen 11:24). (2) The number of years an ancestor lived after the descendant was born is also given. For example, "After he fathered Terah, Nahor lived 119 years ... " (Gen 11:25). In addition, the pre-diluvian genealogy includes the total lifespan of each ancestor, such as, "So Seth lived 912 years and then died" (Gen 5:8).

Because these genealogies list the age of each ancestor at the birth of his descendant, many have attempted to add these numbers together to determine the age of the earth. However, we must exercise some caution in doing this. First, the Hebrew words for *father* (אָב) and *son* (בֵּן) can at times denote *ancestor* and *descendant*. Moreover, the verb translated "fathered" (יָלַד) does not always denote direct fatherhood. The *Theological Wordbook of the Old Testament* notes,

> The word does not necessarily point to the generation immediately following. In Hebrew thought, an individual by the act of giving birth to a child becomes a parent or ancestor of all who are called a son of David and a son of Abraham, *yālad* may show the beginning of an individual's relationship to any descendant.[1]

This can be seen in the genealogy of ten generations from Perez to David in Ruth 4:18–22, where יָלַד is also used. There had to be more than ten generations in this span, given the 837 years between Perez and David. It appears that the author of Ruth purposely omitted some generations so that Boaz would be listed as the honored seventh person in the genealogy, and David would be the tenth generation.

In the same way, we should note that in both the pre- and post-diluvian genealogies there are exactly ten generations. In a study of genealogies that have survived from the ancient Near East, Wilson has noted that genealogies tend to be limited to ten generations at most (many are much shorter). Moreover, it is noteworthy that in the pre-diluvian genealogy, Enoch, who "walked with God" (Gen 5:22, 24), occupies the honored seventh position (cf. Jude 14).

In a few instances it can be demonstrated that these genealogies list father to son to grandson (e.g., Adam to Seth to Enosh, compare Gen 4:25–26 to 5:3–8; see also Lamech as father of Noah, Gen 5:28; see Terah as father of Abram, compare Gen 11:26 to 11:27–32). In at least one case, however, we can be certain that at least one generation has been skipped in the pre-diluvian genealogy (cf. Gen 10:24; 11:12–13; and Luke 3:35–36). In other cases, the context makes it

---

[1] R. Laird Harris, Gleason L. Archer Jr., and Bruce K. Waltke, *Theological Wordbook of the Old Testament* (Chicago: Moody, 1980), §867g.

likely that some generations have been skipped. For instance, if no gaps are postulated in the genealogical record, then many pre-diluvian patriarchs (Enosh, Kenan, Mahalalel, Jared, Lamech, and Methuselah) would have been alive during the time of Noah, but the Bible characterizes Noah as the only righteous man of his time. Likewise, the Bible says that the Israelite "fathers" were idolaters at the time of Abram (Josh 24:2, 14–15). But if there are no gaps in the biblical chronology, many post-diluvian patriarchs (Reu, Serug, Arphaxad, Shelah, Shem, Eber) would have been alive during the time of Abram. As another example, compare the number of generations during the Egyptian sojourn in 1 Chr 6:1–3 (four from Levi to Moses) and in 1 Chr 7:20–27 (twelve from Joseph to Joshua). All this suggests that the pre-diluvian genealogies may skip some generations, making it impossible to assume naively that summing the years of the pre- and post-diluvian ancestors of Abraham will yield the number of years from the creation of Adam to the birth of Abraham.

## DATING THE PATRIARCHS

Using information given in Genesis and knowing the date of the exodus from Egypt, it is relatively easy to establish a timeline for Israel's patriarchs. The most likely date of the exodus is 1446 (see the discussion in chapter 4 on Exodus). Jacob and his family entered Egypt 430 years to the day before the exodus (Exod 12:40–41). Therefore, Jacob entered Egypt on 14 Nisan 1876 (1446 + 430). Jacob was 130 years old when he entered Egypt (Gen 47:9), so he was born in 2006 (1876 + 130). Isaac was sixty when Jacob was born (Gen 25:26), so Isaac was born in 2066. Abraham was 100 years old when Isaac was born (Gen 21:5), so Abraham was born in 2166. Thus, the basic dates for this period are:

### *Basic Chronology of the Patriarchs*

2166 Abram born (Gen 21:5)

2066 Isaac born (Gen 25:26)

2006 Jacob born (Gen 47:9)

1991 Abraham died (Gen 25:7)

1886 Isaac died (Gen 35:28)

1876 Jacob enters Egypt (Exod 12:40–41)

1859 Jacob died (Gen 47:28)

Abraham was born in lower Mesopotamia during the end of the Akkadian Dynasty that had been founded by Sargon the Great (2270–2215). Abraham would have been in Egypt in the First Intermediate Period during the overlapping ninth and tenth dynasties. At the end of the patriarchal period Joseph would have entered Egypt during the Middle Kingdom period and probably served under the pharaohs Sesotris I (1920–1875) and his successor Amenemhet II (1878–1844).

## THEOLOGICAL THEMES IN GENESIS

### CREATION

Genesis's presentation of the creation of the world with humans as the crown of God's creation (Gen 1:1–2:3) ranks as one of the most stirring and majestic passages in all of Scripture. Most striking is God's use of his spoken word to create (Gen 1:3, 6, 9, 11, 14, 20, 24; Heb 11:3). Unlike the pagan myths discussed above, Genesis emphasizes that God alone created the heavens and earth and all that fills them (cf. Rev 4:11; 10:6). God alone was active in the creation of the world, and this is mentioned particularly often by Isaiah (Isa 40:26; 41:20; 42:5; 43:7; 45:7–8, 12, 18; compare Ps 148:5, Eph 3:9; Col 1:16). The opening section of Genesis also emphasizes that the Almighty accomplished his creative activity in six days (Gen 2:1–3), and that human beings are the crown of his creation, made in God's image and likeness (Gen 1:26–27; 5:1–2). The image of God with his hands in the dirt is remarkable (Gen 2:7). This is no naïve theology, but a statement about the depths to which God has entered into the life of creation to create people. The parallel here is that of a governing sovereign who cannot be everywhere present in the realm, but who erects statues of himself as a witness and reminder of who the real sovereign is. By analogue, the invisible God has placed human beings in creation so that, upon seeing the human creature, other creatures are reminded of Yahweh's rule (cf. Ps 8:5). This idea is then used of Christ (John 14:9; Col. 1:15) and of Christians (Col 3:9–10; Eph 4:22–24).

Also in contrast to the Near Eastern creation accounts, God's creation was good and perfect, without strife, conflict, or contention

(Gen 1:4, 10, 12, 18, 21, 25, 31; compare 1 Tim 4:4). Critical scholars believe that, in keeping with ancient mythological thought, in order to create the world, Yahweh had first to defeat chaos. Although Gen 1 is completely free of any pre-creation combat motifs, John Goldingay believes that, just like other ancient Near Eastern deities, Yahweh could not create an ordered universe until first he defeated the forces of chaos. This, then, becomes the pattern for all future salvific acts.

This understanding of Israel's creational theology goes back to Hermann Gunkel who assumed that prophets like Isaiah employed sea-battle imagery to elicit *both* protological *and* eschatological events. In 1895 his book *Schöpfung und Chaos in Urzeit und Endzeit (Creation and Chaos in Primordial Time and the End Time)* argued that the creation account in Gen 1 derived from the Babylonian creation epic, the *Enuma Eliš*. Gunkel coined the term *Chaoskampf* to describe the motif of a primordial battle between Yahweh and chaos in Gen 1:2 that derived from Marduk's conquest of Tiamat.

Since Gunkel, Frank Moore Cross shifted the focus of the discussion from Babylonian to Canaanite origins. Following Thorkild Jacobsen, Cross suggested that "the battle with the dragon Ocean is West Semitic in origin" rather than originally Babylonian, but nevertheless he draws parallels between biblical texts and both Canaanite and Babylonian myths. Whereas Gunkel spoke of *Chaoskampf*, Cross refers more generally to the cosmogonic or creation battle with monstrous Sea. Both of these influential scholars see the *creational/cosmogonic* conquest of Yahweh over the sea wherever Yahweh exerts his power over water in the OT. In his influential Anchor Bible Genesis commentary in 1964, Abraham Speiser likewise argued that the Genesis account of creation is the same as the Babylonian creation myth.

Strife and hostility describe our sin-infected world, but this does not mean they were present from the beginning. The universe came into existence by Yahweh's word, not because he defeated primeval agents of chaos. The presence of evil is often explained with dualism, the belief in two eternal powers, one good and one evil. But Moses' description of matter as initially "without form and void" (Gen 1:2) does not describe Yahweh's battle over unruly forces to create the world. Evil enters the world in Gen 3, through the wiles of Satan, after creation is finished. Conflict with the evil one is not connected to creation. To say so is to revert to a mythic Babylonian or Canaanite worldview.

To emphasize that creation was orderly and not the chaotic process envisioned by the pagan myths, Genesis presents the six days as a progressive and orderly process organized by God, with the six days paired in two sets of three:

### The Days of Creation in Gen 1

| Day 1 | Day 2 | Day 3 |
|---|---|---|
| *Heavens* empty; *light* created | *Expanse of sky* separated from *sea* | *Land* (dry ground) filled with plants |

| Day 4 | Day 5 | Day 6 |
|---|---|---|
| *Heavens* filled with sun, moon and stars to *light* the sky | *Expanse of sky* filled with birds; *seas* filled with creatures | *Land* filled with animals and people |

The term day (יום) is not always used the same way, even in the creation account. In Gen 1:5 and 1:14 what God calls *day* is the period of daylight as opposed to nighttime. Here *day* is something less than a twenty-four-hour day, as the context makes clear. By contrast, in Gen 2:4 the word *day* is used in a phrase to set the temporal context ("in the day" = "when").

The real question, then, is how to understand the phrases in which יום is used to demarcate the stages of creation ("day one," "a second day," and so forth). In the context there are a variety of temporal terms: *start* (i.e., beginning), *evening and morning, day, night, seasons, days,* and *years.* All of these terms have their meaning shaped by the context in which they are used. The terms *day* and *night* suggest that these words are being used in opposition to each other and signal what we normally denote by these terms. Thus, the sun dominates daytime and the moon rules the night (Gen 1:16).

The same is true of "evening and morning" (Gen 1:5, 8, 13, 19, 23, 31). Similarly, *year* and *seasons and years* denote a solar year (365.24218967 days) and its parts (spring, summer, autumn, winter), since the context is the discussion of the way in which these are regulated by the movements of the cosmos (Gen 1:14).

In light of this, the term *day* (יום) is used in phrases that designate the stages of creation to mark off a single cycle of daylight and nighttime. It seems impossible to argue that all of the other terms are used in their common sense to denote ordinary evenings and mornings, seasons and years, but that יוֹם is not. One could, of course, argue this if there were something in the text to suggest it, but lacking that, it is a dubious argument to suggest that יוֹם means anything other than a single rotation of the earth upon its axis.

Gen 1:1–2:3 is a key passage for later OT and NT discussions of the origins of all things, of humans, and of their God-given relationship to all of creation. The commandment concerning the Sabbath refers to the seven days of the creation week (Exod 20:11). God's creation of humankind affords him the relationship of Father of all people (Deut 32:6; Mal 2:10). Moreover, the relationship of man to woman, husband to wife, as partners in sharing dominion over the earth and the responsibility for procreation was established by God (Gen 1:26–29; cf. Gen 2:18–24; Matt 19:4–6; 1 Cor 11:8–12).

The Documentary Hypothesis holds that Gen 1:1–2:3 and Gen 2:4–25 are two different creation accounts with different and even conflicting theological outlooks and goals. The first is assigned to the priestly source (P) during or after the Babylonian captivity, while the second is assigned to the Yahwist (J) with additional material from an Elohistic source (E). This theory holds that the two versions have different and even conflicting theological outlooks and goals as well as different details concerning how creation was accomplished. For instance, in the first creation account animals were formed before humans (Gen 1:24–28), whereas in the second animals were formed after the man (Gen 2:7, 19). In the first story, humans were created to have dominion over the animals (Gen 1:26), whereas in the second, they were to work the garden (Gen 2:15). In the first account, humans as male and female are in the image of God (Gen 1:26), whereas in the second they are created to become one flesh (Gen 2:24).

However, it is not necessary to view the two accounts as at odds with each other. Clearly, Gen 2:4–25 is not a complete creation account: The existence of the heavens and earth is assumed. There is no mention of the sun, moon, and stars. There is no discussion of the creation of sea creatures. Thus, this passage is not a second creation text but an expansion of the description of the creation of humans as male and female.

In addition, the different sequence in the creation of the animals and humans can be explained in complementary ways. For instance, the text relating the sixth day in Gen 1:24–31 may indicate a theological sequence, with humans reserved for last, since they are to be at the pinnacle of God's work as reflections of his image exercising dominion on the earth. The text of Gen 2:17 may record the actual sequence once the reader understands the relationship of the man and the woman to the rest of God's creatures. Conversely, Gen 1 may indicate the proper chronological order, while Gen 2 may speak of the creation of animals only as background to the creation of woman, to illustrate how the previously created animals could never occupy the position for which woman was created.

Moreover, the garden in Eden is introduced to explain the man's occupation and his need for a helper without denying his dominion over the animals or his creation in God's image. Instead, the relation of man to woman as they go about their mutual tasks in the garden is explored. This passage is crucial to understanding marriage as a divinely designed and instituted relationship for mutual comfort and support and for the propagation of the human race. Much of what the rest of the Bible says about marriage and the proper relationship of the sexes to one another is predicated upon this text, especially Gen 2:24 (cf. Matt 19:4–6; Mark 10:6–8; 1 Cor 6:16; 7:10–11; 11:8–12; Eph 5:31, 33).

## THE FALL

The fall of humankind into sin occupies a prominent place in Genesis, immediately following the account of God's creation of man and woman (Gen 3:1–24). One of the results of sin was increased pain (עִצָּבוֹן; Gen 3:16–17). This would characterize a woman's experience in childbirth and a man's relationship with his work. In Gen 6:6 that pain brought grief (verbal root עָצַב) to God, so that sin even impacted him!

The curse upon Adam and Eve for their sin (Gen 3:16–19) was not the end of the matter. The consequences of the fall are emphasized throughout the book. The first murder is related immediately after humans are expelled from Eden (Gen 4:1–16). Sin's effects accelerate so that although Cain was afraid of the consequences of his murderous ways (Gen 4:13–14), his descendant Lamech bragged about his homicidal acts (Gen 4:23–24). When Adam had another son, that offspring was in his likeness—still retaining God's image but now corrupted by sin (Gen 5:3). Moreover, several times Genesis directly states that sin had become permanently attached to human nature (e.g., Gen 6:5; 8:21; cf. Job 15:14; Ps 51:5; Jer 17:9; Matt 15:19; Rom 3:23).

The fall also leads to a renewing and second undoing of creation. The land that emerged from the primeval ocean (Gen 1:9) is submerged in the great flood and re-emerges afterwards. Noah is a kind of second Adam, since all subsequent humanity stems from him. Initially judged to be righteous and blameless (Gen 6:9), he succumbs to sin in an echo of the fall of Adam and Eve (Gen 9:20–27). Whereas Adam's consumption of fruit made him aware of his nakedness so that he tried to cover it up (Gen 3:6–7), Noah's drinking wine from the fruit of the vine led him to uncover himself unwittingly, and his sons had to cover him (Gen 9:23). In Adam's case, the son's behavior is even more reprehensible than the father's. In Noah's case, his son's disobedience leads to dissension among the three brothers. Just as Cain's descendants appear to be the ungodly line in Gen 4, Ham's descendant, Canaan, is cursed by Noah (Gen 9:25).

## GOD'S CHOSEN PEOPLE

Despite the fact that all humans carried the stain of sin from birth, God chose some to be his people through whom redemption for the world would come. This first becomes evident in Noah, whose family Yahweh chose to save despite his conclusion that he had to wipe mankind from the face of the earth (Gen 6:5–8). From Noah's children, God favored Shem (Gen 9:26–27), and his line is traced to Abram (Gen 11:11–32). No reason is given for God's choice of Terah's son—it is simply God's mercy, for Abram would prove to be sinful like the rest of the human race. Yet despite Abram's failing, God repeats his promise to him seven times (Gen 12:2–3 [itself a sevenfold promise]; 12:7; 13:14–17; 15:1–21; 17:1–22; 18:10; 22:15–18). God chose Abram's son Isaac, and Isaac's son Jacob. The choice of this people comes to a climax in Jacob. In addition, the barrenness of Israel's three matriarchs, Sarah (Gen 11:30), Rebekah (Gen 25:31), and Rachel (Gen 29:31), highlight the fact that Yahweh "chooses the foolish things of the world to shame the wise; he chooses the weak things of the world to shame the strong. He chooses the lowly things of this world and the despised things—and the things that are not" (1 Cor 1:27–28).

The name God gives to Jacob, *Israel,* is a mark of Yahweh's covenant grace. He gives this name to Jacob in order to confirm that the promise given to his father and grandfather now passes to him. It designates Jacob, his children, and all their descendants as objects of Yahweh's mercy.

Jacob first receives this name in the momentous wrestling with God (Gen 32:24–32). He asks for a blessing before God departs. In that context of blessing, God renames him *Israel.* Here the meaning of the Hebrew name *Israel* is *he struggles with God* (Gen 32:28). This fits the context, since a wrestling match has just taken place. Because this is meant to be a blessing, one might expect it to denote God's grace (Gen 35:10–13; 2 Chr 9:8; Isa 11:12; 27:6; 44:21; Jer 31:31).

Elsewhere in the OT there is an implied play on words with the name *Israel* in light of the promises of God repeated to Jacob in Genesis. This play on words involves calling the nation of Israel *Jeshurun.* A slight variation of the Hebrew word Israel (ישראל to ישראל) can mean *El (God) has made right,* and the subsequent explanation of the name would be "Because you are right with God, with men you will prevail." The proper noun *Jeshurun* (ישרון) appears in Isa 44:2 and in Deut 32:15; 33:5, 26, while in Num 23:10 Israelites are called *upright ones* (ישרים). Jeshurun is linked with the verb ישר, *be straight, upright.* The ן ending is an affectionate diminutive. *Jeshurun* is parallel with Jacob, *deceiver, liar, trickster,* in Isa 44:2.

Assuming such a play on words in these later texts nicely fits the immediate context of Jacob's naming in Gen 38 as well as the wider context of Genesis (Gen 6:9; 15:6). This name change indicates an act of mercy and redemption by Yahweh. Formerly, he had the name *Jacob,* which means *he deceives.* Now his name is *he struggles with God,* but it can also be used later by Moses and Isaiah to imply a pun on this name: *God has made righteous.* The deceiver stands forgiven and blessed to be an instrument of the promise. It is significant that this act of reconciliation between Yahweh and Jacob accompanies the reconciliation between Jacob and Esau (Gen 33:1–19).

Jacob receives the name *Israel* a second time. "God said to him, 'Your name is Jacob, but you will no longer be called *Jacob*; you will be *Israel*' " (Gen 35:10). The text then includes repetition of the promises of divine favor that he made to Abraham and Isaac: God promises to make his descendants abundant. A great nation and kings will come from him. Yahweh will grant them the Promised Land

(Gen 35:11–13). In such a context the definition of Israel as *God has made righteous* fits well and compliments the strong faith implied in the name which means *he struggles with God*.

After Jacob, Yahweh then carries on the partial fulfillment of the promises of a land, a great nation and many descendants not in one person but in the sons of Israel and their descendants, who also have the designation *tribes* or *children* of Israel. The ultimate fulfillment, however, will come in Christ. Although initially there is a correlation between the name Israel and the bloodline of Jacob, the term *Israel* is not inherently an ethnic designation, and belonging to Israel does not require a certain heritage. Rather, the name is a gift available to anyone. This becomes evident not only by the covenant attached to the name but also by the fact that foreigners can become a part of Israel (e.g., Exod 12:48–49; 20:10; 23:12; Lev 16:29–30; 19:33–34; Deut 29:11; 31:10–13; Josh 8:33; Ps 146:9; Ezek 47:22–23). Essentially, *Israel,* then, is the name for the OT people of God and his NT people, the church (Rom 9–11; Gal 3–4, and esp. Gal 6:16).

## JUSTIFICATION BY FAITH

If Israel is not simply an ethnic designation but can also be used to denote all of God's people, then how does one become part of that people? Genesis addresses this through the subject of justification through faith. Justification involves the declaration of pardon from guilt in an implied courtroom setting. In the Bible, such a declaration comes from Yahweh, who confers this gift upon someone even though, by virtue of sin, it is not deserved or earned. Justification is received through the gift of faith. Faith contributes nothing to the act of justification—it only receives what God has declared. This pardon is free but comes at a high cost to God who declares it. Forgiveness from the guilt of sin is possible, since the punishment is transferred to the promised Savior. In this act of justification, the sinner receives the status of being seen by God as completely righteous. This is not the inherent or natural righteousness which Adam and Eve possessed at creation but lost in the fall. Rather, it is an imputed righteousness, which God graciously credits to a person by the merits of the promised seed, Christ Jesus (cf. Gen 3:15).

Justification through faith becomes particularly clear in the life of Abraham. He believes the gracious promise of Yahweh, particularly that in him and his seed all the nations of the earth would be blessed

(Gen 12:2–3; 17:19; Gal 3:16). Although Abraham does not have all the details regarding this coming Savior, he trusts in the gracious plans of God (Gen 15:5). Through faith in the promise, Abraham receives the gift of justification. "Abram believed Yahweh, and he credited it to him as righteousness" (Gen 15:6). Especially in this example of Abraham, Paul wishes to make clear that faith does not merit anything before Yahweh. Faith is not a way of earning God's favor. This passive righteousness through faith should not be confused with the active righteousness lived out in a believer's life which is always imperfect in any fallen human. Paul excludes human works in the context of justification. Good works do not precede faith (Rom 4:3–25; see Heb 11:8–12). In this way, Paul presents the patriarch Abraham as an archetype of how one may be saved.

While Genesis accentuates justification through faith particularly in the person of Abraham, the book of Hebrews highlights additional persons in Genesis who have this righteousness through faith. Although Genesis says little about Abel, Hebrews indicates that he was righteous through faith. "By faith he was commended as a righteous man, when God spoke well of his offerings. And by faith he still speaks although he is dead" (Heb 11:5). Regarding Noah, after recounting the building of the ark, Hebrews declares: "By faith, he condemned the world and became an heir of the righteousness that comes by faith" (Heb 11:7). Thus, not only Abraham but also other persons in Genesis such as Sarah, Isaac, Rachel, Jacob, Joseph, and Judah exemplify justification through faith.

CHRIST IN GENESIS

## The Messianic Promise

The choosing of Israel as God's people was not simply for their sake, but for the sake of all people. This promise runs throughout Genesis from the first sinners, Adam and Eve, to the last ones in the book—the sons of Israel, especially Judah. God's pledge of a Savior is traced throughout the book as it narrows its focus to Jacob and his sons.

Immediately after Yahweh confronted Adam and Eve about their sin he pronounced a curse on the serpent who tempted them. This curse not only condemned Satan for his role in the fall, but it also contained the first glimpse of a promised Savior who would deliver humans from the curse of sin. God said to the serpent:

> I will put hostility between you and the woman, and between your seed and her seed. He will strike at your head, and you will strike at his heel. (Gen 3:15)

The woman's seed (זרע) is often understood to be a collective—the woman's descendants, since this noun can be used in a collective sense. However, in a study published in 1997, John C. Collins has noted that whenever *seed* is used with singular verbs and adjectives, and especially singular pronouns, it is not collective but singular. In this text the verb *strike* is singular (ישופך). More importantly, it is used with a singular pronoun (הוא), although no pronoun is required by Hebrew syntax in this case. This superfluous use of the pronoun emphasizes that God is promising a particular seed—a single descendant—of the woman who will crush the serpent's head. Therefore, this condemnation of the serpent is also the first Gospel promise in the Scriptures, and has been called the *protoevangelion*. It is humanity's first glimpse of the Messiah.

The word *seed* is important in Genesis. Alexander has noted that it is used fifty-nine times in the book and only 170 times in the rest of the OT. He also observed that the word conveys the concept that there is a close resemblance between the seed and that which produced it. The descendant is like the ancestor. The seed of the woman would be as human as she was. The catchword *seed* is used throughout Genesis to refer to this original promise of the Messiah as this concept is further developed in the unfolding story of God's people.

Eve understood this promise, as shown in her own words. When Cain was born, she named him out of hope that he might be the promised seed from God (Gen 4:1). After Cain's sins demonstrated that he was not the expected seed, she said of her son Seth, "God has given me *another seed* in place of Abel, since Cain killed him" (Gen 4:25).

Seth's line would lead to Noah, where the promise would be handed down through the line of Noah's son Shem. Following the incident of Noah's drunkenness and Ham's role in revealing his father's shame, Noah prophesied about these sons (Gen 9:20–23). A curse was placed on Ham's descendants through his son Canaan (Gen 9:25). However, a blessing was given to Shem through Yahweh, his

God (Gen 9:26). This blessing would be shared with his brother Japheth (Gen 9:27) and is traced through Shem's line to Abram (Gen 11:10–32).

Yahweh's promises to Abraham, Isaac, and Jacob all centered upon the messianic promise. There are several elements to the promises given to Israel's patriarchs, and they are repeated from one generation to the next:

### Yahweh's Seven Promises to the Patriarchs in Genesis

| Promise | Abraham | Isaac | Jacob |
|---|---|---|---|
| **Progeny:** Become a great nation/numerous | 12:2; 13:16; 17:2; 22:17 | 26:4, 26 | 28:14; 46:3 |
| **Reputation:** Have a great name | 12:2 | | |
| **Messianic Seed:** Will be a blessing to the nations through his seed | 12:3; 22:18 | | 28:14 |
| **Protection:** Bless those who bless/curse those who curse; Yahweh will be with him; Will be his God/God of his seed | 12:3; 15:1; 17:7, 8 | 26:4, 26 | 28:15; 31:3; 46:4 |
| **Land:** God will give the land of Canaan to his seed | 12:7; 13:15,17; 17:8; 22:17 | 26:3–4 | 28:13; 35:12 |
| **Influence:** Father of many nations | 17:5–6 | | 35:11 |
| **Royalty:** Will produce kings | 17:6 | | 35:11 |

These promises to the patriarchs in Genesis are foundational to the rest of the Pentateuch and frequently mentioned in the rest of the OT. Their importance and frequency have led Clines to claim that the patriarchal promises of God are the theme of the Pentateuch. More importantly, there are two aspects of these promises that should not be overlooked. First, they are the flowering of the promises and blessings previously given to Adam and Eve (Gen 3:15) and Shem (Gen 9:26). Secondly, all of them are given for the sake of the messianic promise (cf. John 8:56). The making of Israel into a great nation and the promise of protection was for the purpose of their bringing the Messiah into the world. The land of Canaan was given to the seed of the patriarchs so that Israel would have a homeland that would foreshadow the greater land given to all of Christ's followers (Heb 11:8–10). Through faith in Jesus, people from many nations would become children of Abraham (Matt 3:9; 8:11; Luke 3:8; John 8:39; Rom 4:16–17; 9:6–8; Eph 3:6; 1 Pet 3:6).

When God brought Jacob down to Egypt he promised him that there he would become a great nation (Gen 46:3). While in Egypt, all of Jacob's sons would grow to be a large people. However, before Jacob died, he called his sons to him to prophesy what would become of them and their offspring in the last days (Gen 49:1). Joseph received the rights of the firstborn because Reuben had committed adultery with his father's concubine (Gen 49:2–3, 22–26; 35:22; 1 Chr 5:1). Simeon and Levi were cursed because of their double-dealing with the men of Shechem (Gen 49:5–7; cf. Gen 34:1–31). The messianic promise passed to Judah (Gen 49:9–12). He was given the scepter, signifying the royal prerogatives of the Messiah (Gen 49: 10; cf. Mark 15:32; Luke 23:2). More prominently, Judah is depicted as a lion, a symbol that would be ever after associated with the Messiah (Rev 5:5). Later, in Balaam's prophecies concerning Israel, blessing for those who bless the Israelites and curses for those who curse them is linked to their carrying the messianic promise as the lion (Num 23:24; 24:9).

Thus, Genesis traces the promise of the Messiah across the generations as follows:

Eve's seed (Gen 3:15) → Shem (Gen 9:26) → Abraham (Gen 12:2–3, etc.) → Isaac (Gen 26:3–4, 26) → Jacob (Gen 28:13–15, etc.) → Judah (Gen 49:9–12).

## The Messenger of Yahweh

Four times in the accounts of Israel's patriarchs a figure called *the Messenger of Yahweh* (מלאך יהוה) or *the Messenger of God* (אלהים מלאך) appears to someone. (The word translated *angel* in most English Bibles is the Hebrew word for *messenger*. In many Bibles this figure is called *the angel of the LORD*.) The introduction of this Messenger in Genesis prepares for his repeated appearances in the rest of the OT, where he is mentioned forty-seven more times. This is no ordinary angel of God, for in every book of the OT where he is mentioned, he is identified as a manifestation of Yahweh himself.

In Gen 16 the Messenger of Yahweh appears to Hagar near the spring on the way to Shur after she had fled from Sarai's mistreatment (Gen 16:7). This Messenger made a promise that only God can make: "*I* will surely multiply your seed, and they will be so many that they cannot be counted" (Gen 16:10). Moreover, Hagar realized that she had seen God (Gen 16:13), confirming the identity of this Messenger. Later, when Hagar and Ishmael were expelled from Abraham's camp, the Messenger of God called to her and once again promised her concerning her son, "*I* will make him a great nation" (Gen 21:17).

Yahweh's Messenger also spoke to Abraham to stop him before he sacrificed Isaac on Mount Moriah (Gen 22:11, 15). Once again this Messenger is clearly identified as God himself when he makes statements such as "you have not withheld your only son from *me*" (Gen 22:11) and "*I* will surely bless you and make your offspring as numerous as the stars of the sky and the sand on the seashore" (Gen 22:17).

Jacob saw the Messenger of God in a dream, where the Messenger told him, "I am the God of Bethel" (Gen 31:13). Later, near the end of his life, Jacob would refer to this Messenger in his blessing of Joseph's sons, Ephraim and Manasseh:

> The God before whom my fathers Abraham and Isaac walked, the God who has been my shepherd all of my life to this day, the *Messenger* who has redeemed me from all danger: May he bless these boys. (Gen 48:15–16)

Although it does not use the term *Messenger of Yahweh*, the account of Jacob's wrestling with God is another appearance of this divine Messenger according to Hos 12:2–5. Jacob called the site of the wrestling match *Peniel* (i.e., face of God), and said "I have seen God face-to-face, and I have been delivered" (Gen 32:30).

Clearly, the Messenger of Yahweh is a *theophany*, an appearance of God. Such theophanies occur at other vital junctures in the OT story of Israel: at the burning bush Moses saw the Messenger of

Yahweh who will be God calling to him (Exod 3:2, 4; cf. Acts 7:30–34). God, who brings his people out of Egypt, is also this Messenger (Num 20:16). Yahweh's Messenger appeared to the prophet Balaam and his donkey (Num 22). He instructed Balaam to speak only those words which he gave him, which once again demonstrates that the Messenger is God (Num 22:35, cf. Num 23:12, 26; 24:12).

The Messenger of Yahweh appears several times in Judges. In Judg 2 he admonishes Israel for its unfaithfulness when he says, "*I* brought you up from Egypt and led you into the land *I* had solemnly promised to give to your ancestors. *I* said, '*I* will never break my covenant with you . . . ' " (Judg 2:1). Later, Yahweh's Messenger appeared to Samson's mother and father (Judg 13). In this instance, Manoah acknowledged, "We have seen God!" (Judg 13:22).

These and other references to the Messenger of Yahweh in the OT demonstrate God's intimate involvement with his people. On the basis of statements in the NT, many Christians, beginning with the early church fathers, have recognized this Messenger as the pre-incarnate Christ. For instance, John's Gospel says, "No one has ever seen God. The only God who is in the bosom of the Father—he has made him known" (John 1:18).

In addition, the book of Exodus identifies the cloudy pillar that led Israel out of Egypt with the Messenger of God (compare Exod 13:21–22 with 14:19). He is the deliverer of his people, and he threw the Egyptian army into a panic (Exod 14:24). It is no coincidence, then, that when Jesus was transfigured on the mountain and was conversing with Moses and Elijah, he was speaking about "his *exodus* which he was about to fulfill in Jerusalem" (τὴν ἔξοδον αὐτοῦ, ἣν ἤμελλεν πληροῦν ἐν Ἰερουσαλήμ, Luke 9:31). In Jerusalem through his death on the cross and resurrection, Jesus would lead his people out of the bondage of sin and death just as he had led them out of Egypt's slavery. Before doing any of that, he was the Messenger of Yahweh who promised Abraham and Jacob that they would be his ancestors according to his human nature which he would assume in Mary's womb.

## SIN AND GRACE IN GENESIS

As should be evident by the preceding discussion, sin and grace are demonstrated by their constant interplay throughout Genesis. Though humankind fell into sin and deserved to be completely wiped off the face of the earth, in his grace, God promised a Savior to Adam and Eve and later saved the entire human race through the preservation of Noah and his family. Though Abraham's faith in God's promise to bless and protect him wavered when he repeatedly deceived others about his relationship with Sarah (Gen 12:10–20; 20:1–18), God nevertheless was graciously patient with Israel's first patriarch and time and again affirmed his promises to him.

In fact, the sins of willfulness, deception, trickery, and lies would characterize the patriarchal families throughout Genesis. Isaac repeated his father's deceptive ways (Gen 12:11–13) when he lied about Rebekah (Gen 26:6–11). Despite God's pronouncement (Gen 25:23), Isaac insisted on attempting to give the greater blessing to Esau, leading to Rebekah and Jacob's deception and lying (Gen 27). Laban deceived Jacob and gave him Leah for a bride instead of Rachel (Gen 29:13–30). Rachel misled her father when she fled with Jacob from Padan-aram (Gen 31:30–35). Jacob's sons deceived him into thinking Joseph was dead (Gen 37:31–35). When Judah refused to provide a husband for Tamar, his widowed daughter-in-law, she resorted to a ruse in order to bear children for the family line (Gen 38).

Yet despite all of this, God continued to work out his gracious plan for humanity. Through Leah, God would give Judah to Jacob as the bearer of the messianic promise (Gen 29:35; 49:8–12). Through the betrayed Joseph, God would preserve his people even though his brothers acted with evil intent (Gen 50:20). Through one of the twin sons of Tamar—Perez—God would bring forth a line leading to the great king David (Ruth 4:18–22) and to David's greater son Jesus (Matt 1:1–16; Luke 3:23–33).

## CONCLUSION

Genesis not only relates beginnings, but it also serves as the foundation for the rest of the OT. Here Moses first teaches about sin and the promise of redemption of the world through the Savior to come. In its pages, readers can see clearly the contrast between their own fallen nature and the great love, grace, and faithfulness of God.

# SELECT BIBLIOGRAPHY

Alexander, T. Desmond. "Genealogies, Seed and the Compositional Unity of Genesis." *Tyndale Bulletin* 44 (1993): 255–70.

———. "Further Observations on the Term 'Seed' in Genesis." *Tyndale Bulletin* 48 (1997): 363–67.

Batto, Bernard Frank. *Slaying the Dragon: Mythmaking in the Biblical Tradition.* Louisville: Westminster, 1992.

Clines, David J. A. *The Theme of the Pentateuch.* 2nd ed. Journal for the Study of the Old Testament Supplement Series 10. Sheffield: Sheffield Academic, 1997.

Giese, Curtis. "Genesis." In *Called to Be God's People,* 77–117. Called by the Gospel 1. Eugene, OR: Wipf and Stock, 2006.

Hamilton, James. "The Seed of the Woman and the Blessing of Abraham." *Tyndale Bulletin* 58 (2007): 253–73.

Hoffmeier, James K. "Some Thoughts on Genesis 1 and 2 in Light of Egyptian Cosmology." *Journal of the Ancient Near Eastern Society* 15 (1983): 39–49.

Johnston, Gordon H. "Genesis 1 and Ancient Egyptian Creation Myths." *Bibliotheca Sacra* 165 (2008): 178–94.

Lee, Chee-Chew. "גים in Genesis 35:11 and the Abrahamic Promise of Blessings of the Nations." *Journal of the Evangelical Theological Society* 52 (2009): 467–82.

Steinmann, Andrew E. *From Abraham to Paul: A Biblical Chronology.* St. Louis: Concordia, 2011.

Walton, John H. *Ancient Israelite Literature in Its Cultural Context: A Survey of Parallels between Biblical and Ancient Near Eastern Texts.* Grand Rapids: Zondervan, 1989.

Wilson, Robert R. *Genealogy and History in the Biblical World.* Yale Near Eastern Researches 7. New Haven: Yale University, 1977.

Wiseman, P. J. *New Discoveries in Babylonia about Genesis.* London: Marshal, Morgan, and Scott, 1936.

# EXODUS

In Hebrew the name of the second book of the Pentateuch is taken from its first two words ואלה שמות, *and these [are] the names*. This links Exodus with Jacob's ancestors whose lives are a major motif in the book of Genesis. In the LXX the book is called ἔξοδος, which emphasizes Israel's departure from Egypt.

Israel's first moment of settling in a land was when Jacob's sons lived in Egypt under Joseph. They were given the best of the land (Gen 47:6) and dwelt there in security and prosperity (Gen 47:27). Yet this was not *their* land. A Pharaoh arose who forgot Joseph and so he enslaved Israel in his land (Exod 1:8–22). Would God's people ever live in the land he promised to Abraham, Isaac, and Jacob? The book of Exodus answers this question with a resounding "Yes!" God will most certainly set his people free and bring them into the Promised Land!

## AUTHORSHIP

Though Moses is commanded to write in Exod 17:14; 24:4; 34:4, 27–29, and had thirty-nine years to compose the Pentateuch while wandering in the Sinai wilderness, historical critics maintain that Exodus is a creation of anonymous editors who finalized the book after the Babylonian exile.

According to this interpretation, Exod 1–24, 32–34 is likely made up of J and E sources, while chapters 25–31, 34–40 originate from P. Critics also assert that Deuteronomic editing is evident in some passages (e.g., Exod 19:1–8). Understood in this way, the book of Exodus grew over the course of half a millennium or more. It may be likened to a patchwork quilt with various traditions sewn together by post-exilic redactors who were closely associated with P. These authorial issues are discussed in the chapter on the Pentateuch where the argument is made that Moses wrote the book of Exodus.

## LITERARY FEATURES OF EXODUS

The book of Exodus contains theological history. The adjective *theological* does not diminish the noun *history*. Moses wants readers to know that the book's events happened in real space and time. Concurrently, he hopes people will embrace his theological interpretation of this history.

The dominant genre in Exodus is narrative, yet it also displays a wide variety of other genres. A list of names begins the book (Exod 1:1–6), and this is followed by a genealogy (Exod 6:14–25), liturgical rubrics (Exod 12:1–20), a hymn (Exod 15:1–21), and laws (Exod 20–23). The last sixteen chapters include instructions pertaining to the tabernacle (Exod 25–31), and its completion and dedication (Exod 35–40), along with the story of Israel's fall into sin and restoration (Exod 32–34).

The book exhibits several internal linkages that provide overall structure and coherence. For example, Moses' salvation from the Nile River (Exod 2:5) prefigures Israel's deliverance at the Red Sea (Exod 14). Moses' ability to provide water for Zipporah and her sisters (Exod 2:17) foreshadows his water miracles at Marah (Exod 15:23–27) and Rephidim (Exod 17:1–7). The theophany in the burning bush (Exod 3) presages the theophany on Mt. Sinai (Exod 19). Many of the plagues point to greater Egyptian disasters at the Red Sea. For example, Aaron's rod swallows the magicians' rods (Exod 7:12) and the Egyptian army gets swallowed in judgment (Exod 14:16; 15:12). In many ways, the book of Exodus provides its own hermeneutic.

### Outline of Exodus

I.   Israel in Egypt (1:1–13:16)

    A.  Persecution and Moses' early years (1:1–2:25)

    B.  Moses' call and commission (3:1–7:7)

    C.  The plagues and proof of Yahweh's presence (7:8–13:16)

II.  Israel in the wilderness (13:17–18:27)

A.  Leaving Egypt (13:17–24)

B.  Salvation at the Red Sea and celebration (14:1–15:21)

C.  The miracle at Marah and the miracle of manna (15:22–16:34)

D.  Miracle of water and the defeat of the Amalekites (17:1–16)

E.  Getting organized (18:1–27)

III. Israel at Sinai (19:1–40:38)

A.  Yahweh's advent and giving of the Torah (19:1–24:18)

B.  Yahweh's instructions for the tabernacle (25:1–31:18)

C.  Israel's apostasy and restoration (32:1–34:35)

D.  Building the tabernacle and Yahweh's advent (35:1–40:38)

# HISTORICAL, ARCHAEOLOGICAL, AND GEOGRAPHICAL ISSUES

## DATING EVENTS IN THE BOOK OF EXODUS

When we read the pertinent biblical and extra-biblical texts, a fifteenth century date for the exodus becomes the most likely time for Israel's departure from Egypt. Joseph came to power (cf. Gen 41:37–46) during the twelfth dynasty and probably served under the pharaohs Sesotris I (1920–1875) and Amenemhet II (1878–1843) at the end of the Middle Kingdom Period.

Following the fall of the twelfth dynasty, Egypt descended into the Second Intermediate Period, characterized by several competing dynasties. The simultaneous thirteenth and fourteenth dynasties were eventually joined by the fifteenth dynasty headed by Hyksos rulers (c. 1673–1540). (*Hyksos* is the Greek form of an Egyptian word meaning, "rulers of foreign lands," used to refer to Asiatics who ruled over portions of Lower Egypt). When the thirteenth and fourteenth dynasties faded, the Hyksos had to compete with two other native Egyptian dynasties, the sixteenth and seventeenth. However, for many years neither of these were able to oust the Hyksos from the land of the Nile. The Hyksos were violently overthrown by the last Pharaoh of the seventeenth dynasty, Kamose (d. 1540), and Egypt became reunified at the beginning of the eighteenth dynasty under the reign of Kamose's brother, Ahmose I (1539–1515), who may have been the Pharaoh "who did not know Joseph" (Exod 1:8). The events of Exod

1:13–22, 2:1–25 are set during the early years of the Eighteenth Dynasty following the expulsion of the Hyksos.

During this time, the Israelites labored mightily under Ahmose I to build the cities of Pithom and Rameses (Exod 1:11). The only era when God's people could have worked at Pithom was during this period, and it seems evident that Rameses is a scribal update for what was at the time called Avaris and Goshen (cf. Gen 47:11). Such updates appear in other places in the Pentateuch (e.g., Gen 13:18; 14:14 23:19; 37:14; Num 13:22; 14:45; 21:3; Deut 1:44).

Moses was born in 1526. When he was about forty years old, Moses was exiled in Midian for forty years (Acts 7:3; cf. Exod 2:23). Thus, counting back eighty years (Exod 7:7) from the time Moses spoke to Pharaoh immediately preceding the plagues (Exod 7:14–25), Israel's subsequent Exodus (Exod 12:37) can be securely dated to 1446.

According to the Low Chronology, the Pharaoh of the Exodus was Thutmose III (1479–1425), while the High Chronology indicates that Amenhotep II (1454–1428) was the Pharaoh. Those who argue that Amenhotep II was the Pharaoh of the Exodus often cite the Dream Stele of Thutmose III, which indicates he was not the legal heir to the throne (i.e., the legal heir would have died in the tenth plague). However, this is based on speculation about how Thutmose came to power, since Egyptian sources do not tell us why Thutmose ascended to the throne over his siblings. Only Thutmose III ruled for forty years, making him the Pharaoh of the Exodus.

The dating of the Exodus is also connected to 1 Kgs 6:1, which indicates that Israel's departure from Egypt occurred in the 480th year before the month of Ziv during the 4th year of Solomon's reign. Solomon's fourth year was 967, meaning that the Exodus was in 1446, in the month of Nissan (Exod 12:2; Num 33:3).

On the other hand, proponents for a thirteenth century Exodus claim that the 480 years in 1 Kgs 6:1 represent 12 generations of 40 years each. If a generation is twenty years, then Israel's departure from Egypt was in 1208. However, 1 Chr 6:33–37 indicates that there were nineteen generations from the time of Moses to the time of Solomon, not twelve. Further, Steinmann notes that both 1 Kgs 6:1 as well as the Jubilee Years confirm 1446 as the year of the Exodus. He writes:

Those who hold to any date other than 1446 BC for the Exodus, or who maintain that the exodus never happened in any sense as described in the Pentateuch, and as remembered afterward throughout the Old Testament, have to contend that it is a strange coincidence that the date of the exodus as calculated from the Jubilee cycles not only agrees, but *agrees exactly*, with the date of the exodus as calculated from 1 Kgs 6:1.[1]

Dating the Exodus in 1446 is confirmed by Jephthah's statement in Judg 11:26. Probably early in the eleventh century the Ammonites were making hostile advances on Israelite territory in Gilead. Jephthah argues against the Ammonites' aggressive moves on the basis that Israel had a right to the land because they had already occupied it for 300 years. If 1100 is taken as an approximate date for Jephthah's activities, this would place Israel's occupation of the Transjordan under Moses (Num 21) around 1400, about forty years after the departure from Egypt.

Consistent with this view are the pleas for help against the attacks of the Hapiru (perhaps including the Hebrews?) in letters to Thutmose IV (1401–1391) found in the Amarna Letters. Also important is Jericho's destruction that is dated by John Garstang and more recently by Bryant Wood to about 1400. In fact, Bimson claims that a number of cities conquered in Joshua were not standing in the thirteenth century. He thus confirms a fifteenth century period for the Exodus as well as a late fifteenth century date for Joshua's conquest.

The Merneptah Stele also favors a fifteenth century Exodus. Petrie discovered the Merneptah Stele in his excavations in western Thebes in 1896. Merneptah, a Pharaoh of the nineteenth dynasty (1292–1191), subdued several Canaanite cities and defeated an Israelite army. His stele dates to 1211 or 1210. The pertinent line reads, "Canaan is captive with all woe. Ashkelon is conquered, Gezer seized, Yanoam made nonexistent. Israel is wasted, bare of seed."[2] Yet this is not the first extra-biblical reference to Israel in Egypt. Van

---

[1] Andrew E. Steinmann, *From Abraham to Paul: A Biblical Chronology* (St. Louis: Concordia, 2011), 51.

[2] James B. Prichard, ed. *Ancient Near Eastern Texts Relating to the Old Testament* (Princeton: Princeton University Press, 1969), 378.

der Veen, Theis, and Görg maintain that a fragment of a stele, now in Berlin, contains the name *Israel*. The fragment is also from the nineteenth dynasty, but these scholars argue that it was copied from an earlier inscription from the mid-fifteenth century.

In spite of all this evidence, in the 1930s, William F. Albright argued for a thirteenth century date for the Exodus. He believed that this period harmonizes better with archaeological data. Albright maintained, for example, that the cities of Pithom and Rameses, cited in Exod 1:11 (respectively modern Tell el-Maskhouta and Tanis), were not occupied in the fifteenth century. Rameses was built and named for the Egyptian pharaoh named Rameses II who ruled in c. 1279–1213.

Against this position, Bimson maintains that it is very speculative to link Pithom and Rameses with Tell el-Maskhouta and Tanis. It is better, he argues, to associate Rameses with modern Qantir which was occupied in the fifteenth century. Understood this way, Rameses in Exod 1:11 is like Dan in Gen 14:14, a later updating of the text. Bimson further demonstrates that Pithom may be modern Tell er-Retebah or Heliopolis—both are sites connected with activity prior to the thirteenth century.

The second reason some embrace a thirteenth century date for the Exodus is that scholars like Albright, Wright, and Yadin associate Joshua's conquest with the archaeological remains in Canaan that date to the thirteenth century. However, it is just as easy to link these destruction layers with events in the book of Judges. Further archaeological evidence from Jericho, Ai, and Hazor supports a late fifteenth century conquest, therefore pointing to a mid-fifteenth century date for the Exodus. However the greatest obstacle for a thirteenth century Exodus is the fact that this position must condense over 350 years of narrated OT history in the books of Joshua and Judges into 100 years.

Taken together, the cumulative evidence suggests that Pharaoh's interaction with the birth attendants as told in Exod 1:15–22 took place no earlier than after the expulsion of the Hyksos (in the mid-sixteenth century) and no later than the birth of Moses (1526). 1 Kgs 6:1 and 1 Chr 6:33–37 confirm a date of 1446 for the Exodus, while the jubilee data and Judg 11:26 independently converge on a date of 1406 for the beginning of the conquest. The 1406 date is further confirmed by archaeological data from Jericho, Ai (Khirbet el-Maqatir), and Hazor.

## *The Exodus*

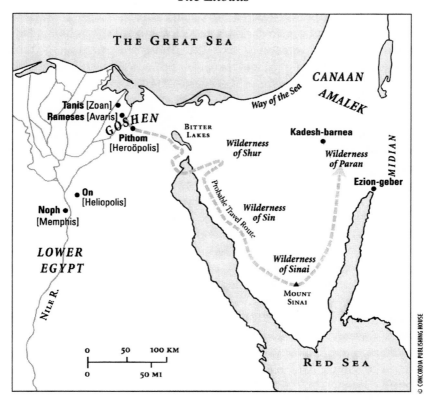

God led His people through the wilderness, not by the Way of the Sea (Exod 13:17–18). Many sites on their route cannot be located with certainty. The Israelites journeyed from Rameses in Goshen to Succoth (12:37), which may be Pithom. They marched to Etham, on the edge of the wilderness (13:20). God ordered them to Pi-hahiroth to bait a trap for Pharaoh (14:1–4). Then God led His people through the Red Sea, trapping the Egyptians under the waters (14:5–31); see *Ant.* 2:315, 324–25. The Israelites traveled into the Wilderness of Shur to Marah (15:22–25) and Elim (15:27). They came via Dophkah and Alush to Rephidim (Num 33:13–14; Exod 17:1), where they defeated the Amalekites (Exod 17:8–16). Through the Wilderness of Sinai, they came to Mount Sinai (Exod 19–40). Israel went to Kibroth-hattaavah, Hazeroth (Num 11:34–35), and then into the Wilderness of Paran (12:16). God commanded Israel to remain in the wilderness for 40 years (Num 14:20–35).

## THE RED SEA

The Hebrew יַם־סוּף is often translated *Red Sea*, a tradition that goes back to the LXX, τὴν ἐρυθρὰν θάλασσαν. It is uncertain where Israel crossed the יָם־סוּף when they left Egypt (e.g., Exod 15:4, 22). Some point out that יָם־סוּף literally denotes *sea of reeds* and reeds don't grow in salt water like that of the Red Sea. Therefore the phrase must refer to a fresh water lake that existed just north of the Gulf of Suez. Caution is in order, though, as יָם־סוּף in 1 Kgs 9:25 clearly refers to the Gulf of Aqaba, which *is* salt water (cf. Exod 23:31). Scholars have proposed various locations like the Bitter Lakes region, Lake Menzaleh, Lake Sorbonis, and the Gulf of Suez as possible sites.

## MT. SINAI

Some have located Mt. Sinai in northwest Arabia, partly on the grounds that they believe a volcano is required to explain the events in Exod 19:16–25. But the smoke, fire, and clouds are better understood as components connected to a miraculous theophany. To be sure, by marriage Moses was related to the Midianites (Exod 3:1; 18:1), whose homeland was considered to be in the region of Arabia, but he was also related to the Kenites who were a nomadic Midianite clan whose presence in the Sinai region is well documented (cf. Judg 1:16; 4:11).

Confirming that Mt. Sinai is not in Arabia but in the Sinai Peninsula, is the fact that the locale was an eleven-day journey from Kadesh-barnea (Deut 1:2). It also took Elijah forty days to reach Sinai from Beersheba (1 Kgs 19:8). It is best, then, to understand that Jebel Musa (Arabic for "Mountain of Moses"), or Mt. Horeb, in the southern Sinai peninsula, is the Mt. Sinai of God's revelation of his Torah to Israel. This has been the Christian tradition dating to the fourth century AD.

## THEOLOGICAL THEMES IN EXODUS

### KNOWING YAHWEH

Pharaoh asks the question, "Who is Yahweh?" (Exod 5:2), and Exodus takes up this theme in a way unlike any other book in the OT. In Exodus we meet Yahweh, the God who is attentive to Israel's pain and singularly against all who oppress his people. Yahweh is awesome, frightening, merciful, jealous, and never to be taken lightly. He is devoted to Israel through thick and thin. In contrast to Pharaoh, whose name is never mentioned in Exodus, thus making evil impersonal, Yahweh can be known. He offers Israel this personal relationship. "I will be your God and you will be my people" (Exod 6:7).

The Tetragrammaton (יהוה) is inextricably linked to the phrase אהיה אשר אהיה, *I am who I am* (Exod 3:14). A common proposal is that the name Yahweh derives from the verb used two times in this verse, היה, *to be*. The initial yod signifies an imperfect verb. Yahweh then means *the One who is*, that is, *the Being One* (thus the Septuagint).

Yahweh is further explained in Exod 6:1–8 where אני יהוה, *I am Yahweh*, appears four times. Elmer Martens contends that this phrase defines the name of Yahweh by setting forth his fourfold plan for Israel: (1) deliverance from Egypt (Exod 6:6); (2) the creation of a covenant people (Exod 6:7a); (3) a relationship whereby Israel may know him (Exod 6:7b); and (4) the gift of the Promised Land (Exod 6:8). The goal of this plan is for the entire world to know Yahweh (e.g., Exod 9:14; 14:4, 18; 18:8–12).

However, the most thorough definition of Yahweh appears following the golden calf apostasy (Exod 32) when Moses pleads for God to continue leading his people. Yahweh indicates that he is willing to stay with Israel, but Moses is not convinced, asking for a sign of divine glory (Exod 33:18). Yahweh then says, "I myself will make all my goodness pass before your face and I will proclaim my name 'Yahweh' " (Exod 33:19). After Moses chisels two new stone tablets, he ascends to Sinai with them in hand. "Yahweh passed before him and proclaimed, 'Yahweh, Yahweh' " (Exod 34:6). The repetition of the divine name appears here and once more in Ps 104:1. Exod 34:6–7, then, is the definitive definition of Israel's God and it subsequently becomes their creed.

> And he called out, Yahweh, Yahweh, the God of compassion and grace, slow to anger and abounding in covenant loyalty and faithfulness. Keeping covenant loyalty to thousands and, lifting up iniquity and rebellion and sin. Yet he will surely not acquit the guilty, visiting the iniquity of the fathers upon the sons and upon the sons of sons up to the third and fourth generation.

These words appear again, with slight variations, in sixteen other passages (Num 14:8; Deut 4:31; Pss 78:38; 86: 5, 15; 103:8; 111:4; 112:4; 116:5; 145:8; Joel 2:13; Jonah 4:2; Hab 1:3; Neh 9:17, 31;

2 Chr 30:9). Yahweh's grace-filled qualities are mentioned first because they are from eternity and last into eternity. His judgment upon sin follows. It appears in time and will end on the Last Day. There exists in Yahweh a tension between tender mercy and stern moral retribution. Out of the two, though, he is inclined more towards showing steadfast love.

Though Yahweh will not give his glory to another (e.g., Isa 48:11), he places his name in his Messenger (Exod 23:21). Who is this Messenger? The epiphany at the burning bush (Exod 3:2–6) makes it clear that Yahweh's Messenger and Yahweh share the same attributes. The Messenger speaks (Exod 3:2), Yahweh speaks (Exod 3:4, 7), and then God speaks (Exod 3:6, 11, 13, 15). This same Messenger goes ahead of Israel to defeat the nation's enemies (Exod 23:20; 32:34). These texts affirm that Yahweh and the Messenger are one. In NT terms, the Messenger "is the image of the invisible God" (Col 1:15), "the radiance of God's glory and the exact representation of his being" (Heb 1:3). Anyone who sees the Messenger sees the Father (John 14:9). The OT Messenger is a pre-incarnate form of the Second Person of the Trinity who became man in Jesus Christ.

## PHARAOH'S HARD HEART

Two verbs are used to describe the hardening of Pharaoh's heart, חזק (Qal e.g., Exod 7:13, 22; 8:19; Piel, e.g., Exod 4:21; 9:21; 11:10) and כבד (Qal e.g., Exod 9:7; Hiphil, e.g., Exod 9:34; 10:1). Both verbs indicate varying degrees of obstinacy, single-mindedness, stubbornness, and lack of regard. Ten times Yahweh is the subject of these verbs, but ten times Pharaoh (or Pharaoh's heart) is the subject. Yahweh hardens Pharaoh's heart (Exod 9:12; 10:1, 20, 27; 11:10), but this happens only *after* the king hardens his own heart (Exod 7:22; 8:15, 19, 32). Yahweh's judgment is to confirm Pharaoh in his sin by hardening the king's heart. Significantly, Yahweh only becomes the subject in the sixth plague (Exod 9:12), while his hardening is anticipated as a future action in Exod 4:21; 7:3. Prior to the sixth plague it is Pharaoh who hardens his own heart. The king's obstinence is due to his own willful resistance of Yahweh's plan for Israel's freedom. Each time Pharaoh refuses to humble himself it becomes easier for him to refuse Yahweh the next time. Yahweh does not originate pharaonic rejection of the divine will, but there comes a point when God seals the fate of this oppressor and makes his fall from power inevitable. It is as though God says to the king, "If that is how you want it, I'll help you along the way."

Throughout this section of Exodus, Pharaoh is not presented as a puppet with no will of his own. He is not an automaton. The struggle is real. Yahweh does not discard him instantly, nor does he relate with Pharaoh in a way in which his will is overpowered. At the same time, Pharaoh is guilty of violating God's ordering of the world. By describing Pharaoh's hardening in these ways, both human guilt and divine sovereignty are emphasized (cf. Rom 1:18–32).

## THE PLAGUES

God's judgments against Egypt are commonly called plagues (from the root נגף). Their movement in chapters 7–12 is from disease and damage to finally darkness and death. The plagues are arranged in the form of three series of calamities comprising three afflictions in each series. The tenth is climactic and lies outside the pattern in that it was the final and most definitive judgment.

The book of Exodus also employs the language of אות, *sign* (e.g., Exod 4:17; 7:3) and מופת, *portent* (e.g., Exod 4:21; 7:3, 9; 11:9–10). Signs and portents are events that prefigure the future (e.g., 1 Sam 2:34; Jer 44:29; 1 Kgs 13:2). As such, the plagues are both acts of judgment in themselves and point toward a future judgment, either the death of the firstborn or Egypt's demise at the Red Sea, or both. By the last plague, Pharaoh and the Egyptians beg Israel to leave (Exod 12:31).

Egyptians worshiped over eighty different gods and goddesses. In Mesopotamia the king was considered the adopted son of the deity, but in Egypt the Pharaoh personified the deity. He was not considered a mere representation of the gods, but was a god himself. Montet observes: "The king was certainly far above ordinary mortals. In official stele he was often called *neter nefer*, the perfect god. A courtier even described him as *neter aa*, the great god."[3] Pharaoh had been begotten by Amon-Re through a queen mother and was deemed to be the god Horus, son of the goddess Hathor.

While Yahweh's plagues serve to demonstrate the impotency of Pharaoh, both as a ruler and as a god, it is not helpful to overly

---

[3] Pierre Montet, *Eternal Egypt* (New York: The New American Library, 1964), 57.

schematize them. They are primarily a judgment upon Egypt's gods (Exod 12:12; 15:11; 18:11). Though Hapi, the fertility god, was closely related to the Nile and Amon/Re was the Egyptian sun deity, specific plagues do not always match up with specific deities in the Egyptian pantheon.

Egyptian magicians duplicated the first sign, turning their rods into serpents (Exod 7:12). They also reproduced changing water into blood (Exod 7:22) and bringing up the frogs (Exod 8:7). The next plagues are lice, insects, pestilence striking the livestock, boils hitting people and livestock, hail striking people, livestock and agriculture, locusts, darkness, and the killing of the firstborn of people and animals (cf. Pss 78:42–51; 105:28–36 for similar lists). The ninth plague was especially devastating in that Amon/Re (the sun) was the Egyptian national god—part of a triad of deities that also included his wife, Mut, and their son, Khons.

Some maintain that the plagues were natural events though extraordinary in magnitude. This naturalistic approach is incorrect for several reasons. It is hardly natural for Moses to strike the ground with his rod and turn it into a snake, and the Nile did not look like blood, it *turned into* blood. Moreover, when the Nile turned to blood, so did the water in vessels throughout Egypt, ruling out a naturalistic interpretation (Exod 7:19–20). Additionally, the plagues were predicted (e.g., Exod 9:5), were discriminate (e.g., Exod 9:26), and in general they move from the least intense to the most intense. The word כל, *all*, is pervasive in these accounts. It is employed over fifty times: for instance, "every tree," "all the fruit," "the whole land." As such, the plagues exceed what is normal at various levels including time, scope, and intensity. To interpret the plagues as only natural occurrences is an idea far removed from the book of Exodus.

## MISSION

At first glance, it doesn't appear as though God's mission to the world is a major theme in Exodus. Yet a closer look uncovers that this is a significant motif. Yahweh's salvation is not for Israel's sake alone, but also for the nations. In Exod 9:14–16, Moses relates these words of Yahweh to Pharaoh:

> Because this time I am sending the full power of my plagues against you and against your servants and against your people, so you may know (ידע) that there is no one like me in

all the earth. For by now I could have sent my hand and struck you and your people with a pestilence that would have wiped you off the earth. But I have raised you up for this, so that I might show you my power and so that my name might be proclaimed in all the earth.

Yahweh expresses his desire that Pharaoh might know (ידע)—here in its fullest covenantal sense—that he is the only God "in all the earth." It is not surprising, then, that when God's people leave Egypt, "a mixed multitude" (i.e., believing Egyptians) departs with Israel (Exod 12:38).

The mission-based patriarchal promises (Gen 12:1–3) provide the foundation for the covenant Yahweh makes with Israel at Sinai (Exod 19–24). Israelites in Egypt are inheritors of the promises given to Abraham, Isaac, and Jacob (Exod 3:15–17; 6:4, 8). Therefore, far from being a distinctly separate covenant, a far less comprehensive creative act occurred at Sinai—and this within an already existing covenant, the one made with the patriarchs. Sinai was a closer specification of what was already entailed in Yahweh's missional promises made in the book of Genesis.

The covenant at Sinai does not establish Israel's relationship with Yahweh. Rather, Sinai's focus is upon the nation's calling as Yahweh's missionary to the world. At Sinai, Israelites are distinctly marked and empowered to be evangelists. This covenant is not a matter of the people's *status*, but of their *vocation*. The flow of thought in Exod 19:5–6 therefore runs like this: "Listen to my voice and do what I command, and in so doing you shall show yourselves to be my people and as for my part, I will be your God and perform the oath sworn to the ancestors. The nations will see this relationship and by faith some will become a part of my chosen people." The phrase in Exod 19:6, "You will be for me a kingdom of priests," announces that Yahweh is recommissioning Israel to be the intermediary between him and the nations. The idea is already hinted at in Exod 4:22: "Then say to Pharaoh, 'This is what Yahweh says: Israel is my firstborn son.'" If Israel is God's firstborn son, that implicitly means there are more children on the way—these family members are the nations that will be blessed through Abraham and his seed. And so at Sinai, Israel's status and vocation were not established for the first time. Instead, they were repeated and renewed. Israel is again commissioned to be the channel through which the gift of salvation will come to all the nations. An example of this appears in Jethro's conversion. Once a priest of Midian (Exod 3:1), after he hears of Israel's salvation at the Red Sea, Jethro confesses, "Now I know that Yahweh is greater than all the gods" (Exod 18:11).

God's redemptive activity on behalf of Israel is not only for Israel and the nations—it also stands in service to the entire creation. In fact, a creation theology is built into the very structure of Exodus. This can be seen in the parallels between Exodus and Gen 1–9. Both share these motifs: (1) a creational setting (Gen 1:28; Exod 1:7); (2) anti-creational activity (Gen 3–6; Exod 1–2); (3) the word תבה which for Noah denotes *ark* (e.g., Gen 6:14), while for Moses it means *basket* (e.g., Exod 2:3); (4) the flood and plagues are ecological disasters; (5) death and deliverance appear in and through water (Gen 6–9; Exod 14); (6) the covenants with Noah and with Israel are confirmed with signs (Gen 9; Exod 24:1; cf. Exod 31:17); and (7) the tabernacle mirrors the days of creation. (See the discussion below.) Yahweh proclaims, "All the earth is mine" (Exod 19:5), and so his actions in the book of Exodus are to restore it *all* rightfully to himself.

### ISRAEL'S LAWS

The Pharaoh calls Israel "a people" (Exod 1:9), but Yahweh calls them "my people" (Exod 3:7). What does it look like to belong to Yahweh? How is Israel to live after their deliverance at the Red Sea? And what will life look like now that they are no longer under the cruel reign of Pharaoh but under the loving rule of Yahweh?

Three months after leaving Egypt, Israel arrives at Mount Sinai (Exod 19:1) where they remain until Num 10:33. While at Sinai, God gives his people the עשרת הדברים, "Ten Words" (cf. Exod 34:28), in Exod 20:1–17, as well as the Book of the Covenant (cf. Exod 24:7) which follows in Exod 20:22–23:14. (The OT has a number of Decalogue-like formulations [e.g., Exod 34:17–26; Deut 27:15–26; Lev 19], but only Deut 5:6–21 is strictly parallel.) The elect people (Exod 3:7) are now the redeemed people (Exod 19:4). Only then is the Torah stated at Sinai. Yahweh saves apart from human obedience.

Divine law given at Sinai stands in continuity with the law observed by people in the book of Genesis. For example, law is assumed in Gen 4:10–13 when Yahweh announces to Cain that he should have known that murder is wrong. Patriarchal narratives also testify to pre-Sinai regulations. One example is in Gen 26:5:

"Abraham listened to my voice and kept my charge, my commandments, my statutes, and my instructions" (cf. also Gen 18:19, 25).

The discovery of the law code of the Babylonian king Hammurabi (c. 1700)—who lived long before Moses—has silenced many critics who maintained that the complexities of Israel's laws in the book of Exodus reflect a post-exilic period. Hammurabi's law code, engraved on a piece of black rock, was discovered at Susa in 1902 and contains 282 laws. Their purpose was not to promote godliness, but rather regulate social relationships.

## THE TABERNACLE

The overall movement in the book of Exodus is from slavery to Pharaoh to the worship of Yahweh. Liturgical rubrics appear in Exod 12, a song is sung in Exod 15:1–18, while Moses and others eat and drink in God's presence in Exod 24:9–12. However, the most obvious worship concerns in the book take place with the building of the tabernacle. Almost one-third of Exodus is devoted to issues regarding its construction. The question of Exodus is not only Whom will Israel serve—Yahweh or Pharaoh? but also, How will Israel worship—according to Yahweh's desires by means of the tabernacle or according to their own desires by means of the golden calf?

Tabernacle-like structures appeared in Egyptian wall-paintings as early as the First Dynasty (c. 3000–2800). Based on these and other artifacts, Kitchen concludes that "most of the biblical tabernacle's technology was literally as 'old as the Pyramids,' in fact older."

God came down to call Moses from the burning bush (Exod 3:8). He also descended upon Sinai to give Moses the Ten Commandments as well as the Book of the Covenant (Exod 19–24). But because Yahweh wanted to live among the Israelites in a permanent way, he told Moses, "Have them [the Israelites] make me מקדש, *a sanctuary*, so that I may dwell among them" (Exod 25:8). Out of ninety-three occurrences of the root קדש, *holy*, in the book of Exodus, seventy-eight of them are connected with the tabernacle. The sanctuary/tabernacle was patterned after the heavenly temple (Exod 25:9, 40) and allowed Yahweh to take up permanent residence in the midst of his people.

In Exod 25–31 Yahweh instructs Moses on *how* to build the tabernacle, while Exod 36–40 reports *that* they built it. These last chapters are slightly abbreviated, but in other aspects they mirror the earlier instructions. In between the tabernacle's planning and execution is the golden calf apostasy and its aftermath (Exod 32–34).

Just as there are creational links between Gen 1–9 and the book of Exodus (see above), there are connections between the construction of the tabernacle and the creation of the world. They are as follows: (1) the Spirit hovers over the creation (Gen 1:2), while Bezalel and the other workers on the tabernacle are given the Spirit to complete the work (Exod 31:20); (2) just as Yahweh created a world in which he would dwell (e.g., Ps 104:1–4; Isa 40:22), Israel's craftsmen re-create a place for Yahweh to dwell (Exod 40:34); (3) the dedication of the tabernacle occurred on New Year's day (Exod 40:2, 17), thus corresponding to the first day of creation; (4) Yahweh's directions to Moses come in seven movements (Exod 25–31) which correspond to seven acts of Moses (Exod 40:17–33), and these "sevens" are parallel to the seven days of creation (Gen 1:2–2:3); (5) both Gen 2:1–2 and Exod 31:17 express concern over keeping the Sabbath; (6) the sequence in Gen 1–3 is creation, fall, and re-creation and this is mirrored in the building of the tabernacle (Exod 25–31), Israel's fall (Exod 32), and the people's re-creation (Exod 33–40); (7) Yahweh looks at his finished creation and declares it "very good" (Gen 1:31), and this corresponds to Moses "seeing" and evaluating the finished work of the tabernacle (there are eighteen references in Exodus 39–40); and (8) an act of blessing occurs in both Gen 2:3 and Exod 39:43.

Additionally, some scholars have argued that the tabernacle is a partial recapturing of Eden. It is like the garden Yahweh planted (Num 24:5–6). Note these connections: Both are places where Yahweh walks among his people (Gen 3:8; Lev 26:11–13; Deut 23:14). The menorah (Exod 25:31–35) has tree-like qualities, evoking the trees in the Garden of Eden (Gen 2:16–17). Eden and the tabernacle are entered from the east (Gen 3:24; Exod 27:13). Finally, Eden is guarded by cherubim (Gen 3:24), who also guard the ark (Exod 25:10–22).

What are we to make of these connections between creation and the tabernacle? Fretheim observes, "The tabernacle is a realization of God's created order in history; both reflect the glory of God in their midst." Indeed, the glory of God fills the tabernacle (Exod 40:34) just as the heavens declare the glory of God (Ps 19:1; cf. Isa 6:3). Levenson states:

The function of these correspondences is to underscore the depiction of the sanctuary as a world, that is, an ordered, supportive, and obedient environment, and the depiction of the world as a sanctuary, that is, a place in which the reign of God is visible and unchallenged, and his holiness is palpable, unthreatened, and pervasive.[4]

The tabernacle was a microcosm of creation (e.g., Ps 11:4; 78:69; Isa 66:1–2). It is the world order as Yahweh intended, reduced in size for Israel.

The golden calf apostasy in Exod 32, sandwiched between Yahweh's instructions to Moses about the tabernacle (Exod 25–31) and the tabernacle's construction (Exod 35–40), is Israel's alternative to a world-ordering divine presence. Everything is undone as the people become like the god(s) they worshiped (cf. Ps 115:8; 135:18). Calves are stubborn and prone to run away. Just so, Israel becomes "a stiff-necked people" (Exod 32:9b) and turns aside quickly (Exod 32:8a).

Aaron created the calf with a writing tool (Exod 32:4), while in Exod 31:18, Yahweh's finger writes on the tablets of the Ten Commandments. Only when the calf is destroyed (Exod 32:20) does Yahweh rewrite his word (Exod 34:1–4). Fretheim compares and contrasts the two building narratives:

### Comparison between the Building of the Tabernacle and the Construction of the Golden Calf

| Tabernacle | Golden Calf |
|---|---|
| Yahweh's initiative | Israel's initiative |
| People freely give to its construction | Aaron demands gold |
| Detailed preparations | No planning |
| Lengthy building process | Lightning-fast assembly |
| Guard Yahweh's holiness | Instant accessibility |
| Yahweh is the invisible God | The calf is a visible god |

---

[4] Jon Levenson, *Creation and the Persistence of Evil: The Jewish Drama of Divine Omnipotence* (San Francisco: Harper & Row, 1988), 86.

| Yahweh is personal | The calf is an impersonal object |

The contrast between the two could not be drawn any more sharply.

The tabernacle was designed to have different levels of holiness. Concerning the metals, the posts holding up the courtyard curtain were silver hooks and rings (Exod 27:10–11). The frames that constituted the walls were silver (Exod 26:19–21). Inside the tabernacle, most of the furnishings and appointments were pure gold (e.g., Exod 25:24–31).

The levels of the tabernacle's accessibility are as follows: Outside of Israel's camp was the realm of the nations, the ritually unclean. Only Israelites who were ritually clean could inhabit space inside the camp. The courtyard was dominated by priests and Levites, though laypeople could enter this area with their sacrificial animals. Only priests and Levites could enter the tabernacle, while inside the Holy of Holies, only the high priest could enter once a year (Lev 16).

The curtains also demonstrate these grades of holiness (Exod 26:1–14). The outermost curtains were "fine goatskin leather" or "the hide of sea porpoise, or dolphin." The innermost curtain was made out of "blue, purple, and scarlet thread with skillfully embroidered cherubim" (Exod 26:1).

Once all of this was in place, God descended from the mountain and entered the sanctuary (Exod 40:34). Israelites no longer needed to go up to Yahweh, since he came down to them. "But Moses was not able to enter the tent of meeting because the cloud dwelled upon it, and the glory of Yahweh filled the tabernacle" (Exod 40:35). No one was able to enter the tabernacle—not even Moses! Thus, the book of Exodus ends with a paradox. God resides on earth, but people are unable to access the forgiving power of his holiness. The solution comes in the office of the priesthood, described in Exod 28–30, although the ordination rite does not take place until Lev 8–9.

## CHRIST IN EXODUS

The verb גאל, often translated *redeem*, first appears in the OT in Exod 6:6. It denotes making a payment for a family member. Someone who acts as a redeemer therefore does so because he has a family connection with the person who is in debt or some other kind of need. Yahweh's decision to redeem Israel was based upon the fact that they were his fellow family members—indeed, they were his firstborn son (Exod 4:22). In a similar way, Jesus is our Redeemer. As our Brother (Rom 8:29) who shares our human nature (Heb 2:14), he has paid off our debt of sin (Col 2:14) and we are free (e.g., Gal 4:5; Tit 2:14).

Christ is also prefigured in the book of Exodus because he shares many of Israel's characteristics. Jesus is *the* firstborn Son in both creation and redemption (Col 1:15, 18), he was called out of Egypt (Matt 2:15; cf. Hos 11:1) and tempted in the wilderness (e.g., Matt 4:1–11). Christ not only celebrates the Passover (e.g., Mark 14:12–25; cf. Exod 12), he is the final Passover Lamb (1 Cor 5:7). He is the Rock that followed Israel in the desert (1 Cor 10:4; cf. Exod 17:1–7), and he assumed the role of Moses as both the final interpreter of the Torah (Matt 5–7) and as the world's greatest intercessor (e.g., Luke 23:34; Heb 7:25; cf. Exod 32:11–14).

John's Gospel contains several Christological allusions to the book of Exodus, the primary one is Christ's tabernacling among us to demonstrate God's presence and glory (John 1:14). John highlights the Passover in his Gospel—more so than the synoptic Gospels (John 2:13, 23; 6:4; 11:55; 12:1; 13:1; 18:28, 39; 19:14). Jesus is the Passover Lamb (John 1:29, 36), and his crucifixion coincides with the Jewish Passover (John 19:14). The Fourth Gospel also accents Yahweh's "I am" (Exod 3:14) by recording Christ's "I am" statements (e.g., John 6:35; 8:12; 10:11; 14:6).

Alexander notes that John's seven signs comport with the signs in Exodus as both sets are given for people to know the true God (e.g., Exod 9:29; John 20:30–31). But the signs also contrast with each other. Water turns to blood in Exodus while in John water is turned to wine (John 2:1–11). In Exodus the last sign is the death of the firstborn. However, in John the last of Jesus' signs is the resurrection of Lazarus.

## SIN AND GRACE IN EXODUS

The name *Moses* appears 770 times in the OT and roughly a third of these occurrences are in the book of Exodus. Moses, then, is closely related with almost all of the sin and grace texts in the book. He approaches sinful Pharaoh and repeatedly delivers God's message: "Let my people go" (e.g., Exod 5:1; 10:3). Moses and Israel, though, are far from perfect. Moses balks at God's call on his life (Exod 3–4), while Israel complains about their lack of water (Exod 15:23–27;

17:1–7). But Israel's chief sin is committing idolatry. Impatient Israelites prompted Aaron to build a golden calf (Exod 32).

Grace abounds in the book of Exodus. Its four notable epiphanies demonstrate divine mercy: (1) with Moses at the burning bush (Exod 3); (2) with Israel at Sinai (Exod 19–23); (3) with Moses, Aaron, Nadab, Abihu, and the seventy elders on the mountain (Exod 24:9–11); and (4) with Moses again on Sinai when God forgives the people and pledges his loyalty to them (Exod 33–34).

## CONCLUSION

In the book of Exodus, Israel moves from bondage to freedom, from despair to praise, from Egypt to Sinai, and from serving Pharaoh by making bricks to serving Yahweh by building his tabernacle. Yahweh seems completely absent in Exod 1, as Pharaoh's genocidal policies become agents of horror and hell. Yet, by the end of the book, Yahweh is fully present as his glory fills the tabernacle.

The verb עבד, *serve*, appears ninety-seven times in Exodus and, while it can denote *slave labor* (e.g., Exod 1:14; 2:23; 6:6), when applied to Israel after the Exodus it means *service* to Yahweh (e.g., Exod 27:19; 36:1, 3, 5; 39:32, 42). The book of Exodus, then, describes Israel's movement from serving one master to another. One kills and destroys. The other liberates and loves.

Israel's Exodus salvation (Exod 14) is the primary way to express deliverance in the OT and reverberates in the NT. From Isaiah's new exodus from Babylon (e.g., Isa 43:16–21), to Christ's Easter exodus on the third day (e.g., Luke 9:31), Israel's departure from Egypt is the arch that spans the rest of the biblical narrative. John likens God's final act of deliverance to the song of Moses and the Lamb (Rev 15:3), when the divine Warrior (cf. Exod 15:3) returns victoriously on his white horse to be called the King of Kings (Rev 19:16; cf. Exod 15:18).

## SELECTED BIBLIOGRAPHY

Alexander, T. D. *From Paradise to Promised Land: An Introduction to the Pentateuch.* 3rd ed. Grand Rapids: Baker, 2012.

Bimson, J. J. *Redating the Exodus and Conquest.* Journal for the study of the Old Testament: Supplement Series 5. Sheffield: JSOT, 1978.

Davis, John. *Moses and the Gods of Egypt*. 2nd ed. Winona Lake, IN: BMH Books, 1986.

Fretheim, Terrance. *Exodus*. Interpretation: A Bible Commentary for Teaching and Preaching. Louisville: Westminster, 1991.

Kitchen, Kenneth. *On the Reliability of Old Testament*. Grand Rapids: Eerdmans, 2003.

Levenson, Jon. *Creation and the Persistence of Evil: The Jewish Drama of Divine Omnipotence*. 1st ed. San Francisco: Harper and Row, 1988.

Montet, Pierre. *Eternal Egypt*. New York: The New American Library, 1964.

Sarna, Nahum. *Exploring Exodus: The Origins of Biblical Israel*. New York: Schocken Books, 1986.

Steinmann, Andrew E. *From Abraham to Paul: A Biblical Chronology*. St. Louis: Concordia, 2011.

Stuart, Douglas. *Exodus*. The New American Commentary, Vol. 2. Nashville: Broadman and Holman, 2006.

van der Veen, Peter, Christoffer Theis, and Manfred Görg. "Israel in Canaan (Long) Before Pharaoh Merenptah? A Fresh Look at Berlin Statue Pedestal Relief 21687." *Journal of Ancient Egyptian Interconnections* (2010) 2.4:15–25.

5

# LEVITICUS

> If you read people passages from the divine books that are
> good and clear, they will hear them with great joy. . . . But
> provide someone a reading from Leviticus, and at once the
> listener will gag and push it away as if it were some bizarre
> food. He came, after all, to learn how to honor God, to take in
> the teachings concerning justice and piety. But instead he is
> now hearing about the ritual of burnt sacrifices![1]

These words come from the pen of Origen, a famous Father of the
Church (AD 185–254). He notes that for most people, the book of
Leviticus is difficult to appreciate. After all, in chapter after chapter,
passages describe in great detail how animals are to be sliced and
severed and then sacrificed. There are also parts that seem like they
come from another planet: things like Urim and Thummim (Lev 8:8),
"unauthorized fire" (Lev 10:1), and bright skin (Lev 13:2). No
wonder so many "gag and push it away." Ironically, though, some of
Origen's greatest theological writings derive from the book of
Leviticus.

The first word in Leviticus is ויקרא, "and he called," and serves as
the book's title in Hebrew. This imperfect, *waw*–consecutive verb
connects Leviticus with the book of Exodus. For instance, in Exodus,
God tells Moses that the Israelites are a priestly nation (Exod 19:6),
and Leviticus lays out many priestly regulations. In the book of

---

[1] Origen, *Homily 27: Numbers 33:1–49*, quoted in Ephraim Radner, *Leviticus* (Grand
Rapids: Brazos, 2008), 17.

Exodus, the design for the tabernacle is revealed (Exod 25–31), while much of Leviticus explains how it is to function as a means of grace and therefore serves as the tabernacle's user's manual. At the end of Exodus, Yahweh's presence descends upon the tabernacle (Exod 40:34). In Leviticus, the implications of his presence are spelled out. The main link, though, between Exodus and Leviticus is blood. Moses mediates a covenant of blood (Exod 24:1–8) and explains its significance throughout the book of Leviticus.

## AUTHORSHIP

Critics maintain that before the Babylonian exile, Israel had little need for priests and sacrifices, because a doctrine of sin had not yet been developed. It was only after the exilic debacle that Israelites saw their sin and felt a need for forgiveness. At this time the priestly writers arose, with their heavy accent on sacrifices and atonement, to offer a system that imparted God's forgiveness. Critics call these writings P (for priestly) and view it as offering a stilted and bureaucratic religion. P represses the earlier "heart religion" represented in J and E. The priestly writings, critics maintain, are composed of Lev 1–16, along with Exod 25–31, 35–40 and much of the book of Numbers. In 1877, August Klostermann theorized that Lev 17–26 was earlier than P and so called these chapters *Heiligkeitsgesetz*, "Holiness Code" or H, a designation that is still popular today. Some have even gone so far as to assign Ezekiel as its author.

To be sure, Leviticus never claims Mosaic authorship, but its contents testify that the book was mediated through Moses to Israel. It opens with the statement, "And Yahweh called to Moses" (Lev 1:1), and the phrase "Yahweh said to Moses" appears throughout the text (e.g., Lev 4:1; 5:14; 11:1; 13:1; 16:1 24:1; 27:1). Yahweh repeatedly commands (צוה) Moses to pass on divine words to Israel (e.g., Lev 7:37–38; 27:34), and Moses obeys (e.g., Lev 8:1–5; 23:44; 24:23). Therefore, Leviticus places a heavy emphasis on its divinely authorized teaching that God gave to Moses who then delivered it to Israel. To accent this idea, the book begins with Yahweh speaking to Moses in the tent of meeting (Lev 1:1) and ends with him speaking to Moses on Sinai (Lev 27:34).

In Mark 7:10, Jesus confirms that Moses spoke about punishment by death to those who belittle their parents (Lev 20:9). He also affirms that Moses commanded in Lev 14:2–32 that a healed leper needs to present himself to the priest as well as make an offering for his purification (Matt 8:4; Mark 1:44; Luke 5:14). For a further defense on the Mosaic composition of Leviticus, refer to chapter 2 on the Origin of the Pentateuch.

## LITERARY FEATURES OF LEVITICUS

Leviticus is divided into two major sections that are separated by chapter 16, which deals with the annual Day of Atonement. Chapters 1–15 deal with priestly holiness, for they give instructions about sacrifices and rituals which ceremonially relate to holiness in life with Yahweh. This section is much like Exod 20:22–24:2; 25:1–31:17. Lev 17–26 deals more with practical holiness that is worked out in daily life with people. Everything in the book hinges on the Day of Atonement in Lev 16 and its prescriptions on how to cleanse the sanctuary. The book's structure therefore links sacrificial rituals with godly personal ethics and peaceful communal life. Most consider Lev 27 as serving as an appendix. Unlike any other book in the Bible, Leviticus is full of lists—liturgical observances, civil, and moral commandments, instructions on food, and so forth. It is peppered with only a few narratives (Lev 8:6–10:20; 16:1; 24:10–23).

### Outline of Leviticus

I.   Israel's Worship (1:1–15:33)

    A.  The Manual of Offerings (1:1–7:38)

        1.  Voluntary God–pleasing Offerings (1:1–3:17)

        2.  Mandated Offerings for Atonement (4:1–6:7 [MT 5:26])

        3.  Eating the Holy Food (6:8–7:38 [MT 6:1–7:38])

    B.  The Inauguration of Worship (8:1–10:20)

        1.  Consecrating the Priests (8:1–36)

        2.  Aaron's Offering (9:1–24)

        3.  Penalties for Disobedience (10:1–20)

    C.  The Manual for Purity (11:1–15:33)

        1.  Clean and Unclean (11:1–47)

        2.  Impurity from Childbirth (12:1–8)

        3.  Diagnosing Skin Diseases (13:1–59)

# THEOLOGICAL THEMES IN LEVITICUS

## SACRIFICIAL TERMS

By virtue of being first on the list in Lev 1, the עלה, *burnt offering*, was the most important sacrifice at Israelite festivals (cf. Num 28–29). It was different from all other sacrifices because the entire animal was burnt upon the altar. The burnt offering was offered twice a day, once in the morning and once in the evening (Num 28:1–8). Lev 1:4 states the key idea: "And he [the worshiper] shall place his hand upon the head of the burnt offering and it will be acceptable for him to make atonement for him." The death of the animal stands for the death of the sinner.

The מנחה, *grain offering*, in Lev 2:1–16; 6:14–23 was made chiefly from fine flour. Since it was not a sacrifice using blood, no atonement language is connected with it. A part of it was burned on the bronze altar and the rest was consumed by the priests.

The שלם, *fellowship offering* (sometimes called *peace offering*), outlined in Lev 3:1–17; 7:11–38, was intended mostly for fellowship with Yahweh. This is what set it apart from other sacrifices. In this corporate meal, Yahweh received some of the offering (Lev 3:3–4) and so did the priest and the worshipers (Lev 7:31–36). Important to note is that the fat of the peace offering was placed on top of the whole burnt offering. Atonement precedes fellowship.

The first three sacrifices were voluntary, while the חטאה, *purification offering* (sometimes called *sin offering*), and אשם, *guilt offering*, were mandated by certain conditions. For that reason, the focus in the first three sacrifices is on procedure, while the last two spotlight occasions that call for the offerings. Both of these sacrifices were specifically for שגגה, *a sin committed in error*, as detailed in Num 15:22–31. The word שגגה seems to imply a lack of premeditation, a kind of stumbling into trouble. It is the opposite of sins committed "with a high hand" (Num 15:30). The latter clearly refers to blatant, premeditated acts, for which the sin and guilt offerings did not help. The purification offering is discussed in Lev 4:1–5:13; 6:24–30. Its distinctive nature is that the animal's blood was used to cleanse sacred items within the tabernacle.

The אשם, *guilt offering*, is defined in Lev 5:14–6:7; 7:1–10. It was a payment to compensate for harm done. This is why some prefer to translate אשם as *reparation offering* or *compensation offering*. Sinners were to restore the principle amount plus a penalty of twenty percent to the people they harmed. This payment was unique to the guilt offering. Additionally, a verbal confession acknowledging guilt was needed (e.g., Lev 5:5). Milgrom writes, for "involuntary sin *'sm* and remorse alone suffices; it renders confession superfluous. But for deliberate sin there is the added requirement that remorse be verbalized; the sin must be articulated and responsibility assumed."[2]

---

[2] Jacob Milgrom, *Cult and Conscience: The Asham and the Priestly Doctrine of Repentance* (Leiden: Brill, 1976), 109.

### *The Offerings of Israelite Laypeople*

| Type of Offering | Offering | Focus of Enactment | Purpose |
|---|---|---|---|
| **Burnt offering** | • Young bull (Lev 1:3–9)<br>• Male sheep or goat (1:10–13)<br>• Turtledove or pigeon (1:14–17) | • Production of a pleasing aroma with the smoke from the whole animal | • Access to God's favor<br>• Acceptance by God |
| **Grain offering** | • Fine flour with olive oil and frankincense (Lev 2:1–3)<br>• Unleavened bread with olive oil (2:4–10)<br>• Roasted fresh grain with olive oil and frankincense (2:14–16) | • Production of a pleasing aroma with the smoke from the token portion | • Provision of most holy bread for the sanctification of the priests<br>• Acceptance by God |
| **Peace offering** | • Bull or cow (Lev 3:1–5)<br>• Sheep (3:6–11)<br>• Goat (3:12–16) | • Production of a pleasing aroma with the smoke from the fat, the kidneys, and the lobe of the liver | • Provision of holy meat for the priest's family and the Israelite family for holy communion with God as His guests<br>• Acceptance by God |
| **Sin offering for unintentional sins** | • Young bull for the congregation (Lev 4:1–21) | • Atonement with blood in the Holy Place | • Cleansing of the unclean congregation and forgiveness by God for admission into His presence |
| | • Male goat for a leader (Lev 4:22–26)<br>• Female goat or sheep for other layperson (4:27–35) | • Atonement with blood on the altar for burnt offering | • Cleansing of the unclean sinner and forgiveness by God for admission into His presence |

| Graded sin offering for some intentional sins | • Female sheep or goat (Lev 5:1–6)<br>• Two turtledoves or pigeons for a poor person (5:7–10) | • Atonement by confession of sins and application of blood to the altar for burnt offering | • Cleansing of the unclean sinner and forgiveness by God for admission into His presence |
|---|---|---|---|
| | • 10th of an ephah of flour for an impoverished person (5:11–13) | • Atonement by confession of sins and production of smoke from the token portion | |
| Guilt offering | • Ram for unintentional or suspected acts of desecration (Lv 5:14–19) | • Restitution to God by the rite of atonement | • Forgiveness by God for an act of desecration |
| | • Ram for the desecration of God's name by a perjured thief (6:1–7) | • Restitution to God by the rite of atonement | • Forgiveness by God for the desecration of His holy name |

From *TLSB* (St. Louis: Concordia, 2009), 171.

## HOLINESS

The theological significance of rites and rituals is seldom explained in detail in Leviticus. Instead, theological statements in the book provide critical interpretive implications. Lev 10:8–11 is such a statement. This is the only passage where Yahweh gives Aaron exclusive commands. The core is God's mandate to distinguish between the holy and common, between the clean and unclean (Lev 10:10). This lays the theological foundation for much of the book. Kleinig offers an understanding of the degrees of holiness in the book of Leviticus through corresponding places and people:

### *Degrees of Holiness in Leviticus*

| *Places* | *People* |
|---|---|
| Holy of Holies | Yahweh and the high priest (Lev 16:2–17) |
| Holy Place and Altar | Unblemished priests (Lev 21:17–23) |

| | |
|---|---|
| Courtyard | Israel's congregation (e.g., Lev 1:4; 4:14; 9:5) |
| Israelite home | Clean Israelites (Lev 14:8) |
| Israelite camp/town | Israelites and resident aliens (Lev 17:8, 10, 13) |
| Clean dump outside the camp | Ashes and carcasses from sin offerings (e.g., Lev 4:12) |
| Unclean area outside the camp | Unclean people and things (e.g., Lev 10:4; 14:40, 41) |
| Wilderness | Azazel (Lev 16:22) |

Adapted from *Leviticus*, Concordia Commentary (St. Louis: Concordia, 2003), 9.

The root קדשׁ, *holy*, appears 152 times in Leviticus, comprising one-fifth of all occurrences in the OT. Holiness is what makes God God and is what distinguishes him from everything and everyone else in the world. It cannot be illustrated by analogy—therefore every attempt to define holiness is bound to fail because it has to do with God's essence and his very nature. The term has no corresponding idea in Israel's life. It is not metaphorical. Therefore the root קדשׁ comes the closest in describing Yahweh. In the OT he is qualified by the adjective *holy* more often than by all other qualifiers combined.

To be holy means that one is unblemished or unmarred. Holy people experience life in its fullness just as God intended. Holiness, therefore, denotes more than separation, it also means wholeness. We see this in texts where mixed crops, mixed clothing, and mixed marriages are incompatible with holiness (Lev 18:23; 19:19). Priests with physical defects were not allowed to offer sacrifices (Lev 20:17–23) and sacrificial animals had to be without defect (e.g., Lev 1:3, 10; 4:3, 23; 9:2–3; 23:12, 18). Exceptions were made only in the case of a freewill offering (Lev 22:23). On another level, holiness is frequently connected with moral integrity (cf. Lev 20:7; 22:32–33).

Israel's neighbors worshiped gods who were not holy in this sense. Their narratives testify to fragmentation, not wholeness; a symbiotic relationship with creation, not separation; and moral chaos rather than ethical goodness. Nature, the divine, and people were all one and this led to the collapse of distinctions at every level. Mesopotamian and Canaanite religions maintained that everything was part of one great whole. For instance, there were no boundaries between Marduk's defeat of Tiamat and its realization through the *Akitu* festival. Israel's neighbors are often depicted as living with no boundaries between parent and child (incest), members of the same sex (homosexuality), or humans and animals (bestiality). In contrast, Yahweh's holiness implies a worldview that distinguishes between God and nature, married and single, father and daughter, and the like.

The polar opposite of קדש, *holy*, is the root טמא, *unclean*. It appears 132 times in Leviticus, comprising over half of its appearances in the OT. Like holiness, uncleanness is both a power and a state of being. It is connected with sin, sickness, and death. Uncleanness takes the form of eating meat from unclean animals and having contact with animal carcasses (Lev 11:24–28), emitting semen (Lev 15:16–18), and having sexual intercourse with forbidden partners (Lev 18:6–20). Uncleanness blocks access to Yahweh's presence in the sanctuary (Lev 7:20–21; 22:3).

Yahweh did not keep his holiness to himself, nor did he employ it to distance himself from Israel. Instead he descended into the tabernacle to join his people on their journey and share his holiness with them. Israelites did not make themselves holy. Yahweh did it for them (Lev 20:9; 21:8, 23; 22:9, 16, 32). These verses all employ a participle from the root קדש, thus denoting God's continual action. The statement in Lev 19:2 neatly summarizes the theme: קדשים תהיו. The imperfect verb תהיו is ambiguous. In the context of Leviticus it means, "You are / will be / shall be holy." Holiness is therefore an objective truth, a promise, and a command.

Everything that is not holy is חל, *common*, and common things divide into two categories—the clean and the unclean. Clean things become holy when they are sanctified, but unclean objects cannot be sanctified. Clean things may become unclean if they are polluted (the verbal root is חלל). Most things and people are טהר, *clean*, a root that appears 74 times in Leviticus, comprising one-third of all occurrences in the OT. Sanctification elevates the clean into holy while pollution degrades the clean into the unclean.

### THE PRIESTHOOD

Israel's priesthood derives from the entire nation being a "kingdom of priests" and a "holy nation" (Exod 19:6). Yahweh directs his holy nation to set apart some of its members to be priests in order to administer his forgiving presence so that the nation, in turn, could be the channel and conduit of his grace for the world. After the sanctuary is built (Exod 35–39), Yahweh descends the mountain and fills it (Exod 40:34). But then there is a problem: "Moses was not able to enter the tent of meeting because the cloud settled upon it and Yahweh's glory filled the tabernacle" (Exod 40:35). The book of Exodus ends with this dilemma. What good is God's presence in the sanctuary if people are unable to have access to him?

The solution to the problem is the ordination of the high priest. At the end of Exodus, God calls Aaron to work within the sanctuary and mediate his holy presence to Israel through sacred rites. The office of the high priest is described in Exodus 28–30, but his ordination rite does not take place until Lev 8–9.

The office of the high priest is grounded in the divine demand to wear holy clothes. God commands Moses, "You shall make holy vestments for the glorious adornment of your brother Aaron" (Exod 28:2). This focus on clothing underscores the central role of the priest to mediate God's holiness to Israel. The vestments serve to protect Aaron. They also transform him so he is capable of bridging the gap between God and Israel.

But the vocation of the high priest is not simply an instance of "the clothes make the man." Aaron was to undergo a process of purification and become holy (Lev 8). We may think of this separation as hierarchical and, as such, a position of power and privilege. However, when the office of priest is viewed as a license for personal promotion, it results in death. This is illustrated in the story of Aaron's two eldest sons, Nadab and Abihu (Lev 10:1–2). God kills them for offering אש זרה, *unauthorized fire*, at the altar. The text is vague about their exact actions, but the rebuke of Moses to Aaron suggests that the two priests were viewing their office as one of privilege, rather than of service (Lev 10:3).

God's intention is for priests to lose their freedom for the sake of the larger community. Individual priests are called to give up their autonomy and become mediators of God's holy presence in the setting of the sanctuary. To do so, priests offered whole burnt offerings, sin offerings, guilt offerings, and peace offerings (Lev 1–7; see above). The transfer of God's blessing to Israel is another aspect of the priests' mediatorial role. Aaron assumed this aspect of his office when he blessed the camp from the door of the sanctuary (Lev 9:22–24; Num 6:21–26). The priests were also responsible for

teaching Yahweh's decrees (Lev 10:11; cf. Hos 4:6–9). The title הכהן
המשיח, *the anointed priest*, only appears in Lev 4:3, 5, 16; 6:22.
Although every priest was anointed, most believe that this designation
only refers to the high priest who received a special anointing from
God (cf. Num 35:25).

## THE DAY OF ATONEMENT

Lev 16 begins with an address to Moses, "And Yahweh spoke to
Moses after the death of Aaron's two sons when they approached
Yahweh's presence and they died" (Lev 16:1). We would expect the
next few verses to discuss the deaths of Nadab and Abihu, their
unauthorized fire, and the like (cf. Lev 10:1–2). Instead, Lev 16:2
introduces another one of Yahweh's speeches to Moses. This double
introduction happens only here in the book of Leviticus and, as such,
distinguishes chapter 16 from every other divine oracle. Additionally,
out of the book's thirty-six speeches, Lev 16:1–34 is the eighteenth,
making the Day of Atonement both the literary and theological
centerpiece of Leviticus which, in turn, stands at the center of the
Pentateuch. The day consisted of three main parts: (1) purifying the
sanctuary, (2) sending away the scapegoat, and (3) presenting two
burnt offerings.

Number symbolism is an important feature in Lev 16. Blood is
sprinkled seven times (Lev 16:14, 19). Both the Holy Place (Lev
16:2, 3, 16, 17, 20, 23, 27) and mercy seat (Lev 16: 2 [twice], 13, 14
[twice], 15 [twice]) are mentioned seven times. The חטאת,
*purification offering*, appears fourteen times in Lev 16 and the key
verb בוא, *enter*, is used ten times. The most important theological
word in Lev 16, however, is כפר, *atone*. Lacking any numeric
symbolism, the verb appears sixteen times, but it is why the day is
called the Day of Atonement in Lev 23:27, 28; 25:9.

The Day of Atonement ritual cleansed Israelites from all their sins
(Lev 16:16, 34). It further purged the sanctuary from the types of
impurities discussed in chapters 11–15. The high priest, normally
dressed in colorful robes, ornate jewelry, and gold intricate
embroidery (Exod 28) were all removed. Instead of looking like a
king, he took on the appearance of a slave. The priest was to sprinkle
blood seven times on and in front of the כפרת, *mercy seat*, the very
place of Yahweh's dwelling (Lev 16:14). The goat that carried the

pollution away, עזאזל (e.g., Lev 16:10), is frequently translated *goat of removal* or *scapegoat*.

Once the Day of Atonement rites were completed, Israelites could continue offering sacrifices to Yahweh through the priesthood, as indicated in Lev 8–10, and so have access to divine forgiveness and grace. The day's rituals also empowered God's people for their life of holiness, as outlined in chapters 17–27.

## LEVITICUS 25: LIFE IN CANAAN

Lev 25 anticipates life in Canaan and legislates three interrelated institutions: the Sabbatical year, the Jubilee, and the redemption of the land with its tenants. All of these are part of Israel's agricultural and liturgical calendars.

In the Pentateuch, Sabbath rest begins with Yahweh (Gen 2:1–3), moves to people (Exod 20:11), involves worship (Lev 23:3), includes animals (Exod 20:10; 23:12; Deut 5:14), and even involves the land (e.g., Lev 25:4, 11). The Jubilee year, connected with the Sabbath, goes even further. It proclaims דרור, *liberty*, to all (Lev 25:11). Named after the יובל, *horn*, that was used to inaugurate it, the Jubilee brought liberty not only for Israelites (e.g., Lev 25:15, 28, 33, 50, 54), but also for foreigners (Lev 25:40). The blowing of the ram's horn at the beginning of the seventh Sabbatical year announced freedom from slavery (Lev 25:54) as well as a return of land to its owner (Lev 25:28). (Lev 25 is the only place in the OT where the Jubilee year is discussed, though it is mentioned in passing in Lev 27:17–25; Num 36:4.)

The Jubilee was announced on the Day of Atonement (Lev 25:10), and this is a significant point. Cancelling the debts of fellow Israelites flowed out of God's cancelling their debts to him. Social and economic justice issue forth from divine mercy. The Jubilee year was also a holiday from agricultural work. All of the people would eat from what the land naturally produced (Lev 25:11, 12). Lev 25:14–17 considers cases when people sell their land, while Lev 25:18–22 discusses the Sabbatical years. In the last half of the chapter (Lev 25:23–55), Moses institutes the right of redemption for Israel's land and its tenants. In this way, the chapter develops a rich theology of the land, indicating how Yahweh, Israel, and the land are all interconnected. Yahweh, who delivered his people from slavery in Egypt, continues to do it every fifty years. They are to live as his servants in the land and belong to no one else (Lev 25:55). Israel was an Exodus people who must never return to a system of permanent slavery (Lev 25:42).

The root גאל, *redeem*, appears twenty-one times in Leviticus, but only in chapters 25 and 27. Lev 25:48 lists a brother, uncle, cousin, or other close relative as examples of a near-kinsman redeemer. These people would act (1) to recover property (Lev 25:24–34), (2) to reclaim certain cultic offerings (unclean animals, a house, a field, and the tithe of land; Lev 27:9–34), and (3) to rescue family members from permanent slavery (Lev 25:39–55).

## LAWS IN LEVITICUS

The book of Leviticus does not teach a distinction between ceremonial holiness and civilian holiness. While Moses notes the differences between clean and unclean, holy and profane, he does not distinguish between the sacred and the secular. Holiness should be seen in the tabernacle and in the fields, in the sacrifices and in the workplace. God's ritual and sacrificial, vocational and ethical stipulations are holistically intertwined.

Most of the laws in Leviticus are concerned with how the actions of a person or a group affect the whole. The book repeatedly addresses how both holy and unholy living impacts Israel's communal health. Love for my neighbor (Lev 19:18) cannot be understood apart from this emphasis. "You shall surely correct your neighbor lest you incur sin upon yourself" (Lev 19:17). To love my neighbor is to reprove my neighbor, lest that neighbor's sin defile the entire community. Sin adversely pollutes the sanctuary and people unless it is dealt with swiftly, correctly, and completely. In some cases even the Day of Atonement is not the answer to maintaining communal well-being. Exclusion or execution is the only proper response. Transgressions in this category include some sexual sins (Lev 18:20, 23–25, 27–30), idolatry (Lev 20:2–5), cursing parents (Lev 20:9), and profaning the holy (e.g., Lev 7:19–21; 22, 3, 9).

Four different types of explanations have emerged regarding the distinctions between clean and unclean animals. They are (1) arbitrary, known only to God, (2) cultic, the unclean animals were used in pagan rites, (3) hygienic, the unclean animals were carriers of disease, or (4) symbolic and therefore illustrations of how Israel was called to live separate from the nations. Douglas has had a significant impact on the study of Leviticus and has argued for the fourth interpretation. Although many of her points have been modified since her first publication on the topic in 1966, her main thesis is still valid.

Douglas maintains that the concepts of purity and pollution in the book of Leviticus are not primitive ideas. Rather they reveal a complex and ordered system. She goes on to argue that the food regulations in Leviticus are not arbitrary, but that only animals fully conforming to each of creation's realms—sky, land, sea—are fit for consumption. *This is because holiness means more than separation; it is tied to wholeness* (see above). So, for instance, Israelites were not to eat pigs, because, unlike other four-footed domestic land animals, they do not chew the cud. God's original intent was also that no creature would eat meat (cf. Gen 1:29–30). Therefore many of the animals that are declared unclean have one feature in common—they are carnivorous. For example, the birds listed in Lev 11:13–19 are unclean because they eat the meat of other animals. Douglas writes, "The dietary laws would have been like signs which at every turn inspired meditation on the oneness, purity and completeness of God." The NT also appears to regard Israel's food laws as symbols that separated Jews from Gentiles. Their abolition under Christ is part of breaking down the wall of partition (cf. Mark 7:19; Eph 2:14–16).

Since death most definitely does not conform to God's ordering of the world, many of the laws in chapters 12–15 that deal, for example, with childbirth, diseases, and discharges, attempt to rectify several symbolic encounters with death. This explains why someone with a serious skin disease becomes impure (Lev 13–14).

Wenham, in his commentary on Leviticus, takes this discussion one step further. He sees three categories: unclean (i.e., some animals, Israelites who are defiled in some way), clean (i.e., some animals, most Israelites), and holy as a subset of the clean (sacrificial animals, priests). This, he says, reminded Israel of these grades of holiness: Gentiles are unclean, Israel is clean, and Israel's priests are holy. He then interprets Acts 10–11 along these lines.

### CHRIST IN LEVITICUS

In one sense, many of the rituals in Leviticus are obsolete for Christians who are interested in the sacrifice of Christ, not in animal sacrifices. But in another sense, the Levitical ceremonies are still of immense relevance for today's church. It was in terms of these sacrifices that Jesus himself and the early church understood his atoning death. The sacrificial system of Leviticus was established by the same God who sent his Son to die for the world. In rediscovering the principles of OT worship mandated in Leviticus, we learn how to gain access to a holy God through the shed blood of Christ.

Biblical typology involves recapitulation, along with escalation. The antitype is always bigger and better than the type that foreshadows it. Therefore, when the book of Hebrews compares Jesus with the high priest on the Day of Atonement, it amplifies Christ's ministry in at least four significant ways. First, the high priest entered the earthly sanctuary once a year (Heb 9:7), while Jesus entered the heavenly sanctuary once for all, at his ascension to the Father's right hand (Heb 9:12, 24). Second, the high priest offered the blood of animals to make atonement (Heb 9:7, 25). Christ, on the other hand, offered his own blood (Heb 9:12). Third, the high priest sprinkled blood on the burnt offering and incense altars (Heb 9:21), while Jesus sprinkles the heavenly tent and its utensils with his blood (Heb 9:21) as well as the hearts and minds of believers (Heb 9:13–14; 10:2, 22). Fourth and most unexpectedly, Israel's high priests were the only people allowed in the Holy of Holies, but Jesus opened up a new and living way for all believers to gain this same access to the Father (Heb 4:16; 10:20).

In Rom 3:25 Paul likewise alludes to the Day of Atonement when he describes Christ's death using the term ἱλαστήριον, *mercy seat*. The same word appears again in 1 John 2:2; 4:10.

The verb נזה, *sprinkle*, appears twenty-four times in the OT, with twenty of them appearing in the books of Leviticus and Numbers. NT writers often employ the action of sprinkling to denote Christ's work as our great High Priest (e.g., Heb 9:13, 19; 10:22; 12:24; 1 Pet 1:2). Jesus is the culmination and consummation of every blood sacrifice in the book of Leviticus.

The Jubilee release in Lev 25 points toward Isa 61:1–3, where the Suffering Servant declares that Yahweh anointed him to enact an extraordinary and ongoing Jubilee. Dan 9:24–27 picks up the idea and develops it further. The messianic era—when God will deal with iniquity, put away sin, atone for wickedness, and usher in righteousness—will begin on the tenth Jubilee after Jerusalem's rebuilding (49 x 10 = 490). Luke 4:16–30 announces that Jesus is this

Servant/Messiah and in this way Isa 61:1–2a, with its Jubilee background, becomes programmatic for Luke's gospel.

## SIN AND GRACE IN LEVITICUS

Sin and grace permeate the book of Leviticus. Sin makes people unclean and unfit to stand before a holy God. In some cases it brings death (e.g., Lev 10:1–2; 20:2, 10–15). Yet Yahweh provides a means whereby sinners are cleansed and made holy, through the sacrificial system. God also shows great pity upon people who become economically enslaved and so gives instructions for their release on the Jubilee Year (Lev 25).

Sin and grace also come into sharp focus in the arrangement of the tabernacle's furniture which provides the foundation for many of the divine speeches in the book of Leviticus. The incense altar, located in the Holy Place, was in front of the curtain to hide the ark of the covenant. God is holy and inaccessible to sinful human beings. The altar for burnt offerings was located in the outer court and was the first piece of furnishing encountered after entering the tabernacle. This was where burnt offerings were administered twice a day, thus providing access to God's gracious presence.

## CONCLUSION

Leviticus used to be the first book Jewish children studied in the synagogue. In the modern church, it tends to be the last part of the Scriptures anyone cares to look at. For some, Leviticus is the "liver and onions" book of the Bible: It must be good for us, but we just don't seem to have a taste for the stuff. Although it is frequently overlooked, Leviticus is the backbone of the Pentateuch and provides the NT, especially the book of Hebrews, with the vocabulary and theological categories to understand Christ's forgiveness. Leviticus is dominated by holiness. Yahweh is holy and he graciously empowers Israel to walk in his holy ways.

Sacrificial blood is a major motif in Leviticus. For instance, blood is sprinkled seven times before Yahweh at the sanctuary (Lev 4:6) as well as on the front of the mercy seat (Lev 16:14). It is placed on the lobe of Aaron's right ear, the thumb of his right hand, and on the big toe of his right foot (Lev 8:23). Why all the blood? Shed blood reconciles people with God. "Without the shedding of blood there is no forgiveness of sin" (Heb 9:22).

# SELECTED BIBLIOGRAPHY

Douglas, Mary. *Purity and Danger: An Analysis of Concepts of Pollution and Taboo.* London: Routledge, 1966.

Kleinig, John. *Leviticus.* Concordia Commentary. St. Louis: Concordia, 2003.

Milgrom, Jacob. *Leviticus: A Book of Ritual and Ethics.* Continental Commentaries. Minneapolis: Fortress, 2004.

Watts, James. *Ritual and Rhetoric in Leviticus.* Cambridge: Cambridge University, 2007.

Wenham, Gordon J. *The Book of Leviticus.* New International Commentary on the Old Testament. Grand Rapids: Eerdmans, 1979.

# 6

# NUMBERS

The Hebrew title for Numbers is במדבר, or *in the wilderness*, which is the book's fifth word. It does not denote a place of blowing sand and occasional palm trees. Rather, מדבר is a locale unable to provide enough resources to sustain people. The noun appears 271 times in the OT and forty-eight of them are in the book of Numbers. The LXX title is Ἀριθμοι, emphasizing the lists of numbers recorded in the book (e.g., Num 1–4; 26). The Vulgate followed this Greek title and named the book *Numeri* from which the English acquired the name Numbers. Like the books of Exodus and Leviticus, Numbers begins with a conjunctive *waw*, וידבר, *and he said*, indicating that we are to read Numbers in light of the greater Pentateuchal narrative.

Although Yahweh's theophany at Sinai (Exod 19–Num 10) is at the heart of the Pentateuch, Sinai was not Israel's final destination. God's promise that his people would one day live in Canaan (e.g., Gen 15:16; Exod 3:8) kept driving Israel forward toward the land of milk and honey. Preparing to live in this land, along with the journey towards it, are the chief concerns in the book of Numbers.

## AUTHORSHIP

The book of Numbers does not tell us who its author is. However, Moses' writing activity is recorded in it (Num 33:1–2), and the book is full of passages where Moses receives revelations from God. The expression "Yahweh said/spoke to Moses (and Aaron)" appears over sixty times (e.g., Num 1:1; 2:1; 4:1; 5:1; 21:8; 27:6; 35:1). These statements are more than literary conventions. They describe historical facts.

However, this has not stopped critical scholars from denying Mosaic authorship. Because Numbers doesn't appear to have any clear sense of narrative movement or direction and contains disparate genres such as lists, narratives, and legislation, critics argue that it is unhelpful to call Numbers a book that has been composed by one author. They view it, instead, as a loose amalgamation of literary strata which they assign to J, E, D, and P. Critics further maintain that dividing Genesis–Deuteronomy into five books was a later imposition driven mostly by the desire to have five fairly equally-sized scrolls. After all, they point out that Israelites are camped at Sinai in three different books. The people arrive in Exod 19 and don't leave until Num 10. Therefore the book of Numbers, critics maintain, is an artificial construction by those who were responsible for the final editing of the OT. Moreover, prior to that, Numbers went through a long period of redactional changes. Over one hundred years ago, George Gray summarized this understanding of Numbers: "The book of Numbers is a section somewhat mechanically cut out of the whole of which it forms a part; the result is that it possesses no unity of subject."[1]

Today critics argue that Numbers' function is to join the priestly material in Leviticus with the book of Deuteronomy. Therefore D and P are the dominant theologies in the book. Many critics further assert that Numbers, which they believe achieved its final form after the exile, mirrors the Second Temple community in Persian Yehud. Issues like Korah's opposition to Aaronic leadership (Num 16) reflect post-exilic disputes over priestly control of the temple. For a further discussion on the authorship of Numbers, see chapter 2 on the Origin of the Pentateuch.

## LITERARY FEATURES OF NUMBERS

### Outline of Numbers

Providing an outline for Numbers is a daunting task. Olson looked at forty-six commentaries on the book and found twenty-four different outlines. The most common suggestion is based on Israel's movement from Sinai to the Plains of Moab. It is reflected below.

---

[1] George B. Gray, *Numbers* (Edinburgh: T & T Clark, 1903), xxiv.

I.   Israel Prepares to Leave Sinai (1:1–10:10)
    A.   The first census (1:1–54)
    B.   Tribal camps and leaders (2:1–34)
    C.   Organizing the Levites (3:1–4:49)
    D.   Various laws (5:1–31)
    E.   Nazarite vows (6:1–27)
    F.   Dedicatory offerings (7:1–8:26)
    G.   Keeping the Passover (9:1–14)
    H.   Yahweh promises to guide Israel (9:15–10:10)

II.  Israel's journey from Sinai to the Plains of Moab (10:11–22:1)
    A.   Leaving Sinai (10:11–36)
    B.   Events along the way (11:1–12:16)
    C.   The spies' mission and report (13:1–33)
    D.   Israel's lack of faith (14:1–45)
    E.   Various laws (15:1–41)
    F.   Korah's rebellion (16:1–51)
    G.   Aaron's rod (17:1–13)
    H.   Priestly duties and portions (18:1–32)
    I.   Purifying the unclean (19:1–22)
    J.   The last events at Kadesh–barnea (20:1–13)
    K.   The journey from Kadesh–barnea to the Plains of Moab (20:14–22:1)

III. On the Plains of Moab (22:2–36:13)
    A.   Balak and Balaam (22:2–24:25)
    B.   Apostasy at Baal Peor (25:1–18)
    C.   The second census (26:1–65)
    D.   Zelophehad's daughters (27:1–11)
    E.   Joshua, Moses' successor (27:12–23)
    F.   Festal offerings (28:1–29:40)
    G.   Women's vows (30:1–16)
    H.   Vengeance against Midian (31:1–54)
    I.   Land for the Transjordanian tribes (32:1–42)

J.  Reviewing Israel's travels (33:1–56)

K.  Israel's boundaries (34:1–29)

L.  Levitical cities (35:1–34)

M.  Zelophehad's daughters and women's inheritance (36:1–13)

The first third of the book is set in the Sinai wilderness (Num 1:1–10:10). The second part of Numbers describes Israel's travels (Num 10:11–21:35). The last third of the book is set on the Plains of Moab, opposite the Jordan River from Jericho (Num 22:1–36:13). Within its dominant genre of narrative, Numbers exhibits a wide variety of literary types, including lists (e.g., Num 1, 26, 33), a blessing (Num 6:24–26), a prayer (Num 12:13), legislation (e.g., Num 15:7–21; 27:1–11), a diplomatic letter (Num 21:14–19), and even a few snippets of poetry (e.g., Num 21:14–15, 17–18, 27–30; 23:19–24).

## TEXTUAL, ARCHAEOLOGICAL, AND HISTORICAL ISSUES

### DATING

The Passover occurred on the fourteenth day of the first month in the year 1446. Israel departed from Egypt on the next day (Num 33:3; cf. Exod 12:2, 6). The tabernacle was erected at Mount Sinai one year after the Exodus (Exod 40:2, 17). One month later the nation prepared to leave Sinai for the Promised Land. This was on the first day of the second month in 1445 (Num 1:1). On the twentieth day of the second month of this year the cloud went up from over the tabernacle and Israel began their journey from the wilderness of Sinai to Canaan (Num 10:11–12).

The book of Deuteronomy opens with a reference to the first day of the eleventh month in the year 1406, thirty-nine years, eight months, and ten days after the nation had departed from Sinai (Deut 1:3). Therefore, the book of Numbers covers the period of time which lasted thirty-nine years, nine months, and ten days. Although Numbers records events that occurred during this time, the coverage is uneven. Num 1–10 narrates developments that fall within a two-month period. Num 11–24 documents the next thirty-nine years of life in and around Kadesh-Barnea (probably modern Ain Qudeis). Num 25–36 concentrates on what happened in the thirty-eighth year after the Exodus.

## *Wilderness Wanderings*

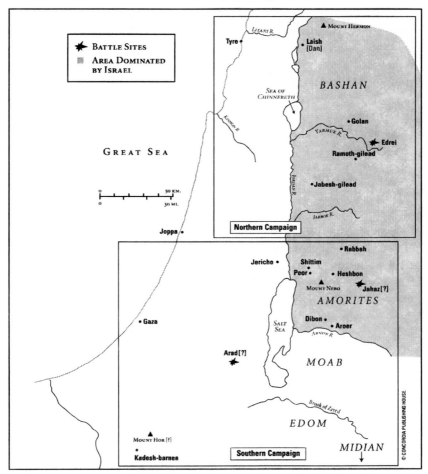

God delayed the conquest of Canaan for 40 years (Num 13–14; Deut 1:19–46). Israel often stayed near Kadesh-barnea (Num 33:36). Aaron died on Mount Hor (Num 20:22–29; 33:37–39). Israel destroyed Arad and surrounding cities (Num 21:1–3). Edom refused passage to the east (Num 20:14–21), so the Israelites went perhaps as far south as Ezion-geber to skirt Edom (Num 21:4; Deut 2:8). They camped in the Valley of Zered and along the Arnon River (Num 21:12–13). At Jahaz, they defeated the Amorites who had occupied part of Moab (Num 21:21–30; Deut 2:24–37). They defeated Bashan at Edrei (Num 21:31–35; Deut 3:1–7). Next they camped east of Jericho at Shittim (Num 25). After they defeated the Midianites (Num 31), Israel controlled the Transjordan from the Valley of the Arnon to Mount Hermon (Deut 3:8–10). Moses died on Mount Nebo (Deut 34).

## NUMBERS IN NUMBERS

Two censuses are taken in Numbers, in chapters 1 and 26. The first census was held in the second month of the second year after the Exodus (Num 1:1), numbering the first generation of post-Exodus Israelites. The second census occurred in the fortieth year after the Exodus to count the second generation of post-Exodus Israelites (Num 33:38). Both censuses were of Israelite men who could engage in battle and who were twenty years of age and older (Num 1:1–4; 26:1–4).

The first census in Numbers totals 603,550 Israelite men who were able to go to war (Num 1). This indicates that the total number of people was close to three million, thus raising several questions. How could only two midwives care for all of these Hebrews (Exod 1:15)? Why would such a vast amount of people have feared Pharaoh's army of roughly 20,000 men? How could such a multitude, along with their livestock (Exod 12:38), have left Egypt in one night? How could all Israel gather at the tent of meeting to hear Moses (e.g., Exod 16:9; 19:17; 33:17)? How did it happen that all the people could march around Jericho seven times in one day (Josh 6:15) and still have enough time in that same day to engage in war? What do we make of the statement that in Canaan there are "seven nations mightier and more numerous than you" (Deut 7:1)? Or how shall we interpret ". . . you were the fewest of all peoples" (Deut 7:7)?

These questions have been answered in four different ways. The first is to take the numbers in Num 1 and 26 literally—after all, God promised Abraham that he would become a great nation (e.g., Gen 12:2; 17:5–6). While in Egypt, "the Israelites were fruitful and greatly increased . . . so that the land was filled with them" (Exod 1:7). Pharaoh was afraid that the rapidly expanding Hebrews would overrun his country (Exod 1:9–12). A literal understanding of the numbers also harmonizes with the earlier census taken during the first year in the wilderness (Exod 30:12–16; 38:26), as well as with other texts that address the number of adult males who left Egypt (Exod 12:37; Num 11:21).

The second way of interpreting the large numbers is to interpret them as describing Israel's population at the time of the monarchy. They are misplaced lists from the time of David, for example 2 Sam 24:9 reports that there were 800,000 warriors in Israel and 500,000 in Judah.

A third way to explain the numbers is to translate אלף (e.g., Num 1:21, 23, 33, 35) not as *thousand*, but as *tribes* or, with a slight modification, *chieftains* (cf. Gen 36:15; Judg 6:15; Zech 9:7). Then Reuben's 46,500 become 46 families, totaling 500 men (Num 1:21). Petrie was the first scholar to suggest this interpretation that leads to 5,550 men in 598 groups in Num 1 and 5,730 men in 596 groups in Num 26. This lowers the total Hebrew population to about 72,000 people. Proponents of this interpretation then argue that these drastically reduced figures are more consistent with the available historical and archaeological data regarding population patterns during the time of the Exodus.

However, this approach does not work for the Levites who would then have twenty-two groups and no men. To translate אלף in a way other than *thousand* creates further problems. It assumes a misunderstanding in the population lists in Exodus, Numbers, and in many other texts. Moreover, the LXX and Samaritan Pentateuch agree with the MT.

A fourth way to interpret the numbers is to take them as indicating an epic style of narrative that is intended to express the wholeness of Israel and the enormity of God's deliverance of the people. The numbers, then, are a literary exaggeration intended to convey a theological point.

While the numbers are often a source for skepticism, there is little to recommend the readings that understand them not to be literal numbers. While a literal reading will always have its detractors, the text of Numbers is clearly seeking to portray the results of the two censuses taken under the authority of Moses.

## FOREIGNERS IN THE BOOK OF NUMBERS

Although the book of Numbers is mainly concerned with Israel's preparations to enter the Promised Land, it also includes narratives involving non-Israelites. The book discusses Midianites, the inhabitants of Canaan, Edomites, and of course Moabites and their king Balak who hired Balaam to curse Israel. Moses evaluates these foreigners using the grid of Gen 12:3: Those who bless Israel are blessed while those who curse God's people are cursed.

## Midianites

In Num 10:29–32 Moses meets Hobab the Midianite. Their discussion is analogous to the one between Moses and Jethro in Exod 18. In both cases, Midianites, whose land was in the northwestern region of the Arabian peninsula, acknowledge Yahweh's goodness and assist Israel in their journey. However, later in the book of Numbers, Midianites are hostile towards God's people. They join Moabites in an effort to thwart Israel's success (Num 22:4, 7; 31:1–54).

In another narrative, some Midianite women, along with Moabites, lead many Israelites to commit apostasy at Baal Peor (Num 25:6–9). There are several similarities between the golden calf episode (Exod 32) and this sin at Baal Peor: (1) both involve the worship of other gods, (2) both times God's wrath is averted by executing the culprits, and (3) in both events Levites execute the idolaters (Exod 32:26–28; Num 25:7–8).

## The Inhabitants of Canaan

Num 13:29 lists the following ethnic groups living in the Promised Land: Amalekites, Hittites, Jebusites, Amorites, and Canaanites. According to Gen 14:7, in the early part of the second millennium, the Amalekites lived in and around Beersheba. Later Israel defeated them at Rephidim (Exod 17:8–16). They regained their power, though, to the point that Israel was told to avoid them (Num 14:25). The Hittites were also contemporaries with Abraham (Gen 23) while the Jebusites lived in the region of Jerusalem (e.g., 2 Sam 5:6–7).

Though the term *Amorite* is sometimes employed as a collective title for all of the inhabitants of Canaan (e.g., Gen 48:22; Josh 24:15; Judg 6:10; 2 Sam 21:2), in the book of Numbers Amorites are distinguished from Canaanites. Israel defeated two Amorite kings, Sihon and Og, who ruled in the Transjordan (Num 32:33). Canaanites lived along the Mediterranean Coast as well as by the Jordan River (Num 13:29).

## Edomites

In Num 20:16, Moses informs the king of Edom that the Israelites are on their border and want to pass through. The country was located south of the Dead Sea on both sides of the Wadi Arabah, and its major trade route was the Desert/King's Highway. This highway ran from the Gulf of Aqaba north through the land of Edom. Edomites rejected Moses' request and did not allow the Israelites to pass through their territory. Their king even threatened to confront Israel with a sword (Num 20:18; cf. Amos 1:10–11). Moses decided not to pursue the issue further and led Israel around by another way (Num 20:21). Balaam therefore curses Edom in his fourth oracle. "Edom will be dispossessed, Seir dispossessed by its adversaries. But Israel is triumphant" (Num 24:18).

## Moabites and Balaam

Moab was located east of the Dead Sea, with Ammon to the north and Edom to the south. Moabites fought with Israel over the former land of the Ammonites, which was claimed by Reuben and Gad (Num 21:24–30; 32:1–5; 33–38). Moabite women seduced Israel into apostasy at Baal Peor (Num 25:1–9).

But Moab's chief experience with Israel in the book of Numbers was through Balaam. Though this prophet was hired by the Moabite king Balak to curse God's people, he ended up blessing them (Num 23:7–10; 23:18–24; 24:3–9; 24:15–19; cf. Num 22:12; Neh 13:2). In doing so, Balaam picks up several themes from the book of Genesis: "Who is able to count Jacob's dust?" (Num 23:10; cf. Gen 13:16; 15:5); "Yahweh their God is with them" (Num 23:21; cf. Gen 17:8); "May those blessing you be blessed and those cursing you be cursed" (Num 24:9; cf. Gen 12:3); "A star will come from Jacob, a scepter will arise from Israel" (Num 24:17; cf. Gen 49:10). In spite of Balaam's blessings for Israel, Israel executed him with a sword (Num 31:8), because he prompted Moabite and Midianite women to seduce many of Israel's men into apostasy at Baal Peor (cf. Rev 2:14).

Knowledge about Balaam has been enhanced by an archaeological discovery in 1967 at Tell Deir 'Alla in the Jordan Valley, which would have been part of ancient Ammon. The fragmentary plaster revealed an inscription dating to about 750 BC. It begins with these words:

> [The sa]ying[s of Bala]am, [son of Be]or, the man who was a seer of the gods. Lo! Gods came to him in the night [and spoke to] him according to these w[ord]s. Then they said to [Bala]am, son of Beor. Thus: "Let someone make a [ ] hereafter, so that [what] you have hea[rd may be se]en!" And

Balaam rose in the morning [ ] right hand [ ] and could not [eat] and wept aloud. Then his people came in to him [and said] to Balaam, son of Beor, "Do you fast? [ ] Do you weep?"[2]

The inscription goes on to discuss death and desolation, the overturning of the natural world, and the fertility gods Sheger and Ashtar.

## THEOLOGICAL THEMES IN NUMBERS

### THE ROLE OF THE LEVITES

Prior to the book of Numbers, the Levites are only referred to several times in the Pentateuch. Their devotion to Yahweh is noted in Exod 32:26–28, and they are briefly mentioned in Exod 38:21 and Lev 25:32–33. The initial chapters in the book of Numbers, though, focus largely upon God's mandate to set apart the Levites for sacred service. This is clear in a number of ways. The tribe of Levi is not required to take part in the census because they are to oversee the tabernacle and its furnishings (Num 1:47–53; cf. Num 2:33). Moses presents the Levites to Aaron as the high priest's helpers (Num 3:6–9). He also connects Levitical service with God's sparing of the firstborn in Egypt (Num 3:11–51; cf. Exod 13:1–16). In theory, then, the Levites were to be sacrificed to Yahweh (Exod 13:2). The laying on of hands in Num 8:10 symbolizes this. The Levites, in turn, laid their hands on the heads of two bulls to make atonement for themselves (Num 8:12).

A lengthy discussion on the Levites occurs also in Num 4:1–49. This passage sets aside three Levitical clans and assigns them duties linked to caring for the tabernacle. They were also to encamp around the tabernacle in a square formation. (The priests were the fourth group that guarded the entrance.) The Gershonites (Num 4:21–26) were to camp behind the tent on the west side and their job was to carry the outer tent coverings, pegs, hangings, screens, and ropes. Kohathites (Num 4:27–32) were to camp on the south side, and they were to transport the most holy things such as the ark, table,

---

[2] William W. Hallo, K. Lawson Younger, Jr., eds. *The Context of Scripture, Volume 2: Monumental Inscriptions from the Biblical World* (Leiden: Brill, 2003), 140–45.

lampstand, altars, and vessels (Num 4:4). Though this was a more privileged duty, probably because Aaron and Moses were descendants of Kohath (Exod 6:16–20; 1 Chr 6:2–3), the Kohathites could only pack and unpack the sacred objects. They could not look upon them (Num 4:20), and they certainly could not touch them. This duty was reserved for the priests (cf. 1 Sam 6:19–20; 2 Sam 6:6–7). The Merarites (Num 4:33–37) were to camp on the north side and were commissioned to carry the tabernacle's parts: frames, bars, pillars, bases, and so forth. Since transporting the tabernacle and its equipment was both dangerous (due to the proximity of divine holiness) and heavy, men had to retire at fifty years old (Num 8:24–25).

The Levites were not accorded the same status as that of the priests. Though they could serve in the sanctuary, they were not allowed, for instance, to offer sacrifices or preside over the sacred rites in the tabernacle (e.g., Num 3:38; 8:26; 18:1–32). As a Levite, Korah rejected these distinctions, arguing that "the entire congregation, all of them, are holy" (Num 16:3). Korah and his followers, especially Dathan and Abiram, maintained that the priests had no divine right to their special status. Though Korah and his kindred carried the most holy things (Num 4:1–20), they wanted more. The Korahites were allowed to test their claim by bringing holy incense but their unholiness was confirmed by God's consuming fire (Num 16:35), thus validating the distinctions between priests and Levites. Korah and his associates are punished with death (Num 16:32–33). God gave priests to Israel (Exod 28–29), and they were ordained by divine mandate (Lev 8–9). To usurp priestly authority was to reject the way Yahweh had chosen to deliver forgiveness and blessing to his people.

## THE TWO GENERATIONS OF ISRAELITES

Olson divides the book of Numbers into two parts: the death of the old generation (Num 1:1–25:19) and the birth of the new (Num 26:1–36:13). The two census reports (Num 1, 26) accentuate this analysis of the book. The first generation is a failure while the second has a future.

The older generation repeatedly demonstrated their contempt for Yahweh and his servant Moses. The optimism of Moses urging Hobab to accompany Israel to the good land in Num 10:32 is quickly replaced by the Exodus generation's accusations and complaints that begin in Num 11. The pattern is as follows:

1.  Divine anger is aroused because of murmuring (Num 11:1; 11:20, 33; 12:9; 21:5).

2.  God punishes his people (11:1, 33; 12:10; 21:6).

3.  Moses intercedes for Israel (11:2; 12:13; 21:8–9).

4.  The punishment is curtailed (11:2; 12:13; 21:8–9).

5.  Frequently the place of complaint is named; e.g., Taberah or "Burning" (11:3), Kibroth–hattaavah or "Graves of Desire" (11:34), and Meribah or "Quarreling" (20:13).

But the most pivotal sin of the Exodus generation comes when the twelve spies return from scouting Canaan and affirm that the land "does flow with milk and honey" (Num 13:27), but nevertheless counsel against trying to take the land for themselves: "The land we explored devours those living in it. All the people we saw there are of great size. We saw the Nephilim there (the descendants of Anak come from the Nephilim). We seemed like grasshoppers in our own eyes, and we looked the same to them" (Num 13:32–33). However Joshua and Caleb dare to say, "If Yahweh is pleased with us, he will lead us into that land, a land flowing with milk and honey, and he will give it to us" (Num 14:8). The people, still intent on returning to Egypt (Num 14:1–4; cf. Num 11:20), decide to rebel (Num 14:7–9). Yahweh then rendered his verdict. Everyone twenty years old and older, with the exception of Caleb and Joshua, will die in the desert. The Exodus generation must sojourn in the wilderness for forty years—one year for each of the forty days which the spies spent in Canaan (Num 14:29–35).

This generation therefore is remembered for its two massive moral failures: the golden calf apostasy (Exod 32–34) and its unwillingness to enter the Promised Land (Num 13–14). These are the only sins singled out when Moses reviews Israel's time in the wilderness (Deut 1:22–45; 9:12–25). And these are the only sins that provoke God to threaten to annihilate his people and begin anew with Moses (Exod 32:10; Num 14:12).

Aaron's death on Mount Hor and God's appointment of Eleazer (Num 20:23–29) anticipate not only the death of the old Israel and the transfer of the promises to a new Israel, but they also foreshadow

Moses' death and the designation of Joshua to be his successor (Deut 34:1–12). Whereas Num 11–25 describes the Exodus generation's death, Num 26–36 does not record any deaths of the new generation. Even when these Israelites engage in combat with the Midianites, no Israelite soldiers are killed (Num 31:49).

The successes of the new Israel are highlighted in the book's last eleven chapters. Military engagements succeed (Num 28), potential problems are solved (Num 32), and legislation looks to the nation's future life in the Promised Land (Num 34). Out of all the people who left Egypt as adults, only Joshua and Caleb would enter the land flowing with milk and honey (Num 26:64–65).

### WHAT WAS MOSES' SIN?

Even Moses didn't make it into the Promised Land. What sin did he commit that was so serious that barred him from entering Canaan? When he tried to give water to thirsty people, Moses usurped God's glory. He claimed the miracle for himself and Aaron: "Shall *we* bring water for you out of the rock?" (Num 20:10). Moses should have said, "Must *he* (God) bring you water . . . ?" Additionally, God instructed him to speak to the rock (Num 20:8), but instead, in anger, Moses struck it twice (Num 20:9–11; cf. Ps 106:32–33). He was therefore barred from entering the Promised Land. But there is more to this story.

Pagan magicians (as in Egypt) manipulated the gods by incantations and actions (cf. 2 Kgs 5:10–13). In contrast, Moses, prior to Num 20, always *silently* performed miracles in order to distance himself from pagan practices. Although people were told what miracle Yahweh would do, when the time came, no words were spoken, showing that the miracle was not a pagan magical incantation but a demonstration of Yahweh's power (e.g., Exod 7:15–20; 8:1–6). Even when Pharaoh asked Moses to implore Yahweh to stop a plague, Moses did so in private, after leaving Pharaoh's presence (Exod 9:28–29). In the miracles of manna, quail, and the rock at Rephidim (Exod 16–17), each time Moses reported what God would do, but there were neither gestures before the people nor were words spoken when the miracle happened.

Since Israel was influenced by Egyptian/pagan practices, Moses had to be silent when performing miracles unless he was specifically commanded by God to do otherwise (cf. Exod 17:6). In Num 20:11—

contrary to the divine mandate only to speak (Num 20:8)—Moses hit the rock twice in the presence of the entire congregation. He did what he had up to this point avoided—linking Yahweh's miracles with pagan religion. And so he would only see the Promised Land from a distance and then die on Mount Nebo (Num 20:12; Deut 34).

## CHRIST IN NUMBERS

In Num 11:6–9, Israelites chafe at God's provision of manna. Many of the Jews also grumbled upon hearing Christ's claim that he was the Bread of Life sent from heaven (John 6:33–58). Whereas Israel failed miserably in the wilderness due to their constant complaints and unbelief, Jesus overcame temptation in the wilderness by relying on God's word (Matt 4:1–11; Luke 4:1–13).

Remarkably, the first time Israelites acknowledge their sin in the book of Numbers is in Num 21:7. Yahweh then directs Moses to place a bronze serpent upon a pole so that those bitten by the poisonous snakes may look at the serpent and live (Num 21:9). This foreshadows Christ's death on the cross (John 3:14–15).

Balaam's oracles contain several references to Christ. In his first oracle, Balaam alludes to the patriarchal promise (Num 23:10; cf. Gen 13:16; 28:24), which included the messianic promise. The second oracle is about Israel's king (Num 23:21; cf. Gen 17:6, 16; 35:11), and Balaam refers to the messianic lion of Judah from Jacob's prophecy (Num 23:24; cf. Gen 49:9; Amos 1:2; Rev 5:5). In his third oracle, he speaks of the greatness of the messianic king (Num 24:7) and connects the messianic lion of Judah to the promise to the patriarchs (Num 24:9; cf. Gen 12:3; 49:9). Balaam's final oracle speaks directly of the Messiah as "not near" (Num 24:17). When he arrives, however, he will be a star from Jacob (cf. Matt 2:2; Rev 22:16) and have a royal scepter (cf. Gen 49:10). He will also defeat Israel's enemies (cf. Gen 49:9; Rev 19:11–21).

## SIN AND GRACE IN NUMBERS

Israel's fervent desire to return to Egypt (e.g., Num 11:4–5; 20:5; 21:5) prompted the people to repeatedly grumble and complain. The chief sin in the book of Numbers—Israel's refusal to enter the Promised Land—was spurred by this longing for Egypt (Num 14:2–4). At one point the people even went so far as to call Egypt "a land flowing with milk and honey" (Num 16:13).

God's grace is manifold in Numbers. His ark leads his people (e.g., Num 10:33–36), he allows Moses to intercede successfully for the Israelites (e.g., Num 14:13–20; 21:7–8), and in spite of the people's rebellion, God repeatedly provided for them (e.g., Num 11:9; 20:11). Yahweh's ongoing gift of peace came through the Aaronic benediction (Num 6:22–27). A partial quotation of this benediction, written on two silver plaques dating from around 600 BC, was found in 1979 at a tomb at Ketef Hinnom on the outskirts of Jerusalem.

## CONCLUSION

The book of Numbers includes stories about Yahweh's cloud and pillar of fire, sending spies into Canaan, water from the rock, the bronze serpent, and Balaam and his donkey. However, the book has a less glamorous side to it. There are lengthy censuses and a list of way stations in the desert. Legislation, both civil and cultic, is scattered throughout Numbers, most of the time without any discernible logic. The book's story line meanders to and fro, most of the time without any sense of direction. Along the way, Israelites demonstrate callous ingratitude, perpetual complaining, and blindness to God's ongoing mercy. Longing to go back to Egypt, they are unwilling to endure current hardship. They also reject Moses' leadership, have little faith in divine promises, and even get caught up in worshiping other gods. Yet Yahweh continues to put up with the people, pinning his hopes on the next generation. Though not perfect, the second generation emerges in the book of Numbers as a formidable nation, ready to enter the Promised Land.

## SELECT BIBLIOGRAPHY

Ashley, Timothy. *The Book of Numbers*. New International Commentary on the Old Testament. Grand Rapids: Eerdmans, 1993.

Budd, Philip. *Numbers*. Word Biblical Commentary 5. Waco: Word, 1984.

Mendenhall, George. "The Census Lists of Numbers 1 and 26." *Journal of Biblical Literature* 77 (1959): 52–66.

Olson, Dennis. *The Death of the Old and the Birth of the New: The Framework of the Book of Numbers and the Pentateuch.* Brown Judaic Studies 71. Chico, CA: Scholars Press, 1985.

Petrie, W. M. Flinders. *Researches in Sinai.* London: Murray, 1906.

Wenham, Gordon. *Numbers: An Introduction and Commentary.* Tyndale Old Testament Commentaries 4. Downers Grove: InterVarsity, 1981.

# 7

# DEUTERONOMY

Deuteronomy brings the Pentateuch to a significant climax. The book begins on the Plains of Moab on the first day of the eleventh month of the fortieth year after Israel's Exodus from Egypt, or January/February [Shebat] 1, 1406 (Deut 1:1–3). What should have been an eleven-day journey took Israel almost forty years.

The English title *Deuteronomy*, however, is a misnomer. It derives from the LXX of Deut 17:18, δευτερονόμιον, *second law*, which is an incorrect translation of the Hebrew משנה התורה הזאת, *a copy of this Torah*. Contrary to the LXX, the book does not simply repeat earlier Torah. Rather it clarifies and explains for a new generation of Israelites what Yahweh delivered to Moses on Mt. Sinai. Therefore the Hebrew title is more accurate, אלה הדברים, *these are the words* (cf. Deut 1:1), as Deuteronomy is more about words than any other book in the Pentateuch. In fact, the only action in Deuteronomy is Moses' death in Deut 34. By accenting the role of God's words, the book prepares Israel to conquer Canaan and live long in the Promised Land.

## AUTHORSHIP AND DATING

Deuteronomy indicates that Moses is its author. The book begins with the statement that "These are the words Moses spoke . . . " (Deut 1:1), and includes comments like, "this is the Torah that Moses set before Israel" (Deut 4:44), "Moses called all Israel and said to them . . . " (Deut 29:2), and "so Moses continued to speak . . . " (Deut 31:1). Throughout the book, Moses refers to himself as among the people, using the first-person pronouns "we" (e.g., Deut 1:19; 2:1; 3:1), "me" (e.g., Deut 1:14, 17; 2:9 17; 4:5; 6:1; 10:11; 18:15), "our" (e.g., Deut 1:6; 5:2, 3; 9:10), and "us" (e.g., Deut 1:20,25; 3:1; 5:2). As Deuteronomy concludes, it frequently refers to Moses' writing activity (Deut 27:3, 8; 28:58; 29:21, 29; 30:10, 19; 31:24). In some places the NT simply calls the Pentateuch "Moses" (e.g., Luke 16:29; 24:27; John 1:45) thus indicating that Moses authored Deuteronomy.

It is likely, however, that several sections of Deuteronomy were composed by someone other than Moses. Texts that update or clarify geography include Deut 2:10–11, 20–23; 3:9, 11, 13–14. New historical information is added in Deut 10:6–9. Both Deut 1:1 and Deut 34 indicate that they were composed after Moses' death.

Critics nevertheless believe that Moses did not write anything in Deuteronomy. Wilhelm Martin Leberecht de Wette (1780–1849) first proposed that the book was composed during Josiah's reform (621) and was the Book of the Torah found by Hilkiah the high priest (2 Kgs 22:8). Deuteronomy was written, critics maintain, to prop up the king's reform efforts and legitimate his reign. Its "discovery" therefore coincided with the time of its composition. Critical opinions differ as to who was responsible for writing the book. All of the authority figures in Deuteronomy—Levites, prophets, elders, and royal sages—have been proposed as its possible authors. At any rate, the composition is believed to be a literary and theological vehicle written hundreds of years after Moses to validate Josiah's kingship.

There are several good reasons for believing that the Torah scroll found during Josiah's restoration of the temple was the book of Deuteronomy. The following connections are noteworthy: (1) the book presented to Josiah contained curses (2 Kgs 22:13, 19; cf. Deut 28:15–68), (2) Josiah destroys Canaanite high places and makes Jerusalem Judah's worship center (2 Kgs 23:4–14; cf. Deut 12:5, 14; 17:8), (3) the king celebrates the Passover in the temple courts (2 Kgs 23:21–22; cf. Deut 16:1–8), (4) Josiah removed those who practiced magical arts (2 Kgs 23:24; cf. Deut 18:14–22), and (5) the king ruled according to the scroll of the Torah (2 Kgs 22:2–3; cf. Deut 17:18–19). These common features do not mandate, however, that Deuteronomy must be a product of the seventh century.

One argument against taking Deuteronomy as a seventh-century document employed to legitimate Josiah and his choice of Jerusalem as the only valid place of worship is the fact that Shechem is mentioned in Deut 11 and 27 as another orthodox place to praise

Yahweh. Another problem with the critical understanding of Deuteronomy is the fact that the book is patterned after second millennium Hittite treaties that were only used between 1400 and 1200 BC. If Deuteronomy was composed during Josiah's reign, then we would expect it to reflect an Assyrian milieu. However, Assyrian treaties share very few features with Deuteronomy. They do not contain a historical prologue, they do not mandate storing the covenant document, rereading it, nor do they promise blessings to those who faithfully live by it. All of these components appear in the book of Deuteronomy (see below). Further complicating matters for critics is the fact that at least half of the curses in Deut 28 go back to the early part of the second millennium—ten connect with Hammurabi's law code and five with legal codes from Mari, which was destroyed in 1759. Out of the twenty-five curses in Deut 28, only seven correlate with Assyrian maledictions. And Assyrians only pledge curses for covenant unfaithfulness. They do not offer blessings to the vassal if he loves his suzerain. If Deuteronomy is a literary product of the Assyrian period, why is it so out-of-step with the treaties from that era?

In 1943, Noth published a book contending that Deuteronomy–Kings is primarily the work of one author, writing in the exile. This de facto led to the belief in a Tetrateuch. Genesis–Numbers is one corpus because Deuteronomy functions as an introduction to the Deuteronomistic history, Joshua–Kings. This analysis has gained widespread acceptance among critics.

There is no doubt that Deuteronomy had a great influence upon the theology and vocabulary in Joshua–Kings. However, this does not mean that Noth's dating of the books is correct. It only suggests that he has shed light upon the theological connections between Deuteronomy and subsequent historical books. For a further discussion on the authorship of Deuteronomy, see the chapter on the origin of the Pentateuch.

## LITERARY FEATURES OF DEUTERONOMY

Both Moses' life and Israel's wilderness wanderings come to an end in Deuteronomy. Knowing that he is barred from entering the land (Deut 1:37; cf. Num 20:10–13), Moses leaves Israel with three lengthy speeches (Deut 1:6–4:40; 5:1–28:68; 29:2–30:20). Deuteronomy, then, is a collection of sermons. This is highlighted by the ongoing use of היום, *today*. The word appears over sixty times in Deuteronomy and accents Moses' homiletical strategy of applying divine torah for the present moment (see below).

Each of the three sermons are linked with short narratives (Deut 1:1–5; 4:41–49; 29:1) that describe Moses' location—"east of the Jordan in the land of Moab" (Deut 1:5), "east of the Jordan in the valley opposite Beth Peor" (Deut 4:44), and "in Moab" (Deut 29:1). The speech markers are helpful, but it is also significant that chapters 1–11 and 27–34 provide the frames for the discussion of the torah in Deut 12–26. This middle section has been likened to Israel's constitutional law. Still another way to outline the book is to note that in Deut 1–4 Moses recapitulates events in Numbers, while in Deut 5–28 his focus is upon life in Canaan. Deut 29–32 is a covenant renewal ceremony and the book ends with Moses' death (Deut 33–34).

Kline and Kitchen both outline Deuteronomy along the lines of an ancient Near Eastern treaty between a sovereign and his vassal. They point out that these second-millennium treaties typically display the following features: (1) a preamble introducing the treaty as well as its participants, (2) a historical prologue reviewing prior highlights of the relationship, (3) stipulations setting out covenant expectations (frequently with general and specific commands), (4) preservation and rereading, (5) a listing of witnesses to the covenant, and (6) blessings and curses. Using this model, Deuteronomy may be delineated as follows:

## Outline of Deuteronomy

I.   Preamble (1:1–5)

II.  Historical prologue (1:6–3:29)

   A. Yahweh's guidance (1:6–46)

   B. Israel's involvement with other nations (2:1–3:11)

   C. Moses, the suffering servant (3:12–29)

III. General stipulations (4:1–11:32)

   A. The call to faith (4:1–49)

   B. Introduction and the Ten Commandments (5:1–21)

   C. The *Shema* and its implications (6:1–25)

   D. Israel's election (7:1–26)

   E. Yahweh's provisions in the wilderness and gift of land (8:1–20)

    F.  Israel's stubbornness (9:1–29)

    G.  Moses' intercession (10:1–22)

    H.  Summary of the Torah (11:1–32)

IV. Specific stipulations (12:1–26:19)

    A.  Worshiping the one God (12:1–32)

    B.  Purging false prophets and idolaters (13:1–18)

    C.  Diet and tithing stipulations (14:1–29)

    D.  Sabbatical release (15:1–23)

    E.  Leaders and institutions (16:1–19:21)

    F.  Warfare (20:1–20)

    G.  Various laws (21:1–25:19)

    H.  Worship regulations (26:1–15)

    I.  Concluding the covenant (26:16–19)

V.  Preservation and rereading (27:1–26)

VI. Blessings and curses (28:1–68)

VII. Witnesses and provision for the covenant's continuity (29:1–33:29)

    A.  Covenant renewal (29:1–30:14)

    B.  Moses passes the mantle to Joshua (31:1–30)

    C.  Moses' song (32:1–47)

    D.  Moses' final Blessing (33:1–29)

VIII. Moses' death (34:1–12)

While this outline reflects ancient Near Eastern treaty influences upon Deuteronomy, these features do not appear in the book in a black-and-white manner. Note, for instance, that a historical prologue appears not only in Deut 1:6–3:29 but also in Deut 9:7–10:11, while a description of depositing the covenant is in Deut 10:1–5 as well as in Deut 31:24–26.

Other scholars, while acknowledging the influence of ancient Near Eastern covenants upon Deuteronomy, take a more cautious approach. For instance, some suggest that the laws in Deut 12–25 are organized sequentially around the Ten Commandments so that Deuteronomy may be regarded as an early exposition of the Decalogue.

# THEOLOGICAL THEMES IN DEUTERONOMY

## THE CRITICAL UNDERSTANDING OF DEUTERONOMY'S THEOLOGY

The consensus of critical scholarship—led in large part by Weinfeld—interprets the book of Deuteronomy as a radical shift from the theology presented in Genesis through Numbers. This view maintains that those who composed the book sought to correct outdated views of God such as his descent upon a mountain (Exod 19:18–20), his appearance to Moses, Aaron, Nadab, Abihu, and the seventy elders of Israel (Exod 24:9–11), and his need for a tabernacle (Exod 25–40). Deuteronomy, say most critical scholars, seeks to repudiate these earlier anthropomorphic ideas. It does this, for example, by indicating that Yahweh is not seen but heard (e.g., Deut 4:33; 5:24–26). And if earlier Pentateuchal texts proclaim "the glory of Yahweh" (e.g., Exod 16:7; 40:34–35), Deuteronomy's repeated refrain of "the place where I cause my name to dwell" (e.g., Deut 14:23; 26:2) combats the belief that Yahweh actually dwells upon the earth. Another outdated view Deuteronomy corrects is that altars may be built in multiple locations (Exod 20:24–25). Instead, Deuteronomy maintains that there should be one central place for worship (Deut 12). In these ways, critics maintain, Deuteronomy demythologizes, centralizes, and secularizes earlier Israelite politics, theology, worship, and morality.

One of the main problems with this position is that it is based upon an inaccurate interpretation of Genesis through Numbers. Milgrom specifically argues that since Weinfeld holds to wrong beliefs concerning Israel's earlier sources, his entire understanding of Deuteronomy is incorrect. For instance, Milgrom maintains that there is no need to set up a chasm between the terms "Yahweh's glory" and "Yahweh's name" as they appear in the Pentateuch. Moreover, Deut 12 stresses the sovereignty of Yahweh in determining where he will be worshiped, rather than restricting the number of permitted worship sites. The text argues for a central—but not sole—sanctuary. And rather than repudiating the crude concept of Yahweh's real presence, Deut 4:39 describes Yahweh's presence as being both in heaven and with Israel. Earlier Pentateuchal texts do not need a Deuteronomic reinterpretation.

## THE ROLE OF THE TORAH

The word תורה, *torah*, derives from the verb ירה which denotes *teach, instruct*. *Torah* refers generally to God's word of both judgment and grace. Rarely does תורה mean *law*. Misunderstandings began when the LXX translated the word as νομός, *law*, and this was followed by the Vulgate's translation as *lex*. Perhaps transliterating it as torah is the best way to avoid confusion.

Torah plays a significant role in Deuteronomy. Deut 1:5 states that Moses באר את־התורה הזאת, *explained this torah*. The rare verb באר denotes *make clear, interpret*, or *explain*. It appears again only in Deut 27:8 and Hab 2:2. Why is this verb an important insight into the book's presentation of the torah? Moses does more than merely promulgate the torah in Deuteronomy. He explicates it so that Israel will live, possess the land, and obey God (e.g., Deut 4:1–2; 6:3, 17–19, 24–25; 8:1; 10:12–11:32). In this way Israel will not be judged but blessed by Yahweh in the land (e.g., Deut 7:4, 9–16; 15:4–6, 10).

Though Moses set the book of the Torah before all Israel (Deut 4:44), the teaching must not stop with him. Future kings are to copy the Torah and read it all the days of their life (Deut 17:18–20). Subsequent prophets like Moses will continue speaking torah to Israel (Deut 18:14–22). It is to be discussed in the family (Deut 6:7, 21–25; cf. 4:4; 11:18–21; 31:9–13) as well as in worship settings (Deut 31:13). Each new generation must know Yahweh through his torah which narrates the great things he has done for his people. There is no other book in the OT that stresses transmitting the faith as Deuteronomy does.

The book also accents the enduring truth of Yahweh's Torah. Moses tells the people to inscribe the Book of Torah on plaster-coated stones on Mount Ebal (Deut 27:1–8) as well as to place a copy of it beside the ark of the covenant (Deut 31:24–26). One dare not add to or take away from the Torah (Deut 4:2; cf. Rev 22:18–20), and the last of the Levitical maledictions states, "Cursed be the one who does not uphold the words of this Torah by doing them" (Deut 27:26).

The torah in Deuteronomy is preached torah. Several of the book's features reflect this homiletical thrust: (1) the frequent use of היום *today* (e.g., Deut 1:10; 2:18; 6:6; 8:11; 13:18; 29:10); (2) the emphasis on "we" (e.g., Deut 2:33; 3:3; 12:8; 26:7); (3) the numerous usages of second-person pronouns; (4) the repeated summons to "hear" (e.g., Deut 6:4; 9:1; 32:1; 33:7); (5) actualizing the present moment (Deut 5:2–3); (6) appeals to blessings that come through belief and curses that follow unbelief (Deut 28); and (7) the emphasis on choosing life today (Deut 30:19).

Deuteronomy is structured in such a way that it frequently integrates torah with redemptive history. The shape that the torah takes emerges out of Yahweh's acts of salvation. In this way divine torah is presented as a gift for people's well-being rather than a burden. For example, the narrative account that "Yahweh set his heart in love on your fathers ... " (Deut 10:15), is followed by the command, "Love the alien ... " (Deut 10:19). The nation's obedience is not a response to the torah as law, but is an act of love motivated by Yahweh's deliverance of Israel from Egypt (e.g., Deut 6:21–25). The torah therefore is not a means to achieve salvation. Rather, the motivation for obedience is drawn from Israel's experience of Yahweh's grace and mercy.

One aspect of the torah is its emphasis on generosity toward society's most vulnerable members. The alien, orphan, and widow are grouped together, for example, in Deut 10:18; 14:29; 16:11, 14; 26:12–13; 27:19. In some cases Levites, who were dependent upon the generosity of others, are mentioned with them (e.g., Deut 14:29; 16:14; 26:12–13). Yahweh loves these people (Deut 10:18). Moses exhorts Israelites to be generous to the poor (Deut 15:7–9) and adds the promise that Yahweh will bless this benevolent action (Deut 15:10). Similar statements are found throughout Deuteronomy (e.g., Deut 7:12–15; 14:29; 15:4, 18).

The central thrust of the torah is Israel's loyalty to Yahweh. Without this, Israel ceases to be Israel. The First Commandment reflects this negatively (Deut 5:7) and it is positively stated in the *Shema*, "Hear O Israel, Yahweh is our God, Yahweh alone" (Deut 6:4). Though it is not possible to outline the book of Deuteronomy by means of the *Shema* or the Ten Commandments (Deut 5:6–21), this torah forms much of the vocabulary in the book. It is most evident in Deut 1–11. Note, for example, the following expressions: (1) "Yahweh your God" and "other gods" (Deut 6:13, 14; 7:4; 8:19; 11:16, 28); (2) "brought out of the land of Egypt, the house of slaves" (Deut 6:23; 7:8, 19; 8:14; 9:26, 28, 29); (3) "with all your heart and all your soul" (Deut 4:29; 10:12; 11:13; 13:3; 26:16; 30:2, 6, 10); and (4) "hear ... love" (e.g., Deut 10:17–18, 19–20).

The word אהב, *love*, frequently denotes ideas associated with feeling, and within the context of Deuteronomy this feeling is bound up with a solemn, public commitment of fidelity that covenant partners make to each other. Loyalty to Yahweh is expressed in Moses' sermons (e.g., Deut 6:10–15; 9:1–10:11), legislations (e.g., Deut 12:2–3), and in his song (Deut 32). Turning to אלהים אחרים, *other gods* (a frequent phrase in the book, e.g., Deut 6:14; 8:19; 11:28; 28:14), is to be disloyal and break Yahweh's torah (Deut 31:16). It is punishable by death (e.g., Deut 17:2–7; 18:20).

Idolatry, then, is a major theme in Deuteronomy. Israel is not to עבד, *serve/worship*, other gods (e.g., Deut 7:4; 11:16; 17:3; 28:36, 64). The people were also prohibited from giving their allegiance to anything Yahweh had made, like the sun, the moon, and the stars (Deut 4:19; 5:8–9; 17:3). To worship anything in the created order is to partake in what is detestable and repugnant to Yahweh (e.g., Deut 12:31; 13:14; 17:4; 20:18). This is why Moses instructs Israel not only to tear down pagan religious shrines (Deut 7:5; 12:2–3), but also to destroy the idolaters themselves (Deut 7:16; 20:17–18). Individuals guilty of idolatry are to be put to death (Deut 6:15; 7:4; 13:15) and so are entire communities (Deut 13:12–16). If Israel as a whole becomes enmeshed in worshiping other deities, then they will be exiled from the land (Deut 4:26–28; 28:36, 64).

The nations were able to judge if Israel's torah was good or not (cf. Deut 4:6; 29:24–28; cf. Jer 22:8–9). This implies that in many ways the torah conformed to a standard other than "God said so." Israel's laws reflect Yahweh's existing moral order which may be discerned, in part, by the nations. And this means that even though the nations do not belong to Israel, they are still subject to creational laws or what is often called general revelation (as opposed to specific revelation that only comes through divine torah). This is why the inhabitants of Canaan are to be exterminated (e.g., Deut 7:1–5; 9:3). Their sins are an abomination to Yahweh (Deut 18:10–12).

## ELECTION

The book of Deuteronomy accents Israel's elect status before Yahweh more so than any other book in the Pentateuch (Deut 4:27; 7:6–7; 10:15; 14:2). The word most frequently employed to express this election is בחר, *choose*. Yahweh not only chooses the nation, but also its king (Deut 17:15), priests (Deut 18:5; 21:5), as well as the place where he will place his name (sixteen times in Deut 12–26, e.g., Deut 12:5; 14:23; 16:11).

Israel is chosen because of Yahweh's love for this people (Deut 7:7–8). The nation is not Yahweh's acquaintance, his business partner, or his associate. He calls them his סגלה, *treasured possession* (Deut 7:6; 14:2; 26:18). In other texts the term denotes royal jewelry and valuable objects (1 Chr 29:3; Eccl 2:8). Israel is also declared to be a holy nation (Deut 7:6; 14:2, 21; 26:19; 28:9) as well as ישרן, *Jeshurun* or *Just One* (Deut 32:15; 33:5, 26). This name derives from the verb ישר, *be straight, upright*. The Israelites were never upright in themselves but were deemed so by Yahweh. Deuteronomy vigorously challenges any teaching that attributes Israel's righteousness as the reason for Yahweh's election (e.g., Deut 9:4–6).

The book of Deuteronomy does not teach a doctrine of rejection parallel to its doctrine of election. His initially exclusive election of Abraham (Deut 1:8; 29:13; 30:30; 34:4) was for the sake of a maximally inclusive end. God's election of Israel did not stem from his indifference toward other nations. Rather, it arises from his love for the entire world. His plan is that Israel will be a conduit and channel of his grace to all people (e.g., Deut 4:6–8; cf. Gen 12:1–3).

## THE LAND

In the book of Deuteronomy—more than at any other moment in Israel's history—there was a long reflective pause, for the nation needed to make final preparations to enter the Promised Land. The question, then, driving much of the book is: After the death of the generation that came out of Egypt, will the new generation, like their parents, fail to trust in Yahweh's promises? Or will they believe in God's power and cross over the Jordan River to enter the Promised Land?

As Israel stands on the Plains of Moab listening to Moses, his speeches pulsate with the rhythmic repetition that the land is a pure gift, flowing from Yahweh's grace (e.g., Deut 1:35; 6:10; 10:11; 12:10). But the people must be on their guard. The land will tempt them to forget Yahweh and his goodness (e.g., Deut 8:7–20). If the land is not to be lost, Israel must remember barrenness and birth (e.g., Gen 11:30; 21:1–3), slavery and freedom (Exod 1–14), water from the rock (Exod 17:1–7; Num 20:1–12), and hunger and manna (Exod

16). In short, the nation must remember Yahweh's grace, a theme that Moses accents especially in Deut 1–4.

The land belongs to many nations (Deut 7:11; 9:1; 11:23) and will become Israel's only because of Yahweh's promise to the patriarchs (Deut 7:8). Deuteronomy includes eighteen of these promises and in many places the recipients of the land coalesce. They include the ancestors, those entering the land, and subsequent generations who read the book (e.g., Deut 1:8).

Conquering the land will not be by Yahweh's action alone. Deut 7:1–2 juxtaposes God's bringing Israel into the land with Israel's entering the land, as well as God's giving the land and Israel's defeat of enemy nations to secure the land. The idea is best stated in Deut 9:3:

> And know today that Yahweh your God, he is the one going before you. He is a consuming fire. He himself will annihilate them and he himself will subdue them before you. But you will dispossess them and you will destroy them quickly just as Yahweh spoke to you.

Canaan is described primarily as (ה)טובה (ה)ארץ, *a/the good land* (e.g., Deut 3:25; 6:18; 8:7; 11:17). It is full of great cities, cisterns, vineyards, and olive trees (Deut 6:10–11), and most certainly it is "flowing with milk and honey" (e.g., Deut 6:3; 26:9, 15; 31:20). Yahweh will give his people rest in the land (Deut 3:20; 12:10; 25:19) and promises to bless the land (Deut 15:4; 23:20; 28:8; 30:16). A host of ordinances are linked to the land—for example, the year of release (Deut 15:1–6), cities of refuge (Deut 19:1–3), the abolition of removing landmarks (Deut 19:14), and the prohibition against leaving a man's body hanging on a tree (Deut 21:22–23). Israelites were to bring the firstfruits of their land and offer them to Yahweh (Deut 26:1–11).

Israel did not earn the land or deserve the land. It was God's gift. They could, however, lose the land. Just as the nations forfeited their right to live in Canaan due to their wickedness (Deut 7:1–5; cf. Gen 15:16), Israel could lose their land privileges through persistent idolatry (e.g., Deut 4:26–27; 28:64).

## CHRIST IN DEUTERONOMY

The only OT books referred to more often in the NT than Deuteronomy are Psalms, Isaiah, and Genesis. It is not surprising, therefore, that Jesus often cites Deuteronomy. For instance, when an expert on the law asks Christ, "What is the greatest commandment?" (Matt 22:36), Jesus refers to Deut 6:5. He also quotes from Deuteronomy to defeat the devil's temptations (Matt 4:1–11; cf. Deut 6:13, 16; 8:3).

Israel is chosen in spite of the fact that the nation is the smallest and weakest among the nations (Deut 7:6–7). Climactically, Jesus is the Elect One (Luke 9:35), the Stone that the builders rejected but who is chosen and precious to God (1 Pet 2:4–8). As Israel-reduced-to-one, Jesus did what the nation was unable to do. He lived by every word that comes from God's mouth and in doing so accomplished life and salvation for the world.

In the book of Deuteronomy, Moses is presented as a suffering servant (Deut 3:12–29), intercessor (Deut 9:25–29; 10:10–11), teacher (Deut 5:1–5, 22–23; 6:1–3), and prophet (Deut 18:9–22). The NT announces that Christ is similar to Moses, yet greater (e.g., Heb 3:3). Jesus is a Servant (e.g., Phil 2:7), Intercessor (e.g., Heb 7:25), and Teacher (e.g., Matt 4:23; 9:35; 26:55). And whereas prophets who followed in Moses' footsteps include Samuel (1 Sam 3:20), Elijah (1 Kgs 18:36), and Elisha (1 Kgs 19:16), Jesus is Israel's final and definitive Prophet, fulfilling the promise made through Moses in Deut 18:15–18 (John 1:21, 25; 6:14; 7:40; Acts 3:22; 7:37).

Moses employs a variety of body parts when he instructs Israel in Deut 15:1–18 on how to care for the less fortunate. *Hand(s)* appear in Deut 15:2, 7, 8, 11; *heart* in Deut 15:7, 9, 10; and *eye* in Deut 15:9, 18. The intention (heart) and attitude (eye) is to prompt loving assistance (hand). God wants people to relate to the needy with their entire lives. Jesus is the full embodiment of this care. Throughout his ministry he provided for the hungry, the destitute, the sick, and the needy.

## SIN AND GRACE IN DEUTERONOMY

When Israel was tested in the wilderness (Deut 8:2–5), they rebelled (Deut 1:26–46; 9:7–24). If it had not been for Moses' intercession, Yahweh would have utterly rejected the nation (Deut 9:18–20, 25–29; 10:10). Moses even says, "You have been rebels against Yahweh since the day I knew you" (Deut 9:24). And when Moses foresees the future he envisions Israel's continual inability to walk in the way of Yahweh's commandments (e.g., Deut 31:16–18; 32:15–35).

The Israelites were not chosen to be Yahweh's light to the world because they were more important, elite, or upright than the other nations. Neither were they elected because they were more numerous, mighty, or powerful (Deut 7:7–8). God chose Israel because of his grace-filled oath to the patriarchs (Deut 7:8; 9:5; cf. 4:31; 6:18, 23; 8:1; 13:17; 19:8; 31:20; 34:4). Yahweh is the God who repeatedly gives gifts to his people. The verb נתן, *give*, appears 167 times in the book of Deuteronomy. Of these, 131 have Yahweh as their subject.

## CONCLUSION

The book of Deuteronomy prepares Israel for life without Moses (Deut 16:18–18:22), warfare in Canaan (e.g., Deut 7:1–5; 9:1–3; 20:1–20), and life in the Promised Land. It may be summarized as Moses' plea for one God, one Torah, and one people.

Deuteronomy plays a pivotal role in the OT with theological motifs flowing into and out of the book. The book draws heavily upon earlier Pentateuchal themes like the patriarchal promises, the Exodus and Sinaitic Torah, and the wilderness wanderings. And because so many subsequent books employ these themes from Deuteronomy, scholars frequently label them "Deuteronomic," while Noth famously called Joshua–Kings the "Deuteronomic History." Most agree that the only subsequent OT books not influenced by Deuteronomy are Joel, Obadiah, Jonah, Nahum, and Habakkuk.

The Pentateuch ends in the same way it begins. Just as Adam and Eve stand before God in Gen 2, in the book of Deuteronomy, a new generation of Israelites stands before God on the plains of Moab. Adam and Eve were created in the image of God and were commanded to have dominion over creation (Gen 1:28), so also Israel, as God's covenant partner, is given responsibilities by Moses in Deuteronomy to subdue the land. Adam and Eve were faced with a decision regarding the tree of the knowledge of good and evil (Gen 2:16–17). In like manner, this moment parallels Moses' words to Israel about the Torah. "See I am placing before you today life and good, death and evil" (Deut 30:15). He goes on to say, "Choose life so that you and your offspring may live" (Deut 30:19).

## SELECT BIBLIOGRAPHY

Brueggemann, Walter. *The Land: Place as Gift, Promise, and Challenge in Biblical Faith.* 2nd ed. Minneapolis: Augsburg Fortress, 2003.

Craigie, Peter. *The Book of Deuteronomy.* New International Commentary on the Old Testament. Grand Rapids: Eerdmans, 1976.

Kitchen, Kenneth. *On the Reliability of the Old Testament.* Grand Rapids: Eerdmans, 2003.

Kline, Meredith. *Treaty of the Great King: The Covenant Structure of Deuteronomy; Studies and Commentary.* Grand Rapids: Eerdmans, 1963.

Milgrom, Jacob. "The Alleged 'Demythologization and Secularization' in Deuteronomy." *Israel Exploration Journal* 23 (1973): 155–67.

Noth, Martin. *The Deuteronomistic History.* 2nd ed. Sheffield: Sheffield Academic Press, 1981.

Vogt, Peter. *Deuteronomic Theology and the Significance of Torah: A Reappraisal.* Winona Lake, IN: Eisenbrauns, 2006.

Weinfeld, Moshe. *Deuteronomy 1–11: A New Translation with Introduction and Commentary.* Anchor Bible 5. New York: Doubleday, 1991.

# 8

# JOSHUA

One of the best-known stories from ancient Israel's history is the conquest of Jericho under the leadership of Joshua. As a result, this book is often associated with Israel's conquest of the land promised to Abraham, Isaac, and Jacob (e.g., Gen 12:7; 13:15, 17; 28:13; 50:24). While the story of Israel's entry into the land and its initial battles to drive out its inhabitants occupy a large part of this book, there are other important aspects to it: the division of the land among Israel's tribes, Israel's recommitment to God's covenant given at Sinai, and the passing of leadership from Moses to Joshua at the beginning of the book (Josh 1:1–9) and from Eleazar to Phinehas (Josh 24:33; cf. Josh 22:13, 30–32; Judg 20:28) at the book's end.

## AUTHORSHIP, COMPOSITION, AND DATE

Traditionally, Joshua has been understood to be the author of the book that bears his name. The Talmud states that "Joshua wrote his own book" (*B. Bat.* 15a) but later qualifies this by stating that Eleazar wrote the account of Joshua's death and Phinehas wrote about Eleazar's death. Certainly, the book claims that Joshua wrote some of its contents—probably most of Josh 24—when it states, "Then Joshua wrote these words in the Book of the Torah of God" (Josh 24:26). Few scholars in recent years have held to Joshua's authorship of the book, although Harstad has defended this view with the possibility that there may have been minor editorial additions after Joshua's death. He argues, however, that the book in its present form dates from the period of the Judges and adduces internal evidence that

Joshua must have been composed before David's conquest of Jerusalem in 1002 (e.g., Josh 15:63; 18:16, 28).

However, the vast majority of scholars do not believe Joshua could have authored the book as we have it. For instance, they point out the frequent use of the phrase "to this day" (Josh 4:9; 5:9; 6:25; 7:26; 8:28–29; 9:27; 13:13; 14:14; 15:63; 16:10). For instance, "the Jebusites dwell with the people of Judah at Jerusalem to this day" (Josh 15:36). Such notices appear to place some distance in time between the events of the book and the time of its writing. Moreover, older place names are consistently explained by new ones (Josh 11:10; 14:15; 15:8, 9, 10, 13, 15, 25, 49, 54, 60; 18:13, 14, 28; 20:7; 21:11), indicating that the author, though perhaps relying on older source texts, updated these for his audience. Finally, it should be noted, the author tells us that Joshua's prayer about the sun standing still in the sky is contained in the book of Jashar (Josh 10:13). Since the book of Jashar also contained the poem written by David to mourn the deaths of Saul and Jonathan in 1009 BC (2 Sam 1:18), it appears that the book of Joshua had to have been written, at the earliest, sometime during David's reign in Hebron. However, the author also depicts Gezer as a Canaanite city, not an Israelite royal city (Josh 16:10). Therefore, it would appear that he was writing before Solomon's Egyptian father-in-law exterminated the Canaanites in that city (1 Kgs 9:16–17). Since the conquest of Gezer had to have taken place before Jerusalem's temple was completed in 961 BC (1 Kgs 3:1; 9:16–17), the composition of the book of Joshua occurred in the first part of the tenth century. Since the author appears to have had access to older records about the dividing of the land among Israel's tribes, he perhaps was a scribe in David's court.

## HIGHER CRITICAL THEORIES ON THE COMPOSITION OF JOSHUA

During the halcyon days of the Documentary Hypothesis in the early to mid-twentieth century, a number of critical scholars sought to find traces of the supposed Pentateuchal sources (J, E, D, and P) in Joshua. These scholars spoke of a *hexateuch*—the five books of the Pentateuch plus Joshua. The logic of this position depended largely on the premise that the narrative about the promise of the land in the Pentateuch must have been completed by Joshua's account of taking possession of it. Usually Josh 1–2 was assigned to the Elohist source, since it was assumed that Judg 1 presented the Yahwist's alternate view of the conquest of the Promised Land. The Priestly source was supposedly behind the chapters detailing the allotment of the land among Israel's tribes (Josh 13–21).

Critical scholarship in the last three decades has largely abandoned the search for Pentateuchal sources in Joshua. Instead, it is common to speak of a *Deuteronomistic History* that includes Joshua, Judges, Samuel, and Kings and supposedly builds on the ideology found in the book of Deuteronomy, especially the dual concept that Israel would experience blessing in the land for its faith as demonstrated by keeping the Sinaitic covenant but would experience God's wrath if it abandoned it. This emphasis, especially prominent in Josh 22–24, is the reason Joshua is considered part of this complex of books that supposedly originated from the same school that produced Deuteronomy toward the end of the seventh century. This view of the former prophets as a Deuteronomistic History was first developed by Noth in the mid-twentieth century and has become an accepted interpretation among critical scholars.

Noth treated Deuteronomy, Joshua, Judges, Samuel, and Kings as a unified history of Israel which he called the Deuteronomistic History. According to his theory, the corpus was written by the Deuteronomist, an author in the Babylonian exile. The Deuteronomistic History was composed to explain the exile as God's rejection of Israel, and it contained a negative message: that there was no hope for Israel's future. The Deuteronomist used earlier sources, but according to Noth, the book of Samuel contained some material that was simply composed by the Deuteronomist himself as well as insertions made after the time of the Deuteronomist (e.g., the supposed appendix, 2 Sam 21–24). Ultimately, however, Noth emphasized the unified character of the Deuteronomistic History. Other critics propose several redactions to this corpus.

Noth's concept of a Deuteronomistic History was widely adopted, and much of critical scholarship to this day still refers to Deuteronomy–Kings as the Deuteronomistic History. However, subsequent studies have pointed out that God's eternal promise to David is an important theme throughout this corpus, calling into question Noth's assertion that there is no hope offered to Israel in these books.

Later critics sought to modify Noth's theory. Cross proposed that the Deuteronomistic History has two redactional layers. The first came from the time of Josiah in support of his reforms. This layer was optimistic about Israel's future. The second layer originated in the exile by a redactor who emphasized the conditions placed on the Davidic covenant. This layer was more pessimistic in outlook. Cross's theory has influenced further work by American scholars.

In Europe a group of scholars in Göttingen, Germany proposed that the Deuteronomistic History had three redactional layers. The first layer (DtrG) provided the basic historical framework and was optimistic, assuming the conquest of the land of Canaan had been successfully accomplished. The next redaction (DtrP) added prophetic narratives. The final layer (DtrN) inserted legal ("nomistic") material. This redactor portrayed the conquest as incomplete and Israel's hold on the land of Canaan as precarious.

While these approaches continue to have their adherents, they remain problematic. All of them rely on assertions that there are competing and conflicting interests evident in the texts of the books that comprise the Deuteronomistic History. Often, however, the presence of these supposedly incompatible ideologies stems from purposeful disharmonization of passages that do not on their face require such readings. Moreover, each of them assumes that there are multiple theologies embedded in books like Samuel. These hypothetical theologies are rather one-dimensional and pedestrian, devoid of nuance and subtlety. In contrast, a holistic reading of a book such as Samuel without preconceived notions of redactional layers could lead one to see a multi-dimensional theology full of nuanced views of God and humans often portrayed with wonderful subtleties in style and substance. Such a holistic approach can appreciate the skill of the author as he delves into the complicated events of God's history in dealing with Israel and the multifaceted motivations of kings and commoners alike. As a result, Joshua, Judges, Samuel, and Kings should be seen as giving a realistic picture of humans and a reliable picture of God's interaction with them.

Noth's approach does not preclude theories that look for underlying sources in Joshua. Nelson, for instance, believes that editors who shaped the Deuternomistic History have used such sources to shape the final form of Joshua. Nevertheless, he, like many critical scholars, views Joshua as primarily a theological and literary creation that offers little, if any, factual historical material about Israel's past. Instead, it supposedly stems from a seventh century author who shaped his portrait of Joshua to be similar to the life of Josiah. This book was later supplemented by an editor during the Babylonian exile.

Without denying that theological currents found in Deuteronomy play a large part in the worldview of the authors of books like Joshua, Judges, Samuel, and Kings, the critical view that Joshua is simply a theological narrative of what Israel thought its history should have been is doubtful and driven more by the ideology of critical scholars than by evidence from the text or from extra-biblical sources. Such critical reconstructions assume that any historical writing that has a theological viewpoint cannot be historically accurate—a common but dubious assumption among critical scholars. Moreover, by placing the composition of Joshua so late in Israel's history, these theories fail to explain many of the features of the book that point to a much earlier date for its writing. For instance, why did the author depict the Canaanites as living in Gezer (Josh 16:10), when other supposedly Deuternomistic editors claimed that the Canaanites had been exterminated from the city (1 Kgs 9:16–17)? How is it that Hurrian names such as Hoham, Piam, Sheshai, and Talmai (Josh 10:3; 15:14) are preserved in Joshua when Hurrian culture had disappeared by the tenth century? Why does Joshua depict Sidon, not Tyre, as the primary Phoenician city (Josh 11:8; 13:4, 6; 19:28), when Tyre had been the most prominent Phoenician metropolis for some centuries before Josiah's day when the Deuteronomistic History was supposedly taking shape? (Tyre is mentioned only at Josh 19:29.) These issues are often overlooked or ignored by critical scholars because of their assumptions that lead them to conclude that Israel could not have accurately preserved its early history in the land.

## LITERARY FEATURES OF JOSHUA

Much of Joshua describes the conquest and occupation of the Promised Land. This narrative highlights God's work in giving the land to Israel as he had promised to Abraham, Isaac, and Jacob.

The beginning of the book relates the first days of Joshua's leadership—a leadership established by God (Josh 1:2–9). Immediately Joshua implemented plans for invading Canaan. The account of the crossing of the Jordan River emphasizes God's commissioning of Joshua as Moses' successor as the Jordan was parted much like the parting of the Red Sea when Israel left Egypt (Josh 3:14–17; cf. Josh 1:17).

A second section of the book recounts the military campaigns led by Joshua. Here the reader sees Israel's successes granted by God and the people's failures when they rely on their own resources or disobey God's commands (Josh 7:1–26; 9:1–27). This theme is reinforced by reciting the blessings and curses on Mount Ebal as commanded by Moses (Josh 8:30–35; cf. Deut 11:26–32; 27:1–8).

Several non-narrative chapters list in detail the dividing of the land among Israel's tribes (Josh 13–21). This brings to a close Joshua's service as Israel's leader of the conquest. The tribes are to complete the conquest of their own allotted territory (cf. Josh 13:1–7; 21:43–45).

The final section of the book tells of Joshua's last words to Israel, his charge to them to trust in Yahweh, his ominous warning that they are not capable of keeping God's commands (Josh 24:19–20), and the pledge of Joshua and the people to obey God. Finally, the book closes with notices of the deaths of Joshua and the high priest Eleazar.

## Outline of Joshua

I.  Joshua's Initial Words to Israel and Preparation for the Conquest (1:1–5:15)

    A.  God commissions Joshua (1:1–9)

    B.  Preparations for crossing the Jordan (1:10–18)

    C.  Spying out the land with the help of Rahab (2:1–24)

    D.  Crossing the Jordan River (3:1–4:24)

    E.  Circumcision at Gilgal (5:1–15)

II. Military Campaigns in Canaan (6:1–12:24)

    A.  The capture of Jericho (6:1–27)

    B.  The capture of Ai (7:1–8:29)

    C.  Blessings and Curses at Mount Ebal (8:30–35)

    D.  Deception by the Gibeonites (9:1–27)

    E.  Joshua's campaign in southern Canaan (10:1–43)

    F.  Joshua's campaign in northern Canaan (11:1–15)

    G.  Summary of Joshua's campaigns (11:16–12:24)

III. Dividing the Land among the Tribes of Israel (13:1–22:34)
   A.  Joshua's instruction for making the division (13:1–7)
   B.  Land for the tribes east of the Jordan River (13:8–33)
   C.  Land for the tribes west of the Jordan River (14:1–19:51)
   D.  Cities of Refuge (20:1–9)
   E.  Cities for the Levites (21:1–45)
   F.  Eastern tribes allowed to occupy their territory (22:1–34)
IV. Joshua's Final Words to Israel and the end of his era (23:1–24:33)
   A.  Joshua's charge to Israel's leaders (23:1–16)
   B.  Joshua presents God's challenge to Israel (24:1–28)
   C.  The death of Joshua, the internment of Joseph's bones, and the death of Eleazar (24:29–33)

## HISTORICAL AND ARCHAEOLOGICAL ISSUES

### COMPLETE OR PARTIAL CONQUEST?

Does the book of Joshua present the account of a complete subduing of Canaan by Israel or does it depict Joshua as leading a first strike and turning the land over for individual tribes to subdue? Scholars have pointed to some texts that appear to portray a complete conquest (Josh 11:23; 18:1; 21:43–44). For instance, Josh 21:44 states, "Yahweh had given all their enemies into their hands." Other passages suggest that Joshua's campaign simply eliminated the main opposition to the Israelites' entry into the land, leaving the rest of the work to individual tribes who would subdue the land over time (Josh 10:40–43; 15:13–19, 63; 16:10; 17:11–13; 19:47; cf. Judg 1:1–36). These texts have led some critical scholars to posit various sources behind the book of Joshua, with references to a complete conquest coming from the idealist language of a Deuteronomistic editor in the seventh century BC. More recently, however, Clarke has observed that the supposed statements of a complete conquest are always qualified in their context in order to limit the invasion to certain regions, kings, or cities that were conquered. For example, when Josh 10:40 states that "Joshua struck . . . all *their* kings," it is referring only to the five kings mentioned in Josh 10:1–22.

Given this evidence, as well as the frequent references to the work that will be left to individual tribes, it is best to view Joshua's military campaigns as only the first phase of the land's conquest. The second phase was entrusted to individual tribes after they were allotted their land and was met with varying degrees of success (Judg 1:1–36).

### WAS THERE A CONQUEST?

While the book of Joshua presents Israel as having carried out a plan to conquer and occupy the Promised Land, many critical scholars have found this account difficult to accept on its face. Much of the impetus for this skepticism came from the supposed tension between passages depicting a total conquest and those depicting a partial one. Instead of viewing the conquest as a large invasion, these scholars have developed other models.

### *Peaceful Infiltration*

This model first was developed by Alt and expanded by Noth in the first half of the twentieth century. Instead of staging an invasion, Israel entered the land through a gradual, peaceful infiltration. These migrants purportedly came to the land during Egypt's New Kingdom period (sixteenth–fourteenth centuries) when Egypt no longer maintained a strong interest in Canaan. Without Egypt's support the native population in the land could not withstand the infiltration and eventual rise of an Israelite kingdom.

This view discounts any historical claims made in Joshua. In addition, it is based on mere sociological speculation and is to this day unsubstantiated by any data, biblical or extra-biblical.

### *Peasant Revolt*

In the early 1960s, Mendenhall first proposed that Israel originated from native Canaanite peasants who had been reduced to slave labor by the feudal rulers of Canaan's great cities. These peasants allied themselves with other oppressed groups, rose up and overthrew their masters, and adopted the Yahwistic religion as an expression of their egalitarian hopes for freedom. Mendenhall's model was further developed by Gottwald, who saw this uprising as the first great socialist revolution.

Based largely on socio-political models and Marxist ideology— Gottwald admits that his political views favor socialism—there is little, if any, backing for this opinion in the biblical text and nothing in extra-biblical sources. Rather, this approach appears to be constructed in order to make Israel's history conform to the political and social views of the scholars who support it.

### ARCHAEOLOGY AND THE CONQUEST OF JERICHO

As argued earlier (see chapter 4 on Exodus), Israel's departure from Egypt took place in 1446. This places the invasion of Israel forty years later, beginning in 1406. However, the evidence for the conquest of Jericho around 1400 is controversial.

Garstang, who excavated Jericho from 1930 to 1936, found signs of collapsed walls, and he dated this destruction of the city to about 1400 at the time of Joshua. Kenyon, who excavated at Jericho from 1952 to 1958, concluded that this destruction of the city occurred too early for Joshua's conquest, dating it to between 1580 and 1550. Wood subsequently argued that Garstang was correct, and Kenyon was wrong. Most recently, published carbon-14 dating results from six grain samples from Jericho associated with the city's disputed destruction layer date these grains to the mid-sixteenth century, seemingly confirming Kenyon's dates.

But the evidence is not as convincing as it might first appear. There is a continuing controversy over the calibration of radiocarbon dating in the eastern Mediterranean basin concerning the accuracy of the calibration scale for carbon-14 dating for this period. Radiocarbon dating after the mid-second millennium BC agrees quite well with other chronological determinations used by historians and archaeologists. In contrast, radiocarbon-determined dates before this time, especially for the fifteenth century, disagree quite sharply with other chronological determinations showing a discrepancy of about 170 years. If we subtract 170 years from Kenyon's dates of 1580 to 1550, then the resulting date agrees quite well with a conquest at the very end of the fifteenth century (i.e., a conquest lasting from 1406 to 1399).

### ARCHAEOLOGY AT HAZOR AND THE DATING
### OF THE CONQUEST

The Canaanite city of Hazor was built on two levels. The lower Canaanite city of Hazor has three primary strata, each ending with a destruction layer. The second layer dates to about 1400, the time of Joshua's campaign, if the exodus took place in 1446. The third destruction layer dates to about 1230, and there is no subsequent urban occupation at Hazor until Solomon's time in the tenth century (1 Kgs 9:15).

## *The Conquest of Canaan*

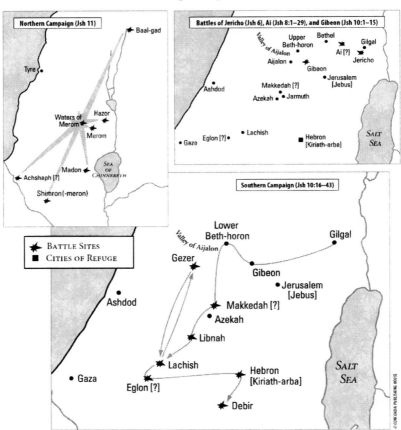

Joshua succeeded Moses for the conquest of Canaan (Num 27:12; Deut 31:14), yet the real general was the Lord (Josh 5:13–15). God delivered Jericho (Josh 6) and Ai (Josh 8) into Israel's hand. God permitted the Gibeonites to become the servants of Israel at Gilgal (Josh 9). Five kings attacked Gibeon, and God gave Israel victory at Gibeon and in the Valley of Aijalon when the sun stood still (Josh 10).

After defeating the northern alliance under Hazor at the Waters of Merom, Israel destroyed those cities allied against it (Josh 11). Israel systematically destroyed the southern towns in the hill country and slopes (Josh 10:16–43).

Other cities conquered included Arad, Adullam, Aphek, Carmel, Dor, Geder, Goiim, Hepher, Hormah, Jokneam, Kedesh, Lasharon, Makkedah, Megiddo, Tappuah, Taanach, and Tirzah.

Cities that the Israelites failed to take were Jerusalem, which David would later conquer, and the five Philistine cities: Ashdod, Ashkelon, Ekron, Gath, and Gaza.

One might be tempted to assign the 1230 destruction to Joshua, thereby supporting the late-date theory for the exodus (i.e., an exodus in the mid-thirteenth century). However, Judg 4:24 implies that in the period following Barak's victory at the Wadi Kishon over the forces of King Jabin of Hazor, the Israelites conquered Hazor. Therefore, the 1230 destruction layer cannot be assigned to Joshua, because this would leave no later conquest as depicted in Judges or any city for Jabin to have ruled, since Hazor would not see any major occupation again until Solomon's reign.

Therefore, the second destruction layer at Hazor appears to confirm that Joshua conquered the city as reported in Josh 11:1–13. Recently Petrovich has argued that this is the most logical conclusion to draw from both the biblical, archaeological, and epigraphic evidence.

## THEOLOGICAL THEMES IN JOSHUA

### HOLY WAR AND THE EXTERMINATION OF THE INHABITANTS OF THE LAND

In Deuteronomy, Moses delivered God's principles for war by which Israel was to conquer the Holy Land (Deut 7:1–26; 20:1–20; 21:10–24). The inhabitants of Canaan were placed under the ban (חרם) and were to be totally exterminated. The justification given in Deuteronomy for this practice is that the Canaanites would lead Israel into apostasy if they were allowed to continue to occupy the land with Israel (Deut 7:4, 16). Moreover, while the Hebrew word חרם sometimes denotes devoting something to extermination because it is abominable (Deut 7:26; 13:12–18), at other times it signifies something that is devoted and consecrated to God and is, therefore, set apart from humans. Such things must be holy (Lev 27:21, 28–29). The principle that unites these two meanings into one word is the shared concept that both what is an abomination to God and what is God's possession must be removed from human access and use.

Joshua carried out these divine mandates during his campaigns (e.g., Josh 6:17–18). Later, when Israel failed to carry out these instructions, God's anger burned against them (Josh 7:1; cf. Judg 2:1–5). Clearly, the book of Joshua depicts God as supporting the extermination of the pagan inhabitants of the land.

Later readers of Joshua have been troubled by these reports of mass killings of the Canaanites and God's support of it. Moreover, some Christians have used these passages in Deuteronomy and Joshua to justify genocide. For instance, Thelle has noted that the Puritan preacher Cotton Mather advocated genocide of Native Americans on the basis of these passages, and Afrikaners used them to justify the system of apartheid in South Africa.

These abuses of the concept of the ban in Joshua resulted from a failure to understand the reason behind God's command: Israel was to remain uncorrupted by the idolatrous practices of the pagan inhabitants of Canaan. God intended for them to be a people set apart for him so they could be the people through whose flesh the Messiah would be brought into the world. Because of the presence of sin in the world, oftentimes two commands of Yahweh clash with one another. In this case the First Commandment (placing God above all else) and the Fifth Commandment (respect for human life) were in conflict. In such cases the First Commandment always takes priority, because all of the other commandments flow from it. The sins of the Canaanites against the First Commandment were not to be tolerated or allowed to be perpetuated in the land, and especially not among the Israelites, the bearers of the Messianic promise (Gen 15:16).

Thus, Joshua cannot be used as a pretext for genocide or unjust discrimination against any community. With the advent of the Messiah in the birth, life, death, and resurrection of Jesus, God's people are no longer the physical line through whom the Messiah is to come into the world. Instead, Christians are called to live among unbelievers, but to avoid being joined with them in their sins (2 Cor 6:14–7:1). At the same time, Christians are still engaged in a battle, but not against "flesh and blood" (Eph 6:12). Rather, they fight against "the rulers, against the authorities, against the cosmic power over this present darkness" (Eph 6:12). In this sense, Christians continue the spiritual battle Israel fought in Canaan. Israel battled spiritual enemies through the divine mandate to exterminate idolatry from the land of Canaan. Later Deborah's song in the book of Judges indicates that God's battles took place on two levels: one on earth (Judg 5:19) and the other in heaven (Judg 5:20). The battle continues for Christians on the heavenly level.

## CHRIST IN JOSHUA

Joshua often depicts God as fighting for Israel (see esp. Josh 23:10). Of particular interest in this regard is the appearance of the Commander of Yahweh's army (שר צבא יהוה) to Joshua just before the conquest of Jericho (Josh 5:13–15). The text gives a couple of indications that this is not simply an angel, such as the archangel Michael, who is sometimes called a commander (שר; Dan 10:21; 12:1). One piece of evidence includes the fact that Joshua is standing on holy ground—a place made holy by the presence of the holy God (Josh 5:15; cf. Exod 3:4–5). Another is that the Commander allows Joshua to worship him, something God's holy angels would never allow (Rev 19:10; 22:9), but is acceptable and appropriate for God himself. Thus, this commander is God.

Moreover, Josh 6:2–5 should be understood as further instructions by the Commander to Joshua, and in this case the Commander is called Yahweh. He is the one who has handed Jericho over to Joshua and his armies—a prerogative elsewhere ascribed only to God in the book (Josh 6:2; cf. Josh 6:2; 8:1, 7, 18; 10:12, 19, 30, 32; 11:8; 24:8, 11). Joshua's orders for the attack on Jericho, therefore, come directly from God.

This Commander is depicted already in Exodus as the Messenger who will go before Israel, bring them into the land, and send hornets against their enemies (Exod 23:20–30; cf. Josh 24:12). He also had the power and authority not to forgive their sins because he bore the name of God (Exod 23:21). Beginning in Genesis, this figure is called Yahweh's Messenger (Gen 16:7, 9, 10, 11; 22:11, 15).

This appearance of God as Commander, therefore, ought to be understood as a manifestation of the pre-incarnate Christ. Not only is Christ depicted in Scripture as the Leader of the heavenly armies (Rev 19:11–16), but also it is only through Jesus that people see the Father (John 1:18; 14:9; Col 1:15).

This also means that the conquest of Canaan is the work of Christ. He briefly appears to Joshua. However, his work in giving the land to Israel is ongoing throughout the book.

## SIN AND GRACE IN JOSHUA

### *The Land as God's Gift to Israel*

One of the clearest ways in which God's grace is shown in Joshua is in the fulfillment of the promise to give Israel the land of Canaan. This is highlighted in Josh 13–22 where the dividing of the land among the tribes and the borders of each tribe's territory is related in great detail (cf. Josh 21:43–44). Divine grace is also underscored at the very beginning of the book when God tells Joshua that he will be his instrument for giving Israel the land that God promised them (Josh 1:6). In a more bittersweet way it is mentioned at Josh 5:6 during the account of the circumcision of Joshua's army. Here the reader is reminded that the previous generation did not inherit the land because of their rebellion in the wilderness (cf. Num 13–14). Clearly the land was God's gift, and the only impediment for Israel receiving and enjoying that gift was their sin and rejection of Yahweh, especially in serving other gods (Josh 23:7, 16; 24:14–16, 20, 23).

God's gracious gift of the land is also emphasized in the promised rest he gave to Israel in the land. At the beginning of Joshua, this is the goal toward which God is working (Josh 1:13, 15), and at the end of the book, God has provided that rest (Josh 21:44; 22:4; 23:1). In a greater way God gives his people rest through the work of Jesus, his Son (Matt 11:28) and will one day bring God's true Israel to perfect rest (Heb 3–4; Rev 14:13).

### *God Grants Israel Victory*

Dovetailing with God's gift of the land is his promise to fight for Israel and give them victory over their enemies (cf. Josh 1:1–9). Joshua repeatedly emphasizes that Yahweh handed land and the peoples of Canaan over to Israel (Josh 6:2; 8:1, 7, 18; 10:12, 19, 30, 32; 11:8; 24:8, 11). The fall of Jericho dramatically demonstrated that Israel's battlefield success was God's doing, as the fall of the city's walls came about by God's work. The well-known incident of the sun standing still in the sky (Josh 10:12–14) states that "Yahweh fought for Israel." However, when Israel failed to trust Yahweh, their victory was not assured, since unbelief was rejection of God's promises. This is shown most vividly in the failure to capture Ai because of Achan's sin (Josh 7:1–9).

## The Twelve Tribes

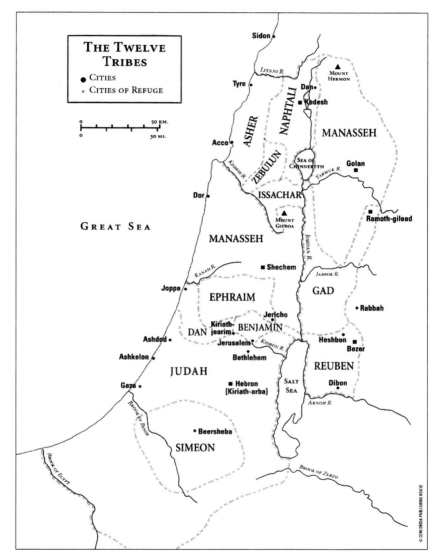

## *God's Covenant with Israel*

The covenant God made with his people at Mount Sinai came from his gracious choice of Israel, and had nothing to do with their earning God's favor (Deut 7:6–8). Israel was empowered to show its response to God's grace and their gratitude for being his chosen people by keeping the laws given by Moses. The people are depicted as doing this throughout Joshua. For instance, Achan's punishment accords with Deut 13, and Joshua led Israel in the covenant ceremony commanded by Moses (Josh 8; cf. Deut 27:1–8). Yet Israel did not always remain faithful to God: Achan disobeyed the ban placed on Jericho; Joshua did not consult God before making a covenant with the Gibeonites (Josh 9:1–27). Despite these failings, God continued to keep his covenant with Israel first given to Abraham, Isaac, and Jacob. His grace was evident in his longsuffering.

At the end of the book, Joshua called on Israel to keep God's covenant given at Sinai. He set forth God's generous blessings to Israel, but also warned them of curses that they would bring on themselves if they abandoned Yahweh (Josh 23:1–16; cf. Josh 24:14–28). For the reader of Joshua this emphasizes the sharp difference between God's love, fidelity, and grace and Israel's inability to remain faithful. It serves as a call to repentance for all readers so that they might also be led to rely on divine mercy and forgiveness.

## CONCLUSION

The book of Joshua begins with the fulfillment of God's promises to Israel's patriarchs, especially in giving the land to their descendants. However, it is only a beginning. Israel would fail to keep the provisions of the Sinai covenant and would eventually be taken from the land. Yet God's promises would endure. Through Christ, God would ultimately fight for his people and conquer sin and death, so that they might look forward to a greater land, one which includes the eternal Jerusalem (Heb 11:8–10; 13–16; 12:22–24; 13:14).

## SELECT BIBLIOGRAPHY

Alt, Albrecht. *Essays on Old Testament History and Religion.* Oxford: Blackwell, 1966 (First published as *Kleine Schriften zur Geschichte des Volkes Israel,* 1953–59).

Clarke, T. A. "Complete v. Incomplete Conquest: A Re-examination of Three Passages in Joshua." *Tyndale Bulletin* 61 (2010): 84–104.

Garstang, John, and J. B. E. Garstang. *The Story of Jericho*. 2nd ed. London: Marshal, Morgan and Scott, 1948.

Gottwald, Norman K. *The Tribes of Yahweh: A Sociology of the Religion of Liberated Israel*, 1250–1050 B.C.E. Maryknoll: Orbis, 1979.

Harstad, Adolph L. *Joshua.* Concordia Commentary. St Louis: Concordia, 2002.

Kenyon, Kathleen. *Archaeology in the Holy Land.* 4th ed. London: Ernest Benn, 1979.

Mendenhall, George E. *The Tenth Generation.* Baltimore: Johns Hopkins University, 1973.

Nelson, Richard D. *Joshua.* Old Testament Library. Nashville: Westminster, 1997.

Noth, Martin. *The Deuteronomistic History*. Journal for the Study of the Old Testament Supplements 15. Sheffield: Journal for the Study of the Old Testament, 1967. Translation of the first half of *Überlieferungsgeschichtliche Studien.* 2nd ed. Tübingen: Max Niemeyer, 1967.

Petrovich, Douglas. "The Dating of Hazor's Destruction in Joshua 11 by way of Biblical, Archaeological, and Epigraphic Evidence." *Journal of the Evangelical Theological Society* 51 (2008): 489–512.

Thelle, Rannfrid I. "The Biblical Conquest Account and Its Modern Hermeneutical Challenges." *Studia Theologica* 61 (2007): 61–81.

Wood, Bryant G. "Did the Israelites Conquer Jericho? A New Look at the Archaeological Evidence." *Biblical Archaeology Review* 16.2 (1990): 44–58.

———. "Dating Jericho's Destruction: Bienkowski Is Wrong on All Counts." *Biblical Archaeology Review* 16.5 (1990): 45–49, 68, 69.

# 9

# JUDGES

The English title *Judges* is based upon the Vulgate *Judices*. The Hebrew name of the book, שפטים, is derived from the verb שפט which denotes *rule, govern*, or *exercise leadership*. More narrowly, however, when describing someone conducting a nation's internal matters, שפט means *judge*. When depicting someone's action in external affairs it is best translated *deliver*.

This second sense of שפט describes the following judges when they engage in battle with outside enemies: Othniel (Judg 3:10), Tola (Judg 10:2), Jair (Judg 10:3), Jephthah (Judg 12:7), Ibzan (Judg 12:8, 9), Elon (Judg 12:11), Abdon (Judg 12:13, 14), and Samson (Judg 15:20; 16:31). Only Deborah is described as a שפט while functioning in a judicial capacity (Judg 4:4–5). That שפט predominantly means *deliver* in the book of Judges also becomes evident in Judg 2:16 where שפטים appears together with ויושיעום, *and they saved them*. In fact the verb ישע, *save, deliver*, describes Othniel (Judg 3:9), Ehud (Judg 3:15), Shamgar (Judg 3:31), Gideon (Judg 6:15; 8:22), Tola (Judg 10:1), Jephthah (Judg 12:3), and Samson (Judg 13:5).

The book of Judges, therefore, is primarily concerned about people who save Israelites from external threats rather than with magistrates who function within the nation. Perhaps the best title of the book then is "Tribal Saviors," as the judges function more like military heroes. The last five chapters, however, abandon this motif all together as Israel's history spirals out of control with one horrific event after another.

## AUTHORSHIP, DATING, AND TEXT

Judges is an anonymous book. The Rabbis attributed authorship to Samuel (*B. Bat. 14b*) and Christians down through the ages have followed suit. The book contains a series of explanatory comments (Judg 1:11; 1:23; 3:1–2; 19:10; 20:27–28) as well as seven chronological notes which conclude with the expression עד היום הזה, *until this day* (Judg 1:21; 1:26; 6:24; 10:4; 15:19; 18:12; 19:30). Cumulatively, these passages point to a composition either late in Samuel's life or after the death of Samuel but before David's day. Judg 1:21 notes, "the Jebusites have lived with the sons of Benjamin in Jerusalem to this day." This statement indicates a time of composition before 1002, when David conquered the city.

It also appears that Judges must have been composed before the Babylonian exile. An exilic author would not have seen the presence of a king as a solution to Israel's problems (cf. Judg 17:6; 21:25). Moreover, the phrase "until the exile from the land" (Judg 18:20) is best understood as referring to the Assyrian conquest of Dan in 734–732. Judg 18:20, therefore, was written sometime in the late eighth or any time in the seventh century.

This leaves two options for the composition of Judges: Either it was composed in the eleventh century and Judg 18:20 is a later scribal gloss, or it was composed in the late eighth to early seventh centuries, and the author used sources from the eleventh century.

Both Ruth 1:1 and 2 Kgs 23:22 indicate that the era of the judges was well defined. It was the time between Joshua's death (Judg 1:1; cf. Judg 2:6–10) and the rise of Israel's monarchy. In determining exact dates, though, it is important to note that several of the judgeships chronologically overlapped. This is indicated by the fact that the expression אחריו, *after him*, connects successive judges only in Judg 3:31; 10:3; 12:8, 11, 13. Therefore, some of the judges were contemporaries who served in different places. Working from the figure of 480 years in 1 Kgs 6:1, the period is summarized as follows:

### *Chronology of the Judges*

| |
|---|
| 1406–1400 Joshua's conquest |
| 1399–1379 Period for the deaths of Joshua and the elders |
| 1378–1371 Oppression by Cushan-Rishathaim |
| 1371–1332 Othniel/Rest for the land |

| | |
|---|---|
| 1332–1315 Oppression by Eglon | |
| 1315–1236 Ehud/Rest for the land/Shamgar | |
| 1236–1217 Oppression by Jabin | |
| 1217–1178 Deborah | |
| 1178–1172 Oppression by the Midianites | |
| 1172–1133 Gideon/Rest for the land | |
| 1133–1131 Abimelech | |
| 1131–1109 Tola | |
| 1109–1088 Jair | |
| 1088–1071 Oppression by the Midianites | |
| | 1088–1083 Jephthah |
| 1088–1049 Oppression by the Philistines | |
| | 1083–1077 Ibzan |
| 1068–1049 Samson (?) | 1077–1068 Elon |
| | 1068–1061 Abdon |

Archaeologists have discovered remains that point to Eglon's occupation of Jericho (Judg 3:13), Israel's victory at Hazor (Judg 4:1, 17, 24), Shechem's destruction (Judg 9:45), and Dan's destruction of Laish (Judg 18:27).

The critical understanding of Judges has been shaped largely by Noth who called the exilic author of Judges "the Deuteronomist" and argued that the book evolved through a series of postexilic revisions and expansions. Some of Noth's work on Judges has become passé, e.g., his understanding that pre–monarchial Israel could be likened to a Greek amphictyony where the tribes gathered periodically at a central shrine. Other parts of his analysis have undergone refinements and revisions. However, the general contours of Noth's interpretation continue to serve as the foundation for any critical investigation in Judges.

Frank Cross revised Noth's interpretation of Judges by postulating a first edition (Dtr 1) published in the seventh century that added Judg 2:1–3:6 to an earlier core as well as a conclusion to condemn the worship cites at Dan and Bethel (Judg 17:1–18:31). Then an exilic author (Dtr 2) added Judg 1:1–36 as a new introduction as well as the civil war account at the end in Judg 19:1–21:25.

Because dissecting the book of Judges in search of earlier sources is an enterprise fraught with subjectivity, an analysis that considers the book's unity and coherence is more fruitful. Consider these literary connections: The two-part introduction (Judg 1:1–36; 2:1–3:6) matches the book's two-part conclusion (Judg 17–18; 19–21). Judg 1:1–2 is similar to Judg 20:18 as both highlight Judah's primary role in warfare. The amputation of a king's thumbs and big toes (Judg 1:6–7) foreshadows the dismemberment of a woman's body (Judg 19:29). And chapters 2 and 17–18 focus on idolatry. These links demonstrate that Judges contains a high amount of symmetry, unity, and balance. Recognizing this, recent studies in Judges have shown less interest in its compositional history and instead have focused more on synchronic issues.

The number of narratives that include women in Judges have made it a favorite for feminist interpretations. Note the following passages that significantly feature women: (1) Deborah urges Barak (a man) to put Sisera to death, while Jael (a woman) is the one who kills him (Judg 4:1–31), (2) Abimelech is killed by "a certain woman" (Judg 9:50–57), (3) Jephthah's daughter dies due to his rash vow (Judg 11:29–40), (4) Delilah proves to be Samson's undoing (Judg 16:4–21), (5) a Levite's concubine is raped and her body is dismembered (Judg 19:22–30), and (6) women are given to men in Benjamin to prevent the tribe from extinction (Judg 21:15–25).

The textual tradition of Judges contains two Greek recensions. The evidence from Qumran indicates that both are probably dependent upon variations in the Hebrew tradition. The older Greek uncial, Alexandrinus, is the prototype for the majority of LXX manuscripts. It, however, diverges more from the Masoretic Text than the later recension represented by codex Vaticanus.

## LITERARY FEATURES OF JUDGES

Judges has three parts. The first section summarizes Israel's conquest and settlement of Canaan, revealing that God's people did not drive out all of their enemies (Judg 1:1–36). Because these Canaanites seduce Israelites into worshiping fertility deities, God disciplines his people by sending foreign armies.

The book's second section narrates Israel's laments over enemy occupations and God's gift of judges to deliver them (Judg 2:1–16:31). Albrecht Alt was the first to employ the terminology of major and minor judges in this part of the book. The former have longer narratives concerning their exploits whereas the latter do not. There are six major judges: Othniel, Ehud, Deborah, Gideon, Jephthah, and Samson. (In the outline below these major judges are in **bold**). There are also six minor judges: Shamgar, Tola, Jair, Ibzan, Elon, and Abdon. (In the outline below these minor judges are in *italics*). Six, of course, is one less than seven. It therefore connotes imperfection. The era of the judges therefore does not reflect Yahweh's plan for Israel. This will only be accomplished through the monarchy. The number six also means that most of the judges were far from perfect. In fact, each judge is worse than the last (cf. Judg 2:19). Adding to the central role of the number *six* in Judges, is the fact that the following refrain appears six times, "the Israelites [again] did what was evil in Yahweh's eyes" (Judg 3:7, 12; 4:1; 6:1; 10:6; 13:1).

As Judg 2:1–16:31 unfolds, Israel's leadership deteriorates to the point that the third part of the book testifies to rampant religious and social anarchy (Judg 17:1–21:25). With its fourfold refrain, "there was no king" (Judg 17:6; 18:1; 19:1; 21:25), this last section points to the root of the problem: without the monarchy all was lost.

## Outline of Judges

I.   Israel's conquest and settlement of Canaan (1:1–36)

    A.  The Southern Tribes: Judah, Simeon, and Benjamin (1:1–21)

    B.  The Central Tribes: Ephraim and Western Manasseh (1:22–29)

    C.  The Northern Tribes: Zebulon, Asher, Naphtali, and Dan (1:30–36)

II.  The period of the judges (2:1–16:31)

    A.  Yahweh's Messenger (2:1–5)

    B.  The new generation's apostasy (2:6–15)

    C.  A theological overview of the era (2:16–21)

    D.  Yahweh uses nations to test Israel (2:22–3:6)

    E.  **Othniel** of Judah (3:7–11)

    F.  **Ehud** of Benjamin (3:12–30)

    G.  *Shamgar* (3:31)

    H.  **Deborah** of Ephraim (4:1–5:31)

I.    **Gideon** of Manasseh (6:1–8:35)

J.    King Abimelech of Shechem (9:1–57)

K.   *Tola* of Issachar (10:1–2)

L.   *Jair* of Gilead (10:3–5)

M.  Reiterating the spiritual problem (10:6–17)

N.  **Jephthah** of Gilead (11:1–12:7)

O.  *Ibzan* of Bethlehem (12:8–10)

P.   *Elon* of Zebulon (12:11–12)

Q.  *Abdon* of Ephraim (12:13–15)

R.  **Samson** of Dan (13:1–16:31)

III. Anarchy abounds (17:1–21:25)

    A.  Micah's idol and his Levite priest (17:1–13)

    B.  The Levite priest and the tribe of Dan (18:1–31)

    C.  Another Levite and the tribe of Benjamin (19:1–30)

    D.  Intertribal warfare (20:1–21:25)

While the book of Judges consists mostly of historical narratives, it also includes the following genres: (1) conquest annals (Judg 1:1–36), (2) hymnic poetry (Judg 5:1–31), (3) an etiology (Judg 6:28–32), (4) a riddle (Judg 14:10–20), and (5) a fable (Judg 9:7–15).

## HISTORICAL ISSUES

### CANAANITE FERTILITY RELIGION

The book of Judges begins with the tenfold repetition of the phrase "did not drive them out" (Judg 1:19, 21, 27, 28, 29, 30, 31, 32, 33; 2:3). Israel's failure to drive out the Canaanites sets the tone for the rest of the book as the author evaluates Israel's spiritual condition by using the sevenfold refrain (with variations), "The sons of Israel did evil in Yahweh's eyes; they forgot Yahweh and served the Baals and Ashterot" (Judg 2:11; 3:7, 12; 4:1; 6:1; 10:6; 13:1). Gideon's father even has an altar to Baal in his backyard (Judg 6:25).

Baal and Asherah were part of a highly developed religious system that prevailed in Canaan, one that was to be a constant threat to Yahwistic faith. The discovery of the Ras Shamra texts in Northern

Syria in 1929 and subsequent years has greatly increased our knowledge of this religion.

The Canaanite pantheon was led by the creator god El and his wife Athirat, who appears as Asherah in the OT. (The plural, Ashterot is in Judg 2:13; 10:6.) Together, El and Athirat are said to have had seventy children. Their most famous son was the storm god Hadad (better known as Baal), and the couple's most influential daughter was Hadad's bloodthirsty sister, Anat.

The first part of the Baal cycle depicts conflict between Baal and Yam, the god of the sea, in which Baal is victorious and exalted as king. The struggle has its setting in the late fall, during the early part of the rainy period in Canaan. At this time the sea becomes so rough that the ancients feared to sail. With waves beating against the shore and threatening to flood the lower areas, Yam was waging war as a chaotic power. His other name, Nahar, or River, probably refers to the bedlam which results from violent rainstorms or melting snow turning riverbeds into destructive torrents. The combination Yam/Nahar would seem to represent all water which threatens—rather than contributes to—vegetation and human survival. But he is no match for Baal.

Baal not only defeats Yam/Nahar, but he also brings life-giving rain which results in the growth of vegetation, at least until the summer drought. The second part of the drama narrates Baal's conflict with the god of the underworld, Mot. Baal is swallowed by Mot, resulting in the cessation of rain. Anat then unleashes her violent power and defeats Mot, and this brings Baal back to life. This presages rain's return and guarantees fertility. Tied to nature, this drama endlessly repeats itself in the cycles of the seasons.

By engaging in sex at a high place, Canaanites believed that they could manipulate Baal and Asherah into having sexual relations in the heavens. This would then produce rain that would water the people's crops. Israelites indulged in these practices, too; several times the book of Judges employs the verb זנה, *become a prostitute*, to describe this act of apostasy (e.g., Judg 2:17; 8:27, 33).

### THE SEA PEOPLES

The Sea Peoples, also known as the Philistines, are prominent in several events in the book of Judges. Deborah's song mentions Shamgar ben Anat (Judg 5:6), who killed six hundred Philistines

(Judg 3:31), while Samson's exploits indicate intensified conflict between Israel and the Sea Peoples (Judg 13–16).

Toward the end of the second millennium, the Hittites and Egyptians lost their longtime grip on the ancient world. The most prominent group to fill this vacuum was the Sea Peoples. Leaving their coastal homelands in and around Greece, including the Aegean Islands and Crete, they defeated the Hittite and Ugaritic kingdoms. In about 1180 they were repelled in Egypt by Rameses III. However, the Sea Peoples met little or no resistance in Canaan (cf. Amos 9:7), and so they settled along the coastal plain and in the Shephelah. These non-Semitic people established five cities—Gaza, Ashdod, Ashkelon, Gath, and Ekron (the so-called Philistine Pentapolis).

Philistines had iron technology before Israel (cf. 1 Sam 13:20–22). Israel would require more than tribal judges to compete. God's people would need the various accoutrements of government that would give them a national identity and make them a people, not just a group of loosely affiliated tribes. They would also need the visible symbols of that power in the form of monumental architecture (e.g., palace, temple, city walls). In short, Israel needed a monarchy. This becomes most evident towards the end of Judges (Judg 17:6; 18:1; 19:1; 21:25).

## THE JUDGES

During the wilderness generation, the Spirit was present with Bezalel (Exod 28:3) as well as with Moses and the elders (Num 11:17, 25). In the book of Judges, however, Yahweh's Spirit plays a more prominent role. He comes upon Othniel (Judg 3:10), Gideon (Judg 6:34), Jephthah (Judg 11:29), and Samson (Judg 13:24–25; 14:6, 19; 15:14–15).

Though militarily successful through God's Spirit, none of the leaders in the book of Judges launched a crusade against Israel's idolatry. (The only judge to do that was Samuel [cf. 1 Sam 7:1–11].) Appeals for repentance and faith come from Yahweh's Messenger (Judg 2:1), a prophet (Judg 6:7–10), and Yahweh (Judg 10:10–16).

### Othniel

Othniel is not only the first judge, he is also the only one who is not critiqued by the book's author. Othniel comes from the tribe of Judah, which, in chapter 1 of Judges, is presented as much more successful than the other tribes in claiming its tribal allotment. He fights with king Cushan-rishathaim of Mesopotamia (Judg 3:10). Later judges are concerned only with Israel's near neighbors such as the Moabites, Philistines, and Canaanites. Therefore, both Othniel's Judean pedigree and his battle with a distant leader give him an aura suggestive of the later Davidic dynasty. Adding to this interpretation is that the closing chapters of Judges castigate the tribe of Benjamin and in particular the town of Gibeah. In fact, the men of Gibeah are shown to be even worse than the men of Sodom. The latter were at least frustrated in their plan to rape the angels who visited Lot (Gen 19:1–16), while those in Gibeah gang-raped the Levite's concubine all night, and she died in the morning (Judg 19:22–26). Why do these narratives conclude the book of Judges? They discredit Saul and his sons, who come from Benjamin and Gibeah. These pro-Davidic and anti-Saul passages validate the Davidic monarchy, and we catch a glimpse of this through Othniel, Israel's first judge.

## Ehud

The account of Ehud is rich in narrative color and detail. Although he hailed from the tribe of Benjamin—which means *the son of my right hand*—Ehud was "a man restricted in his right hand" (Judg 3:15). Ehud is also described as agile and quick-witted—in direct contrast to his enemy Eglon king of Moab, who is depicted as slow and gullible. In fact, his name עגלון, is the diminutive form of עגל, *calf*, and a near homonym of the adjective that denotes *round* or *rotund*. Eglon is an "extremely fat man" (Judg 3:17). Indeed, he is a fattened calf ready to be butchered by the wily Ehud.

Armed with his short dagger, Ehud told Eglon, "I have a דבר for you, O king" (Judg 3:19, 20). This phrase is ambiguous because though דבר can mean *word* or *message*, it can also denote *thing* or even *experience*. Little did Eglon know that the דבר was Ehud's sword, wielded with an unsuspected left hand. And it sank deep into Eglon's fat (Judg 3:21–22). Commentators strive to maintain restraint while conveying the graphic details. "[Eglon's] fat closed in upon the handle" of Ehud's sword, writes John Lawrenz, but the tip of the sword "found the exit point of Eglon's overused digestive system. The king fell, fouled by his own filth." Crude as they are, these details are significant to the plot line. Eglon's death is a literary lampoon against one of Israel's most hated enemies—Moab.

## Deborah

Judg 4 introduces Deborah who is called a prophetess and described as having judged Israel (Judg 4:4–5). Although demonstrating from the start a more forceful personality than Barak, Deborah did not lead the troops into battle but urged him to take that responsibility. When Barak objected that he would not go into battle unless she went with him, Deborah replied that for that reason the honor for the upcoming victory would go to a woman. As the story unfolds it becomes clear that the honor will go to Jael, the wife of Heber, who welcomed the enemy general Sisera into her tent and gave him milk to drink that caused him to fall asleep. She covered him with a blanket and then nailed his head to the ground with hammer and tent peg (Judg 4:21).

Deborah's judgeship is a negative reflection on Israel as it demonstrates the loss of male spiritual and military leadership. The nation was filled with weak-willed men. After Othniel, the first and ideal judge, the next three judges are Ehud (a man restricted in his right arm); Shamgar ben-Anat (because of the four-consonant root of his name and his connection to the Canaanite deity Anat, he is assumed not to have been an Israelite); and Deborah (a woman). Things are getting worse.

## Gideon

Globe argues that Judges is a series of ring structures that unify the book. Within this chiasm he observes that the Gideon narrative (Judg 6:1–8:32) stands at the center. A summary of Globe's outline is as follows:

### Globe's Outline of the Gideon Narrative

Introduction: Part I (1:1–2:5)
Introduction: Part II (2:6–3:6)
    Othniel (3:7–11)
        Ehud and Shamgar (3:12–21)
            Deborah, Barak and Jael (4:1–5:31)
                Gideon (6:1–8:32)
            Abimelech, Tola and Jair (8:33–10:5)
        Jephthah, Ibzan, Elon and Abdon (10:6–12:15)

Samson (13:1–16:31)

Epilogue: Part I (17:1–18:31)

Epilogue: Part II (19:1–21:25)

Gideon's judgeship, then, is the turning point in the book. With him, Israel's spiritual life begins to go radically downhill. Though Gideon destroys an altar belonging to Baal (Judg 6:25–32), he also creates an image out of gold that leads people into idolatry (Judg 8:22–28). After the initial successes of Othniel, Ehud, and Deborah, following Gideon, Israel's faith in Yahweh grows progressively weaker. He is the last judge described with the words, "Yahweh was with [someone]" (Judg 6:12, 16). The result is that the last judge, Samson, is described only as "*beginning* to deliver Israel from the power of the Philistines" (Judg 13:5). King David would have to finish the job (1 Sam 17).

The Gideon narrative is the longest in the judges section. It is one hundred verses (Judg 6:1–8:35). The next closest is Samson with ninety-six verses (Judg 13:1–16:31). Dispirited, depressed, and threshing wheat in the more protected and less visible surroundings of a winepress rather than the out-in-the-open locale of a threshing floor, Gideon is greeted by Yahweh's Messenger, who says, "Yahweh is with you, mighty warrior" (Judg 6:12). Immediately he challenges the Messenger, questioning how Yahweh could be with Israel at all, given their sorry state of oppression under the Midianites and peoples from the east.

Surprisingly, Gideon then musters enough courage to tear down Baal's altar and an Asherah pole, yet he did so during the night out of fear of the townsfolk and members of his own family (Judg 6:27). Though the Spirit of Yahweh came upon him, and though willing soldiers from nearby tribes arrived to support him, Gideon still requested not one but two additional signs. In the first sign he proposed that he would place a woolen fleece on the threshing floor; if the fleece alone was wet with morning dew while the surrounding hard floor remained dry, Gideon would be assured that Yahweh intended to save Israel by his hand. The sign occurred as Gideon prescribed—but then Gideon asked for a second sign, the reverse of the first—which, again, took place as he had asked (Judg 6:36–40). After all of this, he struck down 120,000 Midianites at one time (Judg 6:16; 7:23–25).

## *Jephthah*

Even within the fraternity of the judges, Jephthah was a rough character. His mother was a prostitute, making him a social outcast. His father had a legitimate wife who also bore him sons, and when grown, they drove Jephthah away (Judg 11:1–2). He attracted a group of misfits—perhaps outlaws—who were attracted to his leadership (Judg 11:3). Despite such adverse circumstances, however, Jephthah showed his familiarity with Israel's covenant history and spoke with eloquence about how Yahweh granted Jacob's descendants the land they had been living in for three centuries (Judg 11:14–27). He and his army won convincing victories—devastating twenty towns (Judg 11:33). Jephthah led Israel six years before he died (Judg 12:7).

Jephthah's success, though, is tarnished by the one story for which he has become famous. One day before he left for battle he said to Yahweh, "If you give the Ammonites into my hands, whatever comes out of the door of my house to meet me when I return in triumph ... will be Yahweh's, and I will sacrifice it as a burnt offering" (Judg 11:31). Victorious, he returned, and the first thing to come running out to meet him was his daughter—a יחידה, his *only child* (Judg 11:34).

The word יחיד is also used of Isaac (e.g., Gen 22:2), while each child is also called a עלה, *a burnt offering* (Gen 22:2; Judg 11:31). These connections invite a comparison between the children's fathers, Abraham and Jephthah. Abraham is commanded by Yahweh to offer up Isaac (Gen 22:1); Jephthah takes matters into his own hands. Yahweh delivers Isaac and commends Abraham for his faith (Gen 22:15–18). Though the text in Judges is ambiguous regarding the fate of Jephthah's daughter, the flippant father is subtly condemned for his rash vow.

Jephthah is certainly no Abraham. Though he lamented over having made such a vow, he told his daughter, who is never named, that he must keep it (Judg 11:35). After spending two months in the hills weeping with her friends, she returned, and her father "did to her as he had vowed" (Judg 11:39). Did he sacrifice her or didn't he? Most commentaries say he did. Others note—and this is a good point—that his daughter did not bewail her impending death but her unending virginity. "Give me two months to roam the hills and weep with my friends, because I will never marry" (Judg 11:37). This seems to be a curious comment if shortly thereafter she was put to death. But if the remark was meant to indicate that she remained a virgin all her life after her father fulfilled his vow, it seems to make more sense. Either way, though, she would die childless. The story ends by reporting that it came to be a custom in Israel that young women would go out for four days each year to commemorate the daughter of Jephthah the Gileadite (Judg 11:40).

If Jephthah did sacrifice his daughter, would we expect women to mark the anniversary of such a wretched event? However if he devoted her to a lifetime of service at the sanctuary, which was not entirely unusual (e.g., Hannah and Samuel in 1 Sam 1), would such a commemoration have arisen at all? This account must be included in the story of Jephthah regarding the question, Did he or didn't he sacrifice his daughter?

## Samson

When Yahweh's Messenger told Manoah's wife that she would conceive and bear a son, she repeats to her husband almost word-for-word all the terms of the divine promise, but she significantly changes the final phrase of the annunciation. The Messenger says, "The child will be a Nazarite to God from the womb, and he will begin to save Israel from the Philistines" (Judg 13:5). But in her repetition she concludes, "The child will be a Nazarite to God from the womb *until the day of his death*" (Judg 13:7). It is telling that the promise which ends in liberation abruptly concludes with death. The woman's silence on the explicit promise of salvation and counterpoising it with the phrase "until the day of his death" is a hint of what kind of future lies before Samson. This dissonance of a single phrase subtly sets the scene for a powerful but spiritually dubious judge of Israel who will end up sowing as much destruction as he does salvation.

The account of Samson's life, the last of the six cycles of major judges, least fits the paradigm of Judg 2:11–3:6. His exploits do not describe his leadership for Israelite tribes against their enemies but recount a series of battles in which he seeks personal revenge against the Philistines. What other Israelite hero is so immune to law, morality, and dangerous situations? He is both wild man and trickster, frequently outsmarting his enemies.

The Samson narrative is regarded as one of the most artfully composed sections in the OT. Episodes mirror one another: the dimness of Manoah and the Philistines as well as the rituals conducted for both Yahweh and Dagon. The story abounds with wordplays, riddles, and clever inversions. Samson tears a lion apart with his bare hands, slays a thousand men with the jawbone of a donkey, evades capture at Gaza (where he had gone to visit a Philistine prostitute), and pulls up the city gates and carries them forty miles away. Most surprisingly, Yahweh stirs up Samson's actions (Judg 13:25), fuels his passion for the Timnite woman (Judg 14:4), empowers Samson to kill both the lion and the Philistines, and is involved in Samson's final act of revenge (Judg 16:28–30). Samson was strong enough to defeat the most powerful men, yet humiliated by the weakest of women. He is an anti-hero, an Ishmael or an Esau instead of a Joseph or Moses.

### CHRIST IN JUDGES

Judg 2:1, as part of the prologue to the cycle of the judges, describes Yahweh's Messenger. He brings a stern warning to Israelite leaders assembled at Gilgal. In Judg 6:12 he makes a dramatic appearance to Gideon and throughout Judg 13 this same Messenger appears to the husband and wife who became Samson's parents. This Messenger is unlike other angelic beings in the OT. He displays divine attributes, actions, and names. He is even worshiped. The NT calls him Jesus (e.g., Gal 4:14; Rev 20:1–3).

Despite Gideon's admirable deferral of kingship (Judg 8:23), Israel desperately needed a king (Jud 17:6; 18:1; 19:1; 21:25). And it could not be the pompous Abimelech (Judg 9). Israel required a monarch who would bring political stability as well as spiritual commitment. They needed a king who would bring about comprehensive peace and ensure Yahweh's rightful place among his people.

The NT announces that Jesus of Nazareth is this longed-for and perfect King. The reign of God (by David's house) arrives in Jesus (Matt 1:1–17; Luke 1:32–33; Rom 1:3) yet his rule comes to an ironic fulfillment at the cross. There he is mockingly proclaimed as "King of the Jews" (Matt 27:29, 37). This humble, servant-king of David's line (Matt 21:4–5) embodies the coming of Israel's king to Zion (Zech 9:9). And when history is consummated, Christ, who rose again on Easter morning, will reign forever and ever (Rev 11:15).

## SIN AND GRACE IN JUDGES

Judges opens with the question: "Who shall go up first for us against the Canaanites, to fight against them?" Then God replies, "Judah shall go up" (Judg 1:1–2). Almost the same question is asked in Judg 20:18: "Which of us shall go up first to battle against the Benjamites?" And Yahweh says, "Judah shall go up first." The slight change from "Canaanite" to "Benjamite" grabs our attention. The nation that began by fighting external foes ends up in a civil war. The movement is from tribal brotherhood to tribal bedlam.

A host of other sins are chronicled in between Judg 1:1–2 and 20:18. They include (1) failure to drive out the Canaanites (Judg 1:18–36), (2) the unsuccessful passing on of the faith to the next generation (Judg 2:10), (3) worshiping Gideon's ephod (Judg 8:27), (4) replacing Yahweh with Baal-berith (Judg 8:33), (5) establishing private pagan cults (Judg 17:1–13; 18:14–31), and (6) violence to the Levite's concubine (Judg 19:22–30) as well as to the daughters of Shiloh (Judg 21:19–24). The morally degenerate situation is summarized with these words, "In those days there was no king in Israel and everyone did what was right in his own eyes" (Judg 17:6; 21:25; cf. Judg 18:1; 19:1).

The book of Judges is not a memorial to Israel's heroes of yesteryear as much as it is a testimony to Yahweh's gracious resolve to preserve his people by answering their cries of distress and providing for their salvation. God could not rescind Israel's election because of his promises to the patriarchs; as he says, "I will never break my covenant with you" (Judg 2:1). Yahweh's love is irrevocable and so he is Israel's Savior (Judg 3:9; 6:36, 37; 7:7; 10:13).

## CONCLUSION

Judges may be likened to a musical score. It begins with an overture (Judg 1:1–3:6), is followed by variations (Judg 3:7–16:31), and ends with a coda (Judg 17:1–21:25). Many of the judges are unusual. Ehud is a left-handed secret agent. Deborah is a woman who commands a male warrior. Gideon is the least in his family and most of the time an outright coward. Jephthah is an illegitimate child who can't put a lid on his mouth and Samson is a sex-addicted Nazirite. This is an odd group of people! God, however, delights in choosing the weak and despised to accomplish his saving purposes (1 Cor 1:26–28).

Judg 2:11–3:9 is the theological center of the book. Its message may be illustrated using A, B, C, and D: **A**postasy, Israel sins (Judg 2:11); **B**attering, Yahweh disciplines his people (Judg 2:14); **C**rying out is Israel's only hope (Judg 3:9); and **D**eliverance, Yahweh raises up judges to save his people (Judg 2:16). Tragically, this sequence repeats itself over and over again. The only solution is God's gift of the monarchy. This becomes the main theme in 1 and 2 Samuel.

## SELECT BIBLIOGRAPHY

Block, D. I. *Judges, Ruth.* New American Commentary 6. Nashville: Broadman and Holman, 1999.

Bolling, Robert. *Judges: Introduction, Translation, and Commentary.* Anchor Bible 6A. New York: Doubleday, 1975.

Davis, D. R. *Such a Great Salvation: Expositions of the Book of Judges.* Grand Rapids: Baker, 1990.

Dumbrell, W. J. " 'In Those Days There was No King in Israel; Every Man Did What Was Right in His Own Eyes': The Purpose of the Book of Judges Reconsidered." *Journal for the Study of the Old Testament* 25 (1983): 23–33.

Globe, Alexander. "Enemies Round About: Disintegrative Structures in the Book of Judges." In *Mappings of the Biblical Terrain.* V. Tollers and J. Maier, eds. Lewisburg, PA: Bucknell University Press, 1990, 233–51.

Lilley, J. P. U. "A Literary Appreciation of the Book of Judges." *Tyndale Bulletin* 18 (1967): 94–102.

Noth, Martin. *The Deuteronomistic History.* 2nd ed. Sheffield: Sheffield Academic Press, 1981. (German original, 1943.)

Webb, B. G. *The Book of the Judges: An Integrated Reading.* Sheffield: Sheffield Academic Press, 1987.

Schneider, Tammi. *Judges.* Berit Olam. Collegeville: Liturgical, 2000.

Steinmann, Andrew E. *From Abraham to Paul: A Biblical Chronology.* St. Louis: Concordia, 2011.

# 10

# RUTH

Set during the time of the judges (Ruth 1:1), this short book is one of
the most loved in the OT mainly because of its depiction of family
relationships—Ruth's love and faithfulness toward her mother-in-law
Naomi; the marriage of Boaz and Ruth; Naomi as advisor to Ruth;
Naomi is blessed with a grandchild she never expected to have. In
addition to these touching vignettes, Ruth is an important book
because it not only reveals the family history of Israel's great king
David, but it also points forward to Christ through the promise given
to David (2 Sam 7; Matt 1:5).

## AUTHORSHIP, COMPOSITION, AND DATE

Ruth, like many OT books, does not name its author, and none can be
proposed with certainty. However, the date of the book's composition
can be determined with more confidence. Clearly, it cannot have been
written before David's reign, since the genealogy at Ruth 4:18–22
appears to have been included expressly to culminate with David.
Moreover, the emphasis on Israel as a nation in Ruth 4:7, 11, 14
points to a time before the dissolution of the united kingdom
following the death of Solomon. Note that the genealogy ends with
David and appears to be motivated at least partly as an apologetic for
David's kingship (cf. Ruth 4:14–17). It does not seek to legitimate
Solomon as David's successor (as does 1 Kgs 1–2 and 1 Chr 22:2–19;
28:1–29:25). Most likely, then, the book was written sometime during
David's reign (1009–969).

Higher critical scholars have traditionally dated the composition
of Ruth much later, usually to the post-exilic period. Two primary

arguments have been used to support this view. One is the presence of words that appear to be of Aramaic origin. It was thought that the Aramaic influence on Hebrew was late. However, more recent scholarship suggests that Aramaic was more widespread at an early period than had been previously suspected. A second argument was that the story of the marriage of a Moabite woman into the family that would become the royal line of Israel was composed to counter the movement led by Ezra and Nehemiah to dissolve marriages to non-Israelites (cf. Ezra 9–10; Neh 10:28–30; 13:23–27). However, it is unlikely that Ezra and Nehemiah and others in the post-exilic era would have been opposed to Judeans marrying women who pledged to become part of the people and to worship Israel's God as Ruth did (Ruth 1:16). Instead, their concern was intermarriage to women who remained devoted to their pagan gods and did not raise their children to renounce pagan worship (see especially Neh 13:23–27). So, Ruth could not have served as a counterbalance to the efforts of Ezra and Nehemiah, and there is no reason to date its composition as late as after the Babylonian exile.

## LITERARY FEATURES OF RUTH

Ruth is a skillfully told story of a family from Bethlehem. The author has constructed the narrative plotline with several crises—the death of Naomi's husband and sons, the redeemer who stands in the way of Boaz redeeming Naomi's field, and the lack of a husband for the young widow Ruth. The story also has a stunning resolution—the cleverness of Boaz in obtaining the right to redeem Naomi's field as well as his marriage to Ruth and the birth of an heir. Studies by Bertman, Bovell, and Green, among others, have explored the skillful literary devices used by the author to relate the account of Ruth, Naomi, and Boaz. The author employs literary symmetry and plot development to involve the reader in the story and to highlight its important themes.

### Outline of Ruth

I.   Ruth becomes devoted to Naomi (1:1–22).

    A.  Famine and death affect Naomi's family (1:1–5)

    B.  Ruth pledges her faithfulness to Naomi, Naomi's people, and Naomi's God (1:6–22)

II. Ruth cares for Naomi and for herself (2:1–23).

    A. Ruth gleans in Boaz's field (2:1–17)

    B. Boaz provides for Naomi and Ruth (2:18–23)

III. Naomi's plan for Ruth (3:1–18).

    A. Naomi advises Ruth (3:1–6)

    B. Ruth proposes marriage and redemption to Boaz (3:7–18)

IV. Boaz provides a son for Ruth and an heir for Naomi (4:1–22).

    A. Boaz takes action in order to keep his promise to Ruth (4:1–12)

    B. Boaz and Ruth provide an heir for Naomi (4:13–17)

    C. The family history of Boaz and Ruth culminating in David (4:18–22)

## HISTORICAL ISSUES

### LEVIRATE MARRIAGE AND THE OBLIGATIONS OF A REDEEMER

One of the most obscure passages in Ruth is the discussion between Boaz and the other relative of Elimelech, Naomi's husband, who is responsible for acting as a kinsman redeemer and for purchasing the field which has now become Naomi's (Lev 25:23–34). In Ruth 3–4 this is intertwined with the law of the levirate (from Latin *levir* meaning "brother-in-law") marriage—the requirement that in the event that a man died without an heir, one of his brothers was to marry the widow of the deceased man and have children who would inherit the dead brother's land (Deut 25:5–10). Interestingly, neither Boaz nor the unnamed redeemer in Ruth 4:1–12 are required to marry Ruth. The levirate law applied only to brothers-in-law, and Ruth's only brother-in-law had died in Moab. Nevertheless, Boaz agreed to "redeem" Ruth—to perform the levirate duty, thereby demonstrating his compassion on this young widow.

When Boaz confronted the redeemer, he asked him whether he would buy Naomi's field as the one who had the first right to do so. The man intended to do this until Boaz raised the issue of marriage to Ruth. In many English translations Boaz is quoted as saying that the redeemer must marry Ruth as part of the deal (Ruth 4:5). This understanding follows the *qere* (the Masoretic correction to the text) and many ancient versions. However, there are problems with this reading. First of all, nowhere in the Pentateuch are the redemption of land and the levirate obligation connected to one another. Secondly, the redeemer ceded his rights to Boaz because he would endanger his own legacy to his children if he redeemed the land (Ruth 4:6). However, it is not clear how the unnamed redeemer's marriage to Ruth would have endangered his legacy. Had he married Ruth and had a child, the land would have borne Mahlon's name and be given to the child of Ruth and the unnamed man when he died.

On the other hand, following the suggestions of Green and Wilch, if we adopt the reading of the *ketiv* (the uncorrected text), Boaz tells the redeemer that when the redeemer acquires the land, Boaz intends to acquire Ruth as his wife and raise up an heir for Ruth's dead husband (Ruth 4:5). This reading does not require connecting the redemption of land and the levirate obligation and is, therefore, in harmony with the Pentateuch which also does not require such a connection. Moreover, with this reading it becomes clear as to how the redeemer's legacy would be endangered: the land he would purchase would not go to his heirs if Ruth bore a child to Boaz. Instead, it would become the legacy of Ruth's dead husband, and go to any sons of Boaz that Ruth bore. Thus, the *ketiv* is most likely the correct reading and solves the conundrum presented by this enigmatic exchange between Boaz and the redeemer.

## THE SANDAL CUSTOM

During the narration of the exchange between the redeemer and Boaz, the author explains a custom used as legal attestation for an exchange regarding the redemption of land (Ruth 4:7). The person waiving the right of redemption would give one of his sandals to the person acquiring that right. This is the action taken by the redeemer when he gave his sandal to Boaz (Ruth 4:8). When including this explanation the author of Ruth tells his readers that this is an outmoded custom. This indicates that Ruth was written sometime later when other methods of attestation—most likely written records—had replaced this custom. The sandal custom probably predated the rise of a widespread scribal class in Israel. Royal scribes were most likely deployed around Israel with the rise of the monarchy under Saul and David. Thus, the book of Ruth is looking back from David's day to a less literate society.

The sandal custom is important for another reason—a similar, but distinct, procedure was required when a man refused to perform his levirate duty to marry his deceased brother's wife (Deut 25:9). In case of neglected levirate responsibility, however, the man did not remove his own sandal, but the widow whom he refused to marry was to remove his sandal and spit in his face. This different sandal enactment probably led later readers of Ruth to link the redemption of the land and the levirate obligation and most likely was one of the factors that led to the *qere* at Ruth 4:5 that explicitly connects the two (see above). However, the shoe removal enactment for reproaching a man who would not perform his levirate duty is not the same as the shoe removal custom that attested to a transaction, and the confusion of the two has resulted in obscuring the climax in the narrative in Ruth.

### DAVID'S GENEALOGY

The genealogy from Perez to David that rounds out Ruth (Ruth 4:18–22) lists ten generations. This genealogy is obviously selective, and some generations were skipped by the author in order to arrive at the number ten, which here denotes perfection and symmetry. Moreover, Boaz is the seventh entry in the list, and seven is another important symbolic number in many biblical passages. The genealogy lists five generations from Salmon to David. Salmon married Rahab, the prostitute from Jericho who helped the spies that Joshua had sent in preparation for Jericho's conquest (Josh 2). It was hardly possible that there were only four more generations from Salmon's marriage about 1405 BC to David's birth in 1039 BC.

## THEOLOGICAL THEMES IN RUTH

Ruth begins with a reference to the "days when the judges ruled" and assumes that the reader knows about those times. This explicit setting of the story by the author indicates that he expects his audience to read Ruth's story in light of the events of the days of the judges, and most likely in contrast to the book of Judges itself. Many of the themes in Ruth appear to be chosen to contrast directly with Judges.

### FIDELITY

One stark contrast between Ruth and Judges is the issue of the fidelity of God's people to him and his word. In Judges the people of Israel repeatedly abandon God, and his response is to give them into the hands of oppressors. God never abandons Israel, however. When they repent, he raises up judges to deliver them (Judg 2:16). In contrast to this, the book of Ruth portrays some of God's people who remain faithful despite the general apostasy of Israel during this era. For example, Ruth pledges her fidelity to Naomi and her people, becoming one of them. Most important, Ruth pledges faithfulness to Naomi's God (Ruth 1:16–17). She stands in contrast to her sister-in-law Orpah who returns to Moab and perhaps to its pagan practices (Ruth 1:14–15).

Boaz is faithful to the law of God as given through Moses. He stands in contrast to the nearer kinsman redeemer who forfeits his rights to redemption. Yahweh's response to the faithfulness of Ruth and Boaz is an outpouring of his blessings culminating in David.

## THE PROVIDENCE OF GOD

God's blessings are shown most clearly in Ruth through his providence for the welfare of his people. The book begins with what appears to be a lack of God's care—there is no food in the land, and then there are no husbands for Naomi, Ruth, and Orpah. However, with these crises, God begins to move in the lives of his people. As Bovell points out, only two things are directly noted to be God's doing in the book of Ruth. However, both are acts of providence. He gives his people food (Ruth 1:6). God also gives Ruth the ability to conceive (Ruth 4:12). Yet his providence is not limited to these direct acts. God also provides through the faithful acts of his people. He provides for Naomi through Ruth's gleaning in Boaz's field. That Ruth happened to glean in Boaz's field (Ruth 2:3) is no mere happenstance. It was God's work, though unnoticed by Ruth and Boaz at the time. God provides for Ruth and Naomi through Boaz's generosity. This culminates in Yahweh providing for the nation of Israel by raising up David.

Bovell has argued that Ruth was intended by its author to be read as a Davidic document that supports David's house as legitimately chosen by God, and that this is signaled not simply by the closing genealogy but also by the opening verses. There Naomi is left without sons (Ruth 1:5). Through Ruth, who is better than seven sons (Ruth 4:15), she will once again have a son, Obed (Ruth 4:17). Obed would become the grandfather of David.

Moreover, the beginning of the book begins with a lack of food—including seed from barley and wheat. By the end of the book, God has restored the seed in the barley harvest (Ruth 1:22; 2:17, 23; 3:2, 15, 17), but more importantly, God has given the promise of descendants—Hebrew *seed* (זרע)—through Ruth (Ruth 4:12). This is the only explicit mention of seed in the book, but is a direct reference to the promise of seed in Genesis (e.g., Gen 3:15; see the discussion in chapter 3 on Genesis). God provides King David for Israel through the actions of Naomi, Ruth, and Boaz. This is, of course, in keeping with God using similar circumstances to provide for his people. The famine in Egypt and Canaan brought Jacob's family to Egypt (Gen 42–47; cf. Gen 50:19). Even earlier, famine led Abram to Egypt, and despite Abram's lack of trust in God to protect him, Yahweh brought him out of Egypt a rich man (Gen 12:10–20).

### CHRIST IN RUTH

As noted above, the author of Ruth most likely wanted his readers to understand his narrative in light of the book of Judges. If, as seems probable, the author wrote during David's reign, he probably also wanted them to understand his reference to David in the last verse in light of God's great promise to David that he would be the ancestor of the Messiah (2 Sam 7; 1 Chr 17). Christ is the ultimate goal of the narrative in Ruth through the implied messianic hope in David which would provide not only for Israel, but for all mankind.

Perhaps we should also see Boaz in his role as redeemer of the land and as the ancestor of David and Jesus as prefiguring God's work of redemption in Christ. As Rossow has noted,

> Neither Boaz nor Christ was obligated to redeem, yet both did so—voluntarily and graciously and at great personal cost. As Boaz was Ruth's kinsman, so Christ became our kinsman, becoming bone of our bone and flesh of our flesh, "for which cause He is not ashamed to call [us] brethren" (Heb 2:11). Even Boaz's marriage to Ruth foreshadows the relationship of our Redeemer Christ to the Church, He being the Bridegroom and the Church being His bride. The character,

role, and activity of Boaz are a superb microcosm of the Gospel-event.[1]

## SIN AND GRACE IN RUTH

Sin, especially sin against the First Commandment, is placing one's ultimate trust in someone or something other than God. This is the root of the sins to which the book of Ruth alludes. The trouble in the beginning of the book started when Elimelech and his family left the land of God's promise for pagan, idolatrous Moab. The contrast between Ruth and her sister-in-law Orpah is highlighted when Orpah returned to her family and perhaps to Moab's idols (Ruth 1:15). Even the kinsman redeemer who ceded the right to redeem Elimelech's field by purchasing it from Naomi is ultimately breaking the First Commandment. He valued his wealth, which would have been at risk had he redeemed the field, more than he valued fidelity to God and his command. He not only refused to place God's will above his own desires, but his sin also was in effect a refusal to provide for his kinswoman Naomi who would have obtained funds to support herself.

God's grace is shown in contrast to these sins. Although Elimelech took his family out of Israel where there was death, God brought Naomi back as a result of the news that the famine had ended through God's providence (Ruth 1:6). In addition, he graciously gave Ruth—who was better than seven sons—to Naomi (Ruth 4:15) as well as a new son in Obed (Ruth 4:17). The redeemer failed to do his duty to God and Naomi, but God in his grace provided Boaz as a redeemer for Naomi and a husband for Ruth.

Finally, we should observe that the provision of David for Israel as noted at the end of Ruth is God's gracious act of love despite Israel's constant sin of idolatry under the judges. During the time of the judges, "there was no king in Israel, and everyone did what was right in his own eyes" (Judg 17:6; 21:25). But in the days of the judges God was already laying the groundwork for the rise of Israel's great king, a gift to his people who would become the ancestor of his greatest gift, his very own Son in the flesh, Jesus Christ.

---

[1] Francis C. Rossow, "Literary Artistry in the Book of Ruth and Its Theological Significance." *Concordia Journal* 17 (1991): 17.

## CONCLUSION

In the short four chapters of Ruth, God's grace is highlighted through his work in the lives of Naomi, Ruth, and Boaz. Here the reader sees how God preserved a faithful remnant among his people even during the darkest days of the era of the judges. Moreover, we are pointed to God's gift of Israel's great king David and through him to the greater king, the coming Messiah.

## SELECT BIBLIOGRAPHY

Bertman, Stephen. "Symmetrical Design in the Book of Ruth." *Journal of Biblical Literature* 84 (1965): 165–68.

Bovell, Carlos. "Symmetry, Ruth and Canon." *Journal for the Study of the Old Testament* 28 (2003): 175–91.

Green, Barbara. "The Plot of the Biblical Story of Ruth." *Journal for the Study of the Old Testament* 23 (1982): 55–68.

Prinsloo, W. S. "The Theology of the Book of Ruth." *Vetus Testamentum* 30 (1980): 330–41.

Rossow, Francis C. "Literary Artistry in the Book of Ruth and Its Theological Significance." *Concordia Journal* 17 (1991): 12–19.

Wilch, John R. *Ruth.* Concordia Commentary. St. Louis: Concordia, 2006.

# 11

# SAMUEL

The book of Samuel relates the history of Israel's transition from a tribal confederacy designed to live under divine rule to a monarchy established and supported by God. As Israel failed to honor Yahweh and turned to the gods of the native Canaanite peoples (as related in the book of Judges), the people sought to be more like the nations among whom they lived. This eventually led them to ask for a king "like all the nations" (1 Sam 8:5). One of the longest books in the OT, Samuel spans the era of this shift from the last judges (Eli and Samuel) to the first kings (Saul and David). In English Bibles, the book of Samuel is divided into two volumes, a division that most likely first appeared when Samuel was translated into Greek sometime before Christ. The last years of the judges and the reign of Saul are covered in 1 Samuel, while the reign of David is depicted in 2 Samuel.

## AUTHORSHIP, COMPOSITION, AND DATE

### THE COMPOSITION OF SAMUEL

Like many of the historical books of the OT, Samuel does not name its author. Clearly the writer composed his narrative based on sources. While some of them may have been oral, written records played a major part, as indicated, for instance, by the various lists of David's officials (2 Sam 8:15–18; 23:8–39). Perhaps books by the prophets Samuel, Gad, and Nathan were also employed (cf. 1 Chr 29:29).

Though the book is named after Samuel, he could hardly have been its author. All of the events related after 1 Sam 25:1 take place following his death. A clue to the writer's own time may be his frequent noting of events that led to situations that are still present in Israel "to this day" (עד היום הזה; 1 Sam 5:5; 6:18; 27:6; 30:25; 2 Sam 4:3; 6:8; 18:18). The most telling of these is the note that the city of Ziklag belongs to the kings of *Judah* "to this day" (2 Sam 27:6). Tsumura argues that Samuel was composed during the reign of Rehoboam (932–915 BC), but this is probably too early, especially since 2 Sam 27:6 refers to the *kings* of Judah, implying that several monarchs had occupied the throne.

On the other hand, it is common for critical scholars to date Samuel to the post-exilic period as part of the Deuteronomistic History. This dating, however, is probably too late, and there is little evidence in the Hebrew text to support it. For instance, the name *David* is always spelled דוד in Samuel, and the *plene* form דויד, so common in books from the post-exilic period (e.g., Chronicles, Ezra, Nehemiah, Zechariah), is never found in Samuel. Therefore, although books such as Joshua, Judges, Samuel, and Kings display clear affinities to the theological accents found in Deuteronomy and might be called part of a Deuteronomistic History, that does not thereby make them late compositions.

It is best, therefore, to view Samuel as a pre-exilic book written sometime after the death of Solomon—probably several generations removed from Solomon's era—but before the Babylonian exile (587 BC). A more specific date cannot be determined for the composition of this OT book.

## CRITICAL THEORIES OF SAMUEL'S COMPOSITION

### Source-Critical Theories

Early critical theories of Samuel's composition often sought to find sources behind the book, much akin to the search for source documents proposed for the Pentateuch. These scholars perceived numerous repetitions, doublets, and contradictions. Among these were issues such as: When was Saul first introduced to David and when was David recruited to serve Saul? Was it as a court musician (1 Sam 16:14–23) or during the challenge from Goliath (1 Sam 17:32–38)? Who killed Goliath—David (1 Sam 17:50) or Elhanan (2 Sam 21:19)?

The most important of these issues was the supposed tension between two sources, one displaying a positive attitude toward the monarchy (e.g., 1 Sam 9:15–16) and one portraying a negative evaluation of kings and kingship (e.g., 1 Sam 12:16–19). Julius Wellhausen thought this tension represented two sources: a pro-monarchial source that was pre-exilic and an anti-monarchial source that reflected disillusionment with the monarchy brought about by the experience of the Babylonian exile. Therefore, he dated the final form of Samuel to the post-exilic period. Later scholars thought the tension may have come from various pre-monarchical movements in Israel, dating back to the days of Gideon, that reflect a debate about the merits of having a monarchy (Judg 8:22–9:27).

Ultimately, these source-critical approaches indicate more about the expectations of the critics as they approach the text than they do about the formation of Samuel. Their theories shed little light on the composition of the text itself. Since they reflect the biases and perspectives of each individual critic, these proposed theories of Samuel's formation have largely fallen out of favor.

## Tradition-History Theories

Instead of arguing for two intertwined sources that lay behind the present text of Samuel, scholars who used tradition-historical approaches sought to isolate original collections of narratives organized around various themes that were used by the final author or editor to construct the book's history. The most influential of these theories is that of Rost, who identified three large blocks of material that were supposedly incorporated into Samuel: an ark narrative (1 Sam 4:1–7:1), a history of David's rise (1 Sam 16:14–2 Sam 5:10), and a succession narrative (2 Sam 9–20 and 1 Kgs 1–2). Subsequent to Roth's investigation, others proposed additional sources such as an account of Samuel's childhood (1 Sam 1–3) or an appendix of material from David's reign (2 Sam 21–24) that became an intrusion into the succession narrative.

Recent currents in scholarship have called into question the concept of such independent sources. Bodner examined the work of a dozen scholars to demonstrate that there is now widespread skepticism about whether an independent ark narrative ever existed. He points out that Yehoshua Gitay argued that the ark narrative is inseparable from the rest of Samuel, and Graeme Auld noted that it is tightly integrated with its antecedent material. A similar analysis by Firth of the account of David's rise argued that this block of material, too, was so linked by literary ties to the rest of Samuel that the text should be read as a coherent whole. Frolov's analysis of the succession narrative and its seamless integration into the book of Samuel led him to conclude that "a large, continuous, self-contained, and distinctive 'document' underlying 2 Sam 1–1 Kgs 2 is a figment of scholars' imagination."[1]

This, of course, leads one to question whether independent sources such as the ark narrative or the account of David's rise actually ever existed. If the book of Samuel is a tightly integrated, inseparable whole, then isolating underlying sources becomes more a matter of how a particular scholar reads, understands, and ultimately divides the text of Samuel. It is not a reliable method for isolating sources underlying the received text.

This is not to assert that the author of Samuel had no sources for his work. Clearly, he must have had access to earlier documents to write a history, since history cannot be written without access to sources that relay information about past events and people. Most likely passages such as 2 Sam 21:15–22 and 2 Sam 23:8–39 indicate that the author used records from David's court. However, there should be a healthy skepticism about the ability of scholars to confidently isolate various sources behind the now skillfully integrated narrative of the book of Samuel. Except when the author indicates the origin for his material (cf. possible source references in 1 Sam 10:25; 2 Sam 1:18), it is best to read the narrative as a whole and not speculate on theories of composition that rely on reconstructed sources that are very dubious.

## Redaction-Critical Theories

Some scholars, building on tradition-historical theories, identify distinct editorial layers within the text of Samuel as well as within Joshua, Judges, and Kings. For instance, one editorial layer attempted to justify Josiah's reforms (2 Kgs 22:1–23:7). The final redaction was supposedly done in the exile and holds out hope for a return to the Promised Land (2 Kgs 25:27–30). Supposedly the book of Samuel

---

[1] Serge Frolov, "Succession Narrative: A 'Document' or a Phantom?" *Journal of Biblical Literature* (2002): 103.

was also part of this process of producing the history of Israel from after the death of Moses to the Babylonian captivity. Critics who posit several redactions to these books claim that telltale signs of this process remain embedded in the final text. Foremost among these are supposedly competing and even contradictory theological outlooks.

While these approaches continue to have their adherents, they remain problematic. All of them rely on assertions that there are competing and conflicting interests evident in the texts of the books that comprise Deuteronomistic History (see the discussion in chapter 8 on Joshua). Often, however, the presence of these supposedly incompatible ideologies stems from purposeful disharmonization of passages that do not on their face require such readings. Moreover, each of these interpretations assumes that there are multiple theologies embedded in books like Samuel. These hypothetical theologies are rather one-dimensional and pedestrian, devoid of nuance and subtlety. In contrast, a holistic reading of a book such as Samuel without preconceived notions of redactional layers could lead one to see a multi-dimensional theology full of nuanced views of God and humans often portrayed with wonderful subtleties in style and substance. Such a holistic approach can appreciate the skill of the author as he delves into the complicated events of God's history in dealing with Israel and the multifaceted motivations of kings and commoners alike. As a result, Samuel should be seen as giving a realistic picture of humans and a reliable picture of God's interaction with them.

## LITERARY FEATURES OF SAMUEL

Samuel is primarily narrative history. Although it contains poems (notably 1 Sam 2:1–10; 2 Sam 1:19–27; 22:2–51; 23:1–7) and other materials, even these were included by the author in the service of the narrative that runs from Samuel's birth to the end of David's reign. Samuel itself covers three main eras: the end of the period of the Judges when Israel had no king (1109–1048; 1 Sam 1–8), the reign of Saul (1048–1009; 1 Sam 9–2 Sam 1), and the reign of David (1009–969; 2 Sam 2–24).

Given the narrative history in Samuel and its two long treatments of the reigns of Saul and David, it is not surprising that this has given rise to a number of studies that seek to produce biographical character studies of these kings. There are fewer of these on Saul, but most of them view him in some way as a failed king at the head of a failed experiment in monarchy. Perhaps only Sellars attempts to view Saul in a somewhat positive light, and this only in that he is obedient to the people of Israel, though disobedient to God.

A number of recent biographical studies of David have sought to cast David or God in a less than flattering light. Some, such as Gunn or Brueggemann, have concluded that Saul was a victim of God's favoring David, and David was the recipient of an inscrutable divine blessing. Halpern and McKenzie, on the other hand, assume that the book of Samuel seeks to rehabilitate David from what he actually was—a scheming, petty, and violent despot who pushed aside his predecessor to seize the throne and who eliminated some of his sons in order to cling to his crown. The story of David in Samuel is simply too good to be true, and getting behind the text's portrait of David reveals him as simply another minor Near Eastern potentate. Polzin goes even further, claiming that the text of Samuel itself mainly portrays David in a negative light, consistently condemning him through explicit and implicit characterizations.

On the other hand, Borgman argues that David is gradually revealed to the audience as a complex person whom God chooses over Saul because of David's grasp of the moral imperatives of the world which he inhabits and because of David's delight in God and his mercy, something that Saul consistently lacks. According to this view, David's God is not the inscrutable and arbitrary deity that many scholars perceive in the book of Samuel, but a God who makes excellent sense in a more subtle and complex way than is often grasped by many contemporary biblical scholars.

What all of these treatments of Saul and David perhaps lack in some way—although Borgman comes closest—is the recognition that the narrative of Samuel is knit together not by the human characters but by Yahweh. The book's literary goal is to portray God as the one who deals patiently and mercifully with sinners—Israel as a whole as well as its leaders—Eli, Samuel, Saul, David, and to a lesser extent Jonathan, Abner, Joab and others. The skillful literary weaving together of the events of Israel's history is designed to show the readers that their God is gracious despite human failings, joyful when humans respond to his love in faith and obedience, and long-suffering with human failures and recalcitrance.

# Outline of Samuel

I. Israel without a king (1 Sam 1:1–8:22)

    A. Samuel is dedicated to God's service (1 Sam 1:1–2:11)

    B. The unfaithfulness of Eli's house (1 Sam 2:12–36)

    C. Yahweh calls Samuel to be a prophet (1 Sam 3:1–4:1a)

    D. The ark's journeys and Eli's death (1 Sam 4:1b–7:2)

    E. Samuel delivers Israel (1 Sam 7:3–17)

    F. Israel asks for a king (1 Sam 8:1–22)

II. Israel's first king, Saul (1 Sam 9:1–2 Sam 1:27)

    A. Transition to a monarchy (1 Sam 9:1–12:25)

        1. Saul chosen to be king (1 Sam 9:1–10:16)

        2. Saul publically made king (1 Sam 10:17–27)

        3. Saul saves Jabesh Gilead, confirming his selection as king (1 Sam 11:1–15)

        4. Samuel's warning about the monarchy (1 Sam 12:1–25)

    B. Saul's reign (1 Sam 13:1–2 Sam 1:27)

        1. Saul's first Philistine campaign (1 Sam 13:1–14:46)

        2. Saul's military successes (1 Sam 14:47–52)

        3. The Amalekite campaign—Saul rejected as king (1 Sam 15:1–35)

        4. David anointed king and receives God's Spirit (1 Sam 16:1–13)

        5. David in Saul's service (1 Sam 16:14–19:17)

            a. Saul given a tormenting spirit from God (1 Sam 16:14–23)

            b. David and Goliath (1 Sam 17:1–58)

            c. David and Jonathan's friendship (1 Sam 18:1–5)

            d. Saul's jealousy of David (1 Sam 18:6–19:17)

        6. David flees Saul (1 Sam 19:18–26:25)

            a. David in Naioth (1 Sam 19:18–24)

            b. Jonathan warns David (1 Sam 20:1–42)

            c. David in Nob, Gath, Adullam, and Moab (1 Sam 21:1–22:5)

     d.   Saul kills the priests at Nob (1 Sam 22:6–23)

     e.   David rescues Keilah (1 Sam 23:1–13)

     f.   David in Ziph and Maon (1 Sam 23:14–29)

     g.   David spares Saul's life in Engedi (1 Sam 24:1–22)

     h.   Samuel's death (1 Sam 25:1a)

     i.   David marries Abigail (1 Sam 25:1b–44)

     j.   David spares Saul's life in Ziph (1 Sam 26:1–25)

   7. David in the Philistines' service (1 Sam 27:1–2 Sam 1:27)

     a.   David in the service of Achish of Gath (1 Sam 27:1–12)

     b.   The final Philistine campaign of Saul (1 Sam 28:1–31:13)

       i.   Saul and the medium at Endor (1 Sam 28:1–25)

       ii.   The Philistines dismiss David from battle with Saul (1 Sam 29:1–11)

       iii.   David rescues his wives from the Amalekites (1 Sam 30:1–31)

       iv.   Saul dies in battle (1 Sam 31:1–13)

     c.   David learns of Saul's death (2 Sam 1:1–27)

III. Israel's great king, David (2 Sam 2:1–24:25)

  A.  David's reign over Judah (2 Sam 2:1–4:12)

    1. David made king of Judah (2 Sam 2:1–7)

    2. Conflict between David and the house of Saul (2 Sam 2:8–3:5)

    3. Abner defects and Joab kills him (2 Sam 3:6–39)

    4. Ishbosheth murdered (2 Sam 4:1–12)

  B.  David's reign over all Israel (2 Sam 5:1–16)

    1. David made king over all Israel (2 Sam 5:1–5)

    2. A summary of David's reign over Israel (2 Sam 5:6–16)

  C.  The successes of David's reign (2 Sam 5:17–10:19)

    1. David defeats the Philistines (2 Sam 5:17–25)

    2. David brings the ark to Jerusalem (2 Sam 6:1–23)

    3. God's Covenant with David (2 Sam 7:1–29)

4. David's victories (2 Sam 8:1–14)

5. David's officials (2 Sam 8:15–18)

6. David remembers his promise to Jonathan (2 Sam 9:1–13)

7. David defeats the Ammonites (2 Sam 10:1–19)

D. David's failures and struggles (2 Sam 11:1–20:26)

  1. David during the Ammonite War (2 Sam 11:1–12:31)

  2. Amnon rapes Tamar (2 Sam 13:1–22)

  3. Absalom murders Amnon and flees Israel (2 Sam 13:23–14:33)

  4. Absalom's rebellion and its aftermath (2 Sam 15:1–19:43)

  5. Sheba's rebellion (2 Sam 20:1–26)

E. David—the faithful warrior and king (2 Sam 21:1–24:25)

  1. David and the Gibeonites (2 Sam 21:1–14)

  2. David defeats the Philistine giants (2 Sam 21:15–22)

  3. David's song of deliverance (2 Sam 22:1–51)

  4. David's last words (2 Sam 23:1–7)

  5. David's mighty men (2 Sam 23:8–39)

  6. David's census leads to repentance and a place to build the temple (2 Sam 24:1–25)

# TEXTUAL, HISTORICAL, AND ARCHAEOLOGICAL ISSUES

## THE TEXT OF SAMUEL

Samuel contains more text critical problems than perhaps any other book of the OT. The LXX appears at times to have followed a different Hebrew text for the basis of its translation, and the writer of Chronicles, who incorporated large sections of Samuel into his work, also seems to have had a text that in some places had different readings from the current MT of Samuel. The ancient manuscripts from Qumran appear to confirm that there were variant manuscript traditions for Samuel. Fragments of three scrolls were found in cave 4 at Qumran. 4QSam[a] supports readings found in the LXX and Chronicles whereas 4QSam[b] and 4QSam[c] generally follow the types of readings found in the MT.

These divergent texts are quite strikingly different. For instance 1 Sam 14:41 is much longer (and more understandable) in the LXX than the same verse in the MT. 1 Chr 21:16 reports that David saw Yahweh's Messenger standing over Jerusalem with a sword in his hand. This notice is missing from 2 Sam 24:16, but is included in 4QSam^b, a manuscript that generally supports the MT readings, which may indicate that the MT is deficient at 2 Sam 24:16.

Several other important passages appear to have been damaged in the transmission of the book of Samuel. For instance, 1 Sam 13:1 contains information on Saul and his reign: "Saul was . . . years old when he became king. He ruled . . . and two years over Israel." Unfortunately, neither the LXX nor other traditions preserve the numbers that apparently have been lost from this verse.

Other passages show signs that they may have been damaged due to scribal mistakes, especially when a scribe's eye may have skipped from one word in one line of text to an identical or similar word in a following line. Among these is 1 Sam 14:41, when Saul calls on the high priest to use the Urim and Thummim. This verse is very difficult in the MT, but in the longer LXX it is much more understandable. Another example is in 1 Sam 11:1, which introduces the account of the Ammonite king Nahash's attack on Jabesh Gilead. The MT, though understandable, is somewhat laconic. However, both 4QSam^a and Josephus in book 6 of his *Antiquities of the Jews*, include a longer reading which explains Nahash's activity in Israelite territory east of the Jordan River. The omission of this longer reading is sometimes explained by positing that a scribe's eye skipped from a word in one line to the nearly identical word in a subsequent line, thereby inadvertently shortening the MT text of 1 Sam 11. However, neither 4QSam^a nor Josephus contains the hypothetical longer original reading posited by some scholars. Thus, while there may have been a textual corruption at this point, we cannot be certain if this is the case.

Caution must also be exercised in the use of the LXX when making text-critical decisions. It has long been recognized that the surviving LXX text of Samuel derives from two different translations, usually called the Old Greek and the Kaige translations. The latter's name derives from its tendency to translate Hebrew וגם as καὶ γε. The Old Greek tends to be a more dynamic, idiomatic translation whereas the Kaige is a much more word-by-word formal correspondence translation that yielded a much more awkward Greek. Scholars usually hold that 1 Sam 1:1–2 Sam 11:1 is from the Old Greek, and the rest of 2 Samuel is from the Kaige recension. This means that one has to take into consideration two different sets of translation characteristics when considering the LXX of Samuel.

The variations in the text of Samuel among the MT, the LXX and other traditions have led to some extreme views of its textual history. Some critical scholars favor the LXX in nearly every place where it disagrees with the MT. At the other extreme, Tsumura seeks to defend the MT in almost every instance, even when it appears to be hopelessly corrupt. Perhaps the best approach is to weigh each case of textual variation in its own context and make decisions according to which variant best explains the rise of the others.

## THE HISTORICITY OF DAVID

In the late twentieth century, a number of biblical scholars known as minimalists, or members of the Copenhagen School, held that the Israelite kingdom of David and Solomon was an invention of exilic or post-exilic Judean writers. Other scholars maintain that David and his son Solomon were rulers of a kingdom, but that it was much more modest in size and in influence than depicted in the books of Samuel and Kings. Recent archaeological finds, however, cast doubt upon these theories.

### The Tel Dan Inscription

In 1993 and 1994 excavators at Tel Dan, the site of the biblical city of Dan in northern Israel, discovered three fragments of a stele apparently erected by the Aramean king Hazael (or, less probably, by Hazael's son Bar Hadad). In the Aramaic inscription on this stele the Aramean king claims to have killed both Joram, the king of Israel (מלך ישראל), and Ahaziah of the house of David (ביתדוד). However, according to 2 Kgs 8:29, Hazael merely wounded Joram. Both Joram and Ahaziah were killed by Jehu (2 Kgs 9:14–28).

Most importantly though, in this inscription, Ahaziah is identified as a descendant of David, thereby confirming the accounts in Samuel and Kings that David founded a dynasty. When the Tel Dan inscription was first published, a number of minimalist scholars attempted to argue that the phrase ביתדוד, written without a word divider, should not be read as "house of David." Instead, while conceding that the first element in the phrase was indeed *house* (בית),

199

## *Kingdom of David*

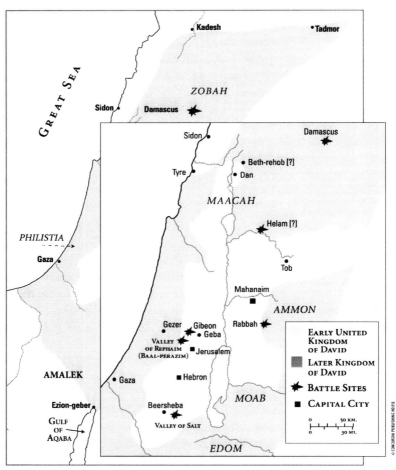

David ruled Judah for seven years at Hebron (2 Sam 5:5; 1 Chr 29:27). Saul's son Ish-bosheth ruled Israel from Mahanaim for two years (2 Sam 2:10). David's men scored a victory over Ish-bosheth's force at Gibeon (2 Sam 2:10–3:1). David conquered Jerusalem and ruled all Israel from there for 33 years (2 Sam 5:1–10; 1 Chr 11:1–9). He defeated the Philistines at Baal-pera zim and routed them from Geba to Gezer (2 Sam 5:17–25; 1 Chr 14:8–16). David had victories against the Philistines at Metheg-ammah (location uncertain); against Edom in the Valley of Salt; and against Moab, Zobah, Damascus, and Amalek (2 Sam 8; 1 Chr 18). He also defeated the Syrians and the Ammonites at Helam (2 Sam 10; 1 Chr 19) and the Ammonites at Rabbah (2 Sam 12:26–31; 1 Chr 20:1–3).

they argued that the second element (דוד) might be understood as "beloved," or a place name (i.e., Dod), or something else. Such arguments were quickly dismissed by the majority of scholars who demonstrated the faulty logic used to support them. Moreover, Andre Lemaire re-examined the Mesha Stele, an inscription first discovered in 1868 at the site of ancient Dibon in Moab. He found that it also contained the phrase "house of David," though written as two words (בית דוד). As a result, there is now general agreement that these two inscriptions confirm the presence of a kingdom ruled by a dynasty established by David.

## *The Khirbet Qeiyafa Inscription*

Khirbet Qeiyafa overlooks the Elah Valley in southwest Israel near the site that 1 Sam 17 describes as the setting for the contest between David and Goliath. This location, which housed no more than about 500–600 people inside a fortified wall, gives evidence for a strong central government that could construct such a city during the late eleventh or early tenth century BC.

During excavations at Khirbet Qeiyafa in 2008, a pottery shard with a faint inscription was discovered. It subsequently proved to be in Hebrew, and therefore at the time of its discovery became the oldest known Hebrew inscription, dating to about the early tenth century. In addition, two burned olive pits were found below the foundation of a city gate, making them no earlier than the construction of the city walls. Subsequent carbon-14 dating of the pits indicated a date of 1051–969, a date consistent with pottery found at the site. It appears that the location was abandoned before the middle of the tenth century, probably sometime during the latter part of David's reign. Subsequent statements by the excavators and others have said that this site must have been an outpost built by the kingdom ruled by David and Solomon. However, the dates are too early for Solomon and actually appear to be confirmation of an outpost guarding Israel's border with Philistia during the reigns of Saul and David.

The presence of an inscription at Khirbet Qeiyafa most likely indicates royal scribal activity. Coupled with the proximity to Saul's confrontation with the Philistines that led to David's slaying of Goliath, the discoveries at Khirbet Qeiyafa provide support for the biblical depiction of a substantial kingdom ruled by Saul and later by David. This kingdom was powerful enough to organize, build, and support an outpost at this location. While some critical scholars have tended to minimize David's kingdom and claim that he was in reality only a local chieftain, the evidence from Khirbet Qeiyafa would suggest that Saul and David were rulers of a realm with enough logistical, political, and financial resources to have built an impressive outpost such as Khirbet Qeiyafa.

# THEOLOGICAL THEMES IN SAMUEL

The book of Samuel is so large that it is difficult to speak of only a few theological themes that characterize it. However, several stand out among the many that are found within this work.

## PROSPERITY AND SUCCESS COME ONLY FROM GOD

The book of Samuel repeatedly emphasizes that God provides prosperity and success and that when humans look to their own devices, they are turning their backs on God and will ultimately fail. This is seen first in the acts of Eli's sons who corrupt the sacrifices and the priesthood (1 Sam 2:12–17), seeking to provide for themselves and satisfy their desires by their own efforts. Eli, who refused to discipline his sons (although he did rebuke them; 1 Sam 2:22–25), received a prophecy that he and his sons would die and the high priesthood would be taken away from his family (1 Sam 2:27–36).

Saul's initial success came from God's work in him (1 Sam 11:6). His ultimate lack of prosperity also is ultimately tied to God. When God's displeasure over Saul's refusal to exterminate the Amalekites is announced by Samuel (1 Sam 15:1–31), the reader is being prepared for the fall of Saul's house that eventually leads to David's installation as king over Israel. It is because Yahweh was no longer with Saul that Saul would give way to David (1 Sam 16:14; 18:12). Saul's ultimate demise is prefixed by Samuel's condemnation of him for his unfaithfulness in consulting a medium (1 Sam 28), again pointing out that without God, Saul cannot succeed.

David was successful because "God was with him" (1 Sam 16:13, 18; 18:12, 14, 28; 2 Sam 5:10). Moreover, God remained with the repentant David, despite his sin with Bathsheba and against Uriah. David specifically acknowledged this in his last words (2 Sam 23:1–7). Noting that when one rules with יראת אלהים, "the fear of God"—that is, in a relationship characterized by divine favor and by one's repentance and trust in God—he brings prosperity to his people. This happened because of God's promise of an everlasting covenant with David (2 Sam 23:5).

## PROPHECY

The role of prophets and prophecy in Samuel is limited, but often noted at important junctures in the narrative. The culmination of Samuel's rise to prominence is marked by his acknowledgement as a prophet (1 Sam 3:20). God's choice of Saul as Israel's first king is confirmed by Saul's prophesying (1 Sam 10:10–13). God's covenant with David is announced by the prophet Nathan (2 Sam 7:1–17). The punishment on Israel for David's sin in connection with the census is announced by the prophet Gad (2 Sam 24:11–13).

Prophets were also called רעה, *seers* (1 Sam 9:9, 11, 18, 19; 2 Sam 15:27; 24:11), presumably because they often received Yahweh's word through visions (1 Sam 3:1, 15; 2 Sam 7:17). In addition, prophecy was manifest in ecstatic activities that involved music and dancing (1 Sam 10:5–13; 19:19–24). Because Saul engaged in such activities when God's Spirit came upon him, the question was raised about Saul being among the prophets (1 Sam 10:11–12; 19:24).

Prophets mentioned by name in Samuel are Samuel (1 Sam 3:20), Gad (1 Sam 22:5; 2 Sam 24:11), Nathan (2 Sam 7:2; 12:25), and even the high priest Zadok (2 Sam 15:27). David, also, was a prophet through whom God's Spirit spoke (Acts 2:30; cf. 2 Sam 23:1–2).

## THE SPIRIT OF YAHWEH

Closely associated both with kings and their successes and with prophets speaking God's word is the Spirit of Yahweh. The "Spirit of Yahweh" or the "Spirit of God" is mentioned fifteen times in Samuel. Five of these are associated with prophesying and three with the success or failure of kings (1 Sam 11:6; 16:13, 14). Clearly, God's work through both prophets and kings is carried out by his Spirit's presence in the lives of his people. He also sent רוח רעה, a harmful or tormenting spirit used to hasten Saul's downfall and David's rise (1 Sam 16:14, 15, 16, 23; 18:10; 19:9). (Note that 1 Sam 16:23 specifically calls this רוח אלהים, "a spirit of/from God.")

## CHRIST IN SAMUEL

From the reign of David onward, the most common association of the promised Messiah in the Psalms and prophets was with David (e.g., Ps 18:50; 89:3–4, 20, 35–36, 49; 132:10–18; Isa 11:1–16; 55:3; Jer 23:5–6; 30:9; 33:15–18; 34:23–24; 37:24–25; Hos 3:5; Amos 9:11–15; Mic 5:2). This connection was prompted by the events related in 2 Sam 7. The chapter opens with David relating to the prophet Nathan his desire to build a house for God, which Nathan initially approves. However, that night, God revealed to Nathan that David was not to build a house for God, but that God would build a house (i.e., dynasty) for David (2 Sam 7:5–16). This oracle given to Nathan is the basis for the messianic hope connected with David and his house. Especially important are the last words of this oracle: "Your house and your kingdom will be secured forever before me, and your throne will be established forever" (2 Sam 7:16). This promise to David came as partial fulfillment of God's promise to Abraham that kings would come from him (Gen 17:6). Moreover, God had provided regulations for kings in the laws given by Moses (Deut 17:14–20). Therefore, the promise of a kingdom to David and his house was not a new plan, but was part of God's plan beginning with the patriarchs.

In many ways this oracle is the high point of David's reign, and, therefore, also of the book of Samuel. Although David would sin and bring misery to himself and his kingdom, nevertheless, God's promise remained with David, and David remained confident of God's promise to him, even in his last words (cf. 2 Sam 23:5). In the Gospels, when some call Jesus "son of David," they are making the connection between 2 Sam 7 and Jesus as the Messiah (Matt 1:1; 9:27; 12:23; 15:22; 20:30–31; 21:9, 15; Mark 10:47–48; Luke 18:38–39; cf. Rev. 3:7; 5:5; 22:16). Moreover, the Gospels affirm that the general opinion of the Pharisees and scribes in the first century was that the Messiah would be David's descendant (Matt 22:42; Mark 12:35).

Luther held that David understood this oracle as being about the Messiah, noting that in his response to Nathan's oracle, he said, "This is the manner of the man" (וזאת תורת האדם; 2 Sam 7:19). Luther understood "the man" to be the promised Messiah. Perhaps there is support for this interpretation in the parallel in 1 Chr 17:7, which could be read to say, "You have seen me according to the search for the exalted man" ( וראיתני כתור האדם המעלה) meaning that God saw in David the longing to see the Messiah, the "exalted man."

On the other hand, many scholars understand "the man" (האדם) to be used in a generic sense to mean "mankind." David, then, comprehended this oracle as a "covenant/charter for mankind." This passage would then point forward to God's work through the house of David that would bring the kingdom to all people, something that was fulfilled in Jesus, who announced the kingdom of God. According to this understanding, David's words continue to be relevant through the mission of the church to bring the Gospel of Christ and his kingdom to the world.

## SIN AND GRACE IN SAMUEL

With the possible exception of the prophet Samuel, the author of Samuel points out the sins of every major character in the book. Most obvious of these are Eli's sin of not disciplining his sons (1 Sam 2:22–36; 3:11–14), Saul's repeated lack of trust and confidence in God (1 Sam 13:1–15; 15:1–35), and David's sins, both his adultery with Bathsheba (2 Sam 11:1–12:15) and his mistake in taking the census (2 Sam 24:1–25). All of these transgressions lead to consequences as God judges the sin and as the sinner sets into motion a chain of disasters triggered by his sins. Even David's repentance does not prevent an elaborate sequence of incidents that stem in some way from his adultery: the death of the child conceived with Bathsheba, the rape of Tamar, the murder of Amnon, and the rebellions of Absalom and Sheba. Clearly, the writer of Samuel wishes to demonstrate that sin often brings unintended and unanticipated consequences to the sinner and frequently to those around him. Even when the sinner repents and is forgiven and delivered from eternal death, the consequences of disobedience in this life are not always ameliorated (cf. Gal 6:7–8).

Another aspect of sin that is highlighted in Samuel is that of accountability: God holds those whom he has placed in positions of authority especially accountable for their sins because their actions affect those whom they rule. Thus, Saul's decisions have dire consequences for all Israel. His failure of leadership, largely due to his lack of confidence in God, leads Israel astray and ultimately to defeat in battle against the Philistines. Because of Saul's sin, God punishes him, first with an evil spirit that vexed him (1 Sam 16:14–

23; 18:10–11), then by giving the kingdom to young David (1 Sam 16:1–13). Finally Saul dies in battle (1 Sam 31:1–13).

It could be argued that Eli's poor supervision of his sons not only leads to their death but also to the capture of the ark by the Philistines and a long, dark period in Israel's history (1 Sam 7:2) that only ended with Samuel's intervention (1 Sam 7:3–13). God held Eli accountable for his sin (1 Sam 3:11–14), and Eli's pitiable death (1 Sam 4:18) is the beginning of God holding him and his house accountable.

Even David, the greatest of Israel's kings, is judged for his actions. Because of his improprieties with Bathsheba, God humiliated him in the sight of all Israel (2 Sam 12:9–12; cf. 2 Sam 16:20–22).

Despite the many sins of Israel and its leaders chronicled in Samuel, Yahweh continued to be merciful and gracious to his people. When Eli's leadership failed, he raised up Samuel to prophesy and to deliver Israel. When the people rejected God as their king and requested a human king to rule over them so they could be like the nations, God was patient and granted their request (1 Sam 8:7). Through David he blessed Israel with victory over all the surrounding nations and ushered in a period of extended peace.

Most importantly, God never forgot his ultimate gracious pledge to Israel—the Messianic promise. Hope for this promise is evident in Hannah's prayer at the beginning of the book: "Yahweh will judge the ends of the earth; he will give strength to his king and lift up the horn of his anointed one" (i.e., his Messiah; 1 Sam 2:10). The Messianic promise given to David in 2 Sam 7 is the focus of David's last words: "he has made an everlasting promise to me, with every detail arranged and secured" (2 Sam 23:5).

God's grace is especially evident in Samuel because of his blessings on the lowly. Hannah is given a child, and God supports her through the loving words of her husband Elkanah (1 Sam 1:23). The boy Samuel, a mere servant in the tabernacle, is called to be prophet. David, the youngest of Jesse's sons and a common shepherd boy, is chosen to be king.

This gracious blessing of the poor and humble is explicit in Hannah's prayer. By including this petition at the beginning of his work, the writer of Samuel is setting the tone for this theme in the rest of the book: "Yahweh kills, and he makes alive. He brings down to the grave, and he raises up" (1 Sam 2:6). In this way the book of Samuel points toward God's grace in Christ, whom he sacrificed for the sins of the world, but made alive again for the saving of many that they might inherit a glorious throne in his eternal kingdom (2 Tim 2:11–12; cf. Rev 20:6).

From Hannah in 1 Sam 2 to David's census in 2 Sam 24, Yahweh frequently reverses what is expected. Consider these events: Hannah overcomes ridicule and barrenness (1 Sam 1). The young man Samuel replaces Israel's supreme religious leaders, Eli and his wicked sons Hophni and Phinehas (1 Sam 3). Unbelieving Philistines gain a military victory over God's people because they are in such a woeful spiritual condition (1 Sam 4). The idol of Dagon, the Philistines' god of grain who is credited with the triumph over the Israelites, falls flat on his face before Yahweh's ark (1 Sam 5). Because of their renewed trust in Yahweh, Israel defeats the Philistines, who have a superior military (1 Sam 7). Saul, a fearful man, becomes the first king in Israel (1 Sam 9–11). Jonathan, Saul's son, is distinguished over his father in battle (1 Sam 14). Israel's king Saul is embarrassed by Samuel, a mere prophet, who announces that Yahweh has taken the kingdom from Saul's hand (1 Sam 15). David, the youngest son of Jesse, is anointed to serve as Israel's second king (1 Sam 16). The shepherd boy David, with just a sling and a stone, is triumphant over the mighty Goliath (1 Sam 17). Saul, the king of Israel and Yahweh's anointed one, dies and is mocked by the Philistines at Gilboa (1 Sam 31). He is even beheaded (1 Sam 31:9).

This motif of reversal continues during David's reign: Michal, the powerful daughter of Saul, never has children (2 Sam 6). Mephibosheth, the crippled son of Jonathan, is given a seat at King David's table (2 Sam 9). Uriah, a Hittite soldier in the Israelite army, is more righteous than King David (2 Sam 11). The prophet Nathan dares to condemn King David for his sin (2 Sam 12). The wise woman from Tekoa knows more about the king's family troubles than David does (2 Sam 14). Finally, David confesses that when God's people are in the dark, Yahweh will light their way (2 Sam 22:29). These reversals are all anticipated in Hannah's observation: "Yahweh makes poor and makes rich; he brings low and he exalts" (1 Sam 2:7).

This is not a new theme in the OT. Sarah (Gen 11:30), Rebekah (Gen 25:21), and Rachel (Gen 30:1) at one time were all barren. They went on to become Israel's beloved matriarchs. The people of Israel, who had been slaves in Egypt, saw Pharaoh's army drowned while they escaped from his mud pits and straw bins (Exod 14:28).

Moreover, in the NT, Paul picks up this motif again: "God chose the foolish things of the world to shame the wise; God chose the weak things of the world to shame the strong. He chose the lowly things of this world and the despised things and the things that are not to nullify the things that are" (1 Cor 1:27–28).

This theme is most evident in Jesus and his ministry: He chose fishermen instead of Pharisees, sinners instead of Sadducees, and prostitutes instead of the princely line of Herod. Ultimately, Jesus wore thorns instead of silver and gold for a crown. His choices led to torment and torture, darkness and death.

Jesus' work led to the greatest inversion of all. Christ rose and overturned death, replacing it with resurrection life. His ministry continued through his apostles, of whom some Jews in Thessalonica declared, "These men who have turned the world upside down have also come here" (Acts 17:6).

## CONCLUSION

Although for some readers the book of Samuel is a simple narrative of events of Israel's history from the days of Eli to the days of David, it is actually a sophisticated and complex account of God's dealing with Israel to establish a king and kingdom that foreshadows Christ's eternal reign. The book has been subjected to critical scrutiny and at times suffered some textual disruption during its scribal transmission. However, despite these difficulties, it continues to be a witness to God's continuing grace to his Israel, not only in its OT form, but also to the NT Israel of God (Gal 6:16).

## SELECT BIBLIOGRAPHY

Arnold, Bill T. *1 and 2 Samuel.* New International Version Application Commentary. Grand Rapids: Zondervan, 2003.

Baldwin, Joyce. *1 and 2 Samuel: An Introduction and Commentary.* Tyndale Old Testament Commentaries 8. Leicester: InterVarsity, 1988.

Bodner, Keith. "Ark-Eology: Shifting Emphases in 'Ark Narrative' Scholarship." *Currents in Biblical Research* 4 (2006): 169–97.

Borgman, Paul. *David, Saul, and God: Rediscovering an Ancient Story.* Oxford: Oxford University, 2008.

Brueggemann, Walter. *David's Truth: In Israel's Imagination and Memory.* Philadelphia: Augsburg Fortress, 1985.

Chisholm, Robert B. Jr. "Yahweh versus the Canaanite Gods: Polemic in Judges and 1 Samuel 1–7." *Bibliotheca Sacra* 164 (2007): 165–80.

Cross, Frank Moore. *Canaanite Myth and Hebrew Epic.* Cambridge: Harvard University, 1973.

Firth, David G. "Shining the Lamp: The Rhetoric of 2 Samuel 5–24." *Tyndale Bulletin* 52 (2007): 203–24.

———. "The Accession Narrative (1 Samuel 27–2 Samuel 1)." *Tyndale Bulletin* 58 (2007): 61–81.

Frolov, Serge. "Succession Narrative: A 'Document' or a Phantom?" *Journal of Biblical Literature* (2002): 81–104.

Gunn, David. *The Story of King David: Genre and Interpretation.* Journal for the Study of the Old Testament Supplement Series 6. Sheffield: JSOT Press, 1978.

Halpern, Baruch. *David's Secret Demons: Messiah, Murderer, Traitor, King.* Grand Rapids: Eerdmans, 2001.

Luther, Martin, "Treatise on the Last Words of David: 2 Samuel 23:1–7." Trans. Martin H. Bertram. *Luther's Works* 15: 265–352; St. Louis: Concordia, 1972.

McCarter, P. Kyle Jr. *I Samuel: A New Translation.* Anchor Bible 8. Garden City: Doubleday, 1980.

———. *2 Samuel: A New Translation with Introduction, Notes, and Commentary.* Anchor Bible 9. Garden City: Doubleday, 1984.

McKenzie, Steven L. *King David: A Biography.* New York: Oxford University, 2000.

McLean, Paul D. "The Kaige Text of Reigns: To the Reader." In *A New English Translation of the Septuagint and the Other Greek Translations Traditionally Included under That Title.* Edited by Albert Pietersma and Benjamin G. Wright, 271–76. New York: Oxford University, 2007.

Miscall, Peter D. *1 Samuel: A Literary Reading.* Bloomington: Indiana University, 1986.

Noth, Martin. *The Deuteronomistic History*. Journal for the Study of the Old Testament Supplements 15. Sheffield: Journal for the Study of the Old Testament, 1967. Translation of the first half of *Überlieferungsgeschichtliche Studien*. 2nd ed. Tübingen: Max Niemeyer, 1967.

Polzin, Robert. *David and the Deuteronomist: A Literary Study of the Deuteronomic History*. Part 3, 2 Samuel. Bloomington: Indiana University, 1993.

Provan, Iain, V. Philips Long, and Tremper Longmann III. "The Early Monarchy." Chapter 8 in *A Biblical History of Israel*. Louisville: Westminster, 2003.

Rost, Leonhard. *Succession to the Throne of David*. Michael D. Rutter and David M. Gunn, trans. Sheffield: Almond, 1982. Translation of *Die Uberlieferung von der Thronnachfolg Davids*. Beiträge zur Wissenschaft vom Alten und Neuen Testament 42. Stuttgart: Kohlhammer, 1926.

Steinmann, Andrew E. *From Abraham to Paul: A Biblical Chronology*. St. Louis: Concordia, 2011.

Sternberg, Meir. *The Poetics of Biblical Narrative*. Bloomington: Indiana University, 1985.

Stirrup, A. "'Why Has Yahweh Defeated Us Today before the Philistines?' The Question of the Ark Narrative." *Tyndale Bulletin* 51 (2000): 81–100.

Taylor, Bernard A. "The Old Greek Text of Reigns: To the Reader." In *A New English Translation of the Septuagint and the Other Greek Translations Traditionally Included under That Title*. Edited by Albert Pietersma and Benjamin G. Wright, 244–248. New York: Oxford University, 2007.

Tsumura, David Toshio. *The First Book of Samuel*. New International Commentary on the Old Testament. Grand Rapids: Eerdmans, 2007.

# 12

# KINGS

The books of Kings document Israel's history from David's last days (1 Kgs 1:1–2:10) to the catastrophic endings of the northern and southern kingdoms (2 Kgs 17; 2 Kgs 25:1–26). Second Kings ends with a faint whisper of hope—Jehoiachin's release from a Babylonian prison (2 Kgs 25:27–30). Other highlights include the building of Solomon's temple as well as the dynamic ministries of Elijah and Elisha. Two of the main motifs in Kings—God's promises to David and the sins of Jeroboam ben Nebat—are consolidated in the reign of Josiah, who is the ideal Davidide as well as the grand purger of Jeroboam's sin.

The Talmud refers to 1–2 Kings as one book (*B. Bat.* 14b–15a) and credits Jeremiah as its author—probably because 2 Kgs 25:27–30 is parallel to Jer 52:31–34. In the history of the text's transmission, a decision was made to divide the book based upon the amount of material that could fit upon one scroll. This is reflected in the Greek tradition where Samuel and Kings are separated into four books called "Kingdoms." The Vulgate and subsequent English versions follow suit, albeit with different titles. The chapter divisions between these four books are arbitrary. For example, the Lucianic recension divides 2 Samuel from Kings at 1 Kgs 2:11.

## AUTHORSHIP, DATING, AND TEXT

Kings is an anonymous composition. However since the seminal work of Noth, it is almost universally acknowledged that Joshua, Judges, Samuel, and Kings were composed by someone who was heavily influenced by the book of Deuteronomy. For that reason these books are frequently referred to as the Deuteronomistic History. In Kings, key transitions are marked by Deuteronomistic speeches and summary comments. The most notable are Solomon's prayer at the temple's dedication (1 Kgs 8:14–61), the split between the northern and southern kingdoms (1 Kgs 11:31–39), Jeroboam ben Nebat's death (1 Kgs 14:7–11, 13–16), the end of the northern kingdom (2 Kgs 17:7–23), and Judah's demise (2 Kgs 21:10–15; 22:15–20).

While Noth embraced the idea that there was one author for Deuteronomy–Kings, Weinfeld envisioned three stages of development in the Deuteronomic School. In the latter half of the seventh century, the book of Deuteronomy was composed; in the first half of the sixth century, the books of Joshua–Kings were written; and in the second half of the sixth century, Jeremiah's prose sermons were added.

Without denying the earlier work of Noth and Weinfeld, Cross and Nelson maintain that Kings underwent two additional redactions. Their theory of a double-redaction is based upon the fact that a number of texts assume Jerusalem's fall (e.g., 1 Kgs 5:4; 9:1–9; 11:9–13; 2 Kgs 17:19–20; 20:17–18; 22:15–20; 23:26–27). They argue that these passages must have been added to an earlier pre-exilic, Deuteronomistic composition during the Babylonian exile. Others envision that Kings grew gradually over time through a much more complex process.

In terms of dating Kings, the last event recorded is in 2 Kgs 25:27–30. This passage describes Jehoiachin's discharge from prison during the thirty-seventh year of his imprisonment. Because he was exiled in 597, his freedom came in 560, which then marks the earliest date that Kings could have been completed. And since there is no mention of a return to Jerusalem after the captivity, it is probable that the book was composed before Cyrus's decree in 538. This marks the latest date that Kings could have been published.

Textual problems in Kings come not from the Hebrew, but from Greek additions. For instance, after 1 Kgs 2:35 and 1 Kgs 2:46, the Greek inserts "Miscellanies" that pertain to Solomon's reign. Additional Greek sections appear after 1 Kgs 12:24 with information pertaining to Jeroboam ben Nebat. Further additions are scattered throughout 1 Kgs 2–11.

## Literary Features of Kings

The foremost literary feature in Kings is its frequent use of chronological markers. The building of Solomon's temple is connected with Israel's Exodus (1 Kgs 6:1) and the corpus ends with references to Babylonian regnal years (2 Kgs 24:12; 25:8). In between, Judean and Israelite kings are introduced and summarized according to the number of years they reigned. These passages cite the length of the king's reign and include a synchronic note regarding the regnal year of his contemporary in the neighboring kingdom. For Judean monarchs the king's age at his accession and mother's name are usually recorded.

Kings also employs the literary strategy of analogy. The reign of each king, with a similar introduction and conclusion, is analogous to every other king. Several narratives are also similar: (1) two mothers and their sons (1 Kgs 3:16–28; 2 Kgs 6:26–31), (2) a queen's death (2 Kgs 9:30–37; 11:13–16), (3) Solomon's theophanies (1 Kgs 3:4–15; 9:1–9), (4) visits by foreigners (1 Kgs 10:1–13; 2 Kgs 20:12–19), (5) resurrections from the dead (1 Kgs 17:17–24; 2 Kgs 4:18–37), (6) the reforms of Jehoiada (2 Kgs 12:4–16) and Josiah (2 Kgs 22:3–7), (7) Manasseh is Judah's Ahab (2 Kgs 21:3), and (8) the confessions regarding Elijah and Elisha (2 Kgs 2:12; 13:14). Moreover, David and Jeroboam ben Nebat are employed as templates to critique or praise kings that come after them. All of these connections supply an inner hermeneutic whereby a text is enlightened and interpreted by its mirror-text.

## Outline of Kings

I.   Succession to David's Throne (1 Kgs 1:1–2:46)

   A.   Solomon Is Designated David's Successor (1 Kgs 1:1–53)

   B.   Solomon Defeats His Opponents (1 Kgs 2:1–46)

II.  Solomon's Reign (1 Kgs 3:1–11:43)

   A.   Wisdom from Above (1 Kgs 3:1–5:18)

   B.   Building the temple (1 Kgs 6:1–7:51)

   C.   Dedicating the temple (1 Kgs 8:1–66)

   D.   Yahweh Appears to Solomon (1 Kgs 9:1–9)

   E.   Solomon's Buildings and Naval Fleet (1 Kgs 9:10–28)

F.   Solomon's Glory (1 Kgs 10:1–29)

G.   Solomon's Demise (1 Kgs 11:1–43)

III.  The Divided Kingdom (1 Kgs 12:1–2 Kgs 17:41)

A.   Jeroboam ben Nebat (1 Kgs 12:1–14:31)

B.   Judean and Israelite Kings from Asa to Ahab (1 Kgs 15:1–16:34)

C.   Elijah of Tishbi (1 Kgs 17:1–2 Kgs 1:18)

D.   Elisha of Abel–meholah (2 Kgs 2:1–8:29)

E.   Jehu's Revolt (2 Kgs 9:1–10:36)

F.   Judah and Israel up to Samaria's Fall (2 Kgs 11:1–17:41)

IV.  Judah's Last Years (2 Kgs 18:1–25:30)

A.   Hezekiah's Reign (2 Kgs 18:1–20:21)

B.   Josiah's Reformation (2 Kgs 21:1–23:30)

C.   Judah's Downfall and Destruction (2 Kgs 23:31–25:30)

Several sources were used to construct Kings. One is called the "Book of the Acts of Solomon" (1 Kgs 11:41). Another is the "Book of the Chronicles of the Kings of Israel," which is mentioned seventeen times in 1 Kgs 14:29–2 Kgs 15:31 and is used for all but two of Israel's kings, Joram and Hoshea. The third source employed in Kings is called the "Book of the Chronicles of the Kings of Judah" (1 Kgs 15:23). It is referred to fifteen times and is used for all but five rulers—Ahaziah, Athaliah, Jehoahaz, Jehoiachin, and Zedekiah. There are no substantial differences between these northern and southern annals. Both record regnal wars and building projects, conspiracies against the crown, as well as monarchial apostasy and faithfulness.

Other documents that are not specifically mentioned, but are proposed by many scholars, include (1) "David's Court History" (1 Kgs 1:1–2:11), (2) an "Elijah-Elisha Prophetic Cycle with the House of Ahab" (1 Kgs 16:29–2 Kgs 13), (3) an "Isaiah Source" (2 Kgs 18:13–20:19; cf. Isa 36:1–39:8), (4) a temple source (e.g., 1 Kgs 6–8; 1 Kgs 14:25–26; 2 Kgs 25:13–17), and (4) two concluding historical abstracts (2 Kgs 25:22–26, 27–30; cf. Jer 52:28–34).

# HISTORICAL ISSUES

Chronological problems in Kings are well known and have been addressed in a variety of ways. Three features make it very difficult to date the kings' reigns. First, while in Judah the New Year began in Tishri (the first month of autumn), in Israel it started in Nisan (the first month of spring). Second, Judah initially employed *accession-year reckoning*, which treats the first partial year of a king's reign as his accession year, and the next year as his first year of reign. At its inception, however, Israel used *non-accession-year reckoning*, which treats the first partial year of a king's reign as his first year of reign, and the next year as his second year of reign. Further complicating matters, for a time Judah changed to non-accession year reckoning and then switched back to its previous way of counting regnal years, while Israel changed from non-accession-year reckoning to accession-year reckoning for its last decades. Finally, compounding the confusion is that Kings does not present events in a strictly chronological manner. For example, Jehoshaphat's death is recorded in 1 Kgs 22:50, but he marches into battle in 2 Kgs 3:9.

Extra-biblical sources shed light on this chronological quandary. Mesopotamian and Egyptian records confirm the following dates: (1) Ahab fought at the Battle of Qarqar in 853, (2) Jehu paid tribute to Shalmaneser III in 841, (3) Jehoash of Israel paid tribute to Adad-nirari III in 796, (4) Menahem (738), Ahaz (733/32), and Hoshea (731) paid tribute to Tiglath-pileser III, (5) Shalmaneser V conquered Samaria in 723, (6) Josiah died at the Battle of Meggido at the hand of Pharaoh Necho in 609, and (7) the Babylonian Chronicles provide dates for Nebuchadnezzar's campaigns in Judah. Based upon these dates, the chronology of kings is as follows:

### *Reigns of the Kings of Judah*

| King | Began Coregency | Began Sole Reign | End of Reign | Official Reign | Total Years |
|---|---|---|---|---|---|
| Rehoboam | | 932t | 914n/914t | 932t–915t | 17 |
| Abijah | | 914n/914t | 912t/911n | 915t–912t | 3 |
| Asa | | 912t/911n | 871t/870n | 912t–871t | 41 |
| Jehoshaphat | 873t | 871t/870n | 848n/848t | 873t–849t | 25 (24) |
| Jehoram | 854t | 848n/848t | 841n/841t | 849t–842t | 8 (7) |
| Ahaziah | | 841n/841t | 841n/841t | 842t | 1 (0) |
| Athaliah | | 841n/841t | 835n/835t | 842t–836t | 7 (6) |

| | | | | |
|---|---|---|---|---|
| Joash | | 835n/835t | 796n/796t | 836t–797t | 40 (39) |
| Amaziah | | 796n/796t | 767n/767t | 797t–768t | 29 |
| Uzziah | 791t | 767n/767t | 740t | 791t–740t | 52 (51) |
| Jotham | 750n/750t | 740t | (735n/735t) 732t | 751t–736t | 16 (15) |
| Ahaz | 735n/735t | 732t | 716t/715n | 732t–716t | 16 |
| Hezekiah | 729t/728n | 716t/715n | 687t | 716t–687t | 29 |
| Manasseh | 697t | 687t | 643t | 697t–643t | 55 (54) |
| Amon | | 643t | 641t | 643t–641t | 2 |
| Josiah | | 641t | Tammuz 609 | 641t–610t | 31 |
| Jehoahaz | | Tammuz 609 | Tishri 609 | 610t–609t | 3 months |
| Jehoiakim | | Tishri 609 | 21 Marcheshvan 598 | 609t–598t | 11 |
| Jehoiachin | | 21 Marcheshvan 598 | 2 Adar 597 | 598t | 3 months 10 days |
| Zedekiah | | 2 Adar 597 | 9 Tammuz 587 | 598t–588t | 11 (10) |

## Reigns of the Kings of Israel

| King | Overlapping Reign | Began Sole Reign | End of Reign | Official Reign | Total Years |
|---|---|---|---|---|---|
| Jeroboam I | | 931n | 910t/909n | 931n–910n | 22 (21) |
| Nadab | | 910t/909n | 909t/908n | 910n–909n | 2 (1) |
| Baasha | | 909t/908n | 886t/885n | 909n–886n | 24 (23) |
| Elah | | 886t/885n | 885t/884n | 886n–885n | 2 (1) |
| Zimri | | 885t/884n | 885t/884n | 885n | 7 days |
| Tibni | | 885t/884n | 880n/880t | 885n–880n | |
| Omri | 885t/884n | 880n/880t | 874t/873n | 885n–874n | 12 (11) |
| Ahab | | 874t/873n | 853n/853t | 874n–853n | 22 (21) |
| Ahaziah | | 853n/853t | 852n/852t | 853n–852n | 2 (1) |
| Joram | | 852n/852t | 841n/841t | 852n–841n | 12 (11) |
| Jehu | | 841n/841t | 814t/813n | 841n–814n | 28 (27) |
| Jehoahaz | | 814t/813n | 798n/798t | 814n–798n | 17 (16) |
| Jehoash | | 798n/798t | 782t/781n | 798n–782n | 16 |
| Jeroboam II | 793n | 782t/781n | Elul 753 | 793n–753n | 41 (40) |
| Zechariah | | Elul 753 | Adar 752 | 753n | 6 months |
| Shallum | | Adar 752 | Nisan 752 | 753n–752n | 1 month |
| Menahem | | Nisan 752 | 742t/741n | 752n–742n | 10 |
| Pekahiah | | 742t/741n | 740t/739n | 742n–740n | 2 |

| Pekah | Nisan 752 | 740t/739n | 732t/731n | 752n–732n | 20 |
|-------|-----------|-----------|-----------|-----------|-----|
| Hoshea | | 732t/731n | 723n/723t | 732n–723n | 9 |

## SOLOMON'S KINGDOM

Critical minimalists like Lemche and Davies have argued that Solomon and his kingdom are literary fabrications drawn up by authors in Persian Yehud. They contend that, had Solomon really existed, extra-biblical accounts would have mentioned him. However, Kitchen maintains that the absence of evidence is not the evidence of absence. He also offers indirect evidence that argues for the existence of Solomon's kingdom. For example, there was a power vacuum in the ancient Near East during the tenth century. Egypt and Assyria were weak at this time and the Hittite kingdom had recently collapsed. In fact, no Assyrian rulers had direct contact with Palestine before 853, so they could hardly mention any Israelite kings in their writings.

Into this power vacuum arose a number of mini-empires such as Carchemish and Tabal. Solomon's political structure is very similar to these kingdoms as he, like them, did not rule directly over all land from the Sinai to the Euphrates, but ruled thru vassal states and allied kingdoms.

Additionally, although no gold from Solomon or a rich tenth century kingdom has been excavated, Pharaoh Shishak (945–924) took away all of the temple's treasures (1 Kgs 14:25–26). And Shishak's successor Osorkon I gives an unprecedented 383 tons of gold to his gods. Epigraphic evidence for Solomon's dynasty (vis-à-vis his father David) includes a text from the tenth century Pharaoh Shishak who refers to the "Heights of David" and the Tel Dan Stele from the ninth century that mentions "the House of David."

Why doesn't Jerusalem yield any evidence for Solomon or his kingdom? It is because ancient Jerusalem lies under a modern city making it is as difficult to excavate as Damascus. Therefore, there are no royal inscriptions from tenth century Jerusalem (nor are there any from tenth century Byblos or Damascus; for that matter, there are none from Herod the Great). Moreover, the fact that nine out of fourteen kings of Israel in the OT are attested in extra-biblical writings strengthens Kings' reliability. This written witness, plus a strong collection of indirect evidence, reinforces that Solomon and his kingdom existed as they are described by the biblical historian.

## Kingdom of David and Solomon

*Detail of Judah*

David experienced civil war in his later years. His army defeated his rebel son Absalom at Mahanaim (2 Sam 17:24–18:18) and the rebel Sheba at Abel of Beth-maacah (2 Sam 20).

David and his men undertook campaigns against the Philistines at Gob and Gath (2 Sam 21:15–22; 1 Chr 20:4–8) and at Lehi, Adullam, and Bethlehem (2 Sam 23:11–17; 1 Chr 11:12–19).

Solomon secured what David had won, taking Hamath and building Hazor, Megiddo, Gezer, Upper and Lower Beth-horon, Baalath, and Tadmor (1 Kgs 9:15–19; 2 Chr 8:3–6). He built a fleet at Ezion-geber (1 Kgs 9:26; 2 Chr 20:36) and sealed pacts with Tyre (1 Kgs 5:1–12; 10:22; 2 Chr 2:3–16; 9:21). Solomon's kingdom stretched from Tiphsah on the Euphrates in the north to Gaza in the south (1 Kgs 4:24).

Solomon's later apostasy caused God to raise adversaries in Hadad of Edom; Rezon of Damascus and Zobah; Pharaoh Shishak of Egypt; and finally Jeroboam, who would rule Israel over against Rehoboam, Solomon's son, who would rule Judah (1 Kgs 11).

## THE NORTHERN KINGDOM

Solomon died before Tishri of 931 and then the kingdom was divided between Rehoboam of Judah and Jeroboam ben Nebat of Israel (1 Kgs 12). The account of the divided monarchy is in 1 Kgs 12–2 Kgs 17.

As the upstart ruler of a newly created kingdom, Jeroboam ben Nebat needed to secure his subjects' allegiance. Clearly this would not occur as long as northerners continued to worship in Jerusalem. The prestige of Jerusalem/Zion had to be neutralized. Toward that end, Jeroboam appropriated the ancient holy sites at Bethel and Dan, where he built new temples, erected golden calves, reorganized the religious calendar, and replaced the hereditary priesthood with a different priestly order loyal to him. In this way, Jeroboam created an effective alternative to the established worship in Jerusalem. Instead of the Solomonic temple, with its great festivals and pilgrimages, the Northern Kingdom had a separate religious structure of its own, closely identified with the new dynasty.

All of the nation's kings are judged negatively because they continued in the sins of Jeroboam ben Nebat, though there is some softening with Jehoram (2 Kgs 3:2) and Hoshea (2 Kgs 17:2). The only king not described as doing evil is Shallum, who ruled for just a month (2 Kgs 15:10–15). Even Jehu, who rose to power on the platform of a return to Yahweh, is rejected (2 Kgs 10:30–31).

The Northern Kingdom, existing as an independent nation for over two hundred years, showed little awareness of its theological connections to Moses and David. The triumph of Canaanite fertility religion suggests that the people had very little sense of self-identity or covenant calling. Apart from some external religious accoutrements, the north all but jettisoned Yahwistic faith. Even so, Yahweh preserved a faithful remnant, "seven thousand who did not bow to Baal" (1 Kgs 19:18).

A king's average reign was eleven years and there were nine different ruling families. Charisma was as important as ancestry to take the throne. The fate of some kings was tragic; seven were assassinated, one committed suicide, one was struck down by God, and one was taken captive to Assyria.

Samaria became the capital city of the Northern Kingdom during the ninth century reign of Omri (1 Kgs 16:24). It was the nation's third capital, after Shechem (1 Kgs 12:1, 25) and Tirzah (1 Kgs 16:6, 8, 9, 23–24). Omri bought the land and built Samaria, which was about forty-two miles north of Jerusalem. It was located on a hill about three hundred feet above a valley and was readily defensible, well located along major trade routes, and within a fertile region cultivated with olive orchards and vineyards.

## *Israel and Judah*

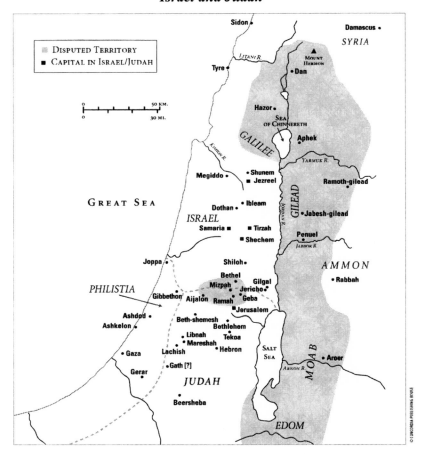

Solomon's son Rehoboam caused Israel to split from Judah; Israel then made Jeroboam its king (1 Kgs 12:1–24; 2 Chr 10:1–11:4). Jeroboam established Israel's capital first at Shechem (1 Kgs 12:25), but later apparently moved it to Tirzah (1 Kgs 14:17). Jerusalem remained the capital of Judah (1 Kgs 12:18). Periodic coups in Israel destroyed the dynasties of Jeroboam (1 Kgs 15:27–30), Baasha (1 Kgs 16:8–13), Zimri (1 Kgs 16:15–22), Omri (2 Kgs 9:14–10:14), and Jehu (2 Kgs 15:8–12). Omri moved Israel's capital to Samaria (1 Kgs 16:23–24); Jezreel apparently served as a secondary capital (1 Kgs 21:1). Moab, and then Edom and Libnah, rebelled against Judah (2 Kgs 3; 8:20–22). Control of territory east of the Jordan passed back and forth between Israel and Syria (2 Kgs 10:32–33; 13:14–25; 14:23–29). A chaotic succession of kings heralded the fall of Israel to Assyria in 723 BC (2 Kgs 15:8–17:23).

Israel's geography made it more exposed to foreign aggression than its southern neighbor Judah. Serious problems for Israel began when Syria attacked Baasha (1 Kgs 15:16–22). Syrian aggression intensified during the reign of Ahab and his successors as the narratives in 1 Kgs 20, 22; 2 Kgs 1–10, 13 are told against this backdrop. All of this happened during the time when Assyria was dormant.

In the middle of the eighth century, the political future of the Northern Kingdom was repeatedly threatened as Assyria began to flex its muscles. Assassinations and political instability began to erode the North's stability, especially after the death of Jeroboam ben Joash in 753. The reigns of those who followed him—Zechariah, Shallum, Menahem, Pekahiah, and Pekah—are described in 2 Kgs 15:8–31. The Assyrian King Shalmaneser V (726–722) adopted Tiglath-pileser III's policy of westward expansion and made King Hoshea of Israel his vassal (2 Kgs 17:3). Hoshea, much like his ancestors, looked to Egypt for military aid, but help never arrived. In a punitive action, Shalmaneser V attacked Samaria, and after a three year siege the city fell in 723, bringing Israel to an end (2 Kgs 17:5–6). Sargon II was primarily responsible for the exile of its citizens as well as the city's repopulation program. He describes the fall of Samaria with these words:

> The ruler of Samaria [King Hoshea], in conspiracy with another king, defaulted on his taxes and declared Samaria's independence from Assyria [cf. 2 Kgs 17:4–6]. With the strength given me by the divine assembly, I conquered Samaria and its covenant partner, and took . . . prisoners of war [cf. 2 Kgs 17:23; 18:11] . . . I conscripted enough prisoners to outfit fifty teams of chariots. I rebuilt Samaria, bigger and better than before. I repopulated it with people from other states that I had conquered, and I appointed one of my officials over them, and made them Assyrian citizens.[1]

The end of Sargon's boast indicates that, in order to squash future revolts, his regime removed populations of rebel kingdoms and mixed them with other exilic groups along with the indigenous population

---

[1] As quoted in Victor Matthews and D. C. Benjamin, *Old Testament Parallels: Laws and Stories from the Ancient Near East* (2nd ed.; Mahwah, NJ: Paulist Press, 1997), 175.

(2 Kgs 17:24–41). Extra-biblical documents attest to this as lists of Israelite names have been found in Assyrian military and economic documents from the eighth and seventh centuries. The collective memory of these people lived on for some time; note the reference to exiles from the Northern Kingdom in the deuterocanonical book of Tobit.

### Assyrian Exile of Israel

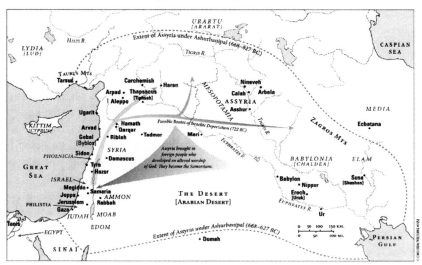

Assyria was the largest empire since the Old Babylonian dominance of Sumer and Akkad before Abraham. It deported people from Galilee and east of the Jordan as early as 733 BC and crushed Syria in 732 BC. God permitted Assyria to destroy idolatrous Israel in 723 BC; Israelites were deported and assimilated into upper Mesopotamia (2 Kgs 15:8–17:23). Assyria resettled other peoples into Israel (2 Kgs 17:24–41). Assyria menaced the entire Near East, at times exacting tribute from the Phoenician cities, Judah, Edom, Moab, and Ammon, and crushing Israel and Philistia. Assyria checked the power of Egypt and even incorporated Egypt into its empire for a time. Borders fluctuated with the power of the kings. Ashurbanipal held a great area, yet Assyria fell to Babylon about 25 years after his death.

## THE SOUTHERN KINGDOM

The Southern Kingdom, meanwhile, demonstrated more faithfulness to Yahweh. And because of its Davidic kings, Judah was more stable than her northern neighbor. Athaliah, however, a worshiper of Baal, successfully reigned for seven years (2 Kgs 11). And when kings belonging to the line of David were assassinated, it was to replace them with more faithful Davidides (2 Kgs 12:20–21; 14:19–21;

21:23–24). A single dynasty lasted from David to Zedekiah for a period of more than four hundred years.

The reign of Judah's nineteen kings and one queen averaged more than seventeen years each. (From Rehoboam to Josiah the average was twenty years.) But southern kings also experienced tragic fates: five were assassinated, two were stricken by God, and three were exiled to foreign lands. The following are given qualified approval: Asa (1 Kgs 15:11–15), Jehoshaphat (1 Kgs 22:43–44), Joash (2 Kgs 12:2–3), Azariah (2 Kgs 15:3–4), and Jotham (2 Kgs 15:34–35). Hezekiah (2 Kgs 18:3–7) and Josiah (2 Kgs 22:2) receive unqualified approval. Both tore down Canaanite high places, something no other kings did.

The Babylonian empire was an alliance of two disparate peoples, the Medes in the Zagros Mountains to the east and the Chaldeans in southern Mesopotamia. After the coalition overthrew the Assyrian Empire with its defeat of Nineveh in 612, Babylon inflicted four deportations upon the people of Judah: (1) 605, in the third year of Jehoiakim (Dan 1:1–7), (2) 598, during the reign of Jehoiachin (2 Kgs 24:10–17), (3) 587, during the rule of Zedekiah (2 Kgs 25:1–21), and (4) 582, when Nebuchadnezzar dispatched Nebuzaradan (Jer 52:30). These expulsions were a mammoth rupture in Judah's life.

Perspective on these Babylonian exiles comes by considering how the Assyrians repopulated lands they conquered. Assyria practiced cross deportation (e.g., 2 Kgs 17:24) because their goal was to establish economically productive provinces throughout their empire. On the other hand, the Babylonian policy may be likened to "slash and burn." The demographic movement was one way—to the heartland of the empire. Babylonians did not invest time and effort in creating productive provinces. Instead, they engaged in military campaigns in those regions to secure tribute and to support construction in their urban centers.

This difference in the practice of exile by the two Mesopotamian empires can be underscored by attention to the numbers of Israelites and Judeans taken in their respective exiles. As for that of Samaria, the author of Kings offers no comment about the number of Israelites taken, other than the statement that "Yahweh rejected all the descendants of Israel" (2 Kgs 17:20). Fortunately, Assyrian inscriptions offer greater detail. The so-called Sargon II Display inscription reports, "I besieged and conquered Samaria. I carried away 27,290 people who lived in it." Another text, the Sargon II Nimrud Prism, puts the figure at 27,280. On the other hand, according to Jer 52:30, the total number of Babylonian deportees was 4,600. This probably denotes only men. Adding women and children brings the aggregate number to around 15,000. Others estimate that the total number exiled was between 20,000 and 25,000. At any rate, there is good reason to believe that far fewer people were taken into exile by the Babylonians than were captured by the Assyrians. The Babylonians removed only members of certain specialized or elite classes—royalty, warriors, skilled workers, scribes, and the like.

Beginning in the twelfth century, and extensively from the ninth century forward, Assyrian sources depict their massive destruction of nature, often called ecocide. Targeting a conquered people's agriculture served as punitive action, intended to inflict long-term economic and psychological pain. The Babylonians likewise destroyed ecosystems as a means of warfare, yet they differed from the Assyrians in one significant way. Whereas, after time, Assyria restored cities and lands devastated by war, the Babylonians adopted a scorched-earth policy. In the sixth century, when the army marched into Judah, it left vast swaths of land dilapidated so as to create a buffer of wastelands between Babylon and Egypt.

## Prophets in Kings

Prophets play a major role in Kings; e.g., Ahijah of Shiloh (1 Kgs 11:29–39; 14:1–18), Shemaiah (1 Kgs 12:21–24), a Judean man of God and an old prophet from Bethel (1 Kgs 13:1–32), Jehu ben Hanani (1 Kgs 16:1–4), Micaiah ben Imlah (1 Kgs 22), Jonah ben Amittai (2 Kgs 14:25), Isaiah ben Amoz (2 Kgs 19–20), Huldah (2 Kgs 22:13–20), and those who prophesied during the reign of Manasseh (2 Kgs 21:10–15). More extended sections document the ministries of Elijah (1 Kgs 17:1–2 Kgs 1:18) and Elisha (2 Kgs 2:1–10:36; 13:14–21).

Kings often employs the title איש האלהים, *a man of God*, to describe prophets. Though the roles of a man of God and a prophet overlap, they are not synonymous. A prophet was an official charged with a specific task, that of announcing the divine word. The man of God, on the other hand, was characterized by supernatural gifts. Both Elijah and Elisha, though prophets, are each called a man of God (e.g., 2 Kgs 1:9; 4:9). The list of their miracles is impressive. Ravens bring food (1 Kgs 17:1–8); bread and oil multiply (1 Kgs 17:9–16); fire and rain appear (1 Kgs 18); wind, an earthquake, and fire are present (1 Kgs 19:11–12); fire comes down from heaven (2 Kgs 1:10, 12); the Jordan is parted and a whirlwind carries Elijah to heaven (2 Kgs 2:1–14); water is purified (2 Kgs 2:19–22); bears kill young boys (2 Kgs 2:23–24); oil is multiplied (2 Kgs 4:1–7); stew is purified (2 Kgs 4:38–41); bread is multiplied (2 Kgs 4:42–44); and an ax-head floats (2 Kgs 6:1–7).

The expression *sons of the prophets*, בני הנביאם, indicates a professional status rather than biological descent. It often appears in texts that designate prophetic guilds (e.g., 1 Kgs 20:35; 2 Kgs 2:3, 5, 7, 15; 4:1, 38; 5:22; 6:1; 9:1).

Kings narrates several confrontations between prophets and their rulers, including Elijah and Ahab (1 Kgs 18) and Joram's attempt to kill Elisha (2 Kgs 6:31). Another explosive encounter occurred between Ahab and Micaiah ben Imlah when the king tried to muzzle this prophet (1 Kgs 22). This is what happened: Ahab killed Naboth in order to confiscate a plot of land (1 Kgs 21). Four hundred prophets then went along with Ahab's reign of terror (1 Kgs 22:6), but Micaiah refused to live the lie. 1 Kgs 22:10 describes one of the most extreme exhibits of royal rule in the OT: "Now the king of Israel [Ahab] and Jehoshaphat the king of Judah were sitting on their thrones, arrayed in their robes, at the threshing floor at the entrance of the gate of Samaria, and all the prophets were prophesying before them." What more could be done to intimidate Micaiah into submission? However, the prophet would not back down. Micaiah describes another assembly and another King (1 Kgs 22:19). Earthly power and authorities are penultimate to the majesty and rule in the divine realm. Ahab's reign is nothing compared to the alternative governance, headed by Yahweh. The wise person will recognize this and not be led astray by the lie (1 Kgs 22:22–23). Ahab, however, refused to humble himself before Yahweh's mighty hand and it cost him his life (1 Kgs 22:29–37).

Yahweh's prophets held the ultimate power in Israel over against kings with their horses, chariots and military hardware. In fact, Elijah and Elisha are called רכב ישראל ופרשיו, *the chariotry of Israel and his horses* (2 Kgs 2:12; 13:16). Rejecting these prophets was one of the primary reasons why Israel and Judah were exiled (e.g., 2 Kgs 17:13).

## ARCHAEOLOGY AND INSCRIPTIONS

Archaeological discoveries shed light on several texts in Kings. For example, unearthed floor-plans of an ancient Israelite four-room house adds to the interpretation of Elisha's "small roof chamber" as part of the house in Shunem (2 Kgs 4:10). Horned altars have been found (cf. 1 Kgs 1:50; 2:28), and Solomon's temple is similar to other Syro-Phoenician shrines. The gateways excavated at Hazor, Megiddo, and Gezer—though the dating is disputed—appear to be Solomonic (1 Kgs 9:15).

Extra-biblical documents also assist in the interpretation of Kings. These include the blessing found at Kuntillet 'Ajrud, "YHWH of Samaria and his Asherah," that sheds light on syncretistic practices (e.g., 2 Kgs 21:7). The following military campaigns are found in extra-biblical reports: Pharaoh Shishak's raid (cf. 1 Kgs 14:25) as well as the victories of Tiglath-pileser III (2 Kgs 15:29), Sennacherib (2 Kgs 18:13–19:36), and Nebuchadnezzar (2 Kgs 24). The Moabite Stone (or Mesha Inscription) interfaces with the expeditions of Joram, Jehoshaphat, and the king of Edom into Moab as recorded in 2 Kgs 3. Jehu's submission to the Assyrians appears on the Black Obelisk of Shalmaneser III (841). Shalmaneser's Monolith Inscription mentions "Ahab the Israelite" who met the Assyrian king at the battle of Qarqar. And Hezekiah's Siloam inscription intersects with the Assyrian crisis in 701 (2 Kgs 18–19).

## CHRIST IN KINGS

Kings repeatedly documents how Judean and Israelite monarchs fall short of their intended goals. Solomon begins his reign with great humility and wisdom (1 Kgs 3), but falls away from God for at least part of his life (1 Kgs 11). Jehu's reform founders because he did not turn aside from the sins of Jeroboam ben Nebat (2 Kgs 10:28–31). Joash's restoration of Davidic glory ends in a near disaster when finances intended for the temple's restoration are used to pay off a foreign invader (2 Kgs 12:17–18). Hezekiah's great faith in the face of the Assyrian army (2 Kgs 18–19) dissipates when he shows the kingdom's treasures to Babylonian envoys (2 Kgs 20:12–19). And even the reformer Josiah dies an untimely and unnecessary death at the hand of Pharaoh Necho (2 Kgs 23:28–30).

Jesus began his reign with great determination when he conquered Satan's lies and deceptions (Matt 4:1–11; Luke 4:1–13).

But, unlike many of his predecessors, he remained faithful to the end. In spite of the torture and torment of the cross, Christ let out a triumphant cry, "It is finished" (John 19:30). The veil was rent. The blood was poured. The curse was removed. Death was defeated and Paradise was restored. Jesus is the only true and faithful King—he both began and finished strong. This is why he is called the King of Kings (1 Tim 6:15; Rev 19:16).

Not only is Jesus greater than Solomon (Matt 12:42) and all of Israel's other kings, he is also greater than Solomon's temple (Matt 12:5). This temple was built on Mt. Zion and was twice as big as the tabernacle. According to its description in 1 Kgs 6, Solomon's edifice was ninety feet long and thirty feet wide, having a total interior of 2,700 square feet. The Holy of Holies was thirty feet long, thirty feet wide and thirty feet high—a perfect cube. When the temple was complete, Yahweh's glory filled it (1 Kgs 8:11). Yet Jesus is the final and definitive temple where heaven and earth meet (John 2:19–22; 14:9). He forever reflects divine glory (John 1:14).

### SIN AND GRACE IN KINGS

Solomon's kingdom fell apart due to his belief in non-Israelite worldviews. The author of Kings connects Solomon to Pharaoh by way of marriage (1 Kgs 3:1; 7:8; 9:24; 11:1). In one generation he managed to confiscate Israel's freedom and reduce social order to a situation that was analogous to Egyptian slavery (1 Kgs 9:20–22).

Another narrative that depicts the propensity of kings to live outside of divine Torah is in 1 Kgs 21. The relation of Naboth and his land is not owner to property (the belief of Ahab and Jezebel), but rather heir to inheritance (Yahweh's will). Elijah entered the scene after Naboth had been murdered and his land taken. The prophet asserted that it was covenant word and not royal power that governed the land (1 Kgs 21:17–29).

The monarchs' repeated moral failures led to the final debacle in the book of Kings—Babylon's assault on Jerusalem. In 597 Nebuchadnezzar imprisoned Jehoiachin (2 Kgs 24:10–12). Zedekiah, Judah's last king, was captured in 587. At Riblah, Nebuchadnezzar slaughtered his sons and then blinded Zedekiah (2 Kgs 25:6–7). It appeared as though God's oath to the house of David had come to a horrific end. But the almost-too-good-to-be-true fact is that Evil-merodach (562–560), the king of Babylon, freed Jehoiachin from prison and gave him a seat of honor (2 Kgs 25:27–30). The ending of Kings indicates that God's gracious promises to the house of David will not end.

## CONCLUSION

During the Davidic/Solomonic era, Israel was on top of the ancient Near Eastern world. God's people wielded great political power. The nation appeared to have everything. But the ironic twist about Israel's history is that, as liberated slaves from Egypt, they began to enslave each other. The oppressed in Egypt became the oppressors in the Promised Land. They neglected the needs of the orphan, the widow, and the alien in the gate. In many ways, and especially beginning with Solomon, Jerusalem became the new Egypt, and everything began to fall apart.

The book of Kings reviews this slow, painful death. The final verdict was the Babylonian exile in 587 as God enacted Sinaitic covenant curses (e.g., Lev 26; Deut 28) to bring his people to their senses, purge the nation of idolatry, and renew its mission to the world. The narrator employs a masterful use of interconnecting scenes and phrases to juxtapose his two major themes—judgment and grace. Though both North and South are unbelieving and idolatrous, 2 Kings ends with a hope and a future for David's throne and for God's people.

## SELECT BIBLIOGRAPHY

Cross, Frank M. *Canaanite Myth and Hebrew Epic: Essays in the History of the Religion of Israel*. Cambridge, MA: Harvard University Press, 1973.

Davies, Philip R. *In Search Of "Ancient Israel."* Journal for the Study of the Old Testament Supplement Series 148. London and New York: T & T Clark, 1992.

DeVries, Simon J. *1 Kings*. Word Biblical Commentary 12. Waco: Word, 1985.

Hobbs, T. R. *2 Kings*. Word Biblical Commentary 13. Waco: Word, 1985.

Jones, Gwilym H. *1 and 2 Kings*. 2 vols. New Century Bible. Grand Rapids: Eerdmans, 1984.

Kitchen, Kenneth. *On the Reliability of the Old Testament.* Grand Rapids: Eerdmans, 2003.

Lemche, Niels Peter. *The Old Testament between Theology and History: A Critical Survey.* Louisville: Westminster, 2008.

Nelson, R. D. The *Double Redaction of the Deuteronomistic History.* Journal for the Study of the Old Testament Supplement Series 18. Sheffield: Sheffield Academic Press, 1981.

Steinmann, Andrew E. *From Abraham to Paul: A Biblical Chronology.* St. Louis: Concordia, 2011.

# 13

# CHRONICLES

Of the historical books of the OT, Chronicles is probably the least appreciated and read. In the LXX the book is called Παραλειπομένων, *omitted things*, as if it were merely a supplement to the books of Samuel and Kings. Modern readers often find the first nine chapters tedious and not worthy of reading or studying, since they contain genealogies, many of which are drawn from earlier books of Scripture. Moreover, since Chronicles is one of the latest books in the OT and removed in time from the events it narrates, critical scholars have often viewed its historical accuracy with a considerable amount of skepticism. However, recent scholarship has paid more attention to this book, not only discovering it to be a work constructed with literary flair but also learning to appreciate Chronicles' unique theological outlook as an important contribution to the OT.

## AUTHORSHIP, COMPOSITION, AND DATE

The author of Chronicles does not identify himself, and scholars often simply refer to him as "the Chronicler." Chronicles is clearly a post-exilic book, since it ends with the decree of Cyrus allowing the Judeans in Babylon to return to Jerusalem and rebuild the temple (2 Chr 36:22–23; cf. Ezra 1:1–3a). In addition, Chronicles mentions the Persian coin called a *daric*, named after Darius I (521–486 BC) and first minted in 515 BC. Even more tellingly, Chronicles lists seven post-exilic generations of David's line, beginning with Zerubbabel (1 Chr 3:17–4; cf. Ezra 2:2; Neh 12:1) and continuing with Hananiah, Shecaniah, Shemaiah, Neariah, Elioenai, Hodaviah. If we estimate about twenty-five years per generation (i.e., from a father to birth of his son), then Chronicles could not have been written before about 400 BC during the reign of Artaxerxes II (404–359 BC). For these reasons, most place its composition sometime during the last seventy years of the Persian Empire. Some critical scholars would date its composition even later, in the early Hellenistic period, but there is little to recommend this. The book demonstrates no familiarity with Hellenistic history or customs and contains no Greek loan words.

## LITERARY FEATURES OF CHRONICLES

Chronicles appears to be the work of a single author. His vocabulary shows consistency throughout the book. He regularly maintains the same theological outlook and accents. For instance, one of his favorite ways of characterizing the piety of faithful Israelites is to say that they "seek (root דרש) Yahweh." The verb דרש occurs over forty times in Chronicles' narrative chapters, beginning in 1 Chr 10 and extending almost to the end of the book in 2 Chr 34. The author uses the related verb בקש in a similar manner.

Though the Chronicler has his own outlook and understanding of Israel's history, his work is highly dependent on earlier sources. The genealogies in 1 Chr 1–7 are clearly based upon the Pentateuch. The author quotes the Psalms when relating scenes of Israel's worship and also appears to allude at times to Joshua and Judges. If Chronicles was written after Ezra, it is possible he drew on Ezra 1:1–3a for the closing of his book (2 Chr 36:22–23). More than half of Chronicles appears to rely upon Samuel and Kings, often incorporating passages nearly word-for-word. In later portions of his book the Chronicler also depends on Isaiah and Jeremiah for their historical insights into kings such as Hezekiah and Josiah (compare 2 Chr 32:9–14, 31 with Isa 36:2–4, 7; 36:18, 20; 37:36–38; 2 Chr 36:11–14 with Jer 52:1–3; 28:1).

Like the author of Kings, the Chronicler refers to "the book of the kings of Israel and Judah" (1 Chr 9:1; 2 Chr 27:7; 35:37; 36:8), "the book of the kings of Judah and Israel" (2 Chr 16:11; 25:26; 28:26; 32:32), and "the book of the kings of Israel" (2 Chr 20:34; cf. e.g., 1 Kgs 14:19, 29; 15:7, 23, 31; 2 Kgs 1:18; 8:23; 10:34; 12:19). He also employs quite a few other sources:

"The book of the chronicles (דברי הימים) of King David" (1 Chr 27:24)

"The words of the seer Samuel" (1 Chr 29:29)

"The words of the prophet Nathan" (1 Chr 29:29; 2 Chr 9:29)

"The words of the seer Gad" (1 Chr 29:29)

"The prophecy of Ahijah the Shilonite" (2 Chr 9:29)

"The visions of the seer Iddo" (2 Chr 9:29)

"The words of the prophet Shemaiah and the seer Iddo" (2 Chr 12:15)

"The annotations of the prophet Iddo" (2 Chr 13:22)

"The words of Jehu, son of Hanani" (2 Chr 20:34)

"The annotations of the book of the kings" (2 Chr 24:27)

"The words of Jehu, son of Hanani" (2 Chr 24:27)

"The words of Hozai" (2 Chr 33:19)

"The laments" (2 Chr 35:25)

In at least one of these cases, it appears that the source may be part of the larger "book of the kings of Israel" (2 Chr 20:34). This probably indicates that these sources cite Samuel or Kings under the name of a prophet who was active during the reign of the king being discussed. Support for this comes from the fact that, with the exception of 2 Chr 35:27, these source citations always appear at the same point in the narrative where the parallel passage in Samuel or Kings refers to the records of the kings of Israel or Judah.

While the Chronicler clearly drew on a number of earlier documents to construct his history, he did not feel constrained by them. His text perhaps differed from them for any number of reasons: stylistic and literary needs, theological concerns, application to his post-exilic audience, and perhaps other reasons known only to him. In addition, the Chronicler is primarily concerned with the history of Judah, so he seldom treats events from the history of Israel (cf. 2 Chr 9–13 for a rare exception).

The relationship of Chronicles to Ezra and Nehemiah occupied discussion among scholars in the nineteenth and twentieth centuries, with one theory holding that the Chronicler was also the author of Ezra-Nehemiah (see the discussion in chapter 14 on Ezra and

Nehemiah). However, recent scholarship has tended to dismiss this concept. Instead, it is likely that the Chronicler wrote his history after the book of Ezra had been completed and perhaps even after the completion of the book of Nehemiah, making it the last of the historical books of the OT, and possibly the last OT book to be written.

## Outline of Chronicles

I. Israel's origin as the people of God (1 Chr 1:1–9:34)

   A. From Adam to Jacob (1 Chr 1)

   B. David's genealogy and descendants (1 Chr 2–3)

   C. The descendants of Jacob's sons (1 Chr 4–7)

   D. Saul's genealogy (1 Chr 8)

   E. The exiles who returned from Babylon (1 Chr 9:1–34)

II. David's reign and the ark of the covenant (1 Chr 9:35–17:27)

   A. The end of Saul's reign (1 Chr 9:35–10:14)

   B. The establishment of David's administration in Jerusalem (1 Chr 11–12)

   C. David's reign: The ark and God's covenant with David (1 Chr 13:1–17:27)

III. David's military triumphs (1 Chr 18–20)

IV. David makes preparations for the building of the temple (1 Chr 21–29)

   A. David prepares a place for the temple (1 Chr 21–22)

   B. David organizes temple worship (1 Chr 23–26)

   C. David leaves the kingdom to Solomon (1 Chr 27–29)

V. Solomon's reign (2 Chr 1–9)

   A. Solomon's early reign (2 Chr 1)

   B. The temple built and dedicated (2 Chr 2–7)

   C. Solomon's later reign (2 Chr 8–9)

VI. The decline of the Davidic dynasty under Rehoboam (2 Chr 10–12)

VII. The Davidic dynasty without renewal of worship in the temple (2 Chr 13–28)

VIII. From Hezekiah's renewal to Josiah's renewal (2 Chr 29–35)

IX. The final decline of David's dynasty and the destruction of Jerusalem (2 Chr 36:1–21)

X. The hope for a new temple (2 Chr 36:22–23)

### *Babylonian Exile of Judah*

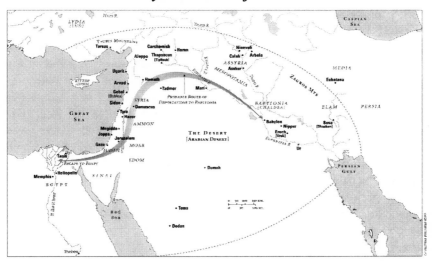

Babylon rebelled against Assyria under Nabopolassar in 626 BC. He and his son Nebuchadnezzar crushed opposition, leading to decisive victories at Carchemish and Hamath in 605 BC, which firmly established the Neo-Babylonian Empire. In that year, Nebuchadnezzar also besieged Jerusalem, deporting Daniel and other Judeans (Dan 1:1–7). After his father's death in 604 BC, King Nebuchadnezzar solidified his gains against Egypt, marked by the deportation of Jehoiachin and other Judeans in 597 BC (2 Kgs 24:8–17; 2 Chr 36:9–10). A third deportation occurred in 587 BC, after Jerusalem was destroyed (2 Kgs 24:18–25:21; 2 Chr 36:11–21). Other Judeans escaped to Egypt after further unrest (2 Kgs 25:22–26), which resulted in a further deportation to Babylonia around 582 BC. The Judeans lived in refugee colonies near Babylon and were not assimilated. The increasing corruption of Babylonia's King Nabonidus—who moved to the Arabian oasis town of Tema, leaving his son Belshazzar as regent (Dan 5:1–4)—hastened its fall to the Persians in 539 BC.

## TEXTUAL AND HISTORICAL ISSUES

### THE TEXT OF SAMUEL AND KINGS USED BY THE CHRONICLER

When comparing Chronicles to parallel passages in Samuel and Kings, it appears at times that the Chronicler is citing a version of those books that varies from the MT. Especially for parallel passages in Samuel, it seems that the text used by the Chronicler was similar to the one that lay behind the LXX version. Many of these readings are also found in Qumran manuscripts of Samuel. Since these texts are located in scrolls from antiquity, this may indicate that the text of Samuel used by the Chronicler and the translators of LXX Samuel is not a recent innovation but may represent a version that had been in existence for some time before the composition of Chronicles.

## THE HISTORICITY OF EVENTS RELATED IN CHRONICLES

Since the Chronicler appears to be selective in his use of material from Samuel and Kings—he omits almost all discussion of the sins of David and Solomon—and since he cites a number of prophets not mentioned elsewhere in the OT (e.g., Iddo [1 Chr.6:21; 27:21; 2 Chr 9:29; 12:15; 13:22], an unnamed prophet [2 Chr 25:15]; Zechariah [2 Chr 20:14]; and Hozai [2 Chr 33:19]), critical scholars have often dismissed the book as unhistorical, containing contrived accounts meant to reinforce the Chronicler's theological outlook. Some go so far as to call Chronicles a "utopian" view of Israel's past, not because it paints Israel's past as uniformly good, but because it presents an unrealistic and idealized view of Israel's heritage in order to present a specific theological and social agenda for the post-exilic community in Jerusalem and Judah.

This rejection of Chronicles' accuracy rests on several assumptions: that the book is too far removed from the actual events it narrates to be an accurate reflection of Israel's history; that the Chronicler could not have possibly had access to factual records or sources; that pressing his theological outlook was more important to him than an accurate portrayal of Israel's past.

On close inspection, none of these assumptions can bear the weight placed upon them. If distance in time makes historical accounts less accurate, then Parson Weems's fanciful biography of George Washington with tales of cutting down cherry trees and throwing silver dollars across the Potomac is a more accurate biography of America's first president than those written by historians in our day. There is no proof—only assumption—that the Chronicler did not have access to various records that could have survived from Judah's monarchy. Nor is there any evidence that the Chronicler was so committed to his theological views that he would have distorted past events or even invented incidents in order to further his own agenda.

Merrill, in a study of two accounts from David's life that appear both in Samuel and Chronicles, has argued that the Chronicler, though possessing a particular theological perspective, cannot be accused of distorting history. He concludes:

> Just as all individuals differ in appearance, personalities, preferences, and perspectives, so authors differ in literary style. The chronicler, like any other researcher, depended on his sources but felt free to use them in a way that reflected his own peculiar circumstances, heritage, experience, and objectives. Differences between him and his sources are therefore not indicative of sloppiness or revisionism on his part; instead they contribute to the veracity and effectiveness of the account while reflecting the chronicler's own unique personality and situation.[1]

## THE CHRONICLER AS SELECTIVE HISTORIAN

All history writing is selective by necessity. The writer must sift through events and decide what he considers to be most important and salient before constructing a narrative and analysis of the past. The Chronicler was no exception to this. In his case we have at least a partial insight into his work because of the many parallels between his text and that of his sources in Samuel and Kings. In recent years, many studies of the Chronicler's view of David have attempted to compare parallel passages of the king's activities in order to characterize the Chronicler as a historian *and* theologian.

Edenburg examined David's conquests in Samuel and Chronicles and came to the conclusion that David is portrayed in Chronicles as the ideal king. (After all, the Chronicler skips over David's great sins of adultery and murder in silence.) All following kings fell short of David's ideal, leading God to rescind the dynastic promise given to David. Besides reducing the Chronicler's work to a decidedly flat two-dimensional portrait of Israel and its kings, Edenburg's analysis runs counter to the evidence in Chronicles itself. David has his flaws and is far from ideal, even in Chronicles. Israel's great king, for instance, cannot build the temple because, according to the Chronicler, he is someone who has shed blood (1 Chr 28:3). Murray has proposed that this statement about David is rooted in Num 31:19

---

[1] Eugene H. Merrill, "The Chronicler: What Kind of Historian Was He Anyway?" *Bibliotheca Sacra* 165 (2008): 412.

and Num 35:30, 33–34, making the king ceremonially unclean and, therefore, unworthy to build the temple. Thus, David is hardly a king with all virtues and no vices.

In contrast, Hoglund concentrates on the Chronicler's presentation of David as a man whose passion is the praise and service of God. He notes that a comparison of the travel accounts of the ark of the covenant to Jerusalem highlights this aspect of David's personality. According to Hoglund, the Chronicler chose to focus upon David's praise and service to God in order to call his readers also to delight in worship of God. This fits well with the Chronicler's frequent mention of the temple, his unique inclusion of David's role in organizing the priests and Levites for service, his expansion of the narratives of Hezekiah's reform, and Josiah's cleansing of the temple.

Gard, on the other hand, while acknowledging that David is often presented as a model king in Chronicles, does not see him as ideal in the sense of a sinless or utopian monarch. He notes that David is portrayed as a sinner in the Chronicler's account of the census (1 Chr 21). The king is especially characterized by the Chronicler as rejecting God and relying instead on the size of the army that he potentially could bring to the battlefield (implied by placing the census after David's military campaigns in 1 Chr 19–20). The king spurns Joab's doubts about the wisdom of conducting a census when Joab asks David why he seeks (root בקש) this, implying to readers that David should have sought Yahweh instead. However, when confronted by God for his sin, David takes responsibility for his action and repents without blaming anyone else, even though the Chronicler has told his readers that it was Satan who incited David to take the census. Here David is presented as the ideal king not because he is without sin, but because he is a repentant sinner. Thus, the Chronicler has shaped his presentation of David to move his readers to similar humble attitudes before God.

What these studies of the Chronicler's shaping of his history demonstrate is not that the book is an unreliable, tendentious history of God's people, but that it is a history written as are all histories—to persuade readers that a particular rendition and construal of past events is relevant to them. Thus, far from making the Chronicler's historiographical method suspect, these studies of synoptic passages in Samuel, Kings, and Chronicles (and Isaiah and Jeremiah) show us that the Chronicler was an accurate historian, albeit one with a particular message for his audience—as is true of all historians.

## THEOLOGICAL THEMES IN CHRONICLES

### WORSHIP AND PRAISE OF GOD

Clearly, one of the great themes of Chronicles is the joyful worship and praise of God as the focus of Israel as a community. Not only is much of David's reign in Chronicles organized around his care for the ark and later his preparation for the building of the temple, but also Solomon's reign is dominated by the account of the building and dedication of the temple. Many of the kings are judged on the basis of their willingness to "seek Yahweh" and by their dedication to true worship. Chronicles' unique use of quotations of the Psalms during scenes of worship highlights the book's emphasis on thanksgiving and praise (e.g., 1 Chr 16:8–36; compare Pss 105, 96, 106; 2 Chr 6:41–42; compare Ps 132:8–10). The reforms under the faithful kings Hezekiah and Josiah further accent the book's emphasis on worship.

Throughout Chronicles, kings are characterized by their attitude toward God-pleasing worship: Do they seek Yahweh? Do they remove the high places? Do they honor the temple as God's chosen place to meet with his people? However, thanksgiving and praise do not begin with the effort of the people or their kings. Instead, it is God who provides for his people's worship, and he is the one who graciously makes a way for Israel to be in his presence. When David first attempts to bring the ark to Jerusalem, he fails because it was not done the way God commanded. In 1 Chr 15:1–24, a passage without a parallel in Samuel, David notes that the failure of his first attempt happened because the Levites did not carry the ark in a God-pleasing manner by following the instructions God had provided for its movement from one place to another (Exod 25:14–15). The effort to bring the ark to Jerusalem was ultimately God's doing, not David's.

The role David played in organizing worship in the temple and planning its construction portrays him as fulfilling the role God had given him (1 Chr 28:19). The temple is God's gift to his people, not simply the desire of David's heart. This is why Israel's great king, a shedder of blood, was prohibited from building it. Even the temple's location came from God's revelation to David (cf. 1 Chr 22:1; 2 Chr 3:1).

Finally, we should note that at the very end of Chronicles, after the temple has been destroyed and the people removed from the land, it is God who stirred up Cyrus and gave hope for a new temple (2 Chr 36:22–23). This notice that God was the one who graciously brought his people into his presence reminded the Chronicler's post-exilic readers that they, too, were his people for whom he provided a place of worship where sinners may be forgiven and cleansed of their iniquities.

## PROPHETS AND PROPHECY

The presence of prophets and prophecy in Chronicles is one of the features that make it stand out from the parallel history of Israel in Samuel and Kings. While both of those earlier books know of prophets such as Samuel, Nathan, Elijah, and Elisha, Chronicles has a unique perspective on these spokesmen of God. First of all, prophets in Chronicles are often depicted as interpreters of events showing kings and people how God views their acts, and they prophesy what God will do in response. Elijah, in his one appearance in the book, is not the miracle-working, Baal-defying prophet of Kings (1 Kgs 18), but instead the one who characterizes Jehoram's evil behavior and prophesies its consequences (2 Chr 21:12–15). The prophet Oded plays a similar role when prophesying to Samaria's returning army (2 Chr 28:8–11).

Secondly, prophets' activities are portrayed more in written communication than in Samuel and Kings. For instance, Elisha sends a letter (2 Chr 21:12). In addition, many prophets leave their words in written records pertaining to events during the reigns of various Judean kings (1 Chr 29:29; 2 Chr 9:29; 12:15; 13:22; 26:22; 32:32).

For the post-exilic community of Jerusalem and Judah for whom the Chronicler wrote, these emphases spoke to their situation. God was no longer sending prophets. They were at least a generation removed from the days of Haggai, Zechariah, and Malachi, and no more prophets were arising. The texts of Moses and the prophets were their only source of divine revelation. Moreover, they needed to see God's response to their behavior in the written words of the prophets just as the prophets had responded to the behavior of Israel and its kings in the past. Prophecy continued to be important to the Judeans in the post-exilic era, but they had to hear the prophets from a distance.

## CHRIST IN CHRONICLES

Apart from the promise to David, repeated in 1 Chr 17 from 2 Sam 7, there is little direct reference to this messianic promise. However, in 2 Chr 21:7, following the notice that Jehoram followed the ways of the kings of Israel, the Chronicler notes that even this was not enough to have David's dynasty removed from the throne of Judah (as many kings had been removed from Israel—see the authorization of Elijah to remove the Omride dynasty in favor of Jehu; 1 Kgs 19:15–28). This is because "Yahweh had promised to give a lamp to [David] and his sons forever." The divine promise to David of the lamp who would become the light of the New Jerusalem (Rev 21:23) lived on in the messianic hope of the post-exilic community.

In addition, David's descendants are unique in that only they out of all Israel are traced for seven generations following the exile (1 Chr 3:19–24). The hope of Israel was still in Yahweh's promise to David, and his genealogy above all others was to be recorded as a reminder of this enduring grace (e.g., Matt 1:1–17; Luke 3:23–38).

## SIN AND GRACE IN CHRONICLES

Scholars have noted that Chronicles has a rather stark theology of reward and retribution. Kings who seek Yahweh, humble themselves, and follow his ways are prosperous. If they go to war, God gives them victory even when the enemy's troops vastly outnumber their own. They pursue building programs and have popular support. Moreover, the Chronicler skips over the more obvious failings of David and Solomon, the planner and the builder of the temple, in order to emphasize the blessing that God bestowed upon them and Israel for their faithfulness. In contrast, kings who abandon Yahweh suffer defeat on the battlefield. They are afflicted with various illnesses. They do not have great building projects, large numbers of wives, or many children.

This meting out of blessing in response to faithfulness and punishment in response to sin for each generation was a reminder to the post-exilic people that they should not become complacent or arrogant in their faith and piety. Instead, they were called to repentance continually, just as the prophets had called Israel and its kings to repentance before the exile. Yet, the Chronicler's view of the blessing granted by God to the faithful among Israel was not that blessing was earned or deserved. If it were, God would not have stirred up the spirit of Cyrus to bring his people back to the Promised Land, nor would he have permitted David to prepare to build a temple when Satan incited him to take a census. The blessings were not earned by the faithful kings, but were a tangible sign of God's grace to repentant sinners.

## CONCLUSION

Chronicles, though often discounted as a late book and mere supplement to Samuel and Kings, contains much worth studying and many lessons for a people who do not live in a theocratic kingdom but want to learn from God's work during the time when Israel lived under that type of government. It is a book rich in theological reflection on God's work among Israel and application to his continuing work among the new Israel of God in Christ Jesus.

## SELECT BIBLIOGRAPHY

Beentjes, Pancratius C. "Isaiah in the Book of Chronicles." In *Isaiah in Context*. Edited by Michaël N. van der Meer, et al, 5–25. Leiden: Brill, 2010.

Edenburg, Cynthia, "David, the Great King, King of the Four Quarters." In *Raising Up a Faithful Exegete: Essays in Honor of Richard D. Nelson*. Edited by K. L. Noll and Brooks Schramm, 159–75. Winona Lake, IN: Eisenbrauns, 2010.

Gard, Daniel L. "The Chronicler's David: Saint and Sinner." *Concordia Theological Quarterly* 70 (2006): 233–52.

Hoglund, Kenneth G. "The Priest of Praise: The Chronicler's David." *Review and Expositor* 99 (2002): 185–91.

Klein, Ralph W. "Psalms in Chronicles." *Currents in Theology and Mission* 32 (2005): 264–75.

Kleinig, John W. *The Lord's Song: The Basis, Function and Significance of Choral Music in Chronicles*. PhD Thesis—University of Cambridge, 1990.

Merrill, Eugene H. "The Chronicler: What Kind of Historian Was He Anyway?" *Bibliotheca Sacra* 165 (2008): 397–412.

Murray, Donald F. "Under YHWH's Veto: David as Shedder of Blood in Chronicles." *Biblica* 82 (2001): 457–76.

# 14

# EZRA AND NEHEMIAH

Ezra and Nehemiah are often remembered as books about building projects: the building of the temple in Ezra and the rebuilding of Jerusalem's wall by Nehemiah. However, these books are more than simply accounts of building projects. They show us the lives of two extraordinary individuals whom God raised up to lead his people as they waited for the promised Savior. They also display how God works through many others who supported Ezra and Nehemiah. Numerous great prayers of repentance demonstrate the fervent faith of those who lived during these days (Ezra 7:27–28a; 9:6–15; Neh 1:5–11a; 4:4–5; 5:19; 6:14; 9:5– 38; 13:14, 22, 29, 31).

## AUTHORSHIP, COMPOSITION, AND DATE

There is little consensus among scholars as to the authorship of these two books. Four major theories dominate the discussion.

### EZRA WROTE EZRA, NEHEMIAH, AND POSSIBLY CHRONICLES

One traditional view, dating back to the Talmud and held by many Christians and Jews over the centuries, is that Ezra wrote Ezra, Nehemiah, and Chronicles (*B. Bat.* 15a). The attribution to Ezra as the author of Chronicles, Ezra, and Nehemiah is based on several characteristics that these books share: they use source materials, they clearly were composed after the Babylonian exile, and the last verses of Chronicles are identical to the opening verses of Ezra. Since Ezra is often depicted as a scribe (e.g. Ezra 7:6, 11), he would have been capable of writing these books. Many scholars, including quite a few evangelicals, still defend this view.

However, there are several difficulties with this position. Ezra's authorship of Chronicles in its present form is almost impossible to hold when chronological factors are considered. The genealogies in Chronicles appear to trace family lines down to about 400, the most probable date for the book's composition. Ezra began his ministry in 458 BC in the seventh year of Artaxerxes I (Ezra 7:7; see also the discussion of the historical setting below). He was mature enough at that time—perhaps thiry or fourty years old—to be trusted by Artaxerxes to carry out the task he was assigned. In 400 BC, when the book of Chronicles was written, he would have been almost ninety or perhaps even almost one hundred years old, assuming he had lived that long. For this reason, it would be highly unlikely that Ezra wrote Chronicles.

Another chronological difficulty involves Neh 12:1–11 which appears to be a list of high priests after the exile. It ends with Jaddua, who most likely began his service as high priest about 370 BC. It is doubtful that either Ezra or Nehemiah would have been alive at that time, since both would have been over one hundred years old. This appears to rule out either Ezra or Nehemiah as the author of Nehemiah.

Finally, we should note that Ezra 7:27–8:34 and 9:1–15 are written in the first person, but other narratives about Ezra in Ezra 10 and Neh 8 and 12 are written in the third person. While it would theoretically be possible for Ezra to have switched from first person to third person to relate events in which he participated, there is no good literary reason to suspect that he did so. A more logical conclusion is that a later author wrote Ezra and Nehemiah, but had access to first-person memoirs of both of these great leaders. (Neh 1:1–7:5 and 13 are written in the first person and appear to be from Nehemiah's personal memoirs.)

## EZRA WROTE EZRA, NEHEMIAH WROTE NEHEMIAH

Early Jewish and Christian interpreters and even some recent scholars have advocated this position. However, like the previous view, it is problematic due to the chronological difficulty surrounding Neh 12:1–11 and the objection concerning the switch from first-person narration to third-person narration. This theory is also implausible.

## THE CHRONICLER WROTE EZRA-NEHEMIAH

Two German scholars, Leopold Zunz and Franz Carl Movers independently came to the conclusion in the 1830s that Chronicles and Ezra-Nehemiah were one continuous work that was later split into two (Ezra and Nehemiah being considered one book). Unlike the more traditional theories, this proposal did not consider Ezra to be the author of this book, but authorship was attributed to an unknown writer called the Chronicler. This view became widely adopted by both conservative and critical scholars through the end of the nineteenth century and into the mid-twentieth century. The theory is based on four major arguments:

First, the opening verses of Ezra are identical to the last verses of Chronicles. This repetition was a conscious retention in both books to indicate their original unity. However, this position is heavily dependent on the assumption that 1 Esdras correctly preserves the original form of the supposed Chronicles-Ezra-Nehemiah book. (1 Esdras is a Greek paraphrase of 2 Chr 35:1–36:23, Ezra, and Neh 7:73–8:12. It also contains additional material not found in the OT.) However, that assumption is questionable (see below), and there are many other explanations for why the end of Chronicles and the beginning of Ezra are identical.

Second, the apocryphal book of 1 Esdras begins with 2 Chr 35 and continues through Ezra 10. Then Neh 8 is appended. This is an argument for the original unity of Chronicles and Ezra-Nehemiah. It also indicates that Neh 8 was displaced in the Hebrew text, supposedly having been moved from an early edition of Ezra to Nehemiah. This assertion, though, rests on a frequent assumption typically encountered in higher-critical approaches to Scripture—that the parallel historical information in the canonical books of the OT is suspect, but that extra-canonical texts are generally more reliable in this regard. There is no warrant for this viewpoint, however, and more recent studies have cast doubt upon the factual accuracy of the portrayal of events in 1 Esdras. In addition, recent studies have concluded that 1 Esdras is a reworking of earlier material, mostly from Ezra with some from Chronicles and Nehemiah. It shows signs of rearrangement of the accounts in Ezra that can only be explained if Ezra was composed earlier than 1 Esdras.

Third, Chronicles, Ezra, and Nehemiah share common vocabulary and syntax, indicating common authorship. This argument has been disputed by several scholars, most notably Japhet, who notes that the vocabulary and syntax of Chronicles, Ezra, and Nehemiah is also shared to a great extent by other OT post-exilic books. In addition, arguments based on linguistic evidence are notoriously difficult to prove and cannot be taken as convincing evidence of common authorship.

Finally, Chronicles and Ezra-Nehemiah share the same themes and an identical theological outlook. However, it should be noted that several motifs in Chronicles are absent or peripheral to Ezra and Nehemiah. For instance, Chronicles places a heavy emphasis on the Davidic kingdom and the office of prophets. These are secondary to Ezra and almost completely missing in Nehemiah.

Perhaps the most elaborate scheme concerning the composition of Chronicles-Ezra-Nehemiah based on this theory was one proposed by Cross that involves numerous suppositions about the author's compositional method. Because of its highly speculative nature, Cross's theory is a doubtful reconstruction of the chronology of this period in Judean history.

While the position that the Chronicler wrote Ezra-Nehemiah still has adherents, it has become a minority opinion among contemporary biblical scholars. Although it was dominant among critical scholars until the mid-twentieth century, it has waned in popularity as more recent studies have challenged all four of the arguments on which it was built. None of them are convincing. Therefore, this view can be safely discarded.

## AN UNKNOWN EDITOR OR EDITORS COMPILED EZRA AND NEHEMIAH

In recent decades many scholars have held that an unknown editor or editors composed Ezra and Nehemiah, relying heavily on source documents, including Ezra's and Nehemiah's personal memoirs. This seems to be the most likely origin of these books. It is highly improbable that Ezra or Nehemiah composed the books that bear their names, and it is impossible to prove that the same author wrote Chronicles. Moreover, it is unlikely that the books of Ezra and Nehemiah were ever part of Chronicles.

## ONE BOOK: EZRA-NEHEMIAH—OR TWO: EZRA AND NEHEMIAH?

Ezra and Nehemiah are counted as two books in the Christian OT canon. However, since ancient times, the two have been treated as one book and continue to be reckoned that way in the Jewish Bible.

### Theories Concerning the Unity of Ezra-Nehemiah

The theory that Ezra and Nehemiah were originally one book enjoys wide acceptance among contemporary scholars. Those who consider Ezra-Nehemiah to be originally one volume point both to the Masoretic and other Jewish traditions as well as to the most ancient LXX tradition. In the oldest surviving LXX codices, Ezra-Nehemiah is treated as one book called Εσδρας B. (Εσδρας A is 1 Esdras.) Only later LXX codices split the two, calling Ezra Εσδρας B and Nehemiah Εσδρας Γ. Jerome also indicates that, in his day, Jewish tradition considered Ezra-Nehemiah to be one book, although in the Vulgate he treated them as two—a tradition maintained in Christian Bibles to this day.

A second argument used to support the unity of Ezra-Nehemiah is that Ezra is mentioned in both Ezra (Ezra 7–10) and Nehemiah (Neh 8, 12). Duggan holds that both books are needed to provide a complete narrative. In addition, he points out that the two books use certain technical terms found nowhere else in the OT. These include נתינים, *temple servants* and the phrase יד־אלהים־על, *the hand of God (was) upon* . . . As a result of these arguments, Eskenazi proposed that Ezra-Nehemiah is written in three major sections and that the center section spans both books:

1. Ezra 1:1–4: the decree to build God's house

2. Ezra 1:5–Neh 7:73: the building of God's house

3. Neh 8:1–13:31: celebrating the completion of God's house.

Eskenazi's theory relies heavily on the assertion that the concept of "God's house" is expanded in Nehemiah to include the entire city of Jerusalem. However, many scholars have demonstrated in various ways that this assertion is doubtful.

## Objections to the Unity of Ezra and Nehemiah

While the theory that Ezra and Nehemiah were originally one book enjoys widespread acceptance, it has not gone unchallenged. First of all, the evidence from the LXX as well as Masoretic and Jewish traditions is removed by some centuries from the composition of Ezra and Nehemiah, making it possible that the two books were combined into one later, perhaps during the process of canonization. Moreover, that Ezra the priest and scribe appears in both Ezra and Nehemiah is hardly proof that these were one book—Joshua appears in Exodus, Numbers, Deuteronomy, and Joshua, yet no one today argues that Joshua was originally part of the Pentateuch. Ezra and Nehemiah can be read as separate accounts, and Nehemiah is not necessarily needed to complete the narrative of Ezra. In addition, the technical terms Duggan cites appear primarily in the source materials used by the author or authors, not in the connecting narratives, making this argument less than persuasive. Finally, we should note that Eskenazi's analysis of Ezra-Nehemiah has multiple detractors, including Kraemer and VanderKam.

In arguing that Ezra and Nehemiah are separate compositions, scholars note that the first verse of Nehemiah is a rather abrupt introduction that seems inappropriate if Nehemiah is a continuation of Ezra. In addition, VanderKam and Kramer point out a number of differences between the two books, including vocabulary, style, theme, and ideology.

## One or Two Books?

In the final analysis there is very little definitive evidence to establish whether Ezra and Nehemiah were originally one book or two. In fact, so much of these books contain source materials that were incorporated into the narrative, that the brief connecting narratives from the author or authors leaves little data to analyze to determine whether or not they share a common author or whether they were composed as one volume or two. For both books the author or authors were more akin to editors who linked together pre-existing material.

For these reasons, it is probably best to interpret each book on its own. However, one must also be aware that Ezra and Nehemiah are connected to one another in various ways (e.g., Ezra appears in both) and have been treated as a set since antiquity.

## DATE OF COMPOSITION

A date sometime after the beginning of the high priesthood of Jaddua during the reign of Darius III (336–331 BC) is the most likely date of composition of Nehemiah (Neh 12:10–11; 10:21). Ezra could have been composed any time after the last events in the book, which took place on March 27, 457 BC (Ezra 10:17).

## HISTORICAL SETTING

The events in Ezra and Nehemiah took place during the first half of the Achaemenid Persian Empire. Several chronological difficulties in Ezra and Nehemiah must be resolved in order to place each book in its proper historical setting.

### The Persian Empire

The empire founded by Cyrus II "the Great" is called the Achaemenid Persian Empire to distinguish it from the later Parthians and Sassanids, also based in Persia. This was one of the largest empires of the ancient world, exceeding both the Roman Empire and the empire of Alexander. Persia had been subject to Media. Cyrus defeated Media, Lydia, and Babylon, casting himself as the savior of conquered nations and allowing religious tolerance. Cyrus also allowed exiles from Judah to return to their homeland.

The early period of the Persian Empire (559–485 BC) consisted of expansion under Cyrus II, Cambyses II, and Darius I "the Great," including the annexation of Egypt. The middle period (485–358 BC) saw culture flourish under Xerxes I, Artaxerxes I, Darius II, and Artaxerxes II. During this time, the Persians fought the Greeks in the Greco-Persian Wars and then alternately supported feuding Greek city-states in the Peloponnesian War. The decline of the Persian Empire (358–330 BC) came under Artaxerxes III and Darius III.

## THE DATE OF THE FIRST RETURN FROM THE EXILE

### Dating the Return

Ezra depicts the initial arrival of Judeans to Jerusalem as a response to the decree of Cyrus allowing them to return and rebuild the temple (Ezra 1). This decree was issued in Cyrus's first year, 538. Many commentators assume that the Judean homecoming took place that same year, but the text of Ezra 1 does not fix the date. Based on the cycle of post-exilic sabbatical years, Steinmann has proposed that the return took place in 530.

### Sheshbazzar and Zerubbabel

Another related topic is the identity of the two men who appear to be leaders of the returning Judeans: Sheshbazzar and Zerubbabel. Medieval rabbis simply equated these two men with each other, a view that has little support among contemporary scholars. Others have argued that these men were leaders of two early groups of Judeans who returned to Jerusalem. Such theories are often adopted upon the underlying assumption that 1 Esdras, which appears to narrate two early returns, is more historically accurate than Ezra. Advocates of this position also interpret the prophecies of Haggai and Zechariah in 520 as implying that Zerubbabel had just recently come to Jerusalem (cf. Hag 1:1 and Zech 4:6). Recent studies have cast doubt upon the reliability of 1 Esdras, noting that it appears to be a reworking of Ezra in order to accommodate other narrative interests of its author. Moreover, there is nothing in either Haggai or Zechariah that implies that Zerubbabel or other Judeans had just recently arrived in Jerusalem in 520.

Instead, it appears from the text of Ezra that Sheshbazzar was the initial leader of the returning Judeans and served as the first governor of the Persian province of Yehud, the area around Jerusalem (Ezra 1:8, 11; 5:14, 16). Zerubbabel appears to have been a prominent leader among these Judeans. His position of leadership was most likely a consequence of his direct descent from David through Jehoiakim, one of the last kings of Judah (1 Chr 3:17; Matt 1:11–12). Zerubbabel would later become governor of Jerusalem, perhaps succeeding Sheshbazzar. In addition, he led the effort to complete the reconstruction of the temple (Ezra 5:2; cf. Hag 1:14; 2:2).

## THE DATE OF EZRA'S ARRIVAL IN JERUSALEM

Ezra 7:7 states that Ezra returned to Jerusalem in the seventh year of Artaxerxes. There were three Persian kings named Artaxerxes, and all of them reigned more than twenty years. It follows that there have been a number of proposals as to when Ezra returned to Jerusalem.

### The Traditional View

The book of Nehemiah places Ezra in Jerusalem with Nehemiah. Since extra-biblical evidence indicates that Nehemiah came to Jerusalem in the twentieth year of Artaxerxes I (445; see below), Ezra must have returned to Jerusalem in the seventh year of Artaxerxes I, 458. In addition, Ezra was accompanied by Hattush (Ezra 8:2–3), the great-grandson of Zerubbabel (1 Chr 3:17–22), making 458 a reasonable date for Ezra's return to Jerusalem. This was the most commonly held view before the rise of critical theories that attempted to place Ezra's return at a later date. The majority of recent scholarship, however, has supported the earlier date of 458 for Ezra's arrival in Jerusalem.

### The Van Hoonacker Theory

This view holds that Ezra came to Jerusalem in the seventh year of Artaxerxes II, 398. First proposed by Maurice Vernes, this position was developed by Albin van Hoonacker in the early twentieth century. It was very popular among critical scholars until the mid-twentieth century and continues to have a few adherents. The Van Hoonacker hypothesis relied heavily upon higher critical assumptions about the unreliable nature of OT historical narratives. It also overestimated the ability of critical scholars to reconstruct theoretical earlier stages of the text and to detect later editors' supposed rearrangement and displacement of textual material.

The most important contention on which this theory is based is that the narrative in Neh 8, which mentions Ezra reading the Torah, was displaced from its supposed original position somewhere in Ezra. It is further held that Neh 12:26, 36 contain later glosses that insert Ezra's name where it was not originally found. If these assertions are accepted, then it follows that Ezra and Nehemiah were not contemporaries, and that Nehemiah never mentions Ezra. Additional support for this theory is found in 1 Esdras which moves from the account of the banishing of foreign wives (1 Esd 8:88–9:36; cf. Ezra

10:1–44) to Ezra's reading of the Torah (1 Esd 9:37–55; cf. Neh 7:73–8:12). 1 Esdras appears to end rather abruptly after Ezra's public reading of the Torah. So, proponents of the Van Hoonaker Theory hold that the end of 1 Esdras was lost, but the material is preserved in Ezra 8. Van Hoonaker also gave a number of other supporting arguments for this hypothesis. For instance, little or no interaction between Ezra and Nehemiah is recorded in these books, making it unlikely that they were contemporaries.

Although the Van Hoonaker Theory was very popular for about forty years, it has been largely rejected because, upon close inspection, none of its supporting arguments are plausible. There is no evidence that Neh 8 was originally part of Ezra. The mention of Ezra at Neh 12:26, 36 cannot simply be eliminated as a gloss, since this would leave one of the processions along the wall of Jerusalem at its dedication without a leader. Recent studies of 1 Esdras have demonstrated that it is unlikely to be more original than Ezra and Nehemiah, and it appears to make selective use of materials from both 1 Chronicles and Nehemiah while rearranging the material in Ezra for the author's own purposes. Even the supporting arguments have been demonstrated to be unconvincing. For instance, Haggai and Zechariah were contemporaries, prophesying at the same time in Jerusalem on the same subject. Yet neither prophet mentions the other. Thus, it is of little consequence that Ezra does not mention Nehemiah, and Nehemiah refers to Ezra only in Neh 8 and 12.

## The Mediating Theory

In an attempt to keep Ezra and Nehemiah contemporaries, yet place Ezra's arrival in Jerusalem after Nehemiah's, some critical scholars have proposed that there is a scribal corruption in the text of Ezra 7:7–8. First suggested by Josef Markwart in 1896, this view holds that the text originally read "thirty-seventh year," placing Ezra's arrival in 428 BC, after Nehemiah's arrival in 445 BC. A scribe's eye saw the שׁ (shin) in "year" (שׁנת), and then skipped over the word thirty (שׁלשׁים), which also begins with a שׁ. This theory has several weaknesses. First, there is a complete lack of manuscript evidence for such a corruption in the text of Ezra 7:7–8. Second, this hypothesis cannot account for Ezra 7:8, which uses an ordinal number השׁביעית, *the seventh*, making it impossible that the number *thirty* was omitted. In Hebrew there are no distinct ordinal numbers above ten, so the number for thirty-seventh would not employ the ordinal form שביעית but the cardinal form שבע. Thus, a scribe would not only have had to accidently omit the number "thirty," but would also have had subsequently to adjust "seven" to "seventh." This is highly unlikely.

## Conclusion

The traditional theory best accounts for the evidence preserved in Ezra and Nehemiah concerning Ezra's arrival in Jerusalem. He came to Jerusalem in 458 and was still there in 445 when Nehemiah completed the rebuilding of Jerusalem's wall.

### THE DATE OF NEHEMIAH'S ARRIVAL IN JERUSALEM

Nehemiah came to Jerusalem in 445 and served as governor until 433. Neh 5:14 says that he was governor from Artaxerxes' twentieth year to Artaxerxes' thirty-second year. Although both Artaxerxes I and Artaxerxes II ruled for more than thirty-two years, extra-biblical evidence establishes that Neh 5:14 must be referring to Artaxerxes I. Two Aramaic papyri from Egypt preserve drafts of a letter dated to 407. These letters name Johanan/Jehohanan as high priest at Jerusalem in 407. Johanan was grandson of Eliashib and son of Joiada, the high priests in Nehemiah's day. Therefore, Nehemiah had to have come to Jerusalem before 407, making his arrival during the reign of Artaxerxes I (464–424). (Artaxerxes II reigned from 404 to 359.) Moreover, the letter mentions Delaiah and Shelemiah, sons of Sanballat, governor of Samaria. From this extra-biblical context it appears that Sanballat was an old man in 407, and his sons had taken over his administrative duties. Sanballat was an active governor in Nehemiah's day (Neh 2:10, 19; 4:1, 7; 6:1–2, 5, 12, 14; 13:28), confirming that Nehemiah must have arrived in Jerusalem in the twentieth year of Artaxerxes I.

In addition, an inscribed silver bowl from Lower Egypt discovered in 1947 mentions the son of Gashmu, king of Qedar. This Gashmu is mentioned at Neh 6:6 (and at Neh 2:19; 6:1–2 as Geshem). The bowl dates to about 400. This places Gashmu a generation earlier. Since he was an opponent of Nehemiah during his time as governor, this evidence also confirms that Nehemiah came to Jerusalem in 445.

Finally, the Greek historian Plutarch, writing in the late first or early second century AD, mentions that Artaxerxes I outlawed flogging or plucking of beards to punish nobles. Thus, this practice would have been illegal if Nehemiah did it during the reign of Artaxerxes II (Neh 13:25). However, it appears as if Nehemiah carried out this punishment during the reign of Artaxerxes I before it was outlawed.

## THE ARAMAIC DOCUMENTS FROM ELEPHANTINE

One of the more important extra-biblical sources relating to Ezra and Nehemiah is the cache of Aramaic documents found at Elephantine, an island in the Nile just north of the first cataract. In the Babylonian and Persian periods, a colony of Judean mercenaries was stationed there maintaining its own temple. In the late nineteenth and early twentieth centuries, a large number of papyri from this colony were discovered and sold on the antiquities market. These documents date from the fifth century BC and include letters as well as legal, administrative, and economic texts. The importance of these documents for Ezra and Nehemiah is twofold. First, the so-called Passover Letter of 407 is preserved in two drafts from Elephantine. It contains information that securely dates Nehemiah to the reign of Artaxerxes I (see above). Second, the Aramaic of these letters is the same type of Imperial Aramaic as found in Ezra 4:8–6:18; 7:12–26. There are numerous linguistic and stylistic parallels between the Elephantine documents and the Aramaic portions of Ezra, confirming that the Aramaic texts in Ezra are genuine Persian-era compositions and not later inventions by the author of Ezra. This is important evidence, since it rules out the contention of some critical scholars who have place the composition Ezra and Nehemiah in the Hellenistic era.

## LITERARY FEATURES OF EZRA AND NEHEMIAH

One of the most notable features about Ezra and Nehemiah is the extensive use of source documents. These include letters and official reports of the Persian authorities, various Judean records, as well as first-person memoirs of Ezra and Nehemiah. When taken together, these source documents make up almost eighty percent of Ezra and over ninety percent of the text of Nehemiah. The author or authors of Ezra and Nehemiah supplied narrative material that links together the various extracts from the sources they incorporated into the text. Most of these are in Hebrew. However, two important documents in Ezra originated from the Persian court and are Aramaic—a report by the officials Bishlam, Mithredath, and Tabeel (Ezra 4:8–6:18), and a decree of Artaxerxes I authorizing Ezra's mission to Jerusalem (Ezra 7:12–26). The language of these documents is Official Aramaic, the kind employed during the Babylonian and Persian imperial dominance of the Ancient Near East.

## Outline of Ezra

I.  Exiles in Babylon become a worshipping community in Jerusalem (1:1–6:22)

   A.  Returning to Jerusalem (1:1–2:70)

      1.  Cyrus's decree and preparations for the return (1:1–11)

      2.  List of men who returned to Jerusalem (2:1–70)

   B.  Construction of the temple (3:1–6:22)

      1.  The construction is begun (3:1–13)

      2.  Opposition to the project is overcome (4:1–6:22)

II.  The first year of Ezra's ministry in Jerusalem (7:1–10:44)

   A.  Ezra is sent by Artaxerxes I to Jerusalem (7:1–8:32)

      1.  Ezra and his mission (7:1–28)

      2.  List of heads of families who returned with Ezra (8:1–14)

      3.  Ezra's account of the journey to Jerusalem (8:15–32)

   B.  Ezra implements his mission (8:33–10:44)

      1.  Ezra's first actions upon arriving in Jerusalem (8:33–36)

      2.  Ezra deals with Judeans who had intermarried with foreigners (9:1–10:44)

## Outline of Nehemiah

I.  Rebuilding Jerusalem's wall (1:1–6:19)

   A.  Nehemiah's reaction to distressing news from Jerusalem (1:1–11)

   B.  Nehemiah receives a commission from Artaxerxes I (2:1–10)

   C.  Nehemiah inspects Jerusalem's wall (2:11–20)

   D.  Leaders of work crews who rebuilt the wall (3:1–32)

E. The construction continues despite opposition and threats (4:1–23)

F. The work is threatened by internal dissention (5:1–19)

G. A plot to assassinate Nehemiah (6:1–14)

H. The wall is completed (6:15–19)

II. Providing for a newly secure Jerusalem (7:1–13:31)

    A. Appointment of gatekeepers (7:1–3)

    B. Nehemiah plans to repopulate the city (7:4–73a)

        1. Nehemiah's plans for a registration of the people (7:4–5)

        2. The record of the first men to return to Jerusalem (7:6–73a)

    C. A public reading the Torah of Moses (7:73b–10:39)

        1. Ezra reads the Torah of Moses (7:73b–8:18)

        2. A day of confession, fasting, and a solemn agreement (9:1–10:39)

    D. New residents for Jerusalem (11:1–36)

    E. Lists of God's servants in Jerusalem's temple (12:1–26)

    F. Dedication of the wall of Jerusalem (12:27–47)

    G. Nehemiah enforces the stipulations of the solemn agreement (13:1–31)

## THE LITERARY METHOD OF THE BOOK OF EZRA

Ezra consists of two main sections. Ezra 1–6 relates the initial return of Judeans to Jerusalem that culminates in the building of a new temple. Ezra 7–10 tells of Ezra's mission to Jerusalem to establish trust and obedience to the Torah of Moses. The author of Ezra has arranged these two sections to be parallel to each other. Each begins with a decree of a Persian king (Ezra 1:1–4; 7:11–13) followed by details of a movement to Jerusalem, including lists of items sent by the king and a list of people who made the journey (Ezra 1:7–2:67; 7:15–8:14). When the Judeans arrive, they offer gifts to God (Ezra 2:68–69; 7:35). Then the mission in Jerusalem begins (Ezra 3:1–13; 8:33–36), and a crisis is encountered but overcome through the aid of men raised up by God (Ezra 3:1–6:22; 8:33–10:44). This careful authorial arrangement of the material demonstrates that Ezra is not simply a stitching together of various source documents, but it is a purposeful use of sources to demonstrate how God was working among the Judeans who returned to Jerusalem after the Babylonian captivity.

## THE LITERARY METHOD OF THE BOOK OF NEHEMIAH

The book of Nehemiah can also be divided into two main sections. Neh 1–6 tells how Nehemiah secured Jerusalem from its enemies by the rebuilding of its wall. Neh 7–13 continues Nehemiah's work by providing for a stable Jerusalem populated with a people pledged to be faithful to God. The first section emphasizes the wall, with the concerns of the Judean people playing a minor role. The second reverses this with the concerns of the people becoming more prominent and the wall playing a minor role. The change highlights the book's movement from temporal concerns to spiritual ones. This development is also shown by the active opposition to Nehemiah from external enemies in the first section. In the second section these enemies are much less prominent, and the only danger from them is their challenge to the spiritual well-being of Judeans (Neh 13:4–9; 23–31).

The author of Nehemiah has united his book by depicting all of the events revolving around Jerusalem. For instance, it is the wall of Jerusalem that protects the city and its temple while the faithful people in the city repent of their sins (Neh 9:1–10:39). They promise to keep the Torah of Moses, especially by providing for the temple and the priests and Levites who serve there. By choosing to narrate the events relating to Nehemiah's service in Jerusalem, the author demonstrates that God continues to provide for the physical and spiritual welfare of his people.

## THEOLOGICAL THEMES IN EZRA AND NEHEMIAH

The narrative of the books of Ezra and Nehemiah is centered on events in Jerusalem. Therefore, it is not surprising that the theological themes in these books also derive from this geographic orientation. Three major motifs surrounding the religious life of the Judeans in Jerusalem are prominent in these books: worship, Scripture, and marriage.

## WORSHIP

Many of the high points in Ezra and Nehemiah revolve around worship during festivals commanded in the Pentateuch (Ezra 3:4–6; 6:19–22; Neh 8:13–18). Several lists of temple personnel also highlight the importance of worship activity in Jerusalem. Moreover, building projects are sanctified by worship services of dedication (Ezra 3:10–13; 6:16–18; Neh 12:27–43).

While both Ezra and Nehemiah mention worship frequently, they differ as to its locus. Ezra focuses on the temple itself, whereas Nehemiah emphasizes the city as a whole. For instance, when mentioning the Festival of Booths, Ezra discusses only the required sacrifices (Ezra 3:4; cf. Num 29:12–38). In contrast, Nehemiah reviews the construction of booths and the study of Scripture (Neh 8:13–18). Ezra is focused on the worship revolving around the temple and the sacrifices. Nehemiah is more broadly concerned about the entire city's holiness.

### Worship at Jerusalem's Temple

The temple is a hub of much activity in Ezra. The first part of the book relates the rebuilding of the temple, and when Ezra arrives in Jerusalem, he brings items for use in the temple. In various ways the book ties the new sanctuary to Solomon's temple: construction on both was begun in the second month and led by a descendant of David (Ezra 3:8; cf. 1 Chr 3:1–19). The same song of praise is used at both dedications (2 Chr 5:13; 7:3; Ezra 3:11). When the new temple was consecrated, some worshipers cried because they remembered Solomon's temple, whereas others shouted for joy (Ezra 3:12). This joining of the old and new temples signals continuity also in God's grace and forgiveness. The place chosen by God to be with his people and grant them forgiveness through sacrifices he instituted (Lev 4:26, 35; cf. Deut 12:5–7) was again operative.

### Prayer

Prayer is important for both Ezra and Nehemiah. Three prayers of confession are particularly prominent in these books: Ezra's prayer upon learning of intermarriage with foreigners (Ezra 9:6–15), Nehemiah's prayer when he was informed about Jerusalem's condition (Neh 1:5–11), and the prayer led by the Levites (Neh 9:5–38 [MT 9:5–10:1]). All of these begin with the assumption that God has invited his people to pray—that prayer begins with God and his mercy toward Israel. Supplication in these books is not a way of obtaining God's favor, but a response to his abiding love.

## *The Wall of Jerusalem in Nehemiah's Day*

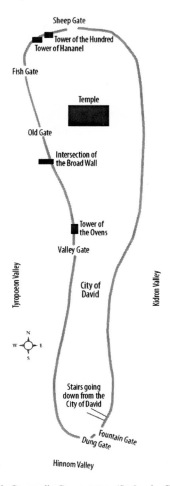

From *Ezra and Nehemiah*, Concordia Commentary (St. Louis: Concordia, 2010), 416.

### *The New Jerusalem*

Closely connected with worship in Ezra and Nehemiah is the rebuilt city of Jerusalem and its holy sanctuary. Ezra 1–6 relates the struggles of the Judeans to rebuild the temple. Ezra arrives in

Jerusalem with gifts of silver and gold for the worship of God (Ezra 8:31–36). He initiates his reforms with a prayer in the temple (Ezra 9). Nehemiah's first concern was for the city and its security (Neh 1:3), leading him to go to Jerusalem and rebuild its wall. Upon his second arrival in Jerusalem he took a number of steps to purify the temple and its priests and to ensure that Jerusalem remained a holy city on the Sabbath (Neh 13:6–30).

The events in Ezra and Nehemiah stand in partial fulfillment of the words of God's prophets in the eighth century who envisioned a rebuilt city. They include Amos (Amos 9:11–15) and Hosea (Hos 3:1–5). However, Isaiah is a proponent of a renewed Jerusalem. The Holy City is an ongoing theme throughout his book. Days are coming when all nations will stream to it because Yahweh will send forth his Torah from Jerusalem (Isa 2:2). Toward the end of this book the prophet increasingly describes the future grandeur of Jerusalem (e.g., Isa 60–62). But there is more building to come (cf. Heb 11:16). God's promises to Isaiah are not completely fulfilled in Ezra and Nehemiah. They will reach their consummation when Christ comes again to usher his people into the New Jerusalem that will shine with everlasting glory (Rev 21).

## Scripture

Ezra and Nehemiah refer to Scripture at least twenty-nine times. All but one of these are references to the book associated with Ezra—the Pentateuch. Even the one exception includes the Pentateuch: Ezra himself mentions Scripture as coming from God's servants, the prophets (Ezra 9:10–11). He then refers to the Scriptures using thoughts and phrases drawn from Leviticus, Deuteronomy, 2 Kings, Isaiah, and Ezekiel.

When referring to the Pentateuch, Ezra and Nehemiah can call it the Torah of God or the Torah of Moses. In this way the divine inspiration of the human author is subtly affirmed (see especially Neh 8:1). Moreover, the written nature of God's revelation is emphasized by frequent references to the scroll (or "book") of the Torah, and the repeated noting of Ezra as a scribe of the Torah. Because of this permanent written nature of God's Word, Ezra and Nehemiah treat the Scriptures as the only sure source and norm for the faith, doctrine, and life of God's people. Thus, the written word in Ezra and Nehemiah is used to instruct God's people through public reading and study (Ezra 7:10; Neh 8:2–3, 5, 8, 13, 18; 9:3; 13:1). The reading of God's Word led to the joyous celebration of the Festival of Booths (Neh 8:13–18).

Interestingly, neither Ezra nor Nehemiah is ever depicted as a prophet in these books, although later traditions treat both of them this way. (The only prophets of God mentioned are Haggai and Zechariah; Ezra 5:1; 6:14.) Instead, both Ezra and Nehemiah are much like Christians today—men of God's Word—who read, study, and use the Holy Scriptures.

The emphasis in these two books, therefore, is on the *written* word instead of the prophesied word. Because it is inscribed on a scroll (e.g., Ezra 6:18; Neh 8:1, 3, 5, 8, 18; 9:3; 13:1), it is enduring. Holy Writ is the permanent source of truth, power, and light. It guides Jerusalem's community to offer acceptable sacrifices (Ezra 3:2), regulate ministries (Ezra 6:18; Neh 12:44), live faithfully (Ezra 7:26; Neh 8:9), and repent of their sins (Ezra 9:10–12). God's living word brings great joy (Neh 8:10). This is why Judahites publically read and study it (Ezra 7:10; Neh 8:2–8; 13:1).

## MARRIAGE

A third important theme in Ezra and Nehemiah is marriage. Both Ezra and Nehemiah had to deal with exogamy: Judeans, especially leaders among them, had intermarried with the neighboring pagan peoples. This problem occupies the last two chapters in Ezra and crops up again in Neh 10 and 13. The dissolution of these marriages is an aspect that many readers of Ezra and Nehemiah find troubling. Marriage is not to be dissolved lightly, since it is a divinely established estate (Gen 2:24; cf. Matt 5:32; 19:3–9; Mark 10:2–9; 1 Cor 7:10–17). Moreover, several prominent marriages of Israelites to non-Israelite women are mentioned in the OT without approbation (e.g., Ruth 4:13).

The problem, however, was not with exogamy, *per se*, but with the First Commandment. Exogamy led to the reintroduction of pagan practices among the Judeans with the result that many of the children of these marriages were not trained in Israel's faith (Neh 13:25–27). The concern is framed in terms of the תּוֹעֲבוֹת, *detestable practices* or *abominations* of pagan neighbors (Ezra 9:1, 11, 14). These are defined elsewhere in the OT in terms of pagan worship (e.g., Deut 7:25–26; 12:31; 20:18; Jer 16:18; Ezek 4:9, 11; 7:20; 8:6, 9, 13, 15,

17). Thus, the problem was not exogamy, but exogamy to foreigners who continued to practice their idolatry that led some Judeans into apostasy or syncretism (Ezra 9:1; Neh 13:24). These marriages introduced a conflict between the First and Sixth Commandments in the lives of the Judeans.

Since the First Commandment is the key command in the Decalogue, governing the most important of all relationships, it is not surprising that the Judeans led by Ezra and later Nehemiah chose to place obedience to it over the Sixth Commandment. Because of their previous lack of concern for the First Commandment when entering into marriages with their pagan neighbors, some Judeans were eventually faced with the unfortunate choice of which commandment of God they were going to break: the First or the Sixth. This was a serious matter and called for repentance. Ultimately the people decided that their spiritual welfare took precedence over the sanctity of marriage. The lesson from Ezra and Nehemiah is not to choose one command over the other, however. Instead, it is to live one's life in such a way as to avoid such unfortunate situations in the first place. In the final analysis, God's Laws were not the primary concern. Instead, his promises and grace became obscured and even lost by those who involved themselves and their families in pagan worship, which relied on human efforts to please false gods. This concern for ensuring the purity of the good news of God's favor to sinners was the driving force behind the concerns about exogamy in Ezra and Nehemiah.

## SIN AND GRACE IN EZRA AND NEHEMIAH

The struggle of the Judeans to maintain faithfulness to Yahweh in the face of the idolatrous practices of the other ethnic groups in Persian Yehud is a prominent theme in Ezra. This is most obvious in the Judeans' refusal to accept the neighboring people's offer to help rebuild the temple in Jerusalem (Ezra 4:1–3). This proposal from the "enemies of Judah and Benjamin" most likely came from people whose worship was syncretistic (2 Kgs 17:24–41).

Another prominent concern in Ezra is faithfulness to God exhibited by the Judeans' zeal for proper worship. The building of the temple, offering of sacrifices, celebration of the festivals commanded by Moses (Passover and Tabernacles), and concern for the offices of the priests and Levites are scattered throughout the book.

The failure of the Judeans to follow God's Law is not overlooked, however. The older worshippers at the dedication of the temple's foundation wept when they remembered Solomon's magnificent sanctuary. Israel's apostasy had led to God's using the Babylonians to destroy the first temple. The sins of the Judeans after the return from exile—especially the sins associated with intermarriage with the surrounding pagan nations (see the discussion above)—also play a prominent role in the latter chapters of Ezra and prompts Ezra's prayer of confession on behalf of the entire community (Ezra 9:6–15).

Nehemiah as governor is especially concerned about the sins of the people against each other. As someone in authority, he realizes that he is responsible to use his power properly and to ensure that those under him respect God's law as well as the laws of the Persian king. Neh 5 is dedicated to his concern for social justice. It is set in the midst of the project to rebuild Jerusalem's wall, a task that sees Nehemiah faithfully carrying out his duty as governor to provide protection for the people.

In both Ezra and Nehemiah, God's grace is present, though it comes in more subtle ways than in other OT books. God's act through Cyrus to allow the Judeans to return to Jerusalem and build the temple begins Ezra on a note of God's grace. His grace in shaping events so that the temple is eventually rebuilt and in Artaxerxes' appointments of Ezra and then Nehemiah to positions through which they can guide God's people is also important. Divine grace is often characterized by the word חסד, *favor, faithfulness, steadfast love, mercy*. It occurs at important junctures in both books and is also found in the prayers of Ezra and Nehemiah (Ezra 3:11; 7:28; 9:9; Neh 1:5; 9:17, 32; 13:22). Moreover, God's favor is often implicit in Ezra and Nehemiah. Despite Israel's sin, God preserved a faithful remnant of his people and provided for them a new temple in a rebuilt Jerusalem. This is sometimes characterized as God's hand being upon the people or upon Ezra or Nehemiah (Ezra 7:6, 9, 28; 8:18, 22, 31; Neh 2:8, 18).

## CHRIST IN EZRA AND NEHEMIAH

While there are no direct messianic references in Ezra and Nehemiah, messianic hope is important in both books. Jeremiah had prophesied the restoration of Jerusalem (Jer 31:27–40), a promise connected with the establishment of God's new covenant. This new covenant would be established by the Messiah (Dan 9:25–27; Mal 3:1–4). Therefore, the zeal connected with rebuilding the temple, Ezra's desire to keep the Judeans free from idolatrous practices that might creep back into Israel through intermarriage, and Nehemiah's yearning to rebuild Jerusalem and repopulate it all have messianic undertones. Additional suggestive messianic motifs appear in the concern throughout Ezra and Nehemiah for the temple, its rites, its personnel, and its sacrifices, as well as for keeping the Sabbath and the annual festivals, since all of these in some way prefigure the coming Messiah. In these subtle ways, Ezra and Nehemiah are focused on the preservation of a people whose hope is focused on the ancient promises of God to send one who would redeem and deliver Israel. That hope is centered in Jerusalem, the city chosen by God and the city where Christ would be condemned and suffer death for the Israel of God—those who by faith look to him for eternal life. Ezra and Nehemiah show readers a people who looked forward to Christ and whom God moved under the leadership of Zerubbabel, Ezra, and then Nehemiah to maintain their faith in him.

## CONCLUSION

Ezra and Nehemiah were written to show us the struggles of faith in the final period of OT history. The era of the prophets was coming to an end. Haggai and Zechariah would encourage the people to rebuild the temple, but soon God would no longer raise up divinely inspired spokesmen. Instead, men like Ezra and Nehemiah would lead the people in faithful obedience to God as they were motivated by his promises preserved in the written words of Moses and the prophets.

## SELECT BIBLIOGRAPHY

Cross, Frank Moore. "A Reconstruction of the Judean Restoration." *Journal of Biblical Literature* 94 (1975): 4–18. Reprinted in *Interpretation* 29 (1975): 187–203.

Duggan, Michael W. *The Covenant Renewal in Ezra-Nehemiah (Neh 7:72b–10:40): An Exegetical, Literary, and Theological Study.* Society of Biblical Literature Dissertation Series 164. Atlanta: Scholars, 2001.

Eskenazi, Tamara Cohn. *In an Age of Prose: A Literary Approach to Ezra-Nehemiah.* Society of Biblical Literature Monograph Series 36. Atlanta: Scholars, 1988.

Japhet, Sara. "The Supposed Common Authorship of Chronicles and Ezra-Nehemiah Investigated Anew." *Vetus Testamentum* 18 (1968): 330–71.

Kraemer, David Charles. "On the Relationship of the Books of Ezra and Nehemiah." *Journal for the Study of the Old Testament* 59 (1993) 73–92.

Porton, Bezalel, and Ada Yardeni, eds. and trans. *Textbook of Aramaic Documents from Ancient Egypt.* 4 vols. in 7. Jerusalem: Hebrew University, 1986–1999.

Steinmann, Andrew E. *Ezra and Nehemiah.* Concordia Commentary. St. Louis: Concordia, 2010.

———. *From Abraham to Paul: A Biblical Chronology.* St. Louis: Concordia, 2011.

Talshir, David. "A Reinvestigation of the Linguistic Relationship between Chronicles and Ezra-Nehemiah." *Vetus Testamentum* 39 (1988): 165–93.

Tuland, Carl G. "Ezra-Nehemiah or Nehemiah-Ezra? An Investigation into the Validity of the Van Hoonacker Theory." *Andrews University Seminary Studies* 12 (1974): 47–62.

VanderKam, James C. "Ezra-Nehemiah or Ezra and Nehemiah?" In *Priests, Prophets and Scribes: Essays on the Formation and Heritage of Second Temple Judaism in Honour of Joseph Blenkinsopp.* Edited by Eugene Ulrich et al., 55–75. Journal for the Study of the Old Testament: Supplement Series 149. Sheffield: JOST, 1992.

Yamauchi, Edwin M. *Persia and the Bible.* Grand Rapids: Baker, 1990.

# 15

# ESTHER

Perhaps no other book in the OT seems as secular as Esther. There is no mention of worship or God, and no overt acts of piety are recounted in the book. Esther is therefore frequently neglected and is often missing from early Christian lists of the OT canonical books. Not a single copy of Esther has been found among the Dead Sea Scrolls. The ancient Greek version of Esther attempted to correct this lack of explicit religiosity by adding a number of sections that mention God and depict Mordecai and Esther as praying on several occasions. One of the challenges in interpreting Esther, then, is understanding its place in the OT canon and its message as part of God's Word.

## AUTHORSHIP AND DATE

Like most other historical books of the OT, the author of Esther does not identify himself. However, given his knowledge of Judeans and of Persian customs, his emphasis on the establishment of the feast of Purim, the setting of the story in the Persian city of Susa, and the lack of any mention of Judah or Jerusalem, we can conclude that the author was most likely a Judean living in Persia.

Since the events in Esther took place between 483 and 473, the book could not have been written before 473. However, Esth 9:28 seems to indicate that the annual feast of Purim, first celebrated on April 6, 473, had become a permanent custom among Judeans and had been commemorated for some time before the book was written. Moreover, Esth 10, with its summary of the end of the reign of Xerxes and Mordecai's role as second-in-rank to the king, as well as the book's opening (Esth 1:1), implies that it was written after Xerxes' death (465). On the other hand, the author does not appear to be influenced by Greek customs, which quickly spread across this part of the world when Alexander the Great conquered the Persian Empire (331). Therefore, Esther was probably written sometime between 465 and 331, with a date of about 460 being the most likely time of its composition.

The events in the book of Esther take place between 483 and 473 during the reign of the Persian king Xerxes (485–465). Everything in the book centers on the city of Susa, one of four capital cities of the Persian kings. (The others were Ecbatana, Babylon, and Persepolis.) Susa's unique status was that it served as the winter home for the Persian kings. Xerxes made extensive renovations on the palace in Susa, which was set on the city's acropolis or citadel (Esth 1:2). From the author's viewpoint, all other events related in the book—even those that take place in the empire somewhere outside of Susa—are directly a result of events that happened in the capital city.

The Persian king Xerxes (called Ahasuerus in some English Bibles) was one of the most powerful men to rule the Persian Empire. (Both the Greek form of his name [Xerxes] and the Hebrew form [Ahasuerus] are attempts to pronounce the Persian name *Khshayarshan*.) His efforts to conquer Greece from 482 to 479 were largely unsuccessful, yet his reign, like the reign of his father Darius, saw Persia at the height of its power.

Set in Susa and in the court of this king, the book of Esther relates the roles played by Esther, a queen of Persia, and her cousin Mordecai, who became Xerxes' most important official. The earliest event in Esther is Xerxes' lavish banquet that took place sometime in 483 or 482 (Esth 1). The latest is the celebration of the first Purim in February 473 (Esth 9).

### *Events in Esther*

| | | | |
|---|---|---|---|
| 25 Elul 483–30 Adar 482 | Sat, Oct 3, 483– Fri, Apr 2, 482 | 180-day banquet | Esth 1:3 |
| 1–7 Nisan 482 | Sat, Apr 3–Fri, Apr 9, 482 | Seven-day feast | Esth 1:5 |
| Shebat–Tebeth 479 | Feb–Dec 479 | 12-month preparation | Esth 2:12 |

| Tebeth 479/478 | Dec 479/Jan 478 | Esther presented to Xerxes | Esth 2:16 |
|---|---|---|---|
| 1 Nisan 474 | Fri, Apr 5, 474 | Haman casts the Pur | Esth 3:7 |
| 13 Nisan 474 | Wed, Apr 17, 474 | Haman issues edict | Esth 3:12 |
| 23 Sivan 474 | Mon, Jun 25, 474 | Mordecai issues edict | Esth 8:9 |
| 13 Adar II 473 | Thu, Apr 5, 473 | Judeans defend themselves | Esth 3:13; 8:12; 9:1 |
| 14 Adar II 473 | Fri, Apr 6, 473 | Purim celebrated | Esth 9:15; 9:17 |

## LITERARY FEATURES OF ESTHER

The author of Esther is clearly interested in the plight of the Judeans living in Persia. (Many other Judeans had already returned to Jerusalem to rebuild the city.) They are living in a pagan environment and have adapted to it, though the author never implies that Esther or Mordecai have become so assimilated that they have abandoned the God of Israel. Yet, their names reflect their pagan environment. *Esther* probably derives from the Babylonian goddess Ishtar, and *Mordecai* from their chief god Marduk.

In order to demonstrate this adaptation to the Persian environment, the author is quite subtle in the way he develops his themes, especially those that border on religion. For instance, when mentioning the fasting that Esther requested of the Judeans in Susa (Esth 4:3, 16; 9:31), he does not mention prayer, though the two often go together (e.g., Dan 9:3; Jonah 3:5–8). Esther was instructed by Mordecai not to reveal her ethnicity or patrimony to conceal not only her Judean heritage (Esth 2:10), but also her religion.

The author also never mentions God, though in perhaps the best-known passage from the book, he comes close to implying that God is in control of events, when he reports that Mordecai told Esther,

For if you keep silent at this time, *relief and deliverance will rise for the Judeans from another place*, but you and your father's house will perish. *And who knows whether you have not come to the kingdom for a time such as this?* (Esth 4:14)

This control of events by God behind the scenes is emphasized subtly throughout the book: Esther won the approval of the entire royal court (Esth 2:15). Mordecai was in the king's gate at the right time to overhear a plot against Xerxes (Esth 2:21–23). When Haman cast lots to determine the best day to attack the Judeans, the lot indicated a day almost a year away, giving plenty of time for Mordecai to undo Haman's plan (Esth 3:7). When Xerxes had a sleepless night and had the official records read to him, the readers happened to turn to the section that recorded Mordecai saving the king's life (Esth 6:2). When Haman is pleading for his life with Esther, Xerxes enters the room and mistakes Haman's actions as molestation of the queen (Esth 7:8). All of these could be seen as happenstance. However, taken together, they imply that some power behind the scenes was manipulating events. The reader is slowly led to conclude that this power is God himself.

Coupled with this indirect development of themes is the author's use of irony: Mordecai receives the honor that Haman devised for himself (Esth 6:6–11). Haman sought to confiscate Judean property. Instead, Haman's property was given to Esther (Esth 3:7–11; 8:1). Haman's dead body was hung on the pole he had erected for Mordecai (Esth 7:10).

## Outline of Esther

I.   Xerxes' feasts (1:1–2:18)

   A.   The first feast—Vashti is deposed as queen (1:1–22)

   B.   The second feast—Esther becomes queen (2:1–18)

II.  Esther's feasts (2:19–7:10)

   A.   Mordecai uncovers the assassination plot (2:19–23)

   B.   Haman's plot to exterminate Mordecai and the Judeans (3:1–15)

   C.   Mordecai calls on Esther's help (4:1–17)

   D.   Esther's first feast—Haman made bold (5:1–8)

E. Xerxes' sleepless night leads to Mordecai being honored (5:9–6:14)

F. Esther's second feast—Haman executed (7:1–10)

III. The Feast of Purim (8:1–10:3)

A. An edict in favor of the Judeans (8:1–17)

B. The institution of the Feast of Purim (9:1–32)

C. Mordecai as Xerxes' second-in-command (10:1–3)

## TEXTUAL AND HISTORICAL ISSUES

### GREEK ESTHER

Greek Esther survives in two distinct translations: One is labeled *Old Greek* and is considerably longer than the MT of Esther. The other is called the *Alpha Text* and is somewhat shorter than the MT. It is not known which of these translations is older, nor is there any evidence that one is dependent on the other. Both appear to have been based on a text very similar to the MT. The Alpha Text is shorter, mainly because in the latter chapters it eliminates material about Esther in order to magnify Mordecai's role. It glosses over material about the feast of Purim, thereby minimizing it. However, the Alpha Text also contains several short additions designed to elevate the role of the Judeans in defending Xerxes from assassination.

The text of Esther in Greek contains six additional chapters added to expand the narrative in both the Old Greek and Alpha Text translations. Often labeled chapters A–F, four of these expansions give added explanation to items passed over briefly in the Hebrew version. The other two recount a vision given to Mordecai, thereby elevating his status to that of a prophet. These chapters are nearly identical in both the Old Greek and the Alpha Text, making it likely that neither originally were part of the Greek translations in which they now reside. At least five of these chapters indicate that they were originally composed in Greek. Jerome took them out of the positions in the text where they had been inserted and placed them at the end of the book as chapters 11–16, confusing the narrative flow of Esther. These chapters and their positions in the Greek manuscripts are as follows:

## *Additions to Esther in the Greek Text*

| | | |
|---|---|---|
| A | Before Esth 1 | Mordecai has a dream about Israel in chaos; Mordecai hears two eunuchs plotting to assassinate the king |
| B | Between Esth 3:13 and 3:14 | Haman's letter giving instructions to destroy Judeans |
| C | After Esth 4 | Prayers of Mordecai and Esther during the fast requested by Esther |
| D | After C | God gives Esther favor in the eyes of the king as she comes before him with a request |
| E | Between Esth 8:12 and 8:13 | Letter of the king rescinding Haman's letter |
| F | After Esth 10 | Mordecai explains his dream now that it has been fulfilled |

These expansions accomplish a number of things. Sections A and F paint Mordecai as an explicitly religious figure, making him a prophet. They are based on the account in Jer 28 where Jeremiah and Hananiah confront each other within the debate over true versus false prophets. Sections B and E are designed to portray the king as pompous and egotistical, thereby creating a sharp contrast with the righteous behavior of Mordecai and Esther. Additions C and D explicitly introduce religious themes—prayer to Israel's God and God's intervention into the events of the Persian court.

### ESTHER'S HISTORICITY

Many critical scholars consider Esther to be a novella with no historical accuracy. Often evidence is cited from the Greek historians Herodotus and Ctesias that supposedly refute the idea that Xerxes had a queen named Vashti or a later Judean queen named Esther. Both Greeks claim that Xerxes' wife was named Amestris. For this reason Fox and Levenson have argued that Herodotus's chronology makes the marriage of Esther to Xerxes impossible. According to their reading of Herodotus, Amestris accompanied Xerxes to Sardis in 480, and she was made queen at that time. However, according to the book of Esther, Vashti was removed as queen in 482, and Esther became queen in 479. This chronology allows for no queen in 480.

However, Shea argued that Amestris was Vashti. Gordis, on the other hand, argued that Esther may be an apocopated form of the name Amestris. In a more recent study that carefully examines the statements by Herodotus in his *Histories*, Hubbard has demonstrated that the supposed chronological difficulty posed by *Histories* vii.114 is actually a misinterpretation of what Herodotus says, and it does not link Amestris with Xerxes at Sardis in 480. Nor do the other two places where Herodotus mentions Amestris have a bearing on the chronological issue (*Histories* ix.108–113; vii.61). Therefore, Hubbard contends there is no problem with the historicity of the book of Esther. He also believes that Amestris could not be Vashti, but could be Esther. Thus, there are no chronological difficulties with Esther that prevent it from being historically accurate, despite the frequent claims of critical scholars.

## THEOLOGICAL THEMES IN ESTHER

### FEASTS AND CELEBRATIONS

A striking feature of Esther is the large number of parties and celebrations packed into ten short chapters. In fact, the book could be outlined around the feasts in the book:

### *Feasts and Celebrations in Esther*

| | |
|---|---|
| Xerxes' feasts (Esth 1–2) | 1. Party leading to Vashti's removal as queen<br>2. Party celebrating Esther's becoming queen |
| Esther's feasts (Esth 3–7) | 3. First dinner party—Haman made bolder<br>4. Second dinner party—Haman executed |
| Mordecai's feast (Esth 8–10) | 5. The first day of Purim—Judeans in the Provinces<br>6. The second day of Purim—Judeans in Susa |

These many parties and celebrations serve temporarily to take the reader's eyes off of the solemn and serious events in the book. Yet, they also point to God's work. When Xerxes or Haman, Esther or Mordecai seem to be enjoying themselves, it does not mean that God is not present and active. Even at such profane times as the drunken revelry of Xerxes' first feast (Esth 1), God is in the background guiding the events and using them to the best advantage of his people. Thus, Esther teaches us that no matter how secular or immoral society may become, it is still under the control of the holy God who never abandons his people.

In addition, Esther tells us that when God's people pursue supposedly secular vocations without making an overt display of their faith, they are nevertheless doing God's work. He uses his people in everyday circumstances, whether they are in positions of power or in what some would consider lowly positions and occupations.

### ISRAELITES VERSUS THE AMALEKITES

Another theme that the author of Esther has skillfully and subtly woven throughout his book is the continued rivalry between Israelites and Amalekites. Israel first encountered the Amalekites after the exodus from Egypt when they attacked and sought to prevent God's people from journeying toward the Promised Land (Exod 17:8–16). Following their defeat, Moses prophesied that "Yahweh will be at war with the Amalekites from generation to generation" (Exod 17:16). Later, God used Gideon to defeat Amalek when it joined with the Midianites to oppress Israel (Judg 7). Still later, God commanded Saul to attack and defeat the Amalekites, though Samuel had to finish the job by executing the Amalekite king Agag (1 Sam 15).

When we first meet Haman, the writer of Esther tells us that he was "the son of Hammedatha, the *Agagite.*" That is, Haman was a descendant of Agag, the Amalekite king. This little bit of information explains to readers who know the previous books of the OT why Haman had such a hatred of Mordecai and the Judeans. It was part of an age-old feud dating back to the days of Moses. Moreover, Mordecai was especially despised because he was a descendant of Saul's father Kish (1 Sam 9:1) through Shimei, a member of "Saul's house" (2 Sam 16:5; see Esth 2:5)! Haman's disgust ran deep, and his resources as Xerxes' most trusted official were great. Yet, once again the writer of Esther shows us that God kept his promise. He made war again on the Amalekites and defended his people, just as Moses had pledged.

## CHRIST IN ESTHER

### The Judeans Escape an Attempted Genocide

The book of Esther is the account of how Esther and Mordecai worked together to save the Judean people from being exterminated by the powerful Persian court official Haman. Circumstances that arise throughout the book enabled them to rise to the defense of God's chosen people.

This remarkable story of deliverance for God's people celebrates the averting of genocide. To this day, Purim is celebrated every year by Jews with the reading of Esther and joyful festivity. Given the book's theme, it is no accident that it has become one of the more prominent books of the Bible with reference to the German Holocaust of the 1940s. Unlike Esther, the Holocaust saw many lives lost.

More important, Esther shows us God's continued commitment to his promise to bring the Savior into the world through Israel. Jesus could not have been born in Palestine if Haman had succeeded in his plot to exterminate the Judeans throughout the Persian Empire, including those in Palestine. Yet, despite the determination of a powerful enemy, God's promise endured, and nothing, not even the power of the mightiest kingdom of its day, could thwart God's plan and his promise of the Messiah.

### Religion in the Background

Although Judeans faced annihilation, no one—the narrator, Mordecai, or Esther—ever speaks about God. However, piety is implied at times in the book. Mordecai fasts and dresses in sackcloth when he hears about Haman's decree. In the OT, fasting was always accompanied by repentance, meditation on God's word, and prayer. Moreover, when Esther prepares to plead for her people before Xerxes, she requests that all of the Judeans in Susa fast for her for three days. By implication she is also requesting that they pray for her. Purim itself is a religious festival celebrated to this day in synagogues.

But why did the author of Esther not explicitly mention any of these religious connections? The answer lies in his rhetorical strategy.

Instead of mentioning how God arranged events to deliver his people, he more powerfully allows his readers to conclude that the Judeans were delivered only because God was in control of events, even when he is not mentioned or acknowledged. There are too many seeming coincidences in the book for them to be truly coincidental. When we look at all of them together, we have to conclude that God is controlling history even when humans do not acknowledge it.

Are all of these events simply an unlikely string of coincidences or are they something else? Without every one of them happening at the right time and in the right order, the Judeans in the empire might well have perished. However, the reader who knows the rest of the OT cannot escape the conclusion that the writer of Esther wants us to see the hidden but almighty hand of God moving throughout the narrative. Without directly saying it, the narrator of the events in Esther is powerfully telling us, "God will never break his promise to send the Messiah. He will rescue his people so that his pledge to Abraham, Isaac and Jacob can be fulfilled."

Thus, while overt references to piety are in the background in Esther, we should not conclude that it recounts a non-religious, secular tale. Instead, it is a very compelling witness to the ability of God to arrange events in this world for the benefit of his people. By its subtle message it forcefully proclaims the Gospel of God's enduring love for all who trust in him.

### SIN AND GRACE IN ESTHER

Clearly, Esther presents the pagans in Persia in a most unflattering, sinful light. The self-indulgent Xerxes is easily maneuvered into unwise decisions in regard to Vashti and several times concerning Haman. Haman's hatred leads him to foolish behavior, and his self-important attitude is itself a manifestation of sinful pride.

However, the author does not gloss over the failings of Mordecai and Esther. Mordecai's own pride, that will not allow him to bow down to Haman, sets into motion the plot against him and his fellow Judeans. Esther's reluctance to stand up for her people might have led to disaster had it not been for Mordecai's words to her.

Yet, despite the sometimes faltering lives of Esther and Mordecai, God did not forget his gracious promise to his people. He orchestrates events so that they are rescued from an empire-wide pogrom, thereby preserving his promise to the patriarchs. His grace cannot be thwarted by the sins and failings of pagans or Judeans.

## CONCLUSION

On the surface, Esther appears to be a secular story of Judeans in Persia. However, the power in this biblical book is in the subtlety by which it makes its theological points. Had the author been more openly theological in his relating of the events, he could not have led his readers to see how God often works in ways unnoticed and unappreciated by the majority of casual observers of human proceedings. Instead, he gently leads readers carefully to consider the actions of Esther and Mordecai, thereby appreciating all the more God's work in day-to-day events of human society.

## SELECT BIBLIOGRAPHY

Baldwin, Joyce. *Esther: An Introduction and Commentary.* Tyndale Old Testament Commentaries 12. Downers Grove: InterVarsity, 1984.

Fox, Michael. *Character and Ideology in the Book of Esther.* 2nd ed. Grand Rapids: Eerdmans, 2001.

Gordis, Robert. "Wisdom and History in the Book of Esther—A New Solution to an Ancient Crux." *Journal of Biblical Literature* 100 (1981): 359–88.

Hubbard, Robert L. Jr. "Vashti, Amestris and Esther 1,9." *Zeitschrift für die Alttestamentliche Wissenschaft* 119 (2007): 259–71.

Jobes, Karen H. "Esther: To the Reader." In *A New English Translation of the Septuagint.* Edited by Albert Pietersma and Benjamin G. Wright, 424–25. Oxford: Oxford University, 2007.

Levenson, Jon Douglas. *Esther.* Old Testament Library. Louisville: Westminster, 1997.

Shea, William H. "Esther and History." *Concordia Journal* 12 (1987): 234–48.

Steinmann, Andrew E. *From Abraham to Paul: A Biblical Chronology.* St. Louis: Concordia, 2011.

Yamauchi, Edwin. *Persia and the Bible.* Grand Rapids: Baker, 1990.

# 16

# JOB

The book of Job describes an excruciating human experience. In the course of several days, the book's central character, Job, loses almost everything near and dear to him. The drama takes place on two levels. On the earthly plane, the conflict is between Job and his three friends. Eliphaz, Bildad, and Zophar claim that the righteous enjoy temporal blessings and prosperity during this life, while the wicked suffer. Their principle of retribution is so uniform that the converse conclusion may be drawn: those who prosper must therefore be righteous, while those who suffer, as Job does, must be overt, unrepentant sinners.

At the same time there is a parallel conflict on the heavenly level between Yahweh and השטן, *the accuser*—or more freely, *the prosecuting attorney*. Yahweh is confident, contrary to the claims of the accuser, that his servant Job serves him חנם, *freely*, in response to divine grace (Job 1:9; 2:3). The accuser pushes back. He believes Job serves God only for the sake of earthly gain. Because every man has his price, the accuser wagers that acute suffering and loss will cause Job to renounce Yahweh.

These earthly and heavenly conflicts center around one question: Do people serve God because of rewards or out of loving gratitude? The question driving the book therefore is not, "Why do the righteous suffer?" It is rather, "Why are the righteous pious?"

## AUTHORSHIP, DATING, AND TEXT

The book of Job does not indicate who wrote it. However, because events in the book and its composition appear to have happened during Israel's sojourn in Egypt (see below), the Talmud (*B. Bat.* 14b) ascribes authorship to Moses. Yet, due to Job's accent on wisdom, some argue that Solomon wrote the book. The most logical identification of the author, who had knowledge of the events and dialogues described, is Job himself, with the account of Job's death in the epilogue added shortly thereafter.

Though it is not clear who wrote the book of Job, the book's era must be sometime during Israel's time in Egypt. Job's friends included Eliphaz, a descendant to Teman (Job 2:11), Esau's grandson (Gen 36:10–11; 1 Chr 1:35–36), and Bildad, a descendant of Shuah (Job 2:11), Abraham's son by his wife Keturah (Gen 25:1–2; 1 Chr 1:32). In Job we also meet Elihu, a descendant of Buz (Job 2:11), the son of Abram's brother Nahor (Gen 22:21). Since Eliphaz is at least three generations from Esau, it stands to reason that Job is about the same—at least three generations from Esau and Jacob, or during the Egyptian sojourn. Bildad's genealogy suggests the same.

Information on Job seems to confirm this. For example, he lived in the land of Uz (Job 1:1). Places by this name are mentioned twice elsewhere in the OT (Jer 25:20; Lam 4:21). In Lamentations the land of Uz is said to be in Edom. Apparently, this portion of Edom was named after Uz, the son of Dishan, a descendant of Esau (Gen 36:28; 1 Chr 1:42). This location is confirmed by the fact that one of Job's friends, Eliphaz, was a Temanite. A region in southern Edom bore this name and was apparently named after one of Esau's grandsons (Gen 36:11, 15, 42). We can conclude that Job appears to be a wealthy Edomite who lived more than two generations after his ancestor Esau, Jacob's brother. Thus, Job must have lived sometime between the eighteenth and fifteenth centuries, during the time that the people of Israel were in Egypt.

In the prologue, Job functions as the head of his household. He offers sacrifices, intercedes for family members, and carries out the role of a priest—something inconceivable after the divine revelation of Torah on Mt. Sinai when God established the Levitical priesthood. There is no mention of the tabernacle or temple in the book of Job, nor is there any central place of worship such as Jerusalem. Job's great age does not approach that of the antediluvians, but is comparable to, and may exceed, those of the patriarchs. If the 140 years of Job 42:16–17 is twice his age before his affliction, this would mean he died at the age of 210. Abraham lived to the age of 175 (Gen 25:7) and Isaac to 180 (Gen 35:28).

Another argument for the antiquity of the events in the book is that the name איוב, *Job*, occurs in various forms in the Egyptian execration texts (ca. 2000) among the names of Palestinian chieftains. *Job* also appears once in an Amarna letter (fifteenth/fourteenth century) and in second millennium texts from Mari and Alalakh. The other names in the book also fit a second millennium milieu.

Job received money from his friends in the form of a *kesitah* (קשיטה; Job 42:11), a measure of silver that is mentioned elsewhere in the OT only in connection with Jacob (Gen 33:19; Josh 24:32). This makes the Talmud's identification of Moses as the author understandable, though it doesn't prove that Moses wrote it.

If the events in Job happened during Israel's sojourn in Egypt, then when was the book written? Its poetry (chapters 3–41) is archaic and very difficult to translate. The book contains roughly one hundred *hapax legomena*, the enclitic *mem* (מ), old case endings, and many rare words. There is also a certain Aramaic flavor to the language in Job, but this does not indicate a late date of composition as Aramaisms are found in Ugaritic (fourteenth century) and other early texts.

The divine name שדי, *Almighty*, occurs thirty-one times in Job, and only sixteen other times in the rest of the OT, six of which are in Genesis. Exod 6:3 implies that שדי was particularly associated with God's dealings with the patriarchs. The divine name אלוה, *God*, appears forty-one times in Job and elsewhere only sixteen times, mostly in older texts.

In spite of the evidence for an ancient hero of faith who is described in an archaic text, the common critical understanding of Job is that the book was composed during the Babylonian exile and is a parable (of sorts) of a righteous nation suffering unjustly under God's cruel hand. Babylon's massive intrusion brought an end to Israel's earlier belief in an ordered universe of reward and retribution. Job, so critics argue, is like Ecclesiastes. Both books protest the mechanical and legalistic theology that is supposedly linked to Moses.

Cross goes even further. Not only was Job composed in the aftermath of the Babylonian exile, he believes that the god who spoke to Job in a storm (Job 38:1) was not the God of Israel's exodus and land conquest. He was none other than Baal—the Canaanite fertility deity—who defeats Behemoth and Leviathan, the gods of chaos and evil (Job 40–41). Understood in this way, the book of Job repudiates the God of history and brings Israel's religion to an end. History has no rhyme or reason and is beyond understanding.

Such a reading of Job, however, ignores the fact that the book is full of divine names that frequently appear in other OT texts (e.g., Yahweh, Elohim, Eloah, and El Shaddai). Moreover, it is not a novel idea that Yahweh speaks from the storm. For example, he manifests himself in this way in Exod 19; Pss 18, 29; Ezek 1; Nah 1. The book of Job also reflects orthodox Israelite theology as expressed in several passages including Gen 1–2; Ps 8; and Isa 51:9–11.

## LITERARY FEATURES OF JOB

Many critics posit two originally separate stories about Job—a prose account of a steadfast hero and a poetic version of a questioning skeptic. They also believe that a chapter has fallen out of the third cycle of speeches and so they rearrange chapters 26 and 27, assigning Job 26:5–14 to Bildad and Job 27:13–23 to Zophar. Elihu's speech (Job 32–37) is often viewed as inferior and repetitious and therefore seen as a late addition.

But excising some sections and rearranging others is dubious. Habel demonstrates that many themes and words are common in both the prose and poetry sections. For instance, in both, Job is blessed, ברך (Job 1:5; 1:10; 1:11; 1:21; 2:5; 2:9; 3:12; 4:4; 31:20; 42:12). Moreover, both the prose and poetry passages address the motifs of sacrifice and prayer.

The speeches of Job and his friends are almost universally viewed as consisting of three cycles. Job's friends speak and Job replies to them in each of the cycles. However, the third cycle contains no speech for Zophar—though Job has two speeches (Job 26:1–27:23). This problem is solved by claiming a lost speech for Zophar (Job 27:13–23). Another approach is to delete some sections of the third cycle, calling them fragmentary material or additions by a later redactor.

The structure of the book, however, is not based upon three cycles but upon the author's repeated use of fourfold groupings. How is this signaled? There is a close relationship between the prologue (Job 1:1–2:14) and the epilogue (Job 42:7–17). However—and this is the book's literary key—Job 1:6–2:10 has no parallel at the end of the book. This section has four parts: (1) a confrontation between Yahweh and the accuser (Job 1:6–12); (2) Job's first crisis (Job 1:13–22); (3) the second confrontation between Yahweh and the accuser (Job 2:1–6); and (4) Job's second crisis (Job 2:7–10). Additionally, Job's first crisis contains four parts. He loses his cattle, flocks, camels, and children (Job 1:13–19). These features establish the book's fourfold pattern. The speeches of Job and his friends (Job 3:1–27:23) contain two four-speech cycles. They are as follows:

### Four-Speech Cycles in Job

Cycle 1: Eliphaz (Job 4:1–5:27)
> Job (6:1–7:21)
> Bildad (8:1–22)
> Job (9:1–22)
> Zophar (11:1–20)
> Job (12:1–14:22)
> Eliphaz (15:1–35)
> Job (16:1–17:16)

Cycle 2: Bildad (18:1–21)
> Job (19:1–29)
> Zophar (20:1–29)
> Job (21:1–34)
> Eliphaz (22:1–30)
> Job (23:1–24:24)
> Bildad (25:1–6)
> Job (26:1–27:23)

This fourfold structure takes a hiatus with the poem on divine wisdom (Job 28) and Job's last speech (Job 29–31). However, it returns with Elihu (Job 32–37). After the introduction (Job 32:1–5), Elihu gives four speeches (Job 32:6–33:33; 34:1–37; 35:1–16; 36:1–37:24) and Yahweh likewise delivers four oracles (Job 38:1–39:30; 40:1–2; 40:6–41:34; 42:7–8). The repeated fourfold structures point back to the prose introduction (the first use of a fourfold structure) to help define the book's main message—Why do believers serve God?

## Outline of Job

I.  Prose introduction (1:1–2:13)
    A.  Job's prosperity (1:1–5)
    B.  The first accusation and Job's loss (1:6–22)
    C.  The second accusation and Job's further loss (2:1–10)
    D.  Job's friends arrive to comfort him (2:11–13)
II.  Job's crisis (3:1–27:23)
    A.  Job's complaint (3:1–26)
    B.  First fourfold cycle of speeches (4:1–17:16)
    C.  Second fourfold cycle of speeches (18:1–27:23)
III.  Celebrating divine wisdom (28:1–26)
IV.  Towards a solution (29:1–42:8)
    A.  Job restates his complaint (29:1–31:41)
    B.  Elihu's four speeches (32:1–37:25)
    C.  Yahweh speaks four times (38:1–42:8)
        1.  Yahweh's first speech (38:1–39:30)
        2.  Yahweh's second speech (40:1–2)
        3.  Job's reply (40:3–5)
        4.  Yahweh's third speech (40:6–41:34)
        5.  Job's reply (42:1–6)
        6.  Yahweh's fourth speech (42:7–8)
V.  Prose conclusion (42:9–17)
    A.  Job's friends obey Yahweh (42:9)
    B.  Job is restored (42:10–17)

The book of Job naturally fits within the wisdom genre. Job is described in classical sapiential terms (e.g., Job 1:1) and chapter 28 is an exquisite reflection on the inscrutability of divine wisdom. Another genre appearing throughout the book is that of lament, but the overall tone of the book is legal or forensic. In fact, the different sections of the book correspond to different stages of a lawsuit.

Can we say that the genre of history also rightly applies to Job? Job 1:1 is very similar to Judg 17:1 and 1 Sam 1:1, both of which narrate historical events. And Job is referred to as a real person in Ezek 14:14, 20. On the other hand, though the book preserves actual events, the dialogues between Job and his friends do not record the exact words of their debate. They are accurate descriptions of what went on. But because people in pain and turmoil rarely express themselves poetically, the dialogues are not precise, word-for-word attestations of what was said.

## THEOLOGICAL ISSUES

### WHY DO THE RIGHTEOUS SERVE GOD?

The standard approach to the book of Job is to interpret it along the lines of theodicy—how can a just God allow a righteous person to suffer? While the accuser, Job and his wife, Bildad, Zophar, Eliphaz, and Elihu take up the issue of suffering, in his speeches at the end of the book God does not. This suggests that Job's suffering is a foil for something bigger. But what is that issue? It is Job's struggle to serve and trust in God.

Although Job confesses that God is the one who "gives and takes away" (Job 1:21), his friends insist that it is human beings who control God's giving and taking by their own righteous or unrighteous lives. They believe that the righteous always prosper and the wicked always suffer. In doing so, the three friends unconsciously align themselves with the accuser's position that human beings serve God only because it gets them something. Job, however, argues that this is not true.

Does this mean that the book has nothing to say about the theodicy of suffering? On the contrary, it is only when the central concern of the book is understood that its teaching on theodicy becomes clear. And it is this: Job demonstrates that theodicy is an irrelevant exercise. People cannot explain God's actions because they do not have access to his wisdom in the heavenly court. They can only make guesses that, in the end, are as unreliable as those made by Job's friends.

Therefore, the overarching dialectic in the book of Job is between a false faith (the accuser and the three friends) and a true faith (Job, Elihu, and Yahweh). Those with false faith serve God only because of temporal benefits. Everything is *quid pro quo*. This faith operates with a mechanical view of retribution: good works earn rewards and prosperity, while evil works bring punishment and suffering. God automatically makes this happen, so he is more like a vending machine than a person (e.g., Job 4:7–9; 5:11–16; 8; 11; 15; 18; 20).

Eliphaz responds to Job's plight with a sympathetic appeal to Job's former piety, automatically and perhaps unconsciously assuming that Job must have had a serious lapse which has occasioned his present sufferings. According to his principle of retribution, the upright never perish (Job 4:7), while those who sow trouble reap it (Job 4:8). Two more examples illustrate the friends' approach to serving God. Eliphaz describes how upon seeing a "fool taking root," God "quickly cursed his household" (Job 5:3). Temporal prosperity for the ungodly is utterly intolerable and retribution must be immediate, not eschatological. Bildad, who generally lacks the tact of Eliphaz, epitomizes the friends' counsel to the bereaved Job: "If your sons sinned against him [God], then he gave them over to the hand of their transgression" (Job 8:4). For Bildad the only explanation for the tragic death of Job's children is open sin against God. His approach adopts an aloof, Stoic attitude toward others in their suffering and grief. The three friends never address God, they never pray to God for Job or for themselves. They do not suffer, but claim that they still know just as much about Job's plight as Job himself (Job 15:9).

It is surprising, the friends assert, that Job does not suffer more (Job 11:6). What he needs to do is stop claiming that he is righteous in God's sight and, instead, repent (Job 5:17; 8:5–6; 11:13–20; 22:1–30). Elihu says something similar, but he does not operate with the same mechanical view of retribution, and he considers God's ultimate purpose in allowing suffering to be salvation, not merely punishment (Job 33:22–30; 33; 34:31–37; 36:1–33).

The friends' understanding is incorrect for two reasons. First, it assumes that the relationship between God and people is based on human achievement. Second, it lacks a doctrine of justification for sinners. Their approach believes that God rules with retributive righteousness. Their piety affirms that God is good, but it cannot affirm that God accepts sinners. That's why no one listens to Job's laments (Job 5:1).

Eliphaz, Bildad, and Zophar embrace the idea that if people sin they will suffer. The Sinaitic covenant curses in Lev 26 and Deut 28 say as much. However, the friends go further and argue that if people suffer, then they have sinned. By reversing the cause and effect, they maintained that all suffering can be explained by sin. And since Job suffers, he has sinned.

Though Job agrees with Bildad that no one stands righteous before God based upon what they do (Job 9:2), he argues that he must be suffering for a reason other than his sin. Job waits for God's vindication and, in spite of his pain, he makes several startling affirmations of faith; Job 13:15–16 (the confession that salvation will come despite death); Job 14:7–17 (belief in an afterlife); Job 16:18–22 (hope for a mediator and afterlife); and Job 19:24–25 (hope for a redeemer and resurrection). Job offers a different motivation for why he serves God—justification by faith and eternal life.

Job contemplates the tree, which has hope since if it is cut down it can sprout again (Job 14:7–9). Though he sees no visible evidence for the hope of an afterlife for people (Job 14:10–12), his faith overcomes human reason: "If a man dies, shall he live again? All the days of my service I will hope, until my renewal comes" (Job 14:14). The noun חליפתי, *my renewal*, derives from the verb חלף. Job uses it to describe a tree sprouting in Job 14:7, leaving little doubt that with the term *renewal* he is thinking of an afterlife. Justification is a possibility, for God will overlook his sin, seal up his transgression in a pouch, and plaster over his iniquity (Job 14:16–17). In his theophanies, God speaks to Job and confirms that which before he only believed on faith—there is order and beauty in the world (Job 38–41).

## JOB'S MEDIATOR/REDEEMER

Job does not serve God for rewards. Belief in a Mediator/Redeemer is the key to his faith. Though God is not a man (Job 9:32) and his judgment is too powerful for people to have any hope, Job longs for a מוכיח, *umpire* or *referee*, who "would put his hand on the two of us" (Job 9:33). This mediator will enable Job and God "to go to court together" (Job 9:32) and settle their differences in a just and equitable manner.

Job makes another startling assertion: "Even now I know that עדי, *my witness*, is in heaven, שהדי, *my testifier*, is on high; מליצי, *my mediator*, is my friend, while my eye weeps to God" (Job 16:19–20).

Job again thinks of justification in legal, forensic terms in contrast to the legalistic conception of justification with which the friends operate. The function of the witness is crucial for Job's eschatological hope. He describes the activity of the witness as litigating with God for the sake of people (Job 16:21).

Job's beliefs in chapters 9 and 16 find their fullest expression in chapter 19 which means that Job 19 is more like a peak in a range of mountains rather than an isolated summit. Yet the affirmation does mark a turning point. Job asserts, "I myself know that גאלי, *my redeemer*, lives" (Job 19:25). The following verses express his belief in the resurrection. Job is emphatic that with his own eyes he will see God, and he yearns for that time (Job 19:26–27).

Furthermore, Job's reference to the redeemer standing "on the earth" (Job 19:25) refers to the public nature of his acquittal. He wants his justification to be made known in space and time, rather than it being a secret declaration by God in heaven which nobody else knows about. Job likely wants his friends' charges to be publicly disproven.

There is good reason to believe that Job is thinking of a single person, rather than of a separate figure in each of the oracles in Job 9:32; 16:19–20; 19:25–27. There are two interpretations of the identity of this figure. Some argue that he is a person other than God, such as an angel, or a lower, imminent "personal god" who negotiates with the higher, transcendent God. This understanding appeals to Eliphaz' reference to the "holy ones" in Job 5:1. These beings appear to be a group of intercessors who can be appealed to for help by those in distress. Elihu likewise refers to a "mediating angel/messenger," who is "one of a thousand" (Job 33:23). If the *min* (מן) in Job 33:23 is partitive, this indicates that Elihu believes that there is a large number of such mediating angels who could deliver Job.

Against this view that the mediator is someone other than God, it may be argued that Job's view is not the same as that of his friends, just as his understanding of justification and the afterlife is radically different. In Job 33:23, Elihu's speech does not necessarily imply belief in the existence of a thousand such mediators. And Job consistently addresses his pleas and complaints directly to God. While he takes comfort in the existence of his redeemer/ mediator/witness, Job never appeals to or invokes this figure as someone who clearly is not God or who is a lesser god or angel.

Therefore Job appeals to God himself. Though he addresses the redeemer as someone distinct from God (as in Job 9:33 where the mediator is between God and Job), Job appeals to God against God. That is to say, Job appeals to God's grace against God's judgment. In support of this interpretation, note Job's consistent recognition of God as the ultimate arbiter in all matters of justice. In chapter 9, for example, Job reflects on the inability of anybody to persuade God to alter his plans. God does whatever he wants to do, and no one can turn back his wrath (Job 9:3–24). In Job's mind, there is no person or force who can deliver people from God other than God himself. Many other passages can be cited as evidence of this point (e.g., Job 12:14–25). Yahweh himself confirms this belief in chapters 40 and 41, where he shows Job his complete mastery over the supernatural figures Behemoth (Job 40:15–24) and Leviathan (Job 41). These are characters that Job is utterly impotent to deal with. It is important to note that in Job's final plea of chapter 31 he leaves his legal case solely in the hands of God, without invoking any other person.

## THE ELIHU SPEECHES

Elihu's introduction is unique in Job in a number of ways. It lists his genealogy (Job 32:1), his purposes for speaking (Job 32:2–3), the reasons for his former silence (Job 32:4), and why he finally chose to speak (Job 32:5). None of this information is given before the speeches of Eliphaz, Bildad, or Zophar. It may be concluded, therefore, that the author is signaling that Elihu's reply to Job's plaint will lead to a resolution of the problem, whereas the previous replies of Job's friends do not. Seen in this light, the Elihu speeches form a bridge between the earlier deadlocked dialogues and the solution announced in Yahweh's oracles.

Elihu describes a possible explanation for the reason God allows suffering. Pain and agony are the way God reveals himself (Job 33:14–16). God uses adversity to keep people from pride (Job 33:17), and save them from the pit (Job 33:18, 22). The theme of the mediator then reappears. Elihu speaks as if a suffering person is on trial, with the מליץ, *intercessor* or *mediator*, as his defense attorney. The use of the word מליץ in Job 33:23 picks up on the term in Job 16:20. While Elihu stresses the value of suffering, he assumes that the person in anguish must repent of sin (Job 33:27).

Yet Elihu introduces some important themes in his discussion of the mediator. In Job 33:24, the peculiar form פדעהו is probably from פדה, *ransom*, which occurs in Job 33:28. The word כפר, *atonement, ransom price*, in Job 33:24 indicates that the mediator finds atonement for sin (cf. Ps 49:7). He restores the suffering person to health (Job 33:25) and this is accompanied by God's favor or grace (Job 33:26).

Elihu, then, provides a significant advance over the theology of the friends. He maintains that God's goal in permitting people to suffer is to bring them to everlasting life (Job 33:29–30). Elihu sees suffering not as simply punishment for sin as the friends do, but as serving the cause of faith.

## THE YAHWEH SPEECHES

Throughout the book, Job wants God to respond and answer him. The silence of God, with his seeming indifference, is a major problem (e.g., Job 9:11, 32–35; 10:8; 14:14–15; 16:18–22; 19:23–27; 31:35). Beginning with Job 38:1, the hidden God becomes the revealed God whose message is clear. Job is not in a position to question Yahweh. Yahweh is the only legitimate Questioner who begins with a bold challenge to Job's wisdom: "Who is this who darkens counsel, with words without knowledge?" (Job 38:2). The counsel which Job obscured is God's eschatological goal of salvation through suffering. There were moments when Job thought God was dealing with him according to judgment and not grace. Job interpreted God's will for himself as for evil, rather than for good.

In his speeches, Yahweh refuses to be drawn into Job's demands. He offers no explanation of suffering. Rather, the text portrays a larger vision of God's power and mystery. After each speech, God pauses, lets his message sink in, and then gives Job a chance to respond, which he does in Job 40:3–5; 42:1–6. But Yahweh does not use his wisdom to humiliate or overpower Job, as easy as that would be. Rather, he patiently instructs Job as to the complexities of the universe and the extreme attention to every detail that is necessary to govern it well.

People are nowhere to be found in these chapters. The thinking of Job and the three friends had become anthropocentric. Theodicy is anthropocentric because it demands that God justify himself and his ways to people. The real issue in the book is not how God may be justified, but how people may be justified—by grace or by works. Yahweh leaves people out of the picture to show Job that Yahweh, not people, is the center of the universe. And Yahweh is a God who justifies people by grace alone.

In Job 3, Job is curved in on himself. He uses images of enclosure. The whole world is collapsing, contracting in on him, and restricting him (e.g., Job 3:23). In the Yahweh speeches, God opens up the entire universe to Job. God expands Job's horizons and discloses to him new vistas, so that he sees from horizon to horizon. In Job 3 his gaze was inward, myopically focused on his own suffering, and downward toward death and the underworld. In the Yahweh speeches, God leads him to look outward toward life all around him and upward toward God in heaven.

Even though people are absent, Yahweh's oracles suggest an analogy from the natural world to the human sphere. If God governs the natural world and keeps it in such a balanced state of harmony and order, how much more does he govern the human world according to his own lofty standards of harmony, justice, and order?

While creation is ordered according to divine wisdom (Job 28), Behemoth and Leviathan are present as well (Job 40–41). Are these natural or supernatural creatures? Natural beasts are partly in view, whatever their exact identity may be. However, they are also transcendent and supernatural agents of evil. Their presence means that life can be unpredictable, unfair, capricious, and seemingly futile.

The word בהמות normally denotes *animals* or *beasts*. However, in Job 40:15–24, it is a proper name in the form of an intensive or abstract plural. *Behemoth* is the abstract and intensified epitome of beastliness and ungodly strength. He is a sort of beast *par excellence*.

Leviathan breathes fire like a dragon (Job 41:10–11) and inhabits the sea (Job 41:23–24), which in Job is the locus of chaos and evil (Job 9:8; 26:12–13; 38:8–11). He rules over all the worldly "sons of pride" as their king, and "on earth is not his equal" (Job 41:25–26). Leviathan appears earlier in the book (Job 3:8), while Rahab (apparently an epithet for Leviathan) is mentioned in Job 9:13; 26:12.

Behemoth and Leviathan are potentially devastating, since Yahweh repeatedly points out to Job that people cannot protect themselves against these beasts, let alone control them. But God subdues them with the greatest of ease. He takes Behemoth by his eyes and pierces his nose with a snare (Job 40:26). Yahweh keeps

Leviathan like a harmless pet on a leash (Job 40:26), or like a fish in a bowl, since Yahweh has set limits for the sea, its home (Job 38:8–11). Just as Yahweh is sovereign over the natural world, he is victorious over wickedness in the heavenly realm.

## Job's Repentance

The only solution that resolves the conflict in the book of Job is the fact that Yahweh alone defeats the forces of evil, Behemoth and Leviathan. The recognition of this reality moves Job to repentance and faith in Yahweh as his Vindicator and is followed by the condemnation of the friend's false theology.

But why did Job need to repent (Job 42:6)? It was because he falsely accused God of injustice. For example, Job describes God in vivid detail as assailing him, shattering him, seizing him by the neck and crushing him, using him as an archery target (Job 16:7–14). With biting sarcasm, Job says God governs the world as if his purpose is to promote chaos and injustice: God uses waters to destroy, not for fertility. God deceives, strips counselors, mocks judges, shackles kings, and destroys the wisdom of elders (Job 12:13–25). In essence, Job accuses God of being a chaos monster like Behemoth or Leviathan who is out to hurt people, rather than working for their salvation. For all of this, Job repents.

Job's repentance, however, is not a capitulation to the theology of his friends. He does not confess that he had committed a grievous sin which precipitated his suffering as punishment. Rather, Job regrets his foolish accusations that God is unjust. He had thought that God was cruel because he had misinterpreted his sufferings as punishment rather than as an opportunity for the exercise and increase of his faith in God's grace (Job 42:5). Job had failed to perceive what the reader knows from the prologue, namely, that it was not his sin which occasioned his suffering, but rather his exemplary faith in God's grace, which was being tested and proved (cf. Job 23:10).

When Job repents, he acknowledges that he has no right to expect God to preserve his prosperity and shield him from all suffering. He has no claim on God. Job realizes he is totally at divine mercy, and it is at this point that God, out of his grace, chooses to show just how merciful he is by restoring Job twofold (Job 42:10).

## CHRIST IN JOB

Job was singled out by God and persecuted by the accuser precisely because he was an exemplary man of faith (Job 1:8–12). A major issue in the book of Job, then, is the problem of the righteous sufferer. The NT repeatedly announces that Christ is the ultimate expression of a righteous suffer (e.g., Luke 23:47; 1 Pet 2:22).

There is also similar imagery between Job 16:7–17 and the passion narratives of Christ. The sufferer is attacked mercilessly while onlookers mock him (Job 16:10; e.g., Mark 15:31; Luke 23:11), and he laments that he has been abandoned into the hands of evil men (Job 16:11; Matt 27:46). The construction in Job 16:17, "although violence is not in my hands," is similar to the description of the Suffering Servant in Isa 53:9. Anderson writes, "That the Lord himself has embraced and absorbed the undeserved consequences of evil is the final answer to Job and all the Jobs of humanity."

In fact, Hartley believes that Job was one of the models employed by Isaiah when the prophet wrote about the Suffering Servant (e.g., Isa 50:4–9; 52:13–53:12). Both Job and Jesus make it clear that a righteous person can suffer the worst afflictions possible and still trust in God.

Job is also a type of Christ when he offers sacrifice not for his own sin, but for the sin of others. In the prologue, he offers sacrifices for his children's sin (Job 1:5). In the epilogue, he offers sacrifices for the sin of the three friends, and God favorably receives Job's prayer on their behalf (Job 42:8).

The book of Job likewise points to Christ by means of the theme of the mediator/redeemer which runs through the book (Job 5:1; 9:32–35; 10:4–5; 13:15–18; 14:7–17; 16:18–22; 19:23–27; 33:23–28). Jesus is our Advocate before the Father (1 John 2:1) who was delivered over to death for our sins but raised again for our justification (Rom 4:25).

## SIN AND GRACE IN JOB

The issue in the book of Job is whether the relationship between God and people is rooted in judgment or grace. If, as the accuser and friends argue, it is based on works and rewards, then people serve God solely to obtain temporal prosperity and a "righteous sufferer" is a contradiction of terms. If, however, as Yahweh contends, the relationship is based on grace, then temporal suffering will not abrogate faith in God, but will instead serve to exercise and strengthen faith that trusts in God's eschatological restoration. The chief sin in the book, then, is the dependence upon human righteousness to gain God's blessings rather than seeing them as gifts of divine grace.

Even though Job was at a loss to explain how a gracious God could permit him to suffer, he never renounced his belief in God's mercy, and so in the end he left his legal case in the hands of God (Job 31). The strong affirmations of a personal mediator, witness, and redeemer, as well as everlasting life and resurrection, were forged in the furnace of suffering. In the end, Job serves God חנם, *freely*, in joyful response to Yahweh's grace. The accuser lost his bet and Yahweh won. "It was not that this man sinned, or his parents, but that the works of God might be made manifest in him" (John 9:3).

## CONCLUSION

A likely etymology for איוב, *Job*, is that it derives from the root איב, *enemy*. Job employs the word איב when he announces that God is his enemy (Job 27:7) as well as when he describes God as treating him as his enemy (Job 13:24), which also is quoted by Elihu (Job 33:10). Job therefore stands as the representative of every believer who, in moments of suffering, weakness, or doubt, considers God to be his enemy, or who feels that God is treating him as an enemy.

Job, a man of faith, tries to reconcile his trust in a gracious God with his experience at the hands of a God who lets him suffer. The theophanies resolve Job's conflict (Job 38:1–42:7). God confirms that which Job previously believed only by faith. Yahweh has power over the forces of evil—Behemoth and Leviathan. In the end God sets everything right (Job 42:10). Job's conception of justice and justification therefore operates on an entirely different plain than that of his friends (Job 13:15–16; 14:7–17; 19:23–27). His hope for justification is not limited to this life, and his faith has an eschatological perspective which is totally lacking in his friends.

Finally, the book of Job is a microcosm of the biblical narrative. Both begin in an idyllic way (Gen 1–2; Job 1:1–3), testify to a diabolical intrusion (Gen 3:1; Job 1:6), describe a fall of unfathomable proportions (Gen 3; Job 1:13–19; 2:7), announce God's intervention (Job 38:1; John 1:14), and picture an ending that is much like the beginning, only greater (Job 42:10–17; Rev 21–22).

# SELECT BIBLIOGRAPHY

Anderson, Francis I. *Job: An Introduction and Commentary.* Tyndale Old Testament Commentaries 14. Downers Grove: InterVarsity, 1977.

Cross, Frank M. *Canaanite Myth and Hebrew Epic: Essays in the History of the Religion of Israel.* Cambridge, MA: Harvard University Press, 1973.

Habel, Norman. *The Book of Job.* Old Testament Library. Philadelphia: Westminster, 1985.

Hartley, John E. *The Book of Job.* New International Commentary on the Old Testament. Grand Rapids: Eerdmans, 1988.

Mitchell, Christopher. "Job and the Theology of the Cross." *Concordia Journal* 15.2 (1989): 156–80.

Steinmann, Andrew. "The Structure and Message of the Book of Job." *Vetus Testamentum* 46 (1996): 85–100.

# 17

# PSALMS

The Psalter was Israel's hymnal. Its title in Hebrew is תהלים, *Praises*. Though the book is chock full of laments, its overall movement is from despair to praise. Based upon the Psalter's frequent use of מזמור, *a song accompanied with a musical instrument*, the LXX title of the book is ψαλμοι, *Psalms*. Through the ages, Psalms has exerted a tremendous impact upon the hymnody, liturgy, and devotional lives of the faithful.

The NT includes more than 400 quotations, illusions, and echoes from the book of Psalms. Ambrose (c. AD 330–397) went so far as to refer to the Psalter as "a gymnasium for the soul," where believers daily exercise their faith. Luther maintained that the Psalms "might well be called a little Bible. In it is comprehended most beautifully and briefly everything that is in the entire Bible."

## AUTHORSHIP, DATING, AND TEXT

The talmudic tractate *B. Bat.* 14b–15a states that "David wrote the Book of Praises," admittedly with help from others like Asaph and the sons of Korah. But did David really compose the seventy-three psalms attributed to him in the Psalter? Critics doubt it, pointing to circumstantial evidence that the psalmic superscriptions were late additions. Chiefly, they argue, is that while the MT has seventy-three psalms attributed to David, in the LXX the number is much higher. A more conservative position regards the superscriptions as reliable early witnesses to the authorship and historical settings of the psalms.

The issue also revolves around the translation of לדוד. The *lamed* (ל) may denote *to, for, on behalf of,* or *about.* Or it may be understood as a *lamed* of authorship. In this case it is translated *by*. The *lamed* functions this way in Isa 38:9 and Hab 3:1 and, more importantly, in Ps 18:1 (MT) where the context of לדוד makes it clear that the psalm was composed by David (cf. 2 Sam 22:1). There is no textual evidence that the psalms ever lacked their superscriptions and texts like 1 Sam 16:14–23, 2 Sam 23:1, and Amos 6:5 support the idea that David was Israel's best-known psalmist. Moreover, the NT assumes that the superscriptions are correct (e.g., Mark 12:35; Acts 1:16–20; 2:25–28). It is therefore best to maintain that the psalmic introductions are part of the inspired text.

In addition to David, the following contributed to the Psalter: Asaph (twelve psalms), the sons of Korah (eleven psalms), Jeduthun (four psalms), and Solomon (two psalms). Moses, Heman, and Ethan contributed one psalm each.

### Names in the Psalms

Nearly two-thirds of the Psalms have names of OT figures associated with them. However, scholars cannot always tell whether they were written by these persons, for these persons, or about these persons. The chart below shows the names associated with various psalms.

| Name | Psalm Association | Contribution |
|---|---|---|
| **Moses:** died c. 1406 BC. Prophet who led Israel out of Egypt and received God's Law. | 90 | Moses led or provided for leadership in worship at the beginning of Israel's independence (Exod 15). |
| **David:** 1040–970 BC. Second king of Israel; warrior, prophet, and poet. | 3–9; 10?; 11–32; 34–41; 51–65; 68–70; 86; 101; 103; 108–10; 122; 124; 131; 133; 138–45 | David appointed 4,000 singers and musicians for the tabernacle. About half of all the psalms are attributed to David. |
| **Jeduthun (Ethan):** Time of David; family of Merari? | 39 | Levites/prophets appointed by David for praise at the tabernacle (1 Chr 25:1–3, 6). |
| **Heman:** Time of David; family of Kohath. | 88 | They used harps, lyres, and cymbals as accompaniment. |
| **Asaph:** Time of David and Solomon; family of Gershon. | 50; 73–83 | Different family groups cast lots to determine when they would serve. |
| **Sons of Korah:** Time of David and Solomon. | 42; 44–49; 84–85; 87–88 | Doorkeepers and musicians of the tabernacle and temple. |
| **Solomon:** died 931 BC. Israel's third king; wrote Proverbs, Song of | 72; 127 | Builder of the first temple; 3,000 proverbs and 1,005 songs, but very few psalms, are |

| Solomon, and Ecclesiastes. | | attributed to Solomon. |
|---|---|---|
| **Ethan:** Time of Solomon. | 89 | An Ezrahite, renowned for wisdom (1 Kgs 4:31). |
| **Anonymous:** Some of these psalms connect with the psalm that precedes them. Most anonymous psalms are in Book Five of the Psalter. | 1–2; 10?; 33; 43; 66–67; 71; 91–100; 102; 104–7; 111–21; 123; 125–26; 128–30; 132; 134–37; 146–50 | Pss 113–18 form the "Egyptian Hallel" of later Jewish liturgy, used at festivals. Pss 120–36 form the "Great Hallel." |

"Names in the Psalms" is from *TLSB* (St. Louis: Concordia, 2009), 840.

Because the Psalter is an anthology of prayers that were written by many people—from Moses (Ps 90) to those who lived after the Babylonian exile (e.g., Ps 126)—it is difficult to discuss the book's dating. Moreover, many of the psalms are historically nonspecific. Based upon the superscriptions, however, Craigie suggested that the book developed in four stages; (1) a psalm was composed, (2) it was joined together with similar psalms, (3) several smaller collections were brought together to form bigger units, finally (4) the Psalter emerged after various additional psalms were added by the final editors (e.g., Ps 1). Examples of intermediate-sized collections include Davidic psalms (Pss 3–41), psalms of ascent (Pss 120–134), and the hallelujah psalms (Pss 146–150). The overall shape of the Psalter, with its five books, reflects the Pentateuch. While an earlier edition of the Psalter only included Davidic psalms (Ps 72:20), the final composition took place after the Babylonian exile (cf. Pss 74, 89, 137).

At least thirty-nine Psalms manuscripts have been found at Qumran. The most important is the Psalms Scroll (11QPs[a]) which includes both canonical and extra-canonical psalms. Individual psalms are ordered differently in this manuscript.

## LITERARY FEATURES OF THE PSALTER

### POETRY

The psalms are poetic texts. In fact, roughly one half of the OT is couched in poetry. But how shall we define Hebrew poetry?

If we put aside preconceived definitions of biblical poetry and prose and look at different parts of the OT to see what distinguishes these genres from each other, it becomes apparent that there are not two modes of speech, but many different elements which elevate style and provide formality and strictness of organization. To use the categories of poetry and prose when studying the OT is to describe sections of the skyline as consisting either of "building" or "no building;" it is an oversimplification of the texts. Besides, Hebrew does not have a word that stands for "poetry" over against "prose." Kugel therefore attacks the whole notion that one can distinguish Hebrew poetry from prose. Rather he sees the two as existing on a continuum.

This is confirmed by Freedman who has argued that in standard prose the particle frequency (i.e., frequency of small words such as לא, אם, or כי) is fifteen percent or more, whereas in poetry the frequency is five percent or less. For a text to be strictly poetic, if it has one hundred words, then the particles את (the direct object marker), אשר (the relative pronoun), and words beginning with the definite article (ה) comprise five or fewer of the words. Texts using these particles between five percent and fifteen percent of the time fall somewhere in between poetry and prose.

The presence of meter in Hebrew poetry has been hotly debated. Josephus attempted to find Greek forms of meter in the OT. Freedman counted syllables and others counted Massoretic accents (neither of which is likely to have been the same when Hebrew poetry was first composed). Most scholars, therefore, believe that meter (as we know it from other forms of poetry) does not exist in Hebrew poetry. The most we can speak of is rhythm.

There is a scholarly consensus that parallelism is the main feature of Hebrew poetry. In 1753 Robert Lowth explained the three basic types of Hebrew poetic parallelism: (1) synonymous, the same thought is repeated; (2) antithetical, opposites are set alongside of each other; and (3) synthetic, an additional thought (neither synonymous nor antithetical) is added in the second or subsequent line. Kugel prefers to analyze Hebrew poetry even more simply as "A is so, and what's more, B." That is, the second line further defines or intensifies the previous thought. Along with parallelism, Hebrew poetry frequently employs alliteration, wordplays, gapping (or ellipsis), similes, and metaphors.

In addition to these features, Hebrew poetry frequently employs stanzas or strophes. Though quite flexible, the use of סלה, *Selah*, may denote refrains. Major thought units are also demarcated by means of a line like "Yahweh of armies is with us" (Ps 46:7, 10) or "Revive us, O God, let your face shine that we may be saved" (Ps 80:3, 7, 19). Acrostic settings (e.g., Pss 37, 119) are another way that psalmists employ strophes.

## The Psalter's Design

Up to the 1990s the dominant tendency was to study psalms individually in relation to their literary form (*Gattung* or genre) and worship setting (*Sitz im Leben*). It was assumed that psalms were contextless compositions—hermetically sealed literary units that did not communicate with their surrounding material. This approach, championed by Hermann Gunkel and his student Sigmund Mowinckel, remain part of the analysis but they now compete for attention alongside a growing interest in the structure of the Psalter as a whole.

The publication in 1985 of Gerald Wilson's Yale dissertation, *The Editing of the Hebrew Psalter*, was a landmark study and provided the framework in which macrostructural work on the Psalter could unfold in a systematic way. His foundational idea was that psalms are not randomly placed, something that Gunkel's form criticism largely presupposed. Based upon the study of other psalm-like depositories in the ancient Near East (e.g., the Sumerian Hymn Collection and the Qumran Psalm Manuscripts), Wilson laid the foundation for the investigation of the Psalter as a book in its own right with a plot, characters, and narrative movement. Wilson, who was heavily influenced by the canonical criticism made famous by his teacher Brevard Childs, argued that there are signs of deliberate ordering that reflect the theological concerns of the book's final editors.

Wilson organized his study around the use of frames. He pointed out the royal covenantal frame that consists of Pss 2, 72, 89, and 144 as well as a final wisdom frame that brought the entire book together. This is made up of Pss 1, 73, 90, 107, and 145 which are the first psalms of Books I, III, IV, and V, along with the final psalm of Book V proper. Taken together, these royal and wisdom frames mean that the Psalter is a book about Yahweh's gift of the monarchy that is the source of instruction for the faithful. Wilson and others assign a pivotal role to Ps 73 which stands just across the divide between Books II and III. If the final *Hallel* is omitted (Pss 146–150), then Ps 73 stands at the exact center of the remaining 145 psalm collection, suggesting that it serves as a paradigm that moves readers from lament to praise by way of candor and close communion with Yahweh.

Wilson further employed the vocabulary of "psalm seams" to denote the importance of psalms that appear at the beginning or ending of the Psalter's five books. For example, Ps 90 comes at a seam between Books III and IV and so is a significant piece to the Psalter's story. After Ps 89 has introduced the failure of the Davidic monarchy, Ps 90 is a prayer of Moses. While this psalm comes from a much earlier time than the exile, it is the voice of Moses that intercedes for Israel in her time of distress after the Babylonian devastation of 587. The compilers of this section of Psalms divert attention away from the monarchy—which had failed so miserably—and back to the intercession of Moses whose ministry saved the nation in an earlier time of Yahweh's judgment (cf. Exod 32–34). Moses' name appears seven times in Book IV (Pss 90–106), thus causing the interceding voice of Ps 90 to continue. This diversion from the fallen monarchy becomes even more evident in the "enthronement of Yahweh" psalms (Pss 93, 95–99), also appearing in Book IV. The thrust of this section of the Psalter is to turn Israel's eyes from the transient earthly monarchs to the eternal heavenly King—Yahweh. Moses pleads for Yahweh to relent (נחם) in Ps 90:13 (cf. Exod 32:12) and this is what God does in Ps 106:45. Therefore Book V begins with exuberant praise (Ps 107:1). Yahweh is gathering the exiles from the four corners of the earth (Ps 107:3).

Wilson further understands that the first three books (Pss 1–89) have a different editorial history than Books IV–V. Books I–III trace the Davidic monarchy from its institution (Ps 2) to its demise (Ps 89). Books IV–V reassert the kingship of Yahweh as a basis for life in a post-exilic community that lacks a Davidic king. Wilson also understands Ps 1 as an introduction to the Psalter which is very much in line with Childs's view.

Integrating the Psalter—as opposed to atomization—yields further interpretive insights. Two royal psalms, Pss 72 and 89, close their respective books, stamping a royal seal on those collections. Perhaps as much as anything, these royal psalms, once the Davidic dynasty had fallen, helped keep alive the hope that it would rise again. Messianic psalms (e.g., Pss 2, 16, 18, 20, 21, 22, 45, 72, 89, 101, 110, 118, 144) are therefore deliberately placed throughout the book in order to give structure and form to the Psalter that points readers to Israel's coming Messiah.

The last five psalms (Pss 145–150) are also strategically placed at the end of the book—and it is no coincidence that they are psalms of praise. Ps 149:6–7 states: "May the praises of God be in their mouths and a double-edged sword in their hands to inflict vengeance on the nations and punishment on the peoples." These verses suggest that praise is a weapon that brings Israel's enemies to their knees. For a people whose armies had been humiliated and their kings deposed, the powerful weapon of worship would accomplish the task of vengeance which the military and monarchy could never do (cf. Pss 8:3; 20:7).

## SUPERSCRIPTIONS

Superscriptions in the LXX often vary significantly from the MT. For instance, the MT has thirty-four psalms without titles, while the LXX only has two. Many of the superscriptions are general, e.g., שיר, *song*, and תפלה, *prayer*. Others are more obscure, e.g., מכתם (e.g., Pss 16; 56–60) and משכיל (e.g., Ps 32). Some superscriptions apparently denote melodies, e.g., שמינית (e.g., Ps 6), ששנים (e.g., Pss 45, 60, 69, 80), and אילת השחר (e.g., Ps 22). Fifty-five times psalms begin with למנצח, *to the director of music*, and fourteen times psalms tell us the occasion when David authored the psalm (e.g., Pss 3, 18, 51). The most famous obscure word in the Psalms is סלה, *Selah*. It is used seventy-one times in thirty-nine psalms (although never in a superscription) and most frequently appears at the close of a strophe.

## PSALM TYPES

Reading the Psalter holistically means that form critical categories, championed by Gunkel, are largely passé. It is now widely acknowledged that relatively few individual psalms fit neatly within Gunkel's genre categories. Many psalms feature two or more genres.

Brueggemann, therefore, provides a helpful way of looking at psalm types. There are psalms of orientation (e.g., Pss 8, 33, 37, 104, 145), disorientation (e.g., Pss 13, 35, 74, 79, 86, 88), and new orientation (e.g., Pss 23, 30, 34, 40, 124, 138). Additional psalm types include the following: Torah psalms (Pss 1, 19, 119); imprecatory psalms (e.g., Pss 35, 69, 79, 109, 137); psalms of trust (e.g., Pss 23,

27, 62, 63, 71, 131); creation psalms (e.g., Pss 8, 104, 148); and acrostic psalms (e.g., Pss 9–10, 25, 34, 37, 111, 112, 119, 145).

Because psalms of lament are the most frequent type of prayer in the Psalter, they deserve an extended discussion. Psalmists often acknowledge the raw experiences of feeling abandoned. They cry out to Yahweh, "How long?" (e.g., Pss 6:3; 13:1–3), "Where is God?" (e.g., Pss 42:3; 44:24; 79:10), "Why?" (e.g., Pss 10:1; 22:1; 43:2; 74:1), "Are you asleep?" (e.g., Ps 44:23), "Wake up!" (e.g., Pss 35:23; 59:4), and "Listen!" (e.g., Pss 17:1; 27:7; 30:10). These writers were transparent before Yahweh and were honest when they were grieved by life's catastrophes.

Laments express Israel's fury over the deep fissures of life. People frequently blame God for everything that is wrong. The principle complaint, though, is divine absence, often called "the dark night of the soul." Yahweh claims to have power over massive injustice, but the converse appears to be so. He is far away. Present realities negate his promises.

Such prayers exhibit a thoroughgoing candor about life's desperate moments and a profound honesty regarding deep pain. Heart-wrenching questions permeate Israel's laments. Why did this happen? Why did God allow it? Who is responsible? Is there any order in the world? Is Yahweh really the Creator and Redeemer? Will he deliver on what he said? How shall we live now that the future has been foreclosed? Such questions regard the abyss as perpetual, a world without end. For instance, Ps 88, surely one of the bleakest of the laments, ends with the word מחשך, *darkness* (Ps 88:18). Hopelessness defines everything.

The Psalter's laments, at the same time, tenaciously refuse to let go of God. They cling to him, no matter what, for driving these prayers are Yahweh's unconditional promises to Abraham, Isaac, and Jacob. Petitioners trusted that in his time God would turn wailing into dancing, remove their sackcloth, and clothe his people with joy (Ps 30:11).

## Outline of the Psalter

IV. Book Three: The Assyrian/Babylonian crisis (Pss 73–89)

V. Book Four: Introspection about the exile (Pss 90–106)

VI. Book V: Praise and reflection on the return to Judah and the new era (Pss 107–145)

VII. Conclusion: The Hallelujah Chorus (Pss 146–150)

Each of the Psalter's five divisions concludes with a doxology (Pss 41:13; 72:18–19; 89:52; 106:48; 150:1–6). The first three doxologies end with "Amen, amen," and the last two conclude with "Hallelujah." The last psalm, Ps 150, closes the Psalter with commands to praise Yahweh with unbridled joy.

Related psalms are often grouped together. They include Pss 9–10 (a semi-acrostic); Pss 42–43 (the same refrain); Pss 93, 95–99 (Yahweh is King); Pss 113–118 (the Egyptian Hallel); Pss 120–134 (Psalms of Ascent); Pss 146–150 (the Hallelujah Chorus). The Asaph Psalms include Pss 50, 73–83, while the Korah Psalms are Pss 42–49, 84–85, 87–88. The divine names appear in the Psalter with the following frequency:

### Frequency of Divine Names in the Five Books of the Psalms

| | |
|---|---|
| Pss 1–41 | Yahweh 273 times and Elohim fifteen times |
| Pss 42–72 | Elohim 164 times and Yahweh thirty times |
| Pss 73–89 | Yahweh forty-four times and Elohim forty-three times |
| Pss 90–106 | Yahweh 103 times and Elohim zero times |
| Pss 107–150 | Yahweh 236 times and Elohim seven times |

## THEOLOGICAL THEMES IN THE PSALTER

### THE TORAH AND MESSIAH

There is a scholarly consensus that Pss 1 and 2 introduce the Psalter with their twin themes of the Torah and Messiah. That these psalms should be interpreted together becomes clear through the words that they have in common: אשרי, *blessed* (Pss 1:1; 2:12); דרך, *way* (Pss 1:1; 2:12); הגה, *meditate* (Pss 1:2; 2:1); and אבד, *perish* (Pss 1:6;

2:12). Both psalms are also untitled. Pss 1–2, then, provide an orientation for reading the book of Psalms.

Although many of his ideas have not gained significant traction, Childs's canonical understanding of the Psalter has an abiding significance. He points out that the use of Torah in Ps 1:2 transforms the prayers in the Psalter from human words addressing Yahweh to Yahweh's words spoken to people. Since we do not know how to pray (cf. Rom 8:26), God graciously gives us the words.

While Ps 1 sets the agenda for the Psalter by contrasting the way of the righteous and the way of the wicked, along with its emphasis on the Torah, Ps 2 moves the focus to the Davidic king. Yahweh says to him, "You are my son; today I become your father." Ps 2, then, describes the inauguration of the Davidic covenant, Ps 72 reflects the transition of this covenant to successive kings, and Ps 89 laments Yahweh's apparent rejection of the Davidic covenant. All three psalms appear in seams (see above).

Why did the post-exilic editors of the Psalter retain these and other royal psalms when there was no king? The prayers were retained because of Israel's belief in an eschatological David (e.g., 2 Sam 7; 1 Chr 17; Hos 3:5; Ezek 34:23–24). All of the messianic psalms, when seen in this light, point to the coming of Christ.

The Torah and the Davidic monarchy are not only connected vis-à-vis Pss 1 and 2. The next royal psalms (Pss 18, 20, and 21) revolve around Ps 19, a Torah psalm. The third and last Torah psalm, Ps 119, is preceded by Ps 118 which depicts a king leading his people in an act of antiphonal worship. The monarch is the rejected stone who has become the cornerstone (Ps 118:22). These close links between the Torah and monarchy become stronger in light of Deut 17:14–20 which states that the king was to read a copy of the Torah "all the days of his life." The eschatological Davidic king, then, will keep Torah piety in an ultimate way.

While there are only a handful of royal psalms, the Davidic King subtly dominates the Psalter—and not only because seventy-three psalms are attributed to David. The book never gives up on David as a sign of divine presence and justice. After Ps 89, which laments what looks to be the end of the monarchy, the Psalter follows with messianic prayers that include Pss 101, 110, 132 and 144. Moreover, the pairing of Ps 144, which is messianic, with Ps 145, which maintains that Yahweh is King, suggests that human and divine rule are combined in Israel's eschatological hopes.

## THE RIGHTEOUS AND THE WICKED

Not only does Ps 1 set a major agenda for the Psalter through its focus on the Torah, but its accent on the righteous and the wicked provides a key to the book's message. A word count confirms that one of the Psalter's chief concerns is how the righteous will fair in light of the wicked ones' ongoing assault against them. For instance, צדיקים, *the righteous*, and related words (e.g., דל, *poor*, אביון, *needy*) appear 125 times in the book, while the root רשע, *wicked*, occurs eighty-two times in the Psalter, more than in any other OT book.

The wicked don't believe God notices them (Pss 14:1; 73:11) and in the end, the book promises that they will get their wish (Pss 1:6; 92:7–8). They can be likened to oxen (Ps 22:12, 21), lions (Ps 22:13, 20), and dogs (Ps 22:16, 20). The wicked, both personally and nationally, are rarely named, and concrete issues are not lodged against them. It is significant that the last phrase of the Psalter, before the book concludes with the hallelujah psalms (Pss 146–150), speaks to the different destinies of the righteous and the wicked (Ps 145:20–21).

A word related to צדק is ישר, *upright*. It frequently appears in the Psalms—twenty-five times. The righteous are also called עבדים, *servants* (e.g., Ps 90:13, 16), and עני, *afflicted* (e.g., Pss 34:6; 37:11). The godly actions of the righteous derive from their forgiven relationship with God and not from a state of their moral perfection. No one is righteous before Yahweh (Ps 143:2). This is why the plea goes out to God, "Deliver me in *your* righteousness" (Ps 31:1; cf. Pss 4:1; 5:8). The righteous embrace their need for God's grace, protection, and guidance. They are therefore typically pictured as humble, lowly, and needy (e.g., Ps 131) and express their relationship with Yahweh most frequently by means of praise. Their passive righteousness, conferred as a gift by Yahweh, propels them to live with integrity (e.g., Ps 15).

Being close to God is what the righteous yearn for the most and "refuge" is the most common idea that expresses this desire (e.g., Pss 2:12; 11:1; 37:40). The statement, "I shall not want" (Ps 23:1) demonstrates that their longing is only for Yahweh (cf. Ps 73:28). "One thing I ask from Yahweh; this is what I seek, that I may live in

Yahweh's house all the days of my life" (Ps 27:4). Indeed, better is one day in Yahweh's courts than a thousand elsewhere (Ps 84:10). Yahweh mercifully grants this longing of the righteous. He transplants them by canals of water (Ps 1:3)—that is, in his holy temple (Pss 46:4; 52:8; 93:12–13).

David is the paradigmatic righteous person in the Psalter. In the twelve psalms that present details in his life that led to the psalm's composition (Pss 3, 7, 18, 51, 52, 54, 56, 57, 59, 60, 62, 142), most frequently he laments the fact that the wicked are persecuting him but acknowledges that Yahweh will deliver him.

## THE PSALMS AND ISRAEL'S WORSHIP

The current emphasis on the Psalter's final form is so pronounced that it is easy to overlook how some psalms functioned earlier in Israel's worship life. Creach, for instance, notes that Num 10:35–36 depicts the ark moving from place to place with the words, "Arise, O Yahweh . . ." and "Return, O Yahweh . . ." Hence, when psalmists pray, "Arise, O God . . ." (e.g., Pss 10:12; 68:1; 82:8) or "Return, O Yahweh . . . " (e.g., Ps 132:8), he argues that they should be heard as part of a procession of the ark as it brings victory over God's enemies (Ps 24:7–10).

This is why Broyles posits the idea that even after the ark of the covenant was installed in Solomon's temple it was still used in festal and military processions. In Samuel, Kings, and Chronicles the ark goes by several different titles—for example, "strength," "cherubim," "throne," "footstool," "splendor," "glory," and "thick darkness." When these words are employed in psalms they often make reference to the ark (cf. e.g., Pss 68:24; 105:4; 132:8). The command, "Seek Yahweh and his strength, seek his face continually" (Ps 105:1), indicates more than just a pious wish. The plea instructs worshipers to orient themselves towards Yahweh's real presence in the ark. It is otherwise difficult to explain why the Chronicler used Ps 105:1–15 to describe David bringing the ark into Jerusalem (cf. 1 Chr 16:8–22).

The Psalter also witnesses to ritual acts in worship. For example, it mentions playing instruments (e.g., Pss 81:2–3; 144:9; 150:3–5), clapping and shouting (Ps 47:1), dancing (Ps 149:3), making sacrifices (Ps 118:27), and processing into the holy place (Ps 132:7). Several psalms include antiphonal aspects (Pss 118, 136).

## PSALMS AND MISSIONS

The Psalter has a universal scope. It contains over 175 references to the nations of the world. Yahweh's name is, for example, "majestic in all the earth" (Ps 8:1, 9), and the heavens declare his glory to the ends of the earth (Ps 19:1–6). He is exalted among the nations and in the earth (Ps 46:10). Yahweh is the Great King over all the earth (Ps 47:2) and is to be praised from the rising of the sun to where it sets (Ps 113:3). He rules from "sea to sea, from the River to the ends of the earth" (Ps 72:8). God has set his throne in heaven and his kingdom rules over all (Ps 103:19).

Yahweh's universality extends throughout eternity: "Yahweh is King for ever and ever" (Ps 10:16) and he is God "from everlasting to everlasting" (Ps 90:2). His kingdom is eternal and his dominion endures through all generations (Ps 145:13).

The vastness of Yahweh's creation and the complexities of the operations of nature demonstrate his universal rule. By his Word the heavens and their hosts were made (Ps 33:6). Yahweh is the maker of heaven and earth, the seas and everything in them (Ps 146:6). He does what he pleases in the heavens and the earth, in the seas and their depths. He sends lightening with the rain and brings the wind out of his storehouses (Ps 135:6–7). Yahweh makes grass grow on the hills and provides food for the cattle and the young ravens, for he is great and mighty in power and his understanding has no limit (Ps 147:5–9).

Because Yahweh is so vast in his universality, Israel is called upon to "proclaim among the nations what he has done" (Ps 9:11), indeed, to "sing of him among the nations" (Ps 108:4). Israel is to sing of his abundant goodness and joyfully celebrate his righteousness (Ps 145:1–7), with the goal that "all people are to extol him" (Ps 117:1).

Several psalms accent Israel's centrifugal missional emphasis. "I will make confession about you, O Yahweh, I will sing of you among the nations" (Ps 57:9). "Our mouths were filled with laughter, our tongues with songs of joy. Then it was said among the nations, 'Yahweh has done great things for them' " (Ps 126:2–3). "They will tell of the glory of your kingdom and speak of your might, so that all people may know of your mighty acts and the splendor of your kingdom" (Ps 145:11–12). The expected result is that all the ends of the earth will turn to Yahweh and all the families of the earth will bow down to worship him (Pss 22:26; 66:3; 86:8).

A more specific example of the Psalter's missional thrust comes from Ps 87. Ps 87:5 mentions Jerusalem's neighbors from all four points of the compass. Rahab is a symbolic name for Egypt (cf. Isa 30:7). The city of Babylon appears as Daughter Zion's constant adversary in the books of Isaiah and Jeremiah (e.g., Isa 13, 47; Jer 51). Philistia denotes the southwestern shoreline of Canaan and its inhabitants. The city of Tyre represents the Phoenician nation of merchants to the north, while Cush denotes the Ethiopian people, living south of Egypt. All of these nations are born in Zion. Ps 87—compared with other Zion Psalms (e.g. Pss 46, 48)—proclaims not the salvation *of* Zion but the salvation of the nations *through* Zion (cf. Gal 4:26).

## IMPRECATORY PSALMS

"Break the teeth in their mouth, O God!" (Ps 58:6). "The righteous will be glad when . . . they bathe their feet in the blood of the wicked" (Ps 58:10). "Blessed is he . . . who seizes your infants and dashes them against the rocks" (Ps 137:8–9). How did such barbaric words make their way into the prayer book of God's people?

The sentiments of broken teeth, bloody baths, and baby bashing are not confined to a few psalms. In fact, thirty-two of them fall under the ominous title "imprecatory." They are often categorized into three groups: imprecations against societal enemies (Pss 58, 94), imprecations against national enemies (Pss 68, 74, 79, 83, 129, 137), and imprecations against personal enemies (Pss 5, 6, 7, 9, 10, 17, 28, 31, 35, 40, 52, 54, 55, 56, 59, 69, 70, 71, 104, 109, 139, 140, 141, 143).

What are we to make of these prayers? Gen 12:3 is helpful. Here Yahweh promises Abram, "The one cursing you אאר, *I will curse.*" The verb אאר is a Qal imperfect from the root ארר. When the same verbal form—ארור—appears in Israel's cursing texts (e.g., Deut 27), it is a Qal, passive participle. Yahweh curses in the *active* aspect of the verb; Israel curses in the *passive* aspect. This grammar and theology are summed up when Yahweh says, "Vengeance is mine, I will repay" (Deut 32:35; cf. Rom. 12:19).

Yahweh's vengeance arises out of a cultural milieu in which cursing was an integral part of life. Ancient Near Eastern texts are filled with treaty curses, inscriptional curses, and incantations to undo curses. Often these blessings and curses were employed to ensure a vassal's loyalty to his sovereign. While the earthly sovereign played an important role in either bestowing favor or calling down curses upon his subject, most of these texts indicate that it was the god's duty to execute either blessings or curses.

It is out of this mindset that the imprecatory psalms are prayed. When psalmists call down curses it is because enemies have been disloyal to Yahweh's covenant promises to Abraham. As a consequence, the covenant breaker deserves Yahweh's covenant curses (cf. Lev 26; Deut 28).

Several texts from Isaiah exhibit the theology of imprecation in the Psalter. When Yahweh enacts vengeance, "his sword is all blood, it is gorged with fat" (Isa 34:6), but this is because he is "contending for Zion" (Isa 34:8). Without vengeance upon Israel's enemies there can be no salvation for Israel (cf. Isa 35:4). This is why, in times of acute and ongoing distress, psalmists invoke the severity of God as expressed in the imprecatory psalms. It is their way of coming before God and throwing the sword to him, for "the battle belongs to Yahweh" (1 Sam 17:47).

## CHRIST IN PSALMS

While speaking after his resurrection, Jesus teaches that everything written about him in the Psalms must be fulfilled (Luke 24:44). Just as David is both a righteous sufferer and the ideal defender of the lowly and afflicted in the Psalter, Jesus is all of this and so much more. On Good Friday the centurion made the confession that Christ is the Righteous One (Luke 23:47).

But this is just the tip of the iceberg. The book of Psalms prophesies much of our Lord's life and ministry. Consider these connections: Christ's baptism (Ps 2:7/Matt 3:17; Mark 1:11; Luke 3:22); his temptations in the wilderness (Ps 91:11–12/Matt 4:6; Luke 4:10); cleansing the temple (Ps 69:9/John 2:17); teaching parables (Ps 78:2/Matt 13:35); feeding the 5,000 (Ps 78:24/John 6:31); Palm Sunday (Ps 8:2/Matt 21:16; Ps 118:25–26; Matt 21:9; Mark 11:9; Luke 19:38; John 12:13); David's Son and David's Lord (Ps 110:1/e.g., Matt 22:44; Mark 12:36; Luke 20:42–43); the rejected Stone (Ps 118:22–24/e.g., Matt 21:42; Mark 12:10–11; Luke 20:17); betrayal in the Upper Room (Ps 41:9/John 13:18); mocked on Good Friday (Ps 22:7–8/Matt 27:46; Mark 15:34); lots casted for his clothes (Ps 22:18/Matt 27:35; Mark 15:24; Luke 23:34; John 19:23–24);

thirsting on the cross (Ps 69:21/John 19:28–30); forsaken by the Father (Ps 22:1/Matt 27:46; Mark 15:34); committing his spirit to the Father (Ps 31:5; Luke 23:46); none of his bones were broken (Ps 34:20; John 19:36); and, most gloriously, his resurrection from the dead (Ps 16:10/Acts 2:28–31; 13:35). No wonder the Psalter is one of the most loved and treasured books in the OT.

### SIN AND GRACE IN PSALMS

The Psalter, in great detail, describes the sins of the wicked. Ps 36:1–4, for example, offers a most damning description of all evildoers. They repay their friends with evil and plunder enemies without cause (Ps 7:4). Such people use their tongues to slander (Ps 15:3), they take bribes (Ps 15:5), love falsehood (Ps 24:4), are unfaithful to the covenant (Ps 44:17), trust in riches (Ps 62:10), and they sin with their lips, heart, and deeds (Ps 141:3–4). The wicked say there is no God (Pss 14:1; 53:1).

But the book of Psalms also describes the sins of the righteous. After all, if Yahweh would mark iniquities, no one could stand (Ps 130:3). Note the seven penitential psalms (Pss 6, 32, 38, 51, 102, 130, and 143). Within these passages we hear believers confess their sin (e.g., Pss 32:5; 38:8; 51:1, 3) and David even admits that he was conceived in sin (Ps 51:5).

But all the more, the righteous rejoice that Yahweh removes their sins—as far as the east is from the west (Ps 103:12). God pours out this lavish grace because of his חסד, *covenant loyalty* (Ps 103:8). He has ordained it that covenant loyalty should pursue believers all the days of their lives (Ps 23:6). When Ethan the Ezrahite begins his long lament over the downfall of David's house he begins by laying claim to God's covenant loyalty (Ps 89:1). And when Judah is restored after the Babylonian captivity, Ps 136 celebrates God's enduring covenant loyalty twenty-six times. Yahweh has a tenacious love and a ready resolve to remain committed to Israel, come what may.

## CONCLUSION

Paul writes, "Be filled with the Spirit, speaking to one another with psalms, hymns, and spiritual songs, singing and making melody with your heart to the Lord, always giving thanks for all things in the name of our Lord Jesus Christ to God the Father" (Eph 5:18–20; cf. Col 3:16). The apostle invites Christians to reread the Psalter's meditations, cries, shouts, and songs in light of the salvation accomplished by God the Father through the Lord Jesus Christ. Paul encourages a lifestyle of joyous dependence on Christ, living in faith like the psalmists. Examples of the Holy Spirit filling people to speak psalm-like prayers include Mary (Luke 1:46–55), Zechariah (Luke 1:67–80), and Simeon (Luke 2:27–32). The early church also leaned heavily on the psalms in their preaching (e.g., Acts 2:24–36) and their prayers (Acts 4:24–31).

## SELECT BIBLIOGRAPHY

Brueggemann, Walter. *The Message of the Psalms*. Minneapolis: Augsburg Fortress, 1984.

Childs, Brevard. *Introduction to the Old Testament as Scripture*. Minneapolis: Augsburg Fortress, 1979.

Craigie, Peter. *Psalms 1–50*. Word Biblical Commentary 19. Waco: Word, 1983.

Creach, Jerome F. D. *The Destiny of the Righteous in the Psalms*. St. Louis: Chalice Press, 2008.

Firth, David, and Philip S. Johnston. *Interpreting the Psalms: Issues and Approaches*. Downers Grove: InterVarsity, 2005.

Freedman, David N. *Pottery, Poetry, and Prophecy: Studies in Early Hebrew Poetry*. Winona Lake: Eisenbrauns, 1980.

Kugel, James. *The Idea of Biblical Poetry: Parallelism and Its History*. New Haven: Yale University Press, 1981.

Lessing, Reed. "Broken Teeth, Bloody Baths, and Baby Bashing." *Concordia Journal* 32 (2006): 76–79.

Wilson, Gerald. *The Editing of the Hebrew Psalter*. Society of Biblical Literature Dissertation Series 76. Chico: Scholars Press, 1985.

# 18

# PROVERBS

Proverbs is a much-loved book of the Bible, with many Christians turning to it to find practical advice for godly living. The short, pithy sayings that occupy most of the book lend themselves to being treated in just this way. However, Proverbs is more than a biblical self-help book. It is overflowing with divine wisdom that provides a guide to understanding the mind of God as he reveals his will in words that point primarily to his grace while also disclosing his wrath against sinners. Proverbs is not known for great passages that show us God's love, but to read it without this perspective is to misread its message. Nevertheless, there are a few important passages in the book that highlight God's love and grace, and to overlook them is to turn Proverbs into nothing more than another writing about making one's way in life. However, with an understanding of the centrality of the gospel, the sayings in this book reveal life in this world that anticipates the glorious life in the eternal kingdom that God wishes to grant to all people.

## AUTHORSHIP, COMPOSITION, AND DATE

Of all of the wisdom literature of the Bible, the book of Proverbs is most closely associated with Solomon, especially in the popular imagination of most Christians. Yet it would surprise many that some parts of this book are attributed to other authors.

### *The Authors of the Sections of Proverbs*

| | |
|---|---|
| Prov 1:1–9:18 | Solomon |
| Prov 10:1–22:16 | Solomon |

| Prov 22:17–24:22 | Wise people |
| Prov 22:23–34 | Wise people |
| Prov 251–29:27 | Solomon (as copied by Hezekiah's men) |
| Prov 30:1–33 | Agur, son of Jakeh |
| Prov 31:1–9 | Lemuel (or his mother) |
| Prov 31:10–31 | Unknown |

Clearly, Proverbs is a book of composite authorship, having been shaped by a later editor (or editors) into the form that is now preserved in the OT. It likely grew in stages beginning with Solomon's reign (971–932) and ending in Judah's late monarchic period.

### *The Growth of Proverbs*

| | |
| --- | --- |
| Solomon writes Prov 1:1–22:16 and compiles Prov 22:17–24:34 | 971–941 |
| Hezekiah's men compile Prov 25–29 | 716–687 |
| Agur writes Prov 30 | 7th century |
| Lemuel (possibly Hezekiah or Josiah) | 716–687 or 641–610 |
| Final editor writes 31:10–31 | 686–457 |

### AUTHORSHIP OF PROVERBS 1:1–22:16

Critical scholars (and a growing number of evangelicals) often argue that Prov 1–9 was composed later than Solomon's time, usually in the early Persian period or, according to Fox, perhaps as late as Hellenistic times. This position stems primarily from evolutionary assumptions about wisdom literature: that the longer, more extended discussions found in Prov 1–9 must have developed later than the shorter aphoristic wisdom as found in much of the rest of the book. However, there is no sound basis for these evolutionary assumptions. The *length* of a composition is not a reliable indicator of its age in relation to other works in the same genre. For instance, the books of Samuel and Kings are fairly long historical works, but 1 Maccabees, a much later book, is shorter than both. Nor can one argue that since the themes explored in Prov 1–9 are treated in a more complete and thorough way than the subsequent short sayings, these chapters must be a later development. Aphoristic wisdom as found in most of Proverbs was not designed to explore themes in any depth, and this continues to be true: an aphorism coined today would not be as thorough in its exploration of its content as would an essay on the same subject composed decades ago.

There have been several observations by scholars confirming that Prov 1:1–22:16 is Solomon's work. Because of the way it is organized, Kitchen and Garrett have argued that this section of Proverbs follows the generic conventions for wisdom literature of the early first millennium.

### The Organization of Prov 1–24

| | | |
|---|---|---|
| Title | 1:1 | "The proverbs of Solomon, son of David, king of Israel" |
| Prologue | 1:2–7 | |
| Main text 1 | 1:8–9:18 | |
| Subtitle | 10:1 | "The proverbs of Solomon" |
| Main text 2 | 10:1–22:16 | |
| Titular interjection | 22:17 | "Open your ears and listen to the words of wise people . . . " |
| Main text 3 | 22:18–24:22 | |
| Titular interjection | 24:23 | "These are also by wise people" |
| Main text 4 | 24:23–34 | |

Moreover, based on the vocabulary, thought, and style, Steinmann maintains that Prov 1–9 and Prov 10:1–22:16 most likely come from the same author. Since Proverbs identifies that author as Solomon, there is good reason to accept that Israel's wise king wrote this material.

### AUTHORSHIP OF PROVERBS 22:17–24:34

Two collections of sayings from unnamed wise people (cf. Prov 22:17; 24:23) are appended to the proverbs of Solomon in 10:1–22:16. Perhaps these are people mentioned at 1 Kgs 4:29–31 whom

Solomon surpassed in wisdom: men of the east (perhaps in Syria, Assyria, and Babylon), the Egyptians, and some Israelites such as Ethan the Ezrahite, and Mahol's sons Heman, Calcol, and Darda. Since the discovery and publication of the ancient Egyptian *Wisdom of Amenemope* in the 1920s, scholars have been fairly certain that at least some of these sayings originated from this collection of Egyptian wisdom, which probably originates from Egypt's twentieth dynasty during the twelfth century. There are close parallels between *Amenemope* and a number of the sayings in Prov 22–23. That Solomon would cite an Egyptian source as an example of the wisdom of others is not surprising given that 1 Kgs 4:30 compares his wisdom to that of the Egyptians. Moreover, Solomon may have had contact with Egyptian wisdom through his wife (1 Kgs 3:1) and his trading partners (1 Kgs 10:28). Most likely, then, Prov 22:17–24:34 consists of two appendices to Prov 10:1–22:16 penned by Solomon on the basis of wisdom literature produced by others in Israel and the wider ancient Near East.

## AUTHORSHIP OF PROVERBS 25–29

Prov 25–29 begins with a notice that this section was transcribed by "the men of King Hezekiah," perhaps royal scribes or priests in Jerusalem. Hezekiah reigned from 716 to 687 BC. Prov 25:1 says that גם־אלה, *these also*, are the proverbs of Solomon. This notice was probably placed here by the final editor or editors of the book. What cannot be ascertained is whether these proverbs were simply copied by Hezekiah's men or whether they also are responsible for the editing and arrangement of these proverbs.

## AUTHORSHIP OF PROVERBS 30

Prov 30:1 credits this chapter to a certain Agur, son of Jakeh. Since Prov 30:11–33 contains mostly numerical sayings in contrast to Prov 30:1–10 which has no numerical sayings, some have suggested that only Prov 30:1–10 should be credited to Agur and that Prov 30:11–33 comes from an anonymous author. However, Steinmann has argued that all of Prov 30 should be viewed as a single composition from Agur. Since this section follows the proverbs of Solomon copied by Hezekiah's men, and since Agur's words are characterized as משא, *an oracle*, a word commonly used by the Judean prophets of the eighth through sixth centuries (e.g., Isa 13:1; 23:1; 30:6; Nah 1:1), a seventh-century date for Agur's activity seems likely.

### AUTHORSHIP OF PROVERBS 31

Prov 31:1 attributes the book's last chapter to a certain King Lemuel's mother as words she used to discipline him. This applies at least to Prov 31:1–9, though Garrett favors the view that it also pertains to Prov 31:10–31, an acrostic poem about a godly wife. Lemuel cannot be identified, though it may be a throne name for one of Judah's kings, most likely Hezekiah (716–687) or Josiah (641–610). The acrostic poem perhaps comes from the final editor of Proverbs. Its theme of a godly wife is reminiscent of the blessings of marriage and warnings against adultery in Prov 1–9. The godly wife exhibits some of the attributes of Lady Wisdom (Prov 3:14–16, 18), showing that she has received and employed divine wisdom.

## LITERARY FEATURES OF PROVERBS

Since Proverbs is a composite book, it is also not surprising that it contains several different genres. Most readers are familiar with the short aphorisms that make up the bulk of Prov 10–29. These short, pithy statements can be classified into several different types (see below). However, Proverbs also contains extended discourses (Prov 1–9), an acrostic poem (Prov 31:10–31), and prayers (Prov 30:1–10).

### Outline of Proverbs

I.  Solomon's instruction about wisdom (1:1–9:18)
    A.  Superscription and Solomon's preface (1:1–7)
    B.  Discourses on wisdom (1:8–9:18)
        1.  First address to a son: Avoid the company of sinners (1:8–19)
        2.  First poem about wisdom: Wisdom's call and the fate of those who refuse to listen (1:20–33)
        3.  Second address to a son: Wisdom's protection (2:1–22)
        4.  Third address to a son: Wisdom leads to a proper relationship with Yahweh (3:1–20)
        5.  Fourth address to a son: Wisdom leads to a proper relationship with one's neighbor (3:21–35)

6. Address to sons: Solomon's parents taught him to value wisdom (4:1–9)

7. Fifth address to a son: Wisdom teaches the difference between wicked and righteous people (4:10–19)

8. Sixth address to a son: Advice for living a righteous life (4:20–27)

9. Seventh address to a son: Wisdom teaches one to avoid adultery (5:1–23)

10. Eighth address to a son: Wisdom leads away from trouble (6:1–19)

11. Ninth address to a son: A father teaches his son to avoid fornication (6:20–35)

12. Tenth address to a son: Wisdom will keep one from adultery and its final result, death (7:1–27)

13. Second poem about wisdom: God's Wisdom and her invitation to life (8:1–36)

14. Third poem about wisdom: Contrast between Lady Wisdom and Lady Foolishness (9:1–18)

II. Solomon's proverbs (10:1–22:16)

   A. A wise son: Introduction to wisdom and righteousness (10:1–12:28)

   B. A wise son: Wise ways to life (13:1–15:19)

   C. Advice to a wise son (15:20–17:24)

   D. A foolish son: Avoiding fools and foolishness (17:25–19:12)

   E. A foolish son: Dealing with fools and foolishness (19:13–22:16)

III. The words of wise people (22:17–24:22)

IV. More words of wise people (24:23–34)

V. Solomon's proverbs copied by Hezekiah's men (25:1–29:27)

   A. Superscription (25:1)

   B. Advice for kings and leaders (25:2–27)

   C. All about fools (25:28–27:4)

   D. Dealing with family, friends, and other people (27:5–22)

   E. More advice for kings and leaders (27:23–29:27)

VI. Agur's proverbs (30:1–33)

    A.  Superscription (30:1a)

    B.  Agur's prayers and advice (30:1b–10)

    C.  Agur's list proverbs (30:11–33)

VII. King Lemuel's proverbs (31:1–9)

VIII. Acrostic poem about a godly wife (31:10–31)

Understanding proverbs can be challenging, because they often refer to customs in ancient Israel that are no longer part of our society. In addition, as is true of all proverbs in all cultures, the surface meaning does not necessarily indicate the full scope or proper application for a particular proverb. Consider the English adage "a stitch in time saves nine," which on the surface seems to be about keeping one's clothes in proper repair. However, the advice offered by this proverb is really about taking proper action to correct a problem in order to stave off more serious problems in the future.

## WISDOM VOCABULARY

### Wisdom Words

As we might expect, a cluster of words is associated with the description of wisdom and wise ways of living in Proverbs and in other wisdom literature in the OT. This vocabulary not only includes words associated with wisdom, but also embraces words descriptive of foolishness.

In Proverbs, the word חכמה, *wisdom*, is often used in parallel constructions with other words that describe specific aspects of wisdom: דעת, *knowledge*; שכל, *good sense*; בינה, *understanding*; ערמה, *prudence*; מזמה, *insight*; and תושיה, *sound judgment*. In addition, some vocabulary describes training and guidance in wise behavior: מוסר, *discipline*; תחבלות, *guidance*; and עצה, *advice*. All of these words point to a wisdom that ultimately derives from God and is founded upon a positive relationship with him. This is summed up in the phrase יראת יהוה, *the fear of Yahweh*.

### Words Relating to Foolishness

Several words are commonly translated *fool* in most English translations but have differing denotations in Hebrew. כסיל is the generic word for fool, whereas אויל denotes a fool who willfully rejects good and purposely chooses evil, while נבל denotes a fool who rejects God and his ways. Some other words also describe fools and their behavior, including פתי, *gullible person* (often translated *simple*); לץ, *mocker*; חסר-לב, *lacking sense*; בער, *stupid*; and רמיה, *laziness*. All of these describe fools, not simply as simpletons, but as alienated from God and his ways.

## Types of Sayings in Proverbs

Since much of Proverbs consists of short aphorisms—even employing them at times in the longer, extended discourse in Prov 1–9—it is important to understand how these sayings communicate. It is notable, for instance, that some simply observe the way life is in a fallen, sinful world. They are not meant to offer advice. Instead, these proverbs inform readers of what kind of situations they might encounter. For example,

> One person pretends to be rich, but has nothing, another person pretends to be poor, but has great wealth. (Prov 13:7)

However, many proverbs go beyond a simple observation to add a conclusion about what has been observed. These sayings imply that a wise person will note the conclusion and behave accordingly. Sometimes this advice is quite subtle, while in other observation and conclusion proverbs the guidance is much more apparent. One example of an observation and conclusion proverb is Prov 13:20:

> Whoever walks with wise people becomes wise, but a companion of fools will be harmed.

A few proverbs directly commend certain wise actions, while others prohibit acting unwisely. These leave readers little choice in behavior if they wish to behave wisely. Many of these proverbs combine commands and prohibitions:

> Do not love sleep, or you will become poor. Keep your eyes open, and you will have enough to eat. (Prov 20:13)

These differing levels of advice in Proverbs are meant to guide readers as they ponder God's wisdom. Each saying ought to be understood in its own right as falling somewhere on a spectrum of those offering specific guidance and those giving a fair amount of freedom as to how and when to implement the instruction.

# TEXTUAL ISSUES

The text of Proverbs is preserved not only in Hebrew but also in several other ancient versions. Most of these are dependent in some way upon the LXX.

## THE MASORETIC TEXT OF PROVERBS

Most of the MT of Proverbs is well-preserved. However, several places in the MT are extremely difficult and perhaps have suffered from scribal corruption. A prime example is Prov 30:1b: "To Ithiel, to Ithiel and Ucal." This reading, which understands Ithiel and Ucal to be proper names—probably men to whom Agur addressed his wisdom—is highly problematic. The repetition of a proper noun is unusual, and the name Ucal occurs nowhere else. Most likely the text suffered from a problem in its transmission. It appears as if the divisions between some of the words were lost, and when vowel pointing was added later, it was an attempt to make sense of this corrupt text. It is more likely that the LXX has correctly reconstructed this phrase: "I'm weary, God; I'm weary God and worn out." Unlike the repetition of a name, this type of repetition for emphasis occurs elsewhere (e.g., 1 Chr 16:28; Ps 29:1; 96:7; Prov 31:4). Thus, the MT of Proverbs, though often presenting a reliable text, has a few places which call for text critical scrutiny.

## THE SEPTUAGINT OF PROVERBS

The ancient Greek translation of Proverbs was probably produced in the second century BC. While attempting to make Proverbs understandable for a Hellenized audience, the translator often closely followed a text that apparently was nearly identical to the MT. However, at other times he seems to have paraphrased, interpreted, or even rewritten sections in order to make them more relevant to his audience. Moreover, the LXX omits more than a few proverbs found in the MT and adds others. In addition to all of this, the LXX rearranged the end of Proverbs, placing Prov 30:1–14 between Prov 24:22 and 24:23; Prov 30:15–31:9 between Prov 24:34 and 25:1; and Prov 30:10–31 after 29:27. In making these rearrangements, all mention of authors or editors other than Solomon were removed, making the entire book appear to come from the pen of Israel's wise king.

# THEOLOGICAL THEMES IN PROVERBS

Since Proverbs covers nearly every area of ancient Israel's life (except worship, which is barely mentioned), there are a wide variety of themes in the book, including wealth and poverty, work and laziness, honesty and deceit, marital faithfulness and adultery, and most importantly, wisdom and foolishness. Therefore, it is difficult to characterize theological themes and accents for the book as a whole. However, two important motifs should be noticed: how Proverbs portrays the second person of the Trinity, as well as its treatment of human sin and divine grace.

## CHRIST IN PROVERBS

While there are few passages in Proverbs that expressly point forward to the coming Messiah, several speak of God's Wisdom in terms that point to the second person of the Trinity and have been understood this way since the earliest Christian writers. Prov 3:13–20 first introduces Wisdom personified as a woman (taking advantage of the grammatical gender of the word חכמה). In this passage, Wisdom's attributes, value, and benefits are praised. At the very end, however, Wisdom is portrayed as more than simply a personification. She is the instrument through which Yahweh created the world (Prov 3:19–20; cf. John 1:1–3).

Prov 8 further develops this theme. In the first part of this chapter Wisdom herself speaks, calling people to receive her benefits (Prov 8:1–11). Then she describes herself, her power, and her gifts to humans (Prov 8:12–21). Here Wisdom is divine, since she empowers kings to rule (Prov 8:15–16). Finally, Prov 8:22–31 is Wisdom's self-description of her role in creation. Yahweh possessed Wisdom from the very beginning, and she was at creation and participated in it. Based on the content of these passages, the first Christians understood Wisdom in Prov 8 to be the pre-incarnate Son of God. In 1 Cor 1:18–31 Paul is clearly building upon Prov 8 when he declares that "Christ [is] the power of God and the Wisdom of God." The apostle also adopts language from Prov 8 at Col 2:2–3 to describe Christ (compare Prov 8:9–11, 21; cf. 1 Cor 2:7–8). Jesus also identified himself as Wisdom (cf. Matt 11:19; 12:42; 23:34; Luke 7:34–35; 11:31, 49). Based on these passages, many of the early church fathers including Origen, Tertullian, and Cyprian understood Prov 8 as being about the pre-incarnate Son of God. In fact, it can be affirmed that nearly every prominent Christian from St. Paul onward through the fourth century agreed that Prov 8 was about Christ.

This interpretation of Proverbs is also important in the development of the church's historic creeds. Based on Prov 8:22 in the LXX, which reads "God ἔκτισέν, *created*, me at the beginning of his ways . . . " (in contrast to the MT's "God קָנָנִי, *possessed*, me . . . "), Arius held that Christ was not divine from eternity but was a creature of God. The Arian controversy was finally put to rest at the Council of Nicea (325) which affirmed Christ's eternal generation from the Father, a truth still confessed in churches that profess the Nicene Creed.

### SIN AND GRACE IN PROVERBS

Sin, the transgressing of God's Law, and its opposite, obedience to God's will, is an ongoing motif in Proverbs. Many of the aphorisms pay close attention to the principles of life in a fallen world. Quite a few of them are designed to restrain sinful behavior by warning of sin's consequences—often in this life (e.g., Prov 6:32–35), but at times the consequences are eternal (e.g., Prov 7:24–27). A good number of the proverbs, however, are designed to guide the believer toward behavior that is pleasing to God. These presuppose that readers are already in a positive relationship with Yahweh through faith and have received his gift of forgiveness and life. Fewer of the proverbs are overtly designed to drive the hearer to sorrow over sin which might lead to repentance. However, since whenever God's law is invoked it accuses sinners of sin, this function of the law is never completely absent.

While Proverbs does not have a large number of well-known passages that speak of God's grace toward repentant sinners, it nevertheless contains some passages that speak to believers of God's promises of life and salvation. Repentant Israel has been brought by Yahweh into a relationship in which it depends on his mercy and kindness even though it does not deserve such favor from him. In addition, scattered throughout Proverbs are a number of sayings that point to God's goodness and work in the lives of his people, highlighting his grace:

Whoever places his trust in wealth will fall, *but righteous people will sprout like foliage.* (Prov 11:28)

In the path of righteousness there is life, And the way of its pathway is no death. (Prov 12:28)

## CONCLUSION

Proverbs is a collection of God-revealed wisdom sayings from Israel's kingdom period. Much of it comes from Solomon. However, wisdom is a gift that God bestows on all believers, so several other wise men also contributed to this collection. Much of the book concerns the believer's life in this world as a walk with God who calls them from their sinful ways and shows them how to live according to his will. Nevertheless, Proverbs also focuses on God's grace in saving repentant sinners through the work of his Son, who is God's eternal wisdom.

## SELECT BIBLIOGRAPHY

Fox, Michael V. *Proverbs 1–31: A New Translation and Commentary*. Anchor Bible 18A and 18B. New York: Doubleday, 2000 and New Haven: Yale, 2009.

Garrett, Duane A. *Proverbs, Ecclesiastes, Song of Songs*. New American Commentary 14. Nashville: Broadman, 1993.

Kitchen, Kenneth A. "Proverbs and Wisdom Books of the Ancient Near East: The Factual History of a Literary Form." *Tyndale Bulletin* 28 (1977): 69–114.

Longmann, Tremper. *Proverbs*. Baker Commentary on the Old Testament Wisdom and Psalms. Grand Rapids: Baker, 2006.

Overland, Paul. "Structure in *The Wisdom of Amenemope* and Proverbs." In *"Go to the Land I will Show You": Studies in Honor of Dwight W. Young*. Edited by Joseph E. Coleson and Victor H. Matthews, 275–91. Winona Lake, IN: Eisenbrauns, 1996.

Steinmann, Andrew. "Proverbs 1–9 as a Solomonic Composition." *Journal of the Evangelical Theological Society*, 43 (2000): 659–74.

———. *Proverbs*. Concordia Commentary. St. Louis: Concordia, 2009.

———. "Three Things ... Four Things ... Seven Things: The Coherence of Proverbs 30:11–33 and the Unity of Proverbs 30." *Hebrew Studies* 423 (2001): 59–66.

# ECCLESIASTES

People in our day often note the absurdities and futility of human existence. Intellectuals explore dystopian perspectives on society, finding little hope and much despair over the human condition. However, this view of humanity's helplessness in the midst of life and the face of death is not simply our concern. Some of the same themes are explored by Qoheleth in the book of Ecclesiastes.

## AUTHORSHIP, COMPOSITION, AND DATE

### AUTHORSHIP AND COMPOSITION

Much of Ecclesiastes is related in the first person by a figure who calls himself קהלת, *Qoheleth* (cf. Eccl 1:2, 12), a feminine singular participle from the Hebrew root קהל, signifying to gather or assemble people. Thus, *Qoheleth* probably indicates a person who presides over an assembly. It has been variously translated: preacher, teacher, and spokesman. The LXX translated it as ἐκκλησιαστής, *a member of the assembly*, from which the English title of the book is derived.

Qoheleth describes himself as "king over Israel in Jerusalem" (Eccl 1:12), and the book's superscription describes him as "son of David, king in Jerusalem" (Eccl 1:1). While any descendant of David could be called "son of David," only one was king of *Israel* in Jerusalem: Solomon. Traditionally, then, Qoheleth has been identified with Solomon, and the words attributed to him were viewed as penned by Solomon.

However, there are a few third person passages in Ecclesiastes: Eccl 1:1; 7:27; 12:9–14. For this reason, some have thought that a later editor reworked Solomon's words and added these third person passages. Others have defended the entire book, including the third person passages, as Solomon's work. For instance, Bollhagen claims that in Eccl 12:9–14 Solomon, out of modesty, resorts to the third person to summarize his observations in the book's epilogue. However, Bollhagen is forced to admit that Qoheleth displayed no such modesty earlier (e.g., Eccl 1:12–16). Since Bollhagen offers no explanation as to the sudden compulsion to modesty at the very end of Ecclesiastes, this explanation seems forced and doubtful. Moreover, Eccl 7:27 says, " 'See, this is what I found,' said Qoheleth, '[I added] one thing to another to find the scheme of things.' " As Fox has observed, "While one can speak of himself in the third person, it is unlikely he would do so in the middle of a first-person sentence."[1] Fox is arguing that "said Qoheleth" is a strange interruption in this quotation if the author is Qoheleth. Instead, one might expect, " 'This is what I found,' I said [to myself] . . . " or a complete omission of the interposed "said Qoheleth." However, if the author is someone other than Qoheleth, the interruption in the quotation is more reasonably explained.

Added to this are the statements about Qoheleth's identity in Eccl 1:12 and 1:16. Eccl 1:12 is often understood to say, "I, Qoheleth, *was* king over Israel in Jerusalem." The past tense is thought to preclude these from being Solomon's own words, since there was no time during Solomon's life when he had abdicated the throne and could speak of it as a past situation. However, the verb היה, a perfect aspect verb form, does not necessarily correspond to a simple past tense, it could be understood as corresponding to an English present perfect tense: "I have been king," allowing for the statement to have been made by Solomon.

Similarly, at Eccl 1:16 Qoheleth states, "I have surpassed in wisdom everyone who ruled Jerusalem before me." It is often noted that only David ruled Jerusalem before Solomon, unless one includes the Jebusite rulers of the city who reigned before David conquered it (cf. 2 Sam 5:6–7). Since the Jebusites were pagans, many think that Solomon cannot be referring to them. However, the wisdom that Qoheleth talks about throughout Ecclesiastes is very worldly, a

---

[1] Michael V. Fox, "Frame-Narrative and Composition in the Book of Qoheleth." *Hebrew Union College Annual* 48 (1977): 84.

wisdom "under the sun"—that is, it is derived from observing the human condition more than it is from special revelation from God. There is no inherent reason why Qoheleth could not be including Jebusite rulers of the city in his statement about surpassing all of Jerusalem's rulers. This type of wisdom primarily derives from God's general revelation via human observation and reason and was as accessible to Jebusites as it was to Israelites.

For these reasons many scholars, both critical and more conservative ones, have viewed Qoheleth as a persona adopted by the author. For a time in Eccl 1–2 this author adopts the perspective and attitude of Solomon. However, it is then noted that there is little in the text of Eccl 3–12 that comes from a royal perspective, and some of the statements seem to come from someone critically observing the behavior of powerful persons in society. For instance, Eccl 4:1 notes the oppression of the weaker members of society by the more powerful. Eccl 5:7–8 observes this oppression by corrupt government officials who often work in tandem and that at times even the king benefits from this. Eccl 10:20 warns against cursing the king, even in private, because even confidential thoughts might be reported to the throne. This saying appears to be an observation by a courtier or a member of the upper classes of society whose words against the king would be highly scrutinized.

Thus, it is thought that, for the opening chapters, the author assumed Solomon's personality for the purpose of portraying life from the perspective of a king but then dropped that viewpoint in the rest of the book in favor of the perspective of courtiers or even common folk. However, this argument could also be made in the other direction. If a non-royal could adopt Solomon's perspective for literary purposes, why could it not have been the other way around—that in Eccl 3–12 Solomon adopted the mindset of his courtiers and of the commoner? Certainly a wise and competent king would understand the possibilities of oppression and corruption practiced among his officials and influential supporters (Eccl 4:1; 5:7) and seek to hold it in check for the benefit of all of his subjects. Likewise, an insightful king would understand the dynamics of court politics and his role in it (Eccl 10:20). Therefore, it is not entirely impossible that a wise king such as Solomon could have produced such observations.

Another view is that of Longman, who suggests that the body of Ecclesiastes (Eccl 1:12–12:7) contains the first person text from

Qoheleth, but the prologue (Eccl 1:1–11) and epilogue (Eccl 12:8–14) come from one of his acquaintances (cf. Eccl 12:8–12). It is this narrator of the prologue and epilogue who is the ultimate author of the book, and the body of the book amounts to a long extended quotation of Qoheleth. Longman's view is attractive and sufficiently nuanced to be a creditable theory. However, Eccl 12:8–12 does not strictly require that the frame narrative author was acquainted with Qoheleth. He simply may have known him by reputation or through a written text composed by Qoheleth. The frame narrator would not have to have been, therefore, a contemporary of Qoheleth.

It appears the most likely scenario for Ecclesiastes, therefore, is that a later frame narrator assembled the thoughts of Qoheleth. He may have updated the language or even paraphrased some words. At the same time, given Qoheleth's explicit statements about his identity, there is no reason to deny that he is Solomon.

## DATE OF COMPOSITION

Critical scholars are almost universally agreed that Ecclesiastes is a late composition. Some date it to the late Persian era, others place it in Hellenistic times. The latest possible date for the writing of Ecclesiastes is 200 BC, since the book is mentioned in Ben Sira, which was written about that time.

This late dating is based primarily on the peculiar Hebrew language characteristics of the book which are thought to reflect a close relationship to Mishnaic Hebrew and Aramaic. For instance, Ecclesiastes makes exclusive use of the first person singular pronoun אני (never אנכי) and the feminine demonstrative זה (never זאת), both of which are thought to be exclusively late. However, Aramaic influence on Hebrew is not necessarily late: David conquered Aramean lands (2 Sam 8:5–6), and interaction with the Arameans from his time onward could have led to Aramaic intrusions into Hebrew. The pronoun אני is not unknown in earlier Hebrew texts (cf. e.g., Josh 5:14; 23:2; 1 Sam 1:26; 3:13; 17:9, 10, 28), and its exclusive use may simply have been an affectation or dialectical variation of the author. Much the same can be said of זה, which is in exilic and pre-exilic texts such as Josh 2:17; Judg 18:4; 1 Kgs 14:5; 2 Kgs 6:19; and Ezek 40:45. Since זה occurs only six times in Ecclesiastes, it is difficult to make the case that this is late Hebrew as opposed to the author's peculiar dialect or even a conscious decision to use a rare form for effect.

Some have pointed to the occurrence of Persian loan words in Ecclesiastes as another indication of a late date, since it is thought that these could have only entered Hebrew during the Persian imperial era. However, Persia was an ancient land, and given Solomon's far-flung commercial interests it would not be surprising if a few Persian words entered Hebrew in his day. In fact only two Persian loan words appear in Ecclesiastes: the nouns פרדס, *garden, park* (Eccl 2:5), and פתגם, *judicial sentence* (Eccl 8:11). Both of these nouns developed extended or differing meanings in later Hebrew. פרדס occurs in Eccl 2:5 (and Song 4:13) meaning *garden.* However, in the Persian-era book of Nehemiah it appears with the extended meaning of *forest.* The same can be observed with פתגם. It occurs in the Persian era books of Esther (in Hebrew) and Daniel and Ezra (in Aramaic) where it signifies a royal decree, a reply, or an official report, but never carries the meaning *judicial sentence* (cf. Esth 1:20; Ezra 4:17; 5:7, 11; 6:11; Dan 3:16; 4:14).

Some critical scholars claim to have detected the effect of Hellenistic thought and philosophy in Ecclesiastes, mounting another argument for a late date. However, such connections are tenuous and largely in the eye of the beholder. It is equally possible to connect Qohelet's thought to earlier Near Eastern motifs.

Thus, there is no secure anchor for a late dating of Ecclesiastes. While it appears that the book can be no older than Solomon's day, it is equally possible that the frame narrator lived and wrote sometime later, perhaps in the era of the divided kingdom, and that he used Solomon's words and thoughts as the basis for his composition.

## LITERARY FEATURES OF ECCLESIASTES

Even with a quick first reading it becomes obvious that Qoheleth used a number of key terms and phrases that he repeats throughout his monologue. The first of these is the word חבל, *vapor, wind, breath,* which occurs thirty-eight times. Qoheleth uses this word in a metaphorical sense to signify that the human condition in a fallen world is insubstantial, fleeting, frustrating, and transitory. Qoheleth begins with an observation that all of life is a vapor (Eccl 1:2), and he closes with this same thought (Eccl 12:8). Various translations have been used for this word in Ecclesiastes, including *vanity, meaningless*, and *futility*. Often at the conclusion of an observation about life, the author characterizes it as a vapor (e.g., Eccl 2:11, 15; 3:19). חבל, therefore, could be viewed as the theme of much of Qoheleth's wisdom.

Another oft-repeated phrase is תחת השמש, *under the sun*. This is Qoheleth's way of referring to life in the fallen, death-infested world, especially as it is viewed from a human perspective. The expression highlights the sphere of human existence to which God has assigned sinners.

Two related phrases that highlight the futility of human effort to find meaning in life are רעות רוח (Eccl 1:14; 2:11, 17, 26; 4:4, 6; 6:9) and רעיון רוח (Eccl 1:17; 4:16). Both of these expressions are often translated *striving after the wind* or *chasing the wind*.

Like the other wisdom books in the OT, Ecclesiastes defies any precise outlining of its contents. Clearly there are three main parts to the book: a prologue (Eccl 1:1–11), Qoheleth's monologue (Eccl 1:12–12:8), and an epilogue (Eccl 12:9–14). However, the long central section does not easily divide into smaller parts. Like many wisdom writings, the author intentionally runs one topic into the next, expecting readers not only to read linearly through the book, but also presuming that they will note a myriad of relationships that create a web of associations backward and forward throughout the monologue. However, there is general agreement that within the monologue there is a change of tone after Eccl 6. In Eccl 7–12 the phrase "chasing the wind" is not used, and "under the sun" occurs half as frequently as in Eccl 1–6.

## Outline of Ecclesiastes

I.   Prologue: Without God everything is like a vapor (1:1–11)

II.  Only God can give meaning to human existence (1:12–6:12)

    A.  The futility of wisdom (1:12–18)

    B.  The futility of pleasure (2:1–11)

    C.  The futility of human existence in death and life (2:12–23)

    D.  God gives meaning, purpose, and permanence to humans in the midst of futility (2:24–6:12)

III. Divine wisdom enables wise living (7:1–12:8)

    A.  Sin has corrupted human relationships (7:1–9:6)

B. God grants life's pleasures, so seek a relationship with him (9:7–12:8)

IV. Epilogue: Fear God and obey his commands (12:9–14)

## THEOLOGICAL THEMES IN ECCLESIASTES

### LIFE VIEWED FROM AN EARTHLY PERSPECTIVE IS FUTILE AND MEANINGLESS

At the beginning and end of Ecclesiastes we find nearly identical statements:

> "Completely vaporous!" said Qoheleth, "Completely vaporous! Everything is vapor!" (Eccl 1:2)

> "Completely vaporous!" said the Qoheleth, "Everything is vapor!" (Eccl 12:8)

These verses are often said to present Qoheleth's theme. The word *vapor* is often translated *vanity* to signify the futility and meaningless of human existence that Qoheleth sees. Like a vapor, humans often are frustrated that there seems to be nothing permanent that one can grasp and hold and that will never disappoint (Eccl 1:14). Also, life's accomplishments seem as transient as vapors that can vanish into thin air as quickly as they appear (Eccl 2:1, 11). Some experiences of life are disgusting and unjust (Eccl 8:14). Moreover, just as nothing can be done to control a vapor because it eventually disperses into the air, so also death brings all people to the same end, and nothing can be done about it (Eccl 2:15).

However, Eccl 1:2 and 12:8 do not present the entire theme of Ecclesiastes. When Qoheleth says that everything is vapor, he does not mean everything in heaven and earth. This can be seen by the qualifying phrases *under the sun* and *striving after the wind*. Qoheleth is saying, in effect, that every effort in the realm of human existence under the sun is like a vapor. This is the key to understanding the book's message. Qoheleth seeks to find meaning and permanence through human wisdom, work and professional life, joy and pleasure, riches and wealth (Eccl 2:1–11). Yet, each of these fails and proves once again that human life *from a strictly human perspective* is like a vapor.

## DEATH AND POSSESSIONS

Rindge has noted that two important topics running throughout Ecclesiastes—death and possessions—are intimately related and are always discussed in close proximity to each other. The vocabulary of the book supports this. Murphy has noted that there are twenty-five Hebrew roots that occur at least five times in Ecclesiastes. In addition to the expected wisdom vocabulary (e.g., חכם, *wise*; טוב, *good*; ידע, *know*) there are roots related to possessions (e.g., עשה, *work*; אכל, *eat*) and מות, *death*.

Qoheleth notes that death is the determined lot for every human being. Therefore, he argues for the proper use of possessions, including enjoyment of the goods that God has given to people. This gives them a small measure of control in life, but it is limited, because the ability to enjoy one's possessions is ultimately in the hands of God (Eccl 2:24–26; 3:13; 5:17–18; 6:2).

## GOD GIVES MEANING TO LIFE

This leads to another important accent in Ecclesiastes: only God can give meaning to life because he is permanent and unchanging, unlike the vapor of human existence. Note some of the passages in which God alone gives what is worthwhile to humans or does things which cannot be undone:

> There is nothing better for a person than that he should eat and drink and make his life good in his labor. This, also, I saw was from the hand of God. (Eccl 2:24)

> I saw that everything that God has done endures forever. Nothing can be added to it and nothing can be taken away. God has done it so that they will fear him. (Eccl 3:14)

> Consider the work of God, because who is able to straighten what he has bent? (Eccl 7:13)

> Though a sinner does evil a hundred times and prolongs his life, yet I also know that it will be well for those who fear God because they fear him. (Eccl 8:12)

> But all this I took to heart, clarifying all of this, that the righteous and the wise and their deeds are in the hand of God. Whether it is love or hate, a person does not know all that is before him. (Eccl 9:1)

Moreover, human existence is not simply confined to life "under the sun." Qoheleth hints that there is more. Thus, he mentions that all humans will have to face God's judgment. This eschatological note cannot simply be confined to death at the end of one's life "under the sun," since both the righteous and the wicked die, and Qoheleth sees little difference in their death (Eccl 9:5). Instead, he knows that even after death God will call all humans to a final judgment (Eccl 3:17; 11:9). This is confirmed also in the third person comments at the end of the book:

> This is the end of the matter [when] everything has been heard: fear God and keep his commandments, for this is the complete [duty of] humanity. For God will bring every act into judgment, including every hidden thing, whether good or bad. (Eccl 12:14)

God will give meaning to evil through condemnation, but the good things he will remember and bless. Thus, "well for those who fear God because they fear him" (Eccl 8:12). This fear of God in Ecclesiastes, as in other wisdom literature in the OT, denotes more than the fear of God's wrath. It also includes a love for God who gives all good gifts. Therefore, it denotes a *positive relationship* with God borne of faith in the Creator and Redeemer who alone can give meaning to life.

### CHRIST IN ECCLESIASTES

Near the end of the third person frame at the conclusion of Ecclesiastes we are told:

> The words of wise people are like goads. And like nails are plantings [from] masters of collected sayings. They are given by one Shepherd. (Eccl 12:11)

Throughout the OT, God is often depicted as the great Shepherd of his people (e.g., Gen 49:24; Ps 23:1–4; 28:9; 80:1; Isa 40:11; Jer 31:10; Ezek 34:12, 15; Mic 7:14). A few prophetic passages connect this with the Messiah (Ezek 34:23; 37:24; Mic 5:3; Zech 13:7). In the NT the Gospel writers and Jesus himself identify the Savior as the great Shepherd (e.g., Matt 2:6; Mark 14:27; John 10:2–18; Heb 13:20; 1 Pet 2:25; 5:4; Rev 7:17). Thus, at the very end of Ecclesiastes, the words of Qoheleth are placed among those of other wise people and are identified as coming from the great Shepherd who is ultimately revealed in the person of Jesus. Eph 2:4–6 indicates that Christians are given life "above the sun," as it were (cf. Col 3:1). Christ, who ascended into the heavens, now rules all things for the good of believers who, by faith, sit with the Savior in the heavenly realms and are granted this eternal perspective.

### SIN AND GRACE IN ECCLESIASTES

Once the theological themes of Ecclesiastes are understood, the dynamics of God's judgment on sin and his graciousness towards sinners as depicted in the book can be appreciated. Qoheleth uses the effects of sin, especially death, to force readers to see the futility of their situation:

> The wise person has his eyes in his head, but the fool walks in darkness. Yet I know that one fate befalls all of them. (Eccl 2:14)

> I praised the dead who are already dead above the living who are still alive. But better than both is the person who has never been. He has not seen the evil deeds done under the sun. (Eccl 4:2–3)

> Indeed, there is no righteous man on earth who does good and never sins. (Eccl 7:20)

> There is an evil in all that is done under the sun, because there is one fate for all. Also, the heart of the children of Adam is full of evil, and madness is in their hearts during their lives. Afterwards they go to the dead. (Eccl 9:3)

Everything that Qoheleth examines in his wisdom repeatedly leads him to conclude that all people are sinners and all meet the same end: death.

Occasionally, Qoheleth notes that the threat of punishment is needed to curb unrighteous behavior because of the pervasiveness of human sin (Eccl 8:11; 10:18). However, he also observes that the demands of God's commandments can offer a guide for those who seek to please God (Eccl 12:13).

At the same time Qoheleth advises:

> Do not be too virtuous, and do not be too wise. Why should
> you ruin yourself? Do not be too wicked, and do not be a
> fool. Why should you die when it is not your time? (Eccl
> 7:16–17)

Some have thought that this passage demonstrates Qoheleth's
unorthodox understanding of righteousness and sin. However, given
the context of these words (Eccl 7:15, 18–20), it is clear that he is
advising against a fastidious outward religiosity that might lead one to
believe that good works can please God and deliver people from the
effects of sin and death. Instead, true righteousness comes from God
through faith to the person who fears him. This, too, is God's
graciousness toward mankind (Eccl 8:12). As Steele concludes:

> Faith lives life knowing that life will end, and faith finds life
> as a gift from God to be enjoyed. Enjoyment is thus the
> proper, albeit paradoxical, expression of faith of a believer
> living in a penultimate world. Qoheleth asks the question,
> "Who is like the wise and who knows the meaning of the
> saying: 'The wisdom of a man makes his face to shine and
> changes the hardness of his face'?" (8:1). His answer as to
> what it is that can make a man's face shine (with joy) and
> change his countenance is found in God's acceptance of one's
> doings, based upon, as Luther put it, the discovery of a
> gracious God.[2]

God's grace is found in Ecclesiastes through granting rich
blessings and giving meaning to life. Humans cannot find their
significance apart from God, who brings them good things and
blesses them physically and spiritually (Eccl 2:24; 5:18, 20; 8:15; 9:1,
7; 12:7). Thus, God and his grace become the only sure refuge and
hope for humans drowning in a sea of futility and death.

## CONCLUSION

In some ways Ecclesiastes speaks as if its view of life is fatalistic.
Yet, unlike much contemporary thought, Ecclesiastes offers an eternal
ray of hope from God. God gives pleasure to humans in this life.

---

[2] Walter R. Steele, "Enjoying the Righteousness of Faith in Ecclesiastes." *Concordia
Theological Quarterly* 74 (2010): 242.

However, God will judge all people. That judgment can reveal his wrath, but it will also reveal him as a gracious Shepherd who preserves his flock with a verdict of life on their behalf.

## SELECT BIBLIOGRAPHY

Bollhagen, James. *Ecclesiastes.* Concordia Commentary. St. Louis: Concordia, 2011.

Eaton, Michael A. *Ecclesiastes: An Introduction and Commentary.* Tyndale Old Testament Commentaries 16. Downers Grove: InterVarsity, 1983.

Fox, Michael V. "Frame-Narrative and Composition in the Book of Qoheleth." *Hebrew Union College Annual* 48 (1977): 83–106.

———. *Ecclesiastes: The Traditional Hebrew Text with New JPS Translation.* The JPS Bible Commentary. Philadelphia: Jewish Publication Society, 2004.

Longman, Tremper III. *The Book of Ecclesiastes.* The New International Commentary on the Old Testament. Grand Rapids: Eerdmans, 1998.

Miller, Douglas B. *Symbol and Rhetoric in Ecclesiastes: The Place of Hebel in Qohelet's Work.* Atlanta: Society of Biblical Literature, 2002.

Murphy, Roland. *The Tree of Life: An Exploration of Biblical Wisdom Literature.* New York: Doubleday, 2002.

Rindge, Matthew S. "Mortality and Enjoyment: The Interplay of Death and Possessions in Qoheleth." *Catholic Biblical Quarterly* 73 (2011): 265–80.

Steele, Walter R. "Enjoying the Righteousness of Faith in Ecclesiastes." *Concordia Theological Quarterly* 74 (2010): 225–42.

# 20

# SONG OF SONGS

Love between a man and a woman was designed to include sexual expression (Gen 2:20–25). From ancient times it has been noted that Song of Songs features the most frank depiction of sexual attraction between a woman and a man in all of the OT. Although this dimension of the divine plan for humans has been corrupted by the fall into sin, sexuality nevertheless remains part of God's blessing in marriage, and the Song of Songs depicts the main characters—the Shulammite woman (Song 6:13) and her Beloved—as rejoicing in the gifts of love, emotional and physical intimacy, and companionship. At the same time, readers of Song of Songs who know the rest of Scriptures cannot help but ask whether this depiction is also meant to remind them of God's loving relationship with his people (cf. Isa 62:5; Jer 2:2; Eph 5:22–33; Rev 19:7, 21:2, 9; 22:17).

## AUTHORSHIP, COMPOSITION, AND DATE

The Song of Songs opens with the words, "The Song of Songs which is Solomon's" (Song 1:1). This superscription has been traditionally understood to mean that the book is the greatest of Solomon's songs, composed by the wise king himself (cf. 1 Kgs 5:12). This interpretation has been endorsed by Franz Delitzsch and by some recent scholars, including Mitchell in his lengthy commentary on the Song of Songs. Of course, this dates the composition of the Song sometime in Solomon's reign (971–932).

However, many scholars, both conservative evangelicals and critics, believe that the superscription does not imply that Solomon wrote the Song of Songs but that it was dedicated to him or is about him. For instance, both Hess and Longman maintain that the superscription means that the Song "concerns" Solomon in some way, whereas Carr offers possibilities that Solomon edited the work of others or that the book is dedicated to him. This view allows for a wide range of dates for the composition of the Song—anywhere from the time of Solomon or during the divided kingdom (most evangelical scholars) to the Persian or even Hellenistic period (critical scholars).

Much of the debate about authorship turns on the interpretation of the Song and especially the understanding of Solomon's role in the rest of the book. He is mentioned at Song 3:7–11 and Song 8:11–12. Longman understands the first to cast Solomon in a positive light, but in the second he is portrayed negatively. For Longman (who admits that Song 8:11–12 is enigmatic), this indicates that Solomon is not the Beloved of the Shulammite, and therefore he cannot have been the author of the book. Mitchell, on the other hand, understands both texts as stating that the Shulammite and Solomon have comingled their property as man and wife, and that they are tenderly devoted to each other. For Mitchell this confirms Solomon's authorship.

Another issue in the debate over authorship is the relation of the Song to love poetry elsewhere in the ancient world. Some critical scholars compare it to relatively late compositions, which would rule out Solomon as the book's author. Others note that it has affinities to Egyptian love poems from a relatively early period. Since such connections can be seen in both directions, this line of evidence is inconclusive.

Often the book's language has been used to argue for a late date. Except for the superscription, the Song consistently uses the relative prefixed particle שׁ instead of the more common relative pronoun אֲשֶׁר. This at one time was taken to be a sign that the Song was composed relatively late. However, it is now clear that the relative particle was used in early texts. For instance, it occurs at Judg 5:7 in what is acknowledged by most scholars to be a very early poem, dating to the middle of the period of the Judges in the twelfth century.

The Song also contains a number of words that are believed to be Persian and Aramaic loan words, indicating that the earliest date for composition would be sometime during the Persian period. For instance, פַּרְדֵּס, *garden*, and כַּרְכֹּם, *saffron*, are identified as Persian loanwords. However, פַּרְדֵּס may demonstrate the development of its use in later Hebrew. It occurs in Eccl 2:5 and Song 4:13 meaning *garden.* By contrast, in the Persian-era book of Nehemiah it is used with the extended meaning of *forest* (Neh 2:8). Thus, פרדס may have developed an extended meaning over time in Hebrew, indicating it entered the language much earlier than the Persian era. כרכם not only has a cognate in Persian (*kurkum*), but also has cognates in Akkadian (*kurkānu*) and Greek (κρόκος), indicating that this spice from the crocus flower was well known throughout the ancient world. Considering the widespread trading that was characteristic of Solomon's day (e.g., 1 Kgs 9:26–28), it would not be unexpected that this word could have been used by Solomon himself.

A number of passages in the Song appear to contain Aramaic loanwords (Song 1:6, 7, 11, 17; 2:9, 11, 13; 3:2, 8; 5:3; 6:11; 7:3; 8:5). Some of these may not have been borrowed from Aramaic at all (e.g., the verbal root שזף, Song 1:6), but others seem to be (the verbal root נטר, Song 1:6). However, given that Solomon's empire extended through Syria to the Euphrates and that later kings of Israel and Judah interacted with the Aramean kingdom (e.g. 2 Kgs 5, 7), it is not certain that such Aramaic loanwords must be signs of post-exilic Hebrew.

Thus, conclusions about the authorship, composition, and date of the Song will depend on the reader's interpretive choices and presuppositions. Those who understand Solomon as a primary figure in the book tend to attribute the book to him or to someone writing during the divided monarchy. Those who surmise that Solomon may not be the Shulammite's Beloved may nevertheless date the book relatively early, perhaps during the divided monarchy. However, critical scholars tend to date the Song much later, seeing it as a Persian-period composition or, in extreme cases, a work from the Hellenistic era. The uncertainty of much of the evidence used in the arguments about the date and composition has led some scholars to conclude that very little can be said with confidence about the authorship and date or social provenance of the Song. This is perhaps too extreme a conclusion, but it illustrates the difficulties in evaluating the evidence. Perhaps it is best to conclude that the Song, if composed by Solomon, dates to his reign. However, if the book is merely dedicated to Solomon or is simply "the greatest of Songs concerning Solomon," then composition by an unknown author during the divided monarchy is more probable.

## LITERARY FEATURES OF SONG OF SONGS

### LITERARY GENRE AND INTENT OF THE BOOK

Much of the history of the interpretation of the Song involves the interpreter's assumption about the book's genre and its overall intended meaning. Several major approaches to its genre have been proposed.

### *Allegory*

Ancient and medieval Christian and Jewish interpreters understood Song of Songs to be an allegory. This was at least partly motivated by a desire to avoid seeing the book according to what it appeared to be at first glance: a sensual love song between a man and a woman.

Jewish scholars understood the Song either as a historical allegory about redemptive history from the Exodus to the Messianic era or as a mystical allegory representing the union between God and the individual soul. In both interpretive schemes the love expressed is between God and humans, either God's love for Israel as a whole or his love for each individual who seeks him.

Christian allegorical interpretations viewed the Song as an expression of the love between Christ and the church. Some of the most notable Christian allegorical interpretations were produced by Hippolytus (170–235), Origen (195–254), Jerome (331–420), and Bernard of Clarivaux, who delivered eighty-six sermons on the Song between 1135 and 1153.

Some have classified Luther's approach to the Song as allegorical. His comments are preserved in a series of lectures from 1530. Although Luther takes the historical context of the Song into account, he finds it to be about Solomon's kingdom. Yet, instead of being about Christ and the church, for Luther the book depicts the relationship between God and Solomon, forming a kind of political allegory from which Christian rulers can learn to govern rightly.

Early Reformed commentators also understood the Song allegorically, but this approach generally fell out of favor with later Protestants. There are, however, notable exceptions: John Wesley (1703–1791) favored an allegorical interpretation. Among Roman Catholics there remain a minority who continue to advocate a somewhat traditional allegorical reading. In commenting on contemporary interpretations of the Song, Longman notes that "the allegorical approach has gone from being the dominant approach to the interpretation of the Song to almost a kind of eccentric archaism."

The tendentiousness and arbitrary nature of the assignment of meaning to the text's details is the main reason that the allegorical method fell out of favor with most interpreters. For instance, Hyppolytus understood the woman's two breasts (Song 4:5) to symbolize the Old and New Testaments, though one is hard pressed to find any contextual evidence for such an interpretation. Much of the motivation leading to an allegorical reading for ancient and medieval interpreters appears to have been an avoidance of the Song's explicit sexuality, which was thought to be inappropriate for a biblical book. However, modern readers have noted that the Scriptures commend sexual expression between a man and woman in marriage as a gift of God and a blessing from him (Gen 2:24; Prov 5:18–19). Moreover, Paul teaches that the sexual drive implanted in humans by God at creation can be tempted to immoral acts if it is not expressed in the God-given institution of marriage (1 Cor 7:2–9).

## A Love Poem Concerning God's Gift of Marital Bliss

Many modern interpreters understand the Song of Songs to be what it appears to be on its surface: an extended poem about the love between a man and a woman. For many Christians this means that the Song describes the holy expression of love between married partners. At times the Shulammite and her Beloved appear to be expressing their desire to consummate their love while at other times they express their joy in having shared physical intimacy. For instance at Song 1:2 the Shulammite says, "Your love is better than wine," implying that she has already tasted this love.

This Christian view is at least as old as Theodore of Mopsuestia (AD 350–428). However, for Theodore this meant that the Song ought not to be part of the Scriptures, since he considered such expression of sexuality, even within the bond of marriage, was not appropriate for God's Word.

During the Reformation, John Calvin (1509–1564) interpreted Song of Songs as an expression of marital bliss and a form of the divine manifestation of love in the lives of Christians. Many modern Protestants have also advocated this view. They see the book's message of properly expressed emotional and physical intimacy as appropriate for the Holy Scriptures and a celebration of this aspect of human existence as created and blessed by God.

## Drama

Akin to the previous approach to the Song of Songs is the view that it has a plotline similar to that of a drama. This understanding does not advocate that the Song was written as a dramatic play for theater, but rather that it contains the same type of plot development that one would find in a theatrical production. The nineteenth-century Lutheran exegete Franz Delitzsch saw the Song as telling a love story between Solomon and the Shulammite, who he identified as a country maiden of humble origins. Delitzsch divided the Song into six scenes of two acts each. Beginning with the lovers' mutual attraction, and progressing to their marriage, the drama supposedly ends with the pair ratifying their covenant of love.

Others who have followed this understanding have argued that there are actually three major characters in the book. This interpretation was motivated by uneasiness with Solomon's extreme polygamy, seeing him ultimately as unfit to be one who is extolled for his faithfulness in marriage. According to this view, the plot involves a love triangle: the Shulammite loves a country shepherd, but Solomon desires her because of her beauty. She does everything she can to resist Solomon's advances and find her Beloved.

While the dramatic interpretation continues to have its advocates, it has several drawbacks that make most scholars suspicious of it. First of all, the supposed plotline is not immediately obvious. One must struggle to find a narrative line to follow, and advocates of the dramatic interpretation often read into the text in order to maintain a plot. Secondly, it is not always evident who is speaking in the various soliloquies, making it impossible to attribute various words to the characters in the drama. Finally, the three-person love triangle approach suffers from the failure of the text itself to distinguish clearly between Solomon and the shepherd, making it unlikely that there are two different men seeking the Shulammite's affection.

## Wedding Songs

Still another interpretive approach is the view that the Song of Songs is an anthology of love poems appropriate for a wedding celebration. This explanation seeks to focus on the imagery of the poetry and disdains any thought of a narrative line within the text. The anthological view was popularized in the nineteenth century by J. G. Wetzstein, a German consul in Syria, who observed week-long Syrian wedding celebrations where the bride and groom were treated as king and queen, and where descriptive poems (called *wasfs* in Arabic) were sung in their honor (cf. Song 4:1–14; 5:10–16; 7:1–20). While this approach occasionally enjoys a brief revival, its major drawback is that it seeks to explain the Song through the lens of modern Syrian folk practices without any demonstration that similar practices were known in ancient Israel.

## Near Eastern Fertility Cult Poems

The cultic interpretation presupposes that the book had its origin in pagan fertility cults in the ancient Near East. It supposes that the myths and rites of divine marriages between gods and goddesses lies behind the now demythologized text of the Song. The impetus for this approach came from the increasing knowledge of pagan fertility cults afforded by Near Eastern archeological discoveries in the late nineteenth and early twentieth centuries. Advocates of this view, who practice a very extreme kind of historical criticism on the text, claim that it offers the best explanation of what is understood to be erotic imagery in Song of Songs.

The fatal problem for this interpretation is that the Song nowhere indicates that the major characters are gods and goddess. To embrace this view, then, one must maintain that the poetry has been radically demythologized during the course of its transmission. However, if this is the case, the demythologization has been so complete that it has left little if any trace of the original cultic setting, calling into question whether it was present in the first place.

## Analogy

Finally, a number of more conservative Christian interpreters seek to bridge the gap between the allegorical and love poem readings by interpreting the Song of Songs along the lines of a love poem concerning God's gift of marital bliss while maintaining that this love between a man and a woman in marriage is also to be understood as analogous to God's love for his people and their love for him.

It can hardly be denied that Scripture employs this analogy (Isa 62:5; Jer 2:2; Eph 5:22–33; Rev 19:7, 21:2, 9; 22:17; see also Hosea

1–3; Jer 3:10; 31:32; Ezek 16:32, 45), and it is quite natural that those who know the Scriptures well would seek to draw this connection while reading the Song. Indeed, given the use of this analogy in the prophets, it is not inconceivable that God's OT people interpreted the Song this way. It is even more understandable that Christians would find this analogical approach appealing, especially in light of Paul's explicit use of it in Eph 5:22–33.

However, some advocates of the analogical approach have sought to go beyond the analogy to identifying specific items in the text as symbolizing various aspects of Christ's relationship to his church. This can lead to making the analogical approach very much like the allegorical interpretation of the church fathers with all of the subjective problems associated with it. Thus, a more faithful use of the analogical view is to avoid over-interpreting the detailed imagery of the text. Instead, it ought to be understood that the language in the Song is poetic and cumulatively paints a picture of this magnificent divine love. The individual elements are not to be pressed into service to make them symbolic or mini-analogies of various aspects of the Christian's life with Christ. It is better to understand the imagery of the Shulammite and her Beloved as in general demonstrating the love of Christ for his bride, the church, and the church's love for the Savior in response to his.

## FLORAL AND FAUNAL IMAGERY

One obvious feature of the poetry of Song of Songs is its use of imagery drawn from nature. At least a dozen plant species from aloes and apples to mandrakes and pomegranates are mentioned. In addition, blossoms and brambles, flowers and vines are among the more generic floral imagery in the Song. Over a dozen plant products are referenced, including general terms such as fruits, nuts, oils, and spices as well as more specific items such as frankincense, nard, myrrh, and saffron. At least ten different species of animals are mentioned, including doves, foxes, gazelles, lions, leopards, turtledoves, and ravens. Thus, Song of Songs contains perhaps the most concentrated use of floral and faunal imagery in the Bible.

This imagery lends a rustic air to the entire Song which mentions pastoral settings such as hills, valleys, forests, gardens, orchards, and vineyards. In fact, in contrast to many books of the OT, very little of the Song is set in an urban environment (cf. Song 3:1–5; 5:2–8). This is true even though the Shulammite frequently converses with "the daughters of Jerusalem" (Song 1:5; 2:7; 3:5; 5:8, 16; 8:4). In the two city settings, the Shulammite must search for her Beloved. In contrast, the country setting appears to be a way for the poetry to isolate the two lovers from others and highlight their joy in each other. They can enjoy the countryside and rejoice in the natural gifts of their Creator who also made them and gave them the gifts of love—including its sexual expression—that are to be received within the bonds of marriage (cf. Song 3:11; 4:8–12; 5:1; 8:8–10).

## GEOGRAPHY

Despite the relatively short length of the Song of Songs, it contains quite a few geographical references. At least seven different places in Israel are mentioned: Mount Carmel, Engedi, Mount Gilead, Heshbon, Jerusalem, Sharon, and Tirzah (and perhaps Baal-Hamon, Song 8:11). These places encompass Solomon's entire kingdom from Judah in the south (Engedi) to northern Israel (Mount Carmel, the city of Tirzah) and even as far as the Israelite territory east of the Jordan (Gilead). All but Jerusalem are used in descriptions of the Shulammite.

Five locales outside of Israel are also mentioned: Mount Amana, Mount Hermon (also called Mount Senir), Lebanon, and Damascus to the north and Kedar in Arabia to the east. Of these, Lebanon, Damascus, and Kedar are used in descriptions of the Shulammite, and Lebanon is used in a depiction of her Beloved.

This extensive use of places that serve as descriptions of persons is unique to Song of Songs. It is interesting to note that with the exception of Kedar, all of these locales would have fallen under Solomon's dominion at the height of his power. Since the Beloved describes the Shulammite with comparisons to places throughout Solomon's kingdom, the temporal setting of the Song appears to be during Solomon's reign and lends credence to interpretations that equate the Shulammite's Beloved with Solomon. He sees her as being as precious as his entire realm.

However, these geographical references do not necessarily make an argument for Solomon as the author of the Song. While they may indicate Solomonic authorship, it is also possible that a later author who was aware of the extent of Solomon's empire could have incorporated these references when constructing the book's temporal setting.

## STRUCTURE OF SONG OF SONGS

The structure of the Song of Songs is notoriously difficult to discern, and there is no consensus among scholars as to even the major divisions of the book. Exum examined twelve different modern commentaries and discovered twelve different outlines of the book. However, her comparison demonstrates there is some agreement on major breaks in the work. A majority of Exum's sources agree that main sections end at Song 2:7; 3:5; 5:1; 6:3; and 8:4. Moreover, there is universal agreement that Song 1:1 is a separate superscription. The outline below offers one possible organization of the Song based on these generally recognized breaks.

### Outline of Song of Songs

I.   Superscription (1:1)

II.  Readers are introduced to the love shared by the Shulammite and her Beloved (1:2–2:7)

III. The Beloved and the Shulammite seek each other (2:8–3:5)

IV.  The Lovers describe each other's features and consummate their love (3:6–5:1)

V.   The Shulammite longs for her Beloved (5:2–6:3)

VI.  The Lovers express their desire for intimacy (6:4–8:4)

VII. The Lovers express their dedication to each other (8:5–14)

## HISTORICAL ISSUES

One much-discussed topic is the status of Song of Songs within the canon. Should it be included or not? From time to time some have expressed doubts that a book with overt references to sexuality ought to be in the Bible. This was the view of Theodore of Mopsuestia, mentioned above. Moreover, scholars in the nineteenth and twentieth centuries often raised the question about whether Song of Songs was considered a part of the canon by Jews in the first few centuries of the Christian era. This discussion was prompted by a passage in the Talmud that records a discussion among first century rabbis as to whether the Song and Ecclesiastes "defile the hands" (*m. Yad.* 3:5). It was thought that the expression "defile the hands" referred to whether or not a book was part of the canon. However, subsequent examination of all of the passages in the Talmud that use this expression has demonstrated that this passage did not contain a discussion of canonicity, but of whether books of the Scriptures which do not contain the full divine name יהוה had to receive the same special handling as other books of the canon. Thus, doubts cast upon whether Song of Songs was part of the canon from the beginning of the Christian era stemmed from scholars' misunderstanding of the Talmud.

In fact, the earliest evidence testifies that Song of Songs was always considered part of the canon (cf. Josephus [*Ag. Ap.* 37–43] and 2 Esd 14:44–47). It is listed among the canonical books by the Talmud (*B. Bat.* 14b), and it is always included in early Christian lists of the OT canonical books. Canonical lists by Melito (d. 190) and Origen (c. 185–254) include the Song. Later lists by Athanasius (328–373), Cyril of Jerusalem (315–386), Ephiphanius (c. 310–404), Gregory of Nazianzus (329–389), and Aphilochius (c. 340–c. 395) also acknowledge Song of Songs as part of the canon.

## THEOLOGICAL THEMES IN SONG OF SONGS

Song of Songs is not an overtly theological book. Neither the word *God* (אלהים or אל) nor the divine name *Yahweh* (יהוה) is used. This has largely contributed to the numerous approaches to the Song's genre and overall message.

### REFRAIN: DO NOT AROUSE OR AWAKEN LOVE UNTIL IT DESIRES

One refrain is used three times in Song of Songs:

> I place you under oath, Daughters of Jerusalem, [by the gazelles and by the does of the field]: Do not arouse or awaken this love until it desires. (Song 2:7; 3:5; 8:4)

This is the only refrain in the book, and it always occurs after descriptions of the couple sharing physical affection (Song 2:4–6; 3:4; 8:1–3). The meaning of this refrain has been debated. Gault examined eight different proposals and found all but two of them unlikely. It could mean that one is to remain chaste and reserve sexual activity until marriage. The other interpretation considered possible by Gault was that this refrain was a warning not to interrupt lovers when they are sharing intimate moments. He maintained that the latter meaning best fits the context. However, to defend this interpretation he had to argue that תעירו, *arouse*, or תעוררו, *awaken*, love was used in a unique way in these passages. Elsewhere the verbal root עור (for *arouse* and *awaken*) always signals moving something or someone from a state of inactivity to activity. Thus, it would at first blush appear to mean that one should not make love active until it desires, a meaning that is contrary to Gault's interpretation of the refrain. Gault, however, maintains that the verbs actually mean "interrupt [love]." He attributes this peculiar sense to poetic license without further substantiation other than his understanding of the context.

Eschelbach, on the other hand, has argued that the refrain is a warning against arousing love prematurely—that is, outside of marriage. He holds that the addressees of this refrain, the daughters of Jerusalem, are designed by the poet to be figures in the poem through which the Shulammite speaks to the book's audience. That is, the poet is using the Shulammite to address the audience who is in the guise of the daughters of Jerusalem. He places the daughters of Jerusalem— and thereby also the readers—under oath that they will not arouse their own physical expressions of love outside of marriage.

This understanding of the refrain is endorsed by a large number of conservative Christian and Jewish scholars. Moreover, it fits well within the context. In each case this refrain follows descriptions of the Shulammite sharing physical intimacy with her Beloved. Then she places the daughters of Jerusalem under oath that they not experience such love until "it desires," implying that the true and godly desire of this kind of love is expressed within the Creator's design and institution of marriage (Gen 2:24).

This also appears to be supported by the Hebrew use of the word *love* with the definite article (האהבה), which is unique to Song of Songs. The most likely explanation is that the article is used as a demonstrative pronoun, yielding the meaning, "do not awake *this* love." (For other examples of the use of the article as a demonstrative pronoun see Gen 24:42; Exod 9:27; Num 22:8; 2 Kgs 19:29.) Since the Shulammite had just described the sharing of physical intimacy, she then places an oath on her audience not to stir up this kind of love inappropriately.

Thus, the one refrain in Song of Songs is used to point to a theology of marriage and sexuality. These are gifts of God, who created humans to share physical and emotional intimacy between the sexes within the institution of marriage.

## A BLAZE FROM YAH

Another passage closely related to this refrain is Song 8:6–7:

> Set me as a seal upon your heart, as a seal upon your arm, for love is as strong as death, jealousy as unyielding as Sheol. Its flames are fiery flames, a blaze from Yah [or *an intense blaze*]. Many waters cannot quench this love, and rivers cannot drown it. If a man were to give all his household wealth for this love, they would utterly despise him.

This passage, like the refrain (Song 2:7; 3:5; 8:4), uses *love* with the article and may be the only one in Song of Songs to mention God. The word translated "a blaze from Yah(weh)" is שלהבתיה. It has been explained in three ways. Some understand it to be the word שלהבת with an intensive suffix יה, "an intense blaze." Other examples of words with this suffix are found at Jer 2:31; 32:19.

Others interpret יה to be the divine name used to form a superlative, "the most intense of blazes." There are examples of the words for *God* (אלהים or אל) used in this way (Gen 23:6; 30:8 1 Sam 14:15; Ps 36:7; Jonah 3:3).

Although this expression is written as one word in the Ben Asher Masoretic tradition, in the Ben Naphtali tradition it is written as two words: שלהבת יה, "a blaze of Yah." Yah, the shortened form of the divine name Yahweh, appears in poetic texts throughout the OT (e.g., Exod 15:2; Ps 150:6). For this reason some scholars understand it to be a direct reference to God as the one who creates this kind of love and blesses married couples with it.

Longman argues that that the divine name appears nowhere else in Song of Songs and that the refrain at Song 2:7 and 3:5 uses a circumlocution for mentioning God directly: "by the gazelles and by the does of the field" sounds similar in Hebrew to "by [the Lord of] Hosts and by God Almighty." Thus, he thinks it unlikely that God is mentioned at Song 8:6. However, it should be noted that the final occurrence of the refrain at Song 8:4, just before Song 8:6, does not contain the phrase "by the gazelles and by the does of the field."

Thus, it would not be surprising that Song 8:6 either contains the divine name, making it explicit for the first time in the book, or that it employs yet another circumlocution for God by using the intensive suffix to hint at the source of the blaze: Yahweh. In either case, this verse is stating or at least hinting to the reader that God is the author of true marital love and blesses sexual expression of that love between wife and husband.

## CHRIST IN SONG OF SONGS

Although Song of Songs has an implicit theology of marriage, the book contains no explicit theological statements. It should not be surprising, then, that there is no passage that directly points to Christ. However, as noted above, the analogy of marriage being like God's relationship to his people runs throughout Scripture. In the NT, St. Paul specifically says that in speaking about marriage he is speaking about the profound mystery of Christ's love for his church (Eph 5:32). Thus, the deep, passionate desire of the Shulammite and her Beloved for one another in the Song helps readers to understand their loving relationship with Christ.

## SIN AND GRACE IN SONG OF SONGS

The joy, delight, longing, and pleasure that the lovers find in one another are celebrated throughout the Song of Songs. These are received gladly by them, and the reader of the book in its scriptural context cannot avoid seeing it as portraying these as gifts coming from the gracious hand of God. The Song also reminds us of God's love for his people, whom he has redeemed and brought into a loving relationship that can be compared to marriage.

In contrast, the refrain at Song 2:7; 3:5; 8:4 calls on the daughters of Jerusalem to foreswear love until it is properly expressed. To do otherwise would be a misuse of the God-given gift of sexuality, sinning against the Creator who made humans male and female and blessed them (Gen 1:27–28; 5:2).

## CONCLUSION

The explicit portrayal of the love of a wife for her husband and his love for her in the Song of Songs has led to widely divergent interpretations. Some have been embarrassed by its frank depiction of sexuality and offered the opinion that such a book is out of place in the biblical canon. Others have sought to blunt the surface meaning of the text by filtering its message through allegory. Instead, it is best to accept the text as celebrating God's gifts of love, desire, and intimacy in marriage. Christian readers can also see the Song of Songs reminding them of the longing they have to celebrate the marriage feast of the Lamb in his eternal kingdom (Rev 19:9).

## SELECT BIBLIOGRAPHY

Carr, G. Lloyd. *The Song of Solomon: An Introduction and Commentary.* Tyndale Old Testament Commentaries 17. Downers Grove: InterVarsity, 1984.

Eschelbach, Michael A. "Song of Songs: Increasing Appreciation of and Restraint in Matters of Love." *Andrews University Seminary Studies* 42 (2004): 305–24.

Exum, J. Cheryl. *Song of Songs: A Commentary.* The Old Testament Library. Louisville: Westminster, 2005.

Gault, Brian P. "An Admonition against 'Rousing Love': The Meaning of the Enigmatic Refrain in Song of Songs." *Bulletin for Biblical Research* 20 (2010): 161–84.

Hess, Richard S. *Song of Songs.* Baker Commentary on the Old Testament Wisdom and Psalms. Grand Rapids: Baker, 2005.

Longman, Tremper III. *Song of Songs.* The New International Commentary on the Old Testament. Grand Rapids: Eerdmans, 2001.

Luther, Martin. "Lectures on the Song of Solomon." Trans. Ian Siggin. In *Luther's Works,* vol. 15. Edited by Jaroslav Pelikan and Hilton C. Oswald, 191–264. St. Louis: Concordia, 1972.

Mitchell, Christopher W. *The Song of Songs.* Concordia Commentary. St. Louis: Concordia, 2003.

Murphy, Roland E. *The Song of Songs: A Commentary on the Book of Canticles or The Song of Songs.* Hermeneia. Minneapolis: Augsburg Fortress, 1990.

# 21

# INTERPRETING PROPHETIC BOOKS

Israel's prophets are an odd group. Over the course of a sixty-year ministry, Isaiah repeatedly predicts his nation's demise (e.g., Isa 3:1–26; 5:6; 10:1–6), reports seeing God (Isa 6:5), calls kings to account (e.g., Isa 7), and walks around barefoot and naked for three years (Isa 20). Jeremiah buries his underwear and then wears it again (Jer 13:1–11), successfully predicts a false prophet's death (Jer 28:16–17), and dares to flaunt a king's authority (Jer 36). What is more, Hosea marries a prostitute (Hos 1:2), Ezekiel shows no remorse when his wife dies (Ezek 24:16–17), Jonah is swallowed by a great fish (Jonah 1:17), and Zechariah reports bizarre night visions (e.g., Zech 1:8–21). What reading strategies should be brought to these books?

## PROPHETS AND ISRAEL'S WORSHIP

In the past hundred years or so, the relationship between Israel's prophets and the nation's worship life has gone through several different stages of interpretation. The initial critical view promoted the idea that there was an irreconcilable difference between the two. Their argument went something like this. Prophets—especially Amos—were the founders of ethical monotheism. Their goal was to de-ritualize Israel's religion and they sought to accomplish this through a complete denunciation of the nation's worship. Scholars interpreted Isa 1:10–17, Micah 6:1–8, Jer 7:1–7—and texts like them—as though Yahweh did not order Israel's worship life. He was only interested in ethics. The vocation of a prophet was to be anti-liturgy, anti-sacrifice, and anti-priest.

While this position was dominant for several generations, today the strict dichotomy between the word-based prophet and the worship-based priest has softened. Some prophets are understood as associated with the temple (e.g., Habakkuk and Joel), while several prophetic oracles are interpreted as being liturgically grounded and therefore offering a positive view of Israel's worship life. For example, Isaiah's call came when he was in the temple (Isa 6), and he has affirming words about worship in Isa 44:28; 52:11; and 66:20–24. Jeremiah and Ezekiel both follow suit (e.g., Jer 33:11, 18; Ezek 20:40–44; 22:8; 40:1–48:36). The post-exilic prophets Haggai and Zechariah advocate rebuilding the temple and reestablishing its sacrificial system. However, some scholars still point to texts like Amos 5:21–24, Jer 7:22, Hos 6:6, and Joel 2:13 and interpret them as a complete rejection of Israel's sacrifices and liturgy.

What these critics ignore, though, is that sometimes prophets employed the rhetorical strategy of dialectical negation. At times, a prophet appears to place two concepts in opposition to each other as if they are incompatible. But they are not. It is, instead, their way of calling their hearers to compare the two and then understand better how each is important and necessary. Some prophetic texts, then, are best understood as making "both/and" rather than "either/or" propositions.

Awareness of dialectical negation assists in the interpretation of texts like Jer 7:21–23, which may appear to be a wholesale rejection of Israel's worship. However, using a "both/and" strategy, Jer 7:21–23 may be translated as follows:

This is what Yahweh of armies says, the God of Israel: Go ahead, add your burnt offerings to your other sacrifices and eat the meat yourselves! For I did not speak (only) and I did not (only) command in the day I brought you forth from the land of Egypt speaking words of a whole burnt offering or a sacrifice. Rather this word I commanded them saying, "Listen to my voice and I will become your God and you will become my people and walk in all the ways I command you that it may go well with you."

Jeremiah is illustrating the primacy of love and faithfulness toward Yahweh (e.g., 1 Sam 15:21–22), and dialectical negation sharpens his rhetoric. Worship ceremonies were means, while walking in God's ways were ends.

Taken in isolation, some prophetic critiques against Israel's worship life appear to be a total about-face from the Mosaic commands and ordinances. But prophets were against outward sacrifice that did not entail the inward sacrifice of a broken and contrite heart (cf. Ps 51:17). They were no more against sacrifices than they were against prayers (Isa 1:15) or worship songs (Amos 5:23). It is only when the sacrificial system and ceremonial laws became a substitute for morality that the prophets inveigh so heavily against them (cf. Isa 58:6–7). Israel's worship was not the problem—the people in the worship services were often the problem.

## FORM CRITICISM

In the last few centuries, scholars have employed several kinds of reading strategies in their overall attempt to understand Israelite prophecy. The earliest of these was form criticism. Although there were forerunners to this methodology, Herman Gunkel is considered to be the founder of OT form critical work. He was impacted by the philosophical system of Hegelian idealism, with its central idea being the evolution from the simple to the more complex vis-à-vis thesis, antithesis, and synthesis. Gunkel's goal was to apply the Hegelian framework to the study of Israel's prophetic literature. He believed that in ancient Israel an idea could be stated in only one way on any given occasion. Any mixture of genres or grammatical discontinuity was a sign of later scribal additions.

Closely connected to Gunkel's notion that original genres were pure was his belief that initial prophetic oral productions were very brief. They were largely terse, ejaculatory, and often cryptic because prophets were incapable of writing long, well-reasoned compositions, characteristic of modern thinkers. Hence, Gunkel argued, prophetic books are little more than a collection of beads on a string. Because of his belief that prophets were ecstatic figures who delivered short and sporadic oracles, he divided chapters and verses by distributing them among many prophets, disciples, and redactors. Gunkel argued that since the basic forms of prophetic discourse were short and self-contained, the scholar's interpretive goal was to identify and isolate these short units in order to reconstruct the original message of the prophet.

This pursuit of *ganz reinen* ("completely pure") forms meant that stylistic and syntactical changes, discontinuities in perspective, new literary genres, and the like are indications of new prophetic oracles. Consequently, Gunkel's search for the original text, not the canonical form, was the chief focus of his research.

The most influential of Gunkel's students was Sigmund Mowinckel. Mowinckel distinguished four types of prophetic materials: (1) various brief sayings, poems and/or oracles in the first person, representing Yahweh's direct discourse through the prophet and usually genuine; (2) narratives about prophets and thought to be influenced by legend; (3) speeches by the prophet in narrative form, usually composed by the post-exilic community; and (4) hopeful prophecies that were also considered post-exilic and artificial.

The next generation of scholars summarized and expanded these form critical ideas. One of the most influential of them was Hans W. Wolff. For example, in his commentary on Amos, Wolff believes that a disciple added vision accounts (e.g., Amos 7:1–9) and oracles against the nations (Amos 1:3–2:3) to the prophet's original words. He attributes an additional layer to a "circle of disciples" who composed the biographical narrative in Amos 7:10–17, while they also supplemented and reformulated earlier material. He then argued for another editorial layer which supposedly emerged during the time of Josiah, when the king destroyed the sanctuary at Bethel (2 Kgs 23:15). The next layer Wolff called the Deuteronomistic redaction which was intent to show that Judah stood under the same judgment as Israel. These sections include the three hymnic oracles, Amos 4:13; 5:8–9; 9:5–6, as well as Amos 1:1, 9–11; 2:4–5; 3:1–2; 3:7; and 5:25–27. The last stratum was the post-exilic eschatology of salvation in Amos 9:11–15. Wolff labeled all of the additions *Nachinterpretation*, or "afterlife."

This methodology assumes that redactional levels arose as a reaction to specific historical events which necessitated updating the text. Discontinuity in genres, perspectives, vocabulary, and the like signal where to divide the book between its different editions.

The primary goal of prophetic studies at this time was to probe behind the text and discover earlier sources that reveal the prophet's history, religion, sociology, and politics. The fundamental assumption was that the book was not the most fruitful object of extensive study. Rather, the primary value of prophetic books lay in their being depositories for earlier oral materials that are more useful and more interesting. Thus, prophetic books were viewed as an aggregate of literary sources, often not pieced together very well, and easily identified and separated out from later additions by their many literary disruptions.

Those who finalized prophetic books—often called redactors—were viewed as technicians, "scissors and paste men," who added irrelevant comments to the material and frequently distorted its original message by adding ideas that had little theological worth. Prophetic scholarship continued to hold to Gunkel's belief that prophets originally delivered short oracles. Passages were divided based upon the idea that the original text was pure.

# REDACTION CRITICISM

By the mid-1970s a major shift was in the making as form critics began to place more emphasis upon the work of redactors. While the recognition and analysis of the pre-literary materials remained an important aspect of the reading strategy, it became viewed as only a part of the task. There was a growing awareness that the form-critical questions should be applied to all stages of the literature, including material which did not have an oral prehistory.

Prophetic scholarship was being redirected. While still distinguishing between the final text and earlier traditions, the new goal was to place greater value upon the additions. Classical form criticism was evolving into what is now called redaction criticism. The difference is in form criticism's archival text designed merely to preserve the prophet's words and redaction criticism's focus on an exhortational text that employs both the prophet's words and later editors as a means to motivate a community living decades, if not centuries, after the prophet. Whereas Gunkel and those who followed him were determined to locate the original words of the prophet, the work of redaction critics began to move the discussion in the direction of studying prophetic books as a whole.

Wolfgang Richter was an important early redactional scholar who engaged prophetic texts on the basis of both their *Sitz im Leben* and *Sitz im Literatur*. Although he focused largely on the synchronic level, a major goal of Richter's research was to identify discontinuities within texts as a means to reconstruct their diachronic or redaction history. He believed that later editions of prophetic collections reflected the concerns and interests of the receptor community. This way of reading is influenced by the belief that prophetic books were capable of being adapted to new situations and of inspiring fresh oracles modeled on it. Therefore, Richter viewed prophetic oracles as testimonies to a living tradition that continually actualized old texts with new interpretations.

Redaction critics frequently speak of this literary growth of prophetic texts. Some use the concept of "explication," while others prefer the idea of adaptation or interpretation. Whatever term is employed, there is a consensus among redaction critics that prophetic books demonstrate a process of continual realization and actualization beginning with the realm of oral tradition.

With so many additional interpretations placed upon the original text, redaction critics believe that those who read the prophets are not confronted with the historical prophet, but with the "presentation" of the prophet, to use a term coined by Ackroyd. The original quest for the authentic words of prophets, a program that formed the basis for form criticism, is now considered a futile enterprise. As critical scholars assign more work to the redactional process, they leave less assigned to the authorship of the prophet. This yields (according to the hypothesis) less reliable historical data about the prophet. Pushed to its extreme, redaction criticism concludes that any historical reconstruction of a prophet is unrecoverable and that the book is largely an imaginative literary construct.

Redaction criticism does not reject the diachronic methods of form criticism, but it reorders priorities so that biblical texts are examined in their final context as literary wholes. Whereas form criticism understood texts in terms of their *beginning*, redaction criticism understands them in terms of their *end*. This feature distinguishes form criticism from redaction criticism in that the latter does not focus its attention in tracing the first oracle uttered or written by the prophet. Rather, redaction critics seek to discover not only the successive stages in the editorial process, but also more important editorial work of the final text. Thus the form critical method of separating the prophetic core from the scribal husk does not change with redaction criticism. The only difference is that the latter places a higher value on the husk. The focus has shifted from the pursuit of original oral forms to the final literary form, that is, the book.

Consequently, redaction critics jettison form criticism's swift access to the prophet and the marginal evaluation of the books. The view of the prophet as *speaker* that dominated in the era of form criticism no longer serves as the starting point for the question. This shift away from form criticism is to take prophetic books seriously as *books*.

## RHETORICAL CRITICISM

Though there are many problems with form and redactional reading strategies, the chief dilemma is the amount of speculation involved by those who employ these interpretive methods. They frequently supply subjective information that is outside of the biblical text. By linking exegesis to historical reconstructions, these modes of interpretation jeopardize the integrity of prophetic texts and their theological message. Since the reconstructed oracles of form and redactional critics are hypothetical and unverifiable, a more fruitful approach to understanding linguistic discontinuity in the prophets is that of rhetorical criticism.

The rediscovery of rhetoric has had a profound impact upon biblical studies, as seen in the growth in the number of articles, monographs, Festschriften, and conferences addressing themselves to the rhetorical analysis of biblical texts. Muilenburg is universally acknowledged as the leader of the movement. In his 1968 ground-breaking paper, "Form Criticism and Beyond," he criticized form criticism because of its tendency to ignore the artistry and particularity of a text's literary features. Muilenburg maintained that form criticism tends to obscure the thought and intention of writers because it fixates on conventions, slights historical commentary, and separates form from content while isolating small units. It neglects the individual, personal, unique, particular, distinctive, precise, versatile, and fluid features of texts. Whereas form critics look for what is *typical*, Muilenburg argued for an investigation of the *particularities* of a given text. He advocated the study of large unified compositions and component genres which are built together into a rhetorical whole. Muilenburg wanted to overcome the arbitrary and atomistic methods of form criticism. In doing so, he paved the way for a more holistic approach to prophetic texts which is now called rhetorical criticism.

Trible divided the various methods that go by the name rhetorical criticism into two branches. The first would be those that carry out Muilenburg's attention to the structure of a passage, which she called the study of the "art of composition." The second method is represented by Wuellner, and especially Gitay, which Trible named the study of the "art of persuasion." Gitay, for example, outlines the structure of prophetic texts in classical rhetorical terms: thesis, ethos, and pathos. In this move beyond Muilenburg, Gitay highlights not only the *stylistic* features of prophetic texts, but also their *persuasive* aspects as well.

This understanding means that prophetic books are rhetorically charged and are designed to persuade. Even a cursory examination of prophetic literature justifies the conclusion that oral communication was the essential feature of their vocation and work. Furthermore, even if there were no such reports or allusions but only the prophetic words themselves, it is clear from the form, style, and content of those words that the prophets were fundamentally speakers. Calls using the imperative of שמע, *hear*, are common in prophetic books (cf. e.g., Isa 1:2; 7:13; 48:1; Jer 10:1; Amos 3:1; 4:1; 5:1). The frequent use of שמע indicates that prophetic texts were meant to be read out loud. Oral communication was expected.

Gunkel described the oral world as part of an evolutionary hypothesis whereby oral means early and primitive, that is, pre-textual. He believed that oral compositions and their cultures predated the OT. Rhetorical critics are opposed to this understanding. Writing against Gunkel's reconstruction of OT texts, Susan Niditch suggests that the oral world lives in the words of the OT. It is better to understand that, in any writing culture, orality and literacy co-exist and interact as each influences the other. Niditch maintains that the prophets' oral performances could have been written down to be orally performed.

Further evidence of this understanding is confirmed in that there is no distinct vocabulary in the OT for the activity of reading. In both Hebrew and Aramaic, the most common verb used is קרא, *proclaim*. The noun derived from קרא is מקרא, a *reading* or *recitation* (e.g., Neh 8:8). Both terms are highly oral. Reading in the OT was aloud and interpersonal. There was no way of naming a private, silent reading of an OT text. In several prophetic passages, texts are represented as written first and then presented orally. These oracles were written on scrolls on the basis of orality. That is, they were for the *ears*, not for the silent perusal of the *eyes*. The classic example is Jer 36.

Not only does rhetorical criticism unite orality, literary form, and persuasion in its interpretive task, but it also adds the component of historical setting. It is important to capture the original rhetorical situation between the author and his audience within the domain of the historical paradigm. Rhetorical criticism assumes that the text is literary artistry, composed for oral delivery in a specific historical situation, and that prophets have specific persuasive goals in mind.

## CONCLUSION

A rhetorical approach to prophetic texts challenges the assumptions and conclusions of form and redactional-critical work. The judgment that editors and intertextual scribes are responsible for the phenomena of linguistic discontinuity should be withheld. Textual interruptions, rather, reflect the oral performance of the text. Greenberg maintains:

> A universal prejudice of modern biblical criticism is the assumption of original simplicity. A passage of complex structure, or one containing repetition, or skewing a previously used figure is, on these grounds, suspect of being inauthentic. Another widespread prejudice equates authenticity with topical or thematic uniformity. A temporal vista that progresses from present, to penultimate, to ultimate time is considered an artificial result of successive additions to a single-time original oracle. Doom oracles that end with a glimpse of a better future are declared composites on the ground of psychological improbability. Such prejudices are simply *a prioris*, an array of unproved (and unprovable) modern assumptions and conventions that confirm themselves through the results obtained by forcing them on the text and altering, reducing, and reordering it accordingly.[1]

---

[1] Moshe Greenberg, "What are the Valid Criteria for Determining Inauthentic Matter in Ezekiel?" in J. Lust, ed. *Ezekiel and His Book* (Leuven: Leuven University Press, 1986), 123–35, 127.

Form and redaction criticisms' recovery of so-called original versions is an enterprise fraught with perils, obstacles, and difficulties. Any results are partly if not largely informed guesswork. In the end, there is a significant difference between having a tangible text and trying to draw inferences or argue cases on the basis of a reconstructed hypothetical original text. What is reconstructed is finally of the scholar's making.

One must ask whether form and redaction critics have discovered a past reality or whether they have created one. The question of what types of discontinuities are acceptable and those that are not must be answered against the background of prophetic literature's own peculiarities of style and not based *a priori* on stylistic conceptions from the Western world. It is precisely the nature of prophetic discourse to make sudden shifts on all levels of language, including style and imagery, and to juxtapose multiple, divergent, and even dissonant perspectives in much the same way as in poetic parallelism. It is therefore an anachronism to impose upon prophetic books criteria applied to writings intended to be scientific or didactic—clear and distinct ideas, logically ordered.

The debate between form/redaction and rhetorical criticism is important. But there is an additional component that must be brought to bear upon the interpretation of Israel's prophets. The clear witness of the NT is that Jesus Christ is the ultimate interpretive key to all OT prophecy. "The testimony of Jesus is the spirit of prophecy" (Rev 19:10). Prophetic oracles point to Christ and are given direction from him. He is Isaiah's Suffering Servant (e.g., Isa 52:13–53:12) and confirms Jeremiah's new covenant (Jer 31:31–34). Jesus is foreshadowed in Ezekiel's new temple (Ezek 40:1–48:36), Hosea's love for his bride (Hos 3:1–5), Amos's roaring Lion (Amos 1:2), Malachi's Sun of Righteousness (Malachi 4:1–2), and so much more. Christ is the very substance, marrow, soul, and scope of Israel's prophetic texts (cf. 2 Cor 1:20).

## SELECT BIBLIOGRAPHY

Ackroyd, Peter. "Isaiah 1–12: Presentation of a Prophet." In *Congress Volume, Göttingen 1977*, 16–48. Supplements to Vetus Testamentum 29 Leiden: E. J. Brill, 1978.

Gitay, Yehoshua. *Isaiah and His Audience: The Structure and Meaning of Isaiah 1–12.* Studia Semitica Neerlandica. Van Gorcum, Assen/Masstricht: The Netherlands, 1991.

Greenberg, Moshe. "What Are the Valid Criteria for Determining Inauthentic Matter in Ezekiel?" In *Ezekiel and His Book.* Edited by J. Lust, 123–35. Leuven: Leuven University Press, 1986.

Lessing, Reed. "Orality in the Prophets." *Concordia Journal* (April 2003): 152–65.

Mowinckel, Sigmund. *Prophecy and Tradition Prophecy and Tradition: The Prophetic Books in the Light of the Study of the Growth and History of the Tradition.* Oslo: Kommisjon Hos Jacob Dybwad, 1946.

Muilenburg, James. "Form Criticism and Beyond." *Journal of Biblical Literature* 88 (1969): 1–18.

Niditch, Susan. *Oral World and Written Word.* Louisville: Westminster, 1996.

Richter, Wolfgang. *Exegese als Literaturwissenschaft: Entwurf einer alttestamentlichen Literaturtheori und Methodologie.* Göttingen: Vandenhoeck & Ruprecht, 1971.

Smith, Gary V. *An Introduction to the Hebrew Prophets: The Prophets as Preachers.* Broadman Holman: Nashville, 1994.

Trible, Phyllis. *Rhetorical Criticism.* Minneapolis: Augsburg Fortress, 1994.

Wuellner, Wilhelm. "Where Is Rhetorical Criticism Taking Us?" *Catholic Biblical Quarterly* 49 (1987): 451–78.

# 22

# ISAIAH

In the OT, Isaiah is the theologian par excellence. His chief doctrine comes from his name, יְשַׁעְיָהוּ, *Yahweh is deliverance.* The prophet employs the root ישע seventy-two times in his book. For sheer grandeur, majesty, and supreme artistry, no book in the OT comes close to Isaiah. The prophet's saving message, soaring language, and unforgettable imagery are tightly woven into the fabric of Christian hymnody, liturgy, and devotional literature. The book's influence upon the NT is massive. About one out of every seventeen verses in the NT is inspired by Isaiah's pen. And it is primarily through Isaiah that the NT articulates its Christology, ecclesiology, and missiology.

## AUTHORSHIP

The modern critical approach to Isaiah was launched when J. C. Döderlein published his commentary on the book in 1789. These initial buds burst into full bloom under the influence of Duhm, whose 1892 epoch-making commentary on Isaiah has made a lasting imprint. He suggested a division between chapters 1–39, 40–55, and 56–66. An "Iron Curtain" of sorts descended upon Isaiah studies, rendering a holistic reading of the book unimaginable. Isaiah was understood as a collection of texts that have little or no coherence or unity of thought. Interpreters following Duhm may be likened to people on a literary archaeological dig. Scholars attempted to unearth the "real Isaiah" and in doing so divided the book into sources, fragments, glosses, and editorial additions.

A 1979 article by Ackroyd called into question these form-critical presuppositions and the Duhmian consensus began to crumble. In a move that would cause ripple effects throughout the guild, Ackroyd understood that Isaiah was the book's presentation of the prophet, not the prophet's presentation of a book. He argued that the book of Isaiah was not a grouping together of unrelated oracles by the mechanical work of redactors, but rather a collection of texts that had been creatively harmonized to become a redactionally unified whole. While there is still a consensus in critical scholarship that the book of Isaiah is a composite that incorporates material written centuries after the prophet's lifetime, there is a growing interest in the larger unity and coherence of Isaiah as a book in its own right.

From separate volumes partitioned into chapters 1–39, 40–55, and 56–66 with different authors to a single book masterfully brought together by a final editor, work on Isaiah has come almost full circle. Whereas Duhm and those like him pursued the "original Isaiah" by means of their form critical methodologies, resulting in two, three, four, or more "Isaiahs," the interest has shifted to later redactors and editors who brought unity to the book. The history of Isaianic scholarship is therefore best described using the triad, one book–three books–one book.

Higher critical belief in one book, however, does not mean belief in one author. Reading Isaiah holistically does not entail discarding earlier critical understandings about the book's composition. Critics still assume the existence of an "Isaiah-school" that played an important role in the book's final editing. They maintain that a group of disciples, close to Isaiah, continued to exist into the time of the Babylonian exile and Israel's return. These followers continuously updated and expanded upon the prophet's earlier texts.

The contentious issue therefore is no longer Isaianic unity but Isaianic authorship. Are the *words* inspired or was an *author* named Isaiah inspired to compose an inspired text? Those embracing different authors for Isaiah refuse to take into account the witness of the NT. It specifically and repeatedly refers to all sixty-six chapters as coming from the pen of Isaiah. For example, in John 12:38–41, quotations from Isa 6:10 and Isa 53:1 are attributed to Isaiah. Granted, there are some NT texts where the author writes a phrase like, "as it says in the book of Isaiah" (e.g., Luke 3:4), yet in other places NT writers state, "Isaiah prophesied" (e.g., Matt 3:3; 8:17; 12:17). If Isaiah did not write the book attributed to him, the NT witness is false. But of even greater significance is that we are left with a

Christological dilemma, for Jesus himself held that the prophet Isaiah wrote the entire book (e.g., Matt 13:14).

Additionally, the ancient versions show no signs of different authors. 1QIsa$^a$ begins with Isa 40:1 as the first line at the bottom of a column, suggesting that at Qumran the scribes did not believe Isa 40–66 was a secondary addition. In fact, there is no manuscript evidence that the book was ever circulated in parts. Thus, we may confidently affirm that all sixty-six chapters are "the vision of Isaiah" (Isa 1:1) which he saw in the pre-exilic period. But his book serves as Yahweh's word not only in pre-exilic times but also in exilic, postexilic, Christological, and eschatological eras.

## LITERARY FEATURES OF ISAIAH

One of the errors of higher critics is that they fail to see that the book of Isaiah is arranged in a topical manner. This ought to be evident by the placement of Isa 6, the prophet's call. Since this chapter does not occupy the beginning position in the book (in contrast to the calls of Jeremiah and Ezekiel, which are in the lead position in their books), it should be recognized that Isaiah's book is arranged topically, and this—not disparate authorship—accounts for the changes between the major sections (Isa 1–39; 40–55; 56–66).

While the first thirty-nine chapters of Isaiah demonstrate poetic brilliance and artistry, in the last twenty-seven chapters he takes this gift to a higher level. Isa 40–55 is organized like a series of connected, revolving discs, placed side by side. Every section is connected to what precedes and follows, yet each new passage differs from the others. Isa 40 introduces the entire unit, while chapters 41–48 announce Yahweh's plan to stir up Cyrus, who will return the Judean refugees to Jerusalem. Chapters 49–54 declare Yahweh's intention to forgive Israel's sin that got them in Babylon in the first place. Isa 55 summarizes the unit.

Isaiah writes these oracles for the benefit of future generations in Babylon after Jerusalem's demise in 587. These are not prophecies after the fact (*vaticina ex eventu*), as the critics would have it. In fact, Isaiah is specifically told at his call that his contemporaries would not understand his words, but that future generations will comprehend it (Isa 6:9–13; cf. 29:11–24).

In the context of the Babylonian exile—which left Israel staring into the abyss—in chapters 40–55, it was important for Isaiah to anchor himself to older texts. A judicious balance needed to be struck, one in which Isaiah's role as conservator of ancient tradition is blended with that of offering comfort and hope. Repeating earlier texts would not adequately address the new uncertainties brought about by the exile. Yet neither was a completely new message likely to take root in the hearts of those in Babylon. Therefore, Isaiah needed to hearken back to "the former things" (Isa 46:9) "declared long ago" (Isa 48:5). But he also had to set aside the former things in order to declare "a new thing" (Isa 43:19) which was "created now, not long ago" (Isa 48:7). If his oracles were too much like the old word, they would risk irrelevance. If they were too dissimilar, they would risk rejection. This tension is stated in Isa 46:9a, "Remember the former things . . . " and Isa 43:18a, "Do not remember the former things . . . ." Isaiah stands between continuity and discontinuity.

Intertextual interpretations in Isa 40–55 accent not only the prophet's reuse of Pentateuchal texts, including the creation narrative of Gen 1:1–2:4a, the Garden of Eden, Noah, and Abraham, but they especially highlight Isaiah's use of Israel's Exodus from Egypt. It is commonly recognized that Isa 40–55 draws most heavily on the Exodus as the archetypal act of Yahweh's deliverance. While the prophet employs numerous Exodus echoes, this theme is the chief subject in Isa 40:3–5; 41:17–20; 42:14–16; 43:1–3, 14–21; 48:20–21; 49:8–12; 51:9–10; 52:11–12; and 55:12–13.

Unlike Isa 40–55, chapters 56–66 initially appear to be a bewildering collection of oracles that lack any overall coherence or movement. However, first impressions may be wrong, and in this case, they are. Far from being a loose assemblage of prophetic oracles with no rhyme or reason, Isa 56–66 reflects a careful and deliberate arrangement. These chapters contain a high degree of literary sophistication through a chiastic ordering of oracles that places chapters 60–62 at the center. These three chapters are the pivot around which everything else is arranged. The broad pattern is A-B-A; Isa 56–59, 60–62, 63–66. The faithful remnant's glorious future is in the middle, while on either side stand descriptions of the acute divisions within the community. The Fifth Servant Song (Isa 61:1–3) is at the center of chapters 60–62, both literarily and theologically. More specifically, chapters 60–62 stand at the core of Isa 56–66 and Isa 61: 1–3 announces the source of God's salvation.

# Outline of Isaiah

I. Judgment on Judah and Jerusalem (chs. 1–12)
- A. Overview of the book (1:1–31)
- B. The pilgrimage of the nations to Zion (2:1–5)
- C. The Day of Yahweh (2:6–22)
- D. Social and moral chaos (3:1–4:1)
- E. Peace after judgment (4:2–6)
- F. The Song of the Vineyard (5:1–7)
- G. A series of woes (5:8–30)
- H. Isaiah's call (6:1–13)
- I. Isaiah and Ahaz (7:1–25)
- J. Assyrian judgment and the remnant promise (8:1–22)
- K. A new king for a new age (8:23–9:7)
- L. Yahweh's wrath (9:8–21)
- M. More woes against Israel and Assyria (10:1–32)
- N. The peaceful kingdom (11:1–9)
- O. The reunited kingdoms (11:10–16)
- P. Concluding hymn of praise (12:1–6)

II. Oracles about the Nations (chs. 13–23)
- A. Babylon's fall and universal judgment (13:1–22)
- B. Salvation for Jacob (14:1–2)
- C. The king of Babylon is condemned (14:3–23)
- D. Yahweh's plans (14:24–27)
- E. An oracle against Philistia (14:28–32)
- F. Oracles against Moab (15:1–16:14)
- G. The destiny of Syria and Israel (17:1–14)
- H. An oracle against an alliance with Egypt (18:1–7)
- I. An oracle against Egypt (19:1–25)
- J. Isaiah stripped and barefoot (20:1–6)
- K. Babylon's fall (21:1–10)
- L. An oracle against Edom (21:11–17)
- M. The Valley of Vision (22:1–14)

N. An oracle about palace leaders (22:15–25)

O. An oracle against Tyre and Sidon (23:1–18)

III. Cosmic Judgment (chs. 24–27)

    A. A curse on the earth and its people (24:1–23)

    B. The first thanksgiving song (25:1–5)

    C. The eschatological banquet (25:6–8)

    D. The second thanksgiving song (25:9–12)

    E. The third thanksgiving song (26:1–6)

    F. An eschatological psalm (26:7–27:1)

    G. The vineyard revisited (27:2–6)

    H. The final destiny of the city and Yahweh's people (27:7–13)

IV. Samaria and Jerusalem (chs. 28–33)

    A. The future of Samaria and its leaders (28:1–22)

    B. Jerusalem's reversal (29:1–24)

    C. The folly of aligning with Egypt (30:1–5)

    D. An oracle against the Negev (30:6–7)

    E. Written for the ages (30:8–14)

    F. Defeat is waiting but mercy is on every side (30:15–26)

    G. Assyria's final phase (30:27–33)

    H. The alliance with Egypt (31:1–9)

    I. The righteous king (32:1–8)

    J. Lamentations, but not forever (32:9–20)

    K. The tyrant is judged and a psalm (33:1–6)

    L. Social and physical disaster (33:7–13)

    M. Teaching on morality and a future without fear (33:14–24)

V. Judgment and Salvation (chs. 34–35)

    A. Oracle against Edom (34:1–17)

    B. The final journey to Zion (35:1–10)

VI. Isaiah and Hezekiah (chs. 36–39)

    A. Jerusalem threatened and delivered (36:1–37:38)

    B. Hezekiah's sickness and healing (38:1–22)

    C. The Babylonians visit Hezekiah (39:1–8)

VII. Exodus from Babylon (chs. 40–55)

    A.  Prologue: Yahweh's power for Israel (40:1–31)

    B.  The call to Cyrus and servant Israel (41:1–42:9)

    C.  Hymn (42:10–13)

    D.  Servant Israel is deaf and blind (42:14–44:22)

    E.  Hymn (44:23)

    F.  Cyrus will lead Israel out of Babylon (44:24–48:19)

    G.  The command to leave Babylon (48:20–22)

    H.  The Suffering Servant saves the nations (49:1–12)

    I.  Hymn (49:13)

    J.  The Suffering Servant comes to rescue Zion (49:14–52:10)

    K.  The command to leave Babylon (52:11–12)

    L.  The Suffering Servant declares Zion's servants righteous (52:13– 54:17)

    M.  Epilogue: The Creator's everlasting covenant (55:1–11)

    N.  Hymn (55:12–13)

VIII.  Struggles in the Servant's New Community (chs. 56–66)

    A.  Overview of chapters 56–66 (56:1–8)

    B.  Leaders are denounced (56:9–12)

    C.  Judgment on idolaters and assurances for the faithful (57:1–58:14)

    D.  Lament over sin (59:1–15a)

    E.  Warrior Yahweh intervenes for the remnant (59:15b–21)

    F.  Promises of salvation (60:1–22)

    G.  The Anointed Prophet (61:1–3)

    H.  Promises of salvation (61:4–62:12)

    I.  Warrior Yahweh intervenes for the remnant (63:1–6)

    J.  Isaiah's lament (63:7–64:12)

    K.  Judgment on idolaters and assurances for the faithful (65:1–25)

    L.  Leaders are denounced (66:1–4)

    M.  Foreigners are admitted to worship (66:5–24)

Isa 1 lays out the book's overall message, which also reflects the prophet's three main sections: judgment (Isa 1:1–9 for Isa 1–39); salvation (Isa 1:10–20 for Isa 40–55); and the call to respond (Isa 1:21–31 for Isa 56–66). Justice and righteousness are hallmark features of the entire book. The prophet sees none of it (e.g., Isa 1:21–23; 5:7), but is certain that the Davidic Messiah will become the locus of a reformation that empowers Israel to have compassion upon the orphan, widow, and alien in the gate (e.g., Isa 9:7; 11:1–4; 32:1). He is the Spirit-inspired Savior whose death and resurrection ushers in an eternal Jubilee—justice and righteousness for all (Isa 52:13–53:12; 61:1–3).

## TEXTUAL ISSUES

Two copies of Isaiah were discovered in Cave 1 at Qumran. One of them, 1QIsa[a], is virtually intact. The carbon dating on 1QIsa[a] by the Tucson laboratory dates the scroll to 341–325 BC or 202–114 BC. The Zurich laboratory dating is 201–93 BC. The manuscript consists of seventeen strips of leather stitched together to create the oldest complete biblical book in existence.

1QIsa[a] establishes the faithfulness of the MT as aberrations between the two are chiefly morphological and orthographical. Following 1QIsa[a], the most significant Isaianic textual find at Qumran consists of twenty-one separate copies of the book that survived the ravages of time. Of these, the most complete is 1QIsa[b] which contains parts of chapters 41–66. It is also congruent with the MT.

## HISTORICAL ISSUES

When compared with Jeremiah or Ezekiel, Isaiah encompasses a greater chronological sweep. The book's vast historical scale may be symbolized by two names appearing in it: Uzziah (Isa 6:1) and Cyrus (Isa 44:28; 45:1). Uzziah was a king from Judah who reigned from 791 to 740. Cyrus was a Persian emperor who ruled from 539 to 530. Since Isa 6:1 refers to the death of Uzziah, there is a two hundred-year period represented by these two kings, extending the historical horizon of the book from the Assyrian period through the Babylonian and into the Persian.

Isaiah began his ministry during Israel and Judah's "Silver Age," an era inaugurated by Jeroboam ben Joash (793–753) in the north and

Uzziah in the south. The prophet also lived through the Assyrian capture and exile of Samaria (723) and the semi-escape of Judah and the nation's colonial status under the same Assyrian colossus (701). The Judean kings Jotham, Ahaz, and Hezekiah were impacted by Isaiah's ministry. And, although he doesn't include Manasseh (697–643) in his superscription, the prophet most certainly lived during this monarch's time. Isaiah records the death of Sennacherib (681) in Isa 37:38.

Chapters 7–8 reflect the Syro-Ephraimitic crisis of 735–732, whereas chapters 36–38 derive from the Assyrian attack on Judah (701). These accounts highlight the responses of two Judahite monarchs, Ahaz and Hezekiah. The narrative connections between these two kings are as follows: the location described in Isa 7:3—"the conduit of the upper pool on the highway to the Fuller's Field"—is identical with that of Isa 36:2; in both texts, Assyria is the decisive imperial power and in both texts Isaiah speaks directly with a king, first Ahaz and later Hezekiah; in both encounters, Isaiah admonishes a king "not to fear" the military challenge that is before him (Isa 7:4; 37:6); finally in both texts there are overt references to "signs" (Isa 7:11, 14; 37:30; 38:7, 22). These similarities highlight the different ways in which each king responded to an Assyrian threat. Ahaz abandons his trust in Yahweh (2 Kgs 16:7–18), but Hezekiah firmly clings to his God (Isa 37).

In Isa 39, Isaiah appears in Hezekiah's court and promises that Judah will undergo a Babylonian exile but not be annihilated. There will be an end, but the end will be the start of a new beginning. Chapters 40–55, then, naturally follow chapter 39 and fit into Yahweh's judgment against Hezekiah. There are both thematic connections between Isa 1–39 and 40–55 as well as a logical progression.

These links, though, do not abolish the gap between Isa 39 and 40, which represents the defining interruption in Israel's history. A series of events occurred between Isaiah's call in 740 (Isa 6:1) and 539 (Cyrus's defeat of Babylon). The Northern Kingdom fell in 723. Nineveh collapsed in 612 and the Assyrian kingdom was destroyed (cf. Nahum). The disastrous reign of Manasseh hastened Judah's demise (2 Kgs 21:18; Jer 15:4). Josiah died at the battle of Megiddo in 609 (2 Kgs 23:29–30) and the subsequent rise of the Babylonian empire under Nabopolassar (625–605) and his son Nebuchadnezzar II

(605–562) brought with it near-anarchy in Judah. Most importantly, however, was Jerusalem's massive destruction and devastation in 587 (2 Kgs 24:20–25:30). The prophetic word in Isa 39 came to pass. Nebuchadnezzar's forces destroyed the capital city and brought its leaders to the other side of the Fertile Crescent.

The Babylonian empire, however, was a brief blip on the stage of ancient Near Eastern history. By 550, the kingdom of Persia began to eclipse Babylon and became the dominant power until the rise of Alexander the Great (333). Isa 40–55 addresses these times between exilic displacement in Babylon and return under Persian permission. The prophet's words of comfort follow directly upon the heels of his prediction of disaster (Isa 39:5–7). In chapters 40–55, the eighth and early seventh century prophet addresses sixth century postexilic Israel.

In 538, Yahweh's stirring prompted Cyrus's decree (Ezra 1:2). Not only had Babylon fallen to Persia, but Cyrus made it possible for Judeans to rebuild the temple that the empire had destroyed (Ezra 4:3). Historians characterize Cyrus as one of history's greatest liberators and humanitarians who practiced religious toleration. In fact, the Cyrus Cylinder documents the king's policy of currying favor with other Babylonian captives by sponsoring the rebuilding of temples throughout his empire.

# THEOLOGICAL THEMES IN ISAIAH

## GOD'S HOLINESS

Few question that Isaiah's call in chapter 6 becomes one of the paramount features in his theology. The prophet hears the seraphim cry out קדש, *holy*, three times (Isa 6:3), and this propels him to employ the root קדש sixty-nine times in his book. Nineteen times he refers to Yahweh as קדש ישראל, *the Holy One of Israel*. The title appears in both judgment (e.g., Isa 1:4; 5:19, 24) and restoration contexts (e.g., Isa 43:3, 14). It announces that the Transcendent One is also, amazingly, in relationship with *Israel*.

## YAHWEH'S PLAN

Central to the book of Isaiah is the root עצה. As a verb, it means *advise*, *plan*, or *decide*. Of the twenty-seven passages that speak of the plan of Yahweh in the OT, sixteen of them are in Isaiah (e.g., Isa

14:24, 26, 27; 19:12, 17; 23:8, 9; 44:26; 46:10, 11). These last two verses state Yahweh's plan through Cyrus.

The root expresses Yahweh's action in history. In Isa 5:19 it is parallel with עשה, *work*. This plan was meant to be taken over by the Judean monarchy as the foundation of its political planning (Isa 30:1), but it was mocked (Isa 5:19). Yet Yahweh will establish his plan in spite of them. To do so, he must destroy the plans of people (Isa 8:10; cf. 7:7; 19:2, 11, 17). With Ahaz the verb עצה occurs in Isaiah's war oracle (Isa 7:5). The king is not to be afraid of the Syrian and Ephraimite plan to conquer Judah and set a puppet king on the throne. Three times in Isa 14:24–27 Yahweh's plan is articulated against Assyria, indeed for all the nations. In the Hezekiah narrative, the noun עצה comes in the context of the Rabshakeh's military manifesto (Isa 36:4–5).

In Isa 13–23, the prophet offers his most comprehensive plan about the nations. Yahweh's alien or strange work (Isa 28:21) is to destroy the wicked, debase the proud, and defeat the tyranny of Assyria and Babylon. His proper work includes the restoration of Israel to Zion, while also reaching beyond Israel to encompass the nations. They too will look to Yahweh and come to Zion (Isa 2:1–5) and enjoy the protection of Israel's Messiah (Isa 16:3–5; cf. 11:10). In Isa 19:25, Yahweh goes so far as to call Egypt "my people" and Assyria "the work of my hands," along with Israel as "my inheritance." Yahweh's plan is to bring all people into fellowship with him, and this will end every conflict between nation and nation (Isa 2:4). "In the latter days" (Isa 2:2), foreign nations will no longer menace Israel or one another. They will come to Zion and learn Yahweh's Torah.

## THE GOSPEL

In the OT, Isa 40:9 is the first place where the term בשר, *gospel*, appears in a theological sense. The gospel announcement is, "Behold your God" (Isa 40:9). The God to behold is the one who speaks double comfort (Isa 40:1) and who exhibits both a strong and tender arm (Isa 40:10–11). Isa 52:10 reveals the arm of power: "Yahweh will lay bare his holy arm." He rolls up his sleeves, displays his arm, and uncovers bulging biceps! But Yahweh's power is made perfect in weakness (cf. 2 Cor 12:9). Isa 53:1 reveals the arm of compassion: "To whom has Yahweh's arm been revealed?" This compassionate arm is made manifest when it is stripped of its clothing, tied to a Roman whipping post, and hung bleeding upon the empire's instrument of death. Through this Suffering Servant, Yahweh forgives Zion of her sins and declares her righteous (Isa 53:11; 54:17).

The gospel also includes Isaiah's message that by means of the Persian King Cyrus, Yahweh will catch Babylon flat-footed, triumph over the empire's deities (Isa 46:1–4) and its royal power (Isa 47:1–11), and lead the exiles in a joyous, triumphant return to Zion/Jerusalem (Isa 52:11–12). Israel is not forever stuck in Babylon's harsh regime, nor are they mired in the muck of their sin.

## REDEMPTION

The term גאל, *redeemer*, is a prominent title for Yahweh in Isa 40–55 (e.g., Isa 43:14; 44:6, 24; 47:4; 48:17; 51:10; 52:3, 9). It denotes a near relative who is to avenge the blood of a family member who had been murdered (Num 35:12–27), buy back a relative's property or an enslaved person (e.g., Lev 25:24–54), and restore a childless widow (Ruth 3:13). Because of his commitment to his family, the redeemer marshals his superior power and resources to assist those in need. Since Israel is Yahweh's firstborn son (Exod 4:22), and therefore a part of his family, Yahweh stands ready as his people's Redeemer to right whatever has gone wrong. He does this by raising up Cyrus (Isa 41:2; cf. 44:28; 45:10) and giving the Suffering Servant for the sins of the world (e.g., 50:4–9; 52:13–53:12).

## SERVANTS

Isaiah's four Servant Songs are some of the most debated texts in the OT. They appear in Isa 42:1–4; 49:1–6; 50:4–9; and 52:13–53:12. The epilogues for each song are Isa 42:5–9; 49:7–13; 50:10–11; 54.

Who is the Servant? Those who identify him with an individual have named, among others, Hezekiah, Isaiah, Uzziah, Josiah, a leper, Jeremiah, Moses, Sheshbazzar, Zerubbabel, Nehemiah, Jehoiachin, Eleazar, Ezekiel, Cyrus, Job, Meshullam, and Zedekiah. The dominant Christian position until the end of the nineteenth century was that Jesus of Nazareth was the fulfillment of the Servant Songs (cf. Acts 8:32–35). On the other hand, the collective view identifies the Servant as a group of people who are described in individualistic terms. This assembly has been understood to be empirical Israel (the entire nation), ideal Israel, a righteous remnant within the nation

Israel, the Davidic dynasty, the prophetic order, and the priestly order. Many do not view the above categories as mutually exclusive, and often scholars interpret the Servant using a combination of several groups.

Isa 42:1–4 is the First Servant Song and the servant (Isa 42:1) is described in terms similar to Jacob-Israel in Isa 41:8–10. Both are upheld by Yahweh (Isa 41:10; 42:1) and both are chosen (Isa 41:8, 9; 42:1). Further evidence suggests that the servant figure in Isa 42:1 and throughout chapters 40–48 is Jacob-Israel. This servant is blind and deaf (Isa 42:19–20), idolatrous (e.g., Isa 44:9–20), and therefore unable to be a covenant people and light to the nations (cf. Isa 42:7). Yahweh still loves Jacob-Israel, despite the nation's fatal flaws, and so he gives them a replacement Servant.

In chapters 49–55 the term עֶבֶד, *servant*, appears seven times (Isa 49:3, 5, 6, 7; 50:10; 52:13; 53:11). Each occurrence denotes Yahweh's substitute Servant. The literary structures of Isa 42:1–4 and 49:1–6 correspond with one another, indicating that the new Servant shares a similar mission with the failed nation. Both are followed by Yahweh's speech (Isa 42:5–9; 49:7–13) and within each of them are the words, "And I am setting you to be a light to the nations" (Isa 42:6; 49:8). The Servant in the second song is given the additional assignment of restoring Jacob/Israel (Isa 49:5). The point is this: *The servant nation needs the individual Suffering Servant to reconcile them to Yahweh and accomplish what they are unable to do.* The new Servant will not only "raise up the tribes of Jacob, and restore the survivors of Israel" (Isa 49:6). Yahweh will make him "as a light to the nations, so that my salvation may be to the ends of the earth" (Isa 49:6).

It follows, then, that within Isa 40–55, there are two servants: servant Israel and the Suffering Servant. Servant Israel is the nation introduced in Isa 41:8 and Isa 42:1–4. After failing miserably (Isa 42:19–20), the nation is rejected by Yahweh. The people are declared to be Israel in name only, in a statement which divests them of their servant office. Isa 48 plays a pivotal role in Isaiah's presentation of these two servants. Servant Israel is dismissed and the Suffering Servant is introduced. The work of Cyrus, which is at the heart of the message of chapters 41–47, is brought to a close (Isa 48:14–15). He is absent in the rest of the book. Yahweh's attention becomes focused upon Israel's replacement, the Suffering Servant who speaks for the first time in Isa 48:16b, "But now Lord Yahweh sent me endowed with his Spirit." The connections between Isa 48:16b and Isa 49:1–6, as well as with Isa 50:4–9, are clear. "But now" in Isa 48:16b anticipates a similar word usage in Isa 49:4, while the title "Lord Yahweh" appears again in Isa 50:4, 5, 7, and 9. Moreover, the theme of "Spirit" reaches back to the first song in Isa 42:1. Both servant Israel and the Suffering Servant are directed by Yahweh's Spirit. The first is defeated by idolatry, and the second is victorious, winning life for the world.

In Isa 49:4, the Suffering Servant laments that he has not been successful in delivering the people from captivity. Yahweh responds to his cry by promising that his new Servant will not only restore Israel but will also bring salvation to the ends of the earth (Isa 49:6). His mission will be accomplished through acute rejection and suffering (Isa 50:4–9; 52:13–53:12). Because of the Servant's submission, even to the point of death, Yahweh will declare many righteous (Isa 53:11). Servant Israel, spurned in chapter 48, is recommissioned as the "servants of Yahweh," for their righteousness is from him (Isa 54:17c). Isaiah 40–55, then, presents two servants; one who is unfaithful and the other whose loyalty to Yahweh restores the sinful nation. The servant needs *the* Servant. Just as Adam needed a Second Adam (1 Cor 15:21–22, 45), so the servant nation needs a Second Servant.

It is correct, then, to interpret the First Servant Song (Isa 42:1–4) typologically. It initially describes the nation of Israel and foreshadows Christ. However, the Second (Isa 49:1–6), Third (Isa 50:4–9), and Fourth (Isa 52:13–53:12) Servant Songs are rectilinear prophecies pointing only to Jesus.

To describe the servants of the Servant as *righteous* is fitting—a form of the root צדק occurs forty-six times from Isa 54:17 to the end of the book. For instance, those who mourn in Zion will be made glad and be called "oaks of righteousness" (Isa 61:3). Like a decorated bridegroom, the servants will be "robed in righteousness" (Isa 61:10). And Yahweh will cause "righteousness and praise to spring up" before all nations (Isa 61:11).

This group of servants of the Suffering Servant is a major motif in Isa 56–66 (Isa 56:7; 63:17; 65:8–9, 13–15; 66:14). They go by other names: "a people" (Isa 65:2–3, 10, 18–19, 22), "those who tremble at God's word" (Isa 66:2, 5), as well as those who mourn in Zion (Isa

57:18; 61:2; 66:10). In chapters 56–66, the single Servant becomes a plurality of servants. They are his offspring (Isa 53:10). Though by no means blameless, this faithful remnant has sincerely repented of its transgressions, lives in obedience to Yahweh's instruction, and anticipates the fulfillment of Isaiah's vision.

### RIGHTEOUSNESS

The most important feature joining Isaiah's book is the צדק root, *righteousness*. These words appear eighty-one times in Isaiah and are evenly dispersed in the book: chapters 1–39 (twenty-eight occurrences), chapters 40–55 (thirty occurrences), and chapters 56–66 (twenty-three occurrences).

In terms of righteousness, a tension exists between chapters 1–39 and 40–55. In Isa 1:21, Zion is called to be righteous and act in righteousness, but fails miserably throughout Isaiah's first thirty-nine chapters. The nation's abandonment of its calling is a reoccurring theme (e.g., Isa 5:1–7; 6:9–13; 8:11–22; 28:1–4; 39:1–8). In spite of it all, though, Isa 1:26 affirms that days are coming when Zion will be called the city of righteousness. How will this happen? Israel will be restored by God's righteous act and salvation, as explicated throughout Isa 40–55, where Yahweh gives grace and salvation through his Suffering Servant (Isa 53:11; 54:17).

A paradoxical situation arises, then, between the call and failure to be righteous in Isa 1–39 and the promised gift of righteousness in chapters 40–55. This tension is resolved in Isa 56–66, showing it to be a tightly connected unit within the larger theological framework of Isaiah. The programmatic text of Isa 56:1–8 unifies the third part of Isaiah with the first two.

Isa 56:1 pairs righteousness with two words that each reflect a different use of *righteousness* in chapters 1–39 and 40–55. In the first instance, righteousness is paired with משפט, *justice*, which conveys the idea that righteousness is morally correct behavior on the part of Yahweh or his people. In fact, throughout chapters 1–39, righteousness is paired with justice and speaks of that which should be done by Israel. This notion of righteousness is an active work that brings about what is right. Significant to this theme of righteousness is that the pairing of righteousness and justice, so prominent in the book's first thirty-nine chapters, does not appear in chapters 40–55, thereby showing a distinct separation in how the theme of righteousness functions in Isaiah. Righteousness and justice are last coupled together in Isa 33:5 before appearing again in Isa 56:1. Thus the pairing of these two words in Isa 56:1 summarizes the theme of Isa 1–39. Having established the thrust of Israel's charge to be righteous and do righteousness in chapters 1–39, what happens to this motif in chapters 40–55?

In the second part of Isa 56:1, righteousness is connected with ישׁועה, *salvation*, a word pair that occurs throughout chapters 40–55 (e.g., Isa 45:8, 21; 46:13; 51:5, 6, 8) but is never found in Isa 1–39. The significant theme of righteousness in Isa 40–55 is that Yahweh will work righteously to bring salvation to unrighteous Israel (cf. Isa 48:1) through his Righteous Servant (Isa 53:11; 54:17). Chapters 1–39, therefore, detail an active righteousness commanded by Yahweh for Israel to do, while Isa 40–55 offers a passive righteousness as Yahweh's gift received by faith.

As chapters 40–55 end, then, an apparent contradiction arises between Israel's unrighteous behavior (chapters 1–39) and Yahweh's promise of a righteous standing regardless of personal righteousness. Israel is called to be righteous, but fails, for only Yahweh is righteous. Yet, Yahweh promises salvation to the unrighteous. Should Israel, then, continue to sin so that this grace may abound (cf. Rom 6:1)? The answer comes in Isa 56–66.

Because both definitions of righteousness occur in Isa 56:1, as evidenced by its pairings with justice and salvation, two kinds of righteousness are present throughout chapters 56–66. The people's failure at active righteousness is represented by the following examples. Isa 57:1–13a addresses Israel's idolatry and how both the Righteous One and his followers perish (Isa 57:1–2). Isa 58:1–2 describes Israelites who live as if they had not forsaken Yahweh's righteousness and justice even though they do not turn from their sin. The prophet also confesses that both righteousness and justice are far away (Isa 59:9), while in Isa 64:6, he compares human righteousness to a filthy menstrual rag.

Equally prevalent in chapters 56–66 is the theme of Yahweh's gift of passive righteous. For instance, the Divine Warrior puts on righteousness as a breastplate and a helmet of salvation (Isa 59:17). He also speaks in righteousness and is mighty to save (Isa 63:1). Chapters 60–62 declare Yahweh's righteous work for his people. A great reversal takes place as Israel receives righteousness as their taskmaster (Isa 60:17) and God declares his people righteous (Isa 60:21); indeed they are called "oaks of righteousness" (Isa 61:3) and clothed in salvation and righteousness (Isa 61:10). Yahweh will cause righteousness to sprout up (Isa 61:11) and this will result in all-seeing Jerusalem's righteousness (Isa 62:1–2). Both themes of righteousness—the failure of Israel to be righteous and God declaring them righteous—appear intertwined throughout chapters 56–66.

Isa 56:1, therefore, functions as the hinge for chapters 1–39 and 40–55, allowing both kinds of righteousness to stand side by side. This solves the tension between chapters 1–39 and 40–55 and also demonstrates the function of Isa 56–66. To view chapters 56–66 as separate from earlier parts of the book is to misunderstand the theological thrust of righteousness and the overall theological unity of Isaiah.

## CREATION

Creation plays a major role in Isaiah's vision. The world of nature is the prophet's starting point, his defining condition, and the standard according to which he understands life. For example, Isaiah calls attention to the grass and flowers (e.g., Isa 40:6–7), trees (e.g., Isa 41:19), and stars (Isa 40:26). The prophet knows the hot, dry khamsin wind (Isa 49:10), as well as the gentle fall of rain and snow (Isa 55:10). He references mountains and hills (e.g., Isa 40:4; 55:12) and must have marveled at an eagle in flight (Isa 40:31). He could not forget the tenderness and innocence of a lamb (Isa 53:7). The prophet had a deep love for the created order.

Note the variety and frequency of creational verbs in Isa 40–55. They are ברא, *create* (sixteen times), עשה, *make* (twenty-four times),יצר, *form* (fifteen times), פעל, *work* (three times), נטה, *stretch out* (five times), יסד, *found* (five times), רקע, *spread out* (two times), צמח, *sprout* (five times), כון, *establish* (two times), טפח, *extend* (one time), and נטע, *plant* (two times).

People and creation are interconnected throughout Isaiah's book. For instance, in Isa 40:6–8, his comparison between grass and people is one of judgment. In Isa 40:23–24, the prophet employs the same ideas to describe princes and rulers—they wither and are carried off like stubble. What happens to grass and flowers happens to people. They thrive and we thrive. They die and we die. If trees lament (e.g., Isa 33:9), so do people (e.g., Isa 6:5). Conversely, if trees rejoice (e.g., Isa 14:8; 44:23; 55:12), so do people (e.g., Isa 42:10; 51:11). Embedded in plant life is the potential for regeneration. Therefore Isaiah promises that the survivors of the house of Judah will "again take root downward and bear fruit upward" (Isa 37:31).

A primary message in the prophet's vision is that the present creation's time is limited. Because the heavens are pitched like a tent (Isa 40:22; 44:24; 45:12; 48:13) they will wear out. The heavenly lights will grow dim (Isa 13:10; 24:22–23), the sky will be rolled up like a scroll (Isa 34:4), and the earth will be depopulated (Isa 24:1). The heavens will vanish like smoke, the earth will wear out like a garment, and its inhabitants will die like gnats (Isa 51:6). But creation is also summoned to break forth with joy, for when Yahweh restores Israel, he will renew the heavens and the earth (Isa 42:10–12; 44:23; 49:13; 55:11–12).

Isaiah rejects a faith that spiritualizes Yahweh's promises to the point that creation is marginalized. The future will have gardens (Isa 65:21), homes (Isa 65:21), and productive work (Isa 65:23). God's concern for the earth will never diminish. He constantly affirms the goodness of its elegance and beauty. Everything will be made new. Isaiah's hope is not redemption *from* the world but the redemption *of* the world.

## CHRIST IN ISAIAH

In some places, the OT flows like a brook towards its fulfillment in Christ, while other places may be likened to a quiet backwater or small stream. In Isaiah, though, we come upon a rushing river that moves us mightily forward toward the New Testament's proclamation of Jesus Christ as Lord. He is Immanuel (Isa 7:14; Matt 1:23), the Wonderful Counselor, Mighty God, Everlasting Father and Prince of Peace (Isa 9:6), the Shoot that comes forth from Jesse's stump (Isa 11:1), a tested Stone and Cornerstone and a sure Foundation (Isa 28:16).

But Isaiah's Fourth Servant Song has impacted the NT more than any other. The earliest Christian preaching announced that Jesus is the suffering Messiah (e.g., 1 Cor 15:3–4), while Isa 52:13–53:12 is reflected by means of the title τὸν παῖδα, *the child/servant*, for Jesus in Acts 3:13, 26; 4:27, 30. The passive verbs in Isa 53, coupled with the statement that it was "Yahweh's will to crush him" (Isa 53:10) influenced Paul's use of παραδίδομαι, *I deliver*, in e.g., Rom 8:32;

1 Cor 11:23; Gal 2:20; and Eph 5:2. Christ's appropriation of Isa 61:1–2a in Luke 4:18–19 confirms that he is the Messiah (Isa 7:14; 9:2–7; 11:1–9) and the Suffering Servant (Isa 49:1–6; Isa 50:4–9; 52:13–53:12).

## SIN AND GRACE IN ISAIAH

Idolatry is the chief sin in the book of Isaiah. Though the prophet refers to idolatry in Isa 2:8 and 2:20, it is not until chapter 6 that he develops a comprehensive assessment of Israel's chasing after other gods. Israel is blind and deaf (Isa 6:9–10). The nation is insensible. How did this happen? Yahweh follows the judgment of *lex talionis*, "Eye for eye, tooth for tooth, hand for hand, foot for foot, burn for burn, wound for wound, stripe for stripe" (Exod 21:24–25). So in essence, Yahweh says in Isa 6, "An idol for an idol. You are as spiritually insensitive as the idols you adore." Unrepentant Israelites will be unable spiritually to see, hear, perceive, or know Yahweh. This is why, for example, Yahweh calls them blind and deaf (Isa 42:19).

Counterfeit deities had a magnetism that attracted many into abandoning Yahweh. This resulted in the nation's double bondage. In the sixth century they became captive politically to Babylon and spiritually captive to the regime's false gods. Israel, then, needed a double salvation. To free them from Babylon, Yahweh provided Cyrus. To free them from sin, he gives them his Suffering Servant.

This message of judgment and grace also comes into sharp focus when we see that Isa 40 is closely related to Isa 6. The derogatory "this people" of Isa 6:9, 10 becomes "my people" in Isa 40:1. The thrust of Isa 6:9–10 is Israel's inability to see and hear, whereas Isa 40:12–31 implies that this curse has been lifted and the people are once again able to understand and perceive Yahweh's plan. Finally, Isa 6:11 depicts desolated cities, while the gospel in Isa 40:9 is directed to these same cities. Isaiah had a call to condemn in chapter 6 and he had a call to comfort in Isa 40.

Isaiah's remnant motif likewise juxtaposes judgment and grace. Regarding judgment, Israel will be left "like a tent in a vineyard, like a hut in a field of melons" (Isa 1:8), a stump of a tree (Isa 6:13), and a pole on a hilltop (Isa 30:17). Yet a new tree will come forth from the stump (Isa 11:1) and this Messiah will create a purified remnant who will live in "the city of faithfulness, the faithful city" (Isa 1:28).

Isaiah's two children reflect this twofold promise—Maher-Shalal-Hash-Baz, *Speed the Spoil, Hasten the Plunder* (Isa 8:1) and Shear-Yashub, *A Remnant will Return* (Isa 7:3).

## CONCLUSION

Located on the front of the historic Trinity Church in Boston are the sculptures of six men. At the center are four Gospel writers who are flanked on the right by Paul and on the left by Isaiah. Isaiah's presence in this distinguished cloud of witnesses speaks volumes about his importance for the church. Jerome (c. 342–420) wrote of Isaiah, "He should be called an evangelist rather than a prophet because he describes all the mysteries of Christ and the Church so clearly that you think he is composing a history of what has already happened rather than prophesying about what is to come." Likewise, when Augustine (345–430) asked Ambrose (c. 327–400) for his advice on what he should read, the latter suggested Isaiah, "Because, I believe, he is more plainly a foreteller of the Gospel and of the calling of the Gentiles than are the others." The book of Isaiah is truly one of the most theologically significant books in the Bible.

## SELECT BIBLIOGRAPHY

Ackroyd, Peter. "Isaiah 1–12: Presentation of a Prophet." In *Congress Volume, Göttingen 1977*, 16–48. Supplements to Vetus Testamentum 29. Leiden: E. J. Brill, 1978.

Childs, Brevard. *Isaiah.* Old Testament Library. Louisville: Westminster, 2001.

Duhm, Bernard. *Das Buch Jesaia.* Göttingen: Vandenhoeck & Ruprecht, 1892.

Lessing, R. Reed. *Isaiah 40–55.* Concordia Commentary. St. Louis: Concordia, 2011.

Melugin, Roy F., and Marvin A. Sweeney, eds. *New Visions of Isaiah.* Journal for the Study of the Old Testament Supplement Series 214. Sheffield: Sheffield Academic Press, 1996.

Motyer, J. Alec. *The Prophecy of Isaiah: An Introduction and Commentary.* Tyndale Old Testament Commentaries 18. Downers Grove: InterVarsity, 1993.

Oswalt, John N. *The Book of Isaiah: Chapters 1–39.* New International Commentary on the Old Testament. Grand Rapids: Eerdmans, 1986.

―――. *The Book of Isaiah: Chapters 40–66.* New International Commentary on the Old Testament. Grand Rapids: Eerdmans, 1998.

―――. "Righteousness in Isaiah: A Study of the Function of Chapters 55–66 in the Present Structure of the Book." In *Writing and Reading the Scroll of Isaiah: Studies of an Interpretive Tradition.* Edited by Craig C. Broyles and Craig A. Evans, vol. 1, 177–91. New York: Brill, 1997.

Rendtorff, Rolf. "Isaiah 56:1 as a Key to the Formation of the Book of Isaiah." In *Canon and Theology,* translated by Margaret Kohl, 181–89. Minneapolis: Augsburg Fortress, 1993.

Schultz, Richard L. "How Many Isaiahs Were There and What Does It Matter? Prophetic Inspiration in Recent Evangelical Scholarship." In *Evangelicals and Scripture: Tradition, Authority and Hermeneutics.* Edited by Vincent Bacote, Laura C. Miguélez and Dennis L. Okholm, 150–70. Downers Grove: InterVarsity, 2004.

# 23

# JEREMIAH

In terms of words, Jeremiah is the longest book in the Bible. It is also one of the most complex. This is evident in several ways, including its structure and flow of thought, the person of Jeremiah, the historical setting of individual texts, and the book's relationship to a much shorter Greek version. Whether the issue is literary, historical, or theological, Jeremiah taxes one's interpretive capacities at every turn. Yet for all of its difficulty, the book's reflection on divine action and human response, as well as the broad range and rigor of its rhetoric, keeps it very much alive for those who read and study this massive theological masterpiece.

## AUTHORSHIP

The initial critical interpretation—led by Bernard Duhm—maintained that only Jeremiah's poetic texts derive from the pen of the prophet. Sigmund Mowinckel followed suit, offering a more detailed analysis of the book's authorship, breaking it down into four layers: (A) poetry original to Jeremiah, (B) legendary biographical accounts added by a redactor, (C) prosaic sermons attributed to a Deuteronomic source, and (D) oracles of hope composed long after the time of Jeremiah.

More recently, the critical view of Jeremiah is typified by Carroll and McKane whose studies have led to a minimalist view regarding the book's historical claims. These critics believe that the person of Jeremiah is largely a fictitious work of Deuteronomic theologians living after the exile. Because they assign so much of the book to these redactors, Jeremiah the prophet is viewed as a construct of literary imagination. Any access to the real Jeremiah is deemed impossible.

Along these same lines, Fretheim argues that the book of Jeremiah has been shaped to address an exilic audience that has already experienced the fall of Jerusalem. The original audience and the oral qualities of Jeremiah are subsumed by multiple redactional layers. Fretheim privileges the *Sitz im Literatur* over the *Sitz im Leben* because he does not believe that a historical reconstruction of Jeremiah's life and times is possible.

These critical readings of Jeremiah believe that originally oracles consisted of disparate units, but over the course of time they were blended into a book. Readers, then, are not confronted with the historical prophet, still less, the oral communication of the prophet, but rather with a presentation of the prophet. Whereas form critics—as typified by Duhm and Mowinckel—believed that oral utterances lay in, with, and under the received text, redaction critics—led by Carroll and McKane—have essentially abandoned the task of discovering the original prophetic words. They believe that Jeremiah's words have been lost due to the many redactional layers placed over his original text.

The problem with this critical position is that it omits the idea that—versed in an oral tradition—Jeremiah could have written his texts to be *heard* and not only to be *read* (cf. Jer 36). If the Homeric epics in their written form still retain oral structures, it seems worthwhile to attend to this possibility in studying Jeremiah. Lundbom follows this interpretive strategy. His rhetorical approach provides a way to appreciate the book's historical claims. We can therefore trust what the book of Jeremiah asserts—that it is the word of the prophet, from start (Jer 1:1) to finish (Jer 51:64).

## LITERARY FEATURES OF JEREMIAH

Those who pick up Jeremiah for the first time may decide that it was put together by an incompetent committee that could not make up its mind. So much in the book appears to be random. Why doesn't the prophet smooth over the numerous ruptures in his text or at least give it more cohesion to overcome its literary turmoil? O'Connor argues that the book is content to leave us with its disjointed disarray because that is the nature of life in a disaster. The book's literary shapelessness, therefore, mirrors the fragmentary nature of Jeremiah's life with Yahweh.

Poetry and narrative stand by each other and often are not thematically connected. The prophet's sermons appear out of nowhere, stories exhibit little chronological order, words of destruction and hope compete with each other for prominence, and, most notably, the book has multiple endings: chapter 45, chapter 51, and chapter 52, none of which bring any closure. This reflects the fact that disasters rarely resolve themselves in an orderly way. By ending without ending, the book refuses to gloss over the ambiguity and uncertainty of pain and heartache. Jeremiah, then, depicts disaster not only by writing about it, but also by mixing genres and giving us a blurring, swirling presentation. Disaster is never neat and tidy and neither is the book of Jeremiah.

This much is certain, though. The book divides into two major parts: (1) chapters 2–25 and (2) chapters 26–51. Jer 1 is the book's overview while chapter 52 is its epilogue. Poetry dominates the first half of the book and prose the second half. Any outline of the book beyond these basic facts becomes very subjective.

## Outline of Jeremiah

I.   Overview of the book (1:1–19)
   A.  Superscription (1:1–3)
   B.  Jeremiah's call (1:4–10)
   C.  Jeremiah's visions (1:11–19)
II.  Indictment for unfaithfulness and the call to repent (2:1–4:4)
   A.  Israel's unfaithfulness (2:1–3:5)
   B.  Return to Yahweh (3:6–4:4)
III. Yahweh will not turn back (4:5–6:30)
   A.  Disaster is coming (4:5–31)
   B.  Reasons for judgment (5:1–31)
   C.  Jerusalem is warned (6:1–30)
IV.  The Temple Sermon (7:1–8:3)
   A.  Misplaced trust (7:1–15)
   B.  Judgment's inevitability (7:16–8:3)
V.   Judgment and tears (8:4–10:25)

One prominent literary feature in Jeremiah is the prophet's use of doublets and recurring phrases. Over fifty doublets have been counted (e.g., Jer 6:13–15 = 8:10–12; 10:12–16 = 51:15–19; 11:20 = 20:12; 23:5–6 = 33:14–16; 30:10–11 = 46:27–28) and recurring phrases show that early ideas are frequently developed in different ways (e.g., Jer 7:1–5 and 26:1–6; 39:4–10 and 52:7–16).

The book of Jeremiah is full of standard prophetic genres like visions (e.g., Jer 1:11–15; 24:1–10), poetry (e.g., Jer 2:2–37), sign acts (e.g., Jer 13:1–11), promises of hope (Jer 30–33), and oracles about foreign nations (Jer 46–51). What is unique to Jeremiah is that the first half of the book is peppered with his so-called confessions (Jer 11:18–12:6; 15:10–21; 17:14–18; 18:18–23; 20:7–14). Despite attacks on his life (Jer 11:18, 21–23; 12:6; 20:10), his isolation from others (Jer 15:17), his sense of rejection by his community, and, above all, his abandonment by God (Jer 12:1; 15:18; 20:7), Jeremiah stays engaged with Yahweh through his confessions. They demonstrate that the prophet knows God, communes with him, and honestly argues with him. Jeremiah's emotional register is anything but flat.

## TEXTUAL ISSUES

The MT of Jeremiah and the LXX vary widely—more so than any other book in the OT. The LXX is one-eighth shorter than the MT (some 2,700 words) and after Jer 25:13a the passages are ordered differently. A Qumran fragment of Jeremiah reflects the LXX and this has given rise to the theory—championed by Frank Cross—that the LXX is not a later abridgement of the MT. Rather it is a translation of a different Hebrew text that circulated in Egypt. This Hebrew text, it is postulated, was different from the proto-Massoretic text which originated in Babylon. The argument, then, is that Qumran proves that there were two different editions of Jeremiah that existed side-by-side. The LXX is based on an early Hebrew edition that Jeremiah completed while he was in Egypt (Jer 41:16–44:30). Later editors edited the first edition and this is reflected in the MT.

Lundbom argues against this interpretation. He believes that the MT came first and that the LXX is a later and much shorter edition due to its numerous scribal errors. To make his point, Lundbom demonstrates that haplography in the LXX was rampant. The number of Hebrew words lost by bad copyists was 1,715 which is 7.8% of the MT.

# HISTORICAL ISSUES

The prophet's ministry lasted for over forty years (cf. Jer 1:1–3; 25:1–3; 36:1–2). It began in 629, Josiah's thirteenth year, and ended several years after Jerusalem's destruction in 587. Jeremiah probably died in Egypt in about 580 (Jer 42–44). These were some of the most tumultuous times in Judah's history.

For most of the seventh century, Assyria ruled over much of the ancient Near East, including parts of Egypt. The end of the century brought with it massive geopolitical changes. It began when Babylon destroyed Nineveh, Assyria's capital, in 612. Judah, under Josiah, removed itself from Assyrian control and existed as an autonomous state until 609 when Josiah died in a battle with Egypt on the plains of Megiddo (2 Kgs 23:29). An Egyptian army was marching north at the time to help Assyria fight Babylon at Haran. Soon afterwards Egypt gained control over Judah and so Pharaoh Necho replaced Josiah's son, Jehoahaz, with Jehoiakim (who was another son of Josiah) to be a vassal king (2 Kgs 23:34–35). At the same time Egypt plundered Judah's treasuries and took Jehoahaz to captivity in Egypt. Shortly after that, the Egyptian-Assyrian coalition was defeated by Babylon at Haran, so the armies retreated to Carchemish. There, in 605, Babylon finally buried what was left of Assyria and also defeated Pharaoh Necho of Egypt.

At this time, Jehoiakim changed his loyalty from Egypt to Babylon and became Nebuchadnezzar's vassal king (2 Kgs 24:1a). Nebuchadnezzar solidified Babylonian rule by also taking Judean hostages. Daniel was exiled as a part of this deportation (Dan 1:1–6). In 601, Egypt, down but not out, defeated the Babylonians in another battle, so Jehoiakim switched his loyalty from Babylon and back to Egypt (2 Kgs 24:1b). In December of 598 a resurgent Babylon attacked Jerusalem. This led to Jehoiakim's death and the surrender of the city in March of 597 under his successor, Jehoiachin. Nebuchadnezzar replaced Jehoiachin after only three months of reign, deported him and 10,000 other leaders from Jerusalem, looted the city, and placed Zedekiah on the throne (2 Kgs 24:12–16). During Zedekiah's reign, the Judean court was wracked between pro- and anti-Babylonian factions. In fact, Babylon and Nebuchadnezzar are mentioned more than two hundred times in Jer 20–52.

Zedekiah repeated the errors of kings before him. Going against Jeremiah's advice in 589, he was convinced by Egypt to revolt against Babylon and thus joined a coalition of other states (Tyre and Ammon). Nebuchadnezzar responded with vengeance and destroyed Jerusalem in 587. According to Jer 52:30, the total number of Babylonian deportees was 4,600. This probably denotes only men. Adding women and children brings the aggregate number to around 15,000. Others estimate that the total number exiled was between 20,000 and 30,000. Whatever the exact number was, the Babylonian exile left Jerusalem like a ghost town, with few people living in and around its precincts (Jer 40–43). Israelite families were scattered, the royal class had no palace, and priests had no altar.

Lipschits confirms this anguish. He believes that Jerusalem and her neighboring villages at this time declined in population by ninety percent, while the land of Judah fell by seventy percent. The region was not settled again until the Persian period, and even then it recovered only in a limited fashion, indicating the extent of the Babylonian damage. During the Persian era, Jerusalem's population was about twelve percent of what the city and its environs had been before 587.

Jeremiah lived through these topsy-turvy times. After Josiah's death in 609, the prophet was persecuted by the rise of an anti-Babylonian faction in Judah (e.g., Jer 20:2). He was protected some by God-fearing elders and princes after his messages against the nation (e.g., Jer 26). Jehoiakim (609–598) then destroyed Jeremiah's dictated prophecies (Jer 36), while Zedekiah (598–587) allowed the nobles to arrest Jeremiah as a traitor who was urging the nation to submit to Babylon (Jer 38). Although, after the fall of Jerusalem in 587, Jeremiah was offered a place of honor by the Babylonians for urging the Judahites to submit to them, he chose instead to stay with his people in Judah and care for those who remained after the deportation (Jer 40). After the murder of Judah's leader Gedaliah, Jeremiah was taken off to Egypt by fugitive Judahites (Jer 43). The prophet lived a few years in Egypt and then probably died there. He had witnessed the downfall of Judah, the burning of Yahweh's holy city, the destruction of the temple, the loss of the land, and several exiles of his people. Throughout these horrific events, the prophet struggled to be faithful to his vocation and mission.

Jeremiah is not a heroic figure of epic proportions. He is an anguished survivor, wounded, isolated, and broken. His celibacy, for example, echoes the end of domestic life (Jer 16:1–4) when there would be no more giving and taking in marriage and no voices of gladness or of a bride and a bridegroom (Jer 16:9). His repeated captivities (Jer 20:1–6; 26:1–24; 37:11–21; 38:1–6), attacks upon his life (Jer 11:18–19, 21–23; 20:1–6; 26:1–24), and his own exile (Jer 42–44) parallel the people's sufferings.

## THEOLOGICAL THEMES IN JEREMIAH

### SIN

The book of Jeremiah begins and ends with references to the Babylonian exile (Jer 1:3; 51:28–30; 31–34). What brought about this massive rupture in Judah's life? The prophet announced that it was due to the people's ongoing infidelity to Yahweh's covenant (Jer 2:20; 5:5; 11:10) and the dominant metaphor he uses is a broken marriage (e.g., Jer 2:2–7, 25; 5:7–8). Judah and her leaders did not know Yahweh (e.g., Jer 2:8; 4:22; 9:3, 6), for to know him is to know his way (Jer 5:4–5), his ordinances (Jer 8:7), and to display justice for the poor and needy (Jer 22:16). In his temple sermon, Jeremiah notes that Judahites claimed that the temple was a sign of Yahweh's presence (Jer 7:4), but he maintains that it had become a means to escape their responsibilities as God's people. Many in Judah practiced social oppression and then took refuge in worship (Jer 7:6–11).

A compelling question in the book of Jeremiah that regularly punctuates the text either explicitly or implicitly is, Why is the land ruined and laid waste like a wilderness (e.g., Jer 5:19; 9:12; 13:22; 14:19; 16:10; 22:8)? The prophet's answer is popularly understood as "what goes around comes around." For example, God not listening to the people (Jer 11:11–17) corresponds to the people not listening to God. God has forsaken Judah because the people have forsaken him (Jer 2:13, 17, 19). God has abandoned Judah (Jer 7:29) because the people first abandoned him (Jer 15:6). This follows the judgment of *lex talionis* which is stated in Exod 21:24–25.

Fretheim highlights another aspect of sin in Jeremiah—the moral order affects the created order. Every creature is in relationship with every other, such that any act reverberates out and affects the whole, shaking the entire world in varying degrees of intensity. For instance, because of sin, rain doesn't fall (Jer 2:12; 3:3; 14:4), the land becomes desolate (Jer 12:10–11), animals and birds are swept away

(Jer 12:4), and the land is defiled (Jer 3:2, 9; 16:18). Indeed, the heavens and the earth are reduced to primeval chaos (Jer 4:23–26).

God's judgment of sin permeates the book. This becomes evident by the recurring words חרב, רעב, and דבר, *sword, famine,* and *pestilence* (e.g., Jer 14:12, 16; 15:2). They frequently appear individually: *famine* occurs more than thirty times in the book, *sword* more than seventy times, and *pestilence* over twenty times. The people are so set in their sin that the prophet sarcastically writes, "Can the Ethiopian change his skin or the leopard his spots? Neither can you, who are so used to doing evil, do good" (Jer 13:23). Indeed, the human heart is deceitful above everything and beyond cure (Jer 17:9). Therefore Yahweh raises up Nebuchadnezzar, who is the chief agent to enact punishment for Judah's sin. The king is surprisingly called God's servant (e.g., Jer 25:9; 27:6; 43:10).

## GOD'S WRITTEN WORD

Phrases like "the word of Yahweh," "the oracle of Yahweh," or "the word that came to Jeremiah" appear in every chapter of the book, with the exceptions of chapters 41 and 52. As Yahweh's messenger, Jeremiah's vocation was clear: deliver God's word—primarily to Judah but also to the nations of the world (Jer 1:10).

Jeremiah compares this word to a consuming fire and pounding hammer (Jer 23:29). He was overcome by its power and could not hold it inside, even when he tried to do so (Jer 20:8–9). Speaking God's word led to any number of problems for Jeremiah. Sometimes people refused to listen to it (Jer 6:10, 19; 8:9) and at other times they persecuted him because of it (Jer 17:15; 20:8; 38:4). Through it all, Jeremiah was certain that God would be true to his promises. His first vision is a wordplay with the consonants שקד, which may mean *almond tree* or *to watch,* depending on what vowels are used. The almond tree is a reminder to Jeremiah that Yahweh will watch over his word and make sure it accomplishes what it says (Jer 1:11–12).

Yahweh places his words in Jeremiah's mouth (Jer 1:9), but it is not until Jer 15:16 that the prophet eats God's word and calls it ששון ושמחה, *joy and delight*. These two words come together four more times in the book, and on each occasion they are paired with חתן וכלה, *bride and bridegroom* (Jer 7:34; 16:9; 25:10; 33:11). By means of this poetic word association, Jeremiah evokes the connection between eating God's word and the exuberance, the ecstasy, and the sheer excitement experienced by a bride and bridegroom. The divine word, then, is the love of Jeremiah's life.

The prophet's internalization of the divine word is an experience that Yahweh intends for all his people. He promises to put his Torah inside of them and write it upon their hearts (Jer 31:33). It will enable them to break out of their guilt because the cornerstone of God's word is his merciful absolution. Yahweh resolves to "forgive [their] iniquity and remember [their] sin no more" (Jer 31:34). Exiles laden with transgressions are granted clemency. Only then will they find energy to face the challenges that await them in their new lives as survivors.

The prophetic word that authorized the undoing of the community (Jer 25:13) also endorses its future (Jer 26–52). In the second half of the book, the transition from the spoken to the written word emerges at critical junctures. At the start of the second half, officials come to Jeremiah's defense by citing one of Micah's oracles (Jer 26:16–19; cf. Mic 3:12). Their appeal to written prophecy, along with historical precedence, saves the day. Toward the end of his book, Jeremiah commands that a scroll, announcing God's judgment on Babylon, be thrown into the Euphrates River to signify that Babylon will "sink and rise no more" (cf. Jer 51:59–64). The prophet writes on this scroll all of the disasters that will come upon Babylon. In between these two texts, Jeremiah sends letters to Babylonian exiles with the aim of dispelling despair and engendering genuine hope in Yahweh's promises (Jer 29). At God's command, the prophet prepares a written scroll that takes dead aim at heartache and hopelessness (Jer 30–33). Additionally, Yahweh instructs Jeremiah to preserve the written documentation of a business transaction between his cousin Hanamel and himself (Jer 32:6–44). The written materials that Baruch places in an earthenware jar serve as a testimony that God would one day restore his people (Jer 32:14).

But perhaps the best-known example of the power of God's written word is the prophet's confrontation with Jehoiakim (Jer 36). Jeremiah dictates God's word to Baruch, who reads it before the king. Jehoiakim in turn destroys the scroll only to have Jeremiah create another one, which contains "all the words of the scroll that King Jehoiakim of Judah had burned in the fire and many similar words" (Jer 36:32). When all is said and done, the event affirms that this seemingly innocuous scroll trumps the king. The written word is victorious!

## GOD'S ENACTED WORD

Jeremiah's message contains more than words. Like prophets before him (e.g., Isa 20; Hos 1–3), he dramatized God's spoken word with symbolic actions. In this way, Jeremiah's life became a living embodiment and a metaphor of what was about to happen. For example, in Jer 13:1–11 the main symbol is a linen loincloth, appropriate for a priest like Jeremiah (cf. Jer 1:1; Exod 28:39; 39:27–29). After burying the loincloth, sometime later Jeremiah digs it up and its deterioration indicates that Judah, once a priestly and holy people (cf. Exod 19:6), had become nothing more than rotten, stinking, and dirty linen. Another time, the prophet broke an empty clay pot to announce Yahweh's judgment of Judah and Jerusalem (Jer 19). Together with some Rechabites, he once went to the temple to test their commitment not to drink wine—thus giving a lesson on obedience (Jer 35). When he confronted the false prophet Hananiah, Jeremiah wore thongs and yoke bars around his neck, the yoke signifying submission to Babylon just as an ox submits to a yoke to pull a cart or plow (Jer 27–28). In Egypt, the prophet buried stones at Pharaoh's palace at Tahpanhes, symbolizing that Nebuchadnezzar would soon build a throne on the same site (Jer 43:8–13). His celibacy (Jer 16:1–4) and mourning (Jer 16:5–9) were also symbolic actions that announced the coming of the Babylonian onslaught. These acts, just like God's spoken word, brought events to pass. In contrast, the symbolic actions of unfaithful Judahiates such as Hananiah's breaking the yoke bars (Jer 28) and Jehoiakim's slashing of the scroll (Jer 36) had no lasting impact.

Jer 32 perhaps offers the best example of the prophet's strategy of enacting God's word. The chapter is set in 589, when Nebuchadnezzar—the Babylonian king—was establishing his headquarters at Riblah. Having destroyed the Judean fortresses at Lachish and Azekah, his troops began to lay siege to Jerusalem. Inside the city, all commercial enterprises were collapsing. Epidemics and diseases were sweeping through neighborhoods. Property values were plummeting. In the midst of this chaos, God says to Jeremiah, "Buy the field" (Jer 32:25). The field referred to is owned by Jeremiah's cousin Hanamel and is located in the prophet's hometown of Anathoth, just three miles north of Jerusalem. In spite of the immanent devastation of the land, the prophet counts out seventeen shekels of silver, signs a deed to the property, gathers eye-witnesses to the purchase, and then gives a sealed copy to Baruch. But why would someone make such a risky investment? Jeremiah was convinced that Yahweh had a future of שלום, *peace*, planned for his people (Jer 29:11).

## THE LAND

Jeremiah is the prophet of the land par excellence. Three creation hymns celebrate God's goodness and authority over the land (Jer 10:12; 32:17; 51:15), and at one point the prophet cries out, "O land, land, land" (Jer 22:29). The book is also saturated with land metaphors (e.g., Jer 8:6–7; 12:9; 24:1; 31:12).

Canaan was given and maintained by Yahweh (e.g., Jer 2:7; 3:19; 4:3; 33:12), so he has the power to make it desolate (e.g., Jer 4:24–29; 8:13, 20; 22:6). The situation throughout the book is dialectical. Israel's involvement is always with land and with Yahweh. It is never only with Yahweh as though they could live with him apart from the land, and it is never only with land, as though they could live in it apart from Yahweh.

Jeremiah indicates that Yahweh's promises are for landless people (Jer 29). Land promises are for exiles, just as earlier in Israel's history, the sojourning patriarchs were promised the land and the slave people triumphed over Pharaoh in order to receive the land. This is one of the central surprises of the Bible: "The meek shall inherit the land" (Ps 37:11; cf. Matt 5:5).

At the heart of this message is Jeremiah's vision in chapter 24. Set in the years immediately following the second Babylonian deportation in 597, Jeremiah goes to the temple and sees two baskets of figs. In basket number one are the good figs. They are plump and juicy, ripe to perfection, the best of the best. In basket number two are the bad figs. They are stinky and smelly, rotten to the core, the worst of the worst. Like Jeremiah's Judean audience, we might surmise that the good figs are those who managed to avoid Babylonian captivity. After the exile in 597, things continued to function very well for them. This group consisted of Zedekiah, the king of Judah, and his officials. These are Judah's best of the best. We might also think that the bad figs are those who are part of the deportation in 597. They are stinky and smelly because they are landless, homeless, and futureless. Rotten to the core, these people should expect no mercy from Yahweh. These are Judah's worst of the worst.

But Yahweh turns these expectations upside down. He says, "Like these good figs, so I will consider as good the *exiles* from Judah, whom I have sent away from this place to the land of Babylon" (Jer 24:5). And those who remain in the land? God vows, "I will make them a horror to all the kingdoms of the earth, to be a reproach, a byword, a taunt and a curse" (Jer 24:9). The first have become last and the last have become first (cf. Matt 19:30; 20:16). Yahweh gives the land to the marginalized and withholds it from those in positions of power. The central phrase of this new history is "restore the fortunes" (Jer 30:3, 18; 31:7, 11).

## TRUE VERSUS FALSE PROPHECY

Jeremiah maintains that the problem with false prophets is that they have not been in the divine council and were therefore messengers who had not been sent by God (Jer 23:18, 21–22; 29:31). Yahweh's word was not in them (Jer 5:13) so their visions were conceived in their own minds (Jer 23:16–17). The lies of these false prophets multiplied because they were stealing oracles from each other (Jer 23:30).

The main message of the false prophets was that ancient glories will quickly return and the nation will soon be restored. Jeremiah counters this with the command, "Do not listen to the deceptive dreams of prophets" (Jer 29:8) which were typified by the nationalist hopes of Hananiah. This false prophet was certain that Babylon would promptly return the stolen temple vessels and all would be well. According to Hananiah and the Jerusalem establishment, there was little need to let go of the old world, for the Babylonian crisis was understood to be only temporary and, in the long run, inconsequential. After a few difficult years, life would return to normal. With ringing authority Hananiah even gave dates and places (Jer 28:3–4). Two times Jeremiah describes prophets like Hananiah with the words, "They have healed the wound of my people trivially, saying, 'Peace, peace,' when there is no peace" (Jer 6:14; 8:11).

The truth is that everything will be plucked up and torn down— the nation, the kingship, the temple, and the ancient hope for landed security (Jer 1:10). Israel's habitat will be broken, the tent will be destroyed, cords will be snapped, and the children will go into exile (Jer 10:20). The institutions upon which Judah relied in the past were broken beyond repair. Grandiosity and false security therefore have no place in the public square. "Do not listen to the words of the prophets who prophesy to you; they are deluding you. They speak visions of their own minds; they keep saying, 'It shall be well with you ... no evil shall come upon you'" (Jer 23:16–17). In time, Jeremiah's message of Babylonian destruction came true and the prophet was vindicated (Jer 28:8–9, 17; 44:28–30; cf. Deut 18:21–22).

## CHRIST IN JEREMIAH

The motif of the "new covenant" (Jer 31:31) is central to the New Testament's understanding of Christ. Jesus came because God "remembered his holy covenant" (Luke 1:72) and the Savior refers directly to Jeremiah's prophecy when he says that the Holy Supper is "my blood of the new covenant" (Luke 22:20). Christ's covenant blood was shed not because he had been unfaithful (cf. Jer 34:18–20), but because humanity had rebelled against its Creator. His blood is poured out "for the forgiveness of sins" (Matt 26:28). With these words the Savior also links his new covenant with the one described by Jeremiah (Heb 8:8–12; 10:16–17). It is the "blood of the eternal covenant" (Heb 13:20; cf. Jer 32:40).

We can see Christ foreshadowed in Jeremiah in another way. Zedekiah, whose name means "Yahweh is righteous," scattered and destroyed Yahweh's flock (Jer 23:1). In the age to come, God promises a "Righteous Branch," a Davidic leader who "will enact justice and righteousness in the land" (Jer 23:5; 33:15). His name is יהוה צדקנו, *Yahweh is our righteousness* (Jer 23:6; 33:16). Jesus is this righteous king of David's line and his gift of righteousness comes because he laid aside his glory and became sin for us (2 Cor 5:21).

In the book of Jeremiah, Yahweh is anything but detached. Rather, he is torn apart by human pain and burns with a loving desire to be reconciled with his people. In one case he laments, "For the shattering of the daughter of my people I am shattered. I mourn, and dismay has seized me" (Jer 8:21). He cries out again, "Who will make my head waters and my eyes a fountain of tears, that I might weep day and night for the slain of the daughter of my people" (Jer 9:1). While some believe that Jeremiah is the speaker here, elsewhere in the book it is Yahweh who most often employs the terms "my people" (e.g., Jer 8:7, 11; 9:7; 15:7; 23:22) and "the daughter of my people" (e.g., Jer 8:19, 21; 9:1). The God who suffers in the book of Jeremiah all the more suffers through Jesus, the Christ.

Finally, during our Lord's ministry some people associated him with Jeremiah (Matt 16:13–14). Why? Jeremiah faced opposition from every quarter—family and friends (Jer 11:18–23; 12:1–6), kings and their officials (Jer 20:1–6; 26:1–24; 36:1–31), and Judah's remnant (Jer 42–44). The prophet felt as though he was a lamb led to the slaughter (Jer 11:19). Jesus was such a Lamb who was sacrificed for the sins of the world (Isa 53:7; Acts 8:32).

## SIN AND GRACE IN JEREMIAH

The message of sin and grace stands at the center of Jeremiah's book. God appointed him "to uproot, tear down, destroy, and overthrow" as well as "to build and to plant" (Jer 1:10). In various combinations these six verbs wind their way throughout the book (Jer 12:14–17; 18:7, 9; 24:6; 31:28, 38–40; 42:10; 45:4).

In another refrain, Yahweh promises to make the whole land desolate, but it will not be a full end (Jer 4:27; 5:10, 18). While Judah's political, economic, and liturgical institutions will come to an end, God's promises will not. Because he will make an end of the nations that scattered his people, the exiles have a hope and a future (Jer 29:11; 30:11; 46:28). When Babylon comes to an end (Jer 51:13), this will mean life and salvation for the exiles.

In his book of comfort, the prophet offers the clearest expression of God's grace (Jer 30–33). Yet there are no pictures of utopia. There is no idyllic healing and no portrait of perfect peace and happiness. Instead, there will still be the blind and the lame (Jer 31:8) and people will still lament and cry (Jer 31:9). The prophet does not offer pipe dreams when he envisions people returning from captivity. However, Jeremiah does promise new life in a community where individuals will enjoy a close relationship with Yahweh. This is depicted as divine favor and protection (Jer 30:10–11), deliverance (Jer 30:10–11, 18–21; 31:7–14, 23–25), and abounding joy (Jer 30:18–19). These promises are enacted because the Davidic covenant is still intact (Jer 33:14–26) which is grounded in God's commitment to Israel's ancestors (e.g., Jer 7:7; 11:5; 16:15; 30:3).

# CONCLUSION

Judah's trip over the waterfall was certain. Her sin brought the nation to the point of no return. The Babylonian exile of 587 happened—in large part—because of the sins of Manasseh (Jer 15:4). Because of this wicked king, Yahweh judged and deported his people. Jeremiah lived during these tumultuous years that witnessed the collapse of Assyria, the rise of Babylon, the false promises of Egypt, and the demise of Judah. He is the most complex and developed prophet in the OT and is anything but shy and aloof in his relationships. His book repeatedly portrays him as hard as a rock while at the same time torn apart inside. Jeremiah's warnings and promises walk people into, through, and beyond the realities of destruction and exile.

# SELECT BIBLIOGRAPHY

Brueggemann, Walter. *Like Fire in the Bones: Listening for the Prophetic Word in Jeremiah*. Minneapolis: Augsburg Fortress, 2006.

Carroll, Robert. *The Book of Jeremiah*. Old Testament Guides. Philadelphia: Westminster, 1986.

Fretheim, Terence. *Jeremiah*. Smyth and Helwys Bible Commentary 15. Macon: Smyth and Helwys. 2002.

Lipschits, Oded. "Demographic Changes in Judah between the Seventh and Fifth Centuries B.C.E." In *Judah and the Judeans in the Neo-Babylonian Period*. Edited by Oded Lipschits and Joseph Blenkinsopp, 323–76. Winona Lake: Eisenbrauns, 2003.

Lundbom, Jack. *Jeremiah 1–52: A New Translation with Introduction and Commentary*. Anchor Bible 21A, 21 B, and 21C. New York: Doubleday, 1999, 2004.

McKane, William. *A Critical and Exegetical Commentary on Jeremiah*. 2 vols. International Critical Commentary on the Holy Scriptures of the Old and New Testaments. Edinburgh: T&T Clark, 1986, 1996.

O'Connor, Kathleen. *Jeremiah: Pain and Promise*. Minneapolis: Augsburg Fortress, 2011.

# 24

# LAMENTATIONS

Coping with a great loss involves grief, mourning, and pain. The book of Lamentations is a stellar example of Israelite prayers that argue, protest, and complain. As early as the book of Genesis we read that Rebekah cried, "If it is this way, why should I live?" (Gen 25:22; cf. Gen 27:46). Jacob (Gen 37:34–35) and Rachel (Jer 31:15; cf. Matt 2:17–18) refuse to be comforted. Later, when Saul and Jonathan died on Mt. Gilboa, David grieved over his deep and irreversible loss (2 Sam 1:23–27). Israel's king again lamented when his son Absalom was struck down by Joab (2 Sam 18:33). Even after Joab reprimanded him, David continued to mourn publically (2 Sam 19:4). Job, with his ongoing and often strident complaints, is perhaps the most vociferous example of complaints directed to God (e.g., Job 14:20; 30:18–25). These kinds of prayers make up almost one-third of the Psalter (e.g., Psalms 22, 44, 73). At no time, though, was there such acute *communal* suffering as when Jerusalem collapsed to Nebuchadnezzar's mighty hordes in 587 BC. This prompted the book of Lamentations with its stirring and poignant plaints. In synagogues, Lamentations is read each year on the day commemorating the fall of the temple to the Babylonians and later to the Romans. In some Christian churches, Lamentations is read during Holy Week.

## AUTHORSHIP, COMPOSITION, AND DATE

### AUTHORSHIP

Although Lamentations does not mention its author or authors, traditionally it has been attributed to Jeremiah. This may stem from

2 Chr 35:25 which reports that Jeremiah mourned over the death of Josiah and that these oracles were recorded in "the Laments" (הקינות). However, it is unlikely that this verse is referring to the book of Lamentations, since none of the poems in the book mention Josiah.

Nevertheless, Josephus attributes the book to Jeremiah (*Ant.*10:78–79), as does the Talmud (*B. Bat.* 15a). The LXX of Lam 1:1 adds a superscription that credits Jeremiah as the book's author. Some of the early Church Fathers also attributed Lamentations to Jeremiah. In the LXX, this collection of poems was placed after Jeremiah, a position it also occupies in the Christian arrangement of the canonical books. On the other hand, Lamentations is not placed with Jeremiah in the Jewish canon. Instead, it is among the Writings. Yet this may reflect the liturgical usage of Lamentations, since the Writings contain books which are not part of the regular Sabbath lectionary but are read in synagogues on special days or not at all.

Since Lamentations does not name its author or authors, some modern scholars have held that Jeremiah could not have composed it. It is further argued that the prophet could not have written certain statements found in Lamentations. These scholars think that since Lam 2:9 condemns Jerusalem's prophets, it would be odd if it had been composed by the prophet Jeremiah. However, a closer reading of Lam 2:9 shows that it does not reject prophets—it notes that Jerusalem's prophets no longer have visions from God. Moreover, even if Lam 2:9 belittles prophets, Jeremiah also denounced false prophets (e.g., Jer 14:11–16; 23:9–32; 28:1–17; 29:20–23). Similar arguments are often based on these types of one-dimensional readings. When they are put aside there is no statement in Lamentations that is inconsistent with Jeremiah composing the book.

Based on the earlier work of Driver, House lists a number of similarities in theme and language between Lamentations and Jeremiah:

### Comparison of Themes and Language between Lamentations and Jeremiah

*Thematic:*

Judah fell because of sin: Lam 1:5, 8, 14, 18; 3:42; 4:6, 22; 5:7, 16; Jer 14:7; 16:10–12; 17:1–3

Sinful prophets and priests: Lam 2:14; 4:13–15; Jer 2:7–8; 5:31; 23:11–40; 27:1–28:17

Useless confidence in human allies: Lam 1:2, 19; 4:17; Jer 2:18, 36; 30:14; 38:5–10

Jerusalem is a broken virgin daughter of Zion: Lam 1:15; 2:13; Jer 8:21–22; 14:17

Appeal to God to defeat enemies: Lam 3:64–66; Jer 11:20

Judah's enemies will also be desolate some day: Lam 4:21; Jer 49:12

*Phraseology:*

Jerusalem's lovers offer no comfort: Lam 1:2; 1:8b–9; Jer 13:22b, 26; 30:13

Jerusalem's eyes/Jeremiah's eyes running with tears: Lam 1:16a; 2:11a, 18b; 3:48–49; Jer 9:1, 18b; 13:17b; 14:17

Jerusalem's wound is great: Lam 2:11, 13; 3:47–48; 4:10; Jer 6:14; 8:11, 21

Israel's priests and prophets have sinned: Lam 2:14; 4:13; Jer 2:8; 5:31; 14:1–14

Women eat their children during the siege: Lam 2:20; 4:10; Jer 19:9

Terror all around Israel: Lam 2:22; Jer 6:25; 20:10

"I have become a laughingstock": Lam 3:14; Jer 20:7

"Wormwood"/"Wormwood and gall": Lam 3:15; Jer 9:15; 23:15

"Terror and a pit": Lam 3:47; Jer 48:43

"They hunt me": Lam 3:52; Jer 16:16b

"The cup" as metaphor for God's wrath: Lam 4:21; Jer 25:15; 49:12

These connections do not prove that Jeremiah wrote Lamentations. They strongly suggest, however, that whoever wrote Lamentations was familiar with Jeremiah and was allowed to remain in Judah where he could have viewed its ruinous state (Lam 1:1, 4, 12; 2:9–12, 15, 21; 4:11; 5:18). On the other hand, there is nothing in the text of Lamentations that could not have been written by someone else who was familiar with the book of Jeremiah and who mourned over Jerusalem's ruin and confessed Israel's sins that stirred up God's wrath against the city.

## DATE

If Lamentations was written by Jeremiah or someone else who viewed Jerusalem's destruction, then its date of composition would have been shortly after the fall of the city to the Babylonians in 587 BC. On 10 Ab (Monday, 28 August), 587 BC, the Babylonian Nebuzaradan, captain of the guard, plundered Jerusalem (2 Kgs 25:9–19; 2 Chr 36:18–19; Jer 52:12–25). So it is possible that Lamentations was written as early as the second half of 587 BC. (Jeremiah was taken to Egypt in Tishri [October/November] 587 BC [Jer 41–43].)

Although there is no indication exactly when the book was composed, there is near universal agreement that it was written no later than a half-century or so after Jerusalem's fall. Some critical scholars wish to date it near the end of this period. For instance, Dobbs-Allsopp undertook a linguistic analysis of Lamentations and concluded that the book's language suggested a date of 540–520 BC. Thus, according to this theory, Lamentations could have been written shortly after the first Judeans returned to Jerusalem from Babylon and saw its ruins. However, it is doubtful that Hebrew texts can be dated this precisely on the basis of linguistic analysis. Thus, it is best to consider Lamentations to have been written during the Babylonian exile, with a date very early in that period the most likely time of composition.

## LITERARY FEATURES OF LAMENTATIONS

### ACROSTIC POEMS

The most readily-apparent literary feature of Lamentations is the acrostic structure of the first four chapters. Lam 1, 2, and 4 are poems of twenty-two verses, one for each letter of the Hebrew alphabet. Chapters 1 and 2 have three lines for each stanza, with the first line beginning with a successive letter of the alphabet in order from *aleph* (א) to *taw* (ת). Chapter 4 follows this same pattern except that each stanza contains only two lines. Chapter 3, like the first two chapters, contains three-line stanzas. However, in this case, all three lines of each stanza begin with the same letter, once again following the order of the alphabet. There is a slight variation in the order of the alphabet in these poems. Lam 1 places *'ayin* (ע) before *pe* (פ)—much like Ps 119—whereas Lam 2, 3, and 4 have *pe* before *'ayin*, as in Prov 31:10–31.

Lam 5, like Lam 4, has two lines per stanza and twenty-two stanzas, but it is not an acrostic. While there have been some attempts to find a hidden acrostic scheme in this poem (e.g., Guillaume), there is little to recommend this approach, as most of the schemes appear forced and artificial. Better, perhaps, is the suggestion of Grossberg that just as Jerusalem has been broken down and become a forsaken ruin, so also the acrostic form has been abandoned, leading to the plea for God's mercy in the midst of disaster.

The acrostic nature of the poems also leads the reader to see a progression in thought. Lam 1 opens the book with an observation of Jerusalem's misery. This is followed by a poem highlighting the reason for this deep pain—Yahweh's anger against Jerusalem for her sins (Lam 2).

The center poem, Lam 3, is the most developed acrostic in the book and brings the thoughts developed in the first two poems to a climax with the suggestion of a resolution. It is a lament in the first person, picking up this device from the first two poems (Lam 1:12–16; 18–22; 2:22). The narrator sketches his personal affliction, ending the first half of the poem with the observation that Yahweh will not reject his people forever, but will show compassion on them, since he finds no joy in causing human misery (Lam 3:31–33). The second half continues to explore God's wrath, but also calls on his people to repent and seek forgiveness (Lam 3:40–42). Then the narrator notes how his enemies taunt him, concluding with the confident statement that God will destroy those who persecute him (Lam 3:64–66).

Lam 4 appears to be influenced by the themes brought to the fore in Lam 3. Now there are only two lines per stanza, and the last one echoes the middle and final stanzas of Lam 3 (Lam 4:22). Finally, Lam 5 is a plea for restoration and vindication from Yahweh.

## *QINAH* METER

Most scholars recognize a poetic rhythm in Lamentations called *qinah* meter. The term was first coined by Karl Budde in the late nineteenth century to describe the rhythm found in much of the poetry in Lam 1–4. This rhythm, which Budde thought generally characterized a lament (Hebrew קִנָה, *qinah*), features a longer line of poetry followed by a shorter one, usually in a stress pattern of 3:2. The term is a double misnomer, however. Hebrew poetry does not exhibit meter in the classical sense of that term. Moreover, the *qinah* pattern is found in other types of poems which are not laments. Despite this mislabeling, *qinah* continues to be used as a technical term to refer to this poetic device whenever it occurs in Hebrew verse.

This consistent use of *qinah* meter throughout the first four chapters gives Lamentations an artistic unity despite the obvious division into separate acrostic poems. Moreover, just as the acrostic form is absent and abandoned in Lam 5, so also the *qinah* pattern is not found in the final poem.

## Outline of Lamentations

I.   Jerusalem's misery because of her sin (ch. 1)

II.  Yahweh's anger against the Daughter of Zion (ch. 2)

III. Yahweh's discipline and his mercy—a first person lament (ch. 3)

IV.  Jerusalem's punishment has been completed (ch. 4)

V.   Plea: Restore us, O Lord (ch. 5)

## HISTORICAL ISSUES

With the pursuit of archaeology throughout modern Iraq during the nineteenth and twentieth centuries, scholars soon became aware of ancient Sumerian and Babylonian laments, especially laments over cities. They began to compare them to Lamentations in order to find common elements and themes. Some argued that Lamentations was heir to these laments which came from the first half of the second millennium BC. Others have disputed that Lamentations could have been influenced by a literary form that flourished some 1,400 years earlier. Instead, they conclude that Lamentations is more likely to share only common cultural outlooks and some literary features, because no direct dependence of Lamentations on the earlier works can be demonstrated.

House offers a number of interesting observations on the connections between Lamentations and the Mesopotamian city dirges without necessarily holding to any type of direct influence of the earlier laments on Lamentations:

1. Lamentations stands in a long tradition of city laments and demonstrates the Hebrew poet's high regard for Jerusalem that he would place it in the same company as other great cities for which laments were written.

2. Lamentations shares some thematic features with the earlier Sumerian and Babylonian laments, including divine displeasure causing the city's demise, lengthy descriptions of the city's destruction, and cries for divine intervention.

3. Lamentations has a number of important differences from the earlier laments. Especially prominent is Lamentations' strict monotheism in contrast to the polytheism of the Mesopotamian dirges.

4. Little historical or literary evidence exists to link Lamentations to the earlier works, making it likely that there is no direct dependence on these earlier texts, but leading to the conclusion that there is some historical link between the two.

5. The Babylonian and Sumerian laments can be used as a sort of partner in a dialogue between them and Lamentations. This can allow interpreters to explain what the author and audience of Lamentations experienced as they mourned Jerusalem's demise.

## THEOLOGICAL THEMES IN LAMENTATIONS

Three theological themes are prominent in Lamentations: The righteousness of God's wrath against Jerusalem in light of her sins, the vengeance of God against the nations who have cruelly afflicted his people, and the need for humble repentance. These three themes work together to highlight sin and grace in Lamentations.

### SIN AND GRACE IN LAMENTATIONS

#### God's Wrath

Clearly, Lamentations connects Jerusalem's suffering with God's wrath and not simply the result of Babylonian aggression (Lam 1:12–13, 15, 22; 2:1–9, 22; 3:1–18; 4:16). Divine anger even led to his bringing destruction on Jerusalem's temple, priests, and kings, even though these were all chosen by him (Lam 2:6–7).

Yet the poet admits that God is correct in bringing this punishment on the city: "Yahweh is just, because I have rebelled against his command" (Lam 1:18). This is an unquestioned and unquestionable aspect of the poet's faith in God—that all God does is just and right, even when it leads to the overwhelming sorrow and pain the poet and his people are experiencing.

## God's Vengeance on the Nations

The nations may have been God's instrument to execute his wrath against sin among his people, but that does not excuse the animosity and cruelty that characterized their acts (Lam 3:52–54). God will also judge them for their sins while bringing vindication for his people who repent and trust in him (Lam 3:58–66; 4:21–22).

## Repentance

The misery of the poet and his audience is not simply an occasion for mourning and self-pity (Lam 1:14–17). Instead, their current state is intended to lead to their acknowledgement of their sin and a rejection of their former acts and attitudes (Lam 3:27–30; 38–41). Moreover, this repentance leads to appeals for Yahweh's forgiveness and a restored union with him (Lam 5:21). For the writer of Lamentations, as for the rest of Scripture, repentance is not only sorrow and revulsion over one's sins (Lam 5:15–16), it is also faith in a gracious and loving God who alone can forgive transgressions and restore his fallen people to a whole relationship with him (Lam 3:22–33; 55–57).

## CHRIST IN LAMENTATIONS

There are no passages in Lamentations that explicitly reference Christ and his work. However, the mercy of God in the book clearly presages his mercy in Jesus.

The anointed kings of Judah's Davidic dynasty were to be examples of God's greater Anointed One. They were viewed as Judah's very breath of life and the ones who would give Israel protection from the nations in this sin-infested world (Lam 4:20). The priests also were to foreshadow Christ and his work of intercession. Yet God removed this anointed dynasty and the chosen priests when they failed to be a representation of the greater Anointed One to come (Lam 2:6, 9).

Although these precursors of Christ were removed from Judah and carried into exile, there was One who was to come who would be a greater king and priest for his people. For this reason the writer of Lamentations calls on his readers to wait for God to come to them with his deliverance (Lam 3:25). God's promise never to reject his people (Lam 3:31) would be fulfilled in his compassion in Christ where his abundant love is shown most clearly (Lam 3:32), since God's goal is to reconcile all people to himself, not simply to punish them for their sins (Lam 3:33). The poet's abiding confidence is in divine renewal, which cannot be thwarted unless God would completely reject his people, something he has promised never to do (Lam 5:21–22; cf. Jer 33:25–26). Though none of these passages in Lamentations explicitly connects with the promised Messiah, they nevertheless flow out of the messianic hope that runs throughout the OT.

## CONCLUSION

Sorrow and contrition over sin are important in the life of every believer and a necessary part of God's work to restore sinners to a forgiven and blessed relationship with him. Lamentations expresses this sorrow with powerful emotional and evocative language as the poet views the destruction of Jerusalem and the exile of its people. But more importantly, Lamentations also brings the grace and mercy of God to mourning sinners so that they might find hope, peace, and life with their Redeemer.

## SELECT BIBLIOGRAPHY

Berlin, Adele. *Lamentations: A Commentary.* The Old Testament Library. Louisville: Westminster, 2002.

Dobbs-Allsopp, F. W. "Linguistic Evidence for the Date of Lamentations." *Journal of the Ancient Near Eastern Society of Columbia University* 26 (1998): 1–36.

Garrett, Duane, and Paul R. House. *Song of Songs/Lamentations.* Word Biblical Commentary 23B. Nashville: Thomas Nelson, 2004.

Gordis, Robert. *The Song of Songs and Lamentations: A Study, Modern Translation and Commentary.* Revised and augmented. New York: KTAV, 1974.

Grossberg, Daniel. *Centripetal and Centrifugal Structures in Biblical Poetry.* Society of Biblical Literature Monograph Series 39. Atlanta: Scholars, 1989.

Guillaume, Phillipe. "Lamentations 5: The Seventh Acrostic." *The Journal of Hebrew Scriptures* 9. http://www.jhsonline.org /Articles/article_118.pdf.

Harrison, R. K. *Jeremiah and Lamentations: An Introduction and Commentary.* Tyndale Old Testament Commentaries 21. Downers Grove: InterVarsity, 1973.

Hillers, Delbert R. *Lamentations: Introduction, Translation, and Notes.* Anchor Bible 7A. Garden City: Doubleday, 1972.

Huey, F. B. *Jeremiah, Lamentations.* The New American Commentary 16. Nashville: Broadman, 1993.

Linafelt, Tod. "The Refusal of a Conclusion in the Book of Lamentations." *Journal of Biblical Literature* 120 (2001): 340– 343.

Provan, Ian. *Lamentations.* New Century Bible Commentary. Grand Rapids: Eerdmans, 1991.

25

# EZEKIEL

In the book of Ezekiel we meet a priest, Ezekiel ben Buzi, one of the Judean exiles deported along with King Jehoiachin to Babylon in 597. Five years into the exile, in the year when Ezekiel would have begun his duties as a priest at the age of thirty (Num 4:3), he was called to be a prophet. Ezekiel not only lives through the collapse of Judah but also through the undoing of the larger ancient Near Eastern world as he witnesses Assyria's downfall and Babylon's rise.

With equal appropriateness, Ezekiel may be described as either the last pre-exilic prophet or the first post-exilic prophet. His use of poetry and prose, as well as the fact that he prophesied both before and after the destruction of Jerusalem, link him to both periods. In his specific concerns he has much in common with his pre-exilic predecessors. Like them, he addresses a definite historical crisis and denounces moral degeneracy and idolatry. To reinforce his spoken message, he makes extensive use of symbolic actions, just like Isaiah, Jeremiah, and Hosea. However, stylistically, Ezekiel is more akin to the post-exilic prophets. His book employs bizarre images, angelic intermediaries, numerology, and apocalyptic visions—all typical of later post-exilic writings. Ezekiel therefore straddles both the pre- and post-exilic worlds.

## AUTHORSHIP

The following indicate that Ezekiel composed the book that bears his name: (1) all of the prophecies express themselves in a first person, autobiographical style, the only exception being Ezek 1:2–3, (2) the account of the scroll (Ezek 2:9–3:3) suggests that there was an early, written record of his words, and (3) several times Yahweh commands the prophet to record his oracles (Ezek 24:1–2; 37:16). There is also sufficient evidence that extra-biblical ancient Near Eastern prophets, long before the time of Ezekiel, composed words from a deity and then attached their name to the document.

Not content with this evidence, form critics argue that Ezekiel's poetry is genuine but his prose is not. Writing in 1924, Gustav Hölscher, for instance, maintained that only 144 verses—out of 1,273—were penned by Ezekiel. More recent scholars like Georg Fohrer, however, only doubt the authenticity of chapters 38–48, while Blenkinsopp accepts that Ezekiel composed a large part of his book but that later redactors made some changes and contributions. Zimmerli is much more extreme; he posits a lengthy and complicated process of growth for the book.

Not only do critics doubt that the entire book was composed by Ezekiel, some also assert that it was authored in Jerusalem, not in Babylon. They point out that most of the book is directed to Jerusalem's inhabitants, with only a few oracles meant for the exiles (chapters 33, 34, 36, 37). The prophet is intimately familiar with what is going on in the temple (Ezek 8–11). In fact, a prince named Pelatiah falls down dead when Ezekiel utters his curses (Ezek 11:13). Advocates of this view believe that the texts that explicitly or implicitly place the prophet in Babylon (e.g., Ezek 1:1; 3:11; 8:3; 11:24; 33:21; 40:1) are in fact literary fabrications.

However, Ezekiel calls those living in Jerusalem "they" over against the "you" of his main audience in Babylon (e.g., Ezek 12:11; 14:22). And if he were living in the city of David it wouldn't make sense for him to "set his face toward it" (Ezek 21:7). Finally, if it seems strange that, in some texts, Ezekiel addresses people in Jerusalem, this is no different from prophetic oracles about other nations. In both cases, the real audiences are those in the prophet's proximate audience. In Ezekiel's case, this would be exiles living in Babylon.

## LITERARY FEATURES OF EZEKIEL

Ezek 1–24 mostly denounces and condemns, while Ezek 33–48 consists largely of promissory oracles of return and restoration. Chapters 24 and 33 function as key structural markers. Ezek 24 announces the beginning of Jerusalem's siege while Ezek 33 reports the city's capture. Both chapters mention the prophet's call when God made him mute (Ezek 3:24–27). His loss of speech (Ezek 24:25–27) comes to an end when a messenger announces Jerusalem's fall (Ezek 33:21–22). Sandwiched between chapters 24 and 33 are Ezekiel's oracles about foreign nations which, in their present literary arrangement, make the transition from Yahweh's judgment of his people to their salvation. Seen in this way, Jerusalem's destruction is the fulcrum of the book, marking the end of judgment and the beginning of divine mercy.

The book of Ezekiel breaks down into four parts: (1) the prophet's call (Ezek 1:1–3:27); (2) oracles of doom for Judah and Jerusalem (Ezek 4:1–24:27); (3) seven nations are condemned, indicating universal judgment (Ezek 25:1–32:32); and (4) announcements of restoration (Ezek 33:1–48:35). The book is made up of fifty literary units, forty-eight of which are clearly signaled— either by a chronological marker or with the phrase "the word of Yahweh came to me." Because of this high degree of literary coherence, Ezekiel is one of the easiest books in the OT to outline.

## Outline of Ezekiel

I.   Ezekiel's call to be a prophet (1:1–3:27)

   A.  Superscription (1:1–3)

   B.  Ezekiel's inaugural vision (1:4–28a)

   C.  Ezekiel's commission (1:28b–3:11)

   D.  Ezekiel's preparation (3:12–15)

   E.  Ezekiel's loss of speech (3:16–21)

   F.  Ezekiel's initiation (3:22–27)

II.  Signs and visions of judgment (4:1–11:25)

   A.  Dramatizing Jerusalem's fall (4:1–5:17)

   B.  Judgment against Israel's mountains (6:1–14)

   C.  Sounding the alarm (7:1–27)

   D.  Yahweh leaves the temple (8:1–11:25)

III. Prophecies of judgment against Israel (12:1–24:27)

   A.  Signs of the times (12:1–20)

   B.  True and false prophecy (12:21–14:11)

C. The price of treachery (14:12–15:8)

D. The adulterous wife (16:1–63)

E. Oracles of sin and retribution (17:1–22:31)

F. Oholah and Oholibah (23:1–49)

G. The boiling cauldron (24:1–14)

H. Jerusalem's end (24:15–27)

IV. Oracles about nations (25:1–32:32)

A. Judgment against Israel's neighbors (25:1–17)

B. Judgment against Tyre (26:1–28:19)

C. Yahweh's plan for the nations (28:20–26)

D. Judgment against Egypt and Pharaoh (29:1–32:32)

V. Jerusalem's demise (33:1–33)

A. Final summons (33:1–20)

B. Final word (33:21–22)

C. Final disputation (33:23–29)

D. Final vindication (33:30–33)

VI. Ezekiel's gospel (34:1–48:35)

A. Saving Yahweh's flock (34:1–31)

B. Restoring Yahweh's land (35:1–36:15)

C. Restoring Yahweh's honor (36:16–38)

D. Resurrecting Yahweh's people (37:1–14)

E. Yahweh's eternal covenant (37:15–28)

F. Yahweh's defeat of Gog of Magog (38:1–39:29)

G. The new temple (40:1–43:11)

H. The new Torah (43:12–46:24)

I. The new land (47:1–48:29)

J. The new city (48:30–35)

Ezekiel's priestly status (Ezek 1:3) probably explains his unusual vocabulary—the book contains 130 *hapax legomena*. Yet where he was schooled in the genre of apocalyptic (Ezek 38–39) is anyone's guess.

Ezekiel is famous for his propensity to reuse phrases. Note the following examples: בן אדם, *son of man* (93 times); ויהי דבר־יהוה אלי, *the word of Yahweh came to me* (50 times); כה אמר אדני יהוה, *thus said Lord Yahweh* (122 times); נאם אדני יהוה, *the oracle of my Lord Yahweh* (85 times); בית ישראל, *the house of Israel* (83 times); and אני יהוה, *I am Yahweh* (86 times). The prophet also reworks themes like divine glory (Ezek 1:1–28; 8:1–11:25; 43:1–9), the prophet as a watchman (Ezek 3:16–21; 33:1–9), Jerusalem as a pot (Ezek 11:1–12; 24:1–11), personal responsibility (Ezek 18:1–32; 33:10–20), and Israel's harlotries (Ezek 16, 23).

Ezekiel displays a wide variety of genres: legal addresses (e.g., Ezek 14:12–15:8; 20:1–44), woe oracles (e.g., Ezek 13:1–16; 34:1–10), sign-acts (e.g., Ezek 4:1–5:17; 12:1–20; 21:18–27), wisdom proverbs (Ezek 12:22; 16:44; 18:2), and visions (e.g., Ezek 37:1–14). What is distinctive, however, is the prophet's frequent use of allegories (Ezek 15:1–8; 16:1–43; 17:1–24; 23:1–49; 27:1–36; 28:12–19; 31:1–18) and oracles for the dead (Ezek 19:1–14; 26:15–18; 28:11–19; 32:1–16).

Odell believes that the book's design comes from ancient Near Eastern building inscriptions. She maintains that it bears a striking similarity to Esarhaddon's Assyrian inscriptions (c. 680). This becomes most clear in chapters 40–48. Ezekiel's adaptation of this Assyrian genre means the prophet embraced Assyria's pervasive cultural and political influence. This is evident when one compares Isaiah's scathing rebuke of Assyria (Isa 10:5–15; 36:1–37:38) with Ezekiel's favorable evaluation of this massive nation (Ezek 31:3).

The international scope of Ezekiel's book also becomes clear in chapter 27. This prophecy may have originated from a Phoenician poem that glorified Tyre during her golden age from the beginning of the tenth until the second half of the eighth century. So important was this island capital that the sinking of "Ship Tyre" creates repercussions to the ends of the earth (Ezek 27:33, 36).

## TEXTUAL ISSUES

Among the prophets, next to Hosea, the MT of Ezekiel is the most difficult to read. Compounding the problem is that the LXX is shorter than the MT by some five percent. Yet, unlike the case with Jeremiah (see chapter 23 on Jeremiah), scholars do not hypothesize the LXX is based on a different Hebrew *Vorlage*. It does, however, differ from the MT in significant ways. For example, the arrangement in Ezek 7 in the LXX is altered and chapter 36 is significantly longer.

## HISTORICAL ISSUES

Historical markers appear in Ezek 1:1–2; 3:16; 8:1; 20:1; 24:1; 26:1; 29:1, 17; 30:20; 31:1; 32:17; 33:21; and 40:1. The only two oracles that are not in chronological order are against Egypt. The first and sixth oracles against Egypt are placed first (Ezek 29:1–30:19), followed by the second through the fifth Egyptian oracles (Ezek 30:20–32:32). (Some are oracles against Pharaoh, but that is essentially the same as Egypt.) It would appear, then, that Ezekiel's oracles are largely arranged in chronological order, with the exception made with the first and last Egyptian oracles in order to group them with the other oracles against Egypt. Seven out of the thirteen dates in the book are connected to Ezekiel's oracles about nations.

All of these references to time are tied to Jehoiachin's exile with one exception—Ezek 1:1, where the thirtieth year probably refers to Ezekiel's age. If this is the case, the prophet was born in 623. At that time, Assyria was still the dominant power in the ancient Near East, but its demise was on the horizon. This would bring with it an era when Judah was a pawn in a massive battle for control of the Syria-Palestinian corridor.

Assyrian dominos began to fall when Nabopolassar (625–605)—Babylon's founder—rallied the Chaldeans and Medes to form an imposing coalition. He defeated Assyria in the following battles: Asshur (614), Nineveh (612), and finally Haran (609). Babylon then triumphed over Egypt at the battle of Carchemish (605). After this, Nebuchadnezzar (605–562)—Nabopolassar's son—began to exercise his iron grip over the Levant.

Meanwhile, in Judah, King Jehoiakim assumed the role of Nebuchadnezzar's vassal from 604 to 602. Then, relying on Egyptian help, he revolted, but ended up dying on 21 Marcheshvan 598 (Dec 9, 598) before Babylon could respond. When Nebuchadnezzar marched against Jerusalem, the city surrendered on 2 Adar 597 (April 16, 597). Jehoiachin paid dearly for his father Jehoiakim's folly. He was exiled to Babylon, along with Ezekiel and other priests and nobility (2 Kgs 24:11–16). Five years later, Yahweh called Ezekiel into ministry (Ezek 1:2).

Judean deportees were placed into agricultural communities as well as in the city of Babylon. Those who lived in the urban center were possibly enlisted for work in the temple, while the book of Ezekiel attests to another community that was more agrarian. These settlements were by the Chebar River (e.g., Ezek 1:3; 10:15; 43:3), one he calls Tel-abib (Ezek 3:15). According to Ezek 8:14, many of the exiles enjoyed a degree of freedom in their refugee camps. They were able to build homes, cultivate fields, and engage in business. But, lest they get too comfortable, Ezek 37:1–14 indicates that Yahweh's plan is to bring them back to the Promised Land.

The prophet's oracles from Ezek 1:4–29:16; 30:20–33:21 were received 593–574. The last oracle in the book appears in Ezek 29:17–30:16, which was during Jehoiachin's (and Ezekiel's) twenty-seventh year of exile, or 571. Because the prophet never mentions the release of Jehoiachin in 560 (cf. 2 Kgs 25:27–30), it is reasonable to conclude that his messages cover the period from 593 to 571.

## THEOLOGICAL THEMES IN EZEKIEL

### DIVINE GLORY

Yahweh's כבוד, *glory*, is Ezekiel's central theological idea. It first appears in chapter 1 in the form of a man (Ezek 1:26–28). In this chapter, the prophet also sees living creatures with chariot wheels filled with eyes functioning as a platform for Yahweh's throne. The faces of the creatures indicate that God is all-present, the eyes suggest his omniscience, and the numerous wheels signal that Yahweh's presence is not static but mobile. The glory is like a dazzling brightness, a flashing fire, and a gleaming metal.

The second appearance of God's glory comes in Ezek 8–11, where the prophet witnesses Yahweh's withdrawal from the temple. The vision begins with people making an altar in the temple to "the idol that provokes jealousy" (Ezek 8:5). Elders have their own idols (Ezek 8:12), women worship Tammuz (Ezek 8:14), and still others bow down to the sun (Ezek 8:16). Bloodshed and violence fill the land (Ezek 9:9), and these abominations drive Yahweh from his temple (Ezek 8:6).

Leaving in stages like a jilted lover (e.g., Ezek 9:3; 10:4, 18–19), Yahweh finds it heart-wrenching to leave the ones he loves. Even when he finally departs, he does not go far. Yahweh's glory stops moving on the mountain east of Jerusalem (Ezek 11:23). There he stands, in solidarity with the exiles. They are outcast, so is he. They are displaced, so is he. They are faced with unfamiliar surroundings, and so is he. Yahweh is present in the vortex of Israel's loss. Though sovereign and free, his glory affiliates with the marginalized exilic community.

In grace, Yahweh's glory returns from the east to fill the rebuilt temple (Ezek 43:1–5). Ezekiel likens this sound to many waters (Ezek 43:2; cf. 1:24) and goes on to write that this glory is what he saw in chapter 1.

## THE SINAITIC COVENANT

One of the most frequent phrases connected with the covenant Yahweh made with Israel at Sinai is "I will be their God and they will be my people" (Exod 6:7). The book of Ezekiel repeats this several times (Ezek 11:20; 14:11; 34:24, 30–31; 36:28; 37:23). The endearing word עַמִּי, *my people*, appears twenty-five times in the book while בְּרִית, *covenant*, is used seventeen times.

Many Israelites in Ezekiel's day viewed the Sinaitic covenant as unconditional, yet Moses insists that it is based upon hearing/faith (Exod 19:5). Ezekiel uses the first twenty-four chapters in his book to point people back to Moses' words. Israel's lack of faith not only made them "a rebellious house" (e.g., Ezek 2:5; 3:9; 12:3; 24:3), their actions were even worse than their pagan neighbors (Ezek 5:5–7; 16:44–53). Many of God's judgments reflect the Sinaitic covenant curses of Lev 26 and Deut 28. Note, for example, the sword motif of Lev 26:36 appears in Ezek 6:3, and the promise of pestilence in Deut 28:21 is fulfilled in Ezek 12:16. Israelites brought these maledictions upon themselves by ignoring Yahweh's lavish grace (Ezek 16:15–43).

## YAHWEH'S MARRIAGE TO ISRAEL

In chapters 16 and 23, Ezekiel joins other prophets (e.g., Hos 1–3; Isa 61:10–11) who portray Yahweh's relationship with his people as a marriage. The marriage began with great promise. When Yahweh passed by Jerusalem and saw that she was ready for love, he covered her nakedness with his garment and entered into a covenant with her (Ezek 16:8). But after some time, she forgot the days of her youth and committed abominations (Ezek 16:43). Israel became an unfaithful bride who broke the marriage covenant. People played the harlot

(Ezek 16:15, 22, 25–26; 28–31, 34–36, 41; 23:3, 5, 7, 11, 14, 17, 19, 27, 30). They pursued other lovers by worshiping idols and graven images and by depending on other nations, primarily Egypt, Assyria, and Babylon (e.g., Ezek 16:32, 38; 23:37, 43, 45).

Judah's failure to turn from her adulteries resulted in divine judgment (Ezek 16:38; 23:45; cf. Lev 20:10; Deut 22:20). But because Yahweh is steadfastly devoted to his wife, she may anticipate redemption (e.g., Ezek 16:60–63). He will reconstitute the marriage under an everlasting covenant (Ezek 16:60) and Israel will come to "know Yahweh," likely indicating an emotional and intimate knowledge (Ezek 16:8). Come what may, Yahweh is a faithful husband who keeps his covenantal obligations (e.g., Ezek 16:9–14).

## APOCALYPTICISM

Apocalyptic writings include these characteristics: (1) revelation is mediated by heavenly beings to select persons through visions, (2) the context has a temporal axis concerning the past and present with a particular accent upon an upheaval in the future, and (3) it is written in a way that makes it accessible only to people perceived as insiders. Biblical sections that are apocalyptic include Dan 7–12, Ezek 38–39, and Rev 4–22.

The apocalyptic nature of Ezek 38–39, far from being disconnected with the rest of the book, functions as an integral part of Ezekiel. It portrays the land's purification from the defilement of corpses in preparation for the temple's restoration in chapters 40–48. Ezek 38 envisions Gog's defeat while chapter 39 features Gog's disposal.

One explanation for Gog's identity is that it derives from Gyges, the name of a Lydian king mentioned in six inscriptions of Ashurbanipal (668–631). Magog is then a reference to the territory of Lydia in western Anatolia. Meshek (Ezek 38:2) is also known from Assyrian sources and is portrayed in Ps 120:5–7 as a barbaric enemy. During Sargon II's reign (722–705), Meshech was ruled by Lydia/Phrygia. Tubal (Ezek 38:2) is similarly mentioned in Assyrian documents and was the territorial designation of the interior Anatolian kingdom bounded on the west by Meshech. While there is no evidence that Lydia/Phrygia ever ruled over Tubal, Sargon II's annals report that he squelched an Anatolian revolt in which Phrygia was allied with Tubal. It could be that Ezekiel employs these northern names to symbolically accent evil and anti-Yahwistic ways. In other texts, the enemy comes from the north (e.g., Jer 1:13–15; 6:22; Zech 2:6).

Therefore, unlike the foreign nations in chapters 24–32, the references in Ezek 38–39 are employed as cyphers of great evil. Contrary to the Egyptians, Assyrians, and Babylonians, with whom Judah had frequent contact, people in the distant north were shrouded in mystery. The reports of these people groups that filtered down spoke of brutal and barbaric kingdoms. This combination of mystery and brutality made Gog and his confederates perfect symbols of the archetypal enemy rising against Yahweh and his people.

Odell offers another attractive explanation for Gog. She argues that it is an obscure allusion to Babylon. A comparable cryptogram appears in Jer 25:26; 51:41, where Babylon is called Shishak. The cryptogram employed in Jeremiah is called athbash, which is where the first letter in the Hebrew alphabet is replaced by the last, the second by the next to the last, etc. (i.e., b-b-l = s-s-k). The code used in Ezek 38–39 involves a different system of substituting letters (i.e., b-b-l = g-g-m), which are then reversed (i.e., g-g-m = m-g-g, or Magog). Theologically and historically this makes sense when one understands that Ezekiel applies the Gog/Magog oracles to announce that Israel's exile in Babylon is only temporary (Ezek 39:25–29). The regime will be defeated.

## THE NEW TEMPLE

The vision in chapters 40–48 comes to the prophet in 574 (Ezek 40:1). The same guide that met Ezekiel in chapters 8–11 to give him a tour of the doomed city reappears and meets him on a very high mountain (Ezek 40:2). The vision describes the new temple and how it will function in the new era.

Much about this temple is similar to Solomon's temple as it is presented in 1 Kgs 6–8. Perhaps most striking is the threefold structure of the temple outlined in the section extending from Ezek 40:48–42:20; first comes the vestibule, then the nave, and finally the inner room which is the holy of holies.

But there are discontinuities as well. For example, Ezekiel's temple appears to be almost empty. Virtually all of the furnishings in Solomon's temple are missing. The only interior furniture mentioned is the "altar of wood" in front of the inner room (Ezek 41:22). This is

## The Temple and the Altar in Ezekiel

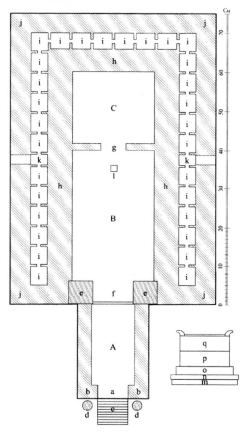

| A | Vestibule (40:48–49) | h | Wall of the temple (41:5) |
|---|---|---|---|
| B | Nave (41:1–2) | i | Side rooms (41:5–7) |
| C | Holy of Holies (41:3–4) | j | Outer wall of side rooms (41:9) |
| a | Doorway of the vestibule (40:48) | k | Entrance of the side rooms |
| b | Doorposts of the vestibule (40:48–49) | l | Table (41:22) |
| c | Steps (40:49) | m | Gutter (43:13–14; perhaps also 43:17) |
| d | Pillars (40:49) | n | Ridge (43:13; perhaps also 43:17) |
| e | Doorposts of the nave (41:1) | o | Smaller, lower ledge (43:14; perhaps also 43:17) |
| f | Entrance of the nave (41:2) | p | Larger, upper ledge (43:14; perhaps also 43:17) |
| g | Entrance of the Holy of Holies (41:3) | q | Hearth (43:15–16) |

From *Ezekiel 21–48*, Concordia Commentary (St. Louis: Concordia, 2007), 1164. Adapted from C. F. Keil, *Biblischer Commentar über den Propheten Ezechiel*, 2nd ed. (Leipzig: Dörffling und Franke, 1882).

distinct from the stone altar of burnt sacrifice that stands outside of the temple (Ezek 40:47; 43:13–27). Most notable among the omissions, however, is the ark of the covenant. Why is this so?

Ezekiel's vision emphasizes Yahweh's all-sufficiency. Within chapter 36, for example, Yahweh acts to restore his people for no other reason than that he may be known as he really is. The book's focus is so much on Yahweh that everything else is finally eclipsed. The city's name at the end of the book is "Yahweh Is There" (Ezek 48:35). What need, then, is there for the ark?

Solomon's great bronze sea of 1 Kgs 7:23 is reworked to become a river flowing from the temple (Ezek 47:1–12). Here Ezekiel's faithful guide points to the water under the threshold of the altar (Ezek 47:1). The prophet describes it as מפכים, trickling. Several verses later, this trickle becomes a surging river of life. The river flows to the Dead Sea which is 1,400 feet below sea level and has a saline content of thirty-five percent. In antiquity it was simply called "the Salt Sea." Ever since divine fire torched Sodom and Gomorrah—the two cities at the southern end of the Dead Sea—the entire area became the ultimate symbol of death (cf. Gen 19:24–25).

The prophet catches up with his guide after a third of a mile and splashes into ankle-deep water. After another third of a mile, Ezekiel wades into water up to his knees. By the time he reaches the mile marker, he can't find a bottom to the river. Afraid to get in over his head, Ezekiel stands on the bank, only to find that both banks are covered with a great number of trees, which, he is told, will miraculously bear fruit every month and always yield leaves that heal. The guide takes him no farther but points eastward and tells the prophet that the river from the temple will transform the Dead Sea into a freshwater lake as rich in fish as the Mediterranean Sea. The river runs all around the Dead Sea, from En-gedi to En-eglaim, which represents a topographical merism, highlighting the totality of the healing waters. Fishermen are at work, spreading their nets and hauling in their catches. "Wherever the river flows everything lives" (Ezek 47:9).

Additional differences between Solomon's and Ezekiel's temple include the fact that Solomon's was one of a number of buildings (e.g. 1 Kgs 6:1–14), whereas the new temple will stand alone (Ezek 43:10–12). As Yahweh's earthly regent, monarchs wielded final authority in sacred as well as civil matters. In Israel's future, Jerusalem's leaders (Ezek 45:7, 8, 13–17) will no longer set "their threshold next to my threshold and their doorposts beside my doorposts, with only a wall between me and them" (Ezek 43:8).

Instead the Davidic prince will be allotted land at the periphery of the city, well away from its sacred center (Ezek 45:7; 48:21–22). Henceforth, the temple mount will belong to the priests (Ezek 45:3–5; 48:9–12).

Additional differences between the old age and the new include the following: (1) the Transjordan will no longer play a role in tribal distribution (Ezek 47:13–20); (2) Judah is placed in the north (Ezek 47:7–8); and (3) the Leah and Rachel tribes are closest to the temple (Ezek 48:1–7).

### CHRIST IN EZEKIEL

Ezekiel envisions a new David who will shepherd and rule his people (Ezek 34:23–24; 37:24–25). In Ezek 34:24 and 37:25 he is depicted as a נשיא, *prince* or *leader*. The leader appears again in chapters 40–48 (e.g., Ezek 44:3; 45:7). Christ is this Good Shepherd who leads his people to find good pasture, that is, abundant life (John 10:1–10).

John's Gospel also accents the motif of Christ as the new temple (e.g., John 1:14; 2:19–22). And, just as Ezekiel's temple flows with living water (Ezek 47:1–12), so John maintains that Christ is the source of this river. It begins with just a trickle. Jesus tells Nicodemus, "No one can enter the reign of God unless he is born of water and the Spirit" (John 3:5). It picks up momentum: "But the water I give will become a fountain of water springing up into eternal life" (John 4:14). And then it becomes a surge: "Whoever believes in me, as the Scripture has said, streams of living water will flow from within him" (John 7:38). But, in an ironic twist for the ages, this raging river completely dries up. Christ laments on the cross, "I thirst" (John 19:28). The Roman spear thrust brought with it a sudden flow of blood and water (John 19:34). Here is *the* temple, crushed and cursed—not by the might of Babylon—but by the sin in people's lives. Yet just as the Spirit entered the dry bones (Ezek 37:1–14) and God's glory returned to Ezekiel's temple (Ezek 43:1–5), this same Spirit and glory returned to the Crucified One. Jesus is alive forevermore.

This death and resurrection motif is central to Ezek 24:15–27. The passage is often understood to be that, just as Yahweh commanded Ezekiel not to mourn his wife's death, Judeans were not to lament the death of Jerusalem. Yet Yahweh's instructions to the prophet to put on sandals and a turban (Ezek 24:17) come from rituals marking status transformation, not acts of mourning. Priests and kings donned turbans when they were installed in office, and marriage rituals involved both sandals and turbans. This means that even in the midst of death (Ezek 24:2), there is new life. The destruction of the old (Ezek 1–24) makes way for the building of the new (Ezek 33–48). Christ's triumphant cry from the agony of the cross surely epitomizes this idea (John 19:30), while his resurrection on the third day indicates that this is how God has chosen to work in the world.

## SIN AND GRACE IN EZEKIEL

Ezekiel frequently alternates between sin and grace, woe and weal. For example, after Yahweh's scathing rebuke in Ezek 16:1–52, the chapter concludes with promises that God will remember his covenant and restore the fortunes of his people (Ezek 16:53–63).

Much has been written about a supposed turn in the OT from generational sin, articulated in the Pentateuch, to a doctrine of individualistic accountability as stated in Ezekiel (Ezek 18:1–32; 33:10–20). Some believe that during the exile the doctrine of individual responsibility began to undermine the understanding of corporate/generational sin. However, Ezekiel is not responsible for an individualism that replaced the previous emphasis of the corporate group. The prophet does not promote a new doctrine of sin. Rather he combats a fatalistic view of life engendered by self-pity and a one-sided emphasis or moral collectivism or corporate solidarity. He calls the people to own up to their sin instead of blaming their parents for the current crisis (Ezek 18:2–3).

The community's culpability was brought about by their fascination with other gods (e.g., Ezek 8). The prophet even speaks of people taking idols into their hearts (Ezek 14:1–11). Ezekiel's most frequent term for idols is גלולים, *fecal deities*. He employs it thirty-eight out of the forty-eight times it appears in the OT (e.g., Ezek 8:10; 16:36; 18:6; 20:8, 24). The noun derives from the verb גלל, *roll*, so it denotes pellets of dung/excrement or something of that sort. Because of this offensive idolatry, Yahweh rejects the intercession of even the most righteous people (cf. Ezek 14:14). There is no room in the relationship for anyone other than Israel and her God. Two's company, three's a crowd.

Yet in spite of their sin of idolatry, Yahweh will shower people with his grace. He promises to gather his scattered people (Ezek

11:16–17; 20:42; 34:11–13), bring them back to the Promised Land (Ezek 11:17–18; 34:14–15; 36:24), give them a new heart and his Spirit (Ezek 11:19–20; 16:63; 34:30–31; 36:25–38; 37:23–24), restore David's dynasty (Ezek 34:23–24; 37:22–25), and establish his presence in the midst of his people (Ezek 48:35). Yet, lest Israel again get puffed up with inordinate pride, Ezek 36:22–32 indicates that Yahweh does all of this because of his own self-regard. It is not based upon any righteousness in Israel.

## CONCLUSION

Ezekiel is the most unusual person among the goodly fellowship of the prophets. He lies immobile for long periods of time (Ezek 4:4–7), is commanded to bake barley cake over human feces (Ezek 4:12), is mute (Ezek 3:24–27; 24:25–27; 33:22), is conveyed to Jerusalem in visions (Ezek 8:1–4), shows no emotion when his wife dies (Ezek 24:15–17), and engages in outlandish behaviors (e.g., Ezek 5:1–4; 12:3–5). Through it all, he sees visions, the people see the prophet, and both see Yahweh, the holy and merciful God of the universe.

## SELECT BIBLIOGRAPHY

Blenkinsopp, Joseph. *Ezekiel*. Interpretation: A Bible Commentary for Teaching and Preaching. Louisville: Westminster, 1990.

Block, Daniel. *Ezekiel 1–48*. New International Commentary on the Old Testament. 2 vols. Grand Rapids: Eerdmans, 1997, 1998.

Davis, Ellen. *Swallowing the Scroll: Textuality and the Dynamics of Discourse in Ezekiel's Prophecy*. Journal for the Study of the Old Testament Supplement Series 78. Bible and Literature Series 21. Sheffield: The Almond Press, 1989.

Greenberg, Moshe. *Ezekiel 1–37: A New Translation with Introduction and Commentary*. Anchor Bible 22 and 22A. New York: Doubleday, 1983, 1997.

Hummel, Horace. *Ezekiel 1–48*. 2 vols. St. Louis: Concordia, 2005, 2008.

Joyce, Paul. *Ezekiel: A Commentary*. Library of Hebrew Bible/Old Testament Studies 482. New York/London: T&T Clark, 2007.

Odell, Margaret. *Ezekiel*. Smyth and Helwys Bible Commentary 16. Macon: Smyth and Helwys, 2005.

Renz, Thomas. *The Rhetorical Function of the Book of Ezekiel*. Supplements to Vetus Testamentum 76. Leiden: Brill, 1999.

Zimmerli, Walther. *Ezekiel 1: A Commentary on the Book of the Prophet Ezekiel, Chapters 1–24*. Hermeneia. Philadelphia: Augsburg Fortress, 1979.

———. *Ezekiel 2: A Commentary on the Book of the Prophet Ezekiel, Chapters 25–48*. Hermeneia. Philadelphia: Augsburg Fortress, 1983.

# 26

# DANIEL

In early 604, King Nebuchadnezzar returned to Babylon with a number of Judean captives, including Daniel. These prisoners were the first wave of what came to be known as the Babylonian Captivity. In 587 Jerusalem would fall, and many Judeans would join Daniel in the captivity. This was a new era for the people of Judah. For the first time since they had entered the land of Canaan in 1406, many of them were living outside the land promised to Abraham, Isaac, and Jacob. This led them to question their relationship with God. Would his promises still hold or were they now abrogated? Would God continue to defend them? Could they rely on him, or had he rejected them forever? Daniel's experiences and prophecies address these issues. Moreover, they point to God's great love that endures even when his people experience turmoil that seems beyond their control.

## AUTHORSHIP, COMPOSITION, AND DATE

Among the prophetic corpus in the OT, no book, with the possible exception of Isaiah, has been more repeatedly denied as the work of its putative author as has Daniel. Critical scholars date its various sections much later than the dates given in the book itself. They view all of the events as fictional accounts written by unknown authors, not the work of Daniel during the Babylonian and Persian periods. Even some scholars who claim to be evangelicals have adopted some form of this critical approach (e.g., Lucas). However, the majority of Christian evangelical scholars continue to accept that Daniel was the author of the book that bears his name.

## DATE AND AUTHORSHIP ACCORDING TO THE BOOK

Dan 1–6 contains accounts of the experiences of Daniel and his friends Azariah, Hananiah, and Mishael (Shadrach, Meshach, and Abednego) under the Babylonian rulers Nebuchadnezzar (605–562) and Belshazzar (553/550–539) as well as the Persian emperor Cyrus the Great (538–530). Dan 7–12 contains visions that are dated to the years of the reigning king. The various chapters can be assigned as follows:

### Chronology of the Events and Visions in Daniel

| Chapter | Date |
|---|---|
| 1 | Summer 605–Spring/Fall 603 |
| 2 | Fall 603 or Winter 603–602 |
| 3 | Late December 594 or January 593 |
| 4 | Probably sometime between 573 to 569 |
| 5 | October 11, 539 |
| 6 | Late October 539–late March 538 |
| 7 | April 7, 553–April 24, 552 or April 5, 550–April 22, 549 |
| 8 | April 16, 511–April 4, 550 or April 13, 548–April 1, 547 |
| 9 | During 538, but after March 24, 538 |
| 10–12 | April 23, 536 |

The book of Daniel cannot have existed in its present form before 536, since that is the date of the final vision. In addition, Dan 1:21 states that Daniel served in the Babylonian court until the first year of Cyrus (spring 538–spring 537). Thus, even the first parts of the book were probably written early in the reign of Cyrus, although they recount incidents from the Babylonian era. This is confirmed by the presence of Old Persian loanwords. Since Daniel was probably in his eighties at the time of composition, it is unlikely that he wrote the book later than about 530.

## CRITICAL THEORIES CONCERNING DATE, AUTHORSHIP, AND UNITY

Higher critical scholarship has long challenged the traditional dating and authorship of Daniel, as well as its unity. Objections fall into two broad categories: historical doubts about the book's authenticity and literary concerns.

Historical uncertainties about Daniel date to the third-century anti-Christian Neo-Platonist philosopher Porphyry. He believed the visions in Dan 7–12 were largely historically accurate, but that they were written *after* the events they purportedly predict. Since the visions largely detail historical activities up to the reign of the Seleucid emperor Antiochus IV Epiphanes (175–164), Porphyry proposed that they were written by a Jew in Palestine about 165 BC. This same approach was revived by higher critics in the early nineteen century and remains the primary historical objection raised by contemporary critical scholars, although they also raise other, more minor historically-related issues. All of them have been addressed by more conservative and evangelical scholars, but the critics remain unconvinced, because they continue to adopt the same controlling assumption as Porphyry: an out-of-hand rejection of genuine predictive prophecy.

Literary concerns traditionally raised by critics include observations about the characteristics of Daniel's language. At the beginning of the twentieth century, Driver asserted:

> The *Persian* words presupposed a period after the Persian empire had been well established: the Greek words *demand*, the Hebrew *supports*, and the Aramaic *permits*, a date *after the conquest of Palestine by Alexander the Great* (B.C. 332).[1]

However, each of Driver's contentions about the language of Daniel has proven to be wrong. Persian loan words are largely confined to administrative terms and are derived from Old Persian, something to be expected if Daniel served in the Persian administration (Dan 1:21; 6:1–28; cf. Dan 10:1). The Greek loan words are only three—all of them are terms for musical instruments, one of which was borrowed

---

[1] Samuel Rolles Driver, *An Introduction to the Literature of the Old Testament* (14th ed. New York: Scribner, 1909), 508.

from Ionic Greek, indicating a date well before 332. Moreover, Yamauchi has demonstrated that there was significant contact between the ancient Near East and Greece long before Alexander. Archer has clearly shown, with the discovery of the Dead Sea Scrolls, that it is apparent that the Hebrew of Daniel is not as late as the second century BC. Finally, studies of the Aramaic of Daniel have concluded that it is Imperial Aramaic, which was current from the seventh century to about 300 BC. Moreover, some of the characteristics of Daniel's Aramaic point to a time during the sixth century, precisely what the book itself indicates.

There are other arguments for the antiquity of Daniel. For instance, Steinmann has established that Ben Sira, written around 180 BC, likely adapted language from Daniel, including the visions which critics date to the mid-second century BC. Moreover, the Dead Sea Scrolls treat Daniel as a prophet on a par with Isaiah and Ezekiel. This would imply either that, despite being a mid-second century forgery, Daniel was rapidly accepted as a genuine prophetic book, or that the traditional date for Daniel is correct. Given the unlikely possibility of any mid-second century book—much less a pseudepigraphal one—being accepted as genuine prophecy by nearly all Jews (as evidenced by the Dead Sea Scrolls, the NT, and Josephus), the logical conclusion is that Daniel is a genuine sixth-century composition.

## THEOLOGICAL PROBLEMS WITH THE CRITICAL DATING OF DANIEL

Clearly, the critical dating of Daniel is a denial of the divine inspiration of Scripture, if one understands the God who inspired the Scriptures to be as trustworthy, truthful, and powerful as the Scriptures portray him. However, there is a greater issue at stake, since the book of Daniel constantly makes the point that God is in control of human history—both in Daniel's day and well beyond it. This overarching worldview supports several themes in Daniel.

One of these themes is the messianic kingdom. If God were not in absolute control of history (as critical theory assumes he is not), then his promise of a messianic kingdom is not assured. In fact, many critical interpretations of Daniel deny that the book contains messianic oracles. Therefore, one might conclude that Christian messianic understandings based on Daniel (including several passages in the NT) are built on a foundation of sand.

Second, the book clearly portrays God as the protector of his people—both in Daniel's day (esp. Dan 1, 3–6) and in the future (Dan 2, 7–12). He is able to offer them this protection because he controls history. If the narratives about God's mastery of history (Dan 1–6) are fabricated and unhistorical and if the visions (Dan 7–12) are not accurate, people have no one to guide and direct their lives.

Third, Daniel often contrasts the powerful God of Israel with the impotence of the false gods of Babylon. If the critics are correct, however, Yahweh's power is illusory, since he is no more able to come to the aid of his people than Babylon's gods could help the Babylonians.

Finally, Daniel clearly encourages the faithful to trust in God in the face of persecution and cultural pressure to abandon their beliefs. If Yahweh is not the God who knows his people's trials and defends them by his almighty power, if the stories of his deliverance (e.g., Dan 1, 3) and promises of future rescue (e.g., Dan 7, 12) are products of wishful but misguided thinking on the part of the author of Daniel, then the book has little to offer its readers other than, perhaps, an interesting but irrelevant story.

## LITERARY FEATURES OF DANIEL

Few books of the Bible are organized into distinct, discernible sections as is Daniel. It consists of ten units, and with the exception of the transition between the fifth and the sixth sections (Dan 5:31), these units are clearly delineated from one another by obvious beginnings and endings.

The first six units in the book are narratives that relate incidents from the lives of Daniel and his three Judean companions in the Babylonian captivity. Arranged in chronological order, these six sections are one chapter each in the English versions of Daniel. These are designed to be read as self-contained units, and their connection to one another is not through a continuing narrative, but is signaled thematically and structurally.

The last four units are visions that once again are clearly delineated from each other and arranged in chronological order, but the first vision is dated before the narrative of Dan 5. Thus, the visions overlap chronologically with the narratives. Each of the first three visions (Dan 7–9) consists of one chapter in Daniel. The last and longest vision is divided into three chapters (Dan 10–12). Like the narratives, the visions are self-contained units whose connection to each other is signaled thematically and structurally.

## Outline of Daniel

| | | |
|---|---|---|
| Introduction 1: Prologue (1:1–21) | NARRATIVE | *Hebrew* |
| A. Nebuchadnezzar dreams of four kingdoms and the kingdom of God (2:1–49) | NARRATIVE | *Aramaic* |
| B. Nebuchadnezzar sees God's servants rescued (3:1–30) | NARRATIVE | *Aramaic* |
| C. Nebuchadnezzar is judged (4:1–37) | NARRATIVE | *Aramaic* |
| C.' Belshazzar is judged (5:1–31) | NARRATIVE | *Aramaic* |
| B.' Darius sees Daniel rescued (6:1–28) | NARRATIVE | *Aramaic* |
| A.' Introduction 2: Daniel has a vision of four kingdoms and the kingdom of God (7:1–28) | VISION | *Aramaic* |
| D. Details on the post-Babylonian kingdoms (8:1–27) | VISION | *Hebrew* |
| E. Jerusalem restored (9:1–27) | VISION | *Hebrew* |
| D.' More details on the post-Babylonian kingdoms (10:1–12:13) | VISION | *Hebrew* |

INTERLOCKED CHIASMS

Daniel's text is in two languages: Hebrew (Dan 1:1–2:4a; 8:1–12:13) and Aramaic (Dan 2:4b–7:28). Both the narratives (Dan 1–6) and the visions (Dan 7–12) make use of these languages. Scholars have often debated the reason for Daniel as a bilingual composition, with critical scholars proposing various redactional schemes or that some chapters may have been written in Aramaic and later translated into Hebrew. However, the key to understanding the author's reason for employing two languages lies in recognizing that Daniel consists of two interlocked chiasms.

Chiasm is the concentric arrangement of parts in a pattern such as ABC:C'B'A'. It is frequently employed as a literary technique in the Bible. One example is Gen 9:6:

> Whoever *sheds* the *blood* of *man*, by *man* his *blood* will be *shed.*

Daniel consists of two interlocked chiasms, each with its own introduction that is not part of this pattern. The first is introduced by Dan 1 in Hebrew, followed by an Aramaic chiasm in chapters 2–7. The second is prefaced by Dan 7 in Aramaic, followed by a Hebrew chiasm in chapters 8–12. Both introductions contain themes developed later in the chiasms: Dan 1 presents the captured vessels from Jerusalem's temple (Dan 1:2; cf. Dan 5), the wisdom of Daniel (Dan 1:4; cf. Dan 2, 4, 5), and Daniel's Judean companions (Dan 1:6–7; cf. Dan 3). Dan 7 introduces the vision genre to the book. It also presents animal imagery (cf. Dan 8) that employs an angelic interpreter in the vision which is a feature used in each of the subsequent visions.

The matching parts of the chiasms are most clearly discerned by their common motifs. However, there are also verbal parallels between these matching parts (compare Dan 2:44 with Dan 7:14, 27; Dan 3:8 with Dan 6:24; Dan 5:18–21 with Dan 4:12–13, 20, 22, 29–30; Dan 8:25 with Dan 11:36).

Thus, the bilingual nature of Daniel is part of its compositional scheme: It consists of a Hebrew introduction to an Aramaic chiasm interlocked with an Aramaic introduction to a Hebrew chiasm. The first chiasm contains both narrative and visionary genres, linking the two together, and implying that the visions are not simply appended to the narratives, but flow from them in order to develop several themes that run throughout the book. Moreover, this interlocked structure highlights Dan 7 with its messianic vision of the Son of Man.

## GREEK DANIEL

The ancient Greek text of Daniel presents several interesting peculiarities. Not only has it been preserved in two different translations, but the extant manuscripts contain various additions to the book.

## OLD GREEK AND THEODOTION

Two major translations of Daniel survive from antiquity: the Old Greek and Theodotion. The Old Greek has been preserved in only a few manuscripts, since at an early time the translation attributed to Theodotion replaced it in the early church. The Old Greek version was probably translated in the last half of the second century BC and differs most often from the MT of Daniel in Dan 4–6. These are probably due to the translator's attempt to clarify certain matters for his readers and reflect theological biases.

In all likelihood, Theodotion's version originated in the early first century AD (and, therefore, was not produced by Theodotion, who lived during the second century AD, although later scholars attributed it to him). Theodotion's Greek often matches more closely to the MT than does the Old Greek, but at times it departs in favor of clarity for its Greek readers.

## GREEK ADDITIONS TO DANIEL

These two Greek versions of Daniel contain three major additions: the story of Susanna, where Daniel as a boy demonstrates his wisdom in acquitting the pious Susanna of the false charges that were brought against her; the accounts of Bel and the Dragon, where Daniel demonstrates the impotence of pagan idols; and the Prayer of Azariah along with Song of the Three Young Men—additions to Dan 3 which depict Shadrach (Azariah), Meshach, and Abednego praying and praising God during their ordeal in the fiery furnace. These additions are intended to reinforce themes already present in Daniel. However, they are clearly Hellenistic compositions, although the presence of several Hebraisms in the Song of the Three Young Men may indicate that it was originally composed in Hebrew. The additions also attest to the popularity of Daniel among God's people during the Hellenistic era. This also led to the composition of other Aramaic Daniel stories as preserved among the manuscripts at Qumran: the Prayer of Nabonidus (4QPrNab ar/4Q242), Pseudo-Daniel (4QpsDan ar/4Q243–245), and perhaps The Son of God Text (4QApocalypse ar/4Q246).

# THEOLOGICAL THEMES IN DANIEL

Daniel presents several important theological themes to its readers. However, all of these flow from one theme and, in turn, support this major message of the book: the promised coming of the Messiah. In fact, all of the key motifs in Daniel find their greatest fulfillment in the Messiah.

## CHRIST IN DANIEL

Most of the messianic passages in Daniel are contained in sections with eschatologically-oriented revelations: Dan 2, 7, 9, and 12. They build upon the OT perspective that the end times will begin with the coming of the Messiah (e.g., Num 24:14; Isa 11:1–9; Jer 23:1–6; Ezek 34:23; Hos 3:5; Mic 4:1; see Dan 2:28; 10:14). However, there are other messianic references throughout Daniel: the stone hewn without human hands (Dan 2:34, 45); the Messiah (Dan 9:25–26); the Most Holy One (Dan 9:24), and a leader (9:25–26). These point to Christ, who will be "cut off and have nothing" (Dan 9:26) at his crucifixion in order "to end transgression, to finish sin, and to atone for iniquity" (Dan 9:24).

The climax of Daniel's messianic revelations is found in the vision of the Son of Man coming before the Ancient of Days (Dan 7). Here the Messiah is not only pictured as having both divine and human natures but also as receiving "dominion, honor, and a kingdom" (Dan 7:14), a kingdom that becomes the possession of his faithful people (Dan 7:27).

### *The Messiah's Enthronement in Daniel 7 and Psalms 2 and 110*

It is appropriate to compare the enthronement of the Son of Man in Dan 7 with other passages in the OT that speak of the enthronement of the Messiah.

Two psalms are particularly relevant, and they follow much the same pattern as Daniel's vision: Pss 2 and 110. Both of these psalms speak of the decree of God concerning the Messiah's installation as king. While not every element in Daniel is present in these two psalms nor is every element in the psalms present in Daniel, these three passages present complementary pictures of the enthronement of the Messiah. Jesus explicitly connects Ps 110 and Dan 7 in Matt 26:64 and Mark 14:62. The heavenly vision of Christ shown to Stephen at his martyrdom (Acts 7:55–56) probably reflects a combination of Ps 110 and Dan 7.

| *Daniel 7* | *Psalm 2* | *Psalm 110* |
|---|---|---|
| A. Four beasts (nations) emerge from the sea to rule oppressively over God's people before the advent of the Messiah (7:1–8, 17, 19–21, 23–25). | A. Nations oppose God and his Messiah (2:1–3). | |
| B. The Ancient of Days convenes his heavenly court (7:8–10). | | |
| C. Decree of the heavenly court: the Son of Man is installed as eternal king over all nations (7:13–14). | C. God's decree: God mocks the rebels and installs his Messiah as King to rule the nations (2:4–9). | C. God's decree: God installs David's Lord as King at his right hand to rule over his enemies (110:1–3). |
| | | D. God's decree: the Messiah is Priest forever (110:4). |
| E. Decree of the heavenly court: the beasts are shorn of power and slain (7:11–12, 26). | E. Admonition to the nations: serve the Lord and kiss the Son or you will perish (2:10–12a). | E. The Lord and his Messiah crush kings and fill nations with corpses (110:5–6). |
| F. The Ancient of Days comes and decrees in favor of his saints; they receive the kingdom for eternity (7:18, 22, 27). | F. Those who take refuge in the Son are blessed (2:12b). | |

"The Messiagh's Enthronement in Daniel 7 and Psalms 2 and 110" is from *Daniel*, Concordia Commentary (St. Louis: Concordia, 2008), 359–360.

## GOD AS PROTECTOR OF HIS PEOPLE

Although the book of Daniel begins with God handing his people over to the Babylonians (Dan 1:1–2), he does not abandon them there. Instead, throughout Daniel, God is the protector of his people. This is seen most clearly when he rescues Daniel from the lions' den (Dan 6) and Shadrach, Meshach, and Abednego from the fiery furnace (Dan 3). However, virtually every chapter emphasizes that God controls the events of human history in order to defend and deliver his people, even in the midst of intense persecution. The visions emphasize God's deliverance, not only in time, but also on the last day. The clearest prophecy in the OT of the resurrection of all people and the eternal glory of God's people is found in Dan 12:1–3.

## THE USELESSNESS OF FALSE GODS AND THE POWER OF THE TRUE GOD

When reading Dan 3, it is impossible to miss the confrontation between those who worship idols and those who cling to the true God. However, this theme is also found throughout the book and dovetails nicely with the theme of God's protection for his people. The power of the true God as demonstrated in Dan 4–6 is at times an implicit judgment on the uselessness of counterfeit gods (although see Dan 5:23, where this is made explicit). Yahweh reveals his gracious nature when he has pity on sinful humans and in his patience deals with them, a point made even to the pagan Nebuchadnezzar in Dan 4. In the visions, God makes known his intention to keep his promises to Israel and the world, especially through the promised Messiah.

## MAINTAINING THE INTEGRITY OF ONE'S FAITH

Throughout Daniel, God's people are encouraged to maintain the integrity of their faith, even in the face of persecution. This ability does not come from within sinful humans, but is itself a gift of God to his people as he strengthens them and remains with them (cf. Dan 1:8–15; 3:25; 11:35). This integrity of faith is not simply the product of belief in an omnipotent God. It derives from faith in a merciful God who will keep his promise in the coming Messiah, who is the culmination of his eternal covenant with his people.

## DANIEL AND THE REST OF SCRIPTURE

Daniel has ties to several other OT books and is frequently quoted in the NT. One of the most noticeable parallels is with the story of Joseph in Genesis. Both Daniel and Joseph are condemned to punishment because of their loyalty to God (Gen 39; Dan 6). Both are servants and advisors to pagan kings (Gen 41:46; Dan 1–6). Both interpret dreams for kings (Gen 41:1–38; Dan 2, 4). Both are promoted to high office (Gen 41:39–45; Dan 2:48; 5:29; 6:1–2). Both are men of wisdom and insight, and even some of the vocabulary of the Joseph stories in Genesis is employed in Daniel to help the reader see these connections. For instance, the Egyptian loanword for *magicians* (חרטמים) occurs in both accounts (Gen 41:39–45; Dan 2:48; 5:29; 6:1–2). Both use the verbal root זעף, *look gaunt* (Gen 40:6; Dan 1:10). Eunuchs (Hebrew סריס) play a pivotal role in the early captivity of both Joseph and Daniel (Gen 37:36; 39:1; 40:2, 7; Dan 1:3, 7–11, 18).

Daniel also shares several features with Esther, since part of Daniel is set under the Persian Empire as is Esther. Moreover, both books show faithful Judeans navigating the difficult waters of pagan society without losing or betraying their God.

Daniel has features also found in the prophetic books of the OT. Like some of the prophets, he had visions and engaged in predictive prophecy (e.g., Isa 6; Amos 7:1–9; Ezek 1). At the same time, Daniel can be linked with the OT wisdom books, employing much of their vocabulary (e.g., בין, understand—twenty-two occurrences in Daniel; חכמה, *wisdom*—ten occurrences; שכל, *have insight*—nine occurrences). Like the wisdom in those books, Daniel demonstrates that his wisdom is not found in the way the world counts wisdom, but in God's ways.

Daniel is frequently quoted in the NT. The most notable of these involve Daniel's messianic prophecies that Jesus claims are fulfilled in himself (Dan 7:13–14 is referenced at Matt 24:30; 25:31; 26:64; Mark 13:26; 14:62; Luke 21:27; cf. Rev 1:7, 13; 13:14). Building upon Dan 9:25–26, Jesus, the expected one who is coming, is referenced at Matt 11:2–3; Luke 7:18–20; Rev 1:4, 8; and 4:8. All in all, there are more than fifty passages in the NT which quote or employ language from Daniel.

## SIN AND GRACE IN DANIEL

The book of Daniel clearly depicts as of prime importance the first commandment and its prohibition of honoring any other god. Moreover, Daniel and his companions maintain faithful worship of God, fulfilling the intent of the Sabbath commandment. At the same time, Daniel honors human authority and acknowledges that it is from God, keeping the fourth commandment (e.g., Dan 2:37–38). In these ways, Daniel not only urges people to live godly lives but also implicitly (and at times explicitly) condemns sinful behavior that would ignore God's statutes and ordinances.

Daniel clearly emphasizes God's grace, not only in the narratives that show divine deliverance, but also in the prophecies of God's future salvation of his people, especially through the work of the prophesied Messiah. The book also frequently accents the establishing of God's eternal kingdom (e.g., Dan 2, 7, 12). This is a gracious gift to his people, those who will be incorporated into his reign. The establishing of the kingdom comes at a price, however, as Daniel prophesies the atoning death of the Messiah (Dan 9:24, 26). Thus, for Daniel, as is true later of Jesus in the Gospels, the cross and atoning death of the Messiah are the foundation of God's triumphant kingdom.

Those who know the true God and his promises are characterized in Daniel as having insight, wisdom, and knowledge. This is God's grace at work in the lives of his people. Although their wisdom may not prevent them from perishing in this world (Dan 11:35), they will rise to life in God's eternal kingdom (Dan 12:1–3).

## CONCLUSION

Daniel is a pivotal prophet who serves to encourage God's people as they transition from living under an established OT theocracy to living in a world of pagan influence and foreign domination. Therefore, his book is in many ways a bridge to the NT where Jesus will minister to Jews living under Roman supremacy and usher in the kingdom of God through his death and resurrection. Daniel's book gave comfort to God's ancient people, but continues to point people today to the work of God in the person of Christ, who began the fulfillment of Daniel's prophecy in his life, death, and resurrection, and will complete that fulfillment on the final day in the resurrection of all people (Dan 12:1–3).

## SELECT BIBLIOGRAPHY

Archer, Gleason L. Jr. "The Aramaic of the 'Genesis Apocryphon' Compared with the Aramaic of Daniel." In *New Perspectives on the Old Testament*. Edited by J. Barton Payne, 160–69. Waco: Word, 1970.

————. "The Hebrew of Daniel Compared with the Qumran Sectarian Documents." In *the Law and the Prophets: Old Testament Studies Prepared in Honor of Oswald Thompson Allis.* Edited by John H. Skilton, Milton C. Fisher, and Leslie W. Sloat, 470–81. Nutley, NJ: Presbyterian and Reformed, 1975.

Collins, John J. *Daniel with an Introduction to Apocalyptic Literature.* Forms of the Old Testament Literature 20. Grand Rapids: Eerdmans, 1984.

————. *Daniel: A Commentary on the Book of Daniel.* Hermeneia. Minneapolis: Augsburg Fortress, 1993.

Lucas, Ernest C. *Daniel.* Apollos Old Testament Commentary 20. Downers Grove: InterVarsity, 2002.

Payne, J. Barton. "The Goal of Daniel's Seventy Weeks." *Journal of the Evangelical Theological Society* 21 (1978): 97–115.

Steinmann, Andrew. *Daniel.* Concordia Commentary. St. Louis: Concordia, 2008.

Yamauchi, Edwin M. "The Greek Words in Daniel in the Light of Greek Influence in the Near East." In *New Perspectives on the Old Testament.* Edited by J. Barton Payne, 170–200. Waco: Word, 1970.

————. "Daniel and Contacts between the Aegean and the Near East before Alexander." *Evangelical Quarterly* 53 (1981): 37–47.

# 27

# THE BOOK OF THE TWELVE

The final section of the latter prophets is normally called the Minor Prophets, a phrase that bears a derogatory tone, especially when it is compared to the title given to Isaiah, Jeremiah, and Ezekiel who are called the *Major* Prophets. The Book of the Twelve is a better and even more historically accurate title for the books from Hosea through Malachi.

Although this is a slight change, calling these books The Book of the Twelve places them in a position comparable to their prophetic peers—Isaiah, Jeremiah, and Ezekiel. A rough comparison confirms this: Isaiah consists of 105 pages in BHS. Jeremiah is the longest as it occupies 116 pages, whereas Ezekiel is the shortest with 95 pages. The Book of the Twelve stands in between, with 96 pages. So in terms of length, the Book of the Twelve, considered as a unit, belongs in the same category as the Major Prophets.

The belief that these twelve prophets cohere as a book is an ancient one. The collection predates Sirach's prayer, "May the bones of the Twelve Prophets send forth new life from where they lie" (Sir 49:10). Both the Qumran library and Josephus count the Twelve as one book. Hosea–Malachi generally appear as the fourth book of the latter prophets in the Hebrew Bible (*B. Bat.* 14b) and the Talmud stipulates that only three lines should separate the individual books of the Twelve whereas four lines should separate other biblical books (*B. Bat.* 13b).

Given this history, it is surprising that neither Jews nor Christians have typically interpreted the Twelve as one book. Until the beginning of the 1990s—apart from a few exceptions—the individual books of the Twelve were treated like other prophetic writings, without considering the possibility that each book should be read and understood in the context of the other eleven. At the end of the last century, however, it became acceptable in scholarly circles to view these books as a literary unit. The idea put forth is that each of the Twelve was constructed by final redactors in such a way that the message of each builds on its predecessors, picking up words and motifs from them. The redactors who combined the writings into one book wanted their readers to look for, discover, and appreciate how the different thematic threads generate a tapestry that reflects Yahweh's message in the corpus.

One motif that occurs with striking prominence in the Twelve is the phrase יום יהוה, *the day of Yahweh* (e.g., Joel 2:31; Amos 5:18–20; Obad 15; Zeph 1:7–16; Mal 4: 5). The expression is explicitly present in all but Jonah and Nahum, and it is implicit in the latter (cf. Nah 1:7). Since the day of Yahweh is relatively infrequent in Isaiah and Ezekiel and non-existent in Jeremiah, its frequency in the Twelve is noteworthy.

Another pronounced theme is that of an earthquake. It begins in Amos 1:1 when the prophet notes that his ministry ended שנתים לפני הרעש, *two years before the earthquake*. Joel, Nahum, Haggai, and Zechariah take up the earthquake motif and adapt it to fit their times and circumstances. Reading the Twelve as a book, we might hypothesize that these prophets intentionally borrowed the earthquake theme as a means to connect themselves to Amos and his bona-fide status in the community. But in borrowing from Amos, these prophets do more than simply repeat the manner in which he employs earthquake theology—they transform and build upon the borrowed text.

For example, unlike Amos's quake, Joel's is specifically connected to the coming Day of Yahweh. Joel 2:2 describes it as "a day of darkness and gloom, a day of clouds and blackness." This is a significant move beyond Amos. A Yahweh-induced earthquake is now eschatologically a subset of the dominant theme in the Book of The Twelve—the Day of Yahweh. One of the central characteristics of this day is the convulsion of the created order. Stars fall from heaven, the sun's light grows dim, the moon turns to blood, and the earth shakes (e.g., Joel 2:28–32). Joel envisions an apocalyptic army: "Before them the earth shakes, the heavens quake" because "the day of Yahweh is great; it is dreadful. Who can endure it?" (Joel 2:11).

Joel's place in the Twelve gives an eschatological perspective on subsequent quakes not only in Amos, but also in Nahum, Haggai, and Zechariah.

Like Joel, Nah 1:5 transforms the earthquake motif for his unique purposes. His shaking will manifest itself in 612 with the fall of Nineveh. Read in light of Joel's eschatological perspective, Nahum's quake against Nineveh foreshadows the day when all of Yahweh's enemies will fall. Haggai then alludes to Amos's quake as a way to indicate that the second temple will not lack the glory and significance of Solomon's former structure (Hag 2:6–7; cf. Hag 2:21). Finally, Zechariah, like Joel, also places the shaking into an eschatological context (Zech 14:5).

That the Book of the Twelve exhibits an overall theme, plot, and/or direction greater than the sum of its parts has been challenged, especially by ben Zvi. His concerns are as follows: (1) the Book of the Twelve does not have a comprehensive heading; (2) the argument that redactors used catchwords to form redactional links between different prophetic books seems to be doubtful, since in many cases the mere fact that the same word occurs in two different literary units may be accidental; and (3) there is the danger that an interpretation on the wider redactional level can conceal the original meaning of a particular book and may lead to its misunderstanding.

Therefore caution is in order. The best way to interpret the Twelve is to utilize a synchronic approach in order to grasp certain elements of literary unity that divulge theological themes—like the Day of Yahweh and divine shaking. However, one must insist on treating the separate books of the Twelve as important in and of themselves and composed by the authors who bear their names before asking questions about how they fit into a larger picture.

There is a final and related issue concerning these books. The Christian canon concludes the OT with the Twelve, placing Israel's prophetic literature at the end. The Hebrew Bible places the Twelve at the end of its second section, the Prophets, and just before the beginning of the last section called the Writings. The result is that the two canons conclude with different books—Malachi and 2 Chronicles—and therefore with different theological emphases.

The Hebrew Bible ends with the exhortation to live in Judah and worship at the temple in Jerusalem (2 Chron 36:23), whereas the Christian OT concludes with the affirmation that Elijah will return to bring about familial harmony (Mal 4:5–6). The former focuses on place, the latter on a prophet and his ability to restore relationships. The placement of the Twelve at one or another point in the canon affects how people view Yahweh's plan for the future. Judaism believes God wants the nation back in the land with life centered and ordered in the temple. Christianity embraces an emphasis on the preparatory role of John the Baptist who, as the Elijah of Mal 4:5 (cf. Matt 11:12–14), is the forerunner of Jesus, Israel's greatest prophet (e.g., John 6:14).

## SELECT BIBLIOGRAPHY

Ben Zvi, Ehud. "Twelve Prophetic Books of 'The Twelve.' A Few Preliminary Considerations." In *Forming Prophetic Literature: Essays on Isaiah and the Twelve in Honor of John D. W. Watts.* Edited by James W. Watts and Paul R. House, 125–56. Journal for the Study of the Old Testament Supplement Series 235. Sheffield: Sheffield Academic Press, 1996.

Lessing, Reed. "Amos and the Earthquake." *Concordia Theological Quarterly*, 74 (2010): 243–59.

Peterson, David. *The Prophetic Literature.* Louisville: Westminster, 2002.

Redditt, Paul L., and Aaron Schart, eds. *Thematic Threads in the Book of the Twelve.* Beihefte zur Zeitschrift für die alttestamentliche Wissenschaft 325. Berlin/New York: Walter de Gruyter, 2003.

# 28

# HOSEA

Hosea's ministry came shortly after the preaching of Amos (c. 765–760), who also prophesied in the Northern Kingdom. Hosea overlaps chronologically with both Micah and Isaiah who prophesied in Judah. Although Hos 1:1 lists only one king from the North—Jeroboam ben Joash—the parallel list of Southern kings includes Uzziah, Jotham, Ahaz, and Hezekiah. Hosea, then, also preached after the death of Jeroboam, ministering from about 755 to 720. It was a stormy time, to say the least, for his nation and his family. Due in large part to his marriage to Gomer and its likeness to Yahweh's marriage to Israel, some of the most moving imagery in the OT is found in Hosea. This, no doubt, is the reason NT writers made frequent use of Hosea, quoting from him some thirty times. Among the prophets, only Isaiah is cited more often.

## AUTHORSHIP

In the heyday of form-criticism, scholars frequently assigned passages of doom to Hosea and oracles of hope to later, post-exilic editors. On this basis, for example, Wolff breaks the book into three parts; Hos 1–3, Hos 4–11, and Hos 12–14. Each section begins with condemnation and ends with salvation. Other critics point out the references to Judah (e.g., Hos 1:7, 11; 6:11; 12:2) and argue for an additional post-exilic Judean redaction.

These diachronic methodologies have yielded to a more synchronic understanding of the book. For instance, ben Zvi reads Hosea holistically, though he doesn't reject earlier form-critical reconstructions of the text's history. As such, his approach to Hosea is one that is common to the critical interpretation of Israel's prophetic corpus as a whole—Hosea is a literary and theological text built upon the social memories agreed upon by people living in exilic Persian Yehud. This group of authors and editors created a literary piece whose events are generally set in the monarchic period. Since ben Zvi does not believe that the book is interested in communicating precise political history, he interprets the lack of specific historical details as proof that the original social setting is mostly erased. Hosea himself is understood to be a literary character, not an historical person.

The book of Hosea then portrays the worldview of exilic Yehud male leaders who lived in a patriarchal society. This means, for example, that the metaphor of husband and wife in Hos 1–3 does not reflect the circumstances governing marriage at any time in Israel, due, in large part, to the fact that "Israel" in the book of Hosea is a "trans-temporal" Israel, that is, an ideological construction of the nation's past. It also follows that the Baalism portrayed in Hosea does not correspond to any historical situation. It is rather an ideological construal that served theological purposes. The intention of these idealizations is to socialize Persian Yehud around the themes of the Jerusalem cult and the Davidic monarchy, led by men.

Thus, ben Zvi argues against those who employ reading strategies that are concerned with the prophet's *ipsissima verba*. In this move beyond historical questions, he posits an interpretation of Hosea that is concerned only with the book's composers and receptor community. Numerous times he seeks to dismantle historical pursuits that attempt to get behind the text.

But if Hosea is only a book that presents a prophetic character—as ben Zvi contends—then we have no way of knowing how, what, and when the prophet spoke. Is this *Sitz im Buch* methodology the best or only way to approach a prophetic text? Is there absolutely no access to the prophet and the events which he describes? The fact is, several sections of the OT indicate prophetic texts were written *first*, and then presented orally. These texts were written on scrolls on the assumption that they would be spoken. That is, they were for the *ears*, not for the silent perusal of the *eyes*. The classic example is Jer 36:2 where Jeremiah tells Baruch, "Take a scroll and write on it all the words I have spoken to you concerning Israel, Judah and all the other nations." If these texts were read aloud or recited from memory before an audience, then the retention of oral and historical features is a practical necessity. The problem is that ben Zvi's analysis of Hosea denies these fundamental aspects of prophetic texts. He turns Hosea into a book that lacks any oral qualities. According to Israel's testimony, if her prophets were anything, they were proclaimers of Yahweh's word to people who lived in specifics times and places.

## LITERARY FEATURES OF HOSEA

Hosea's style is very different from his eighth-century prophetic counterparts—Amos, Isaiah, and Micah. It is rough, disjoined, jagged, and choppy. Jerome famously called it *commaticus*, or broken up with commas. Many believe that Hos 1:1–2:1 and 3:1–5 are prose, while the rest of the book is poetic. However, Anderson and Freedman contend that Hosea's writing cannot be categorized this neatly. Rather, there is a combination of poetry and prose throughout the book.

Hosea is also well-known for his numerous similes. Yahweh is like a destructive moth and dry rot (Hos 5:12), a roaring lion (Hos 5:14; cf. 13:7–8), a trapper (Hos 7:12), a bear (Hos 13:8), and a fertile pine tree (Hos 14:8). On the other hand, Israel is like a stubborn heifer (Hos 4:10), a dove (Hos 7:11), and a treacherous bow (Hos 7:14). Some of the prophet's favorite vocabulary includes שוב, *turn/repent* (twenty-three times); ידע, *know* (eighteen times); אהב, *love* (sixteen times); זנה, *prostitute* (fifteen times); מצרים, *Egypt* (thirteen times); and חסד, *covenant loyalty* (six times).

### Outline of Hosea

I. Superscription (1:1)
II. Hosea's family life (1:2–3:5)
    A. Hosea, Gomer and their children (1:2–2:1)
    B. Yahweh's marriage to Israel (2:2–23)
    C. Hosea restores Gomer (3:1–5)
III. Israel's unstable politics (4:1–9:17)
    A. Israel is unfaithful (4:1–19)
    B. Israel is punished (5:1–15)
    C. The call to repentance is ignored (6:1–7:16)
    D. God punishes Israel for rejecting him (8:1–9:17)

IV. Israel's last days (10:1–14:8)

    A.  Israel's sin reaps destruction (10:1–15)

    B.  Yahweh's love for Israel (11:1–11)

    C.  Israel sins against God (11:12–12:14)

    D.  Yahweh is angry with his people (13:1–16)

    E.  Israel repents and is blessed (14:1–8)

V.  Wisdom colophon (14:9)

The book of Hosea has three parts: (1) the superscription (Hos 1:1), (2) the oracles of the prophet (Hos 1:2–14:8), and (3) a concluding exhortation to its readers (Hos 14:9). Hosea's oracles break down into two sections—the prophet's family life (Hos 1–3) and his oracles of judgment and hope (Hos 4:1–14:8). Beyond these bare essentials, it is very difficult to outline the book, because it lacks clear structural markers such as "thus said Yahweh" or "an utterance of Yahweh." Deciding where one oracle ends and another begins presents enormous challenges. It comes as no surprise, then, that scholarly outlines for the book are anything but uniform.

Yet some believe that Hosea proceeds along historical lines. Chapters 1–3 reflect the reign of Jeroboam ben Joash. This was a time of material abundance that led to spiritual complacency (e.g., Hos 2:5, 8, 13). During this era, Assyria was consumed with political problems on its northern and eastern borders, so it posed no threat to the Syrian-Palestinian corridor. However, after the death of Jeroboam ben Joash, Assyria began its westward expansion, and this brought with it panic and political instability in Israel. Chapters 4–9 were composed at this time when the Northern Kingdom was beset with internal and foreign challenges (e.g., Hos 7:3–7; Hos 7:8–12). A key event during this time was the Syro-Ephraimite war (cf. Isa 7), alluded to in Hos 5:8–6:6. Afterwards, Israel was reduced to an Assyrian vassal state. Chapters 10–14 reflect the anarchy that overwhelmed the Northern Kingdom during the nation's waning years under her last king, Hoshea.

## TEXTUAL ISSUES

No other book in the OT—with the possible exception of Job—has as many textual problems as does Hosea. Chapter 2 is the only part of the book that does not present significant challenges. The rest of Hosea is very difficult to read, probably due to the prophet's northern dialect. The LXX is quite literal and does not expand on the Hebrew as it does in other books of the OT. It can therefore be helpful in making text-critical decisions.

## HISTORICAL ISSUES

Hosea is the first prophet in the Book of the Twelve probably because tradition considered it to be the earliest in this corpus (*B. Bat.* 14b). However, based upon Hosea's list of Judean kings—Uzziah, Jotham, Ahaz, and Hezekiah (Hos 1:1)—his book should be placed after Amos, who only mentions Uzziah (Amos 1:1). Moreover, while Assyria is not mentioned in the book of Amos, the empire is named nine times in Hosea (e.g., Hos 5:13; 11:5; 12:1). This reflects the fact that Assyria did not begin its march toward the Mediterranean Sea until after Amos's ministry. He addresses events in the first half of the eighth century and only mentions that "a nation" will oppress Israel (Amos 6:14). Hosea, on the other hand, shows a much greater awareness of the Assyrian threat. For instance, the reference to שלמן in Hos 10:14 may denote Shalmaneser V, the Assyrian king who invaded Israel in 725–723. Hosea was also aware of the corrupt state of Israel's final monarchs (Hos 7:17; 13:10–11). Though he only mentions Jeroboam ben Joash in Hos 1:1, the prophet most certainly witnessed the reigns of the North's last six kings. Perhaps not mentioning them was his way of showing them distain. (Isaiah treats Manasseh in the same way; cf. Isa 1:1). We know that Hosea married Gomer around 760 because the message in Hos 1:4 announces the end of Jehu's dynasty which happened when Jeroboam ben Joash died in 753. Hosea records events, then, from roughly 760 to about 715.

After the death of Jeroboam ben Joash in 753, political events in the North began to spiral out of control. Six kings followed him in the next thirty years—Zechariah, Shallum, Menahem, Pekahiah, Pekah, and Hoshea. Only two of them—Menahem and Hoshea—were not assassinated by their successors. Assyrian aggression brought on much of this instability. Tiglath-pileser III (745–727) invaded during the Syro-Ephraimitic War of 735–733 and stripped Israel of her outlaying territories in and around the Sea of Galilee (cf. Isa 9:1). Shalmaneser V and Sargon II finished off the Northern capital of Samaria in 723. During these last days, Israel's choices of foreign alliances were hotly debated (e.g., Hos 7:11). The prophet's position was decidedly anti-Assyrian (e.g., Hos 8:9; 10:6; 14:3).

# THEOLOGICAL THEMES

## HOSEA'S FAMILY

Hosea's marriage to Gomer has generated a great deal of speculation. Is this an allegory or does it reflect historical reality? In light of the firm injunctions against prostitution in Lev 19:29 and Deut 23:17, did God really command Hosea to marry a prostitute? Was Gomer a cult prostitute and devotee to Baal or simply an unfaithful wife? Or perhaps she was a prostitute in a spiritual way, just as every apostate Israelite at the time was considered a prostitute to foreign gods. But if Gomer was a prostitute, was she one when Hosea married her or did she later become unfaithful? Were any of the children illegitimate? Is it Gomer that Hosea restores in chapter 3, or someone else? Did Hosea know he was marrying a prostitute, or does the text reflect what he later came to realize? Any answers to these questions must remain speculative. Hosea's marriage and children are so inextricably related to Yahweh's message to Israel that it is difficult to create any kind of family biography—precise data is simply not available. Therefore any attempt to reconstruct the particulars of Hosea's family life is doomed to fail. The book's chief focus is upon Yahweh and his relationship with Israel.

Though some have tried to explain away the shocking command, "Go, take to yourself a wife of harlotries" (Hos 1:2), this much is true: The mandate should be taken at face value and we must conclude that Gomer was sexually involved with other men both before and after her marriage to Hosea. Hosea's life, then, like other prophets, was a living testimony to God's word for his people (e.g., Isa 20; Jer 13:1–11; Ezek 4–5).

The prophet's children were also signs of Yahweh's message to his people (cf. Isa 8:18). The first is called יזרעאל, Jezreel or *God Sows* (Hos 1:4). The name points to Yahweh's judgment upon the house of Jehu, because the king poured out innocent blood in Jezreel when he solidified his political power (2 Kgs 9–10). The couple's second child was called לא רחמה, *No Compassion*. She symbolically announced that God would not have compassion upon his people (Hos 1:6–7). Hosea and Gomer, then, had a third child named לא עמי,

*Not My People.* Yahweh's judgment upon his wayward nation was that they were no longer his people and he was not their God (Hos 1:8–9; cf. Exod 6:7).

### FEMINIST INTERPRETATIONS OF HOSEA

Feminist scholars like O'Brien argue that Hosea is misogynistic. In commenting on Hos 2, she employs a term coined by Athalya Brenner—pornoprophetic. O'Brien concludes that chapter 2 sanctions domestic abuse against women. She writes, "Only if a husband can properly strip, expose, and kill his wife can the threats of [Hosea] chapter 2 carry weight and can the Deity's angry punishment of Israel be justified." O'Brien maintains that Hosea's metaphors accurately present how Israelite families functioned in the eighth century.

However, this line of interpretation ignores OT texts where the beauty of marriage is defined (Gen 2) and celebrated (Song of Songs). It also passes over the injunction to love your neighbor as yourself (Lev 19:18b). O'Brien and feminist interpreters like her do not allow the entire OT canon to form their understanding of marriage and family. They select prophetic metaphors that are employed in texts like Hos 2 and Ezek 16 and 23 and build their interpretation of Israelite marriage solely upon them.

All metaphors have inherent in them continuity with the subject depicted as well as discontinuity. That is to say, every metaphor speaks both a "yes" and a "no"—an "is" and "is not." In the history of interpreting biblical metaphors, the temptation has been to fall off the horse on one side or the other, either taking the metaphors literally in every respect or denying any essential relationship between the metaphor and its subject. O'Brien fails to attend to the "no" of Hosea's metaphor of marriage and attempts to create a one-to-one correspondence between the way human beings and Yahweh function in the world. What is intended to be metaphorical O'Brien literalizes and fossilizes.

### CHRIST IN HOSEA

Christ fulfills Hosea's hopes of a new David (Hos 3:5; cf. Matt 9:27; Mark 11:10; Luke 2:4; Rom 1:3). In Matt 2:12–15, the holy family flees to Egypt in order to fulfill the word of the Lord spoken in Hos 11:1, namely that "out of Egypt I have called my son."

Hosea's understanding of Yahweh's marriage to Israel is taken up in several NT texts that depict Christ's relationship with the church as that of a Bridegroom and his Bride (e.g., Eph 5:22–33). John the Baptist's metaphor of the bride/bridegroom brings clarity to the relationships between himself, Jesus, and Christ's followers. John identifies his role as the "friend of the bridegroom" (John 3:29) who is sent before Christ. Two friends were traditionally responsible for bringing the bride and bridegroom together and for watching over their sexual relations outside the bridal chamber. "The bridegroom's voice" (John 3:29: cf. Jer 7:34; 16:9; 25:10; Rev 18:23) is the triumphant shout that is made to indicate to the friends outside that he is united with a virginal bride. The Baptist is, therefore, the one who leads the bride to her groom and rejoices in their successful union. In the Bible's final vision, John beholds the eschatological marriage between Christ and his church (Rev 19:7–8; 21:2). "Blessed are those who are invited to the marriage supper of the Lamb" (Rev 19:9).

God called Hosea to reestablish his relationship with Gomer even though she had already repeatedly rejected him. The word אהב, *love*, in Hos 3:1 has a broad range of meanings: have sexual relations, fall in love, express deep emotional care, and make an alliance. All of these probably pertain to what Yahweh is telling Hosea to do in chapter 3. The prophet is to act and speak in such a way that he wins over Gomer's affections. Did he do it? "So I bought her for fifteen shekels of silver and about a homer and a lethek of barley" (Hos 3:2). Why did the prophet need to make a payment for someone who was already his wife? Most commentators suggest that Hosea went the extra mile and also paid off Gomer's debts. Just like Hosea, Jesus made similar outrageous loving investments. For instance, he offered living water to a Samaritan woman (John 4:1–44), healed blind Bartimaeus (Mark 10:46–52), gave new life to the desperate Zacchaeus (Luke 19:1–10), and raised Lazarus from the dead (John 11). Why did Jesus make the ultimate investment and die on a Roman instrument of death? It was the only way to restore us to the Father. Hosea writes: "After two days he [Yahweh] will revive us. On the third day he will restore us so that we may live in his presence. Let us acknowledge Yahweh. Let us press on to acknowledge him. As surely as the sun rises, he will appear. He will come to us like the winter rains, like the spring rains that water the earth" (Hos 6:1–3; cf. 13:4).

Hosea's words "on the third day" point to Christ's resurrection which guarantees our eternal redemption.

### SIN AND GRACE IN HOSEA

Stemming in large part from Israel's fascination with Canaanite fertility religion (Hos 2:8, 16; 13:1), the book of Hosea displays a wide variety of words for sin. The prophet lists the following: unfaithfulness (Hos 6:7), shedding blood (Hos 6:8), shameful deeds (Hos 6:9), prostitution (Hos 6:10), deceit (Hos 7:1), evil deeds (Hos 7:2), lies (Hos 7:3), adultery (Hos 7:4), drunkenness (Hos 7:5), deception (Hos 7:6), anarchy (Hos 7:7), apostasy (Hos 7:8), ignorance (Hos 7:9), arrogance (Hos 7:10), senselessness (Hos 7:11), rebellion (Hos 7:13), and false faith (Hos 7:14). This is quite a list, and it comes from only two chapters out of Hosea's total of fourteen! At the root of every sin in the book is Israel's apostasy (e.g., Hos 5:11; 8:6). The priests (e.g., Hos 4:6; 5:1; 6:9) and political rulers (e.g., Hos 5:10; 9:15) led the people astray. But Yahweh does not forever forsake his sinful people. He says, "I will betroth you to me forever. I will betroth you in righteousness and justice, in love and compassion" (Hos 2:19). And the children's names denoting judgment are reversed to announce grace (Hos 1:10–2:1; 2:21–23).

Hosea's twin message of sin and grace reflects that of other pre-exilic prophets: God's judgment because of sin is imminent while his restoration as a sign of divine grace is eschatological, "in that day" (e.g. Hos 2:16, 21) and "afterwards" (e.g., Hos 3:5). The prophet announces this through the lens of Deut 4:20–31, a passage that envision four stages in Israel's history: (1) deliverance from Egypt and the wilderness wanderings (Deut 4:20–23; e.g., Hos 2:16–17; 11:1–4; 13:4), (2) divine judgment because of idolatry (Deut 4:24–25; e.g., Hos 2:3–13; 13:1), (3) exile from the land (Deut 4:26–28; e.g., Hos 9:3), and (4) restoration (Deut 4:29–30; e.g., Hos 1:10–2:1; 2:14–23; 3:5; 6:1–3; 11:8–11; 14:1–8).

## CONCLUSION

Faced with a nation that was worshiping the false gods Baal and Asherah, Hosea was called to announce that the covenant made at Sinai was now broken and Israel would be exiled from the land. At the heart of this covenant was the gracious promise, "I will be their God and they will be my people" (Exod 6:7). The prophet reverses this into a message of doom. His third child is named Lo-Ammi or Not My People (Hos 1:9). While this was a stinging indictment upon the nation's apostasy, God was not finished. The prophet promises that in the coming days, Israel will be called "You are my people," and they will answer "You are my God" (Hos 2:23). This promise of restoration is fulfilled in Christ (1 Pet 2:10) and will be consummated in the new heavens and new earth (Rev 21:3).

## SELECT BIBLIOGRAPHY

Andersen, Francis, and David N. Freedman. *Hosea: A New Translation with Introduction and Commentary.* Anchor Bible 24A. New York: Doubleday, 1980.

Ben Zvi, Ehud. *Hosea.* Forms of the Old Testament Literature 21A/1. Grand Rapids/Cambridge: Eerdmans, 2005.

Hubbard, D. A. *Hosea: An Introduction and Commentary.* Tyndale Old Testament Commentaries 24. Downers Grove: InterVarsity, 1989.

O'Brien, Julia. *Challenging Prophetic Metaphor: Theology and Ideology in the Prophets.* Louisville: Westminster, 2008.

Sweeney, Marvin. *The Twelve Prophets.* Vol. 1. Berit Olam. Collegeville, MN: Liturgical, 2000.

Wolff, Hans W. *Hosea: A Commentary on the Book of Hosea.* Hermeneia. Philadelphia: Augsburg Fortress, 1977.

# 29

# JOEL

The book of Joel is famous for its references to locusts as well as to Yahweh's gift of the Spirit. Although the OT cites a dozen men named Joel, none of them can confidently be associated with the book's author. The superscription in Joel 1:1 does not detail the prophet's historical context. And unlike the books on either side of Joel—Hosea and Amos—no kings are listed. There is no consensus, therefore, regarding Joel's date, the book's unity, its theology, or even the literalness of its message.

## AUTHORSHIP

Since the form-critical work of Bernard Duhm, critics have argued that the prophet Joel only composed the account of the locust plague (Joel 1:2–2:27). The second half of the book (Joel 2:28–3:21) was written by "Deutero-Joel" and considered to be an example of second-century Maccabean eschatological hopes. The editor living at this time, it is argued, combined both parts of the book by adding the Day of Yahweh motif in Joel 1:15; 2:1, 2, and 11. Mason has more recently clarified and advanced this view.

However, the book of Joel is a coherent literary piece in that it presents Yahweh's response to a time of national calamity. Joel 1:2–2:14 is the prophet's call for the people to repent while Joel 2:15–3:21 records the response of God, who promises that the land's fertility will be restored and that enemy nations will be defeated. Joel employs similar vocabulary throughout his three chapters and presents a logical progression—more so than many other prophetic books. It is therefore reasonable to believe that it was composed by one author, Joel the son of Pethuel.

## LITERARY FEATURES OF JOEL

Like many of the prophets, Joel's poetic parallelism is charged with creative metaphors and similes. He has a propensity—depending on when we date the book—to function either as a storehouse of words and phrases for prophets who followed him or to employ motifs and ideas from prophets who preceded him. For instance, Joel 1:15 is almost identical to Isa 13:6, and Joel 3:16 comes very close to Amos 1:2. There are twenty-two parallels in Joel with twelve other prophetic books.

### Outline of Joel

I.   Superscription (1:1)
II.  Catastrophes current and coming (1:2–2:17)
     A.  The current catastrophe: the locust plague (1:2–20)
     B.  The coming catastrophe: the Day of Yahweh (2:1–17)
III. Yahweh's response (2:18–3:21)
     A.  Healing and restoration (2:18–27)
     B.  The gift of the Spirit (2:28–32)
     C.  The defeat of enemy nations (3:1–3:21)

The first part of Joel describes two catastrophes: a locust plague and the Day of Yahweh. The prophet artfully weaves together these two themes throughout this section. The impact of both events is the prophet's call for the people to repent. The book takes a dramatic turn in Joel 2:18 when it states, "Then Yahweh became jealous for his land and had pity on his people." The second half of the book is filled with language that defines this divine jealousy and pity. Yahweh initially attends to the locust plague (Joel 2:18–27). However, he broadens his response to include the promise of his Spirit (Joel 2:28–32) and deliverance from national enemies (Joel 3:1–21).

## TEXTUAL ISSUES

The text of Joel is remarkably well preserved. Joel 2:23, however, is one exception. The phrase את המורה לצדקה, *the early rain for vindication*, was famously understood at Qumran to describe the Teacher of Righteousness.

The Hebrew text is four chapters long, instead of the English three. Joel 2:38–32 in English equals Joel 3:1–5 in Hebrew. The latter textual tradition highlights God's gift of his Spirit.

## HISTORICAL ISSUES

Because locust plagues are relatively common in Joel's part of the world, it is difficult to provide any specific details on his historical situation. Scholars have argued for dating the book anywhere from the ninth to the second century.

It is typical for prophets to cite kings in their superscription (e.g., Isa 1:1; Jer 1:1; Hos 1:1), therefore, it is notable that Joel offers no such list. Leadership in his community is in the hands of priests and elders (Joel 1:2, 13; 2:16). Joel's book, therefore, could have been composed in the ninth century when Jehoiada the priest functioned as Judah's leader after Athaliah's death and before Joash was old enough to rule (2 Kgs 11). And Joel's style reflects that of a pre-exilic Hebrew author. His vivid poetry is very different from the prose of post-exilic prophets like Haggai and Malachi.

On the other hand, Joel could have lived after the Babylonian exile, when there was no monarchy. It appears in the book that the Northern Kingdom is no longer standing. Joel regularly refers to Judah (six times), Jerusalem (six times), and Zion (seven times), but he never mentions Israel. Another useful piece of information is that Joel assumes the existence of the Jerusalem temple (e.g., Joel 1:8–10). This, then, rules out the possibility that the book's events occurred between 587 and 515, since at this time the temple lay in ruins, having been destroyed by the Babylonians (2 Kgs 25).

Additional data includes the fact that the book mentions many of Judah's traditional enemies (Joel 3:4–8). There is, however, no acknowledgement of Assyria or Babylon. Thus, the time from the dominance of Assyria in the Fertile Crescent to the fall of Babylon (the mid eighth century to the late sixth century) is ruled out for the time of the book's composition. A post-exilic date for Joel is buttressed by the fact that his use of the Day of Yahweh motif has an eschatological slant. Earlier prophets like Amos and Isaiah tied the theme to the historical invasions of foreign armies. Joel also assumes the existence of Israelites who have been scattered throughout the nations (Joel 3:1–2). In all likelihood, this indicates a period after the Babylonian conquest and during the Second Temple period. Putting all of these historical considerations together, the events in the book probably occurred after the return from Babylon, sometime between 515 and 400.

Finally, it must be noted that Joel's lack of specificity regarding historical particulars may be due to the fact that he composed the book for liturgical usage. Liturgy, by nature, lacks historical particulars so as to be relevant in all times and in all places.

## THEOLOGICAL THEMES IN JOEL

### LOCUSTS

What is the nature of the catastrophe that the book of Joel describes? Is it a locust plague described as if it were a military attack (Joel 1:4), or is it a military attack described as if it were a locust plague (Joel 1:6)? Because some texts use locusts to describe an army (e.g., Judg 6:5; Jer 51:27), Stuart argues that Joel envisions either the Assyrian assault against Jerusalem in 701 or the Babylonian invasion of Judah and Jerusalem in 589–587. On the other hand, many interpret the locust plague to be an extended metaphor employed to depict the Day of Yahweh. However the best interpretation is to understand that the prophet was deliberate when he did not specify the relationship between the locusts in Joel 1:2–20 and the attacking enemy army in Joel 2:1–11. The ambiguity facilitates the book's usage as a liturgical text.

Joel's ideas about locusts derived from the Sinaitic covenantal curse, where Yahweh says, "You shall carry much seed into the field and shall gather in little, for the locust shall consume it" (Deut 28:38). Yahweh's defeat of the locusts (cf. Joel 2:20) points to God's final day of judgment when all enemies of his kingdom, though fierce and mighty (cf. Rev 9:1–11), will finally and fully be destroyed.

## YAHWEH'S AUTHORITY OVER THE NATIONS

The book of Joel repeatedly accents Yahweh's authority over the nations. The terms גוי, *nation*, and גוים, *nations*, appear in Joel 1:16; 2:17, 19; 3:2, 9, 11, and 12. God exercises dominion over the foe from the north who many consider to be an apocalyptic cypher for his enemies (Joel 2:20). Yahweh will assemble all the nations for judgment in the Valley of Jehoshaphat (Joel 3:12). Yet he also promises grace to the nations. In the last days he will pour out his Spirit upon all flesh (Joel 2:28). Then it will happen that *everyone* who calls on Yahweh's name will be saved (Joel 2:32).

### THE HOLY SPIRIT

Up to this point in the OT, the Holy Spirit comes upon Othniel (Judg 3:10), Gideon (Judg 6:34), Jephthah (Judg 11:29), and Samson (Judg 13:24–25; 14:6, 19; 15:14–15). He imparts the skill necessary to excel in craftsmanship (Exod 31:3; 35:31) and enables Balaam (Num 24:2), Saul (1 Sam 10:10), Asa (2 Chr 15:1), Jahaziel (2 Chr 20:14), Zechariah (2 Chr 24:20), Micah (Micah 3:8), and Ezekiel (Ezek 11:5) to function as prophets. With Joel, however, Moses' wish comes true, namely that all of God's people would be prophets when he places his Spirit upon them (Num 11:29).

Joel 2:28–32 is filled with supernatural language that describes a period much later than the prophet's, as indicated by the word "afterward" (Joel 2:28). Yahweh promises an outpouring of his Spirit upon all people. Cosmic signs are then described and the vision culminates with the salvation of all who call on Yahweh's name. The oracle gives no one a privileged status before God, an idea echoed in Gal 3:28.

### CHRIST IN JOEL

Joel sees the onslaught of locusts and what does he do? He calls the people to prayer, crying out, "Blow the trumpet in Zion" (Joel 2:1, 15). His urgent call is for the Israelites to tremble (Joel 2:1), return to Yahweh with fasting, weeping, and mourning (Joel 2:12), and to rend their hearts and not only their garments (Joel 2:13). The pivotal point, though, is Joel's command for the priests to intercede before Yahweh, saying, "Spare your people, O Yahweh, and make not your heritage a reproach, a byword among the nations. Why should they say among the peoples, 'Where is their God?'" (Joel 2:17). Jesus is our High

Priest who in like manner makes intercession for us (Heb 7:25). Luke 23:34 records Jesus' prayer for the Roman soldiers crucifying him: "Father forgive them for they do not know what they are doing." In fact, Christ continually intercedes for sinners (Isa 53:12; Rom 8:34).

After his death and resurrection, Jesus fulfills another aspect of Joel's book—he breathes on his disciples and says, "Receive the Holy Spirit" (John 20:22). Then, according to Joel's prophecy, Christ sends the Holy Spirit from heaven (Acts 2:17; cf. Joel 2:28). After the Day of Pentecost, Peter announces that calling on the name of Yahweh (Joel 2:32) is tantamount to calling on the name of Jesus. There is salvation in no other name (Acts 4:12).

### SIN AND GRACE IN JOEL

Joel does not specifically cite any of Judah's sins. Nowhere does he indicate what brought about the curse of the locusts. Yet locusts indicate divine judgment (e.g., Deut 28:38; 1 Kgs 8:37), so some transgression lies in the background of the book.

After the people heed the call to repent (Joel 2:12–17), Yahweh responds in grace. First he promises to restore grain, oil, and wine (Joel 2:19) that the locusts had devoured (Joel 1:10). Next he defeats "the northerner" (Joel 2:20), a term that has a supernatural quality to it. The stench that rises from his defeat indicates the complete destruction of all evil. God then promises plenty of rain, restoration from the locusts, and a great agricultural abundance (Joel 2:20–27). In the latter days he will pour out his Spirit (Joel 2:28–32), and this is followed by his defeat of all of his enemies (Joel 3:1–21). Yahweh does all of this because he is "gracious and merciful, slow to anger, and abounding in covenant-loyalty. He relents of evil" (Joel 2:13; cf. Exod 34:6; Ps 86:15; Jonah 4:2).

## CONCLUSION

Joel is the second prophet to appear in the Book of the Twelve and he accents one of its major themes—the Day of Yahweh (Joel 1:15; 2:1, 11, 31; 3:14, 18). The prophet promises salvation for God's people and therefore paves the way for authors of the NT to understand the significance of Christ and his gift of the Holy Spirit for all who repent.

# SELECT BIBLIOGRAPHY

Allen, Leslie C. *Joel, Obadiah, Jonah, and Micah.* New International Commentary on the Old Testament. Grand Rapids: Eerdmans, 1976.

Craigie, Peter. *The Twelve Prophets.* Vol. 1. The Daily Study Bible. Philadelphia: Westminster, 1984.

Crenshaw, James. *Joel: A New Translation with Introduction and Commentary.* Anchor Bible 24C. New York: Doubleday, 1995.

Mason, Rex. *Zephaniah, Habakkuk, Joel.* Old Testament Guides. Sheffield: JSOT Press, 1994.

Stuart, Douglas. *Hosea-Jonah.* Word Biblical Commentary 31. Waco: Word Books, 1987.

# 30

# AMOS

The book of Amos probably constitutes the earliest collection of prophetic oracles that have been preserved as an independent literary work. The prophet has left us not only oracles and speeches but also a series of vision reports (Amos 7:1–9; 8:1–3; 9:1–4). Both his preaching and visions reflect the life of a Judahite cattleman who was called to be a prophet to the Northern Kingdom. But the book is not just about the life and times of Amos or Israel's history in the early eighth century. Its major focus is on Yahweh, who is the God of Israel as well as the God of the universe. In his book, Amos employs ten different names to describe Yahweh for a total of eighty-six times in nine chapters. This God sends fires and earthquakes, locusts and drought, famine, disease, and an army bent on the complete annihilation of Israel. What unleashed such fury against a nation whom he calls "my people" (Amos 7:15; 8:2)? Is there any future after such devastation? The book of Amos answers these questions with a wide variety of rhetorical features that display a polished style, even as it contains a straightforward, "in-your-face" message.

## AUTHORSHIP

Most critics believe that the majority of Amos's sayings are authentic, yet the following have been questioned: the title (Amos 1:1), the Tyre oracle (Amos 1:9–10), the Edom oracle (Amos 1:11–12), the Judah oracle (Amos 2:4–5), the confrontation between Amos and Amaziah (Amos 7:10–17), the hymns (Amos 4:13; 5:8–9; 9:5–6), and the oracle of salvation (Amos 9:11–15). The underlying criterion embraced by those who believe these texts did not originate with the prophet is the assumption that the book was updated at least a half-dozen times over the course of three hundred years. The prophet's oracles were supposedly made more relevant for later audiences by adding additional material. Therefore, critics hold, Amos is more of a tradition rather than the work of a single author.

Form and redaction critics are not uniform in their analysis, but this much is agreed: Amos 9:11–15 is regarded as the latest addition to the book. Julius Wellhausen's remark regarding this oracle is now classic: "Rosen und Lavendel statt Blut und Eisen,"[1] *roses and lavender instead of blood and iron*. The promise of restoration is unthinkable in the context of the prophet's repeated threats of destruction.

Though there are many problems with these formal and redactional understandings of Amos, the chief dilemma is the amount of speculation involved by those who use these interpretive methods. Rearrangement of materials to fit presupposed historical systems makes understanding them ostensibly easier. But by linking their exegesis to historical reconstructions, these modes of interpretation jeopardize the integrity of the biblical text and its theological message. For instance, when it comes to the integrity of Amos 9:11–15, it is just as easy to believe that if Yahweh could change his course of action before (cf. Amos 7:3, 6), then even if eight times he issued an irreversible judgment (Amos 1:3–2:5), the possibility is held out that he could again change from condemnation to grace. And this is exactly what Amos 9:11–15 announces: the words "building" and "planting" restore the earlier judgment in Amos 5:11; the agricultural bounty in Amos 9:13–14 restores the plagues and drought in Amos 1:2 and 4:6–11; and dwelling in the land in Amos 9:15 restores the exilic threats in Amos 5:5, 27; 7:11, and 17. This kind of internal unity is indicative of one author—a herdsman from Tekoa, turned prophet, named Amos.

## LITERARY FEATURES OF AMOS

Amos employs a number of rhetorical devices. One of his favorites is that of repetition. For instance, Amos 1:3–2:16 contains five

---

[1] Julius Wellhauser, *Die Kleinen Propheten übersetzt und eklärt* (Berlin: Georg Reimer, 1892), 96.

reoccurring phrases: (1) "thus says Yahweh," (2) "because of three crimes and for four," (3) "I will not revoke it," (4) "I will send fire," and (5) "and it will consume her fortresses." The imperative שמע, *hear*, appears as a structuring device in Amos 3:1, 4:1, and 5:1. In Amos 4:6–11, the prophet employs the fivefold statement, "but you did not return to me." The five visions (Amos 7:1–9: 8:1–3; 9:1–4) are each introduced with the same verb ראה, *see*. The first two visions repeat several phrases verbatim (cf. Amos 7:1–6) and this same feature occurs in the second pair of visions (Amos 7:7–9; 8:1–3). Additional rhetorical devices include a riddle (Amos 3:3–8), sound plays (Amos 5:5; 7:7–9; 8:1–3), and rhetorical questions (Amos 2:11; 5:18, 20, 25; 6:12; 9:7).

Amos makes use of the following genres: (1) oracles about nations (Amos 1:3–2:3), (2) graded numerical sayings (e.g., Amos 1:3, 6, 9), (3) woe oracles (Amos 5:18; 6:1), (4) a lament (Amos 5:1), (5) hymns (Amos 4:13; 5:8–9; 9:5–6), (6) a curse formula (Amos 7:17), (7) wisdom argumentation (Amos 3:3–8), (8) riddles (e.g., Amos 2:9; 3:12; 5:24; 6:12; 9:9), (9) visions (Amos 7:1–9; 8:1–3; 9:1–4), (10) a narrative (Amos 7:10–17), and (11) eschatological promises (Amos 9:11–15).

The mention of הרעש, *the earthquake*, in Amos 1:1 sets the primary literary and theological themes for the book: Yahweh's earthquake-like judgment will shake Israel, Judah, and the nations, until everything comes crashing down. The motif of the earthquake is most prominent in the fifth vision (Amos 9:1–4), where the verbal root רעש appears. However, an earthquake is inferred in the following verses: Amos 3:13–15 (Yahweh's command to destroy Bethel and the royal houses); Amos 4:11 (a part of Israel was destroyed like Sodom and Gomorrah); Amos 6:11 (Yahweh will smash all of Israel's houses); and Amos 8:8 (the land will shake). This earthquake eventually moves the land up and down like the Nile (Amos 8:8; 9:5) and destroys the shrine at Bethel (Amos 9:1).

The prophet also has a propensity to take divine promises and turn them into oracles of judgment. One example is in Amos 1:3–2:16, which is a series of oracles about nations. Whether in warfare, public lamentation, court, or worship setting, oracles about nations always boded well for Israel. For example, in 1 Sam 15:2–3 and 1 Kgs 20:26–30, the prophetic proclamation against the enemy is matched with a specific promise of victory for Israel. Amos inverts this genre and adapts it for his own purpose to make a stinging accusation against Israel's elite.

From Amos 1:3 through 2:5 the prophet's audience, in all likelihood, cheered and applauded after each neighboring nation was condemned. "Great preacher, this Amos!" was the mantra of the moment. The sermon builds to a climax as three, four, and five nations are placed under divine fire. With the next judgment pointing to Judah (Amos 2:4–5), the number reaches seven. It was probably time for the Aaronic benediction (Num 6:22–27), a general dismissal, and then the normal post-service discussion about the weather and the events of the week. But Amos was not done preaching. The Lion was still roaring (cf. Amos 1:2; 3:8; 5:19). God's wrath was about to fall upon Israel. This oracle (Amos 2:6–16) came as a shocking surprise. There are seven oracles, beginning with Aram (Amos 1:3–5) and ending with Judah (Amos 2:4–5). Seven is a number commonly used to denote completeness, making an eighth oracle unexpected. Little did the audience (presumably at Bethel) know that the prophet's analysis of the crimes of the nations was in reality a noose that was getting ready to tighten around its neck!

Amos begins a new section with the words, "Hear this word that Yahweh has spoken concerning you, O children of Israel, concerning the entire clan which I brought up from Egypt, saying . . . " (Amos 3:1). The prophet's audience might have concluded that the Exodus was a sign of God's ongoing and eternal favor (e.g., Num 24:8; Judg 6:13; 1 Kgs 8:51–51). It forever guaranteed Israel's favored nation status. In the next verse, however, Amos flatly contradicts these expectations. He quotes God as saying, "You alone have I known from all the families of the earth; therefore I will punish you for all of your iniquities" (Amos 3:2). Just as Amos shocked his unwary audience with the Israel oracle (Amos 2:6–16), so again he overturns expectations by using acts of grace to announce condemnation. These types of inversions continue throughout the rest of the book (e.g., Amos 5:18–20; 9:7).

## Outline of Amos

I.   Superscription and introduction (1:1–2)
II.  Oracles about nations (1:3–2:16)
     A.  Aram (1:3–5)

B. Philistia (1:6–8)

C. Tyre (1:9–10)

D. Edom (1:11–12)

E. Ammon (1:13–15)

F. Moab (2:1–3)

G. Judah (2:4–5)

H. Israel (2:6–16)

III. Declarations concerning Israel (3:1–6:14)

A. Accusations lodged against Israel (3:1–4:13)

B. Lamentation for Israel (5:1–3)

C. Exhortation to seek Yahweh (5:4–17)

D. Judgment on the day of Yahweh (5:18–27)

E. Warning to the secure and complacent (6:1–7)

F. Certain destruction for the prideful house of Israel (6:8–14)

IV. Visions (7:1–9:10)

A. Vision of the locusts (7:1–3)

B. Vision of the fire (7:4–6)

C. Vision of the plumb line (7:7–9)

D. Narrative interlude: Amos versus Amaziah (7:10–17)

E. Vision of the summer fruit (8:1–3)

F. Interlude: Confirmation of judgment (8:4–14)

G. Vision of Yahweh beside the altar (9:1–4)

H. Interlude: Exodus undone (9:5–10)

V. Restoration of David's falling ten (9:11–15)

## HISTORICAL ISSUES

In the last thirty years of the ninth century, the Aramean kingdom repeatedly kept Israel in a defensive mode (e.g., 2 Kgs 13:7; 10:32–33). This changed when the Assyrian king Adad-nirari III (806–783) began his westward expansion that included the conquest of the Aramean capital Damascus (c. 800). The result was a lull in Israelite wars against Aram (or Syria) during the reigns of Uzziah (791–740) and Jeroboam ben Joash (793–753).

Assyria did not attempt any further expansion westward, in part because it was in an alliance with Israel. This agreement dated from the reigns of Jeroboam ben Joash's great-grandfather Jehu (841–814). Living before the westward campaigns of Tiglath-pileser III, both Jeroboam ben Joash and Uzziah were able to take full advantage of this political situation and expand their economic influence.

Early in his rule, Jeroboam ben Joash changed the political map of Israel. Through military conquests, the territories east of the Jordan were recovered and annexed (Amos 6:13), the northern border was extended to Lebo-Hamath and the southern border was enlarged all the way to the Dead Sea (2 Kgs 14:25). The large extent of this kingdom rivaled that of the combined kingdom of David and Solomon during Israel's Golden Age. Israel had reached the summit of its material power, the height of its economic prosperity, and the pinnacle of its territorial expansion. The nation had all signs pointing to Yahweh's unlimited favor, and the future appeared to hold limitless possibilities (Amos 5:18). Yahweh's protection was assumed to be unconditional. The nation felt certain of its future.

The duration of Amos's prophetic ministry cannot be dated with exactness, but he must have completed his mission prior to 753, for his oracles make no reference to the dramatic reversal in domestic political affairs after the death of Jeroboam ben Joash, nor does he give any direct indication that he knows of the westward territorial expansion of the Assyrian empire under Tiglath-pileser III (745–727), which began during this time. Whatever information that may be gleaned from Amos's oracles about the nations (Amos 1:3–2:3) also alludes to events either contemporaneous to the initial stages of Jeroboam ben Joash's reign or, more likely, to historical events prior to Amos's ministry. But by all accounts, they reflect an era before the reign of Tiglath-pileser III. It is safe, therefore, to date the ministry of Amos to an earlier, rather than a later, time in Jeroboam ben Joash's reign.

Also helpful is Zech 14:5, which refers to an earthquake during the reign of Uzziah and is likely the same earthquake mentioned in Amos 1:1. Archaeologists have tentatively located this cataclysm in the first half of the eighth century. Stratum VI at Hazor shows evidence of a great earthquake in about 760. This helps date Amos's ministry to sometime between 765 and 760 BC.

# THEOLOGICAL THEMES IN AMOS

Although Amos comprises only 9 chapters and 146 verses, it has been the subject of voluminous literature. The enormous attention given to the book is not difficult to explain. As the first of the writing prophets, he stands as the originator of a significant movement in Israel's theology. The oracles and narratives of earlier prophets are embedded in other books (e.g., Elijah and Elisha in 1 and 2 Kings), but Amos begins the phenomenon of a prophetic book. Almost every exegetical method or hermeneutical perspective has been used to investigate Amos.

Julius Wellhausen, in his *Prolegomena to the History of Israel* (1883), argued that prophets—and especially Amos—were the originators of ethical monotheism. However, Amos did not initiate Israel's theological reflections. The book is inextricably tied to Pentateuchal blessings and curses. The prophet's ideas and thematic frame of reference come from the Mosaic covenant as it is articulated in the Pentateuch. Amos was not a revolutionary trying to overturn the established order, but a covenant proclaimer who harkened back to Israel's theological beginnings.

## JUSTICE AND RIGHTEOUSNESS

Building upon Mosaic Torah, Amos wants the leaders in Israel to feed the hungry, give water to the thirsty, provide shelter for the homeless, offer clothes to the naked, and look after the sick. He calls this משפט, *justice*, and צדקה, *righteousness* (Amos 5:7, 24; 6:12). The prophet had been in the divine council (Amos 3:7), so he knew that Yahweh earlier had sided with the barren woman (Gen 11:30), rescued slaves and provided for their food, drink, clothing, and shelter (Exod 14, 16, 17; cf. Deut 8:2–4), and then given them the command, "Do not take advantage of an orphan or a widow" (Exod 22:22).

There are two groups in the book of Amos—those responsible for dispensing justice and righteousness and those for whom it was withheld. People who mistreated their fellow Israelites are described as royal and court officials (Amos 2:7; 3:10; 5:10, 12), rich women (Amos 4:1), those who oversaw military engagements (Amos 6:13), religious leaders (Amos 7:10–17), and merchants (Amos 2:6; 8:5–6). These are "all the sinners of my people" (Amos 9:10).

Those who were being denied justice and righteousness are the farmers and workers who were in danger of losing what property they still owned. They were being abused sexually (Amos 2:7), fiscally (Amos 2:8; 5:11), judicially (Amos 5:10), spiritually (Amos 2:12), and vocationally (Amos 4:1; 5:11). This second group are "small Jacob" (Amos 7:2, 5) who also are called (1) אביונים, *needy* (Amos 2:6; 4:1; 5:12; 8:4, 6); (2) דלים, *poor* (Amos 2:7; 4:1; 5:11; 8:6); (3) ענוים, *afflicted* (Amos 2:7; 8:4); and (4) צדיקים, *righteous* (Amos 2:6; 5:12). This is the remnant of Joseph (Amos 5:15) as well as the remnant of Edom (Amos 9:12).

Yet it would be a misreading of Amos to believe that he idealized the poor or their poverty. The poor were not righteous because they had been denied their rights, but rather because Yahweh had reckoned their faith as righteousness (cf. Gen 15:6; Hab 2:4). Responding to their gift of a righteous standing before Yahweh, we may assume that these poor people were faithful to their covenantal calling, whereas the rich were not.

The purpose of Amos's advocacy for justice and righteous, therefore, is not to put the disenfranchised on a pedestal, but to point out that Israel's leaders will have to face judgment because of their treatment of these people (e.g., Amos 4:12). The prophet did not advocate class warfare. Instead, the righteous poor will be vindicated by Yahweh and Yahweh alone. His prophet's oracles call for *conversion*, not *revolution*. Amos does not promote liberation theology.

## THE DAY OF YAHWEH

Chronologically (but not canonically), the phrase יום יהוה, *the Day of Yahweh*, makes its first appearance in the OT in Amos 5:18–20. The oracle addresses those "who long for the Day of Yahweh." This assumes that there were those listening to Amos who could identify with the expression. His rhetorical questions, as well as his repetition of the contrast between "darkness and not light" suggests that the prophet was trying to refute a widely held view that the Day of Yahweh would usher in more divine blessings. Contrary to popular opinion, when Yahweh appears, it will not be a day of national victory and celebration but a night of horrific disaster and defeat. The Northern Kingdom was anticipating deliverance. They were promised disaster instead.

From events narrated in passages such as Exod 14; Josh 6–8; Judg 5, 7; and 1 Sam 15, Israelites were aware of what would happen on Yahweh's day—he would completely defeat his enemies. Therefore the day of Yahweh is another way to say the *battle* of Yahweh. But according to Amos, what Israel understood to be a day of divine grace would turn out to be a day of God's wrath. There would be no escape (Amos 2:14–16; 5:19; 9:2–4). In Amos, this event is also called the "day of battle" and "the day of whirlwind storms and tempests" (Amos 1:14). as well as "in that day" or "days are coming" (Amos 2:16; 4:2; 5:18–20, 20; 6:3; 8:9, 10, 13; 9:11, 13). It is a time of judgment for unbelievers while believers on that day will be saved.

## CREATION

Amos's three creational hymns (Amos 4:13; 5:8–9; 9:5–6) indicate that the world of nature plays a significant part of his prophecy. The book begins with an earthquake and the drying up of the pasturelands as well as Mt. Carmel (Amos 1:1–2). The non-human creation and the human world of politics, religion, war, and business are intimately intertwined. This is the reason, for instance, why both the land (Amos 1:2) and the people mourn (Amos 9:5). The human and nonhuman are so deeply interconnected that human sin has a devastating effect upon the rest of the world. For this reason, Amos repeatedly announces creation's undoing—beginning with the earthquake (Amos 1:1) and ending with the land rising and falling like the Nile (Amos 9:5). In between he sees famine (e.g., Amos 4:6), drought (Amos 4:7–8; 7:4–6), and locusts (Amos 7:1–3). The prophet insists that righteousness and justice in the divine/human sphere brings about harmony and peace for the rest of creation. Everything is interrelated in one universe, and Yahweh's will is to bring about *shalom* for the entire created order. This will happen through his promises to David (Amos 9:11) that are able to reverse the destruction and bring about a new creation (Amos 9:13–15).

## NATURAL LAW

The main gist of Amos's oracles about the nations is that Damascus, Gaza, Tyre, Edom, Ammon, and Moab (Amos 1:3–2:3) have all violated Yahweh's moral law, which they are obliged to keep. Because this law is inscribed upon the hearts of all people, the prophet appeals to an innate order about conduct which is self-evidently right. Amos declares that the perpetrators of evil (e.g., Amos 1:3, 11, 13; 2:1) will not get away with murder. Reality is not shaped by *realpolitik*, nor will the ruthless and powerful finally have their way. In Yahweh's just universe, the wicked will receive their due punishment. While such a confession seems to run smack in the face of a world where plunder, death, injustice, and evil are rampant, it also boldly confesses that exploitation is not the final word. Amos testifies to Yahweh's righteous rule even in the midst of a world gone astray.

Nations are not denounced for sins which they could not have been expected to recognize (e.g., Torah and Sabbath observance), but rather for their crimes against humanity. The prophet preaches against the nations not simply because of their disobedience to Yahweh, but also for failing to follow the dictates of their own God-given moral sense. Although the people Amos addresses are without special divine revelation, they are not exempt from moral responsibility. They do not have the Ten Commandments written in stone, but they do have them written upon their hearts. And because the nations have disregarded these laws, Yahweh will wage war against these war criminals by sending divine fire to consume them (e.g., Amos 1:4, 7, 14; 2:2).

## CHRIST IN AMOS

Amos's phrase, "two years before the earthquake" (Amos 1:1), indicates that two years after his preaching stopped, there was a massive earthquake which vindicated his ministry. Amos was a true prophet (cf. Deut 18:18–22; Jer 28:9; Ezek 12:21–28) because his messages of divine shaking (e.g., Amos 9:1) were followed by Yahweh's definitive action of an earthquake. Christ's ministry is also vindicated by earthquakes: one on Good Friday (Matt 27:51) and the other on Easter (Matt 28:2). The death and resurrection of Jesus announce that he is the new David (Rom 1:3–4) who initiates the new age envisioned in Amos 9:11–15.

As a cattleman, Amos heard the lion's roar when it caught its prey and he saw what a lion could do to its victim (Amos 3:4, 12). The automatic response upon hearing a lion's roar is sheer terror (Amos 3:8). When a lion comes near, the only logical response is to secure safety as soon as possible (Amos 5:19). The imagery of Yahweh as a Lion in the book of Amos indicates that the covenant curse of harm from wild animals (cf. Lev 26:22; Deut 32:24) will be carried out by Yahweh himself. Jesus is called "the Lion of the tribe of Judah" (Rev 5:5) to connect him to God's promises to Judah as well as to David. Unlike the mighty David, though, Christ's great power becomes most perfect in his death on the cross (cf. 2 Cor 12:9).

### SIN AND GRACE IN AMOS

Amos 1:2–9:10 is intended to burn and bury the world of power politics and phony religion as these were known in the prophet's day. Only after sin is exposed is God's grace announced in Amos 9:11–15. This oracle proclaims that the night of judgment is over and the eschatological new day is at hand. Yahweh has torn as a Lion, but he will heal. He has killed, but he will also make alive. Yahweh has a plan for the entire created order, not just for Israel. The remnant of the nations will be restored (Amos 9:12), and the mountains and hills will drip with new wine (Amos 9:13).

Amos does not envision the temple and its worship as the foundation for the new future. Nor are there priests in the restored community. Neither are there kings, military commanders, or armies. Gone are the royal officials (Amos 3:8–15), the judges (Amos 5:10–17), the revelers (Amos 4:1–3; 6:1–7), and the tradesmen (Amos 2:6–8; 8:4–6). The only people remaining are the remnants of Joseph (Amos 5:15) and Edom (Amos 9:12) who are envisioned as peasants planting their vineyards and making gardens (Amos 9:14). Those who, like the prophet (cf. Amos 1:1; 7:14–15), make their living off the land are the ones who are part of Yahweh's future. "The meek will inherit the earth" (Matt 5:5).

## CONCLUSION

Living in a society of haves and have-nots, Amos announces that the lifestyles of the rich and famous were merely an illusion. The high-roller days of Jeroboam ben Joash were about to end. In a few short years the good times would cease to roll. Storm clouds were gathering on the horizon, and soon a succession of great ancient Near Eastern empires would roll over Israel as well as Judah and flatten them like pancakes. It was the task of Amos to announce that the storm was about to strike and to explain why. But divine demolition is penultimate—salvation is ultimate. The new order envisioned at the end of the book announces that there will be no more possibility of death and displacement. Guaranteeing this is Yahweh's word in Amos 9:15: "They will never again be uprooted."

## SELECT BIBLIOGRAPHY

Andersen, Francis, and David Noel Freedman. *Amos: A New Translation with Introduction and Commentary.* Anchor Bible 24A. New York: Doubleday, 1989.

Carroll, M. Daniel R. *Amos: The Prophet and His Oracles.* Louisville: Westminster, 2002.

Hayes, John H. *Amos, the Eighth-Century Prophet: His Times and His Preaching.* Nashville: Abingdon, 1988.

Lessing, Reed. *Amos.* Concordia Commentary. St. Louis: Concordia, 2009.

Motyer, J. A. *The Day of the Lion: The Message of Amos.* The Bible Speaks Today. Downers Grove: InterVarsity, 1974.

Paul, Shalom. *A Commentary on the Book of Amos.* Hermeneia. Minneapolis: Augsburg Fortress, 1991.

31

# OBADIAH

The book of Obadiah is the shortest in the OT and is part of Israel's ongoing protest against the Edomites. Strained relations between the two nations are already reflected in the Jacob-Esau narratives. For example, Gen 25:23 foretells that Edom will either be subject to his brother Israel or in revolt against him (cf. Gen 27:39–40). At the time of Moses, Israelites sought to pass peacefully through the nation on the Kings' Highway but Edom opposed them "with the sword" (Num 20:18, 20). Later, Edomites were subjugated by Israel's first kings (e.g., 1 Sam 14:47; 2 Sam 8:13–14; 1 Kgs 11:15–17; 22:48), but they were able to achieve independence during the time of Jehoram, king of Judah, in the mid-ninth century (2 Kgs 8:20–22). Entering Jerusalem at that time, Edomites plundered the palace and took off with the royal household (2 Chron 21:16–17). When Jerusalem was destroyed in 587, the Edomites cried out, "Tear it down, tear it down to its foundations" (Ps 137:7).

Documenting Israel's grievances against Edomite crimes, therefore, was not a difficult thing to do for any Hebrew writer at almost any point in OT history. In fact, there are more prophetic oracles against Edom than against any other nation (e.g., Isa 34:5–15; Jer 49:7–22; Ezek 25:12–14; 35:1–15; Amos 1:11–12; Mal 1:2–5). Obadiah stands in this long line of prophets who were outraged at Edomite acts of terror.

## AUTHORSHIP

Form and redaction critics frequently divide the book of Obadiah between Obad 1b–14 and Obad 15–21 and postulate separate authors for each section. This is because in Obad 15, the specific oracle against Edom expands to include all the nations. Signaling the break in the text is the word כִּי, *because*. Often critics interpret this as a catchword used by redactors to connect two disparate texts. Raabe considers these and other authorial objections and finds them dubious. He writes, "The approaches that fragment the book into separate, self-contained oracles or that posit several stages of growth for the book seem to impose a western standard of uniformity and self-consistency on an ancient text." Though there are at least a dozen men named Obadiah in the OT, making precision impossible, there is no good reason to doubt that a prophet named Obadiah wrote the entire book bearing his name.

## LITERARY FEATURES OF OBADIAH

Obadiah is an oracle about a foreign nation. This genre appears in every prophetic book, with the exception of Hosea. Large collections of these oracles are in Isa 13–23; Jer 46–51; Ezek 25–32, 35; and Amos 1–2.

The name עֵשָׂו, *Esau*, appears seven times in the book of Obadiah (Obad 6, 8, 9, 18 [two times], 19, 21). Esau is the ancestral father of the Edomites (Gen 36:9) and his name often stands in the place of Edom (e.g., Deut 2:5; Jer 49:8). By repeatedly employing Esau— which in Obadiah is synonymous with Edom—the prophet recalls the strife and contention that existed between Jacob and Esau throughout much of the brothers' relationship (cf. Gen 27:41; 32:1–21), a strife that continued in the later history of Israel and Edom.

### Outline of Obadiah

I.   Superscription (v. 1a)

II.  The first proclamation against Edom: humiliation (vv. 1b–4)

III. The second proclamation against Edom: displacement (vv. 5–7)

IV.  The third proclamation against Edom (vv. 8–18)

    A.  Doom and accusation (vv. 8–14)

    B.  Judgment against the nations (vv. 15–16)

    C.  Restoration for Jacob (Judah) and destruction for Esau (Edom) (vv. 17–18)

V.   Israel's restoration and the kingship of Yahweh (vv. 19–21)

The book of Obadiah consists of two main parts: an oracle against Edom (Obad 1b–14) and a broader oracle of judgment against all the nations which leads to Zion's restoration (Obad 15–21).

## HISTORICAL ISSUES

The phrase עבדיה חזון, *the vision of Obadiah*, is unusually short. Prophetic superscriptions normally include biographical material about the prophet or something about the intended audience (e.g., Jer 1:1; Hos 1:1; Amos 1:1). Obadiah's superscription only identifies the prophet and the book's genre, placing it in the category of other prophetic books that begin with the word *vision* (e.g., Isa 1:1; Nah 1:2).

Because of its lack of historical detail and the ongoing strife between Israel and Edom throughout the biblical period, scholars have dated Obadiah anywhere from 850, when Philistines and Arabs attacked Jerusalem (2 Kgs 8:20), to 450, when Edomites began moving north into Judah.

One helpful point is that Obadiah is closely related to the Edom oracle in Jer 49:7–22. Many of the same motifs and much of the same vocabulary occur in both texts. The closest parallels are in Obad 1b–6 and Jer 49:9–10, 14–16. Raabe maintains that it was Obadiah who modified Jeremiah's oracle and not the other way around. This helps locate Obadiah after Jeremiah, probably sometime in the first half of the exilic period, 585–555. The earliest date for its writing is the fall of Judah and Jerusalem to the Babylonians (587), while the latest date must be before the campaign of Nabonidus against Edom (553).

## THEOLOGICAL THEMES IN OBADIAH

### DIVINE RETRIBUTION

Obad 5–6 describes the humiliation predicted in Obad 1b–4. In contrast to Edom's presumed safety and security high and hidden in the rocks, the nation will be plundered as if by thieves and gleaners. Edom will be destroyed by thieves because they are like thieves (cf. Obad 11). The nation will be plundered just as they themselves have plundered (cf. Obad 15).

This is frequently called *lex talionis*, or the law of retribution, which is stated in Exod 21:24–25. Payback is frequently displayed in prophetic judgment scenes: destroyers will be destroyed (Isa 33:1); devourers will be devoured (Jer 30:16); reproachers will be reproached (Ezek 36:6); and plunderers will be plundered (Hab 2:8). This correspondence pattern depicts the just nature of God's punishment. When he judges, it is not some strange fate coming out of the blue but is rational and appropriate to fit the particular crime committed by the guilty party.

### DIVINE JUDGMENT

The expression ביום ההוא, *on that day*, in Obad 8 is common in prophetic literature. It frequently refers to a future day of judgment for a specific nation (e.g., Isa 13:1, 9; Jer 46:2, 10). The phrase may also refer to the final judgment (e.g., Joel 2:1–11). Obadiah employs the expression to refer both to the historical judgment of Edom as well as to the last day when all unbelievers will be humbled before Yahweh. The prophecy flows seamlessly from the particular in Obad 8 into Obad 15, where the day of Yahweh is a universal day of judgment for all nations. Throughout Obad 8–15, Yahweh speaks in the first person. He himself will carry out judgment upon Edom (cf. Deut 32:35). Even the wise man and the warrior (Obad 8–9) will not be able to prevent their destruction.

### THE CUP OF WRATH

The drinking in Obad 16 is used frequently in other texts as a metaphor for receiving God's wrath. It occurs mostly in poetic and prophetic texts (e.g., Ps 60:3; Lam 4:21; Isa 51:17–23). Judgment is likened to drinking a cup of poisoned wine. For instance, in Jer 25, after the prophet has passed around "the cup of the wine of wrath" (Jer 25:15), he shifts from referring to the deity as "Yahweh the God of Israel" (Jer 25:15, 27) to "Yahweh the God of *Armies*" (Jer 25:27, 28, 29 32). Yahweh the Warrior God (e.g., Exod 15:3) is therefore behind the punishment against Edom: "They will drink and swallow and will be as though they had never been" (Obad 16).

### CHRIST IN OBADIAH

David's military campaigns—as listed in 2 Sam 8—end with his victory over Edom, his last enemy (2 Sam 8:13–14). Obadiah maintains that Edom will once again taste defeat. This will be fulfilled when David's greatest Son, Jesus, returns to destroy "*the* last enemy" (1 Cor 15:26)—death itself.

Obad 17 depicts restoration in terms of the tribal allotments in Josh 13–21. The land will be restored to the people of Israel and the exiles will return to what was promised to them. But this will be more than a restoration to pre-exilic times. It will exceed every previous era of Israelite power, for Yahweh himself will rule, and Israel will face her enemies no more. The final words of Obad 21, "the kingdom will belong to Yahweh," find their consummation in Christ. Rev 11:15 states, "The kingdom of the world has become the kingdom of our Lord and of his Christ, and he will reign forever and ever." This is why the Jews in Thessalonica attacked Paul and Silas saying, "They are all defying Caesar's decrees, saying that there is another king, one called Jesus" (Acts 17:7).

### SIN AND GRACE IN OBADIAH

The picture in Obad 3–4 likens Edom to an eagle who has built her nest high in the mountains, supposedly safe from any threat or danger. This security, however, is false, because Yahweh will bring the Edomites down from their high and presumptuous place. Edom's chief sin is pride. Obad 18 indicates that by means of his people—the houses of Judah and Jacob—Yahweh will judge this sin by burning the house of Esau so that there will be no survivors. In other texts, fire also functions as a means of judgment for unbelievers and redemption for God's elect (Isa 4:4–5; Mal 4:1–3). This salvation is envisioned as Zion's vindication (Obad 17, 21). As Yahweh's dwelling place and fortress against all enemies, divine grace is given to all who take refuge in Zion.

## CONCLUSION

In the book of Obadiah, Edom represents both itself and serves as an illustration of what God intends to do against all unbelieving nations. Because Edom and Adam are spelled using the same consonants, אדם, the nation is uniquely positioned to serve as a symbol for all the prideful nations who exhibit the sin of Adam in Gen 3. The end of Edom, therefore, signifies the end of all of God's enemies and his gift of the new Davidic reign to all believers (cf. Amos 9:12). Jesus, David's greatest Son, was born to rule over "all the nations" (Rev 12:5).

## SELECT BIBLIOGRAPHY

Allen, Leslie C. *The Books of Joel, Obadiah, Jonah and Micah.* New International Commentary on the Old Testament. Grand Rapids: Eerdmans, 1976.

Clark, D. J. "Obadiah Reconsidered." *Bible Translator* 42 (1991): 326–36.

Lillie, J. R. "Obadiah: A Celebration of God's Kingdom." *Currents in Theology and Missions* 6 (1979):18–22.

Ogden, G. S. "Prophetic Oracles against Foreign Nations and Psalms of Communal Lament: The Relationship between Jer 49:7–22 and Obadiah." *Journal for the Study of the Old Testament* 24 (1982): 89–97.

Raabe, Paul. *Obadiah: A New Translation with Introduction and Commentary.* Anchor Bible 24D. New York: Doubleday, 1996.

# 32

# JONAH

Through the ages—whether in art or literature, cartoon or animation—in the biblical firmament, Jonah has been a star of the first magnitude. The book continues to delight and challenge the simple soul as much as the sophisticated scholar. Children commonly love Jonah and many adults are fascinated with it. Outsiders who have minimal knowledge or interest in the Bible know enough about Jonah to laugh at a joke based on the story. This makes the book of Jonah a strong contender for the best-known story in the OT, and it is undoubtedly one of the great literary masterpieces in the Bible. Jesus compares himself to Jonah (Matt 12:41), while drawings of the prophet appear more often in the Roman catacombs than any other biblical figure.

## AUTHORSHIP

The book of Jonah is an anonymous work and its events can be readily dated to the middle of the eighth century. The question regarding authorship, then, is *when* was the book composed. Jonah cannot have been written any later than the third century, as it is mentioned in Sir 49:10 and possibly cited in Tobit 14:4, 8. The upper limit is the identity of "Jonah ben Amittai" (Jonah 1:1) with the prophet of the same name from Gath-Hepher who, according to 2 Kgs 14:25, prophesied to Jeroboam ben Joash (793–753). Dates for the book's composition therefore could range over a span of six centuries.

Many believe Jonah was written in the late fifth or early fourth century. They maintain that the book's implied universalism best accords with a post-exilic date and is a protest against a xenophobic mood prevalent at that time.

Several criticisms have been raised against this view. The primary observation is that there is no substantial historical evidence—apart from a highly irregular reading of Ezra-Nehemiah which overemphasizes putative ethnic conflicts—to substantiate any Israelite particularism in the post-exilic era. Even though this interpretation is rejected in more recent works, the view of Jonah as a corrective against a hypothetical Israelite provincialism is still put forward, albeit in more abstract terms.

When trying to adduce a date for the narrative's composition, many nineteenth- and early twentieth-century scholars judged certain words and terminology to be typical of late Hebrew and Aramaic influence. Some of these include מלח, *sailor* (Jonah 1:5); ספינה, *ship* (Jonah 1:5); עשת, *think* (Jonah 1:6); זעף, *fury* (Jonah 1:15); טעם, *decree* (Jonah 3:7); and עמל, *labor over* (Jonah 4:10). Yet, as early as Hezekiah's reign, Aramaic was the language of diplomats, which even the political and military rulers of Judah understood (2 Kgs 18:26; Isa 36:11). In Jonah's native land of Israel, the early presence of Aramaic forms and expressions is readily explained by the close proximity of Syria and Phoenicia, and particularly by the thirty years of Syrian domination before the rule of Jeroboam ben Joash (2 Kgs 13:1–7, 14–25).

The presence of Aramaisms in Jonah, therefore, may be turned on its head—some words actually make a strong argument for identifying the author of the book with the Jonah of 2 Kgs 14:25 and dating it during the reign of Jeroboam ben Joash. Indeed, the complete lack of Persian or Greek loan words in Jonah, together with the paucity of characteristics distinctive of late biblical Hebrew, suggests not only that the traditional dating of Jonah at the time of Ezra and Nehemiah or later is in error, but also that it is quite unlikely that the narrator, while writing in this period, was deliberately archaizing the language of his story to bring it into conformity with a pre-exilic setting.

If the book of Jonah originated in the Northern Kingdom, it would seem necessary to assume that it was composed prior to the capture and destruction of Samaria in 723. After this time most of the northern population was deported to Assyria and replaced by people from elsewhere (cf. 2 Kgs 17:23–24).

# LITERARY FEATURES OF JONAH

While it is clear that the book of Jonah differs from other prophetic books, it is not apparent how its genre should be classified. Scholars often call Jonah a parable, saga, fiction, folklore, legend, fable, and the like. But it is uncertain that these genres were known in the ancient Near East. Those who describe the genre of Jonah with these terms do not tell us about the actual genre of the narrative. Rather, they express their own lack of confidence in the historical reliability of the book.

The first word of the text is ויהי, *and it came to pass*. This often signals an historical account (e.g., Gen 17:1; 22:1; Exod 32:19; Josh 4:1; 1 Kgs 17:8–9). The beginning of Jonah therefore suggests that the book is intended to be treated as factual. The Hebrew word for *parable*, משל, does not appear in the book.

While Jonah is an accurate report of the prophet's journeys, the book employs irony to satirize him along the way. Note the following ironies: Jonah the prophet abandons the task Yahweh calls him to do (Jonah 1:3); he sleeps during the storm while unbelievers pray to their gods (Jonah 1:5); the unbelieving captain has to urge Jonah, a believing Israelite, to pray (Jonah 1:5); he flees from Yahweh yet confesses him as Lord (Jonah 1:9); Jonah appears to remain unrepentant, while the sailors (Jonah 1:16) and Ninevites repent and believe (Jonah 3:5); his anger over the conversion of Nineveh (Jonah 4:1) occurs just after Yahweh turns his anger away (Jonah 3:10); the sailors and Ninevites perform classic acts of Israelite piety like making vows, sacrificing, and clothing themselves with sackcloth (Jonah 1:16; 3:6–8), while Jonah does none of this, even though he promises to do so (Jonah 2:10). When we put all of this together, Jonah is the opposite of what we would consider a prophet to look like. The function of the final question in the book (Jonah 4:10–11) is to challenge the author's contemporaries, as well as those of all times and all places, who exhibit the sinful characteristics of Jonah.

## Outline of Jonah

I.   Jonah's call and his reaction (1:1–3)

II.  On board ship in the midst of a storm at sea (1:4–17)

III. Inside the great fish (2:1–10)

IV. Yahweh gives Jonah his assignment a second time (3:1–3)

V. Jonah delivers God's message and Nineveh's response to it (3:4–10)

VI. Jonah's prayer in Nineveh (4:1–3)

VII. Jonah sits outside the city of Nineveh and Yahweh teaches him a lesson on mercy (4:4–11)

The overall structure of Jonah can be allocated to two contrasting scenes: at sea (chapters 1 and 2) and in Nineveh (chapters 3 and 4). Schematically, this structure of the book appears as follows:

### Two Scenes in Jonah Compared

| Chapters 1–2 | | Chapters 3–4 | |
|---|---|---|---|
| Word of God to Jonah | 1:1 | Word of God to Jonah | 3:1 |
| Content of the word | 1:2 | Content of the word | 3:2 |
| Response of Jonah | 1:3 | Response of Jonah | 3:3–4a |
| Gentile response | 1:5 | Gentile response | 3:5 |
| Action of the captain | 1:6 | Action of the king | 3:6–9 |
| Sailors and Jonah | 1:7–15 | Ninevites and God | 3:10 |
| Disaster averted | 1:15c | Disaster averted | 3:10c |
| Response of the sailors | 1:16 | Response of Jonah | 4:1 |
| God and Jonah | 2:1–11 | God and Jonah | 4:2–3 |
| God's response | 2:11 | God's response | 4:6–11 |

From this perspective, the function of chapters 1 and 2 is largely preparatory in that they are designed to set the scene and prepare readers for chapters 3 and 4, in which the primary encounter between Yahweh and Jonah takes place.

The root רעע, *evil*, frames the narrative. There is evil beginning with the Ninevites (Jonah 1:2), moving to the sailors (Jonah 1:7), returning to the Ninevites (Jonah 3:10), coming to Yahweh (Jonah 3:10; 4:2), and landing on Jonah (Jonah 4:1). The expression רעה

גדולה, *great evil*, only applies to Jonah (Jonah 4:1). Except in the reference to Jonah, all the evil is taken away. Yahweh tries to save Jonah from his evil (Jonah 4:6), but it appears as though he is unsuccessful (Jonah 4:7–11).

## HISTORICAL ISSUES

For many, the book of Jonah is just another fish story. Skepticism is not confined to the account of the "great fish" (Jonah 1:17). Other historical questions are just as pertinent: Why is the king of Nineveh not named? How could a great city—along with its animals—repent so quickly after just a five-word sermon? And why is there no record of such a massive conversion in Assyrian annals?

Extra-biblical information testifying to the validity of the events recorded in Jonah comes from the Assyrian kings Assur-dan III (773–755) and Assur-nirari V (755–745). Their reigns were times of great political instability brought about by natural and political crises. General anarchy ruled in the empire, and Nineveh at this time was an autonomous city. As a semi-independent city-state, a "decree of the king and its nobles" (Jonah 3:7) comports well with these political realities.

Wiseman documents reasons for Assyria's weaknesses. For example, he cites a total solar eclipse on June 15, 763 that happened during the reign of Assur-dan III. Wiseman then offers a translation of a Ninevite omen which predicts what might occur following this eclipse. Included are the words: "The king will die, rain from heaven will flood the land. There will be famine. A deity will strike the king and fire will consume the land." Not only did Assyrian kings take these types of omens seriously, they may even have abandoned the throne to a substitute monarch until the danger was over. These events may well have rendered the Ninevites and their king open to Jonah's pronouncement that in forty days the city would be overthrown (Jonah 3:4).

Not only has the mass conversion of the Ninevites caused some to doubt the historicity of Jonah, others point to the three-day journey in Jonah 3:3 as an inaccurate account of the size of Nineveh in the eighth century. However, one way of interpreting Jonah's trek is to take it as a reference to Greater Nineveh or the Assyrian Triangle. This interpretation posits that "Nineveh" in the book is meant to include the area surrounding the city, including Dur Sharrakin (present-day Khorsabad) and Calah (present-day Nimrud). An area this large would warrant a three-day journey. The great city of Nineveh (e.g., Jonah 1:2; 4:11) may mean something like the "Nineveh district" (cf. Gen 10:12).

Two problems arise with the title "the king of Nineveh" (Jonah 3:6). First, cuneiform documents never use this phrase to designate the reigning Assyrian monarch and second, the OT elsewhere calls him "the king of Assyria" (e.g., Isa 36:13). Most commentators therefore take the title in Jonah to be a sign that the narrator is not a trustworthy source of history. However, this judgment demands too much historical precision. For example, Egyptian literature does not use the term "pharaoh" as a substitute for the royal name, nor does it use the title attached to a specific name, i.e., Pharaoh Necho. Yet the OT frequently uses the term in this way in contexts that are clearly historical (e.g., 2 Kgs 23:29). And the title "the king of Samaria" occurs twice (1 Kgs 21:1; 2 Kgs 1:3) where it would be more accurate to use the term "the king of Israel." Mesopotamian literature also refers to foreign leaders using less than technical terms.

Laetsch's arguments for the historicity of Jonah build upon Christ's words. Based upon Matt 12:39–42, Laetch states: (1) there is no indication that Jesus is referring to a parable or quoting from a legend, or that the Pharisees regarded the story of Jonah as an allegory or myth; (2) there is no indication that Jesus or his opponents regarded Jonah or the repenting of the Ninevites as less historical than Solomon or the Queen of the South; (3) if Jonah's sojourn in the belly of the fish was non-historical, then according to Christ's own logic, his authenticating sign would be based upon a non-factual event. Laetch concludes:

> As Jesus lay in the grave three days, as Jesus rose again, as these are historical facts, so is the three-day captivity of Jonah in the fish's belly and his deliverance is not a legendary story, a mere parable, but irrefutable fact, historical truth. Else Christ would never have regarded it as a sign and prophecy of His own burial and resurrection after three days.[1]

---

[1] Theodore Laesch, *The Minor Prophets* (St. Louis: Concordia, 1956), 218.

492

There are no valid reasons to reject the testimony of the Old and New Testaments, Assyrian history, and the ancient writings of Jews and the Christian Church—all of which support the historical framework of the Jonah narrative.

## THEOLOGICAL THEMES IN JONAH

The book of Jonah is hardly a theological lightweight. Until recently, it played a part in the major liturgical festivals of three religious traditions. Up to the Second Vatican Council, Jonah was read in the Holy Saturday liturgy of the Roman Catholic Church. It still retains this place in the liturgical calendar of the Greek Orthodox Church. In Judaism, Jonah is the *Haftarah* (prophetic writing) for Yom Kippur.

### DIVINE REPENTANCE

The Ninevites hope that Yahweh will נחם, *change his course of action* (Jonah 3:9). Yahweh does change (Jonah 3:10), and this is what gets the prophet so upset (Jonah 4:2). God's willingness to reverse a prior decision announces the priority of grace in all of his dealings with the world. Divine change enables him to express his primary attributes: his grace, mercy, patience, and covenant-loyalty (Jonah 4:2). The verb נחם in the Niphal reflects the extent to which Yahweh will go in order to execute his uncompromising salvific intentions—even for the wicked Ninevites.

God's change of mind is one of the most neglected themes in biblical studies. He changes his course of action at some of the key junctures in the OT: the flood story (Gen 6:6), the Sinai revelation (Exod 32:12, 14), as well as when the monarchy is instituted (1 Sam 15:11, 29, 35). Most of the time, נחם in the Niphal appears in the context when Yahweh shifts from judgment to grace. However, the statement that he does not change previous decisions appears in eight texts (Num 23:19; 1 Sam 15:29; Ps 110:4; Jer 4:28; 20:16; Ezek 24:14; Hos 13:14; Zech 8:14). Of these, five describe God's refusal to alter his decision concerning Jerusalem's judgment of 587, and one, Ps 110:4, speaks of his unwillingness to change in relation to the eternal priesthood and order of Melchizedek.

The remaining two verses—Num 23:19 and 1 Sam 15:29—appear to place his unwillingness to do an about-face within a standard statement of principle. "God is not a man that he should change his mind." The statement in Num 23:19 appears within a narrative where Balaam seeks to curse Israel. God says he will not let that happen because he has made an unconditional promise to Abraham and his descendants (Gen 12:1–3). 1 Sam 15:29 appears in the context of Yahweh's final rejection of Saul and is connected to the refusal to change to one specific decision—the choice of David as Israel's new king (cf. 1 Sam 13:14). This is also an unconditional covenant (cf. 2 Sam 7). The Davidic and patriarchal promises are the backbone of the NT gospel (e.g., Luke 2:4; Gal 3:29). On this, God will never change his mind.

## YAHWEH'S WORD

In its first verse, the book of Jonah uses דבר־יהוה, *the word of Yahweh* (Jonah 1:1), and it ends with God's words to his prodigal prophet (Jonah 4:10–11). This word not only figures prominently within the narrative of Jonah, but it gains momentum as events unfold. For example, in Jonah 3:1, the prophet's commission is reiterated from chapter 1, but this is added, "Proclaim the message which I am speaking to you" (Jonah 3:2). In Jonah 3:3, the prophet arises and goes to Nineveh according to Yahweh's word which prevails over Jonah's stubborn ways. He then delivers God's word (Jonah 3:4), and the message brings repentance and faith for everyone in Nineveh (Jonah 3:5). When it reaches the Ninevite king, he joins his people by donning sackcloth and ashes (Jonah 3:6). This same powerful word earlier was God's means to convert the sailors (Jonah 1:9, 16).

After God's word changes Nineveh, the prophet counters with his word: "Alas Yahweh, was this not my word . . . " (Jonah 4:2). Jonah, appointing himself as a religious advisor to Yahweh, rails against God. If the prophet's word isn't the final word, he would rather die (Jonah 4:3, 8). The book of Jonah, then, is a contrast between divine and human words. Yahweh's word of forgiveness for the Ninevites finally overrides all other words—even Jonah's!

## CHRIST IN JONAH

"The sign of Jonah" is mentioned three times in the Gospels (Matt 12:39; 16:4; Luke 11:29). It does not refer exclusively to Jonah's deliverance from the fish, for when he is swallowed, Jonah is— paradoxically at the same time—both under Yahweh's judgment and given salvation. When Jesus refers to the sign of Jonah, he is also stating the paradox that he will undergo both judgment and salvation.

The primary meaning of the "sign of Jonah," then, is the correspondence between Jonah's descent into Sheol and our Lord's experience of death; especially when he—like Jonah—is "driven away from Yahweh's presence" (Jonah 2:4; cf. Matt 27:46). Jonah and Jesus had to go through judgment and condemnation before they experienced new life.

### SIN AND GRACE IN JONAH

By word association, *Jonah* would undoubtedly prompt the reaction of *whale*, but a subject that takes up only three verses out of a total of forty-eight cannot be regarded as the book's main concern. Readers sometimes look so intently at the great fish that they fail to see the great God. The name *Yahweh* is mentioned twenty-two times in the book, אלהים or אל, *God*, thirteen times, and the combination *Yahweh God* four times for a total of thirty-nine references to the deity in four chapters. *Jonah* is used only sixteen times. This is clearly a story about the God of Abraham, Isaac, and Jacob, and his grace for all people, even their animals!

Though Yahweh condemns Nineveh for its evil (Jonah 1:2), he brings them salvation and, along the way, the sailors turn to Yahweh and are delivered (Jonah 1:16) while Jonah is saved, both from drowning in the sea, as well as from Sheol (Jonah 2:2). Ironically in the end, even though Yahweh provides a miraculous plant to save Jonah (Jonah 4:6), the prophet appears to thwart the idea. Although justice demands that the idolatrous sailors, the prodigal Jonah, and the evil Ninevites perish—God's grace prevails and grants new life. Indeed ישועתה ליהוה, *salvation belongs to Yahweh* (Jonah 2:9).

## CONCLUSION

By means of only 689 words in the Hebrew text, we meet a huge storm on the Mediterranean Sea, take a tour of Sheol, discover the insides of a great fish, watch a plant come and go in a day, see from a hot east wind over distant lands, and meet repentant sailors and Ninevites. Yet most surprising of all is that we meet the God "who made the heavens and the earth and the dry ground" (Jonah 1:9). This God surprises us again and again with his out-of-this-world love that pursues reluctant and stubborn sinners like Jonah, and like us.

## SELECT BIBLIOGRAPHY

Laetsch, Theodore. *Bible Commentary: The Minor Prophets*. St. Louis: Concordia, 1956.

Lemanski, Jay. "Jonah's Nineveh." *Concordia Journal* 18 (1992): 40–49.

Lessing, Reed. *Jonah*. Concordia Commentary. St. Louis: Concordia, 2007.

Sasson, Jack. *Jonah: A New Translation with Introduction, Commentary, and Interpretation*. Anchor Bible 24B. New York: Doubleday, 1990.

Wiseman, Donald. "Jonah's Nineveh." *Tyndale Bulletin* 30 (1979): 29–51, 47–50.

# 33

# MICAH

Micah is frequently overlooked due to the literary skill and exquisite theology of his fellow eighth-century prophets—Amos, Hosea, and Isaiah. His name, מיכה, means *who is like [Yahweh]?* This forms a bookend with the confession at the end of his book, מי אל כמוך, *who is a God like you?* (Mic 7:18). By affirming Yahweh's uniqueness, Micah produced some of the most well-known texts within Israel's prophetic corpus—Zion's elevation as the highest of all mountains (Mic 4:1–5), Bethlehem's role in the Messiah's birth (Mic 5:2), and the divine plan for all people to exhibit justice, kindness, and humility (Mic 6:8).

Like Amos the Tekoaite (Amos 1:1) and Nahum the Elkoshite (Nah 1:1), Micah is known by his hometown—Moresheth-Gath (Mic 1:1, 14). The village was about twenty miles southwest of Jerusalem along the Shephelah, near the Philistine city of Gath. From his small-town purview, Micah could see through the façades of the rich and powerful in Jerusalem. He drew the line between himself and the big city's false prophets (Mic 2:11) and rejected the idea that he was paid by the establishment to utter oracles in Yahweh's name (Mic 3:5–8).

## AUTHORSHIP

Based upon the assumption that Micah's oracles of restoration and hope are post-exilic, form critics have dissected the book into numerous smaller pieces. Because Mic 1–3 contains judgment (with the exception of Mic 2:12–13), they hold that much of Mic 1–3 derived from the prophet's pen. Conversely, because Mic 4–5 is full of passages of mercy and grace, critics doubt their authenticity. They theorize that the book's final form did not appear until after the Babylonian exile. Critics frequently point to Mic 4:10 as proof of this view, as this verse mentions Babylon. In light of the fact that Micah and Isaiah share many of the same ideas—such as the nations' pilgrimage to Zion (Mic 4:1–5; Isa 2:1–5), woe oracles (Mic 2:1–5; Isa 5:8–30), and the day of Yahweh (Mic 5:9–15; Isa 2:6–22)—Childs believes that Micah was redacted by the same editors who created the final form of Isaiah.

Jeppsen has surveyed this critical approach to Micah and he questions its results. Hagstrom, along with Andersen and Freedman, also argue for the book's unity. If we allow the possibility of predictive prophecy, then there is no reason why Micah from Moresheth-Gath could not have composed all seven chapters.

## LITERARY FEATURES OF MICAH

Martin Luther once wrote: "They [the prophets] have a queer way of talking, like people, who instead of proceeding in an orderly manner, ramble off from one thing to the next, so that you cannot make heads or tails of them or see what they are getting at."[1] Nowhere is this truer than in the book of Micah. Does it exhibit a logical, chronological, or theological structure? It is difficult to say. The prophet's book is a bewildering collection of oracles that acrobatically jump around without telling us how they cohere. The literary term for this is parataxis, which describes a writing that places materials next to each other without giving readers transitional assistance. This characterizes Micah to a tee. So much appears to be random. The book resembles a snowball rolling downhill, picking up loose ends along the way. "Connecting the dots" seems nearly impossible.

We can say, however, that the book divides into three parts: (1) chapters 1–3 generally are oracles of doom against Samaria and Judah, climaxing with the prophet's prediction that Jerusalem will be destroyed; (2) chapters 4–5 contain promises of hope and restoration; and (3) chapters 6–7 begin with prophecies of judgment and end with a divine pledge of forgiveness and salvation. The overall movement in the book of Micah is one of judgment for sin and salvation by

---

[1] Martin Luther, *Luthers Werke: Kritische Gesamtausgabe* (Weimer Ausgabe. Weimer: Herman Böhlau, 1883–1993), 19.350.

grace: (1) Mic 1:2b–2:11 (judgment)/Mic 2:11–12 (salvation); (2) Mic 3:1–13 (judgment)/Mic 4:1–5:15 (salvation); (3) Mic 6:1–7:6 (judgment)/Mic 7:7–20 (salvation).

Micah's superscription includes the verb חזה, *perceive events* (Mic 1:1). Amos, Obadiah, Nahum, and Habakkuk also begin their books with this root. Micah employs a wide variety of genres that include (1) wordplays within a lament for cities (Mic 1:10–16); (2) messianic prophecies (e.g., Mic 5:2–4); (3) a covenant lawsuit (Mic 6:1–6); and (4) psalmody (Mic 7:7–20). Unlike other prophets (e.g., Isa 6–8; Jer 26, 32; Hos 1–3; Amos 7:10–17), Micah does not contain any narrative events about his ministry, though he does tell us that he was filled with Yahweh's Spirit in order to prophesy (Mic 3:8).

## Outline of Micah

I.   Superscription (1:1)

II.  Oracles of judgment (1:2–3:12)

    A.  Samaria's disaster is Jerusalem's warning (1:2–9)

    B.  Judah's disaster is Jerusalem's warning (1:10–16)

    C.  Sins and punishment (2:1–5)

    D.  False prophets (2:6–11)

    E.  Promises of safety and salvation (2:12–13)

    F.  Jerusalem's doom (3:1–12)

III. Oracles of salvation (4:1–5:15)

    A.  The nations journey to Zion (4:1–5)

    B.  Jerusalem's future greatness (4:6–10)

    C.  Jerusalem's enemies are removed (4:11–13)

    D.  The perfect king is coming (5:1–6)

    E.  The future remnant (5:7–9)

    F.  Yahweh's punishment and deliverance of Israel (5:10–15)

IV.  Oracles of doom and restoration (6:1–7:20)

    A.  Yahweh's lawsuit against his people (6:1–8)

    B.  Economic dishonesty and its judgment (6:9–16)

    C.  Lament over a decadent nation (7:1–7)

    D.  Confident hope (7:8–20)

## HISTORICAL ISSUES

Micah indicates in his superscription that his ministry occurred during the reigns of Jotham (751–736), Ahaz (732–716), and Hezekiah (716–687). He also notes that his oracles pertain to both the North (Samaria) and the South (Jerusalem). Anti-Northern passages clearly appear in Mic 1:2–7 and 6:9–16. The former predicts Samaria's fall while the latter indicates that the house of Omri (885–874) is under divine judgment. In only one of two passages in the prophetic corpus where one prophet is specifically cited in another prophetic book, it becomes clear that Micah uttered the passage regarding Jerusalem's doom during the days of Hezekiah (Jer 26:17–19; Mic 3:12; cf. Dan 9:2; Jer 25:11–12; 29:10).

What were these days like? In the late eighth century, Assyrian imperial plans included the permanent possession of western Syria and Palestine. Tiglath-pileser III (745–727), Shalmaneser V (727–723), and Sargon II (721–705) made major advances towards realizing this goal. Assyria's defeat of Samaria in 723 was in keeping with this policy. It brought with it waves of refugees into Jerusalem and surrounding villages. According to archaeological data, the area increased in population three to four times. This, no doubt, brought with it great economic challenges. The demands on goods and property increased while the supply remained about the same. Micah saw how the poor were crushed by these new fiscal realities. Because justice was lacking (Mic 3:1, 8), the strong oppressed the weak (Mic 3:2–3). Micah denounces the "get rich quick" schemes that drove people from their homes (Mic 2:9) and killed innocent people (Mic 3:10). Much of the establishment—magistrates, prophets, and priests—were part of the corruption (Mic 3:9–12). The social and economic fabric that was a part of Israel's charter was being torn apart (Mic 7:1–6). Micah's preaching at this time may have brought about Hezekiah's reform (2 Kgs 18:1–8). But another crisis was looming on the horizon.

The death of Sargon II in 705 on a battlefield in Anatolia and the impossibility of burying him in a royal grave caused a wave of joy throughout the Levant (cf. Isa 14:4–23). This sudden fall led nations—weary of living under the Assyrian boot—to believe that the time had come when they could liberate themselves from the regime's rule. When Sennacherib (704–681) ascended the throne, his annals document that there was widespread mutiny throughout the empire.

In 703, two successive revolts one month apart brought the situation to a climax. The first, led by the Babylonian Marduk-sakir-sumi II, was removed within a few weeks. The second was led by Merodach-Baladan who assembled a large coalition of Chaldeans, Arameans, Babylonians, and Elamites. This rebellion against Assyria also included Judah, as ambassadors of Merodach-Baladan visited Hezekiah to secure his part in the alliance (2 Kgs 20:12–19; Isa 39:1–8; 2 Chr 32:31). Hezekiah became convinced that the time was ripe for a Judean revolt against Assyria.

In 701, Sennacherib arose with vengeance and began to devastate the Levant—and this, of course, included Judah. Most scholars believe that Micah records Sennacherib's march from Lachish to Jerusalem (Mic 1:10–16). The Assyrian strategy was to ravage the Shephelah so as to deprive Jerusalem of this buffer territory, its agricultural produce, and manpower to restock its military. According to Assyrian records, Sennacherib defeated forty-six Judean cities and then laid siege to Jerusalem.

Rather than face the attacking army, Hezekiah paid Sennacherib a large tribute (2 Kgs 18:16). The Assyrian king returned home, boasting that he had penned up Hezekiah "like a bird in a cage." However, this behavior is not consistent with Assyrian policy or with Sennacherib's strategy on this campaign. If any city should have been destroyed and any king deposed, it should have been Jerusalem and Hezekiah. Instead, according to biblical historians, a plague decimated the Assyrian army and forced its general's hasty departure (2 Kgs 19:35–36; 2 Chr 32:21). That Sennacherib did not mention such a disaster is characteristic of the adulatory tone of Assyrian annals. The final success of Hezekiah's rebellion was not due to his trust in foreign alliances, but because "he held fast to Yahweh and did not cease to follow him" (2 Kgs 18:6a).

However, Hezekiah's son, Manasseh (697–643), was nothing like his father. Manasseh launched a massive program to persecute faithful Yahwists (2 Kgs 21:1–18). This is one reason why Micah's oracles include ruin and devastation against Judah (e.g., Mic 3:12).

# THEOLOGICAL THEMES IN MICAH

## THE REMNANT

Just like his fellow eighth-century prophets—Amos (Amos 5:15; 9:12) and Isaiah (e.g., Isa 1:8–9; 7:3; 10:20–22)—Micah promises that God will save a remnant. He foresaw a faithful few who would be spared when Shalmaneser V and Sargon II attacked Israel (723), as well as when Sennacherib advanced against Judah (701) and when Nebuchadnezzar destroyed Jerusalem (587). The common denominator in each era is a remnant that consists of those whom Yahweh helps to live in, through, and after judgment. God's people must experience heaps of rubble before they can sparkle with divine beauty.

After Yahweh judges Israel (e.g., Mic 1:6), Judah (Mic 1:12; 3:12), and the nations (Mic 4:11–12), Micah's remnant promises include this pledge: "A שארית, *remnant*, from Jacob shall be among the nations . . . like a lion among the beasts of the forest" (Mic 5:8). The prophet envisions Zion as the place where these survivors will dwell in peace (Mic 4:1–5), where a new Davidic king will lead them as a faithful shepherd (Mic 5:2–4; cf. Mic 2:12). The last promises in the book are likewise meant only for the remnant (Mic 7:18).

## DISASTER

Yahweh stands over all creation (Mic 1:2–4). His control over every domain is so complete in the book of Micah that even distress and disaster are claimed for divine purposes. He cites Yahweh as saying, "Against this family I am devising רעה, *disaster*, from which you cannot remove your necks" (Mic 2:3). God's plans include judgment against Jerusalem. He will raze it and make the city a rubble (Mic 3:12). Judah has no say in this. Everything is settled on Yahweh's terms for he is without rival, advisor, competitor, or aide. Yahweh alone is in control of every event that shapes world history. Pagan deities are therefore excluded, as is every form of dualism. This is one reason why Micah is so critical of those who worship other gods (e.g., Mic 1:7). There are no counter-powers equal to Yahweh.

In the ancient Near East, a nation's destiny was wrapped up in battles fought by deities. Reality was not united but divided. In this light, Mic 2:3 is a bold confession of faith in the one and only God, Yahweh. To be sure, everything he created is very good (Gen 1:31).

However, in this fallen world and for salvific purposes, Yahweh may decide to inflict misery. He is not the author of evil, nor the source of evil, but in a permissive sense he is responsible for it. By declaring that disaster proceeds from him, Yahweh announces that he is the supreme power in the universe.

## CHRIST IN MICAH

Micah envisions a new David coming from Bethlehem who will "be ruler over Israel, whose origins are from of old, from ancient times" (Mic 5:2; cf. Matt 2:5–6), who "will stand and shepherd his flock in Yahweh's strength" (Mic 5:4). Micah juxtaposes the Messiah's compassion as a Shepherd with his strength as a mighty King. In the wilderness, Yahweh attended to Israel's needs with this same mercy and might (cf. Deut 1:30–31), and the synthesis of Shepherd and Soldier occurs in other texts (e.g., Isa 40:10–11). Yahweh combines toughness and gentleness. There is an authenticity about the gentleness of a tough person as well as an attraction to the toughness of a gentle person. This combination reaches its fulfillment in Christ Jesus. As true Man, he demonstrates solidarity with the weak when he weeps, bleeds, and dies. As true God, Jesus has authority over every evil that threatens his church—including finally his defeat of death.

Christ is also foreshadowed in the book of Micah through the promise of שלום, *peace* (Mic 5:5; cf. Eph 2:14). The Savior promises peace (John 14:27) and imparts it as one of the fruits of his resurrection (John 20:19, 21, 26). Finally, Mic 7:8 is one of only two other places in prophetic literature where Yahweh is called a Light (the others are in Isa 60:19, 20). Christ is the Light of the world. Those who follow him will never walk in darkness (John 8:12).

## SIN AND GRACE IN MICAH

The motif of Yahweh riding upon the heights of the land appears in Mic 1:3 and evokes the power of a mighty warrior gliding upon the clouds and executing judgment against his enemies (cf. Isa 19:1). In his book, Micah bluntly confronts people with the power of this God. He is therefore sometimes referred to as "the Amos of the Southern Kingdom." Note, for instance, what the prophet says when he addresses Israel's preoccupation with alcohol: "If a liar and deceiver comes and says, 'I will prophesy for you plenty of wine and beer,' he would be just the prophet for this people" (Mic 2:11). Yet sometimes

Yahweh's anger over sin can be demonstrated by silence: "Then they will cry out to Yahweh and he will not answer them, and he will hide his face from them" (Mic 3:4). What sins brought this about? They include transgressions related to worship (Mic 1:5–7), economics (Mic 2:1–2), prophecy (Mic 3:5–7), sorcery, misplaced trust in military hardware, and idolatry (Mic 5:10–15).

To announce divine pardon and grace, Micah—like other prophets (e.g., Hos 2:14–15; Isa 43:16–21)—employs the motif of a new Exodus. Just like Pharaoh and his army (cf. Exod 15:5), Israel's sins have been cast במצלות ים, *into the depths of the sea* (Mic 7:19). Yahweh will not only drown and defeat sin, he will gather scattered Israelites and bring them home (Mic 2:12; 4:6).

## CONCLUSION

Micah confirms that pride is the root of all sin—human arrogance unleashes divine wrath throughout his book. Yahweh's goal therefore is for his people to "walk הצנע, *humbly*, before him" (Mic 6:8). This verb appears only here in the OT, yet Prov 11:2 states, "When pride comes then comes disgrace, but with צנועים, *humility*, comes wisdom." Lacking this insight, God's people were bound to be disgraced by enemy nations. But trusting in his unconditional promises to the patriarchs (Mic 7:20), the remnant will most certainly be saved.

## SELECT BIBLIOGRAPHY

Andersen, Francis, and David Noel Freedman. *Micah: A New Translation with Introduction and Commentary.* Anchor Bible 24E. New Haven: Yale University Press, 2000.

Childs, Brevard. *Introduction to the Old Testament as Scripture.* Philadelphia: Augsburg Fortress, 1979.

Hagstrom, D. G. *The Coherence of the Book of Micah.* Society of Biblical Literature Dissertation Series 89. Atlanta: Scholars Press, 1988.

Hillers, Delbert. *Micah.* Hermeneia. Philadelphia: Augsburg Fortress, 1984.

Jeppsen, K. "How the Book of Micah Lost Its Integrity: Outline of the History of the Criticism of the Book of Micah with Emphasis on the 19th Century." *Studia Theologia* 33 (1979): 101–31.

Waltke, Bruce. *A Commentary on Micah*. Grand Rapids: Eerdmans, 2007.

# 34

# NAHUM

Little is known about Nahum. The only biographical information given in the book's superscription is that his hometown was Elkosh, a village whose whereabouts are difficult to pin down. The best guess is that it was located somewhere in southwest Judah. While Jonah preached a message that moved the city of Nineveh to repentance and faith (Jonah 3), Nahum was called to serve at a time when Ninevites would not repent. In 612, his prophecy was fulfilled when a coalition of Babylonians, Medes, and Scythians destroyed the wicked and hard-hearted city.

## AUTHORSHIP

Critical investigations regarding the authorship of Nahum were initially confined to the semi-acrostic poem in Nah 1:3–7. Hermann Gunkel—who believed that the broken poem was added by a post-exilic redactor—tried to restore the text by carrying it into Nah 2:3. Debates among critics then began to rage regarding the role of the poem in the book and how best to restore it. But more heat than light was generated by their investigations. Maier's study—published posthumously—offers a conservative rebuttal against those who separate Nahum into different strata and date the book's final form after the exile. More recently, Christiansen has argued for the semi-acrostic poem's integrity, only amending it in a few verses. He believes in the original integrity of the book and that it was published by Nahum during Ashurbanipal's last westward expansion in 639–637.

## LITERARY FEATURES OF NAHUM

The book of Nahum shares several characteristics with Obadiah: both lack historical specificity in their superscriptions and both are oracles about foreign nations. Nahum's vivid imagery, coupled with his poetic flare, demonstrates his ability to enable his readers to visualize the events that he prophesies. The prophet's literary beauty, though, stands in sharp contrast with his stern message. While reading his book we can almost see the horses galloping into the great city of Nineveh, smell the stench of dead bodies, feel the ground move from onrushing chariots, and hear the cries of those doomed in Nineveh to suffer and die.

In the superscription (Nah 1:1), the book is described as a משׂא, *oracle*, which is a term that often denotes a prophecy against a specific foreign nation (e.g., Isa 13:1; 19:1; Hab 1:1; Zech 9:1). The intention of this kind of prophetic writing is to explain how particular events reveal Yahweh's will at work in current human affairs.

## Outline of Nahum

I.   Superscription (1:1)

II.  The Divine Warrior (1:2–15)

    A.  A partial acrostic poem of Yahweh's wrath and mercy (1:2–8)

    B.  Doom for Nineveh and deliverance for Judah (1:9–15)

III. The future destruction of Nineveh (2:1–3:19)

    A.  Nineveh besieged and pillaged (2:1–10)

    B.  The lion taunt (2:11–13)

    C.  Woe to the city of bloodshed (3:1–3)

    D.  The sorceress-prostitute taunt (3:4–7)

    E.  The comparison with Thebes taunt (3:8–11)

    F.  Final taunts (3:12–19)

Following its chapter divisions, the book of Nahum may be divided into three parts: chapter 1 portrays Yahweh as the Divine Warrior; chapter 2 is a vivid description of the battle of Nineveh along with a taunt; and chapter 3 is an oracle about Nineveh's fate. The symmetry between chapters 2 and 3 is evident. The sequence in chapter 2 is attack (Nah 2:1–5), capture (Nah 2:6–10), and a list of Nineveh's sins (Nah 2:11–13). The pattern in chapter 3 is attack (Nah 3:1–3), a list of sins (Nah 3:4–6), and capture (Nah 3:7–19). The last two ideas in chapter 3 are reversed so as to end the book with the city's demise.

## TEXTUAL ISSUES

Fragments of Nahum discovered at Qumran, along with the LXX, testify to the accuracy of the MT. The MT and English versifications do not coincide with one another in chapters 1–2. The MT of Nah 2:1–14 in English versions is Nah 1:15–2:13.

## HISTORICAL ISSUES

The book of Nahum is concerned with one topic—Nineveh the capital city of the Assyrian kingdom. Artwork and massive sculptures from Assyria portrayed the empire as a ravenous lion. Throughout much of the seventh century, this lion roared and the ancient Near Eastern world trembled at its sound. Aware of this imagery, Nahum writes, "The lion tore enough for his cubs and strangled prey for his lionesses. He filled his caves with prey and his dens with torn flesh" (Nah 2:12). The images of prey and torn flesh allude to the wealth that the Assyrians obtained from their constant conquests.

One example of Assyrian might comes from its defeat of the Northern Kingdom of Israel. After a time of weakness during the early part of the eighth century, under Tiglath-pileser III (745–727), Assyria began again to flex its muscles and expand westward. After the death of Jeroboam ben Joash in 753, the Assyrian resurgence generated assassinations and political instability in the North. The author of Kings narrates the reigns of those who followed him: Zechariah, Shallum, Menahem, Pekahiah, and Pekah (2 Kgs 15:8–31). The last Northern king was Hoshea, who dared to withhold tribute from Shalmaneser V (728–723). The Assyrian king responded with vengeance. Hoshea was imprisoned, Samaria was destroyed, and thousands of people were exiled (2 Kgs 17:1–6).

Nineveh—Assyria's leading city—was revived by Tiglath-pileser III and Sargon II (721–705), who made it his capital. Sennacherib (704–681) enlarged Nineveh's circumference from approximately three miles to about seven miles. His massive construction projects were trapezoidal-shaped fortifications running eight miles around the city's perimeters.

Nahum's prophecy describes Nineveh in graphic detail. It was full of lies and dead bodies without end (Nah 3:1) and was a shapely harlot out to seduce the nations (Nah 3:1–4; cf. Zeph 2:13–15). Nineveh was "a city of crime, utterly treacherous, full of violence, where killing never stops" (Nah 3:1). The book ends with these ominous words: "All who hear the news about you clap their hands over you. For upon whom has not come your unceasing evil?" (Nah 3:19). The prophet celebrates with glee over the imminent downfall of the wicked Assyrians.

How wicked were they? Though Assyrians invented the idea of deporting entire populations to distant lands (2 Kgs 15:29; 17:6; Isa 36:16–17), they are remembered most for their inhumane warfare, as depicted in this battle speech of Ashurnasirpal II (883–859):

> I stormed the mountain peaks and took them. In the midst of the mighty mountains I slaughtered them. I dyed the mountain red like wool with their blood. I darkened the gullies and precipices of the mountains with the rest of them. I carried off their spoil and their possessions. I cut off the heads of their warriors and formed them into a pillar in front of their city. I burned their young men and their maidens in the fire.[1]

Erika Bleibtreu observes, "Assyrian national history, as it has been preserved for us in inscriptions and pictures, consists almost solely of military campaigns and battles. It is as gory and bloodcurdling a history as we know."[2] The empire brought heartache, pain, and death wherever it went. Nineveh was the chief of sinners.

And this is why Yahweh must judge Nineveh and why he sends Nahum to announce the city's doom. The prophet's superscription does not give any explicit historical information about his life, but the book had to be written sometime after the destruction of Thebes (663) and before Nineveh's downfall (612). Although Nahum's superscription

---

[1] Daniel David Luckenbill, *Ancient Records of Assyria and Babylonia* (2 vols.; Chicago: Chicago University Press, 1926–27), paragraphs 443, 447.

[2] Erick Bleibtreu, "Five Ways to Conquer a City," *Biblical Archaeology Review* 16/3 (May/June 1990): 36–44, 42.

does not refer to a Judahite king, it is safe to infer that Josiah, who reigned from 641 to 610, was on the throne while Nahum was active.

The fall of נא אמון, *Thebes* (present-day Luxor in Egypt), is mentioned in Nah 3:8, thus indicating that the book was composed sometime after this watershed event. Though his father Esarhaddon (681–669) had marched into Egypt, Ashurbanipal led Assyria to its imperial summit when he defeated Thebes. Nahum points out the collapse of Egypt's capital city to warn Nineveh that it will experience the same destruction. Both cities were protected by water—Thebes by the Nile River and Nineveh by moats—but in both cases these defenses were not enough to save them.

Major weaknesses in the Assyrian colossus were exposed in 653 when Babylon led an insurrection against the empire. When Ashurbanipal died in 627, Assyria began a much more rapid period of decline. In August of 612, Nabopolassar (625–605) led a coalition of Medes, Babylonians, and Scythians against Nineveh. In a Babylonian text Nabopolassar states: "The city was seized and a great defeat inflicted upon the entire population. . . . The city turned into a ruin, hills, and heaps of debris." Xenophon passed by in 401 with his retreating Greek army and he describes Nineveh as "a great stronghold, deserted and lying in ruins."

## THEOLOGICAL THEMES IN NAHUM

### DIVINE VENGEANCE

Nahum's prophecy of doom begins with a description of God, who is roused to anger as a mighty warrior. Yahweh comes in נקם, *vengeance*, to defeat his enemies (Nah 1:2). He commands the whirlwind and storm, and rebukes waters and makes them dry (Nah 1:3–4). "The mountains quake before him. The hills melt. The earth heaves before him, the world and all who dwell in it" (Nah 1:5). Divine anger is like fire (Nah 1:6) and—switching images—it is like an overflowing flood (Nah 1:8). Yahweh is not a benign God but a forceful agent. He will defeat all who organize and mobilize against his right ordering of the world.

The verb *vengeance* occurs seventy-nine times in the OT and eighty-five percent of them have Yahweh as their subject. Simply mentioning vengeance, however, elicits thoughts of mindless revenge and senseless rage. It is normally understood as a bitter grudge acting itself out to settle the score. But this definition gives a misleading impression regarding *Yahweh's* vengeance which denotes punishment imposed in accordance with his laws and ordinances. It does not mean personal revenge or excessive retaliation. Yahweh's vengeance, in contrast to human vengeance, repays unrepentant sinners according to what they have done to others. It is retaliation for previous sins, demonstrating Yahweh's retribution against his enemies. This, in turn, brings vindication for his people. Isa 34:8 is helpful in this regard. Here "יום נקם, *a day of vengeance*, for Yahweh" is parallel with the "year of restoration for the cause of Zion." When Yahweh comes in vengeance it is to bring down the proud and give grace to the humble. Nahum makes God's vengeance a part of Israel's core confession of Yahweh's attributes (Nah 1:2–3).

Peels maintains that divine vengeance and love do not contradict one another: "God's vengeance has nothing to do with a spontaneous, wrathful or hateful urge to destroy. On the other side, the love of God is not just good affections, but it can be expressed as wrath and jealously; God's love is dynamic, holy love."[3] Yahweh grants grace and judges. He blesses and curses (cf. Gen 12:2–3). While his wrath and anger vary from situation to situation, his mercy endures forever (e.g., Ps 136). Nahum therefore cries out for vengeance—not to satisfy his lust for revenge but for Yahweh's enemies to be judged and for his kingdom to come.

God's vow of vengeance against all of his enemies is fulfilled in Revelation 17–19. Again, Peels writes: "All injustice that is not repaired, all oppression and opposition, all shame, fear and doubt, will be put to an end by God. The problem of evil is completely done away with in the avenging judgment of God. Only after the judgment and fall of the whore can the feast of the Lamb and the bridegroom begin."

## THE GOSPEL

In Nah 1:15, the prophet writes, "Behold, upon the mountains are the feet מבשר, *of him who brings the gospel*, who makes known peace." The religious use of the verb בשר appears in the Psalms and the

---

[3] H. G. L. Peels, *The Vengeance of God: The Meaning of the Root NQM and the Function of the NQM-Texts in the Context of the Divine Retibution in the OT* (Oudtestamentische studiën 31. Leiden: Brill, 1995), 312.

Prophets. For instance, Ps 68:11 describes heralds who joyfully announce Yahweh's saving deeds while its use in Ps 40:9 seeks to awaken joy. Isaiah uses the term seven times (e.g., Isa 40:9; 41:27; 52:7; 61:1). In Isa 52:7, for example, bringing the gospel denotes not just that the Exodus from Babylon is immanent, but that Yahweh's royal reign is coming.

This is how Nahum understands the gospel. He refutes the idea that Yahweh is powerless in the face of Assyrian atrocities. Nineveh's destruction announces the gospel that includes Yahweh's just rule. Matthew sums up the preaching and ministry of Jesus with the formula "the gospel of the kingdom" (Matt 4:23; 9:35; 24:14). In Jesus' ministry, God's end time gospel reign is now active (Mark 1:15). And this is very good news, because all enemies of the kingdom—as typified by Nineveh—will one day be placed under Christ's feet (1 Cor 15:25).

## CHRIST IN NAHUM

Nah 1:7–8 captures the central theme of the book. These verses state, "Yahweh is good, a stronghold in the day of trouble. He knows those who take refuge in him. But with an overflowing flood he will make a complete end of the adversaries, and will pursue his enemies into darkness." This image of the Divine Warrior is a reminder that God does not step back from anyone who inflicts harm upon his people. He will fight for them, in this case, with a massive flood of water.

The book of Revelation makes it clear that Christ also functions as a Divine Warrior. "I saw heaven standing open and there before me was a white horse, whose rider is called Faithful and True. With justice he judges and makes war. . . . He is dressed in a robe dipped in blood, and his name is the Word of God. . . . He treads the winepress of the fury of the wrath of God Almighty" (Rev 19:11, 13, 15). No stone in front of the tomb could hold back the resurrection. And nothing is going to hold back this Second Coming of Christ. On the day when clouds no longer carry nourishing rains but rather bear the Warrior and the thunder of his judgment, every enemy of God's people will be defeated. Satan and his minions will be thrown into the lake of fire (Rev 20:10).

## SIN AND GRACE IN NAHUM

Nahum's name derives from the root, נחם, *comfort*, which is a fitting summation of his book. Yahweh's judgment against Nineveh brings great comfort and consolation for Judah. Nah 1:9–2:2 alternates between this judgment for Nineveh and salvation for God's people as Nah 1:12, 13, 15 are messages of grace placed within harsh judgments against the evil city.

Yahweh's judgment of Nineveh becomes clearer in chapter 2. The prophet writes, "The shield of his mighty men is red, his soldiers are clothed in scarlet" (Nah 2:3). The red shields and scarlet garments foreshadow the bloodshed and death of Nineveh's soldiers. Changing images, Nahum pictures the city as a female who will be stripped and carried off into exile (Nah 2:7). In chapter 3, Nahum pours it on. He writes that Nineveh is a city of blood (Nah 3:1) and will be attacked without mercy. "Horsemen charging, flashing sword and glittering spear, hosts of slain, heaps of corpses, dead bodies without end—they stumble over the bodies" (Nah 3:3). The prophet repeats the announcement that Nineveh will be stripped naked (Nah 3:5) and made filthy (Nah 3:6). He culminates with this statement: "There is no easing your hurt, your wound is grievous" (Nah 3:19). Nineveh's loss is Judah's gain. Out of this bloodthirsty city's death arises vindication and grace for the people of God.

## CONCLUSION

No assessment of Nahum can stop without commenting on its connection with Jonah. Reading the two books together gives a more comprehensive understanding of Nineveh. Both books end with questions regarding the city: "For who has ever escaped your endless cruelty?" (Nah 3:19); "Should I not be concerned about that great city?" (Jonah 4:11). God's mercy led Nineveh to repent when the city heard Jonah's preaching (Jonah 3), while the book of Nahum indicates that Ninevites soon returned to their old ways of violence, bloodshed, and terror. Through the Babylonian king Nabopolassar in 612, Yahweh poured out his vengeance upon the evil and immoral city.

# SELECT BIBLIOGRAPHY

Christiansen, Duane. "The Acrostic of Nahum Reconsidered." *Zeitschrift für die Alttestamentliche Weisenschaft* 104 (1975): 17–30.

——. *Nahum: A New Translation with Introduction and Commentary.* Anchor Bible 24D. New Haven: Yale University Press, 2009.

García-Treto, Francisco. "The Book of Nahum: Introduction, Commentary and Reflections." *New Interpreter's Bible.* Vol. 7. Nashville: Abingdon, 1996.

Luckenbill, Daniel D. *Ancient Records of Assyria and Babylonia.* 2 vols. Chicago: University of Chicago Press, 1926–1927.

Maier, Walter A. *The Book of Nahum.* St. Louis: Concordia, 1959.

Peels, H. G. L. *The Vengeance of God: The Meaning of the Root NQM and the Function of the NQM-Texts in the Context of Divine Retribution in the Old Testament.* Oudtestamentische studiën 31. Leiden: Brill, 1995.

# 35

# HABAKKUK

By making his message plain, Habakkuk enables God's people to understand Yahweh and how his divine power will be working for them (Hab 2:2). Habakkuk's name derives from an Akkadian word denoting some kind of garden plant. The LXX Αμβακουμ confirms this, as it reflects an Akkadian spelling. The prophet was probably involved with livestock and agriculture (cf. Hab 3:16–19) and, because of his psalm in chapter 3, Habakkuk apparently functioned in the temple. (1 Chr 25:1–8 suggests that some prophets were also musicians.) The prophet's oracles were delivered after the fall of Nineveh in 612 and either before or shortly after the fall of Jerusalem in 587. During this time, the Babylonians were on the march, slicing through ancient Near Eastern opponents like a hot knife through butter. Habakkuk asks Yahweh why this is happening and then records God's answers to his heart-wrenching laments.

## AUTHORSHIP

Authorial issues in the book of Habakkuk revolve around the prophet's psalm in chapter 3. Critics point out that it is missing in a commentary (Pesher) found at Qumran (1QpHab). However, all of the complete versions of the LXX contain the entire three-chapter book. Differences between chapters 1 and 2 with chapter 3 have been overstated by critics who want to drive a wedge between these two sections of the book. Note the following similarities: (1) both begin with superscriptions indicating that Habakkuk is the author (Hab 1:1; 3:1); (2) both take up the theme of Yahweh's פֹעַל, *work* (Hab 1:5; 3:2); (3) the motif of foreign invaders appears in both sections (Hab

1:5–17; 2:5–20; 3:12–14, 16); and (4) in the face of overwhelming suffering, both parts express a buoyant confidence in Yahweh (Hab 2:4; 3:17–19).

## LITERARY FEATURES OF HABAKKUK

Just like Nahum, Habakkuk's prophecy indicates that it is a משא, *oracle* (Hab 1:1; cf. Nah 1:1). The genre does not consist of a uniform structure but such texts consider Yahweh's actions with nations in the past and draw conclusions about what he plans to do in the future (e.g., Isa 13:1; Zech 9:1). Within this genre, the prophet also makes use of a lament (Hab 1:2–17) and woe oracles (Hab 2:6–19).

Habakkuk changes genres in chapter 3 as its title is תפלה, *a prayer*, that is to be played upon שגינות, *shiginoth* (Hab 3:1; cf. 3:19). The meaning of this second word is uncertain. Its only other appearance in the OT is in the superscription of Ps 7. Therefore it is likely a musical term indicating that the prophet's psalm is meant to be set to music. Note also Habakkuk's use of these psalm-like terms: סלה, *Selah* (Hab 3:9) and למנצח, *to the choir director* (Hab 3:19).

### Outline of Habakkuk

I.   Superscription (1:1)

II.  The debate between Habakkuk and Yahweh (1:2–2:4)

   A.  The argument about divine justice (1:2–11)

     1.  Habakkuk's first complaint: The lack of justice in Judah (1:2–4)

     2.  Yahweh's response: His plan for avenging evil (1:5–11)

   B.  The second argument (1:12–2:5)

     1.  Habakkuk's second complaint: How can God not act against evil? (1:12–2:1)

     2.  Yahweh's response: He will judge the wicked in his own time (2:2–2:5)

III. Yahweh's justice is certain: Woes to the arrogant oppressors (2:6–20)

   A.  The plunderer plundered (2:6–8)

   B.  The fortified are dismantled (2:9–11)

   C.  The citizens are crushed (2:12–14)

D. The shameless are put to shame (2:15–17)

E. The idolater is silenced (2:18–20)

IV. Habakkuk's psalm of submission (3:1–19)

A. Superscription (3:1)

B. Yahweh's march from Sinai to Zion (3:2–7)

C. Yahweh defeats all enemies (3:8–15)

D. Habakkuk's confession of faith (3:16–19)

## TEXTUAL ISSUES

The major issues regarding the text of Habakkuk have to do with chapter 3, the prophet's psalm, where he employs some very archaic Hebrew. Scholars propose a number of emendations. For example, William Albright made thirty-eight corrections and suggested five additions. Regarding the entire book, there are also significant differences between the MT and LXX. This becomes most apparent when NT authors quote from Habakkuk employing the LXX (e.g., Acts 13:41; Rom 1:17; Gal 3:11).

## HISTORICAL ISSUES

Historical questions in Habakkuk are related to identifying the רשע, *wicked*, in Hab 1:4, 13. Most interpreters understand the first use of the term to refer to unbelievers in Judah and the second use as pointing to the attacking Babylonians. If this is the case, then any time between 609 and 587 would fit the prophet's ministry. He then lived during the reigns of Jehoiakim (609–598), Jehoiachin (598), and Zedekiah (598–588). Habakkuk was a contemporary of Jeremiah, Ezekiel, Daniel, and Zephaniah.

Yahweh responds to Habakkuk's first complaint by announcing, "I am raising up הכשדים, *the Chaldeans*" (Hab 1:6). Chaldeans first appear in the Abraham narratives (e.g., Gen 11:28, 31; 15:7). The term may denote (1) the name of a people, (2) the name of a territory, or (3) a technical term in the book of Daniel for a group skilled in interpretations, that is, astrologers and diviners (e.g., Dan 2:2; 5:4). As a distinct people, the Chaldeans appear in the ninth century in the land lying to the south of Babylon, reaching east to Elam's border. By the eighth century, the words *Chaldean* and *Babylonian* were employed synonymously in both biblical and extra-biblical texts. In terms of language and writing, Chaldea and Babylon had merged into one people.

The Babylonian empire, then, was an alliance of two disparate peoples, the Medes in the Zagros Mountains to the east and the Chaldeans in southern Mesopotamia. Throughout the eighth century, Assyria politically and militarily dominated them. Yet, because of its many marshlands, Chaldea made an ideal center from which to wage guerilla warfare against the Assyrians. This is evident by the strategy of the Babylonian king, Merodach-Baladan II (2 Kgs 20:12–19 and its parallel at Isa 39:1–8).

Babylon overthrew Assyria with the defeat of Nineveh in 612. However, the dynasty's moment in the sun was fleeting. The kingdom began with Nabopolassar's ascension to the throne (625–605), shined most brightly during Nebuchadnezzar's rule (605–562), and ended with the invasion of Babylon by Cyrus the Great in 539.

## THEOLOGICAL THEMES IN HABAKKUK

### WHY DO THE RIGHTEOUS SUFFER?

Habakkuk doesn't mince words. When faced with the colossal collapse of his world, he cries out, "How long, O Yahweh, must I call for help, but you do not listen? Or cry out to you, 'Violence!' but you do not save?" (Hab 1:2). Denial was impossible. Past glories would not return, nor could the prophet hope for a quick fix.

Habakkuk faced at least two disasters. The first one was the breakdown of fair play and righteousness in his country. He laments, "The wicked surround the righteous, so justice goes forth perverted" (Hab 1:4). Ironically, Yahweh's response brings with it Habakkuk's second catastrophe. Instead of providing comfort for his prophet, God promises to destroy Judah through a "bitter and hasty nation." Yahweh asserts, "I am raising up the Chaldeans, that bitter and hasty nation who march through the breadth of the earth, to seize dwellings not their own" (Hab 1:6). Now the prophet faced two issues, one internal and the other external. Both were threatening to destroy Judah. This prompts Habakkuk to complain, "Why then do you tolerate the treacherous? Why are you silent while the wicked בלע, swallow up, those more righteous than themselves?" (Hab 1:13). Habakkuk witnesses a horrific reversal. Moses and his fellow Israelites celebrate that Yahweh swallowed up Egyptians at the Red

Sea (Exod 15:12). Later, the sons of Korah who rebelled against Moses are swallowed up by the earth (Num 16:30). In Isa 25:7–8, Yahweh defeats the "last enemy" by swallowing up death (cf. 1 Cor 15.26). However, instead of enemies being swallowed, God is now sending the enemies of his people to swallow them! Between 614 and 587, the Chaldeans (i.e., the Babylonian Empire) conquered Assyria, Judah, Egypt, and a host of other city-states. Is Babylon to go on "destroying nations without mercy" (Hab 1:17)?

The major issue in Habakkuk, therefore, centers upon the age-old question, "Why do the righteous suffer?" Though he does not answer this question, Yahweh provides the solution through the eventual destruction of the Babylonians (Hab 2:6–19). Indeed, God's agent of judgment is itself judged. Because Yahweh is in his holy temple, the only response is silence (Hab 2:20), that is, faithful watching and waiting (Hab 2:1, 4). The prophet announces that suffering is not understood philosophically or intellectually, but relationally and spiritually by trusting in Yahweh.

At the end of his book, Habakkuk's painful questions fade and the sounds of warfare are over. No further anguish disturbs the prophet's heart. Yahweh's promises have invited him to reassess the nature of divine justice and suffering. *His outward circumstances are no different. What has changed is his perspective.* Having poured out his pain to Yahweh, Habakkuk is now confident that God loves him and is working out his divine purposes (cf. Gen 50:20; Rom 8:28). The prophet then makes one of the greatest statements of faith in all of Scripture. As such, he provides a powerful example of how Israel should pray during the intense suffering that was coming with the final Babylonian assault and capture of Jerusalem in 587.

Though the fig tree should not blossom, nor fruit be on the vines, the produce of the olive fail and the fields yield no food, the flock be cut off from the fold and there be no herd in the stalls, yet I will rejoice in Yahweh. I will take joy in the God of my salvation. (Hab 3:17–18)

## LIVING BY FAITH

Habakkuk, fighting to make sense out of all the evil in Judah as well as Babylon's march toward his homeland, longs for a clear and concise word from God. And so Yahweh delivers it: "Write down the revelation, באר, *make it plain*, on tablets so that it may be read quickly/easily" (Hab 2:2). The verb translated *make it plain* means to make something clear, either by explaining the full content of a message or by writing the message in large, clear letters for everyone to see. The rare verb occurs in Yahweh's command in Deut 27:8: "And you shall *make plain* all the words of this Torah on these stones you have set up." Moses then writes the Torah clearly on stone tablets. Habakkuk likewise has a revelation from God that is to be made clear as crystal. These parallels between Moses and Habakkuk suggest that the prophet's revelation is equal in significance with that of the Torah at Mt. Sinai.

And what could be as important as Yahweh's Sinaitic Torah? "The righteous will live by his faith" (Hab 2:4). Habakkuk wanted God to end injustice and destroy Babylon immediately. Instead, in Hab 2:3, God refers to an appointed time for these things to happen. Since they will not occur all at once, Habakkuk is told to live in faith that the day is coming when evil will be completely and eternally eradicated. When he believes in this coming salvation, God reckons him as righteous.

Six hundred years later, Habakkuk's clear statement of justification by faith is passed on to Paul who makes the message clearer still. Quoting from Hab 2:4, in part, the apostle writes, "For in the gospel a righteousness from God is revealed, a righteousness that is by faith from first to last, just as it is written, 'The righteous will live by faith' " (Rom 1:17). In chapter after chapter of Romans, the apostle makes the revelation of a righteous standing before the Father by faith alone in Christ the clearest it has ever been (e.g., Rom 3:22–24; 4:24; Rom 5:1; Rom 8:33).

## CHRIST IN HABAKKUK

Habakkuk stands in a long line of those who protest Yahweh's actions. The OT is full of national and individual laments. Lamentations is arguably the principle example of the lament genre. Community laments also include Pss 44, 74, 79, 80, and 83. Of course, far more extensive in the OT are the individual laments. Some representative texts include Pss 22, 31, 42–43, 73, 77, 88, and 130. Israelites allowed weeping to endure for the long nights of life, while also affirming that joy will come in the morning (Ps 30:5).

Following in this tradition, Jesus lamented and cried out to his Father. For instance, when Lazarus died, Christ was deeply saddened

(John 11:33, 38). He even wept (John 11:35). Yet it was upon the cross that Jesus protested and cried out most vehemently. On Easter morning, his lament was turned into a song of everlasting deliverance (cf. Ps 22:1, 24–31).

### SIN AND GRACE IN HABAKKUK

In Hab 1:2, the prophet cries out חמס, *violence*. The term encompasses a broad field of meaning, as evidenced by the great number of words that are parallel with it in poetic texts. Violence is parallel with "iniquity" (Hab 1:3), "blood" (Ps 72:14), "ruin" (Ps 55:12), and "wounds" (Jer 6:7).

Yahweh has a plan for punishing the violent sinners in Judah through the powerful Babylonian empire. But the Babylonians, God's instrument of retribution, will not escape his punishment either (cf. Isa 10:5–19 for a similar judgment upon Assyria). Yahweh will judge their hubris, as detailed in Hab 2:6–19. This series of woes against the Babylonians confirms that divine judgment will come to them, too. God will not permit evil to go on flourishing. He will bring it to an end. His goal is for grace to abound, so much so that "all the earth will be filled with the knowledge of the glory of Yahweh as the waters cover the sea" (Hab 2:14).

More grace appears in Habakkuk's psalm when he announces God's march from Teman and Mount Paran (Hab 3:3). Teman was located in Edom, south of Judah (Num 33.37) and Mount Paran (Gen 21:21; Deut 1:1) is in the desert region between Egypt and Canaan. By mentioning these two places, Habakkuk refers to Israel's Exodus from Egypt that resulted in their salvation from oppression and slavery (Exod 14). If Yahweh saved his people once from a powerful empire, he will do it again. In wrath he will remember mercy (Hab 3:2).

## CONCLUSION

Habakkuk is greatly disturbed at the ongoing evil in his country and in God's use of the pagan Babylonians, but he refuses to take matters into his own hands. The prophet is content to wait for an answer. This posture is similar to that of other prophets, like Moses and Elijah, who waited for a revelation from Yahweh (e.g., Exod 33:21–23; 1 Kgs 19:9–13). Instead of engaging in speculation, Habakkuk waits for a concrete answer from Yahweh. And the answer he gets is what marks his ministry. The Talmud (*Mak.* 23b) quotes a rabbi as saying, "Moses gave Israel 613 commandments, David reduced them to ten, Isaiah to two, but Habakkuk to one: *the righteous shall live by his faith*" (cf. Hab 2:4).

## SELECT BIBLIOGRAPHY

Andersen, Francis. *Habakkuk: A New Translation with Introduction and Commentary.* Anchor Bible 25. New York: Doubleday, 2001.

Hiebert, Theodore. "The Book of Habakkuk, Introduction, Commentary and Reflections." *New Interpreter's Bible.* Vol. 7. Nashville. Abingdon, 1996.

Robertson, O. Palmer. *The Books of Nahum, Habakkuk, and Zephaniah.* New International Commentary on the Old Testament. Grand Rapids: Eerdmans, 1990.

Smith, Ralph. *Micah-Malachi.* Word Biblical Commentary 32. Waco: Word Books, 1984

Sweeny, Marvin. *The Twelve Prophets.* Vol. 2. Berit Olam. Collegeville: Liturgical, 2000.

36

# ZEPHANIAH

Zephaniah's name derives from the verb צָפַן, *watch over/protect*, and יה, *Ya* (a shortened [apocopated] form of Yahweh). Together the words mean *Yahweh watches over/protects*. This may reflect the fact that the prophet was born during Manasseh's reign of terror (697–643), when faithful Yahwists were often persecuted. God protected Zephaniah from death when he was a child so that he could grow up to become a spokesman for the truth. Zephaniah's genealogy is unique among the prophets in that it contains four generations. The final name is Hezekiah—the godly Judean king who reigned from 716 to 687—and mentioning him serves to give authority to Zephaniah in perilous times.

## AUTHORSHIP

Form critics argue that Zephaniah was not responsible for both the judgment (Zeph 1:2–3:7) and hope oracles (Zeph 3:8–20) in the book that bears his name. Their belief in pure forms prompts the conviction that different authors can be identified by changes in thematic content. Typical of this view is Neef who maintains that Zephaniah's salvation oracles must be later post-exilic additions. He bases his study upon the criterion that for a text to be considered an original unit, it must display a uniform vocabulary and theme. An author can have only one motif in mind at a given time. On the other hand, Berlin argues for reading Zephaniah holistically. She writes, "Viewing it as a whole yields an interpretation much more interesting and compelling than viewing it as a collection of separate parts." Ball believes that all three chapters are original with Zephaniah and that the book's unity derives from the prophet's rhetorical expansion of Zeph 2:1–7.

## LITERARY FEATURES OF ZEPHANIAH

The book of Zephaniah—composed in excellent Hebrew poetry— features standard prophetic genres that include oracles about nations (Zeph 2:4–15) and promises of restoration (Zeph 3:9–20). Some interpreters maintain that the book of Zephaniah follows a strict outline: (1) judgment against Judah (Zeph 1:2–3), (2) judgment against the nations (Zeph 2:1–15), and (3) salvation for the faithful remnant (Zeph 3:1–20). However, a subtle rhetorical move occurs at the transition between chapters 2 and 3. The conclusion of the oracle against Nineveh appears in Zeph 2:15. Then in Zeph 3:1, in a woe oracle against an unnamed city, Zephaniah offers a withering indictment. Initially the reader may think that the prophet is continuing his tirade against Nineveh. However, by Zeph 3:5, it is clear that Zephaniah is lashing out against another capital, namely Jerusalem! The destiny of Israelite and non-Israelite cites is the same—devastating judgment. For similar texts that convey this literary feature of entrapment, see, for example, 2 Sam 12:1–13; Isa 5:1–7; Amos 1:3–2:6.

### Outline of Zephaniah

I.   Superscription (1:1)

II.  The Day of Yahweh is a day of wrath (1:2–3:8)

    A.  Yahweh's just wrath against Judah (1:2–2:3)

       1.  Yahweh's universal judgment (1:2–3)

       2.  Announcement of condemnation for Judah (1:4–6)

       3.  Yahweh's day is near and hastening fast (1:7–14)

       4.  Description of the day of wrath (1:15–18)

       5.  Judah's last chance to repent (1:19–2:3)

    B.  Yahweh's wrath against the nations surrounding Judah (2:4–15)

       1.  West – Philistia (2:4–7)

       2.  East – Moab and Ammon (2:8–11)

       3.  South – Cush (2:12)

    4. North – Assyria (2:13–15)

  C. Yahweh's wrath and concern for Jerusalem (3:1–8)

    1. The evil of "the oppressing city" (3:1–5)

    2. Yahweh's concern for Jerusalem (3:6–8)

III. The Day of Yahweh is a day of restoration (3:9–20)

  A. The conversion of the nations (3:9–10)

  B. The remnant of Judah is saved and purified (3:11–13)

  C. Judah sings a song of victory because of its restoration (3:14–20)

# HISTORICAL ISSUES

No prophetic books were published between the days of Isaiah and Zephaniah. This means that for much of the seventh century, God's voice was silent. In all likelihood, the evil king Manasseh (697–643) and his wicked son Amon (643–641) were responsible for this censure. Persecution, child-sacrifice, and idolatry were rampant at this time (e.g., 2 Kgs 21:1–9, 16). During these dark days, Judah was in league with Assyria and influenced by the vast empire's pagan gods.

    The Assyrian king Sennacherib (705–681) was murdered by two of his sons in 681 and was succeeded by his youngest son, Esarhaddon (cf. Isa 37:37–38). Under Esarhaddon (681–661), the empire extended as far as Memphis (south of present-day Cairo), while the next king, Ashurbanipal (685–627), strengthened his nation's grip on Egypt by defeating Thebes (present-day Luxor)—a city 440 miles further south of Memphis on the Nile River (cf. Nah 3:8). Assyrian power began to wane when Ashurbanipal died, thus loosening the empire's grip on many countries, including Judah. This opened the door for Josiah who was promised—by name—three centuries before his birth (1 Kgs 13:1–2).

    Josiah came to the throne when he was eight years old, following the assassination of his father, Amon (2 Kgs 22:3). In 623, a scroll was found during the temple's renovations (2 Kgs 22). It contained at least the book of Deuteronomy, if not the entire Pentateuch. The impression of the scroll on Josiah was powerful: "When the king heard the words of the Torah, he tore his robes" and "wept" (2 Chr 34:19, 27). He then crushed the altar that Manasseh had built (2 Kgs 23:12) and demolished the altar and high places at Bethel (2 Kgs

23:13–15). Josiah's destruction was so complete that excavations at Bethel have never uncovered any remains of its sanctuary. But these glorious days of renewal and restoration were cut short. Josiah died at the battle of Megiddo in 609 while fighting the Egyptians (2 Kgs 23:29–30). The subsequent rise of the Babylonian empire under Nabopolassar (625–605) and his son Nebuchadnezzar (605–562) brought with it near-anarchy in Judah.

Zephaniah ministered during Josiah's reign (Zeph 1:1), sometime after the king's reformation was launched. "The remnant of Baal" (Zeph 1:4) indicates that the reform was well underway and that only a few Canaanite fertility worshipers were left. Moreover, Zephaniah was active after Nineveh's downfall in 612, as he records the city's doom (Zeph 2:13–15). The prophet foresees a foreign threat to Judah, but he does not mention Babylon by name (e.g., Zeph 1:4, 10–11; 2:1; 3:1–4). Babylonian incursions into Judah only began after the battle of Carchemish in 605. Putting this data together, it appears as though Zephaniah's oracles were delivered sometime between 611 and 610, shortly before Josiah's death. The prophet's oracles indicate that the king's reformation—though an important turning in the OT—wasn't enough to stem the tide of divine judgment.

## THEOLOGICAL THEMES IN ZEPHANIAH

### THE DAY OF YAHWEH

The book of Zephaniah opens with God's stern words: "I will utterly sweep away everything from the face of the earth" (Zeph 1:2). This is a startling claim. Yahweh plans to rid the world of everything—lock, stock, and barrel. To intensify this threat, in the next verse the prophet repeats God's words, "I will sweep," two more times (Zeph 1:3). The rest of the chapter goes on to describe the Day of Yahweh: "A day of wrath is that day, a day of distress and anguish, a day of ruin and devastation, a day of darkness and gloom, a day of clouds and thick darkness, a day of trumpet blast and battle cry" (Zeph 1:15–16). Zephaniah draws on earlier uses of this motif in, for example, Amos 5:18 and Isa 2:6–22.

Many call Zephaniah the "Prophet of the Day of Yahweh," since the theme dominates his book—especially in Zeph 1:2–3:8. Judgment is coming because of Judah's sin. The list of transgressions includes idolatry, syncretistic worship, and spiritual indifference (Zeph 1:4–6).

The sorry state of affairs came, in large part, through the reigns of Manasseh and his son Amon (2 Kings 21) and continued even after Josiah's reformation.

The phrase יום יהוה, *the Day of Yahweh*, often appears in prophetic texts (Isa 13:6, 9; Ezek 13:5; Joel 1:15; 2:1, 11; Obad 15; Mal 3:23). Closely related expressions include "the day of Yahweh's anger" (Isa 13:13) and "the day of vengeance" (Isa 61:2). In some contexts "in that day" refers to "the Day of Yahweh" (e.g., Amos 2:16; 8:9, 13). "The Day of Jezreel" (Hos 2:2), "the Day of Midian" (Isa 9:4), "the day of Egypt" (Ezek 30:9), and "the Day of Jerusalem" (Ps 137:7) are all days that refer to military action. Therefore, the day of Yahweh is another way to speak of his action as a divine warrior who attacks and defeats evil.

The day is fulfilled in several ways, beginning with the Assyrian destruction of the Northern Kingdom in 723, continuing with the Babylonian devastation of the Southern Kingdom in 587, and finding its climax in the end of the age. While this is frightening, it is not the entire picture. Divine grace also exists with divine fury and, in fact, on this day, mercy is God's last word. Yahweh promises to save a remnant from among the nations (Zeph 3:9–10) as well as from among his own people (Zeph 3:12–13).

Yahweh's final Day of Judgment does not mean that the earth will be destroyed. When Zephaniah quotes God as saying, "I will sweep everything away from the face of the earth" (Zeph 1:2), the prophet is using an image from the Noahic flood (Gen 6–8). Yahweh judged the world then, but he did not destroy it. Afterwards he established an everlasting covenant with creation (Gen 8:21–22). Those who try to qualify this promise by claiming that it includes only destruction by water—as though God only ruled out one form of world annihilation—fail to appreciate that God says לא־אסף עוד, *never again*, to the general references to destruction in Gen 8:21. Yahweh sets aside the option of worldwide annihilation and the sign of the rainbow is given as a reminder of this promise (Gen 9:13–16). God will continue with the world. Neither the substance nor the essence of the created order will be destroyed.

## IDOLATRY

In his first chapter, Zephaniah gets to the heart of Judah's problem—idolatry. His first target is Baal worship (Zeph 1:4), a constant problem for Israelites (e.g., Num 25:3–5; Judg 8:33; 1 Kgs 16:31–32; Jer 7:9). What made these pagan gods so tempting? Mesopotamian empires like Assyria and Babylon thrived off of the Tigris and Euphrates rivers, while Egypt's source of water was the Nile. Judah, on the other hand, was completely dependent upon rain for her source of moisture. This is why Baal and Asherah were so tempting. Extra-biblical texts from Ugarit (northern Lebanon) picture Baal as the provider of rain. He would send it when a man went to a high place, found a sacred prostitute, and had sex with her. This would prompt Baal to engage in sex with Asherah and presto, instant rain. Human action that seeks to manipulate the gods is called *sympathetic magic.* Like all human attempts to coerce divine behavior, even when involving false gods, it is roundly condemned in the Pentateuch and the Prophets.

Next in line for Zephaniah are those who worshipped "the starry host" (Zeph 1:5a). When Judah became a vassal of Assyria, they also adopted the Assyrian astral deities (2 Kgs 21:1–5; 23:4–14). Among them were Sikkuth and Kiyyun (cf. Amos 5:26)—both often associated with Saturn. Like modern-day astrologers, some of God's people adopted the pagan belief that the stars in the heavens directed events on the earth. Zephaniah also points out that there were some taking oaths by Molech (Zeph 1:5b), who is mentioned together with Ashtoret of Sidon and Chemosh of Moab in the account of Josiah's reform measures (2 Kgs 23:13).

Zephaniah's use of both Baal and Molech is telling. The same combination is described in Ezek 16:20–29; 23:39–45. Baal and Molech also appear together in Jer 32:35, while infant sacrifices, normally given to Molech, are offered to Baal in Jer 19:5 (cf. Ps 106:28). All of these texts come from the era of the late Judean monarchy when apostates blended their homage to Molech with fertility worship to Baal.

Josiah was successful in destroying pagan paraphernalia (2 Kgs 23:4), but his reformation failed to bring about lasting change. Idolatry made its way back into Judah's life. It was as if there were no differences between Yahweh and the pagan gods. The holy God of the Exodus and Sinai, beside whom there is no other, whose characteristics are unique among all the other gods of the nations, had become for Judeans just another name in a long list of deities.

## CHRIST IN ZEPHANIAH

In Zeph 1:13, Yahweh pledges that Judahites will build houses but not live in them, plant vineyards but not drink their wine. Because of their disloyalty, these God-given blessings (Deut 6:9–10) are reversed and the people are cursed (cf. Deut 28:30–32). In the final section of his book, however, Zephaniah announces another reversal. This one is from judgment to mercy. The sounds of warfare are replaced with the sounds of triumph. The righteous remnant is saved by Yahweh. They are no longer the object of his wrath and scorn. Central to this new day is God's promise, בְּשׁוּבִי אֶת־שְׁבוּתֵיכֶם, *When I restore your fortunes* (Zeph 3:20). Albeit with slightly different configurations, the phrase appears in, for example, Deut 30:3; Jer 29:14; Ezek 16:53; Amos 9:14; and Ps 126:4. Only in Job 42:10 is the expression employed for an individual. Its usage there indicates that the idea is not restricted to a return from captivity but indicates the reversal of a curse.

This inversion from a curse to a blessing and from death to life—so central to the book of Zephaniah—points to God's greatest reversal of all. On Easter morning, Jesus blew the rock open from the inside. He rolled away the stone. He is Life overriding death and making all things new. "Why do you look for the living from among the dead? He is not here, but has risen" (Luke 24:5–6).

## SIN AND GRACE IN ZEPHANIAH

Yahweh's anger burns against the enemies that surround Judah (Zeph 2:4–12). This list includes Gaza, Ashkelon, Ashdod, Ekron (four of the five cities of the Philistine Pentapolis), Cherethites (people from Crete), Moabites, Ammonites, and Cushites. However, the chief sinner in chapter 2 is Nineveh. The pompous city boasts, "I am and there is no one besides me." The city assumed that there was no authority to which it had to answer. This is a highly optimistic but wholly erroneous view. Every nation must appear before Yahweh's judgment seat (cf. Rom 14:10).

In chapter 3, however, Zephaniah shifts from speaking about Yahweh's impending wrath to the day of salvation (Zeph 3:9–20). The prophet brings a message of grace for all people. The changing of speech (Zeph 3:9) reverses the curse of Babel. This is done so that the faithful may worship Yahweh through calling on his name. The promise is similar to Joel 3:5 that Peter uses in Acts 2:21 to explain Pentecost.

## CONCLUSION

Among his seventh-century peers in the Book of the Twelve—Nahum and Habakkuk—Zephaniah is often neglected. This is unfortunate, because Zephaniah is the prophet's prophet, for his oracles epitomize the entire prophetic corpus. Centered upon the Day of Yahweh, the book announces that the day of wrath is coming upon God's people (cf. 1 Pet 4:17). Zephaniah then states that judgment will also fall upon the nations. The book ends with restoration for the faithful remnant—gathered from among both Israel and the nations—as the prophet envisions Yahweh rejoicing with gladness and celebrating the remnant with loud singing (Zeph 3:17).

## SELECT BIBLIOGRAPHY

Ball, Ivan J. *A Rhetorical Study of Zephaniah.* Berkeley: BIBAL Press, 1988.

Berlin, A. *Zephaniah: A New Translation with Introduction and Commentary.* Anchor Bible 25A. New York: Doubleday, 1994.

Neef, Heinz-Dieter. "Vom Gottesgericht zum universalen Heil: Komposition und Redaktion des Zephanjabuches." *Zeitschrift für die Alttestamentliche Wissenschaft* 111 (1999): 530–46.

Robertson, O. Palmer. *The Books of Nahum, Habakkuk, and Zephaniah.* New International Commentary on the Old Testament. Grand Rapids: Eerdmans, 1990.

Smith, Ralph. *Micah-Malachi.* Word Biblical Commentary 32. Waco: Word Books, 1984.

Sweeny, Marvin. *The Twelve Prophets.* Vol. 2. Berit Olam. Collegeville: Liturgical, 2000.

# 37

# HAGGAI

It is not clear whether Haggai had been a part of the Babylonian exile and had returned or had lived in Jerusalem all his life. We are told nothing about his age or ancestry. Due to his concern about the temple and ritual cleanness, some have argued that he was a priest, but this is speculative. For his part, Haggai is content to say that he was Yahweh's prophet (Hag 1:1) and messenger (Hag 1:13). Prophetic expressions abound in his book. Note, for example, "the word of Yahweh came" (Hag 1:1, 3; 2:1, 10, 20) and "thus says Yahweh of Armies" (Hag 1:2, 5, 7; 2:6, 11). Of first importance for Haggai is that God, after a fifty-year period of silence, had finally spoken.

Living in the Persian province of Yehud, Haggai, along with his fellow prophet Zechariah, served in the midst of a very small community, both geographically and numerically. The Jerusalem temple was still a pile of rubble. The ark of the covenant with its mercy seat and the cherubim were gone forever. The tablets of the Ten Commandments, the manna, and Aaron's rod had been swept away, as had the Urim and Thummim and the continual fire on the altar. In 587, the year Babylon destroyed Judah and Jerusalem, everything was gone with the wind. During the second year of Darius (520), Haggai steps into this dismal situation and stirs the people into rebuilding the temple.

## AUTHORSHIP

Because the book of Haggai is written in the third person, a number of scholars believe it was compiled by the prophet's followers.

Ackroyd, for instance, holds that the book was not only composed by some of Haggai's disciples, but that the prophet's oracles were published at least a century after the events narrated in the book. Meyers and Meyers, on the other hand, date the book with the dedication of the second temple, in 515. This, coupled with the fact that a narrative couched in the third person is common in the OT (e.g., the books of Moses) as well as in other ancient Near Eastern literature, makes it reasonable to believe that Haggai composed the book that bears his name.

## LITERARY FEATURES OF HAGGAI

Unlike other prophetic books, Haggai does not begin with a superscription. Instead, he provides the dates of his oracles within the book itself. While Ezekiel lists more dates, the book of Haggai, for its size, contains a greater density of chronological markers. All of the dates appear within a four-month time span.

Haggai writes in prose, though some passages have a poetic quality to them (Hag 1:4, 6–11; 2:4, 8). His lack of poetry—so prevalent in pre-exilic prophetic texts—demonstrates the cultural rupture that had taken place with the Babylonian exile.

### Outline of Haggai

I.   The command to rebuild Yahweh's temple (1:1–11)

II.  The people obey (1:12–15)

III. The glory of this temple will surpass Solomon's (1:16–2:9)

IV.  A faithful response to Yahweh will remove the people's defilement (2:10–19)

V.   Zerubbabel is Yahweh's chosen leader (2:20–23)

## HISTORICAL ISSUES

The rebirth of Judah, promised by Jeremiah and Ezekiel, meant that the end was not actually *the* end. The warnings of Moses' Torah (e.g., Lev 26 and Deut 28) and of other eighth-century prophets (e.g., Isa 3:1–4:1; Micah 3:9–12) had come true. But gospel oracles were also fulfilled. Yahweh gave assurance that he would stand by David's household and backed up this pledge with "forever," "forever," and "forever" (2 Sam 7:13, 16; 23:3). This guaranteed resurrection and new life.

Jeremiah declared how it happened. "Yahweh has stirred the spirit of the kings of Media [the people to which Cyrus's mother belonged], for his intention regarding Babylon is to destroy it. For this is Yahweh's revenge, his temple's revenge" (Jer 51:11). In 538, Yahweh's stirring prompted Cyrus's decree that allowed Judeans to return to the Promised Land and rebuild the temple (Ezra 1:1–4; 2 Chr 36:22–23).

However, to speak of the return from exile in 538 is not correct. First, both 2 Kings and Jeremiah indicate that most Judahites were never exiled in the first place. Second, those who were exiled to Babylon, in all likelihood, died there. Third, it is not a return because most of the people who made the journey had never lived in Judah. They were probably descendants moving to the land of their fathers and mothers. Fourth, it is not *the* return because there were *several* subsequent returns, not least of which was the one led by Ezra who guided about 50,000 people back to Judah in 458 (Ezra 2:64–65). Finally, Judeans in Babylon did not travel to Judah until several years after Cyrus's decree. Probably the first group to journey to Jerusalem from Babylon made the trip in 533.

Although Cyrus permitted Judahites to travel to their ancestral homeland and authorized the reconstruction of the temple in Jerusalem (Ezra 6:3–5), the efforts stalled because of opposition and apathy (e.g., Ezra 3:12–13; 4:4–5; Zech 4:10). Sheshbazzar laid the foundation for the temple in 532 but was unable to finish (Ezra 5:16). It wasn't difficult to delay construction. Judah had been devastated by the Babylonians. People needed to devote their time and energy to the task of sheer survival. Who had time to worry about religion? The rag-tag group was buried in what seemed to be the task of never-ending nation building.

Little was done under the reign of Cambyses (530–522), who died while on a military campaign near Mt. Carmel. In the aftermath of Cambyses' death, a certain Gaumata instigated a revolt. Other Persian districts, especially in Babylon, also began to rebel against Achaemenid rule. Darius (522–486) therefore began his reign with a full-blown crisis on his hands. By 520, he was able to squelch most of the uprisings, except in Egypt.

Meanwhile, some of the richer members in Jerusalem were living comfortably in "paneled houses" (Hag 1:4), but most of the Judeans were enduring poverty, scarcity, and hopelessness. Drought had brought with it crop failure (Hag 1:10–11), leading to inflation and acute hunger. Haggai summarizes this sorry state of affairs by depicting a person earning his wages, only to put the money in a purse full of holes (Hag 1:6). Life was now dictated by famine, fate, and foreign oppression. Where was God? He was speaking through Haggai. The prophet's first date—"the second year of King Darius in the sixth month, on the first day of the month"—corresponds to August 29, 520 (Hag 1:1). It is one of four dates listed in the book, the last one being the equivalent of December 18, 520. Though Haggai's ministry lasted a little more than four months, he is mentioned with Zechariah in Ezra's account of building the second temple. Both prophets address Zerubbabel, the governor of Yehud, and Joshua, the high priest (Ezra 5:1; 6:14).

Zerubbabel was the grandson of Jehoiachin (1 Chr 3:17–19)—the last Davidic king taken to Babylon (2 Kgs 24:8–17; cf. 2 Kgs 25:27–30). When Zerubbabel and Joshua were prompted to begin rebuilding the temple, a certain Tattenai, the governor of the Persian province "Beyond the River" (which probably included Samaria and Judah), along with another official named Shethar-bozenai, tried to discourage the project (Ezra 5:3). These Persian leaders sent a letter to Darius (Ezra 5:7–17), who responded by locating a scroll in the royal archives that authorized the endeavor (Ezra 6:1–5). The king then sent notification to the local officials that they should do everything possible to assist the Judeans in their work (Ezra 6:6–12). The temple was finished on the third day of Adar, in the sixth year of Darius's reign (i.e., March 12, 515; cf. Ezra 6:15).

## THEOLOGICAL THEMES IN HAGGAI

### YAHWEH OF ARMIES

The title צבאות יהוה, *Yahweh of Armies*, is prominent in Haggai's book. It appears in Hag 1:2, 5, 7, 9, 14; 2:4, 6, 7, 8, 9 (two times), 11, and 23 (two times). This name emphasizes God's power and authority, especially as a warrior on behalf of his people (cf. Exod 15:3). He commands heavenly (e.g., Josh 5:14; 2 Kgs 6:17) as well as earthly armies (e.g., Isa 13:4). Haggai uses the title to describe how

Yahweh's domain extends over the entire world, including the Persian Empire.

It would have been easy for Haggai and his community to believe that Persia was absolute and therefore eternal. Pragmatists perhaps decided to accommodate to the new realities, including the worship of Persian gods and conformity to the religion of the day. After all, Persia was not only a political-military superpower. It was also an advanced, sophisticated, winsome culture.

Haggai, though, maintains that the Persian kingdom, indeed, all the kingdoms of this world, are temporal and will quickly pass away. Yahweh of Armies is going to shake, rattle, and roll *everything* so that finally only his kingdom will stand (Hag 2:6–7). The prophet goes on to describe another earthquake that will not only shake the nations, but even heaven and earth (Hag 2:20–22). Yahweh of Armies will one day overthrow all kingdoms. There is a counter-governance in the world that the would-be autonomous nations and states do not acknowledge but cannot escape. Haggai is a prophet of this universal God who is the judge of all the earth.

Some clarification is in order regarding Yahweh's pledge, "I will shake all nations ובאו חמדת כל־הגוים, *and the desired of all nations will come*" (Hag 2:7). The Vulgate understood that Christ is the desire of all the nations. In 2 Chr 36:10, however, חמדת refers to the precious vessels of Yahweh's house—that is, the temple's liturgical vessels (see also 2 Chr 32:27; Jer 25:34; Dan 11:8). Moreover, the verb ובאו, *will come*, is plural, indicating that the singular *desired* is probably to be understood as a collective noun for all of the vessels. Through Haggai, then, Yahweh of Armies promises that when he shakes the nations, the vessels taken by Nebuchadnezzar from Solomon's temple in 587 will return to their rightful domain—the rebuilt courtyard and Holy Place in Jerusalem's temple.

## CHRIST IN HAGGAI

The people in Yehud were discouraged. When they began rebuilding the temple, it appeared to be a poor replacement for what had once been the nation's pride—Solomon's temple with all its glory (cf. 1 Kgs 6–8). The prophet asks, "Who is left among you who saw this house in its former glory? How do you see it now?" (Hag 2:3). Since Solomon's temple had been destroyed seventy years earlier (2 Kgs 24:8–9), few of the people would have actually seen it. However, its reputation surely survived. The ruins had even become a site for pilgrimages (Jer 41:5). The prophet acknowledges the poor condition of the temple and then uses it as a stepping stone to promise its future glory. Christ is this new temple (Matt 12:5), for from him radiates divine glory (John 1:14; Heb 1:3). And, just as Israel's temple was resurrected in the days of Haggai, so Christ rose from the dead. Death has no more dominion over him (cf. John 2:19–22; Rom 6:9).

Christ is also foreshadowed in Haggai through God's promises to Zerubbabel, who hailed from David's line. In Hag 2:23, the prophet emphasizes that Yahweh is responsible for his appointment as governor. God calls him "my servant" and "a signet ring." The word servant is an allusion to the promise of a new David (Ezek 34:23–24) who is Jesus our Lord. But what is a signet ring? In ancient times, a king or a noble would wear a ring that acted as a stamp. When issuing decrees, commandments, and resolutions, the king would seal the scroll with clay or wax with the royal signet or emblem authenticating the message. How does this relate to Christ? In *the* descendent of David (e.g., Matt 1:12, 13), Yahweh's presence is authenticated. When we see Jesus, then we see the Father (John 14:9).

## SIN AND GRACE IN HAGGAI

Haggai criticizes the people for having self-serving priorities. They were so worried about possessions and money that this eclipsed their faith and service of God (cf. Matt 6:31–33). Judahites claimed that there was not enough time to rebuild Yahweh's house. In response, the prophet condemns their actions and commands them to rebuild the temple. "These people" (Hag 1:2) expresses divine anger over sinful priorities. Yahweh refuses to call them "my people" (cf. Exod 6:7; Isa 40:1). Therefore the Judeans in Yehud experienced frustrated labor, famine, drought, and poor harvests. Haggai explains that this happened because of their neglect of the temple. Their problems derive from breaking the Sinaitic covenant (cf. Deut 28:38–40).

In the past, God's people often treated prophets with apathy or even contempt (e.g., Isa 30:10–11; Ezek 33:30–33). However, Haggai's message is met with belief and action twenty-four days later. The Judean's repentance brings divine grace. In Hag 1:14, God calls them "the remnant" instead of "these people," thus showing that they are now in a reconciled relationship with him (cf. Isa 10:20–22; 37:31–32; Jer 23:3; Mic 5:8; Rom 9:27; 11:5).

## CONCLUSION

As one reads the book of Haggai, the differences between the present reality and future glory are striking. The present reality was a desolated land under Persian rule. The temple was in ruins. Zerubbabel was a powerless Persian governor even though he was in the line of King David. Yahweh makes grand promises about his people's future and they are fulfilled in multiple ways. Zerubbabel was able to lead the people of Judah and the temple was rebuilt. And Christ, who descended from Zerubbabel and David, will return at the end of the age. Then God will shake the heavens and the earth one final time in order to give the faithful a kingdom that can never be shaken again (Heb 12:26–28).

## SELECT BIBLIOGRAPHY

Ackroyd, Peter. *Exile and Restoration*. Old Testament Library. Louisville: Westminster, 1968.

Meyers, C. L., and E. M. Meyers. *Haggai: Zechariah 1–8: A New Translation with Introduction and Commentary*. Anchor Bible 25B. New York: Doubleday, 1987.

Steinmann, Andrew E. *From Abraham to Paul: A Biblical Chronology*. St. Louis: Concordia, 2011.

Taylor, Richard. *Haggai, Malachi*. The New American Commentary 21A. Nashville: Broadman and Holman, 2004.

Verhof, Pieter A. *The Books of Haggai and Malachi*. New International Commentary on the Old Testament. Grand Rapids: Eerdmans, 1987.

# 38

# ZECHARIAH

Zechariah's oracles are not only the most obscure in the Book of the Twelve, they are also the longest. Both the book's lack of clarity and its length have given rise to any number of theories concerning its date, authorship, unity, and meaning. Several things are clear, though. Zechariah was a prophet (Ezra 5:1; 6:14) and he returned from Babylon in 533, along with Joshua the high priest (Neh 12:4). Because the postexilic community had failed to rebuild the temple (Ezra 3:8–13), the prophet's first order of business was to encourage the people to complete it. Once the temple is finished, Yahweh promises to usher in his kingdom and reign from Zion, thereby attracting all the nations to his cosmic rule (e.g., Zech 2:11; 8:22).

## AUTHORSHIP

The authorship of the book of Zechariah has been contested since the beginning of the critical era. Matthew attributes Zech 11:12 to Jeremiah (Matt 27:9) and this, say critics, is the best evidence that even in antiquity the book's authorship was in question. But this can be explained in another way. While the first quotation in Matt 27:9–10 is similar to the passage in Zechariah, the second quotation—"and they gave them for the potter's field, as the Lord directed me"— alludes to Jer 32:6–9. Though Matthew alludes to Jer 32:6–9, another cluster of relevant images derives from Jer 19:1–13 as well as from Jer 18:2–3. It is because Jeremiah is the longer book that Matthew attributes the entire prophecy to him. Mark does the same thing when he combines Isa 40:3 with Mal 3:1 and attributes the quote to Isaiah (Mark 1:2).

Another reason form and redaction critics doubt that Zechariah composed all fourteen chapters is that there is a marked difference between chapters 1–8 and 9–14. Many go further and divide the last six chapters between Zech 9–11 and 12–14. This, for example, is the position of Meyers and Meyers who argue that at least three different authors composed the book. They call them Proto (Zech 1–8), Deutero (Zech 9–11), and Trito Zechariah (Zech 12–14). Meyers and Meyers make this decision on the basis of the structural markers at Zech 9:1 and 12:1, where they believe the expression משא דבר יהוה, *an oracle of the word of Yahweh*, breaks the last section of the book into two distinct parts.

However, based upon what she believes to be chiastic arrangements in Zech 1–8 and 9–14, Baldwin makes the case that the prophet Zechariah composed all fourteen chapters. And, though Childs does not embrace the idea that one author composed the entire book, he points out several features that exhibit Zechariah's unity: (1) divine protection for the New Jerusalem (Zech 2:5; 9:8; 14:11); (2) Eden-like fertility (Zech 8:6; 14:6, 8); (3) covenant promises (Zech 8:8; 13:9); (4) the curse of Zech 5:3 is removed in Zech 14:11; (5) God's judgment of the nations (Zech 2:1–2; 14:6); (6) gathering exiles (Zech 8:7; 10:9–10); (7) new worship rites for the new age (Zech 8:18–19; 14:20); (8) the outpouring of the Spirit (Zech 4:6; 5:4; 12:10; 13:3); and (9) a meek messianic figure (Zech 3:8; 4:6; 9:9).

## LITERARY FEATURES OF ZECHARIAH

Since Zechariah was both a prophet and a priest, it comes as no surprise that his visions are concerned with priestly ideas. Note, for example, an altar (Zech 1:18–21), the priesthood (Zech 3:1–10), the menorah (Zech 4:1–14), and divine holiness (Zech 14:20–21). Within this priestly framework, the prophet displays a wide variety of literary features that include exhortations (e.g., Zech 1:1–6), visions (Zech 1:7–6:8), and prophetic sign acts (Zech 6:9–15).

A much debated issue is whether the book of Zechariah contains apocalyptic passages. The discussion is largely driven by the definition of apocalyptic—something that is far from being settled. However, the scholarly consensus appears to be that Zechariah's apocalyptic elements (e.g., visions, angels, symbolic language, and the reinterpretation of earlier texts) are midway between the apocalyptic texts in Ezekiel (Ezek 38–39) and those in Daniel (Dan 7–12).

## Outline of Zechariah

I. Superscription (1:1)

II. Opening oracle (1:2–6)

III. Eight night visions (1:7–6:8)

    A. A man on a red horse (1:7–17)

    B. Four horns (1:18–21)

    C. The measuring line (2:1–13)

    D. Accusing the high priest (3:1–10)

    E. The golden lampstand (4:1–14)

    F. A flying scroll (5:1–3)

    G. A woman in an ephah (5:4–11)

    H. A chariot and the four winds (6:1–8)

IV. Crowning Joshua (6:9–15)

V. Fasting and morality (7:1–8:23)

    A. Fasting (7:1–6)

    B. Reiterating the prophetic word (7:7–14)

    C. Ten promises (8:1–23)

VI. The first oracle (9:1–11:17)

    A. Yahweh's kingdom in Syria, Phoenicia and Philistia (9:1–8)

    B. The coming of the King (9:9–10)

    C. Freeing the captives (9:11–17)

    D. Prophetic admonition (10:1–2)

    E. Restoration of Judah and Joseph (10:3–12)

    F. Taunting the tyrants (11:1–3)

    G. Rejecting the Shepherd (11:4–17)

VII. The second oracle (12:1–14:21)

    A. An attack against Jerusalem (12:1–8)

    B. Weeping over the one who has been pierced (12:9–14)

    C. Cleansing Jerusalem (13:1–6)

D. A smitten Shepherd and remnant spared (13:7–9)

E. The New Jerusalem (14:1–21)

Many have noted a chiasm in the prophet's night visions. Visions one (Zech 1:7–17) and eight (Zech 6:1–8) contain four multicolored horses and both are concerned with Yahweh's plan for the nations. The links between visions two (Zech 1:18–21), three (Zech 2:1–12), six (Zech 5:1–4), and seven (Zech 5:5–11) are not as clear. However, they are all concerned with obstacles facing the exilic community. For example, visions two and three address Gentile opposition, while visions six and seven discuss sin in the congregation. The central visions—four (Zech 3:1–10) and five (Zech 4:1–14)—are set within the temple and both make use of the theme of Yahweh's seven eyes (Zech 3:9; 4:10). The concentric pattern, then, begins with Gentiles (visions one and eight), moves to Jerusalem (visions two, three, six, and seven) and centers in the temple (visions four and five).

## HISTORICAL ISSUES

The three dates in the book of Zechariah (Zech 1:1, 7; 7:1) place his prophecies in the second and fourth year of Darius who reigned over Persia from 522 to 486. Although Cyrus (559–530) had authorized the construction of a temple in Jerusalem (2 Chr 36:22–23; Ezra 1:1–11), under Sheshbazzar's leadership only the altar had been rebuilt (Ezra 5:6–17). After the unexpected death of Cyrus's son and successor Cambyses in 522, the empire was rocked by turmoil because there was no clear successor. Darius, a general under Cambyses and a member of the Achaemenid royal family, was installed on October 5, 522. After a herculean effort, he was able to bring about stability throughout most of the kingdom by 520. Egypt was subdued in 518.

During these turbulent times, Zerubbabel was appointed by Persian officials to serve as a governor in Yehud (Hag 1:1). He oversaw a remnant community that was beset by opposition from the outside (Ezra 3:8–4:5, 24; 5:1–6:22) and discouragement from within (Hag 1:5–11; 2:15–19; Zech 8:9–13). The chief problem, though, was that construction on the second temple had stalled. Compared to Solomon's temple, this building was far less impressive (Hag 2:3). It didn't have Solomon's silver and gold or the ark of the covenant. Its altar was made of stone, not bronze. In comparison to Solomon's architectural wonder, Zerubbabel's looked like just a little bit of nothing. No wonder Zechariah reminded the governor not to despise small beginnings (Zech 4:10).

Zechariah began his ministry during the eighth month of the second year of Darius (Zech 1:1). This would have been in October/November of 520 and just a month before Haggai gave his last two oracles (Hag 2:18, 20). Zechariah's second date is the "twenty-fourth day of the eleventh month," which is the month of Shebat, in the second year of Darius (Zech 1:7) and this corresponds to February 15, 519. The prophet cites one more date, the fourth year of King Darius on the fourth day of the ninth month (Zech 7:1), which would have been December 7, 518.

While the first eight chapters focus on events in the here and now, the last six are much more apocalyptic and eschatological. This is evident by the fact that Zech 1–8 cites the names of people like Zerubbabel, Joshua, Helem, Tobiah, and Jedaiah. On the other hand, Zech 9–14 lists no personal names. And, in terms of chronological markers, chapters 9–14 are also much different. Months and years are not cited. The temple is standing (Zech 9:8; 11:13–14; 14:21), but the community is divided (e.g., Zech 10:1–3), while one shepherd is rejected and another is accepted (Zech 13:7–9). Days of political peace in Zech 1–8 have given way to times of turbulence and upheaval in Zech 9–14.

Given the lack of historical citations in chapter 9–14, a good measure of restraint is in order. However, historical critics frequently argue that Zech 9:1–8 reflects the ongoing conflicts between Persia and Greece—beginning with Darius's attacks against Thrace and Macedonia in 516—and that the rest of Zechariah describes military activities until Alexander's overthrow of the Persian empire in 333. Others maintain that the last six chapters of Zechariah depict Alexander the Great's conquest of Canaan in 333, and what follows describes events in the latter part of the fourth century.

However, any historical reconstruction of Zech 9–14 is to read against the text. An overzealous search for chronological details is a futile endeavor. Why, over forty different people have been proposed for the three shepherds in Zech 11:8 alone! The issues of dates and times must be subordinated to Zechariah's overarching theological concerns.

## Theological Themes in Zechariah

### Divine Justice

Zechariah responds to questions regarding fasting with these words: "This is what Yahweh of Armies says: 'Administer משפט אמת, *true justice*' " (Zech 7:9). The picture that the word *justice* brings to mind is that of a blindfolded woman holding a set of balances. It is often understood to be a static concept describing the achievement of fairness and equality and symbolized in the state of balance where all is at rest. But Zechariah's justice is a call actively to protect widows, orphans, immigrants, and the poor (Zech 7:10). The prophet's command for justice is a call to marshal resources so that people are housed, fed, clothed, and incorporated into the economic fabric of Judah's post-exilic community.

In doing so, Zechariah rejects a type of dualism where spiritual issues are divorced from political and social concerns. He demonstrates that a spiritual person is not one whose inner eyes are always cast heavenward in prayer and contemplation, focusing on the joys of the life to come. To live spiritually does not mean a passive detachment from this world, a transcending of the self to a higher, more sublime world.

Zechariah challenges the people in Persian Yehud to renounce the type of thinking where spiritual goals are divorced from social concerns, as if the latter were of no spiritual significance, and as if Yahweh had no better vision to offer the world. Assisting the poor, working toward fairer wages, and so on, do not save people eternally. Moreover, solving social issues brings only provisional order and peace. By anticipating another kingdom throughout his book, Zechariah undercuts the morally ambiguous kingdom of this world and its pretentious estimation of itself. He announces that it is best to confront injustice by being different, but not separate, from the world.

### God's Holiness

In Zechariah's third night vision (Zech 2:1–13), he sees Yahweh providing a fire around Jerusalem to protect the city. Divine glory is no longer confined to the Holy of Holies. The entire city becomes his dwelling place. This previews the book's ending.

Zechariah closes his book with a vision of perfect holiness where even the bells on horses and mundane cooking utensils are קדוש

ליהוה, *holy to Yahweh* (Zech 14:20–21). This description recalls the same inscription upon the high priest's turban (Exod 28:36–38; 39:30–31). The designation is also applied to sacrifices offered or dedicated to Yahweh (Lev 23:20; 27:30, 32), silver and gold vessels used in the temple (Ezra 8:28), and the spoils of holy war (Josh 6:19).

Excluded, though, from the holy city is the כנעני, *trader*. This is how the several English versions translate the word. Although it can refer to a merchant or trader (e.g., Prov 31:24; Ezek 16:29; Zeph 1:11), in Zech 14:21 it is better to transliterate the Hebrew and render the word *Canaanite*. Why? Yahweh has nothing against those who buy and sell in the marketplace. However, he has everything against pagan Canaanites.

The transgression of Noah's youngest son, Canaan (Gen 9:25), launched a line of people whose sin and sexual depravity grieved Yahweh. Canaanites polluted the Promised Land with their idolatry and immoral lifestyles (e.g., Exod 34:11–16; Lev 18:2–5; Deut 7:1–6). Zechariah uses the term *Canaanite* in his context, not to refer to a specific nationality, but to denote all unbelievers whose lives and commitments demonstrate the exact opposite of Yahweh's holiness.

## CHRIST IN ZECHARIAH

In the center of the first vision (Zech 1:7–21) is a man riding on a red horse who is מלאך יהוה, *Yahweh's Messenger* (Zech 1:11; cf. Zech 12:8). Early Christian commentators like Justin Martyr and Eusebius recognized this to be the second person of the Trinity, our Lord Jesus Christ. And what does this Messenger do? He intercedes for Israel: "Yahweh of Armies, how long will you withhold mercy from Jerusalem and from the towns of Judah?" (Zech 1:12). Jesus likewise intercedes for the Roman soldiers crucifying him. "Father forgive them for they do not know what they are doing" (Luke 23:34). The Spirit of Jesus also intercedes for the baptized (Rom 8:26–27).

While the Branch motif in other prophetic texts is concerned with the king (e.g., Isa 11:1; Jer 23:5–6; 33:15–16), Zechariah calls Joshua the high priest, Yahweh's Branch (Zech 3:8; 6:12–15). Ps 110 also combines the offices of king and priest and this becomes foundational to understanding Jesus in the book of Hebrews (e.g., Heb 7).

Passages from Zech 9–14 are cited more often in the passion narratives of Jesus than any other section in the OT. For example, the prophet writes, "Rejoice greatly, O Daughter of Zion! Shout,

Daughter of Jerusalem! See, your king comes to you, righteous and being saved, gentle and riding on a donkey, on a colt, the foal of a donkey" (Zech 9:9; e.g., Matt 21:5). Again, he says, "So I took the thirty pieces of silver and threw them into Yahweh's house to the potter" (Zech 11:13; Matt 27:9). And again, "They will look on me, the one they have pierced" (Zech 12:10; John 19:37). A final quotation is "Strike the Shepherd, and the sheep will be scattered" (Zech 13:7; Matt 26:31).

Zechariah's Shepherd is none other than Christ our Lord whose mission was singular. He came to rescue, bind up, and bring home lost sheep (Matt 9:36; 10:6; 15:24; 18:10–14). Jesus says, "I am the good shepherd. I know my sheep and my sheep know me. Just as the Father knows me and I know the Father and I lay down my life for the sheep" (John 10:14–15).

Next to Ezekiel, Zechariah's visions had a greater impact on Revelation than any other book in the OT. His influence is evident in, for instance, the pierced Messiah (Rev 1:7; Zech 12:10), the vision of the four horsemen (Rev 6:1–8; Zech 1:7–8), the two olive trees (Rev 11; Zech 4:12–14), and the vision of the New Jerusalem (Rev 21–22; Zech 14). All of these texts announce the coming of Christ's eternal kingdom.

## SIN AND GRACE IN ZECHARIAH

In Zechariah's first vision, Yahweh expresses his wrath over how other nations had sinfully treated Israel (Zech 1:15). In his second night vision (Zech 1:18–21), God reveals how he will deal with these nations, symbolized by four horns. He will send four craftsmen against his adversaries, and they will execute judgment. For every enemy fighting his people, God raises up a counteracting power to destroy it. While the rebel nations must face judgment due to their sin, if they join themselves to Yahweh they will be called "my people" (Zech 2:11; cf. Exod 6:7).

More divine grace becomes evident in Zechariah's third vision (Zech 2:1–13). Here he sees a man measuring Jerusalem, a scene that evokes the first vision (cf. Zech 1:16). The city will have a vast population, and it will be protected by Yahweh. The "wall of fire" is much like the pillar of fire that accompanied Israel through the wilderness and separated the Egyptians from the Israelites at the Red Sea (Exod 14:19–24). Further, the return of God's glory in the midst of Jerusalem (Zech 2:5) recalls the time when Yahweh left the temple during the Babylonian conquest of 587 (Ezek 9:3; 10:19; 11:23). Now he will return (cf. Ezek 43:1–7). Yahweh will be present to protect his people, forever (Zech 14).

## CONCLUSION

Zechariah begins his book with a series of visions announcing the triumph of Yahweh's kingdom that will be initially manifested through Jerusalem's rebuilt temple. The prophet ends by telling the despondent people about a coming day. "It will be a unique day, without daytime or nighttime, a day known to Yahweh. When evening comes, there will be light" (Zech 14:7). Zech 14:6–11 presents a sequence of five statements that progressively depict how nature, as well as Jerusalem, will be transformed. The polarities of the first creation will cease to exist (day and night, cold and heat, summer and winter). The pinnacle of this renewal is an immense display of light. Darkness will be forever banished. And this, Zechariah maintains, is the motivating power behind his call to finish construction on Yahweh's temple and become a community marked by mercy and justice.

## SELECT BIBLIOGRAPHY

Baldwin, Joyce. *Haggai, Zechariah, Malachi: An Introduction and Commentary*. Tyndale Old Testament Commentaries 28. Downers Grove, IL: InterVarsity, 1991.

Childs, Brevard. *Introduction to the Old Testament as Scripture*. Philadelphia: Augsburg Fortress, 1979.

Meyers, Carol L., and Eric M. Meyers. *Haggai; Zechariah 1–8: A New Translation with Introduction and Commentary*. Anchor Bible 25B. Garden City: Doubleday, 1987.

———. *Zechariah 9–14*. Anchor Bible 25C. New York: Doubleday, 1993.

Smith, Ralph. *Micah-Malachi*. Word Biblical Commentary 32. Waco: Word, 1984.

# 39

# MALACHI

Malachi's central motif is Yahweh's gift of his covenantal promises to the patriarchs (Mal 1:2–3), the tribe of Levi (Mal 2:8; cf. Num 3:5–13), and the men and women who enter into marriage (Mal 2:10–16). Because these are not embraced by everyone in the community, God will tear it apart. The community is split into the arrogant and evil doers on one side, and all who fear Yahweh on the other (Mal 4:1–2).

Malachi's superscription is extremely brief. No information is stated, such as the prophet's ancestry, location of preaching, or historical context. The book does not mention Judahite officials, high priests, or foreign rulers. However the issues in Malachi—such as the need for a purified priesthood, the importance of paying tithes, and concern for the Levites—are very similar to those addressed in the fifth century by Ezra and Nehemiah. In light of these connections, the book of Malachi probably has its origins at this time in Persian Yehud.

## AUTHORSHIP

Who wrote the book of Malachi? The answer revolves around the interpretation of מלאכי (Mal 1:1). Does this reflect the prophet's name or is it best rendered *my messenger*? Those arguing that it is a title and not the author's name point out that the expression משא דבר יהוה, *an oracle of the word of Yahweh*, only appears in Zech 9:1; 12:1; and Mal 1:1. It is assumed, therefore, that the last redactor of the Book of the Twelve pasted these three sections to the end of the corpus. The first two oracles were assimilated into Zechariah while the third one gained an independent status and became Malachi. The collection then became twelve books so as to mirror the twelve tribes of Israel and give it a sense of unity and completion. Confirming the book's anonymity, so the critics argue, is that the LXX took it as a title with a *third*-person suffix, ἀγγέλου αὐτοῦ, *his messenger*.

Yet those who promote this interpretation fail to see that, unlike Zech 9:1 and Zech 12:1, Mal 1:1 adds the term ביד, *by the hand of*. This expression appears frequently in texts that describe God speaking through prophets (e.g., 2 Kgs 14:25; Isa 20:2; Hag 1:1; Zech 7:7). In addition, Malachi reads more like an independent literary unit rather than like a hodgepodge of late oracles added by a clumsy redactor. Bearing the stamp of a coherent composition, its claim that it was written by an Israelite named Malachi should be embraced.

## Literary Features of Malachi

Just like Nahum and Habakkuk, the book of Malachi identifies itself as משא, *an oracle*, an explanation of how Yahweh is going to intervene in human affairs. Within this genre, Malachi employs twenty-two rhetorical questions in fifty-five verses. Some have therefore called the prophet's style catechetical, Socratic, or didactic. However, most scholars label the book's genre as a disputation. Much like Micah (e.g., Mic 2:6–10) and Jeremiah (e.g., Jer 28:1–11; 29:24–32), Malachi takes issue with those in his community that have a false understanding of God's will and ways. He does this by presenting an idea that seeks to correct an aberrant belief or behavior (thesis). This is followed by the people's rationale for their sin (antithesis). The prophet concludes with evidence showing the people their sin (defense). The outline below therefore follows the majority of scholars who describe Malachi in terms of six arguments by Yahweh, structured in terms of an introduction, question, and answer. The prophet's concern, though, is pastoral: Malachi wants people to repent and embrace Yahweh's mercy and love.

Is Malachi poetry or prose? BHS considers it poetry while most English versions present it as prose. The prophet's style appears to reflect something in the middle. Some scholars therefore call Malachi's prose poetic while others stress that his poetry is prosaic. At any rate, the debate demonstrates how difficult it can be to define Hebrew poetry.

# Outline of Malachi

I. Title (1:1)

II. God's love (1:2–5)

    A. God loves Jacob (1:2)

    B. Yahweh defeats Judah's enemies, especially Edom (1:3–5)

III. Condemnation of the priests (1:6–2:9)

    A. Yahweh is Father and Master of all (1:6a)

    B. "How have we despised your name?" (1:6b)

    C. Condemnation

        1. Priests have placed defiled food on the altar (1:7–14)

        2. Priests "have caused many to stumble by your instruction" (2:1–9)

IV. The people must be faithful through proper marriage practices (2:10–16)

    A. Yahweh is the Father and Creator of all (2:10a)

    B. "Why then are we faithless to one another?" (2:10b)

    C. The men have "married the daughter of a foreign god" (2:11–16)

V. Yahweh will establish justice through his messenger (2:17–3:5)

    A. "You have wearied Yahweh with your words" (2:17a)

    B. "How have we wearied him?" (2:17b)

    C. The people claim that Yahweh delights in wickedness (2:18)

    D. God will send his messenger to establish justice (3:1–3:5)

VI. Repentance (3:6–12)

    A. "For I Yahweh do not change" (3:6)

    B. "How shall we return?" (3:7)

    C. "Bring full tithes to the storehouse" (3:8–12)

VII. The command to observe Yahweh's word (3:13–4:6)

    A. "Your words have been hard against me" (3:13a)

    B. "How have we spoken against you?" (3:13b)

    C. The people have said, "It is vain to serve God" (3:14–15)

    D. The ones who fear Yahweh are remembered by him (3:16–4:3)

E. Final words (4:4–6)

   1. A call to observe the Torah of Moses (4:4)

   2. "Behold, I will send you Elijah" (4:5–6)

## HISTORICAL ISSUES

While little is known about the life and times of Malachi, the prophet gives us some clues. In Mal 1:8, he employs the Persian term פחת, *governor*. The temple has been rebuilt (Mal 1:10; 3:1, 10) and has been up and running for some time, as evidenced by the people's disillusionment as well as the priest's weariness and apathy. Edomites have suffered a major setback (Mal 1:3–4) and, though this invasion is difficult to date, it seems likely to have taken place in the middle of the fifth century.

Malachi has a lot in common with the book of Nehemiah. Both address the following issues: (1) tithing (Mal 3:7–10; Neh 10:37–39); (2) divorce and mixed marriages (Mal 2:10–17; Neh 10:30; 13:23–29); (3) the Sabbath (Mal 2:8–9; 4:4; Neh 13:15–22); (4) corrupt priests (Mal 1:6–2:9; Neh 13:7–9); and (5) social ills (Mal 3:5; Neh 5:1– 13). Nehemiah served as governor of Persian Yehud from 445 to 433 and returned to institute further reforms in late 429 or early 428 (Neh 13:6–31).

Because some late Second Temple texts and the Targum identify the author of Malachi with "Ezra the Scribe," some scholars maintain that Ezra took up Malachi's calls for reform. However, this would require that Ezra's arrival postdates that of Nehemiah, which is unlikely (see the discussion of the date of Ezra's arrival in Jerusalem in chapter 14 on Ezra and Nehemiah). In addition, it would ignore the close ties between Malachi and Nehemiah in favor of looser parallels between Ezra and Malachi. A date of 450–430 for Malachi therefore matches all of the evidence.

## THEOLOGICAL THEMES IN MALACHI

### ELECTION

The opening section of Malachi establishes its major premise. God says, "I have loved (אהב) Jacob yet Esau I have hated (שנא)" (Mal 1:2–3). These are startling words. They seem to indicate that God arbitrarily hated Esau. But the verb שנא, *hate*, should not be understood this way. Instead here it connotes that a relationship does not exist between Yahweh and Esau. Confirming this understanding is that in Mal 1:2, אהב connotes Yahweh's covenant that he established with Israel. Jacob and Esau stand for Israelites and Edomites, respectively, since they are the ancestors of each of these nations (Gen 36:15–19, 35–39). As part of this deep love for Jacob/Israel, Yahweh comes to rescue his people and defeat their enemies. And the Edomites were public enemy number one. They were a constant threat and nuisance to Israel (e.g., 1 Sam 14:47; 2 Kgs 16:6; 2 Chr 28:7; Obad 10–11).

The primary accent in Mal 1:2–3 is Yahweh's choice to protect and defend a community living in the distant, out-of-the-way Persian province of Yehud. This is in keeping with his election of the patriarchs who were "perishing Arameans" (Deut 26:5), the matriarchs who were all barren at one point (Gen 11:30; 25:21; 29:31), and Israel who "was the least of all the people" (Deut 7:7). The fall of Jerusalem in 587 did not cancel Yahweh's election nor did it mean that he had permanently rejected his people. The Sinaitic covenant was broken, the patriarchal covenant which is "everlasting" still stood (e.g., Gen 17:7). Yahweh's promise to the patriarchs is the decisive guarantee that he has bound himself to Israel forever.

Confirming this idea is the fact that Yahweh calls these people his סגלה, *treasured possession* (Mal 3:17). This title originally applied to all Israel (e.g. Exod 19:5; Deut 7:6; 26:18). Now the little group of Judahites in the insignificant Persian province of Yehud receives this designation that demonstrates Yahweh's great faithfulness and love for them. The result of this covenant commitment is that the faithful will be spared from the judgment on the Day of Yahweh (Mal 4:1–3).

Malachi does not teach a doctrine of rejection to parallel a doctrine of election. In light of his call of Abraham (Gen 12:1–3), Yahweh's initially exclusive choice was for the sake of a maximally inclusive end. He chose Israel to restore all people to himself. Election is not for the purpose of leaving some out but the means of bringing all in. There is only one blessing (cf. Gen 27:38) so that all may be blessed (Mal 1:11)—including Esau and Edom (cf. Amos 9:12; Acts 15:13–19).

## THE HOME

Malachi points his readers toward home. Some of his last words promise that Yahweh's plan includes turning "the hearts of the fathers to their children, and the hearts of the children to their fathers" (Mal 4:6). A strong sense of community pervades the prophet's understanding of Israelite households. Fulfillment in life, to use a modern expression, would not be achieved individualistically, as, for example, through personal adventure or professional achievement. Nor was it found in the context of some larger community overriding the familial structures, such as citizenship in a state. It meant, instead, to be embedded in the texture of the generations and to participate harmoniously as a member of a family. This was life with a promise and a future.

Archaeology has revealed a common pattern of family life in ancient Israel consisting of two or three families related by kinship and marriage, living in a residential complex of two or three houses connected together. This solidarity continued as deceased members were commemorated as an essential component of the organic whole. This is noted by means of the frequent expression, "to be gathered to one's fathers" (e.g., Gen 25:8, 17; 35:29; 49:29, 33; Judg 2:10). Malachi states the same idea when he promises a "book of remembrance" for the faithful (Mal 3:16). The family endures.

It is sinful to deny that people are created, redeemed, and sanctified to be in relationship with others, beginning with the family. This is why Malachi quotes Yahweh as judging those who take marriage lightly (Mal 2:14–15). God hates divorce, which always includes "breaking faith" (Mal 2:16), and rejects God's design for the two to be one flesh (Gen 2:24). Indeed, to be alone in Israel meant something unusual or threatening was happening. Ps 25:15 states, "My eyes are always toward Yahweh, for he is the one bringing my feet out of the net. Turn to me, and be gracious to me, for I am alone and afflicted." Being alone as a longed-for benefit that gives pleasure is an alien concept in the OT. The sense of identity and self-awareness of the individual living in a network of social relations was significantly different from those of the typical privatized individual of Western post-industrial, urban society. Yahweh's plan for life centers upon the family. "God is the one who causes lonely people to dwell in a household" (Ps 68:6 [Heb. 68:7]). Malachi testifies to this design throughout his book. In fact, those who spurn it are promised a curse (Mal 4:6).

## CHRIST IN MALACHI

Mal 1:11 is one of the most important passages in the book and functions as the central theme of its section. "From the rising of the sun to the place where it sets" is used to show that Yahweh's name will be honored over an area that includes the known and the unknown world. "Will be great" describes the honor given to Yahweh while "among the nations" means that his name will be glorified in a future time by non-Israelites. These promises are fulfilled in Christ Jesus. Following his death and resurrection, the Savior holds all authority in heaven and on earth (Matt 28:18). While Christians now grasp this promise by faith, Paul maintains that the day is coming when we will experience it with our eyes and with our ears. "Every tongue will confess Jesus Christ is Lord to the glory of God the Father" (Phil 2:11). Universal acclaim for Christ will happen when he returns as the "Sun of Righteousness" who will come with perfect healing in his wings (Mal 4:2).

Not only is Christ's universal authority and coming kingdom discussed in Malachi, but so is his forerunner, John the Baptist (Matt 11:7–10). John prepares the way (Mal 3:1a; cf. Mark 1:2) for Jesus who is the Messenger of the new covenant (Mal 3:1b; cf. Jer 31:31–34; Luke 22:20; 1 Cor 11:25; Heb 12:24).

## SIN AND GRACE IN MALACHI

Mal 1:6–2:9 emphasizes the theme of fearing Yahweh who is a Father and Master deserving honor and reverential awe. אדונים, *master* (Mal 1:6) is a plural form connoting that Yahweh is the ultimate Sovereign of heaven and earth. However, the priesthood of Malachi's time no longer stood in awe of this Lord. Instead, they offered impure sacrifices and led the people astray with their teachings. Because the priests dishonored Yahweh, Judahites also fell into sin. They broke the spiritual unity of their national family and severed the bonds of their own families. These sins became manifest when Israelite men married unbelieving Gentiles (Mal 2:11). This was a strictly forbidden practice (Exod 34:16) and the downfall of King Solomon (1 Kgs 11:1–8; Neh 13:23–27).

As the book of Malachi comes to a close, it promises that Yahweh will judge these sins of the apostates but will pardon the transgressions of those who turn to him. In his final section (Mal 3:13–4:6), the prophet describes the two groups. The first one consists of those who speak harshly against Yahweh, while the second includes those who honor and respect him. Throughout this passage, Yahweh contrasts the actions and destinies of these two groups. He promises that people will see this distinction (Mal 3:18) but the prophet also offers grace and mercy. Yahweh will respond in love to those who fear him. Their names will be written in the book of remembrance and God will spare them from judgment (Mal 3:16; cf. Exod 32:33; Dan 12:1; Rev 3:5).

The destinies of these two groups come into even sharper focus in Mal 4:1–3. This section contains images frequently connected with the day of Yahweh. Malachi employs this motif to announce God's just wrath against those who do not believe. Yet the passage goes on to state that those who honor Yahweh will not face his wrath. The Sun of Righteousness will arise with healing in his wings and will enable believers to skip for joy like cattle just released from the stall.

## CONCLUSION

The book of Malachi ends by invoking Moses and Elijah (Mal 4:4–6). Those who believe this is an artificial addition that was added as a summary of the prophetic corpus fail to see how these two heroes of yesteryear represent the goal of Malachi's teaching. He wants Judahites, like these two faithful servants of old, to cling to Yahweh's word. Moses' Torah is central to Malachi's message. His themes in Deuteronomy—such as fear, love, and election—permeate the prophet's book (e.g., Mal 1:2–3, 6; 2:5, 16; 3:5; 4:2). Note also Moses' teaching regarding the Levitical priesthood (Deut 17:9; 18:1; cf. Mal 2:4, 8; 3:3) and the tithe (Deut 14:28–29; 26:12–13; cf. Mal 3:10).

Elijah is the second person Malachi employs to summarize the substance and goal of his book. The mighty prophet from Tishbe is likened to the first messenger who prepares the way for the final Messenger (Mal 3:1; cf. Mark 1:2). Elijah is well-suited for this role. He was a mysterious figure in that he did not die but was taken to heaven in a whirlwind (2 Kgs 2:11). Not being bound by death, Elijah will return and bring with him a new day. This day dawned when

John the Baptist—who served in the spirit and power of Elijah (e.g., Matt 11:14)—pointed to the one who is greater than Moses and all the prophets (e.g., Acts 3:22–26), Jesus Christ our Lord.

## SELECT BIBLIOGRAPHY

Kaiser, Walter. *Malachi: God's Unchanging Love*. Grand Rapids: Baker, 1984.

Hill, Andrew E. *Malachi: A New Translation with Introduction and Commentary*. Anchor Bible 25D. New York: Doubleday, 1998.

Taylor, Richard. *Haggai, Malachi*. New American Commentary 21A. Nashville: Broadman and Holman, 2004.

Verhof, Pieter A. *The Books of Haggai and Malachi*. New International Commentary on the Old Testament. Grand Rapids: Eerdmans.

Peer Reviewed

**Concordia Publishing House**

Similar to the peer review or "refereed" process used to publish professional and academic journals, the Peer Review process is designed to enable authors to publish book manuscripts through Concordia Publishing House. The Peer Review process is well-suited for smaller projects and textbook publication.

We aim to provide quality resources for congregations, church workers, seminaries, universities, and colleges. Our books are faithful to the Holy Scriptures and the Lutheran Confessions, promoting the rich theological heritage of the historic, creedal Church. Concordia Publishing House (CPH) is the publishing arm of The Lutheran Church—Missouri Synod. We develop, produce, and distribute (1) resources that support pastoral and congregational ministry, and (2) scholarly and professional books in exegetical, historical, dogmatic, and practical theology.

**For more information, visit:**
**www.cph.org/PeerReview.**

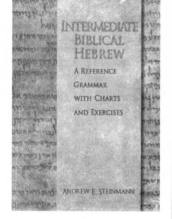

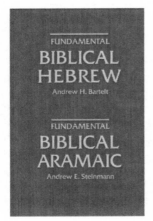

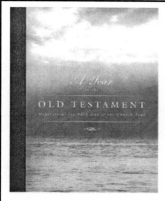

# The Concordia Commentary Series

"I have a great deal of respect for this series. It takes serious regard of the biblical text in its original language, and deals with both textual difficulties and theology—an impressive feat at a time when many commentaries are trying to avoid difficult details."—David Instone-Brewer, University of Cambridge

"Pastors and scholars alike will find plenty of helpful insights . . . in the series as a whole."—Robert B. Chisholm Jr., *Bibliotheca Sacra*

"One of the best commentary series currently available for those seeking an exposition of the biblical text that balances the academic with the pastor."—David W. Jones, *Faith and Mission*, Southeastern Baptist Theological Seminary

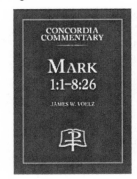

Contributors to the Concordia Commentary series provide greater clarity and understanding of the divine intent of the text of Holy Scripture. Each volume is based on the Hebrew, Aramaic, or Greek with sensitivity to the rich treasury of language, imagery, and themes found throughout the broader biblical canon. Further light is shed on text from archaeology, history, and extrabiblical literature. This landmark work from Lutheran scholars will cover all the canonical books of the Hebrew Scriptures and the Greek New Testament. Two new volumes are released each year.

Concordia
Publishing House

**www.cph.org/commentary • 1-800-325-3040**

CPSIA information can be obtained at www.ICGtesting.com
Printed in the USA
LVOW07*2127020415

432659LV00006B/26/P